The Hour
of Our Death

THE HOUR
OF OUR DEATH

by Philippe Ariès

translated from the French by Helen Weaver

OXFORD UNIVERSITY PRESS
New York   Oxford

Oxford University Press

Oxford   New York   Toronto
Delhi   Bombay   Calcutta   Madras   Karachi
Petaling Jaya   Singapore   Hong Kong   Tokyo
Nairobi   Dar es Salaam   Cape Town
Melbourne   Auckland
and associated companies in
Berlin   Ibadan

First issued as an Oxford University Press paperback, 1991
Published by arrangement with Alfred A. Knopf, Inc.

Oxford is a registered trademark of Oxford University Press

Assistance for the translation of this book was given by the Franco-American
Foundation.

Library of Congress Cataloging-in-Publication Data
Ariès, Philippe.
[Homme devant la mort. English]
The hour of our death / Philippe Ariès ; translated from the
French by Helen Weaver.
p.   cm.
Translation of: L'homme devant la mort.
Includes bibliographical references and index.
ISBN 0-19-507364-9
1. Death.   I. Title.
BD444.A67313   1991   91-17259
306.9—dc20   CIP

ISBN 0-19-507364-9 (PBK.)

2 4 6 8 10 9 7 5 3 1
Printed in the United States of America

Contents

Illustrations   *vii*

Foreword   *xi*

Preface   *xiii*

Book One   *Sleepers of Stone*

Part I THE TAME DEATH

  1 *The Tame Death*   5

  2 *Place of Burial*   29

Part II THE DEATH OF THE SELF

  3 *The Hour of Death: The Final Reckoning*   95

  4 *Guarantees of Eternity*   140

  5 *Tombs and Epitaphs*   202

Book Two   *Death Untamed*

Part III REMOTE AND IMMINENT DEATH

  6 *The Turning of the Tide*   297

  7 *The Vanities*   322

8   *The Dead Body*   *353*

9   *The Living Dead*   *396*

Part IV   THE DEATH OF THE OTHER

10   *The Age of the Beautiful Death*   *409*

11   *The Visit to the Cemetery*   *475*

Part V   THE INVISIBLE DEATH

12   *Death Denied*   *559*

Conclusion   *Five Variations on Four Themes*   *602*

Notes   *617*

Index   *640*

Illustrations

FOLLOWING PAGE 204

The Appian Way, Rome. In the foreground, the tomb of Sesto Pompeo Giusto, Consul (A.D. 14). *Alinari-Giraudon, Paris.*
Christian necropolis around the basilica of Saint-Salsa, Tipasa, Algeria. *Robert Harding Associates, London; photograph by F. Jackson.*

Saint-Bavon, Haarlem, tomb slabs in the floor. *Courtesy of The Courtauld Institue of Art, London.*
Les Innocents in the Time of François I, sixteenth century. *Musée Carnavalet, Paris; Photographie Giraudon, Paris.*

The Christ of the Book of Revelation, with the four winged beasts. Sculpture on the Royal Portal, Chartres, twelfth century. *Courtesy of The Courtauld Institute of Art, London; photograph by George Zarnecki.*
The Last Judgment. Sculpture on the south portal, Chartres, thirteenth century. *Courtesy of the Courtauld Institute of Art.*
Saint Sebastian Interceding for the Plague-Stricken, 1497–9, Josse Lieferinxe, *Walters Art Gallery, Baltimore.*
The tomb of Jean de Lagrange, with representation of decomposing cadaver, 1402. *Musée Calvet, Avignon; photograph copyright James Austin.*
Death, the shop of Hans Memling, late fifteenth century. *Musée de Beaux Arts, Strasbourg; Photographie Giraudon, Paris.*

Danse Macabre, fifteenth century, la Chaise-Dieu. *Photographie Giraudon, Paris.*

The Triumph of Death, Florentine School, fifteenth century. *Pinacoteca, Siena; Anderson-Giraudon, Paris.*

Consular diptych of Flavius Petrus Sabbaticus Justinianus, Byzantine, sixth century. *The Metropolitan Museum of Art, New York. Gift of J. Pierpont Morgan, 1917.*

The tomb of Philippe Pot of Burgundy, fifteenth century. *The Louvre; The Mansell Collection, London.*

Roman sarcophagus, with portrait of a physician seated in front of his cabinet of surgical instruments, fourth century. *The Metropolitan Museum of Art, New York. Gift of Ernest and Beata M. Brummer, 1948, in memory of Joseph Brummer.*

Sarcophagus of Saint Theodechilde, seventh century, Crypt of Jouarre. *Photographie Giraudon, Paris.*

Mural tomb of Guillaume Caucelme de Taillet, thirteenth century, Arles-sur-Tech. *Photograph copyright James Austin.*

Tomb slab of Abbot Isarnus, eleventh century, from the Abbey of Saint Victor, Marseilles. *Courtesy of The Courtauld Institute of Art, London.*

Tomb effigy of Jean d'Alluye, 1248, French. *The Metropolitan Museum of Art, New York. The Cloisters Collection, 1925.*

Tomb effigy of a lady, possibly Margaret of Gloucester, late thirteenth century. *The Metropolitan Museum of Art, New York. The Cloisters Collection, 1953.*

Funerary monument of Louis XII and Anne de Bretagne, sixteenth century, Jean Juste, Abbey of Saint-Denis, Paris. *Photographie Giraudon, Paris.*

Funerary statue of Marie de Barbancon-Cany, attributed to Barthelemy Prieur (d. 1611), Palace of Versailles. *Photographie Giraudon, Paris.*

The tomb of Nicolas Aubry, 1621, cemetary chapel, Saint-Hilaire, Marville. *Inventaire Général Lorraine; photograph by H. Simon.*

FOLLOWING PAGE 428

A row of Hapsburg sarcophagi in the Kaisergruft, the Church of the Capuchins, Vienna: Ferdinand III (d. 1657), Mattias (d. 1619), and Marie Magdalena (d. 1743). *Kunsthistorisches Institut, University of Vienna.*
The Pantheon in the Monastery of San Lorenzo, the Escorial. Engraving by P. de Villafranca, 1654, from *Descripcion del real monasterio de San Lorenzo*, Madrid, 1681. *Arts, Prints, and Photographs Division, The New York Public Library. Astor, Lenox and Tilden Foundations.*

New England burial ground, Wakefield, Massachusetts. *Photograph copyright © 1980 Allan I. Ludwig, all rights reserved.*
New England headstones: Joseph Hickox (detail), 1725, Durham, Connecticut; Jacob Strong (detail), 1749, South Windsor, Connecticut; Sarah Skiner (detail), 1753, South Windsor, Connecticut; William Wolcott (detail), 1749, South Windsor, Connecticut. *Photographs copyright © 1980 Allan I. Ludwig, all rights reserved.*

Brunhilde Watching Watching Gunther Suspended from the Ceiling, 1807, Henry Fuseli. *Castle Museum, Nottingham Castle, Nottingham.*
The Ecstacy of the Blessed Ludovica Albertoni, 1671–4, Gianlorenzo Bernini, Church of San Francesco, Ripa. *Alinari/Editorial Photocolor Archives.*
The Martyrdom of Saint Daniel, 1592, Tiziano Aspetti, *The Metropolitan Museum of Art, New York. Purchase, 1970, The Edith Perry Chapman Fund and The Fletcher Fund.*

Catacombs of the Capuchin Convent, Palermo. *The Mansell Collection, London.*

The Tomb of Spurzheim, Mount Auburn Cemetery. Engraving after a drawing by James Smillie, 1847, from *Rural Cemeteries of America* (Nehemiah Cleveland, *Greenwood Illustrated*, 1847, and Cornelia M. Walter, *Mount Auburn Illustrated*, 1850), New York, 1847, 1850. *Local History and Genealogy Division, The New York Public Library. Astor, Lenox and Tilden Foundations.*
Alley, Pére-Lachaise, Paris. *Photograph by Anne de Brunhoff.*

Diederich M. Havemeyer monument, Greenwood Cemetery, Brooklyn, New York. *Photograph by Edmund V. Gillon, Jr.*

The Little Margaret, funerary portrait sculpted after a photograph, ca. 1900, Green Mount Cemetery, Montpelier, Vermont. *Photograph by Edmund V. Gillon, Jr.*

Pierrette, Woodlawn Cemetery, The Bronx, New York. *Photograph by Edmund V. Gillon, Jr.*

The Tomb of Raffaele Pienovi, 1879, G. B. Villa, Genoa. *Photograph by Anne de Brunhoff.*

Jane My Wife, Griffith family monument, Greenwood Cemetery, Brooklyn, New York. *Photograph by Edmund V. Gillion, Jr.*

Foreword

This is not an introduction. The real introduction to this book was published in 1975 in my *Essais sur l'histoire de la mort*. In that little essay I explained why I had chosen this subject, what was my original point of departure, how I was later drawn to expand my area of investigation both backward and forward in time, and some of the problems that attended an undertaking of such magnitude. I need not repeat those remarks here, for they have been reprinted as the preface to this edition.

I entitled this premature introduction "The Story of a Book That Never Ends," and it was the present volume to which I referred. At that time—1974—the end was so far from sight that I had decided to publish the preliminary outline without further delay. Little did I realize that a stroke of good fortune would soon permit me to accelerate my pace and finish the book sooner than I had hoped. In January 1976, thanks to the good offices of my friend Orest Ranum, I received a six-month grant to work at the Woodrow Wilson International Center for Scholars. During this period I was able to devote all my time and energy to my subject and thus finish, at last, a book that I had been working on for almost fifteen years.

This book owes a great debt to friends and colleagues who became interested in my research and sent me documentation (information about sites, monuments, inscriptions, and texts), references, and newspaper clippings. I would like to express my gratitude to the director of the Smithsonian Institution, James Billington; to Mlles. or Mmes. N. de La Blanchardière, N. Bowker, N. Castan, L. Collodi, M. Czapska, A. Fleury, H. Haberman, C. Hannaway, J.-B. Holt, D. Schnaper, S. Strazewska, and M. Wolff-Terpoine.

Also, to Messrs. G. Adelman, J. Adhemar, S. Bonnet, P.-H. Butler,

Y. Castan, B. Cazes, A. Chastel, P. Chaunu, M. Collart, M. Cordonnier, J. Czapski, P. Dhers, J.-L. Ferrier, P. Flamand, J. Glénisson, J. Godechot, A. Gruys, M. Guillemain, P. Guiral, G.-H. Gy, O. Hannaway, C. Ielinski, Ph. Joutard, M. Lanoire, P. Laslett, I. Lavin, F. Lebrun, G. Liebert, R. Mandrou, O. Michel, M. Mollat, L. Posfay, O. Ranum, D. Stannard, B. Vogler, and M. Vovelle.

The manuscript was very carefully read by Annie François.

To this list I must add the names of a few authors who were particularly rich sources of inspiration or information: F. Cumont, Emile Mâle, E. Morin, Erwin Panofsky, and Alberto Tenenti.

The voyage was long and exhausting, but there were many who helped me along the way. Now, at last, the ship is coming into port. May the reader be unaware of the uncertainties of its course!

Preface

The four lectures I gave at Johns Hopkins University, which have been admirably translated by Patricia Ranum, were intended for an American audience. When they appeared in English in 1974, I thought I had almost finished the book on attitudes toward death that I had been working on for so long. The general outline was completed, and the writing was well under way. Alas! I was forgetting the obligations of a career that had suddenly become much more demanding. I may as well face the fact that the end is not yet in sight.

And yet the subject that I decided to study fifteen years ago in a climate of general indifference is now being hotly debated and has invaded books, periodicals, and radio and television broadcasts. I could not resist the temptation to take part in this debate. Indeed, that is my excuse for presenting to the French public these ideas, for which I shall soon offer further documentation but which will remain essentially unchanged.

Western Attitudes Toward Death came about by accident. Professor Orest Ranum of Johns Hopkins, who is well known to French seventeenth-century scholars for his work on Richelieu and Paris, asked me to lecture on national history and consciousness. I responded by proposing instead the only subject I was capable of talking about, since I was totally absorbed by it. He agreed. This marked the beginning of a book and a friendship.

The preparation of these lectures was by no means marginal to my work. It forced me to make an attempt at synthesis, to discover the broad lines and major volumes of a structure whose slow construction over the

Excerpts from the preface to *Essais sur l'histoire de la mort* (Paris: Editions du Seuil, 1975). This book contains the French version of *Western Attitudes Toward Death* (Baltimore: Johns Hopkins University Press, 1974), plus a dozen articles that appeared between 1966 and 1975.

years has obscured its unity and coherence. It was only after giving these four lectures that I had my first overall view of what I felt and what I wanted to say.

It may seem surprising that it took me so long to reach this point: fifteen years of research and meditation on attitudes toward death in our Western Christian cultures! The slow pace of my progress must not be attributed solely to material obstacles, lack of time, or sheer lassitude before the immensity of the task. There is another, more profound reason, which has to do with the metaphysical nature of death. The field of my research kept expanding just when I thought I had reached the outer limits, and each time I was pushed further, both backward and forward in time, from my point of departure. Let me explain.

My original plan was modest. I had just finished a long study on the sense of family, in the course of which I had discovered that this sense, which was said to be very old and to be threatened by modern life, was, in fact, recent and was associated with a specific phase of modern life. I wondered whether this represented a general tendency, in the nineteenth and early twentieth centuries, to attribute remote origins to collective and mental phenomena that were really quite new. This would be tantamount to recognizing, in this age of scientific progress, the capacity to create myths.

I decided to study modern funerary customs to see whether their history confirmed my hypothesis. I had already become interested in attitudes toward death in my *Histoire des populations françaises*. I was also struck by the importance in the sensibility of the 1950s of the visit to the cemetery, piety for the dead, the veneration of tombs. Every November I was always impressed by the migratory instinct that brought flocks of pilgrims to the cemeteries, in the cities as well as in the country. I wondered about the origin of this piety. Had it existed since the beginning of time? Was it the last link in an unbroken chain, a survival of the funerary rites of pagan antiquity? Something about its style suggested that it was not, and that I ought to look into it. This was the beginning of an adventure. Little did I imagine where it would lead me!

I decided to study the history of the large urban cemeteries: the destruction of les Innocents, the creation of Père-Lachaise, the debates over the relocation of the cemeteries in the late eighteenth century. In order to understand the meaning of these debates and the feelings they expressed, I had to put them in a historical context. I had a stopping point: my own observations on the pilgrimages to the cemeteries of today. But I had to establish a starting point: How were the dead buried before the major decisions were made that still determine the spirit of our legislation with respect to cemeteries?

A rapid survey revealed the ancient funerary practices, so different from our own: the narrowness and anonymity of the graves, the piling up of bodies, the reuse of graves, the storing of bones in charnels—all phenomena that I interpreted as marks of indifference toward the dead. I could give a preliminary answer to the question I had raised. Although there might be a few vestiges of them in our folklore, the funerary cults of antiquity had certainly disappeared. Christianity had disposed of the dead by abandoning them to the Church, where they were forgotten. It was not until the late eighteenth century that a new sensibility rejected the traditional indifference and that a piety was invented which became so popular and so widespread in the romantic era that it was believed to have existed from the beginning of time.

I could have stopped there, but I was not satisfied; I was all too aware of the tentative nature of my conclusions. I had demonstrated the originality of the romantic cult of the dead, but my view of the medieval and early modern indifference toward burial, based on documents of the late eighteenth century and the revolutionary period, seemed a little superficial and simplistic. I decided to take a closer look. Imprudent curiosity!

Wills are the best source of information on the ancient attitude toward burial. My wife and I spent almost three years in the National Archives, researching several collections of Parisian notarial records by spot-checking every twenty years from the sixteenth to the nineteenth century. There was no turning back! I had lost all freedom; from now on I was totally caught up in a search that constantly expanded. I would gladly have limited my attention to choice of burial in wills. But how could I resist all this other fascinating evidence, so varied beneath its deceptive appearance of sameness, as Michel Vovelle has understood? The presence of clauses detailing pious observance led me to become interested in religious services, endowment Masses, funeral processions, and relations with the family, the clergy, and the church council.

But the wills raised more questions than they resolved. They sent me on to other sources: literary, archaeological, liturgical. And each time, I buried myself in a new and fascinating series of documents, which I abandoned whenever they seemed to be repeating themselves.

Take tombs, for example. At first I tried to limit myself to a few books, such as Panofsky's *Tomb Sculpture*. But tombs are just as irresistible as wills! My travels took me to the Catholic and Protestant churches of Italy, Holland, Germany, and England. All the churches of Latin Christendom, except perhaps for those of iconoclastic France, are living museums of personal biography, inscription, and portraiture.

Each body of information sent me on to another. My original purpose had been obscured by other, more essential problems, which led me to the very foundations of existence. I sensed a relationship between attitudes toward death in their most general and common expression and variations in the awareness of self and other, the sense of individual destiny or of the collective destiny of the race. I kept going further and further back in history, happy when I came up against a cultural boundary: burial *ad sanctos,* the frontier of another world. I had already extended the scope of my investigation well beyond the limits permitted by the most liberal historical procedure.

But during my journey through medieval and modern history, a great change was taking place around me, a change that I suddenly discovered around 1965 with the help of Geoffrey Gorer's *Death, Grief, and Mourning in Contemporary Britain.* When I began my research, I thought I was starting with a contemporary phenomenon: the cult of the cemetery, the pilgrimage to the tomb. But the phenomenon that I believed to be contemporary had already been at least partly outmoded before my eyes. The prohibitions surrounding death that were born in the United States and northern Europe in the twentieth century were now invading France. An unforeseen dimension had been added, this time in the present, to a research project that had already extended itself too far into the past.

Moreover, in a final turn of the mad wheel of history, the prohibition had no sooner been imposed on our industrial societies than it was itself violated, not by some obscene transgression but by the serious and admissible ideas of anthropologists, doctors, ethnologists, psychologists, and sociologists. Death is being talked about so much today that I must hasten to emerge from the semiobscurity of my solitary adventure and add my voice to the large chorus of "thanatologists."

A field of study covering more than a thousand years is likely to put good historians on their guard, and rightly so. In my own defense, I shall repeat some remarks I made at a symposium entitled "The Faces of Death in Contemporary Society," held at the Center for Protestant Sociology of the University of Strasbourg in October 1974.

Changes in man's attitude toward death either take place very slowly or else occur between long periods of immobility. Contemporaries do not notice these changes because these periods of immobility span several generations and thus exceed the capacity of the collective memory. If the modern observer wishes to arrive at an understanding that eluded contemporaries, he must widen his field of vision. If he confines himself to too short a time span, although it may seem long according to the classical historical method, he runs the risk of attributing originality to phenomena that are really much older.

The historian of death must not be afraid to embrace the centuries until they run into a millennium. The errors he will not be able to avoid are less serious than the anachronisms to which he would be exposed by too short a chronology. Let us, therefore, regard a period of a thousand years as acceptable. Within this period, how are we to detect the changes that were not noticed by contemporaries?

There are at least two methods of approach, which are not contradictory but complementary. The first is the quantitative analysis of homogenous documentary series. The model has been provided by Michel Vovelle with his studies of southern wills and altarpieces depicting souls in purgatory.

The second approach, which is the one I have used, is more intuitive and subjective, but perhaps more comprehensive. The observer scans a chaotic mass of documents and tries to decipher, beyond the intentions of the writers or artists, the unconscious expression of the sensibility of the age. This method is regarded with suspicion today because it sometimes utilizes material of noble origin, and it is believed that the aesthetic quality attributed to an elite does not express the ideas of the people.

But in reality a theological idea, an artistic or literary theme, in short, anything that seems to be the product of individual inspiration, can find form and style only if it is both very close to and slightly different from the general feeling of its age. If it were very different, it would not even be conceivable by its author, or understandable by the elite any more than by the masses. If it were no different at all, it would pass unnoticed and would never cross the threshold of art. What is similar reveals to us the common denominator of the age. What is different could be either a stray impulse without a future or, on the contrary, a prophetic adumbration of things to come. The historian must be able to distinguish these similarities and differences. If he does so—and the risks are many—he is entitled to take his examples where he finds them in a large and heterogenous body of material, and to compare documents of various kinds.

Particular subtlety is required in the analysis of clerical documents, which constitute an important source of attitudes toward death. The historian of death cannot read with the same glasses as the historian of religion. He must not regard these documents as what they were in the minds of their authors: lessons in spirituality or morality. He must look behind the ecclesiastical language and discover the background of common ideas that was taken for granted and that made the lesson intelligible to the audience—a background that was common to literate clerics and to the people, and that therefore expressed itself in a naïve style.

The Hour
of Our Death

BOOK ONE: SLEEPERS OF STONE

Part I

THE TAME DEATH

I

The Tame Death

The idea of death that I shall use as the point of departure for this discussion is that of the early Middle Ages, as illustrated by the death of Roland. But the idea is older than that: It is the unchronicled death throughout the long ages of the most ancient history, and perhaps of prehistory. Nor did it end with the Middle Ages; we shall meet it again in La Fontaine's woodcutter, in Tolstoi's peasants, and even in an old English lady in the middle of the twentieth century. What makes the early Middle Ages unique is that at that time a knightly aristocracy imposed the imagery of popular and oral traditions on a class of scholarly clergymen who were the heirs and restorers of classical antiquity. The death of Roland became the death of the saint—but not the exceptional death of the mystic, such as Galahad or the Wounded King. The medieval saint was borrowed by monastic scholars from a secular and chivalric tradition that was itself of folkloric origin.[1]

The value of this literature and this period is that it re-creates for us clearly, in texts that are quite accessible, an attitude toward death that is characteristic of a very old and very enduring civilization that goes back to the dawn of history and is only now dying out before our eyes. This traditional attitude will serve as a constant frame of reference throughout this book as we seek to understand each of the changes whose history we are attempting to trace.

The Warning

To begin with, let us ask ourselves quite simply how the knights die in the *Chanson de Roland,* the stories of the Round Table, and the poems about Tristan.[2]

They do not die just anyhow: Death is governed by a familiar ritual that is willingly described. The common, ordinary death does not come as a surprise, even when it is the accidental result of a wound or the effect of too great an emotion, as was sometimes the case. Its essential characteristic is that it gives advance warning of its arrival:

"Ah, good my lord, think you then so soon to die?"

"Yes," replies Gawain, "I tell you that I shall not live two days."

Neither his doctor nor his friends nor the priests (the latter are absent and forgotten) know as much about it as he. Only the dying man can tell how much time he has left.

King Ban has been badly hurt falling off his horse. Ruined, driven from his land and his castle, he runs away with his wife and son. He stops to watch the castle "which had been his great consolation" burning in the distance. He cannot overcome his grief: "King Ban thought about these things. He put his hands over his eyes, and a great sorrow seized him and oppressed his heart. He could not shed a tear, his breath stopped, and he fainted. He fell off his palfrey so hard . . ." People lost consciousness frequently in those days, and even rough warriors, fearless and brave, swooned on every occasion. This emotional susceptibility on the part of men lasted until the baroque period. It was not until after the seventeenth century that it became important for the male to master his emotions. During the romantic era fainting was the exclusive prerogative of women, who abused the privilege. Today it has no significance except as a medical symptom.

When King Ban regained consciousness, he observed that bright red blood was issuing from his mouth, nose, and ears. "He looked up at heaven and said as well as he could . . . 'O lord God . . . help me, for I see and I know that my end has come.'" *I see and I know.*

Both Oliver and Turpin realize that death is upon them, and they express themselves in almost identical terms. "Roland feels death invading his body. From his head it moves down toward his heart." He "knows that his time has run out."

Tristan, wounded by a poisoned weapon, "felt his life spilling out. He knew that he was about to die."

The pious monks behaved no differently from the knights. Raoul Glaber tells how at Saint-Martin-de-Tours, after four years of solitude, the very venerable Hervé knew that he was going to leave the world very soon, and a great many pilgrims hurried there in the hope of some miracle. Another monk, who had some skill in medicine, had to hurry the brothers he was treating, "for he knew that his death was near."[3] An inscription from 1151 at the musée des Augustins, in Toulouse, tells how the great sacristan of Saint-Paul-de-Narbonne also knew that he was going to die:

"Mortem sibi instare cerneret tanquam obitus sui prescius" (He saw death standing beside him and knew that he was about to die).[4] He made his will in the presence of the monks, confessed his sins, went to church to receive the *corpus Domini,* and died there.

Sometimes these presentiments had a supernatural quality. One in particular was unmistakable: the appearance of a ghost, if only in a dream. King Ban's widow had taken vows after the death of her husband and the mysterious disappearance of her son. Years passed. Then one night she had a dream in which she saw her son and her nephews, who were believed to be dead, in a beautiful garden. "Then she realized that our lord had answered her prayers and that she was going to die."

Raoul Glaber describes how a monk named Gaufier had a vision while he was praying in church. He saw a company of solemn men wearing white robes with purple stoles, led by a bishop with a cross in his hand. The bishop walked up to an altar and celebrated Mass. He explained to Frère Gaufier that these were monks who had been killed in battles with the Saracens and that they were going to the land of the blessed. When the monk related his vision to the provost of the monastery, "a man of profound learning," the provost told him, "Take comfort in the Lord, my brother. But since you have seen that which it is seldom given to men to see, you must pay the debt of all flesh, so that you may share the fate of those who appeared to you." The dead are always present among the living, in certain places and at certain times, but their presence is perceptible only to those who are about to die. So the monk knew that his end was near. "The other brothers were summoned and paid him the visit that was customary in such cases. At the end of the third day, as night was falling, he left his body."[5]

Strictly speaking, the distinction we are making here between natural signs and supernatural premonitions is probably an anachronism; in those days the boundary between the natural and the supernatural was indefinite. It is nevertheless remarkable that the signs most often mentioned to indicate imminent death in the Middle Ages were signs that today we would call natural: an obvious, routine observation of the common and familiar facts of everyday life.

It was later, in more modern and contemporary times, that observers who no longer quite believed in them emphasized the miraculous quality of presentiments, which were henceforth regarded as popular superstitions.

This reservation appears by the early seventeenth century in a passage from Gilbert Grimaud, who does not question the reality of the apparitions of the dead, but explains why they are frightening: "What increases this fear is the belief of the common people, which one finds even in the writings of Pierre, abbot of Cluny, that such apparitions are, as it were, the harbingers of death to those to whom they appear."[6] This is not the opinion of people in general, still less of educated people: It is the belief of the common people.

After the split that divided the *literati* from traditional culture, presentiments of death were ranked with popular superstitions, even by writers who regarded them as poetic and venerable. Nothing could be more significant of this than the way Chateaubriand speaks of them, in *Le Génie du Christianisme*, as a charming example of folklore: "Death, so poetic because it touches on the immortal, so mysterious because of its silence, had a thousand ways of making its presence known," but he adds, *"for the people."* It would be impossible to admit more openly that the educated classes no longer perceived the premonitory signs of death. By the beginning of the nineteenth century, they no longer really believed in things that they were beginning to find picturesque or fascinating. For Chateaubriand, the "thousand ways of making its presence known" are all supernatural: "Sometimes death announced its presence by the tolling of a bell that rang all by itself; sometimes the man who was about to die heard three knocks on the floor of his room."

This miraculous quality, the legacy of times when there was no clear boundary between the natural and the supernatural, has prevented romantic observers from seeing the very positive quality of the premonition of death and the way in which it is deeply rooted in daily life. The fact that death made itself known in advance was an absolutely natural phenomenon, even when it was accompanied by wonders.

An Italian text from 1490 shows how spontaneous and natural was the clear recognition of imminent death, and how fundamentally alien to the miraculous or to Christian piety. We are now in a psychological climate very remote from that of the *chansons de geste:* a commercial town of the Renaissance. In Spoleto there lived a pretty girl, young and flirtatious, very much attached to the pleasures of her youth. Suddenly she is struck down by illness. Will she cling to life, unaware of the fate that awaits her? Today any other reaction would seem cruel and monstrous, and the family, the doctor, and the priest would conspire to maintain her illusion. But this young girl of the fifteenth century immediately understands that she is going to die. She sees that death is near: *"Cum cerneret, infelix juvencula, de proxima sibi imminere mortem."* She rebels, but her rebellion does not take the form of refusing to accept her death—that does not occur to her —but of defying God. She has herself dressed in her finest clothes, as if for her wedding day, and she gives herself to the devil.[7] Like the sacristan of Narbonne, the young girl of Spoleto *knew.*

Sometimes it even happened that the premonition went beyond a warning and that, right up to the end, everything took place according to a schedule that was arranged by the dying person himself. In the early eighteenth century, stories like this one were common: "The death [of Mme. de Rhert] was no less amazing than her life. She arranged for her funeral herself, had her house draped in black, had Masses said ahead of time for the repose of her soul, and had her funeral service—all this without feeling the least bit sick. When she had finished giving all the necessary orders to spare her husband the tasks that would have fallen to him without this foresight, *she died on the day and at the hour that she had indicated.*"[8]

Such clairvoyance was not given to everyone, but everyone knew at least that he was about to die, and this recognition took certain proverbial forms that were handed down from one age to the next. "Knowing that his death was near," repeats La Fontaine's plowman.

Of course, some people did not want to see these signs and warnings. La Fontaine again:

How impatient you are, O cruel goddess!

Moralists and satirists made a point of ridiculing those unreasonable persons who refused to face facts and violated the natural order of things. These people no doubt became more common in the seventeenth and eighteenth centuries, and judging from La Fontaine, those who tried to cheat death were found primarily among the old:

He who most resembles the dead is the most reluctant to die.

Eighteenth-century society had little compassion for these old men and women (of fifty!) and mercilessly mocked an attachment to life that would seem quite comprehensible to us today:

Death had the last word.
Come along, old man, and don't argue.

To try to avoid death's warning was to expose oneself to ridicule: Even the mad Quixote, who was actually less mad than the old men of La Fontaine, would not try to escape from death into the dreams in which he had consumed his life. On the contrary, the signs of the end brought him back to reason: "Niece," he said very quietly, "I feel that death is near."

The belief that death sends out a warning has come down through the ages and has persisted for a long time in the minds of ordinary people. It was Tolstoi's genius to have rediscovered it, haunted as he was both by death and by the myth of the people. On his deathbed in a country railroad station, he moaned, "What about the muzhiks? How do the muzhiks die?"[9] The answer is that the muzhiks died like Roland, or the young woman of Spoleto, or the monk of Narbonne: They knew.

In Tolstoi's "The Three Deaths," an old coachman is breathing his last in the kitchen of an inn, near the big stove. Next door, in a bedroom, the wife of a rich businessman is also dying. But whereas death is first kept a secret from the rich woman for fear of frightening her, and then treated like a grand spectacle in the romantic manner, in the kitchen the old coachman understands at once. When a peasant woman asks him kindly how he feels, he answers, "Death is here, that's how it is," and nobody tries to deceive him.

It was the same way with an old French peasant, the mother of M. Pouget, whose biographer was Jean Guitton. "In '74, she contracted a summer cholera. After four days she asked to see the village priest, who came and wanted to give her the last rites. "Not yet, M. le curé; I'll let you know when the time comes." Two days later: "Go and tell M. le curé to bring me Extreme Unction."

An uncle of this same M. Pouget was ninety-six. "He was deaf and blind; he prayed all the time. One morning he said, 'I don't know what's the matter with me, I've never felt like this before; please get the priest.' The priest came and gave him all the sacraments. An hour later he was dead." Jean Guitton comments, "We see how the Pougets in those bygone days passed from this world into the next simply and straightforwardly *observing the signs* [italics added], and above all, *observing themselves.* They were in no hurry to die, but when they saw the time approaching, then not too soon and not too late, but just when they were supposed to, they died like Christians."[10] But non-Christians died just as simply.

Mors repentina

If death was to be known in advance in this way, it could not be sudden: *mors repentina.* When it did not give advance warning, it ceased to be regarded as a necessity that, although frightening, was expected and accepted, like it or not. It destroyed the order of the world in which everyone believed; it became the absurd instrument of chance, which was sometimes disguised as the wrath of God. This is why the *mors repentina* was regarded as ignominious and shameful.

When Gaheris dies of poison after eating a piece of fruit that Queen Guinevere has given him in all innocence, he is buried "with full honors, as befits such a worthy man." But his memory is laid under an interdict. "King Arthur and all who were in his court were so grieved by *such a vile and ugly* death that they seldom mentioned it." Anyone who is aware of the ostentatious displays of mourning that characterized this period can judge the significance of this silence, which seems modern. In this world that was so familiar with death, a sudden death was a vile and ugly death; it was frightening; it seemed a strange and monstrous thing that nobody dared talk about.

But we moderns, who have banished death from daily life, would, on the contrary, be moved by an accident so sudden and absurd and would tend on this extraordinary occasion to suspend the usual prohibitions. The vile and ugly death of the Middle Ages is not only the sudden and absurd death, like the death of Gaheris, it is also the secret death that is without witness or ceremony: the death of the traveler on the road, or the man who drowns in a river, or the stranger whose body is found at the edge of a field, or even the neighbor who is struck down for no reason. It makes no difference that he was innocent; his sudden death marks him with a malediction. This is a very ancient belief. Virgil consigned to the most miserable part of the underworld those innocent people whose deaths had been brought about by false accusations and whom we moderns would wish to rehabilitate. They shared the fate of the children who wept because they had never known the sweetness of life. Christianity tried to combat the belief that a sudden death was shameful, but it did so in a cautious and halfhearted manner. The thirteenth-century bishop and liturgist of Mende, Gulielmus Durandus, betrays his confusion on this question. He thinks that to die suddenly is "to die not for some manifest reason, but solely by the judgment of God." Someone who has died in this manner must not, however, be regarded as accursed. He must be given the benefit of the doubt and receive Christian burial: "Wherever we find a dead man, we must bury him, because we do not know the cause of his death." Indeed, "The just man, no matter when he leaves this life, is saved." But despite this affirmation of principle, Durandus is tempted to give in to the prevailing opinion: "If a man dies suddenly while taking part in some popular game such as ball or bowls, he *may* be buried in a cemetery, because he was not trying to hurt anyone." He *may:* This was merely tolerance, and some canonists set restrictions. "Because he was engaged in the diversions of this world, some say that he must be buried without the singing of psalms or the other ceremonies accorded to the dead."[11]

But if one can argue about the sudden death of an honest player, there is no longer any doubt in the case of a man killed by criminal action. The victim cannot be exonerated; he is inescapably dishonored by the vileness of his death. Durandus compares him to the man who has died while committing adultery or robbery, or while playing a pagan game, that is, any game other than the knightly tournament. (Not all the canonical texts show the same indulgence toward the tournament.)[12] While the popular disapproval that fell upon the victims of a murder did not prevent their receiving a Christian burial, it sometimes entailed the payment of a sort of fine. A canonist named Louis Thomassin, who wrote in 1710, reports that in the thirteenth century the archpriests of Hungary were in the habit "of collecting one silver mark for all those unfortunates who had been murdered by sword, poison, or other similar means, before allowing them to be buried." And he adds that it was necessary to call a council at Budapest in 1279 to restrain the Hungarian clergy from "extending this custom to persons who had been killed by falls, fires, collapsing buildings, and other similar accidents, and to see that they were given an ecclesiastical burial, provided they showed signs of repentance before they died." Thomassin speaks as a man of the eighteenth century when he makes this comment on customs that he found extravagant: "We may well believe that the council confined themselves to opposing the spread of this exaction, since they did not believe they could abolish it entirely."[13] The popular prejudice was still alive at the beginning of the seventeenth century. In their funeral orations for Henri IV, preachers felt obliged to exonerate the king from the ignominious circumstances of his death under Ravaillac's knife.[14]

The death of condemned prisoners was shameful by definition. Until the fourteenth century, they were denied even religious reconciliation: They were damned in the next world as well as in this one. The mendicant friars, with the support of the papacy, succeeded in obtaining from the temporal powers the right to stay with prisoners about to be executed; it was always one of them who accompanied the condemned man to the scaffold.

On the other hand, in a society founded on chivalric and military ideals, the stigma attached to sudden death was not extended to the noble victims of war. In the first place, the death of the knight fallen in single combat among his peers allowed time to carry out the customary rites, albeit in abridged form. Furthermore, the death of Roland, the death of the knight, was regarded by the clergy, as well as by the laity, as the death of a saint. A different spirit, however, appears among the liturgists of the thirteenth century, a spirit that corresponds to a new ideal of peace and order that is further removed from chivalric models. They classified at least some cases of knightly death along with the questionable deaths of the old beliefs. For them, the death of the warrior has ceased to be the model of the good death; at any rate, it corresponds to this model only under certain conditions: "The cemetery and the Office of the Dead," writes Durandus, "are granted without hesitation to the defender of justice or to the warrior killed in a war *whose motive was just.*"[15] The qualification is very significant, and it might have had profound consequences were it not for the fact that in the new states of the period, soldiers in the temporal wars enjoyed the privilege that Durandus of Mende reserved for crusaders—and this, thanks to the perennial complicity of the Church, until World War I.

But because of this aversion to violent death among the clergy, and despite the emergence of a more moral and more reasonable attitude, Durandus continued to invoke the primitive beliefs regarding the pollution of sacred places by the liquids of the human body, blood, or sperm: "Those who have been killed are not brought into the church for fear their blood will soil the floor of the temple of God." In such cases, the Mass and the *Libera* were said in the absence of the body.

The Exceptional Death of the Saint

The death that does give advance warning is not viewed as a spiritual good, as had been propounded for centuries in Christian writing, from the church fathers to the devout humanists. The ordinary and ideal death of the high Middle Ages is not a specifically Christian death. Ever since the risen Christ triumphed over death, the fact of being born into this world is the real death, and physical death is access to eternal life. Thus, the Christian is urged to look forward to death with joy, as if to a new birth.

"Media vita in morte sumus" (In the midst of life, we are in death), writes Balbulus Notker in a tenth-century missal. And when he adds, *"Amarae morti ne tradas nos"* (Do not deliver us to bitter death), the bitter death is sin and not the physical death of the sinner.[16] These pious sentiments are not altogether unknown in medieval secular literature, and we find them in the poems of the Round Table. When the Wounded King is anointed with the blood of the Grail, he recovers "sight and the strength of his body" and the health of his spirit. "The old king sat up in bed, his shoulders and chest bare to the navel, and lifting his hands to heaven, 'Dear Father Jesus Christ,' he said, 'now [that I have confessed and taken Communion] I beseech you to come and take me, for I could not leave this life with greater joy than at this moment. I am nothing but roses and lilies [the old idea that the body of a saint is not subject to decay]. He took Galahad in his arms and clasped him to his breast, and at the same moment our Lord proved that he had heard the king's prayer, for his soul left his body."

Similarly, when Galahad had his vision of the Grail, "he began to tremble, and lifting his hands to heaven, he said, 'Lord, I thank you for granting my desire! I now see the beginning and end of all things. And now, I beseech you to allow me to pass from this terrestrial life to the celestial one.' He humbly received the *corpus Domini.* . . . Then he went and kissed Percival and said to Bohan, 'Bohan, salute my lord Lancelot, my father, when you see him.' After which he came back and knelt once again before the silver table, and soon his soul left his body."

This is the exceptional and extraordinary death of the mystic, whom the approach of the end fills with a "celestial" joy. It is not the secular death of the *chanson de geste* or the medieval romance, the ordinary death.

The Deathbed:
The Familiar Rites of Death

When the dying man felt his end to be near, he made the necessary arrangements. In a world as full of marvels as that of the Round Table, death itself was a very simple thing. When Lancelot, defeated and wandering alone in the deserted forest, realizes that he has "lost even the strength of his body," he believes that he is about to die. He takes off his weapons, lies down quietly on the ground with his arms crossed on his chest and his head turned toward the east, and begins to pray. King Arthur is taken for dead: He is lying down with his arms crossed on his chest. However, he has enough strength to clasp his page "so hard to his breast that he crushes him without realizing it and bursts his heart"! Death is not subject to this sentimental hyperbole; it is always described in terms whose simplicity contrasts with the emotional intensity of the context. When Isolde comes back to Tristan and finds him dead, she lies down next to him and faces east. Archbishop Turpin waits for death: "Over the center of his chest, he has crossed his beautiful white hands." This is the ritual attitude for recumbent figures: Durandus says that the dying man must lie on his back so that his face is always turned toward heaven. This orientation toward the east, toward Jerusalem, was retained for a long time in the burial of the dead. "The dead man must be buried so that his head is to the west and his feet to the east."[17]

Once he has assumed this position, the dying man can perform the last acts of the ceremony. He begins with a sorrowful and sober recollection of the things and people he has loved and a brief account of his life, reduced to its essential images. Roland "called to mind several things:" in the first place, "all the lands he had conquered, that valiant man," next, his beloved France, his ancestors, and Charlemagne, his lord, who had raised him. He does not have a single thought for Aude, his betrothed, who falls dead when she learns of his cruel end, nor for his fleshly parents. The soldiers in our great modern wars always called on their mothers before they died. But

Roland on the threshold of death remembers the things he has possessed, the lands he has conquered, which he regrets as if they were living things, his companions, his troops, and the lord who raised him and whom he served. "He weeps and sighs, he cannot help himself." It is also his lord whom Archbishop Turpin regrets: "How cruel is death! Never again shall I see the mighty emperor."

In the stories of the Round Table, the wife and child have a greater role, but the parents are always forgotten. The heart of King Ban "was so sorely grieved when he thought of his wife and son that his eyes grew dim, his veins burst, and his heart stopped in his breast."

This brief account of the medieval regret for life is intended to convey the subtle ambivalence of a popular and traditional feeling about death, which was immediately betrayed by the expressions of scholarly cultures: the *contemptus mundi* of medieval spirituality and the Socratic detachment or stoical acceptance of the Renaissance.

Naturally, the dying man feels sad about the loss of his life, the things he has possessed, and the people he has loved. But his regret never goes beyond a level of intensity that is very slight in terms of the emotional climate of this age. The same will be true of other periods, such as the baroque, that were also given to inflated expression.

Thus, regret for life goes hand in hand with a simple acceptance of imminent death. It bespeaks a familiarity with death, a relationship that will remain constant throughout the ages.

Achilles did not fear death either, but in the underworld, his shade complained, "I would rather be a stable boy and work for a poor farmer than reign over the dead."

Attachment to a miserable life is inseparable from familiarity with a death that is never far away.

"In cares and pains . . . he lived all his life," says the peasant in Guyot Marchant's fifteenth-century *Danse Macabre*. [18]

> *Many long for death.*
> *Not I! Come wind or rain,*
> *I would rather be*
> *Back in the vineyard again.*

But regret does not inspire him to an act of rebellion. When the woodcutter in La Fontaine's *Fables* "calls for death, it comes without delay." But only to help him load his wood.

The wretch who "called out every day / for death to come his way" sends it back when it arrives: "Come no nearer, O death! O death, leave me alone."

Either "Death comes to cure all our ills" or "It is better to suffer than to die": Here are two statements that are really more complementary than contradictory, two sides of the same coin. The regret for life removes the forced and rhetorical quality that the acceptance of death has in the ethical maxims of scholars.

La Fontaine's peasant would like to avoid death, of course, and since he is an old fool, he even tries to outwit it. But once he realizes that the end is really near, that there is no doubt about it, he stops playing the part of someone who is holding on to life, a part he had to play in order to live, and immediately goes over to the side of death. He adopts the classical attitude of one dying. He gathers his children around his bed for his last instructions and his last farewells, just like all the old people he has seen die.

> *My dear children, he says, I am going to our fathers.*
> *Good-bye, promise me that you will live like brothers.*
> *He takes each one by the hand, and dies.*

He dies like the knight in the *Chanson,* or like those peasants in the heart of Russia whom Solzhenitsyn describes in *The Cancer Ward:* "But now, pacing the ward, he recalled how those old people had died in their villages along the Kama River—whether they were Russians, Tartars, or Udmurts. They did not bluster, fight back or boast that they would never die. They took death *calmly.* Far from postponing the final reckoning, they got ready, little by little, and in good time decided who was to get the mare and who the foal, who the homespun coat and who the boots, then they passed on peaceably, as if simply moving to another cottage."[19]

The death of the medieval knight has the same simplicity. The baron is brave and fights like a hero, with herculean strength and incredible exploits, but his death is in no way heroic or extraordinary; it is just like anyone else's death.

After the regret for life, the dying man of the Middle Ages goes on to perform the customary rites: He asks forgiveness of his friends, takes his leave of them, and commends them to God. Oliver asks Roland to forgive him for any wrongs he may have done him unknowingly: " 'I forgive you here and before God.' As he said these words, they bowed to each other."

Ywain forgives his murderer, Gawain, who slew him without recognizing him: "Fair sir, it is by the will of the Savior and for my sins that you have slain me, and I forgive you gladly."

Gawain is himself killed by Lancelot in fair combat, and he says to King Arthur before he dies: "Dear uncle, I am dying. Send word to Lancelot that I salute him and that I beg him to come and visit my grave after I am dead."

Then the dying man commends all those who are dear to him to God. "May God bless Charles and dear France," prays Oliver, "and above all, Roland, my friend." King Ban commits his wife, Hélène, to God: "Give counsel to her who is bereft." For was it not the worst misfortune to be deprived of counsel, the greatest misery to be alone? "Lord, may you remember my poor son, who is orphaned so young, for you alone can sustain the fatherless."

In the Arthurian cycle we even find an element that is later to become one of the dominant motifs of the will: choice of burial. This was of no interest to Roland and his companions. But Gawain says to the king: "Sire, I ask that I be buried in Saint Stephen's Church in Camelot, beside my brothers . . . and that you have inscribed on my tombstone . . ." Also, in the cycle: "Dear lord, the Maid who never lied asked before she died, . . . I pray you, do not bury my body in this country." So she was laid in a boat without sails or oars.

After his farewell to the world, the dying man commends his soul to God. In the *Chanson de Roland,* where the last prayer is reported at length, it consists of two parts. First comes the confession. Roland prays, "God, forgive me by your grace for my sins, the great and the small, which I have committed from the hour I was born until this day that I have been slain." Archbishop Turpin "made his confession. He raised his eyes to heaven, clasped his hands together, and lifted them up. He prayed to God to grant him paradise." Oliver "confessed his sins out loud, with his hands clasped together and lifted to heaven, and prayed to God that he be granted paradise." This is the prayer of the penitent, the barons to whom Turpin granted a collective absolution, saying, "Confess your sins out loud."

The second part of the last prayer is the *Commendatio Animae.* This is a very old prayer of the early Church, which was handed down through the ages and which gave its name to that category of prayers known until the eighteenth century as Commendations. We find it in abridged form on the lips of Roland: "My true Father, you who never lie, you who raised Lazarus from the dead, you who saved Daniel from the lions, save my soul from all dangers and from the sins I have committed in my life." When King Ban addresses himself to God, his prayer is composed like a liturgical orison: "I thank you, dear Father, that it pleases you that I end my life in indigence and want, for you too have suffered poverty. Lord, who came to redeem me with your blood, do not forget the soul you placed in me, but help me."

In the stories of the Round Table, the arrangements regarding survivors and choice of burial are more precise than in the *Chanson de Roland.*

The prayers, however, were often omitted and replaced with such statements as "He confessed his sins to a monk and received the *corpus Domini.*" Two elements are conspicuous by their absence. There is never any mention of Extreme Unction, which was reserved for the clergy, and no special invocation is addressed to the Virgin Mary. The complete *Ave Maria* did not yet exist.

The acts performed by the dying man, once he has been warned that his end is near, have a ceremonial, ritual quality. We recognize these acts as the still-oral source for what later became the medieval testament, which was required by the Church as a part of the last sacrament: the profession of faith, the confession of sins, the pardon of the survivors, the pious dispositions on their behalf, the commendation of one's soul to God, the choice of burial. The written will seems merely to have formalized and rendered obligatory the instructions and prayers that the epic poets showed as spontaneous impulses on the part of the dying.

After the last prayer, nothing remains but to wait for death, which now has no further reason to delay. It was believed that the human will had the power to gain a few extra moments.

Thus, Tristan struggled to give Isolde time to arrive. When he saw that it was hopeless, he stopped fighting: " 'I cannot hold on to my life any longer.' He repeated three times, 'Isolde, my love.' The fourth time, he gave up the ghost." In the *Chanson*, no sooner had Oliver finished his prayer than "his heart failed, and he fell on the ground. The count died without further delay." If death is slower in coming, the dying man waits in silence; he has no further communication with the world: "He said [his last instructions, his last prayers] and never breathed another word."

The Public Aspect of Death

Familiar simplicity is one of the two essential characteristics of this death. The other is its public aspect, which is to last until the end of the nineteenth century. The dying person must be the center of a group of people. Mme. de Montespan was less afraid of dying than she was of dying *alone*. Saint-Simon describes how "she lay in bed with all her bed-curtains open, candles all around the room, and women keeping vigil around her. She kept waking them up every few minutes; she wanted to find them chatting, primping, or eating, so she could be sure they would not doze off." But on May 27, 1707, when she realized that she was about to die, she was no longer afraid. She summoned all her servants, "down to the lowest one," asked their forgiveness, confessed her sins, and presided, as was the custom, over the ceremony of her own death.[20]

The hygienically minded doctors of the late eighteenth century who took part in the investigations of Vicq d'Azyr and of the Academy of Medicine began to complain about the number of people who invaded the bedrooms of the dying.[21] Their efforts did not meet with much success, for in the early nineteenth century, when the last sacrament was being taken to a sick man, anyone could come into the house and into the bedroom, even if he was a stranger to the family. The pious Mme. de La Ferronays was walking in the streets of Ischl during the 1830s when she heard the church bell and learned that the holy sacrament was about to be administered to a young priest whom she knew to be sick. She had not dared to visit him yet, because she had not met him, but the holy sacrament "brought me there *quite naturally* [italics added]. I knelt down by the main entrance along with everyone else, while the priests went by. Then I went upstairs and watched while he received the last sacrament and Extreme Unction."[22]

Death was always public. Hence the profound significance of Pascal's remark that one dies alone, for at that time one was never physically alone at the moment of death. Today his statement has lost its impact, for one has a very good chance of literally dying alone, in a hospital room.

Some Modern Survivals

Although this simple and public way of leaving after saying good-bye to everyone has become exceptional in our age, it has not completely disappeared. I was surprised to encounter it in the literature of the twentieth century, and not in far-off and still-holy Russia, but in England. In her book about the psychology of mourning, Lily Pincus begins by describing the deaths of her husband, Fritz, and her mother-in-law.

Fritz, who must have been between sixty and seventy years old, was suffering from a cancer that was already very far advanced. He realized it at once. He refused to have the operation and the elaborate, heroic treatments and chose to remain at home. "I had," his wife writes, "the overwhelming experience of life being enhanced by the acceptance of death."

> When Fritz's last night came, he made sure that I shared with him the full awareness of it, and when I could give him this assurance, he said with a smile, "Then all is well." He died a few hours later in complete peace. The night nurse, who had kept watch with me, had mercifully left the room to make her breakfast, so that I was

alone with Fritz in his last, peaceful hour, for which I shall be eternally grateful.

This account of a "perfect death" reveals a romantic sensibility that was not customarily expressed before the eighteenth century.

The death of Fritz's mother, on the other hand, is more consistent with the ancient traditional model. She was an old Victorian lady, superficial and conventional, somewhat frivolous, incapable of doing anything by herself. Suddenly she was stricken with cancer of the stomach, a cruel illness that put her into situations that would have been humiliating for anyone, for she lost control of her bodily functions, without ever ceasing to be the "perfect lady." She did not seem to be aware of what was happening to her. Her son worried about her and wondered how this woman, who had never been capable of facing the least difficulty in her life, would be able to face her death. He was mistaken. The helpless old lady knew exactly how to take command of her own death.

> On the day before her seventieth birthday she had a stroke and was unconscious for a few hours. When she awoke, she asked to be sat up in bed, and then with the most lovely smile and shining eyes demanded to see all the different people in the house. She said good-bye to each individually as if she were going on a long journey, with thank-you messages for friends and relatives and all who had cared for her. She remembered especially all the children who had given her pleasure. When after nearly an hour of this "reception" her strength left her, Fritz and I stayed on with her alone until she bade us farewell most lovingly and said, "Now let me sleep."

But since this was the middle of the twentieth century, the dying person could no longer be sure of being left in peace. Half an hour later the doctor arrived, asked after his patient, and flew into a rage, ignoring the explanations of Fritz and his wife that the old lady had said her last farewells and had asked to be left alone. Angrily he rushed into her room, hypodermic needle in hand, and bent over the sick woman to give her an injection. But just then the woman, who had seemed to be unconscious, "opened her eyes and with the same brilliant smile with which she had said good-bye to us, put her thin arms around his neck and whispered, 'Thank you, Professor.' Tears sprang to the doctor's eyes, and there was no further mention of an injection. He left us as a friend and ally, and his patient continued the peaceful sleep from which she did not awake."[23]

The familiarity and public quality of death is expressed in a proverbial statement that we have already encountered and that has its source in Scripture. Pierre-Henri Simon, recalling a scene from his youth, relates this attempt at humor on the part of his professor, Bellesoort: "I can still hear him, in the honors class in Louis XIV, reading us Bossuet: 'We all die, said that woman whose wisdom Solomon praises in the Book of Kings.' He let his big hand fall on the desk, paused for effect, and remarked, 'She was quite an original thinker, that woman.' "[24]

Bossuet still understood the meaning and importance of the idea that "we all die" within the context of his age. But Bellesoort and his student, despite their education and goodwill, found it pompous and trite. This lack of understanding, which is no longer a novelty, points up the difference between two attitudes toward death. In the poem about Tristan, when Rohalt comes to console Queen Blanchefleur for the loss of her lord, he says, "Is it not true that all who are born must die? May God receive the dead and preserve the living!"

In the Spanish *romancero* of Count Alarcos, which is more traditional, the countess, who has been unjustly sentenced by her husband to be executed, says the words and prayers that prepare one for death. But before the lament of regret for life ("I am sorry for my children, who will be deprived of my company"), she repeats the formula "I am not sorry to die, *since I had to die sometime.*"[25] In another *romancero*, Durandal, fatally wounded, cries, "I am dying in this battle. I am not sorry to meet my death [understood: since we all die], although it comes early. But I am sorry to leave [the regret for life] . . ."[26]

In "The Death of Ivan Ilyich," published in 1886, Tolstoi revives the old idea of the Russian peasants and contrasts it with the more modern ideas that have since been adopted by the upper classes.

Ivan Ilyich is very sick. He is beginning to think he may be dying, but his wife, his doctor, and his family tacitly conspire to deceive him about the gravity of his condition and treat him like a child. "Gerasim was the only one who did not lie." Gerasim is a young servant fresh from the country, and still close to his peasant and rural origins. "It was clear that he was the only one who understood what was happening and did not find it necessary to conceal it. He simply felt sorry for his weak and emaciated master." He is not afraid to show him this pity by performing quite naturally the disagreeable services that very sick people require. One day Ivan Ilyich, touched by his devotion, insists that he take a little rest, go away for a change. Whereupon Gerasim replies, as Rohalt had answered Queen Blanchefleur, "We all die. Why not take a little trouble?" Tolstoi comments, "Gerasim shows that he did not mind this work precisely because he was doing it for a dying man and hoped that when his own time came, someone would do the same for him."

Russia must be a museum, for the proverbial saying reappears in a wonderful story that Isaac Babel wrote in 1920. In a Jewish village in the Odessa region, during the carnival, six weddings were being celebrated at the same time. There was a big party with eating, drinking, and dancing. A widow, Gaza, half-whore, dances wildly, letting down her hair, beating time on the wall with a stick. " 'We are all mortal,' whispered Gaza as she swung her stick." Another day, Gaza walks into the office of the secretary of the executive committee for collectivization, a solemn and conscientious man. She considers trying to seduce him but realizes that it would be wasted effort. Before she leaves, she asks him, in her proverbial manner, why he is always so serious. "Why are you afraid of death? . . . Have you ever heard of a *muzhik* who refused to die?"[27]

In Gaza's primitive code, the idea "we all die" is either an expression of her *joie de vivre* in the intoxication of the dance and the feast or a mark of indifference to tomorrow, an affirmation of living in the moment. According to this code, the fear of death stands for the spirit of caution and organization, a rational and deliberate conception of the world—in short, the modern conception.

By virtue of its familiarity, the idea of death came to be associated in common parlance with the elemental and unthinking life.

Pascal wrote that it "is easier to endure death without thinking about it than the thought of death without the danger of dying." There are two ways of not thinking about death: the way of our technological civilization, which denies death and refuses to talk about it; and the way of traditional civilizations, which is not a denial but a recognition of the *impossibility of thinking about it directly or for very long* because death is too close and too much a part of daily life.

Death as Sleep

The distance between death and life was not traditionally perceived as a "radical metamorphosis," to use Vladimir Jankélévitch's phrase. Nor was it the violent transgression that Georges Bataille compared to that other transgression, the sexual act. The idea of an absolute negativity, a sudden, irrevocable plunge into an abyss without memory, did not exist. Nor did people experience an existential disorientation or anxiety, at least these did not figure in the stereotyped images of death. But neither did they believe in an afterlife that would be a simple continuation of the life that had gone before. It is worth noting that the solemn last farewells of Roland and Oliver make no allusion to some heavenly reunion. Once the period of mourning was over, the other was quickly forgotten. Death is a passing over, an *inter-itus.* Better than any historian, the philosopher Jankélévitch has grasped this quality, which is so contrary to his own convictions. The deceased glides into a world "that differs from this one only in its diminished intensity."[28]

Indeed, Oliver and Roland say good-bye as if each were about to fall into a long sleep of indefinite duration. The belief that the dead are asleep is ancient and constant. As early as the Homeric Hades, the dead, a "dim multitude," "unfeeling phantoms of exhausted humans," "are sleeping the sleep of death." Virgil's underworld is also a "kingdom of shadows," the "abode of sleep," shadows, and "sleep-inducing night." In the place comparable to the Christian paradise, where the happiest shades repose, the light is purple, that is, the color of twilight.

Ovid relates that on the day of the Feralia, the Day of the Dead, the Romans sacrificed to Tacita, the mute goddess, a fish with its mouth sewn shut, an allusion to the silence that reigned among the Manes, or spirits of the departed. This was also the day on which offerings were taken to the graves, for at certain times and in certain places, the dead emerged from their sleep like the unclear images of a dream and sometimes troubled the living.

However, it almost seems as if even the exhausted shades of paganism are a little more animated than the Christian sleepers of the first centuries after Christ. Of course, the latter can also wander invisibly among the living, and we have seen that they appear to those who are about to die. But early Christianity tended to exaggerate the hypnotic insensibility of the dead to the point of unconsciousness, no doubt because their sleep was merely a period of waiting for a blissful awakening on the day of the resurrection of the flesh (see chapters 3 and 5).

Saint Paul teaches the Corinthians that the dead Christ rose and appeared to more than five hundred brothers: Some are still alive; however, others have gone to sleep—*"quidam autem dormierunt"* (1 Cor. 15:6).

Saint Stephen, the first martyr, was stoned to death. The Acts of the Apostles tells us that he fell asleep in the Lord—*"obdormivit in Domino"* (7:60). In inscriptions next to the *hic jacet* (here lies), which one finds much later in the French form *ci-gît*, one often reads *hic pausat, hic requiescit, hic dormit,* or *requiescit in isto tumolo* (here rests or sleeps or in this grave rests). Saint Radegonde asked that her body be buried "in the basilica, where many of our sisters are also buried, in perfect or imperfect repose." It was impossible to guarantee the quality of the sleep in advance.[29]

The medieval and Gallican liturgies, which would be replaced in the Carolingian age by the Roman liturgy, mention the *nomina pausantium* (the names of those who sleep) and invite the faithful to pray *"pro spiritibus pausantium"* (for the souls of those who sleep). The Extreme Unction reserved for the clergy in the Middle Ages was called the *dormientium exitium* (the sacrament of those who sleep).

There is no better illustration of the belief in the sleep of the dead than the legend of the Seven Sleepers of Ephesus. It was so widespread that we encounter it in Gregory of Tours, Paul Diacre, and again, in the thirteenth century, in Jacobus of Varagine.

The bodies of the seven martyrs, who were victims of the persecution of Decius, were placed in a sealed grotto. The popular version of the legend has it that they stayed there for three hundred and seventy-seven years, but Jacobus of Varagine, who knows his chronology, points out that if you add it up, they could not have slept more than one hundred and ninety-six.

Be that as it may, at the time of Theodosus a heresy began to circulate that denied the resurrection of the dead. To confound the heretics, God caused the seven martyrs to rise from the grave; in other words, he woke them up. "The saints rose and greeted each other, thinking they had been asleep for only one night." In fact, they had slept for several centuries, and one of their number, who went into town, found that it had changed completely from the Ephesus of his day. The emperor, the bishops, and the priests were informed of the miracle and joined the throng around the burial cave to see and hear the Seven Sleepers. One of the saints became inspired and explained the reason for their resurrection. "Believe us, it is for your sake that God has raised us up before the day of the great resurrection . . . for we have really been raised from the dead, and we are alive. *For even as the child lives in his mother's belly without feeling any needs, so have we been living, resting, and sleeping, without experiencing any sensations!'* After he had said these words, the seven men laid their heads on the ground and went to sleep, giving up their spirits according to the will of God."[30]

The idea of death as a state of dormancy has resisted centuries of suppression by the literati as we shall see in chapter 5. It is found in the liturgy and in funerary art. It sometimes occurs in wills. In 1559 a priest of Paris contrasted the idea of the *umbra mortis*, the shadow of death, with the *placidam ac quietam mansionem,* the house of repose.[31] And right up to our time, the prayers for the dead would be said for the *repose* of their souls. The idea of sleep is the most ancient, the most popular, and the most constant image of the beyond. Even today it has not yet disappeared, despite competition from other kinds of images.

In a Flower Garden

If the dead slept, it was usually in a garden full of flowers. "May God receive all our souls among his holy flowers," Turpin asks God over the bodies of the barons. Similarly, Roland prays that "he will let them lie in holy flowers." This verse contains both aspects of the state that followed death: lying down, or the sleep without sensation; and holy flowers, or the garden in bloom. The paradise of Turpin and Roland (at least this image of it, for there were others) differs little, except for the presence of light, from the "cool meadows" of Virgil's Elysium, "watered by streams," or from the garden that the Koran promised to believers.

In Homer's Hades, on the other hand, there was neither garden nor flowers. Hades—at least the Hades of Book XI of the *Odyssey*—also lacks the punishments that later, in the *Aeneid*, foreshadow the Christian hell. The distance between the underworlds of Homer and Virgil is greater than the distance between Virgil's underworld and the earliest figurations of the Christian afterlife. Dante and the Middle Ages were not mistaken about this.

In the *Credo* of the old Roman Canon of the Mass, hell refers to the traditional abode of the dead, a place of waiting rather than of punishment. There the just or the redeemed of the Old Testament waited until Christ, after his death, came to deliver or awaken them. It was not until later, when the idea of judgment became predominant, that the underworld became for a whole culture what it had been only in isolated cases, the kingdom of Satan and the eternal residence of the damned.[32]

The Prayer Book of Serapion, a Greco-Egyptian liturgical text of the middle of the fourth century, contains this prayer for the dead: "May his spirit rest in a green and tranquil place."

In the apocryphal Acts of Paul and Thecla, "the heaven that is the resting place of the just" is described as "a place of refreshment, satiety, and joy." It is the *refrigerium*. *Refrigerium* or *refrigere* is used in place of *requies* or *requiescire*. "*Refrigeret nos qui omnia potes!*" (Give us refreshment, thou who canst do all things) reads an inscription in Marseille that may date from the end of the second century.

In the Vulgate, the Wisdom of Solomon (4:7) refers to paradise as *refrigerium:* "*Justus, si morte preoccupatus fuerit, in refrigerio erit*" (The good man, if he was mindful of death, will be in paradise). The word is still used in the same sense in the old Canon of the Roman Mass, in the Memento of the Dead: "*in locum refrigerii, lucis et pacis*" (in a cool place, full of light and peace). The French versions have omitted the image, because according to the translators the idea of coolness does not have the same appeal in the north as it had in the east and in the Mediterranean. I grant that in the urban societies of today, we prefer the warmth of the sun to the coolness of the shade. But by the time of Saint Louis, a pious hermit of Picardy was already contrasting the "dark valley and winter" of this world with the "bright mountain" and "beautiful summer" of paradise.

Paradise ceased to be a cool garden of flowers when a purified Christianity revolted against these sensuous images and found them superstitious. They took refuge among American blacks. The films inspired by Negroes show heaven as a green pasture or a field of white snow.

The word *refrigerium* has still another meaning. It referred to the commemorative meal that the first Christians took on the graves of the martyrs and the offerings they left there. Thus, Saint Monica brought gruel, bread, and wine "to the tombs of the saints, according to the custom of Africa." This act of devotion, which was inspired by pagan practices, was prohibited by Saint Ambrose and replaced by eucharistic services. It has been retained in the Eastern Christian church, and traces of it remain in our folklore. It is curious that the same word signified both the resting place of the blessed and the ritual meal offered at their graves.[33]

The reclining attitude of a guest at a Roman banquet is the one that the Vulgate (Matt. 8:11) attributes to the blessed: *"Dico autem vobis quod multi ab oriente et occidente venient et recumbent cum Abraham et Isaac et Jacob in regno coelorum"* (Moreover, I say to you that many come from both east and west and recline with Abraham and Isaac and Jacob in the kingdom of heaven).

Thus, we find that the words designating paradise are related to three ideas: the cool garden, the funereal rest, and the eschatological feast.

But medieval iconography has shown little liking for these symbols. After the twelfth century it has preferred the throne or the bosom of Abraham.

The throne undoubtedly has its source in Oriental imagery, but it has been transposed into a feudal court. In the paradise of Roland, the dead are "sitting." The bosom of Abraham occurs more frequently. It often adorned the outside wall of the church, the one that looked onto the cemetery. The dead buried there would one day be held like children on the knees of Abraham. Indeed, writers like Honorius of Autun regarded the cemetery *ad sanctos* as the bosom of the Church, into which the bodies of men are entrusted for safekeeping until the Last Day and which holds them like Abraham in his bosom.

The image of the garden full of flowers, although rare, is not altogether unknown; it reappears occasionally in Renaissance paintings, in which the blessed stroll two by two in the cool shade of a wonderful orchard.

But the most widespread and persistent image of paradise is that of the recumbent figure of funerary art, the *requiescens* (see chapter 5).

Resignation to the Inevitable

A study of the legal documents of the late seventeenth century reveals that the popular conception of death was marked by the same compound of indifference, resignation, familiarity, and lack of privacy that we have found in other sources. What Nicole Castan wrote about death in connection with the criminal procedures of the Parliament of Toulouse can be applied equally well to the Middle Ages or to rural Russia in the twentieth century:

"The man of the seventeenth century exhibits a lesser degree of sensitivity [than that of our own] and demonstrates in torture and death a resignation and endurance that we would find astonishing. It may be because of the formality of the official records, but never does a condemned prisoner show any particular attachment to life or express a reluctance to die." This is not for lack of facility with words: "One notes that these people are very skilled in conveying the fascination of money and wealth." But in spite of this love for material things, the criminal "generally is more afraid of the beyond than he is attached to this world."

"The dying man gives the impression that he accepts his fate."[34]

It is illuminating to compare Mlle. Castan's observations on executions in the south of France in the seventeenth century with an account of a hanging in the American South at the end of the nineteenth century.

In *Outre-Mer*, Paul Bourget tells how he happened to witness this incident in the course of a trip to the United States in 1890. A young black man had been sentenced to be hanged. He was the servant of a Mr. Scott, an ex-colonel from the North who had settled in Georgia and to whom Bourget had been introduced. Bourget arrives at the jail and finds the prisoner eating. "I couldn't take my eyes off this criminal who was about to die, whom I had seen defending his life with stubborn courage, and who was now munching the fried fish of this final meal with obvious relish." The condemned man is next handed "the uniform of execution," a new shirt. "He shivered slightly at the contact of the cool fabric, a mark of nervous sensitivity that made the courage this boy of twenty-six displayed in the face of these preparations even more impressive." His former master, Colonel Scott, asks to be alone with him for a few minutes, to prepare him for death and to play the role of confessor that the mendicant friar played in the seventeenth century. They kneel and recite the Lord's Prayer together, and Bourget makes this comment on the scene: "The physical and almost animal courage [he does not understand the immemorial resignation in the face of death] that he had shown by eating with such a hearty appetite was suddenly ennobled by a touch of the ideal." Bourget does not realize that there is no difference between the two attitudes that he contrasts. He was expecting either rebellion or a big emotional scene, but what he observes is indifference. "I thought about the amazing indifference with which this half-breed let go of life, a life that he cared about, since he was sensual and vigorous. I said to myself, 'What an irony that a man of this sort . . . should instinctively arrive at what philosophy regards as the ultimate goal of its teaching: resignation to the inevitable.' "

At the sight of the gallows, Seymour, the condemned man, drops the cigar he has saved. "This nervous gesture was the only sign that he was having an emotional reaction. He mastered it immediately, for as he mounted the wooden steps, his bare feet did not tremble. His manner was so calm, so natural, so completely dignified, even before the horror of his punishment, that silence fell among those coarse spectators." Just before the hanging, his face was covered with a black cloth, and Colonel Scott, still in his role of confessor, made him repeat some pious invocations. "Lord, remember me in your kingdom," repeated the half-breed in his drawling voice. Then after a pause, "I'm all right now," and very firmly, "Good-bye, captain . . . good-bye, everybody": the last farewell.[35]

The best comment on this scene is Nicole Castan's remark, quoted above: "The dying man gives the impression that he accepts his fate."

The Tame Death

The fact that we keep meeting instances of the same general attitude toward death from Homer to Tolstoi does not mean we should assign it a structural permanence that is exempt from historical variations. Many other elements have overlaid this fundamental and ancient background. But it has resisted the pressures of evolution for about two thousand years. In a world subject to change, the traditional attitude toward death is like a bulwark of inertia and continuity.

It has by now been so obliterated from our culture that it is hard for us to imagine or understand it. The ancient attitude in which death is close and familiar yet diminished and desensitized is too different from our own view, in which it is so terrifying that we no longer dare say its name.

Thus, when we call this familiar death the tame death, we do not mean that it was once wild and that it was later domesticated. On the contrary, we mean that it has become wild today when it used to be tame. The tame death is the oldest death there is.[36]

2

Place of Burial

In the last chapter, we noted the persistence of an attitude toward death that remained almost unchanged for thousands of years, an attitude that expressed a naïve and spontaneous acceptance of destiny and nature. This attitude toward death had its counterpart in one toward the dead that expressed the same unconcerned familiarity with the places and artifacts of burial. This mentality is peculiar to a well-defined period of history. It appears clearly around the fifth century A.D., which was very different from the centuries that preceded it, and disappears at the end of the eighteenth century without leaving any traces in the customs of today. Hence, its term —long, but clearly circumscribed—falls within the interminable reign of the phenomenon we have characterized as "the tame death."

It begins with the rapprochement between the living and the dead, the invasion of the towns and villages by cemeteries, which were henceforth surrounded by the habitations of men. It ends when this promiscuity was no longer tolerated.

The Protection of the Saint

In spite of their familiarity with death, the ancients feared the proximity of the dead and kept them out of the way. They honored their burial places, partly because they feared the return of the dead. The reverence they showed to tombs and to the Manes was designed to prevent the dead from "coming back" and bothering the living. Whether they were buried or cremated, the dead were impure; if they were too near, there was danger of their contaminating the living. In order to avoid all contact, the abode of the dead had to be separated from the domain of the living, except on the days of propitiatory sacrifices; this was an unbreakable rule. The law of the Twelve Tables stipulated "that no dead body be buried or cremated inside the city." The stipulation was repeated in the Theodosian Code, which ordained that all mortal remains must be removed from Constantinople: "All bodies contained in urns or sarcophagi on the ground must be removed and left outside the city."[1]

In the words of the jurist Paul, "No dead body may be left in the city, lest the *sacra* of the city be defiled."[2] *Ne funestentur*—"defiled" by death: the word clearly expressed the intolerance of the living. *Funestus*, which is the root of the weaker French word *funeste* (deadly, fatal, baneful), did not originally mean profanation in general but specifically the kind caused by a corpse. *Funestus* comes from *funus*, which means "funeral service," "corpse," and "murder."

This explains why the cemeteries of antiquity were always outside the towns, along roads like the Appian Way in Rome. They were either family vaults constructed on private estates or communal cemeteries owned and managed by associations that may have provided the early Christians with the legal model for their communities.[3]

In the beginning, the Christians observed the customs of their times and shared the prevailing attitudes toward the dead. At first they were buried in the same necropolises as the pagans, then next to the pagans in separate cemeteries, but always outside the towns.

Saint John Chrysostom shared the aversion of the ancients to contact with the dead. In one of his homilies, he calls for a return to the traditional custom. "Take care that no sepulcher be built in town. What would you do if someone were to leave a corpse in the place where you eat and sleep? And yet you leave the dead *(animam mortuam)* not where you eat and sleep but next to the body of Christ. . . . How can one visit the churches of God, the holy temples, when they are filled with such a terrible odor?"[4]

As late as 563 we find traces of this attitude in a canon of the Council of Braga forbidding burial in the basilicas of the holy martyrs: "One cannot refuse to the basilicas of the holy martyrs the privilege that the towns retain inviolably for themselves, of allowing no one to be buried inside their walls."[5]

But this aversion to the proximity of the dead soon gave way among the early Christians, first in Africa and later in Rome. The change is remarkable, for it reflects a profound difference between the old pagan attitude and the new Christian attitude toward the dead, a difference that existed in spite of their mutual acceptance of the tame death. Henceforth and for a long time to come—until the eighteenth century—the dead ceased to frighten the living, and the two groups coexisted in the same places and behind the same walls.

How did people move so quickly from the old repugnance to the new familiarity? Through faith in the resurrection of the body, combined with worship of the ancient martyrs and their tombs.

Things might have proceeded otherwise; some of the early Christians, in order to show their rejection of pagan superstition and their joy in returning to God, attached no importance to the place of their burial. They believed that the pagan worship of tombs was in opposition to the fundamental dogma of the resurrection of the flesh. Saint Ignatius of Antioch hoped that the wild animals would leave nothing of his body.[6] Anchorites in the Egyptian desert asked that their bodies be left unburied and exposed to the voracity of dogs and wolves or to the charity of the stranger who might happen upon them by accident.

"I found a cave," writes one of these monks, "and before going inside, I knocked according to the custom of the brothers." Since there was no answer, he went in and saw a seated monk, who did not speak. "I reached out my hand and touched his arm; it crumbled into dust in my hand. I felt his body, and realized that he was dead. . . . So I got up and prayed, covering the body with my cloak. I dug a hole in the ground and buried him, and left."[7]

Centuries later, Jean de Joinville and Saint Louis, returning from the Crusades, made a similar discovery on the island of Lampedusa. They came upon an abandoned hermitage. "The king and I walked to the end of the garden. Under the first arch we saw a whitewashed chapel and a red earthen cross. We walked under the second arch and found two human bodies whose flesh was all rotted away. The ribs still hung together and the bones of the hands were joined on the breast. They were lying facing the east, in the manner in which bodies are laid in the ground."[8]

This minimal concern for burial might have proved sufficient, and it is true that the Eastern monks, the heirs of the desert hermits, have always professed indifference to the fate of their final remains. In the West, however, the ascetic contempt for the body, living or dead, dis played by cenobites, did not become popular with Christian people as a whole, who were inclined to reconcile the new faith in the resurrection with the traditional worship of tombs. But this reconciliation did not serve to reinforce the ancient fear of the dead; on the contrary, it led to a familiarity that eventually, in the eighteenth century, bordered on indifference.

Christian popular eschatology began by accommodating itself to the old beliefs about the earth. A great many people were convinced that on the Last Day only those individuals would arise who had received a decent burial and whose graves had not been violated: "He who goes unburied shall not rise from the dead." The fear of not rising from the dead was the Christian equivalent of the ancestral fear of dying without burial.[9]

According to Tertullian, only the martyrs, by virtue of their blood, possessed "the sole key to paradise." "No one earns the right of dwelling with the Lord simply by the fact of leaving his body."[10] The dead were waiting for the Day of Judgment, like the Seven Sleepers of Ephesus. Deprived of sensation and memory by the loss of their bodies, they were incapable of feeling either pleasure or pain. Not until the Last Day would the "saints," who had been promised eternal bliss, emerge from the "lower regions" and occupy their celestial abode. Everyone else was condemned to an eternal sleep; the wicked would not rise from the dead. The standard language of curses threatened the damned person with the worst punishment; they deprived him of his resurrection: "He will not arise on the Day of Judgment."

It was popularly believed that violation of the grave jeopardized the awakening of the deceased on the Last Day and consequently his eternal life: "May this sepulcher never at any time be violated, but may it be preserved until the end of the world, so that I may return to life *sine impedimentum* when He comes who is to judge the living and the dead."[11]

Ecclesiastical writers who were more enlightened insisted that the power of God is just as capable of restoring bodies that have been destroyed as it is of creating them in the first place, but their efforts were in vain. They did not succeed in convincing the people, who had a very vivid sense of the unity and continuity of the individual and did not distinguish the soul from the body or the glorified body from the fleshly one. It is possible, therefore, as Dom Leclercq suggests in his article on *ad sanctos* in the *Dictionnaire d'archéologie chrétienne,* that the fear of violation is at the bottom of the custom, which later became widespread, of burying the dead near the tombs of the martyrs. The martyrs were the only ones among the saints (that is, the believers) whose immediate admission into paradise could be depended upon; they would keep watch over the bodies and drive away those who would profane them.

However, burial *ad sanctos*—that is, near the tombs of the martyrs— had another motive. It is clear that the fear of violation that was so keen during the first centuries abated relatively soon, that is, by the early Middle Ages. The fact of the matter is that it no longer had an economic motive; after that, there was nothing to attract looters to the sarcophagi, which no longer contained anything of value. But the fear had also lost its spiritual motive. As long as the bodies remained under the protection of the venerated saint and within the sacred confines of the church, whatever changes might affect them were no longer of any importance. Indeed, how many times would they be "violated," so to speak, by being removed from their original places by the priests themselves, often quite unceremoniously, but without being profaned, since they remained on church land?

The primary motive for burial *ad sanctos* was to obtain the protection of the martyr, not just for the physical body of the deceased but for his whole being, on the Day of Awakening and Judgment.

The Faubourg Around the Cemetery

Religious writers were convinced of the fortunate effects of the physical proximity of the bodies of the faithful to that of the martyr. Maximus of Turin explains, "The martyrs protect us while we live in our bodies and take care of us after we have left our bodies. Here they keep us from falling into sin; there they protect us from the horrors of hell—*inferni horror*. That is why our ancestors took care to place our bodies near the bones of the martyrs. Tartarus fears them, and we escape punishment; Christ illuminates them, and his light drives away the shadows."[12]

The same language often appears in the inscriptions on tombstones. For example, this one on the tomb of a subdeacon: "May the man whose bones lie in this tomb, who deserved to be buried near the sepulchers of the saints, be spared the furies of Tartarus and the cruelty of its torments." Or this one, dated 515, from the tomb of a rich Viennois Christian: "Only under the protection of the martyrs may we look for eternal rest. May the very holy Vincent and the saints his companions and peers watch over this place and drive away the shadows by shedding the light of true light *(lumen de lumine vero)*."[13]

Saint Paulinus had the body of his son Celsus taken to the graves of the martyrs of Aecola, in Spain: "We have sent him to the town of Complutum so that he may lie with the martyrs in the union of the grave, and so that from the blood of the saints he may draw that virtue that refines our souls like fire."[14] We see here that the saints not only grant protection from the creatures of Tartarus, they also communicate to the deceased who is associated with them a little of their virtue, and postmortem, redeem his sins.

Countless inscriptions from the sixth to the eighth centuries repeat the same set phrases: "who deserved to be associated with the sepulchers of the saints," "resting in peace and in the company of the martyrs," "he was laid to rest *ad sanctos*," or "*inter sanctos*." A few are more specific: "at the feet of Saint Martin." Other phrases have become so commonplace that we no longer recognize their original meaning: "*in loco sancto*," "*huic sancto loco sepultus*."[15]

Thus, the tombs of the martyrs attracted other graves, and since the martyrs had usually been buried in the communal cemeteries outside the towns and cities, the old pagan burial grounds provided Christianity with its most ancient and venerated sites.

The custom is generally believed to have originated in Africa and spread to Spain and Rome, and in fact it is in Africa that archaeologists have discovered its earliest manifestations.

The juxtaposition of cemeteries and peripheral churches is obvious to the most casual visitor in all the recent diggings, wherever the ancient site has been completely uncovered and modern towns have not concealed it.

Martyria or *memoriae* were first built on the sites of revered tombs in the cemeteries beyond the walls. Later, a basilica was built next to or in place of the chapel. One often finds that these faubourg sanctuaries have been built around a small chapel of radial design, round or polygonal, in juxtaposition with a large basilica with one or more naves. Basilicas with several naves, preceded by a very large atrium, had in fact become necessary to accommodate the large crowds of pilgrims attracted by the celebrity of the saint. So the "confession," or tomb, of the saint (so-called in commeration of his confession of Christ) determined the site of the basilica in an ancient necropolis. Later the presence of the holy relics attracted no longer just the visits of pilgrims, but the permanent residence of the dead. The basilica became the nucleus of a new cemetery *ad sanctos,* on top of the former dual-purpose necropolis or next to it.

The excavations in the Roman towns of Africa are restoring to our eyes the extraordinary spectacle of disorderly piles of stone sarcophagi surrounding the walls of basilicas, in particular the apse, the part nearest the confession. The tombs penetrate the interior and invade the naves, at least the lateral naves; this is what one finds in Tipasa, Hippo, and Carthage. The spectacle is just as striking in Ampurias, in Catalonia, where the Christian necropolis and its basilicas were built on the ruins of the Greek town, long since abandoned. In Italy, archaeologists had to dig up the Christian cemetery to find the remains of the old Neapolis, which can be seen today amid a confusion of overturned Christian sarcophagi.

The same situation is found in our Gallo-Roman cities, but it is no longer visible to the naked eye and has to be reconstructed beneath the successive deposits of history. The most recent of these, the suburbs of the nineteenth and twentieth centuries, have obliterated the last traces, which were still apparent in the painted or engraved "views" of the late eighteenth century. This is how we know the cemetery and basilica of Saint-Victor, near Marseilles; Saint-Marcel, near Paris; Saint-Seurin, near Bordeaux; Saint-Sernin, near Toulouse; Saint-Hilaire, in Poitiers; and Saint-Rémi, in Reims, among others.

The cemeterial basilica designed for pilgrims and surrounded and invaded by the dead was under the care of a secular or regular community and usually became the center of a powerful abbey of monks or nuns. In the Roman towns of Africa and in Catalonian Ampurias, it looks as if neighborhoods of poor Christians grew up around the extraurban basilicas, although the episcopal see, the *episcopium*, was situated within the town itself, behind the walls. In Gaul, abbeys also constituted the nuclei of suburbs such as Saint-Sernin, in Toulouse, and Saint-Martin, in Tours, which were soon joined to the city and included inside a wall of later construction. The habitations of the dead did not drive away those of the living.

For a long time the cemeterial basilicas were separate from the church of the bishop, the cathedral, which was inside the wall and sometimes on top of it and which contained no tombs. The basilicas, on the other hand, were filled with the dead, drawn there no longer necessarily by the martyrs who were the first to be worshiped there but by famous persons who had been buried near them. In this way more recent saints replaced the titular saints of the most ancient relics in the piety of the faithful and in their choice of burial places.

Relics transported from the site of the martyrdom sometimes took the place of the actual *martyrium*. King Childebert had an abbey built to shelter some relics of Saint Vincent of Saragossa, which he had brought back from Spain himself along with a Toledan cross. He planned to be buried there. He wanted to make the Abbey of Saint-Vincent the necropolis of his dynasty, just as Saint-Denis was for the Capetians. Saint Germain, the bishop of Paris who had consecrated the city, was buried there; the king and the holy bishop both sought the proximity of the relics of Saint Vincent. Saint Germain was not buried in the church itself, but *in porticu*, in a chapel adjoining the church.

The tomb of Saint Germain itself became the object of great veneration. In 755, the body was transferred to the sanctuary, where it was buried under the high altar, and at that time the church took the name of Saint-Germain, our Saint-Germain-des-Prés. Saint Germain subsumed Saint Vincent. Similar substitutions occurred in Paris, where the bishop, Saint Marcel, replaced Saint Clement, one of the first popes, and in Bordeaux, where the name of the church was changed from that of the protomartyr, Saint Stephen, to that of the bishop, Saint Seurin.

When communities of canons were founded in the cathedral churches, the canons, like the bishops, had their tombs in the abbeys of the faubourgs. Hence, the Gallo-Roman cities at the dawn of the Middle Ages featured two centers of Christian life, the cathedral and the cemeterial sanctuary. Here, the seat of the episcopal administration and of a large number of clergymen; there, the tombs of the saints and the crowds of pilgrims. This duality was not devoid of rivalry.

The Dead Within the Walls

Time eventually erased the distinction between the faubourg, where the dead had been buried since time immemorial, and the town, where it was still forbidden to bury the dead. The development of new communities around the cemeterial basilica was the first indication of a great change. The dead, the first occupants, had not prevented the living from moving in next to them. Here we observe, in its first stages, a lessening of the aversion that the dead inspired in antiquity. The advance of the dead past the walls and into the heart of the towns signifies the complete abandonment of the old taboo and its replacement by a new attitude of indifference or familiarity. Henceforth and for a long time to come, the dead completely ceased to inspire fear.

We can imagine how the canonical interdict was circumvented thanks to the example of Arras. Saint Vaast, bishop of Arras, died in 540. He had chosen to be buried in a wooden oratory on the bank of the Crinchon, in accordance with the rule that stated that "no deceased person could be laid to rest inside the walls of a town." But when the time came to take him there, the porters were unable to lift the body, which suddenly became too heavy, as if it refused to be moved. The archpriest lost no time in establishing that a supernatural intervention had occurred and asked the saint to order "that you be carried to the place that we [that is, the clergy] have been preparing for you for a long time." Immediately the body became light, and the porters had no trouble bringing it "to the burial place that was fitting for a servant of God, in the church, on the right hand of the altar where he himself had performed the service of his pontifical see."[16] It is not difficult to understand what lies behind this miracle. The clergy of the cathedral refused to let themselves be deprived of a venerable body or of the prestige and advantages that would accrue to the church. But they could not have circumvented the traditional interdict in this way unless it had already lost much of its force.

The same thing almost happened to Saint Germain. The Parisian clergy had obtained permission to have a church dedicated to him in the Ile de la Cité. This church already contained a relic of the holy bishop, for which Saint Eloi had designed a magnificent reliquary. But the clergy were not content with this and hoped that some day the entire body of the saint could be transferred there, hard by the episcopal sanctuaries. This day never came, and Saint Germain remained in the abbey on the Left Bank of Paris where he had been buried after his death. The clergymen of Paris failed where those of Arras had succeeded, no doubt for lack of sufficient temporal support. The new Carolingian dynasty was less attached than the Merovingians to Paris, its Cité, and its veneration of saints.

Once the body of the saint had entered *in ambitus murorum* (within the walls), it attracted in its turn the tombs of the dead and the visits of pilgrims, and the differences in burial function between the cathedral church and the cemeterial church began to disappear. The dead had already coexisted with the inhabitants of poor suburban neighborhoods; now they were introduced into the historic hearts of the towns. From now on, every church had tombs inside its walls and a cemetery next to it. The osmotic relationship between the church and the cemetery had been definitively established.

The phenomenon claimed not only the new parochial churches of the episcopal city but also the rural churches. Barbarian or Merovingian cemeteries have been found, predictably, at a distance from the villages and inhabited areas, always in open country. In Civaux, for example, one can still see rows of monolithic sarcophagi, single and double, extending over large areas. After the seventh century we observe a change analogous to the one that brought the dead inside the towns. These cemeteries in the open fields were abandoned, covered over by vegetation, and forgotten, or else they were used only occasionally—in time of plague, for example—in which case a chapel of more recent construction, sometimes dedicated to Saint Michael, was added to the burial grounds. On the other hand, this was also the period when the cemetery appeared around the church. Today archaeologists often find beside the church, under its walls, or inside it, sarcophagi identical to those discovered in the country. Either they were transported from the Merovingian necropolis and reused or else they continued to be made after the same model, except that from now on they were intended to be used inside the ecclesiastical enclosure.

This substitution of sites is clearly legible in the excavations at Civaux. Around the church a large cemetery has been found that is several hundred meters away from the Merovingian necropolis, which is located in open country.

The same relationship between church and cemetery has been established at Châtenay-sous-Bagneux with the help of some documents from the eighteenth century, for it is no longer visible under the contemporary houses.[17]

The Gallo-Roman and Merovingian necropolis was not completely abandoned until the end of the Middle Ages. In 1729, it was on the verge of disappearance. "The site was then given over wholly to cultivation, and nothing remains but the name of a place called 'le Grand-Cimetière.'" The persistence of the name and even the preservation of the site at a time when burials had become rare—they may have occurred in time of plague—is explained by the nonfunereal functions of the cemetery, which we shall examine later on.

The outlying cemetery was next replaced by the church and its wall. In the oldest part of the church, the choir, fifteen plaster sarcophagi have been found that are "unquestionably Merovingian." Robert Dauvergne believes that they originally came from the Grand-Cimetière, but he assumes on the basis of funereal furnishings found in these tombs that their reuse in the church dates from the twelfth or thirteenth century. We may assume, however, that there are earlier cases of such reuse.

At Châtenay, for example, there was a period sometime between the eighth and the twelfth centuries when people preferred to be buried in the church or next to it rather than in a remote cemetery in the open country.

In Guiry-en-Vexin, around the carriage path of the château, archaeologists have found about three hundred sarcophagi and some simple graves right in the ground. Funerary artifacts indicate that this necropolis dates from the fifth or sixth century. In the same town, but in the open country, a seventh-century cemetery was recently discovered with forty-seven tombs and ten pits containing the bones of two hundred and fifty bodies.

At Guiry, as at Châtenay, it would seem that the church cemetery was used alternately with the cemeteries in the open fields. The church at Guiry contains several tombs made of gathered stones that seem to be Merovingian.[18] Another example is Minot-en-Châtillonais, which has been studied by Françoise Zonabend[19] and is analyzed at the end of chapter 11 of this book, "The Visit to the Cemetery."

The date of the transfer is often difficult to determine and may vary from one place to another, but the general rule is that in rural areas the dead were at first buried away from the houses, in the open fields, and afterward, in the eighth century or later, they were buried in and around the churches.

Here, no doubt, the determining factor in location was not so much the martyrs and holy bishops of the towns and their faubourgs as their founding lords. In pagan regions conquered by the early Christians and converted en masse, such as Carolingian Germany, abandonment of the pagan cemeteries and burial in or near the churches were imposed by force: "We order that the bodies of Christian Saxons be taken to church cemeteries and not to pagan burial grounds."[20]

In the time of the Byzantine Empire, the rich Gallo-Roman landowner was sometimes buried on his own property. A man from the Vienne region had this inscription, dated 515, engraved on his tomb: "Penthagothus, on leaving this uncertain existence, has not wished to seek a place of burial [in a public cemetery]; he has entrusted his body to this land that belongs to him." But the custom of burial *ad sanctos* had become so widespread that when the dead person did not go to the saint, it was the saint who came to him. Thus, Penthagothus had placed some martyrs' relics in his tomb, according to a practice observed in other Merovingian and Carolingian *Memoriae:* "Only under the protection of the martyrs," he proclaims, "may we look for eternal rest. May the very holy Vincent and the other saints, his companions and peers"—the more saints there were, the better was the protection— "watch over this *domus.*" The use of the word *domus* indicates that the tomb is also a temple, a consecrated place where the liturgy can be celebrated; later it will be called a chapel.[21]

And in the ninth century, Bishop Jonas of Orléans censures those who charge a fee for permission to bury the dead *in agris suis* (on their own land).[22] The burial ground of the rich landowner became *locum publicum et ecclesiasticum,* and the family monument became the rural and parochial church, even the collegiate church or abbey. Such is the origin of the underground chapel of Saint-Maximin, in Provence; those tombs that legend later attributed to Mary Magdalene were family tombs. Similarly, the *memoria* of la Gayolle, a few kilometers from Saint-Maximin, is also a family chapel.

Family burial places like these must often have been the origin of rural parish churches. The lord maintained a chaplain in his villa, and the chapel where he celebrated the Mass might also be the lord's *memoria.*

At Guiry-en-Vexin, a deed that dates from the sixteenth century but that refers to some very ancient documents states that the lords of Guiry, "having adopted Christianity, following the example of Clovis I, . . . began by building a small church or chapel, which they dedicated to God under the protection of Saint Andrew the Apostle. We know that a Gabriel de Guiry was buried there in 818."[23] So this church served as a burial place for its founders and their successors. The case was common and explains why the canonical texts granted the lay founders of churches the same exceptional rights to ecclesiastical burial as were granted to priests and religious, as we shall see further on.

These funerary chapels did not always become parochial churches, but they were always objects of veneration; Mass was celebrated over the holy relics that had been placed there. An example is the subterranean *memoria* of Abbé Mellebaude. It is true that it was not *in agris,* but in an old cemetery *extra muros,* at the gates of Poitiers. Its first discoverer, P. de La Croix, believed it to be a monument to the memory of a martyr. He was probably mistaken, because in reality it was the tomb of an abbot of the late seventh century. But his error is quite understandable, for nothing could be more like the *memoria* of a martyr than this tomb. Before he died, the abbot placed some saints' relics in it. He conceived of his hypogeum as a symbolic representation of the *spelunca,* the grotto of the Holy Sepulcher; and finally, he designed his tomb as a chapel dedicated to the cross of Christ, with an altar for the celebration of the Mass.

The abbot's *memoria* thus became a kind of *martyrium,* but also, like all the churches, in time, a place of burial *ad sanctos.* "The faithful dug graves in its ground and covered them with slabs that they cut out of stones borrowed from the building itself. In them they placed enormous sarcophagi, which can still be seen in place; and in their desire to obtain places in this crypt for themselves and their relatives, they did not hesitate [around the ninth or tenth century?] to tear down a wall or break the step of a sanctuary."[24]

Burial *ad sanctos,* development of faubourgs around the cemeterial basilicas, invasion by tombs of the towns and villages, where they coexisted with the habitations of men—these were so many stages in an evolution that brought together the living and the dead, who had once been kept apart.

The Cemetery
as the Bosom of the Church

It was an evolution not only in practice but also in doctrine and in law. An explicit new conception of the sanctity of the dead replaced that of antiquity. Medieval writers very soon came to feel that their burial customs were in opposition to those of the ancients. For a long time it was believed that the pagans had not reserved a special place for graves. Although Humbert of Burgundy is quite certain that human beings, unlike animals, have always been concerned about burying their dead, he believes that the pagans buried them anywhere at all: "in their houses, in the garden, in a field, or in other similar places."[25] In the early twelfth century a canon of Le Mans talks about "solitary places": *quaedam solitaria loca.*[26] The early writers, and even Sauval in the seventeenth century, were inclined to confuse pagan cemeteries, where they still existed, with the tombs that were lined up along the main roads, beyond the gates of the cities, in other words, with *solitaria loca.* Thus, Sauval admitted, "as long as Paris was under the rule of the Romans, . . . those who died were always buried along the main roads." We can assume that in those days the roads were bad places, frequented by an itinerant and dangerous population of vagabonds and soldiers. "Before this cemetery [les Innocents; that is, a long time ago], fathers and mothers were permitted to bury themselves and their children in their cellars, gardens, and by their private roads," perhaps to avoid the "main roads."[27]

This idea that the ancients buried their dead on their own property persisted until the eighteenth century, and it was in imitation of what was believed to be the ancient custom that the practice of private graves was revived. In the Middle Ages, however, this form of interment was considered unacceptable.

Humbert of Burgundy compared the pagans, who were buried anywhere at all, with the Christians, who were buried only "in venerated and public places designed for that purpose and consecrated to that end."[28] Heretics were blamed for denying the cemetery its requirement of *locum publicum et ecclesiasticum*. The Waldensians and Hussites believed "that it made no difference at all where one buried the dead, whether the land was sacred or profane."[29] The clustering of Christian dead around saints' relics and the churches built around these relics had become a distinguishing characteristic of Christian civilization. A sixteenth-century writer recognized that "cemeteries are not merely burial grounds and receptacles for dead bodies, they are also holy or sacred places, designed to inspire prayers for the souls of the departed who repose there": holy and sacred places, public and frequented by men, not impure and solitary.[30]

The traditional opposition between the dead and the sacred was, therefore, not so much forgotten as inverted. The dead body of a Christian created by its very nature a space if not altogether sacred, at least, according to the subtle distinction of Durandus of Mende in the thirteenth century, religious. A seventeenth-century ecclesiastical writer was struck by the difference between the Christian attitude and the belief in the impurity of the dead that was common to the Jews and the Romans. He attempted to explain it in terms of doctrine: "This notion [on the part of the Romans] was quite pardonable, since the law of Moses made such a point of warning men about the contamination they risked from contact with dead bodies." "Since the Son of God has not only sanctified, but crucified death itself, not only in his own person but in his members, not only by his own resurrection but by the hope he gives to us, by instilling in our mortal bodies his quickening spirit, which is the source of eternal life, the tombs of those who died for him have been regarded as sources of life and sanctity. This is why they have been placed in churches, or basilicas have been built to contain them."[31] Saint Augustine betrayed a certain lack of enthusiasm toward devotions that undoubtedly reminded him of the superstitious funerary practices of Africa. He emphasized the fact that the honors due the dead were primarily intended to console the living. Only prayers had a real propitiatory effect. But these reservations were quickly forgotten in the Middle Ages. People believed, as Saint Julian did, that the prayers of the living were more effective when said near the tombs of the martyrs. "The proximity of the *memoriae* of the martyrs is so advantageous to the deceased that if one commends to their patronage someone who had been buried in their vicinity, the effect of the prayer is increased."[32]

The *Elucidarium*, which is less simplistic, returns, not without hesitations or reservations, to the principles of Saint Augustine. The work of Honorius of Autun, dating from the late eleventh or early twelfth century, it was read and put into practice until the end of the Middle Ages. "It is in no way harmful to the just not to be buried in the cemetery of the church, for the whole world is the temple of God, consecrated by the blood of Christ. Whatever may happen to their bodies, the just will always remain in the bosom of the Church." Having said this out of respect for the church fathers, the author also acknowledges the common belief and practice, and attempts to justify it. "It is profitable, however, to be buried in places that are consecrated by the tombs of certain saints. Those who are still undergoing punishment benefit from the prayers that are said for them by the just buried near them, and also from the prayers said by their relatives when they come to these places and when the tombs call to their minds the memory of the deceased."[33] It will be noted that the intercessions of the dead are placed on the same level with the prayers of the living, and that both are inspired, even compelled, by the physical proximity of the tombs.

According to Honorius of Autun, the proximity of the saints does not provide any protection for the wicked. On the contrary, "the wicked derive no advantage from it. In fact, it is even harmful to them to be united in burial with those who are so far removed from them in merit. We read that there are many whom the devil has dug up and flung far from consecrated land." This last remark is an allusion to some miraculous events reported by Gregory the Great and constantly repeated afterward. The bodies of the wicked defile the church and the cemetery, just as formerly, dead bodies in general defiled the land of the towns. The cemetery is the holy dormitory of the dead and, according to Honorius of Autun, the bosom of the Church, the *ecclesiae gremium,* where she rekindles the souls of those who are dead in body to restore them to eternal life, just as by baptism she revives the dead who are still in this world.

The Burial of the Damned

The situation is already the reverse of what it was in antiquity, or at least in the idea of antiquity that existed then. It is now the solitary grave that inspires dread. It is not impossible that the old habits of burying the dead *in agris suis* persisted; we have seen that Jonas of Orléans was still denouncing them in the ninth century.[34] In 1128, the bishop of Saint-Brieuc was still prohibiting burial at the foot of the crosses at crossroads.[35] But such cases had become exceptional and suspect. Only social outcasts were left in the fields, or, as the place was later called, the dump.

I do declare that if I die
I would not in churchyard lie
But bury me in the fields instead.[36]

Persons who had been excommunicated or prisoners who had been executed and not claimed by their families, or whom the lord in his judicial capacity had refused to reinstate, were left to rot unburied with no more than a block of stone laid over them *(imblocati)* to preserve the appearance of the landscape.[37]

Manfred, the natural son of Emperor Frederick II and an enemy of the pope, died excommunicate in the battle of Benevento in 1266. Dante tells us that he was buried then and there, "at the bridgehead near Benevento, guarded by a big heap of stones," i.e., each soldier threw a stone on his body. But Pope Clement IV would not allow this accursed body to remain inside the kingdom of Sicily, which was a fief of the Church and thus the equivalent of consecrated soil. Therefore, according to a legend adopted by Dante, his bones were dug up again "and now the rain drenches them and the wind blows them out of the kingdom, along the Verde where he [the pope] had them carried without a single torch," at night.

Alain Chartier gives the name "false atrium," that is, false cemetery, to the place where the bodies of outcasts were thrown:

It is a kind of false atrium
And there they throw the bodies of the damned.
I saw more than four of them,
blackened, rotting, left to lie
On the ground, without a grave.[38]

This hellish dump sometimes coincided with the gallows. The bodies of those who had been executed were not taken down but remained exposed for months, even years. On November 12, 1411, Colinet de Puiseux was beheaded and dismembered. Each of his arms and legs was hung from one of the main gates of Paris, and his body, or what was left of it, "put in a sack on the gallows." It was not until September 16, 1413, almost two years later, that "the body of the traitor Colinet de Puiseux was taken down from the gallows and his arms and legs removed from the gates. And yet he deserved to be burned and thrown to the dogs rather than to be laid in hallowed ground; but the Armagnacs had their way with him." According to the *Bourgeois de Paris,* they would have done better to burn him or let him rot at the foot of the gallows, a prey to birds and dogs.[39]

There is a very fine description of a gallows in a text from 1804. In spite of its late date, we may assume that the details had changed very little since the end of the Middle Ages. The book is a novel, Jan Potocki's *Manuscrit trouvé à Saragosse*. The hero, after a night of fantastic adventures, wakes up under the gallows. "The bodies of Zata's two brothers [executed bandits] were not hanging; they were lying beside me." Customarily the bodies of the hanged were either cut down after a while or allowed to fall down of their own weight and rot at the foot of the gallows. "I was lying on some pieces of rope and broken wheels [instruments of torture?], the remains of human bodies, and the unspeakable rags that had fallen away from them as they rotted." Overhead, hanging from the gallows, "the hideous cadavers, buffeted by the wind, swung crazily while horrible vultures pulled them this way and that and tore out shreds of their flesh."[40] Shades of Villon.

The area around the gallows, which was enclosed by a wall, also served as a dump, so that the remains of the executed were covered with garbage. Alain Chartier's "false atrium" may have been around a gallows. In any case, the sinister relationship between the gallows, the garbage dump, and certain insalubrious and nauseating occupations has been noted by Louis Chevalier in connection with Montfaucon.[41]

In principle, however, the bodies of criminals could be buried in holy ground. The Church allowed it, because God does not punish a man twice for the same reason; a man who was executed had paid for his crime. But the Church's instructions were not carried out until the period of the mendicant friars and the religious brotherhoods. The men of the Middle Ages and of early modern times did not believe that the course of justice or of legal action stopped with the death of the defendant. In the case of a suicide, they prosecuted the dead man in court, and his body was ejected from the cemetery. In Brittany at the beginning of this century, according to Gabriel Le Bras, there still existed special cemeteries reserved for suicides, where the coffin was passed over a wall that had no opening.[42]

In the case of an executed criminal, they preferred to let him rot or to burn him and scatter his ashes, which were sometimes mixed with the records of his trial, or criminal writings: "Their ashes, which were thrown to the wind, the air, the water . . ." Agrippa d'Aubigné writes in *Les Tragiques* of Protestants condemned to the stake. When the lepers learn that Isolde has been sentenced by King Mark to be burned alive for adultery, they ask that the unfortunate woman be turned over to them instead. They will be able to provide her with a fate far worse than fire. "Sire, if you wish to throw your wife on the fire, the punishment will be just, but too short. This bonfire will burn her quickly, and the *strong wind will scatter her ashes.*"

Nor does death check the course of vengeance. After Goneval kills Ganelon, the treacherous enemy of his lord, Tristan, he "dismembers him completely [like a beast of venery] and goes off with his severed head." The rest of the dismembered body is left to the animals. He ties the head by the hair to the "leafy bower" where Tristan and Isolde are sleeping, to greet them on their awakening.

In these cases medieval man refused to give his enemy, or the enemy of society, the burial *ad sanctos* that theologians would have tolerated or required. Inversely, in the thirteenth and fourteenth centuries, it sometimes happened that he claimed such burial for his relatives and that the clergy refused it because the deceased was not in good standing with the Church; he had died intestate, excommunicate, and so on. In such cases the family of the deceased who had been excluded in this manner would act as his substitute, when possible, in order to expiate his wrongs and reconcile him with the Church. The operation was sometimes time-consuming, and there is a case on record of an excommunicated prelate whose body lay for eighty years in a lead coffin, stored in a château, waiting for the right to rest once and for all in consecrated ground. When it was not possible to lift the canonical ban, the family would try to obtain access to the *locum publicum et ecclesiasticum* by force. It is said that for lack of a proper grave, coffins were sometimes laid on the tops of trees in the cemetery, which must have been a strange sight! Or else the dead were buried secretly, but the devils or angels did not always allow them to remain undisturbed in the places they had usurped in the holy ground, which they defiled with their presence. Either they dug them up by night and turned them out themselves or else they caused unusual phenomena that alerted the clergy to the fraud. There exist forms that were used to petition the authorities for the right to exhume a corpse and eject it from a cemetery or church.

In all these cases an attempt was made, in the name of personal vengeance or the right of the lord or of the Church, to deprive the victims or culprits of the advantages that automatically attended burial *apud memorias martyrum* (by the graves of the martyrs). And the Church made every effort to reserve the consecrated areas for those who had died in her good graces.

Burial in Church: Law vs. Practice

When religious writers and ecclesiastical law broke with ancient tradition and required burial of the dead near sanctuaries frequented by the living, they were affirming the benefic character of an area regarded by the an-

cients as malefic. The sense of the sacred that the dead inspired had taken
on a new meaning. But to what extent did the sense of the sacred survive
the familiarity of the everyday?

Although church law was in agreement with current practice on the
efficacy of burial *ad sanctos,* it diverged from it in some cases, depending
on whether the term referred to the cemetery next to the church or to
burial inside the church itself.

For centuries the decrees of the councils continued to distinguish the
church per se from the consecrated area around the church. While the
councils decreed the necessity of burial beside the church, they were constantly repeating the prohibition against burial inside the church, subject
to a few exceptions in the case of priests, bishops, monks, and certain
privileged laymen—exceptions that immediately became the rule.

In 563 the Council of Braga forbade burial inside churches. It allowed
graves to be placed near the walls of churches, but only on the outside.[43] This is the rule that the juridical texts kept reiterating until the
eighteenth century, when finally, under the pressure of custom, they were
forced to authorize some departures.

Hence we find the monotonous repetition of these precepts in the
records of the councils of the Middle Ages: "Let no person be buried in
church" (Mayence, 813). "In accordance with the instructions of the
church fathers and the teachings of the miracles [probably a reference to
Pope Gregory's accounts of the bodies of unreconciled criminals being
expelled miraculously from the churches they were defiling], we hereby
decree that henceforth (*deinceps*) no layman shall be buried inside a
church" (Tribur, 895). "We prohibit . . . that any person be buried in
church" (pseudo–Council of Nantes, 900).

The liturgist Durandus of Mende lived in the thirteenth century, an
age when churches were cemeteries. He tried to preserve at least the choir,
which was still the most sought-after place, first, because it contained the
confession of the saint, and second, for the very reason the Church tried
to prohibit its use: "No body should be buried near the altar where the body
and blood of Our Lord are prepared and offered, except the bodies of the
holy fathers."[44] Durandus was merely repeating the prohibition of the
pseudo–Council of Nantes against burying the dead "near the altar where
the body and blood of Our Lord are prepared." The prohibitions of the
councils were full of exceptions: bishops and abbots, priests, or certain loyal
and devoted lay members of the congregation, with the permission of the
bishop, the priest, or the rector (Mayence, 813). Who are these loyal and
devoted laymen? We have met them earlier in connection with the rural
churches where they had their tombs: "lords of the *villae* and patrons of
the churches and their wives, by whom the honor of these churches has

been increased." The beneficent founders of churches, starting with kings, ranked with the anointed priests of the Lord, who were themselves the equals of the martyrs and saints. These consecrated bodies did not defile the church; on the contrary, they were allowed to accompany the body and blood of Our Lord on the altar.

At the end of the Middle Ages, the councils of the Counter-Reformation attempted in their turn to oppose deeply rooted custom and return to the spirit and letter of the ancient law. They invoked the principle *in ecclesiis vero nulli deinceps sepeliantur* (henceforth let no one be buried in church). They expressed outrage that exceptions to this principle were the privilege of noble birth, power, and wealth, instead of being reserved for piety and merit: "that this honor may not be granted for money, but only by the Holy Spirit."[45] The bishops admitted, however, that burial in church was an honor, so they must not have wondered that in those days when men were even fonder of fame than they were of fortune, they sought it so insistently.

The Council of Rouen (1581) gives three categories of persons who are entitled to burial in church: The first two categories are by privilege; the third by choice.

1. "Those who have dedicated their lives to God, especially the men [nuns only in cases of necessity], because their bodies have been chosen as temples of Christ and of the Holy Spirit"

2. "Those who have received honors and dignities in the church [ordained clergymen] or in the world [the rich and powerful], because they are the ministers of God and the instrument of the Holy Spirit", and finally

3. "Those who by their nobility, their actions, and their merits have distinguished themselves in the service of God and of the common good"[46]

All others had to be buried in the cemetery.

The Council of Reims (1683) distinguished the same categories, but defined them in more traditional terms: two categories of privileged persons —priests and the patrons of the church already recognized in the Middle Ages; and "those who, by their nobility, their example, and their merits, have rendered service to God and to religion," the latter being admitted, in accordance with the ancient custom, only by permission of the bishop. Everyone else was buried in the cemetery, which "at one time the most illustrious persons did not hold in contempt."[47]

The persistence of such passages, if interpreted literally, would lead one to believe that burial in church was the exception to the rule. But in reality their repetition with so little variation from the sixth to the seventeenth century, over a thousand years, betrays the extent to which the prohibitions were ignored. In 1581, the church fathers again decreed, *"in ecclesiis nulli deinceps sepeliantur."* But as early as 895 they were already insisting *"ut deinceps nullus in ecclesia sepeliatur,"* for even then their rule was not being observed. And in the late eighth century Bishop Theodulf of Orléans was denouncing the practice as an abuse that was already of long standing: "It is an old custom in this region to bury the dead in churches."[48]

One begins to wonder whether the canonical regulation was ever actually observed. From the first appearance of the practice of burial *ad sanctos,* tombs had invaded the interiors of churches, beginning with the cemeterial basilicas. The churches of Roman Africa in the fourth and fifth centuries were at least partly paved, in their lateral naves, with mosaic tombs that bore epitaphs and pictures of the deceased.[49] In Damous el-Karita in Carthage, the stone covers of the tombs form the paved floor of the basilica. At Alyscamps, in Arles, the church of Saint-Honorat is built on a layer of sarcophagi. The walls rest on top of them, without any foundation. It would appear that burial in church was contemporaneous with the texts that forbade it and that the canonical prohibitions did not prevent its spreading throughout the Christian world over a long period of time.

For until the end of the eighteenth century at least, the practice of burying the dead in churches persisted. In the seventeenth century, the churches were paved with tombs; their floors were composed of tombstones, like those of the basilicas of Roman Africa. In most French churches we can no longer detect the checkered pattern of flat tombstones beneath the floors, which were completely restored in the eighteenth and nineteenth centuries. However, it still exists in places such as Châlons-sur-Marne, for example, where the zeal of lay or ecclesiastical restorers has not been excessive, or in poor and isolated hamlets. It is in regions that were not subjected, as France and Austria were, to the successive purifications of the clergy of the seventeenth and eighteenth centuries, in Catholic Italy or Calvinist Holland, that one can still find the old structures almost intact.

In Saint-Bavon in Haarlem, the seventeenth-century floor, which is composed entirely of tombstones, has been preserved intact. The sight is impressive, because it shows us what has disappeared, or been altered, elsewhere. The whole floor space of the church is a compartmentalized cemetery, and no matter where the faithful turn, they walk on graves.

The large slabs of Saint-Bavon are not cemented together. Each one has a hole carved out in the middle where the gravedigger inserted his crowbar. They are usually numbered with Arabic numerals in the style of the seventeenth century, post-Reformation, like the ground plan of a modern cemetery. This sort of concern for the dividing up of space must have been quite new and indicates a rational organization of the area beneath the floor that did not exist in previous ages. But it also shows that it had become common practice to devote the entire floor of the church to graves. Several of these slabs also bear a monogram, a date, arms (some of them *armes parlantes,* such as a shoemaker's tools),[50] or macabre symbols (death's-heads, skeletons, hourglasses, and the like). A few are more richly decorated, always with heraldic motifs.

Calvinist Holland has preserved to this day the appearance of the old churches with their floors paved with tombs. But this practice of burying the dead in church was not to find favor with the reformers, who would view it suspiciously as a sign of papist superstition. It must have been very deeply rooted in custom to survive.

Dutch painting has depicted scenes of funerals in the interiors of churches as a familiar sight. Emanuel de Witte shows us a funeral in 1655. The funeral procession has entered the church and is making its way toward the choir. Meanwhile, the gravedigger and his helper have been preparing the grave. They have lifted the carved stone slab that sealed the tomb. It was not covering a *cave,* as they called it in seventeenth-century France, that is, a stone-walled burial vault, but simply the bare ground. The grave-diggers must have dug the grave some time ago, since they have taken the trouble to cover it with wooden boards. We know that some graves remained open this way for several days. The earth that has been dug out and piled to one side contains a disorderly collection of bones and skulls, the remains of older graves. Such was the familiar appearance of a Protestant church in the middle of the seventeenth century![51]

So we see that the customary procedure, from Christian antiquity until the eighteenth century, was burial inside the churches, which were veritable cities of the dead. Although the conciliar fathers as a body may have maintained an intransigent juridical position in their statutes, the same pious pontiffs, acting as individuals, were the first to forget this stance in their pastoral decisions.

In the ninth century the Bulgarians wrote to Pope Nicholas asking whether it was permissible to bury Christians in church. The pope replied, citing the authority of Gregory the Great, that it was indeed possible as long as the individuals in question had not committed mortal sins. The justification he gives is that of the *Elucidarium* of Honorius rather than the assurance of salvation through the proximity of the martyrs: The sight of the tomb invites the relatives of the deceased to remember him and to remember him to God each time they visit the holy place. "According to passages from these two popes [Gregory and Nicholas]," comments the eighteenth-century writer Thomassin, "in Italy, it was enough for a layman to have led a Christian life and to have died in a state of grace to render the grave he had chosen in church advantageous and salutary"; this, despite the canonical prohibitions.[52]

At the end of the Middle Ages, Gerson candidly accepted the right to purchase "a safe and honorable place for one's grave" in church. In so doing, the deceased was demonstrating "pious foresight . . . and a good heart."[53]

The only effect of the canonical prohibitions, besides maintaining a principle, was to make the customary practice of burial in church subject to the payment of a fee.

Burial, like the sacraments and the sacramentals, could not be sold. But exceptions to the general rule could be purchased. This is more or less the origin of the burial fees collected by priests and likened at first to offerings, then later exacted as fees and referred to by the ambiguous and rather shameful expression "laudable customs." At least that was how the canonists of the seventeenth and eighteenth centuries explained them. In his book *Ancienne et Nouvelle Discipline de l'Eglise* (1725), the jurist Thomassin entitles the chapter he devotes to burial fees "Concerning Burial Offerings After the Year One Thousand, and the Simony to Which They Sometimes Gave Rise."

"The Church would never have been obliged to repeat the decrees prohibiting the exaction of burial fees so many times if the faithful had all agreed to be buried in the public cemeteries, there to await the resurrection common to them all, and perhaps even more glorious for those less given to the vain and ridiculous pride that seeks to distinguish itself even by its place of burial." This is the opinion of an educated priest in the Age of Enlightenment, a stranger to medieval and popular mentalities. "Apparently," he goes on, "payment was only required for a place more honorable than in the public cemeteries [that is, a place in the church]. There was no charge for burial in the cemeteries. The rich wished to distinguish themselves by being buried in church, their wishes were granted as a reward for their prayers and donations, and in the end these donations became obligatory."[54]

The scale of prices for burial in the cemetery and in the church indicates clearly that the difference between the two was merely a matter of prestige. In the popular mentality of the Middle Ages and the beginning of the modern era, there was really very little distinction between burial in the church or beside it. It is true that there was a hierarchy of honor and devotion that extended from the confession of the saint or the high altar to the edge of the cemetery, but its continuity was not broken by the physical wall of the church. It was as if this wall did not constitute a division, as if all that counted was the distance from the spiritual center of the ecclesiastical complex. *Tumulatio in ecclesiam* or *sepelitio apud martyrum memorias:* The two expressions were used interchangeably.

We are less surprised by the lack of attention paid to the canonical instructions—that was not unusual—than by the persistence and tenacity with which the ecclesiastical authorities maintained for a thousand years a rule that was never observed. The conciliar decrees preserved a theoretical conception of the sacred that was in contradiction with practice. They prolonged, in a world that no longer understood it, the traditional reluctance to defile the sanctity of the temple by the corruption of the dead. Contact with the dead no longer caused either profanation or pollution.

Neither laymen nor even clergymen, in their personal conduct, were influenced by the conception of the sacred that was still embodied in the law. In spite of the canonical texts, they were all naïvely convinced that the sanctity of the church was no more incompatible with the proximity of the dead than it was with the familiar presence of the living. The mental boundary between the sacred and the profane remained somewhat imprecise until the reforms of the sixteenth and seventeenth centuries. The profane was pervaded by the supernatural, and the sacred was impregnated with naturalism.

Churchyard and Charnel

The close relationship between the cemetery and the church can still be seen from the words that referred to them and the ambiguity with which they were used.

If one wished to found a cemetery, one built a church. In a charter of 870, Louis the German recalls that his parents had a church built "in order to have a cemetery for the dead in that place."[55] The basilica of Notre-Dame-de-Tours was built as a burial place for the poor. In Paris, les Champeaux is the very large cemetery of a very small parish church, the church of les Saints-Innocents, although in this case the territory of the parish does not extend beyond the walls of the cemetery. The words *ecclesia* and *cimeterium* are almost synonymous. Charles du Cange defines *cimeterium* as "a church where the bodies of the dead are buried."[56]

However, if it was usual to build a church in order to have a cemetery, it was not so easy to transform a cemetery into a church, for legal reasons of which we are aware. "If bodies have been buried before the church has been consecrated, let it not be consecrated."[57] The Council of Tribur (895) even stipulates that in the event that there are too many tombs, the altar should be removed if one is already there.[58] This is why the Merovingian necropolises were abandoned, for lack of a church inside their walls, in favor of the nearest alternative.

The cemeterial function began inside the walls of the church and continued beyond them, in the space that constituted the *passus ecclesiastici, in circuitu ecclesiae.*[59] Hence, the word *church* did not mean simply the church but the whole of this area. The customary laws of the ancient county of Hainaut define *parish church* as "nave, bell tower, and cemetery."[60] The cemetery proper, in the strict sense of the word, was simply the court or courtyard of the church. *"Atrium id est cimiterium,"* writes Gratian in the commentaries of his *Decretum. Aître* and *charnier* are the oldest words for cemetery in the spoken French language. *Cimetière* is a latinized Greek word that was long restricted to the scholarly language of the clergy.

Turpin urges Roland to sound the horn so that the king and his army will come and avenge them, mourn for them, and "bury them . . . in churchyards." A chronicler reports they "took by force both the churchyard *(aître)* and the church of the town." The expressions *aître Saint-Maclou* and *église Saint-Maclou* were used interchangeably. The word was replaced in French by *cimetière* after the seventeenth century, while the English *churchyard,* the German *Kirchhof,* and the Dutch *kerkhof* have survived.[61]

The part of the atrium that was originally most popular as a burial place was the semicircular area surrounding the apse, *in exhedris ecclesiae.* This part first contained those revered tombs that no one yet dared to place in the choir, *in cancello.* The body of Saint Martin, in Tours, and that of Saint Germain, in Paris, lay in this area in chapels, before being transferred into the sanctuary under the high altar.

The other preferred part was the "vestibule" (uncovered entrance court), also known as the *paradisum,* or parvis. It was here that the body of the first layman to be buried almost inside a church, Emperor Constantine, was placed. The *paradisum* was *impluvium sub stillicidio,* that is, it received the rainwater that had absorbed the sanctity of the church by running down the roof and walls.[62] In French the expression was *"suz la gutiere"* (under the eaves).[63]

In southwestern France, where Constantine was often represented on horseback on the western facade over the vestibule, people also said, "Under the Constantine of Rome, on the right side of the church."

Apart from these preferred locations around the church, the dead were buried *in atrio,* in the courtyard that would later become the cemetery proper.

It will be noted that *aître* has neither the religious meaning of "rest" or "sleep" nor the realistic meaning of "burial," but simply designates the courtyard of the church.

A second word was used synonymously with *aître: charnier* (charnel).

The two words are used indiscriminately in the *Chanson de Roland.* When Charlemagne and his army come to the place where the bodies of Roland and his companions are lying, they pick them up and "to a charnel quickly bring them down." "With pointed stakes they open the charnels." "Afterward the dead [those killed at Formigny in 1450] were buried in vast charnels."[64]

At the end of the Middle Ages it appears that the use of the word *charnier* was very widespread and that it had taken the place of the word *aître,* which was now retained only before the proper name of a saint as part of a place name, as in *aître Notre-Dame, aître Saint-Maclou,* and so on.

According to Antoine Furetière, *charnier* comes from *carnarium,* which "was used by Plautus with the same meaning." The classical Latin *caro* had passed into clerical language with several meanings: "the word was made flesh," "the sins of the flesh," "the flesh is weak." In popular language, the same *caro* has given some words signifying meat: the Italian *carne*.[65]

In Rabelais, as in Plautus, the word *carnier* refers to the pantry where the lard was kept. R.-J. Bernard finds it still in the nineteenth century in Gévaudan, where "it was often located near the master bedroom."[66]

In Old French, the same word *carnier* also signifies the blessed place where the dead lie: *carnarium* or *carnetum,* in the Latin of the clergymen. We have just cited its use in *La Chanson de Roland* with no pejorative connotation. No doubt common usage originally adopted a popular and vulgar word to give a name to something that had no name in polite discourse, except for the word *cimetière,* from the latinized Greek, which was still too scholarly.

Here, however, it is not a case of substituting one word for another but of creating a new word to correspond to a new concept, that of cemetery; and it is this new development that is interesting. To the Romans the *tumulus,* the *sepulcrum,* the *monumentum,* and later the *tumba* had more meaning than the space that the tombs occupied. One might almost say that there was no such thing as a cemetery, there were only tombs placed more or less in juxtaposition.

To the medieval mentality, on the other hand, it is the cemetery that has meaning. By the beginning of the Middle Ages, the tomb has become anonymous and unimportant. What matters is the public and enclosed space for graves, which explains the need to give it a name.

The word *charnier* retained the general meaning of "cemetery," but by the end of the Middle Ages it also designated a particular part of the cemetery, a part so characteristic that it was taken for the whole. This part was the ossuary, and also the galleries where bones were both stored and

displayed. This evolution in language reflects the form taken by the ecclesiastical enclosure, the atrium enclosed by walls.

The dead were buried not only *sub stillicidio* but also *in porticu*: under
porch roofs or galleries built onto the wall of the church, under niches or
enfeux, carved out of this wall and succeeding one another like an arcade.
The porticoes continued along the walls that enclosed the atrium, giving
it the appearance of a cloister. In fact, cloisters also served as cemeteries
for monks or canons. The early cemeteries looked exactly like cloisters
consisting of a single arcaded gallery along the length of the church or
several galleries framing an enclosed courtyard.

Around the fourteenth century it became common procedure to dig
up the more or less dried-out bones in the older graves in order to make
room for new ones and to pile them in the attics of the galleries or above
the arches, if any. Sometimes the bones were concealed. In 1812, in Paris,
on the site of the present Collège de France, a large number of bones were
discovered on top of the arches of a deconsecrated church that was being
torn down. But generally speaking, the bones were visible.

These galleries and the ossuaries that surmounted them, "the place in
the wall of the church that contains the bones of the dead,"[67] were called
charniers (charnels). "At les Innocents," writes Guillaume le Breton in his
Paris sous Charles VI, "there is a very large cemetery surrounded by houses
called charnels in which the bones of the dead are piled."[68]

Le Trésor of Ranconnet-Nicot, dated 1606, defines *charnier* as "the
place where the bones of the deceased are placed, *ossuaria."*[69] According
to Richelet, it is *ossium conditorium,* "the bone yard," "the place in a
cemetery where the bones of the dead are stored in orderly rows," but also
a synonym for *cemetery,* as in *les charniers Saints-Innocents.*[70]

According to these passages, *charnier* refers to the ossuary above the
gallery, as well as to the gallery itself. At les Innocents, each arch of a gallery
had its corresponding covered space, which was known as a charnal. Each
was like a chapel, with the name of its donor carved on the wall: "This
charnel was built and given to the church for the love of God in the year
1395. Pray to God for the dead." "With what was left of his worldly goods,
Armand Estable had this charnel built to shelter the bones of the
dead."[71] And in the seventeenth century, Sauval writes, "The most remarkable feature of this cemetery [les Innocents] is the tomb of Nicolas
Flamel and his wife, Pernelle, which is near the door on the side facing rue
Saint-Denis, under the charnels."[72] In sixteenth- and seventeenth-century
wills, people asked to be buried "under the charnels."

The final phase of this semantic evolution came in the seventeenth
century when the meaning of "ossuary" disappeared from polite usage, if
not from the dictionaries, and the word *charnier* henceforth meant only the

gallery around the church and its courtyard. It quickly became archaic, and it was at this time that the word *cimetière*, derived from church Latin and already in use since the sixteenth century, definitively entered the spoken language.

At least this was the semantic evolution in French. In English, popular use of the word *cemetery* seems to have come even later. *Churchyard* and *graveyard* were not replaced by *cemetery* in current usage until the nineteenth century, and then only to distinguish another kind of cemetery, the "rural cemetery" (see chapter 10).

Words are an accurate reflection of reality; the medieval cemetery was both atrium and charnel.

An atrium is a small rectangular courtyard one side of which coincides with the wall of the church. Its small size distinguishes it from the modern cemetery as well as from the extensive and sometimes ill-defined burial grounds of antiquity. When a medieval cemetery was built on the site of a Gallo-Roman or Merovingian cemetery, it occupied no more than a small part of it. The cemetery grew smaller when it moved inside the ecclesiastical enclosure.[73] It is inconceivable to us (and it was even surprising at the time) how over five hundred years' worth of Parisian dead could have been crowded into the small quadrilateral, not much bigger than the present area of the place des Saints-Innocents, bounded by the rue Saint-Denis, rue de la Ferronnerie, rue de la Lingerie (all of which still exist), and rue aux Fers. These were the old boundaries of the church of les Saints-Innocents and its cemetery, and here, for once, the cemetery was much larger than the church.

A courtyard or atrium is surrounded by charnels, which are at once covered galleries, funerary chapels, and ossuaries. According to Corrozet, the cemetery of les Saints-Innocents "contains eighty arches and charnels under the walls of the church," that is, all around the church.[74] Les Innocents has disappeared, but charnels still exist in Brittany, Rouen, Blois, Montfort-l'Amaury, etc. The spaces under the charnels were funerary chapels, which were almost as sought after as burial places as the interiors of churches. At les Innocents, in the Orgemont and Villeroy chapels, two enlarged charnels on the courtyard side, the price of burial in the seventeenth century was twenty-eight francs. Under the small charnel (short side) the price was even higher, because the demand for burial was excessive in relation to the speed of decomposition: for each tombstone to be lifted, twenty-five francs; for a grave with no tombstone to be lifted, twenty francs. Under the big charnels (the two long sides), for one tombstone to be lifted, eighteen francs, and fifteen francs without a tombstone to be lifted. Elsewhere, but not in the big communal graves, around the edge of the atrium, the price was five and three francs, which no doubt included the coffin. We know the price of burial in Saint-Louis-en-l'Ile in 1697. The gravedigger's bill is twelve francs, to which must be added six francs for parochial fees from the priest's statement, making eighteen francs, a figure comparable to the price of burial in the large charnels of les Innocents.[75]

The Common Graves

Over the galleries, the open garrets were filled with skulls and bones that had dried out and been piled in the open air and were visible from the cemetery.

The space between the charnels was rarely planted with trees but was often overgrown with grass, so that the priest and the community argued over the rights to pasturage and sometimes over the fruits. There were a few visible tombs here and there, an occasional monument of liturgical function—cross, altar, pulpit, or *lanterne des morts* (a hollow stone column containing a lantern)—but most of the interior courtyard was bare and uncovered. This was where they buried the poor, those who could not afford the high price of burial in the church or under the charnels. They were piled in huge common graves, veritable pits thirty feet deep and fifteen by eighteen feet in area, which contained between twelve hundred and fifteen hundred bodies; the smaller ones between six hundred and seven hundred. There was always one open, and sometimes two. After a few years (or months), when they were full, they were covered over and other pits were dug nearby, in the part of the atrium that had been left undisturbed the longest. These pits were barely covered with earth when they were closed, and it was said that during cold winters, the wolves had no trouble digging up the bodies—nor did the thieves who supplied amateur anatomists in the eighteenth century. The use of these pits cannot go back much further than the sixteenth century, and it is reasonable to assume that it became habitual during the epidemics of plague that ravaged the towns, which were already overcrowded from the demographic advance of the thirteenth century. As early as Glaber's time, they were dug in time of famine. "Since it was impossible to bury each body separately because of the great number of the dead, the good souls who feared God built in several places charnels where more than five hundred bodies were placed." In October 1418, according to the *Bourgeois de Paris*, "so many people died in such a short space of time that it was necessary to dig big pits, in each of which were placed thirty or forty persons, piled like bacon, with a few handfuls of dirt thrown on top." It also speaks of big graves in which about six hundred persons were placed: "They had to dig some more big pits, five at les Innocents, four at la Trinité, and in other places."[76]

Sauval also believes that the cemetery of la Trinité dates from the great Black Plague of 1348: "In 1348 Paris was so crowded that the cemeteries were overflowing with bodies. Philippe de Valois was obliged to instruct the merchants' provost to look outside the town for a place to make new ones. So he took a big garden in rue Saint-Denis adjoining la Trinité, after negotiating with the monks."[77]

After the epidemics of 1544, 1545, and 1553, the authorities of Châtelet tried to find "some separate cemeteries apart from the others," further away than rue Saint-Denis, "in which to bury the bodies of those persons who shall hereafter die of the malady of the plague, and also of those who by poverty are wont to be exposed in public without burial. . . . Henceforth the bodies of those who have died in the public hospital of said town would no longer be buried in the cemetery of the orphanage of la Trinité. The cemetery of la Trinité would be devoted to housing the poor children fed and maintained at said orphanage and adapted to their comfort. In place of which cemetery an appropriate and sufficient space will be taken on the island of Macquerelle bounded by the river Seine. . . . But inasmuch as the town, one year later (1555), pointed out that it was to be feared that those who were transporting the bodies there might throw them in the river the sooner to be done with them, no further action was taken."[78]

In the end, these large pits that the texts mention primarily in connection with epidemics were no longer reserved for times of high mortality. After the fifteenth century, and until the end of the eighteenth century, they were the usual place of burial for the poor and for those who died in modest circumstances. In 1763, the report of a commissioner of Châtelet who had been assigned to help conduct an investigation on the cemeteries of Paris described les Innocents as follows:

We also note that there is presently, about twenty feet from the tower known as Notre-Dame-des-Bois, on the north side, a common grave, which the gravedigger tells us was dug in the course of January last, about fifteen by eighteen feet by twenty feet deep, and covered after a fashion with various boards; which grave is capable of containing between six and seven hundred bodies, and in which there were presently five hundred. He added that during the month of May another one would be dug, but he was unable to indicate the site, precisely *because he had no firm idea of the order of these excavations.* This means that sometimes in the course of digging, the gravedigger encounters bodies that have not been consumed, whereupon he stops and either fills the pits with new burials or covers them over and begins again in a different place.[79]

These large pits were not only dug in the old cemeteries that dated from the Middle Ages. In a brand-new cemetery, which the church council of Saint-Sulpice had founded in 1746 in rue de Bagneux, a commissioner, in the course of the same investigation, found a pit fifteen feet by fifteen feet by eighteen feet deep "covered with an iron grille, capable of containing five hundred bodies."[80]

All the evidence seems to indicate that the methods adopted in the thirteenth and fourteenth centuries in the towns in order to bury victims of the plague quickly were retained in the case of all those who could not pay for the right to be buried in the churches or under the charnels.

The common graves justified the epithet "flesh-eating" that was given to les Innocents, but which other cemeteries also deserved. "In this cemetery there are so many bones of the deceased that it is a miracle," says Corrozet, but this was owing to its peculiar virtue: "The soil of which [cemetery] is so putrefying that it will consume a human body in nine days."[81] Alyscamps, in Arles, was also said to possess this property, which was regarded as supernatural. When testators, sometimes bishops, who could not be buried in les Innocents asked that a little of its soil be placed in their coffins, it was no doubt because of this miraculous quality. The bones exposed in the charnels came from these pits. There were two successive operations: The first involved the whole body, and the second involved only the bones, after the flesh had been consumed. We know that this practice of double burial is known in other cultures, such as that of Madagascar, but there it has a different religious significance.

We should mention a special type in Catalonia and in the south of France that differs from the usual custom of charnels. In small Romanesque churches, one finds cavities that have been cut out of the walls and that open toward the outside. They were designed to hold bones and were covered with an epitaph. One can still see examples of these tombs today. It is obvious that they were like second burial places and that they were designed only for bones, for they were not large enough to admit the whole body. The skeleton had been dismantled. Were these tombs reserved for important personages after their flesh had decomposed or had been broken down by boiling, for example? This practice must have developed in places where the canonical interdicts against burial in church were better respected. In such places the dead would have been buried as near as possible to the wall or, better still, inside the wall. In non-Mediterranean France, however, the use of ossuaries has a different meaning; it is a mass phenomenon that became widespread in the fourteenth and fifteenth centuries, at the end of the urban development, when the limited space in the cemeteries was unable to absorb the dead of a growing population that was periodically exposed to the higher mortality rates of epidemics. Space was created by digging up the bones and transferring them wherever possible, that is, to the attics or on top of the arches.

This practice was still followed in the late nineteenth century in Breton cemeteries. Anatole Le Braz tells us that after five years the bones of the last occupant were taken to the charnel to make room for new ones. The gravedigger of Penvenan had "worked over the whole length of the cemetery six times," meaning "that over the years he had buried up to six bodies in the same hole."[82] He was doing his job like all his predecessors, the gravediggers of the sixteenth and seventeenth centuries, whose contracts with the parochial church councils have been preserved in notarial archives. On October 27, 1527, the gravedigger of Saint-Maclou, in Rouen, received three francs "for tidying the cemetery and storing the bones of the dead in the gallery."[83]

"It would be difficult to find a more expert gravedigger," Le Braz goes on. "He could see right through the ground into the graves that he had filled in. To his eyes, the damp earth of the cemetery was as transparent as water." One day the rector asked him to bury one of his parishioners, or rather "to dig a hole for him in the place where big Ropertz was buried five years ago." But the gravedigger knew his cemetery and its inhabitants too well for that. "Over there, you know, the bodies last a long time. I know old Ropertz. By now the worms have barely begun to work on his guts."[84]

Ossuaries

The most striking characteristic of the charnel is the visibility of the bones. For a long time, probably until the seventeenth century or so, the bones came right up to ground level, where they were mixed with stones and pebbles. A stained-glass window from the sacristy of Saint-Denis (1338), which has since been lost, once illustrated the merciful works of Saint Louis. One of these was the burial of the dead, but it was not an interment that was represented but a gathering of bones. Saint Louis is filling a sack with skulls and shinbones while his companions, who are helping him carry the sack, hold their hands over their noses and mouths. Several of Carpaccio's paintings show cemeteries strewn with half-buried pieces of skeletons and even mummies.

In the days of Pantagruel, skulls and bones were lying around everywhere and provided the beggars of les Innocents with something to "warm their bottoms." They inspired the meditation of Hamlet. Painters and engravers depicted them inside the churches or beside them, mixed with the earth that had been dug out of the ground.

Nevertheless, as early as the fifteenth century, and perhaps earlier in the towns, people began organizing this enormous mass of bones that was perpetually being heaved up by the earth. They were displayed artistically on *présentoirs*[85] over the galleries of the charnels, or on the porches of the churches, or in small chapels next to the churches that were designed for this purpose.

There are still a few examples left on the border between France and Luxembourg and in the ossuaries of Brittany. The Breton type do not have a particularly Breton name. They are called *garnals,* a word that recalls the *carnier* of the *Chanson de Roland;* and in fact they are the curious late survivals of the charnels of the end of the Middle Ages and the beginning of modern times.

Le Braz describes them as follows: "Behind the railing of the clerestory mixed with the remains of wooden coffins, the bones are piled in heaps. Sometimes they overflow onto the outer sills of the windows, and outside the church one walks by rows of moss-covered skulls that follow the comings and goings of the passersby with empty eyes." It seems that one night around 1800, "a young man who had had too much to drink brought home a skull that he had stolen from a charnel. After he had sobered up, he was terrified." That was the original story. It gave rise to a legend in which the drunken youth stole what he thought was the fine linen coif of a dead woman who was dancing in the cemetery and whom he had tried to abduct. When he got home, he put it in his wardrobe, but the next day, "in place of the white coif of fine linen, there was a death's-head, and on the head there was hair, long soft hair that proved it to be the head of a girl." The rector who was consulted in the case said that there was nothing for the young man to do but "take it back to the charnel of Pommerie where it came from."[86]

Breton burial customs provide a key to the meaning of the exhibition of bones that was practiced from the middle of the medieval period until the eighteenth century and even later in Brittany, Naples, and Rome. In the nineteenth century this macabre practice of transferring bones to *présentoirs* was prohibited by law, but the government tolerated it in the Breton west, where the custom persisted until World War I. After that, however, a new attitude appeared. The Breton family, moved by a modern concern for personalizing the tomb, abandoned the traditional anonymity of the charnel in favor of a sort of individual miniature ossuary, the "skull box." These boxes had an opening, often in the shape of a heart, through which one could see the skull, just as reliquary shrines were provided with a round window through which to see the saint.[87] These skull boxes were not confined to western France; examples from the same period can be seen in the charnel of Marville, in Meuse.

Le Braz quotes a Breton hymn that invites the faithful to contemplate the bones piled in the charnels:

> *Let us to the charnel, Christians, let us see the bones*
> *Of our brothers . . .*
> *Let us see the pitiful state that they have come to . . .*
> *You see them broken, crumbled into dust . . .*
> *Listen to their lesson, listen well . . .*[88]

It was important to *see.* The charnels were exhibits. Originally, no doubt, they were no more than improvised storage areas where the exhumed bones were placed simply to get them out of the way, with no particular desire to display them. But later, after the fourteenth century, under the influence of a sensibility oriented toward the macabre, there was an interest in the spectacle for its own sake. The bones and skulls were arranged around the courtyard of the church so as to form a backdrop for the daily life of those sensual times.

The Large Open Cemetery

The charnel cemetery lasted until the end of the eighteenth century. But another type of cemetery did exist. Auguste Joseph Bernard, an authority on medieval tombs, has noted that after the twelfth century larger cemeteries start to appear.[89] It was during the same period that people stopped piling sarcophagi on top of one another and that they even stopped using stone sarcophagi altogether. This was also the period of the *lanternes des morts.*

Larger cemeteries also existed alongside the atria with their small courtyards surrounded by charnels. Indeed, Gabriel Le Bras writes, "the old cemeteries were sometimes *enormous*" (emphasis added).[90]

These large cemeteries were always near the churches and inside the ecclesiastical enclosure. We recognize them in the seventeenth century in the Gaignières drawings of towns: Notre-Dame-d'Evreux, Saint-Etienne-de-Beauvais, and the abbey of Saint-Amand in Rouen.[91]

Near Saint-Savin-sur-Gartempe, in the little village of Antigny, there is an example of this other type of medieval cemetery. Next to the church there is a large square covering the old cemetery, where stone sarcophagi of the twelfth or thirteenth century have been dug up and displayed. In the middle is an altar surmounted by a cross.

The plan of these places is no longer geometrical and rectangular like that of the charnels, but vaguely oval, of a loose and irregular shape. There are no more visible galleries or charnels. The cemetery is sometimes enclosed by a low wall edged with trees like a hedge and with large gateways or openings through which carts could pass. This wall defines a vast open space. If Gaignières' draftsman had not written in the word, one would never guess that the space represented a cemetery.

However, if we examine the drawing more closely, we can make out a few crosses and some small rectangles. The rectangles mark the location of the large common graves described above. The crosses are the only ornaments to break this large, bare surface. Sometimes there is only a single monumental cross mounted on a pedestal, a Calvary cross; sometimes there are five. At the cemetery of les Innocents there were fifteen. There were similar crosses in all the cemeteries, but they were few and far between, nothing resembling the dense rows of crosses in our modern cemeteries. At the Grand-Cloître or courtyard of the canons of Vauvert, in the cemetery on your left as you enter the courtyard, there are several crosses, both wooden and stone.[92]

The crosses were donations. Some were intended for liturgical use, like the large Calvary crosses used in certain Breton religious ceremonies. A few smaller crosses marked the sites of graves or served as landmarks; these were erected by the families of those who were buried around them.

The Social Functions
of the Cemetery

The medieval cemetery was not only a place where the dead were buried. As Le Bras has emphasized, the word *cimeterium* also designated a place where the dead used to be buried, and sometimes where no one had ever been buried, but which provided a function common to all cemeteries, including those that were still used for burial.[93] The cemetery, together with the church, was the center of social life. It took the place of the forum. During the Middle Ages and until well into the seventeenth century, it corresponded as much to the idea of a public square as it did to the notion, now become exclusive, of a space reserved for the dead. The word originally had two meanings, only one of which survived the seventeenth century to our own time.

This twofold function is explained by the privilege of the right of asylum, or sanctuary, which had the same motives as burial *ad sanctos*. The patron saint granted a temporal protection to the living who honored him, just as he gave a spiritual guarantee to the dead who entrusted their bodies to his safekeeping. The territory in which the authority of the lay powers could be exercised stopped at the wall of the church and its atrium. Inside those walls, the living were like the dead who rested in the peace of God: *omnino sunt [cimeteria] in pace Domini.*

The first nonfunerary meaning of the word *cimeterium* was "an area of asylum around the church." Du Cange defines it as such.[94] The meaning passed from church Latin into French. Although the definition of *cimetière* in Richelet's dictionary does not give a literal meaning of "asylum" that is as clear-cut as the one in Du Cange's glossary, it nevertheless recognizes that function in its commentaries: "Cemeteries have always been known as places of asylum."[95] A contemporary historian observes that in Brittany, "the word *cimetière* rapidly acquired the meaning of refuge or sanctuary."[96]

An anecdote reported by the Bollandistes illustrates this role of sanctuary: "In England, during a private feud, an enemy troop arrived in a village and immediately began looting even those belongings that the inhabitants had placed in the church and cemeteries for safekeeping. In the latter place, clothing, sacks, and even strongboxes hung from the branches of trees. Some of the robbers climbed the trees, but by the intercession of the blessed patron saint of the church, the branches broke, the robbers fell down, and their bodies, together with the objects that were hanging from the branches, crushed their companions who were waiting for them beneath."[97] We have already seen that the coffins of the excommunicate were also hung from trees, as were the bodies of criminals. Trees were put to many uses in those days!

Under the circumstances we can see how the function of sanctuary sometimes prevailed over the function of burial. Absurd as it may seem to us, there was nothing to prevent the creation of cemeteries in which no one was buried and in which it might even be against the law to bury anyone. In this case, a space that was necessarily surrounded by walls, and usually close to a chapel or oratory, was consecrated *sub priori immunitatis* (primarily for sanctuary). Du Cange gives an example of a cemetery that was *"ad refugium tantum vivorum, non ad sepulturam mortuorum"* (for the refuge of the living, not for the burial of the dead). By founding this cemetery, the bishop of Redon provided the inhabitants of the region with a place of refuge, without depriving the monks on whom the parish depended of any of the income they received for burial in the cemetery of the monastery.[98]

The function of sanctuary transformed the cemetery, sometimes into a place of residence, always into a public meeting place, whether or not it continued to be used to bury the dead.

Sometimes the refugees who asked for asylum in the cemetery settled there and refused to leave. Some were content with rooms over the charnels. Others built houses and thus prolonged an occupancy that the ecclesiastical authorities had intended to be temporary—not because the clergy found it scandalous that people should live in cemeteries but because they wished to control their use.

A Norman council of 1080 ordered that the refugees be expelled after the end of the war: *"de atrio exire cogantur."*[99] It was understood, however, that the oldest residents could remain.

And so the cemeteries came to be occupied by houses built on top of the charnels, some inhabited by priests, others rented to laymen. This is how the word *cimeterium* acquired the meaning of a place that had become inhabited next to the church: *locus seu vicus* (neighborhood, community) *forte prope ecclesiam constitutus.*[100] It sometimes happened that the inhabited island invaded the area of the cemetery to the point where there was no more room for graves. Nevertheless, the inhabited island remained a cemetery, its inhabitants claimed the privilege (which was sometimes contested) of the right of sanctuary, and even later the word persisted, as in *la place du vieux cimetière-Saint-Jean.*

At the beginning of the thirteenth century, a church tribunal considered whether the customary law of the land allowed the *domini villarum*, (lords of the manor) to exact *census, customas, et alia servitia* from the inhabitants of the cemetery. At Sélestat, in the thirteenth century, it was decided that inhabitants of the cemetery indeed enjoyed the privilege of immunity.[101]

The people who lived in the cemetery were utterly oblivious to the sight of burials or to the proximity of the large common graves, which were left uncovered until they were full.

The residents of cemeteries were not the only persons who frequented them without paying attention to the sights and smells of the graves and ossuaries. The cemetery served as a forum, public square, and mall, where all members of the parish could stroll, socialize, and assemble. Here they conducted their spiritual and temporal business, played their games, and carried on their love affairs. Medieval writers were aware of the public character of the cemetery and remarked on the difference between the *locus publicus* of their time and the *loci solitarii* of pagan tombs.

Auguste Bernard, an expert on burial fees in the Middle Ages, writes that the cemetery was "the noisiest, busiest, most boisterous, and most commercial place in the rural or urban community."[102] The church was the town hall,[103] and the cemetery was the public square, in a time when there were no other public places except the street, and no other meeting places, since most of the houses were so small and overcrowded.

In the atrium, the courtyard of the church, people gathered for all those regular ceremonies that the church was too small to contain, such as sermons, processions, and the distribution of sacraments. In 1429 at les Innocents, Frère Richard preached every day for a whole week from five o'clock in the morning until ten or eleven o'clock before a congregation of five to six thousand persons. Five to six thousand in the small space of a cemetery! "He preached from the top of a platform almost a fathom and a half high, his back to the charnels, his face toward the cartwright's workshop, right by the danse macabre."[104]

Some churches, like the one in Guérande, or the cathedral in Vienne, still have a stone pulpit carved out of the facade and facing out, toward the old cemetery, which has now disappeared. The investigations of the second half of the eighteenth century note that the gravedigger of les Innocents lived in a little house that was still known as *le prêchoir*. From the plans, it would seem that originally the "caretaker's house" was built against one corner of a corridor that ran all the way around the church of les Innocents and separated it from the cemetery proper. This house was later enlarged and converted into an office. That must have been when the caretaker's residence was transferred to the *prêchoir* in the middle of the cemetery.

The Palm Sunday procession took place in the cemetery; the large Calvary cross derives its French name, *la croix hosannière,* from this ceremony. On Palm Sunday it served as a temporary altar on which to rest the monstrance in which the Host was carried in procession, and the stone stand that was sometimes added to it held the Gospel during the singing of the Passion. The base of one of these crosses was decorated with a representation of Christ's entrance into Jerusalem.

Even today in our rural communities, Palm Sunday is a feast of the dead; the tombs are decorated with the blessed branches. One wonders whether this custom does not derive simply from the fact that the Palm Sunday procession took place in the atrium, and that the atrium was also used for burial. In the Middle Ages, the dead were included in the paschal liturgy simply because they were there, being trodden underfoot by the living and exposed to their pity. This frequent contact with the dead in the cemetery generally resulted in a casual indifference on the part of the living, except during the climactic moments of a religion of salvation that revived memories of the deceased on the actual sites of their graves.[105]

During pilgrimages the cemetery served as a stopping place for the procession. "Twelve thousand children gathered at the cemetery of les Innocents and walked in a candlelight procession to Notre Dame to give thanks to God for the victory at Formigny."[106] During the religious agitation against the Calvinists in the time of the League, the cemetery was also the meeting place for all kinds of civilian and military processions. In 1588 "at nine o'clock in the evening in the cemetery of les Innocents, there were several colonels and captains from various districts numbering eleven companies."[107]

Some of the residents of cemeteries were quite unusual, like the female recluses who chose to confine themselves there. "On Thursday, October 11 [1442], the recluse of les Innocents named Jeanne La Vairière was moved into a brand-new cottage by the bishop; a beautiful sermon was preached in her presence and before a very large crowd who had come for the ceremony."[108]

Here is the epitaph of another recluse who was confined in 1418:

> Here lies Aliz la Bourgotte
> The recluse, a very devout woman,
> Whose life was dedicated to God.
> She chose to serve him in this place
> Where she reigned in humility
> For forty-six years.[109]

The hermitage in which the recluse was immured had access to both the church and the cemetery. At Saint-Savin, in Basses-Pyrénées, whose cemetery served a whole valley of the mountain, one window looked onto the church. Legend has assigned it to the Cagots (local outcasts, or cretins). Was it not rather the means of communication with the church of a reclusoir?

It sometimes happened that these pious female hermits lived in close proximity with recluses of another type, who were there against their will, prostitutes or criminals who had been sentenced to be imprisoned there in perpetuity. In 1485 a woman who had killed her husband and whose death sentence had been commuted was taken to the cemetery of les Innocents and placed "in a little house that had to be built for her." Women of this sort were confined in a reclusoir the way women who were found guilty of other misdemeanors were sent to convents or public hospitals, for lack of prisons.

The administration of justice occupied an intermediate position between religious demonstrations and secular activities. At once an essential expression of power—much more so than in our modern states—and a popular means of participation in public life—a function that has disappeared today—the administration of justice partook of both the sacred and the profane. Even temporal justice was administered in the church—or rather, in the cemetery, for it was an outdoor activity.

In the Carolingian period, the count, the centurion, and the vicar held their judiciary assembly *(placita)* in the cemetery. The place of the tribunal was at the foot of the Calvary cross. As late as the fifteenth century, Joan of Arc was tried by a church court in the Saint-Ouen cemetery, in Rouen.

When the inquisitorial procedure replaced ordeals and duels, the interrogations and tortures took place indoors, in an auditorium. However, the sentence had to be pronounced publically, on a stone platform built for that purpose in one corner, if not always of the cemetery at least of the square that was an extension of it and that was only separated from it by a wall. Even private legal transactions had not only to go through the notary —or the priest—in the presence of a few witnesses or signatories but had also to be brought to the attention of the community. In the Middle Ages, that civilization of the visible, the legal act was a spectacle that was presented inside the ecclesiastical enclosure. In the Carolingian period, manumissions took place in the church near the altar, and exchanges, donations, and sales, in the atrium, where the community habitually assembled. Most of these operations had nothing to do with the function of burial. However, there was one that mobilized the dead in its dramatic symbolism. Some local customary laws—in Hainaut, for example—provided that a widow could free herself from the debts of her family by a ceremony in the course of which she laid her belt, her keys, and her purse on the tomb of her husband. In the twelfth and thirteenth centuries, the cemetery was also the scene of a ceremony, inspired by the funeral service, that celebrated the civil death of lepers.

In modern times, private cases passed from the cemetery to the notary's offices, just as judicial hearings passed to the rooms of the town hall. But the decisions still had to be read publically in the cemetery before the community of townspeople, who usually gathered there after High Mass. There they deliberated; there they elected their trustees, their treasurer, and their officers. In the nineteenth century, most of the legal functions of the cemetery were transferred to the town hall, which was the seat of the municipal council. But in that museum that is Brittany, some of them have persisted, especially the announcement of private legal transactions, as is shown by this excerpt from a story collected by Anatole Le Braz: "After Mass was over, the town clerk would make the announcements for the week from the top of the steps in the cemetery [that is, from the stations of the cross or from the Calvary cross], read the new laws to the people assembled in the square, and announce on behalf of the notary the sales that would take place during the week." Orators "mounted the cross." In fact, the pedestal of the cross, "which in some places is actually in the shape of a pulpit, is almost always used as a speaker's platform. It is from this position that lay orators [and formerly preachers] address the people." This is the origin of the French idiom *monter sur la croix*, which means "to harangue."[110]

Under the circumstances it is not at all surprising that communal equipment was set up in this popular place, frequented by the whole community. A document from the end of the twelfth century deals with the installation of a communal oven in the cemetery.[111] Seven centuries later, Breton legends still recalled the presence of the communal bakehouse at the cemetery. In the cemetery in Lanrivoiré, they displayed loaves of bread in the shape of stones. The bread had been miraculously changed into stone because the lord who supervised the baking at the cemetery had refused to give a piece of bread to a poor man.[112]

The proximity of the ovens to the graves, in which the dead were buried so close to the surface and from which they were periodically exhumed, and to the ossuaries, where they were indefinitely exposed, may be surprising, even disgusting to the modern sensibility, but it was a matter of indifference to the townspeople from the Middle Ages until the eighteenth century.

The right of sanctuary turned the cemetery not only into a public forum and meeting place but also into a marketplace and fairground. The merchants enjoyed exemption from taxation and profited from the large numbers of customers drawn by religious, legal, or municipal demonstrations. Days of pilgrimage were also fair days.

Certain texts acknowledge the right of persons living in the cemetery to keep shops there. Du Cange quotes one of these to illustrate the definitions he gives of the word *cimeterium*: "The men of the cemetery of Jay sold wine and beer in the cemetery."[113] Tradesmen set up shops along the charnels. The synods of the fifteenth century tried to prohibit secular activities—at Nantes in 1405 and at Angers in 1423.[114] They prohibited lay judges (but not church tribunals) from holding court in the cemeteries and from pronouncing sentence there. They made it illegal to turn the cemetery into a fairground or marketplace or to sell or even display bread, poultry, fish, and other things. A single exception was made in favor of wax, the noble raw material of candles, the precious product of the queen bee, who is honored in the paschal liturgy: *"apis mater eduxit."* They also prohibited workers and harvesters from meeting there and applying for employment during hiring season.

These prohibitions on the part of the councils reflect the same concerns as the prohibitions against burial in churches. They were designed to protect the holy places from tradesmen, just as the other prohibitions were designed to protect the sanctuary from cadavers. They succeeded in some cases, in the sixteenth century, in removing the seat of justice or the marketplace from the ecclesiastical enclosure. But even so, both continued to hug the cemetery, as if they had been separated from it against their will. The covered stalls of the Saint-Germain market were hard by the Saint-Sulpice cemetery; les Champeaux, the central market of Paris, adjoined the cemetery of les Saints-Innocents.

On the whole, the prohibitions of the councils were ineffectual. In practice, no theoretical consideration, no legal or moral authority could prevent the church and the cemetery from serving as a town meeting place so long as people felt the need to come together periodically for the purpose of self-government and also to experience a sense of community.

When the town hall became the seat of an assembly that continued to meet in public, but that was henceforth more isolated by the law from the mass of electors, it lost the popular quality of the church and the cemetery. This was not a consequence of secularization; the positivists were not raving when they called the town hall a secular temple, a role that the church had played to perfection for centuries. No, the real reason for the change was the rise of bureaucratic forms in public life and administration, the disappearance of the sense of shared, communal experience. Formerly the community expressed its collective consciousness on holidays; it released the excess energy of its young in games in the same place where it held meetings of a religious, legal, political, or commercial nature: the cemetery.

The cemetery was the place for strolling, socializing, and merrymaking. It took the place of a mall. It still does in the Brittany of Anatole Le Braz: "It is under the elms or yews of the cemetery, after vespers, that the young man will meet the young woman who strikes his fancy, there that he will wait, on days when there is a processional, to invite her to take a walk or to dance."[115]

The disapproval of the synods, reiterated fruitlessly as it was for centuries, tells us that the cemeteries continued to be used for recreation, and for the games that accompanied the markets and fairs.

In 1231 the Council of Rouen prohibited "dancing in the cemetery or in the church under pain of excommunication." This prohibition reappears almost unchanged in 1405, when it was forbidden for anyone to dance in the cemetery or to take part in any sort of game; or for mimes, jugglers, mummers, strolling musicians, or mountebanks to pursue their dubious professions there.[116] In the seventeenth and eighteenth centuries, les Innocents was a kind of commercial arcade. Idlers strolled there just as they did in the arcades of the Palais-Royal, where there were also booksellers and people selling notions and linens. Both the town hall and the church, being public places, attracted shops and customers. Two out of the four charnels were named after the kinds of business that were done there; the charnel of the linen drapers and the charnel of the writers, that is, the public letter writers: "Under arches a fathom and a half wide . . . there are two rows of shops of writers, linen sellers, booksellers, and dealers in secondhand clothing."[117] A flea market in the cemetery! Berthaud mentioned,

> *The five hundred fooleries*
> *You find in the galleries.*[118]

"In the midst of all this confusion, a funeral was going on. The gravediggers proceeded to open a grave and take out bodies that had not yet decomposed, although even in the heart of winter the soil of the cemetery gave off noisome odors."[119] This passage from 1657 shows that this promiscuity was not always appreciated. Strollers made fun of the picturesque activities of the petty businessmen: "I took him to the charnels of les Saints-Innocents and showed him the famous secretaries of that locality. I gave him the opportunity to hear the reading of a letter in the lofty style of those gentlemen. I pointed out a servant girl who was paying one of them to falsify a bill for shoeing a mule [so she could pocket the difference]."[120]

These promenades were often frequented by undesirable characters. As early as 1186, according to Guillaume le Breton, the cemetery of les Saints-Innocents was known as a place of prostitution *(meritricabatur in illo)*. It was for this reason that Philip the Fair had its wall rebuilt. The reputation of les Innocents had not improved by the time of Rabelais: "[Paris] was a good town to live in, but not to die in," because of the beggars, bums, and derelicts who haunted the cemetery night and day.[121]

We meet them again in the eighteenth century. "The poor people tarried there, depositing their filth, spreading disease and contagion, and indulging in all manner of excesses.[122] Thieves were just as certain of finding refuge there in the evening as in the daytime, courtesy of the unsuspecting residents of les Innocents."[123]

In those days when the police exercised only a poor and intermittent control over the dangerous elements of society, vagabonds sought refuge and profit in public places, churches, and cemeteries, wherever there were taverns and shops.

Marketplace; place for announcements, auctions, proclamations, sentences; scene of community gatherings; promenade; athletic field; haven for illicit encounters and dubious professions—in short, the cemetery was the public square. It had the function of the public square, since it was the public place par excellence, the center of collective life. It also had the form of the public square, the two familiar forms of medieval urbanism and the beginning of modern times: the fairground and the square courtyard.

Undoubtedly it was the appearance of the market in the twelfth and thirteenth centuries that brought about the enlargement of some cemeteries that we noted above on the authority of Auguste Bernard and Gabriel Le Bras. After that they came to resemble the large crossroads of medieval towns, which were dominated by a monumental, central cross: a Calvary cross or crossroads cross.

Was it the cemetery or the cloister that provided the model for the square or rectangular park flanked by shopping arcades: the plaza mayor of Spain, the place des Vosges, or the galleries of the Palais-Royal in Paris? From the sixteenth to the eighteenth century the inhabitants of towns, whether large or small, preferred to carry on their public activities within these enclosed spaces, of which some, like les Innocents, were cemeteries. After les Innocents was destroyed, its recreational functions were taken over by another rectangular courtyard, the one at the Palais-Royal. The galleries of the Palais-Royal were in turn replaced in the nineteenth century by the *grands boulevards,* a sign that urban man and his social life had undergone a transformation. Now he preferred the open and linear space of the boulevard, lined by the terraces of cafés, to the enclosed and square space of the courtyard. Perhaps there is a vestige of the traditional taste in the covered walkways of nineteenth-century towns and cities.

In the bourgs, those little half-rural, half-urban communities, in the seventeenth century, the bailiff's square and the central market were an extension of the cemetery. They were eventually separated from it when a movement that began in the late sixteenth century in some places, and later in others, separated the cemetery from the church, as we shall see in chapter 6 of this book, "The Turning of the Tide." This movement also had the effect of weakening the secular role of the cemetery in places where it was not supported by a powerful tradition, as it was at les Innocents in Paris. In the absence of such support, the function of public place passed from the cemetery to the adjacent square. But for a very long time, before it was isolated from the church, the cemetery was the public square.

The Church
Replaces the Saint

A great deal of what has been said about the cemetery and its public character can also be applied to the church. Each was a house of the dead and of the living. In the beginning, this was because of the devotion to the relics of saints, to their *memoria.* Later, after the twelfth century, the two remained closely connected, but the underlying motive of the devotion had changed. The same feeling that attracted the sarcophagi of the early Christian era to the *martyria* continued to motivate the people of the later Middle Ages to choose to be buried in the church or beside it. However, it was no longer the memory of a certain saint that was now desired but the church itself, because Mass was celebrated there, and the most desirable location was the altar: not the confession of the saint but the table of the eucharistic sacrifice.

Burial *apud ecclesiam* had replaced burial *ad sanctos*. This change is all the more remarkable because at the time it was taking place, devotion to the saints became fashionable once again. Jacques Le Goff has distinguished two phases in the history of the worship of saints, the first in the early Middle Ages, as illustrated by the early, legend-filled hagiographies, and the second starting in the thirteenth century with the *Légende dorée* and the miraculous anecdotes of an art that cultivated the picturesque qualities of folklore.[124] The first period coincides with the popularity of burial *ad sanctos*. The second had no direct effect on burial customs, nor did it influence the attitude toward the dead. If we confined ourselves to the reading of wills, we would not suspect how popular legends about saints had become by the end of the Middle Ages. Only one aspect of this devotion appears in wills: the posthumous pilgrimage.

Sometimes the testator asks that someone hired for the purpose make in his place and for the repose of his soul a pilgrimage that he was unable to make during his lifetime, to a place and for a fee that he specifies. It was customary for the sum to be paid upon the pilgrim's return, on the strength of a certificate made out by the clergy of the church he had visited. The 1411 will of a procurator at the Parliament of Paris provides for "a journey and pilgrimage that my wife and companion and myself had intended to make to Notre-Dame-de-Boulogne-sur-la-Mer and also to Notre-Dame-de-Montfort, Saint-Come, and Saint-Damien-de-Lusarches. Because I have been given to understand that my companion had intended to make a pilgrimage to Santiago de Compostela in Galicia, although she had said nothing about it to me and I had not given my consent, nevertheless I desire that a trustworthy messenger be sent there who will bring back a letter of certification."[125] Anatole Le Braz cites posthumous pilgrimages of this sort in nineteenth-century Brittany.[126]

People still went to pray on the tomb of a saint in the presence of venerated relics, but they were less interested in being buried nearby. This second period of the popular worship of saints did not have as profound an effect as the first on the religious sensibility of the times. No doubt the cult was already giving rise to a reaction of mistrust on the part of the clergy and was beginning to appear suspect. A secretary to Queen Isabeau of Bavaria who was canon of several churches specified in a will dated 1403 what disposition he wished for his body in the event that he should die far away from home. His preferences vary according to the quality of the church in the place of his decease. His first choice is the choir, or if that is not possible, the nave in front of the statue of Our Lady. However, if the church in the place of his decease is dedicated to a saint other than the Virgin Mary, the canon does not ask to be buried near the high altar, the choir, or the chapel of the saint. Instead, he anticipates the reforms by asking to be buried in the nave in front of the crucifix. Thus, the order of preference reads: the choir, the statue of the Virgin Mary, and the crucifix, all of which come ahead of the saint.[127] Less circumspect individuals also stopped seeking the posthumous protection of a saint other than Our Lady or the patron saint of their confraternity. From now on, the church outweighed other considerations. The church was the image that the testator associated quite naturally with his body. A councillor at the Parliament of Toulouse wrote in 1648, "I give my soul to God. My body I leave to the church of the Augustins [and not to the earth] and to the tomb of my family."[128]

This shift in devotion had no effect on the attitude toward the dead or its manifestations; *the church had simply replaced the saint.* The difference is considerable in the history of religious ideas, but it is negligible in the history of ideas about death.

The problem, then, is to determine what motives dictated the choice of a church, a certain location within a church, or a cemetery. Answers to these questions are provided by wills, since the choice of burial place is one of their reasons for being. But the authors of wills were not unaware of certain stipulations of church law.

In the beginning, the cemeterial church was the church of an abbey that was venerated for the saints' relics or tombs that it contained. Later, the importance of the saint declined in favor of the abbey itself. It became customary to be buried in a monastery. This is the only detail that Roland gives when he expresses the hope that Charlemagne will be able to recover his body and the bodies of his companions.

Substantial financial considerations also entered into the picture, for the deceased was soon obliged to provide in his will for legacies in favor of the abbey he had chosen. The bishops also hoped to deprive the abbeys of the monopoly on burials and even to reserve this right for the cemeteries of their cathedral churches, which were first located outside the walls and later adjacent to a parish church or the episcopal church. "The burial of the dead must be performed on the site of the bishop's see." If the episcopal cemetery was too far away from the place of decease, the burial was to take place in a community of canons, monks, or nuns, in order to take advantage of the intercession of their prayers. It was only in the event that neither of these alternatives was possible that the fathers of the Council of Tribur in 895 authorized local burial in the former chapel, now the parish church, where the deceased paid the tithe. Burial in the rural church did not occur until the Church stopped requiring burial in the episcopal cemetery. In the Pyrenees, tradition has preserved the memory of a time when people came from all over an entire valley to bury their dead in a cemetery such as the one at Saint-Savin, near Pau.

And yet the law recognizes that each person has the right to choose the place of his burial. There was some ambiguity in the case of the married woman. According to a decree of Gratian, "the wife must follow her husband in life and in death." But according to a decretal of Urban II, death emancipates the wife from her husband.

The question arose as to what happened when the deceased had not had an opportunity to express his own wishes. In this case the law prescribed that he be buried with his relatives *(in majorum suorum sepulcris jacet)*. In the still-significant case of the married woman, the wife was buried either with her husband or in a place chosen by her husband or else near her own ancestors.

There was some reason to fear that families would claim precedents in order to control their burial place as if it were a possession that could be handed down by inheritance. This is why the choice of the parish church was recommended. Hincmar writes, "No Christian shall presume to dictate the place of his burial as if he owned it by inheritance; but let them be buried in the parish churches in those places assigned by the clergy [the bishops]."[129] The ambiguity surrounding the practice is explained by the desire not to deprive the parish church of its burial fees. The parish church was always entitled to collect a "fair share" determined by custom— sometimes after long negotiations—when one of its parishioners had chosen to be buried in another church. Moreover, after the seventeenth century at any rate, bodies could be exhibited at the parish church before being taken to the church where they were to be buried. In the seventeenth and eighteenth centuries, it was the gravedigger of the parish church who was mentioned in the records if burial took place elsewhere. Church law wavered between according preference to the family and according it to the parish church.

The uncertainty of the law is reflected in practice. In the beginning, the knights of the *Chanson de Roland* and later the knights of the Round Table had no interest in family burial. Neither Roland nor Oliver demonstrated the slightest desire to lie next to his parents, to whom in fact they never gave so much as a thought before they died. The knights of the

Round Table hoped to be buried in the church in Camelot beside their comrades-in-arms.

Beginning in the fifteenth century, most testators ask to be buried in the church or cemetery where members of their families have already been buried, beside their dead husbands, wives, or even children: "In the church of Monseigneur Saint-Eustache, next to my very dear companion and wife and my children, whose souls are with God" (1411). A husband and wife ask to be buried side by side in Saint-Médéric, their parish church (1663). The widow of a shopkeeper, "in the cemetery of Saint-Gervais, her parish church, in the place where her deceased husband is buried" (1604). A parishioner of Saint-Jean-en-Grève, "in the cemetery of les Saints-Innocents, in the place where his deceased wife and children are buried" (1609). A master cobbler of the parish of Saint-Martial "desires that his body be buried in the cemetery of les Saints-Innocents, near the place where his deceased wife and children are buried" (1654).[130]

Some request burial near their parents and spouse at the same time, in a church or cemetery: "in the abbey of Saint-Sernin [in Toulouse], in the grave where our grandfather, grandmother, father, mother, brother, and sister, and my two wives are buried" (1600); "in the church of Saint-Etienne-du-Mont, in the place where her parents and husband are buried and near their children" (1644).[131]

Others request burial near their parents, without reference to the spouse. A councillor to the duke of Orléans, a parishioner of Saint-Nicolas-des-Champs: "in the cemetery of les Saints-Innocents, in the place where his fathers, mothers, and brothers are buried." "In the church of Saint-Séverin, in the tomb of his ancestors" (1690). "In the courtyard of the church of Saint-Germain-le-Vieil, where my two sisters are" (1787). Perhaps the last two were unmarried. However, widows clearly preferred the graves of their parents to those of their husbands: "In Saint-Jacques-de-la-Boucherie, her parish church, in the place where her deceased mother is buried" (1661); ". . . chooses [to be buried in] the cemetery of the church of les Saints-Innocents in Paris, near the place where his father and mother are buried" (1407).[132]

A holograph will dated 1657 illustrates how a testator sometimes hesitated between burial with the spouse and burial with the parents: "I wish that my grave be wheresoever my wife shall desire to be buried." In this case the deceased will be buried in a place to be determined by the survivor, unless circumstances make it impossible, in which case, "in the cemetery, in the place where my father, mother, and distant forebears are buried."[133]

We see that the church was almost always chosen for family reasons, so that one could be buried either beside one's parents or, more often, beside one's spouse and children. The practice became widespread in the fifteenth century, and it clearly expresses the rise of a feeling that transcended death. Indeed, it may have been the moment of death that brought this feeling to full consciousness. In those days the family played a minor role in the normal course of daily life. But in times of crisis, when an unusual danger threatened a person's honor or life, the family recovered its authority and imposed its ultimate solidarity until after death. The family prevailed over the military kinship that had united the knights of the Round Table in their cemeteries; their real family had been their fellow warriors. It accommodated itself, on the other hand, to the trade brotherhoods, because spouse and children were buried together in the chapel of the confraternity.

It sometimes happened that the testator preferred to be buried near someone outside his family. Particularly if he was unmarried, the attraction of the parents was weaker than that of the wife and children in the case of a married man. He might choose, for example, to be buried with an uncle who had been his benefactor, such as the dealer in tapestries of 1659 who wished to lie "in the tomb of his late uncle, M. de La Vigne."[134] Or he might choose a friend; that was Jean Régnier's dream:

> *At the Dominicans is where*
> *I would be buried when I die*
> *For with the brothers of Aucerre*
> *Several of my friends do lie.*[135]

The friend might also be a distant relative. He was a little like the "brother" in the archaic societies. This appears in wills like that of a president of the Parliament of Paris in 1413 who asks to be buried in a chapel in which "his late father and his other friends" are buried.[136] From the fifteenth to the seventeenth century, it was very common for a testator to make pious endowments for the salvation of his soul and of his wife's "conjointly and for the souls of all their friends."

In 1574 a notary chose to be buried "near the grave of the late Maître François Bastoneau, also a notary, his cousin and good friend." In those days friendship was not, as it is among adults of our own time, simply one of the pleasures of social life; it was, as it still is today for the child and the adolescent, a lasting bond comparable to love, so strong that it sometimes even survived death. It is found at all levels of society, even the most humble. The woman who rented chairs at Saint-Jean-en-Grève, the widow of a soldier in the Piedmont regiment, wrote that she wished her body to lie "in the little cemetery near the church of Saint-Jean [a desirable location], next to the grave of Mme. Jacques Labbé, her good friend" (1642).[137]

In preference to the family and or worldly friends, seventeenth-century testators sometimes chose the spiritual friend, the confessor. Not content to favor him with a legacy of some sort, as was the custom, they also chose to lie in his shadow, like the Parisian doctor in a holograph will of 1651 who asked that his body be buried in the church of Saint-Médard, "near the confessional of M. Cardos."[138] Here the confessor of the seventeenth century, who was venerated as a saint during his lifetime, has replaced the saint of the early Middle Ages.

Finally, it sometimes happened that servants asked to remain near their masters after death: "as close as possible to the tomb of the late lord Pierre de Moussey and his wife, during their lives bourgeois of Paris, his master and mistress, may God forgive their sins" (sixteenth century).[139] "In the church of Sainte-Croix-de-la-Bretonnerie, near the grave of her master's daughter" (1644).[140] In most cases the masters are the executors of the wills of their servants, and the servants leave the choice of their burial place up to them.

These earthly, familial, or more traditional loyalties were sometimes overlooked, especially in the seventeenth and eighteenth centuries, in favor of the spiritual family, the parish. This was a result of the Council of Trent, which wished to restore to the parish church a function that it had supposedly had in the Middle Ages, especially in the fourteenth and fifteenth centuries: "I desire that my body be buried in the church of Monseigneur Saint-Jehan-en-Grève, my parish church."

Certain ingenious testators combined the parish church with another church of their choice: ". . . wishes her body to be buried in the collegiate church of Monseigneur Saint-Médéric, in Paris, her parish church, in the choir, in the grave in which her late husband, the very honorable Thibault, is buried." This was a widow who after the death of her husband became "one of the good women of the chapel of Saints-Etienne-et-André." But she must have had a special devotion to the church of Saint-Jean, for she added her "wishes that before her burial her body be taken to the church of Saint-Jehan-en-Grève and that a complete service be said there, and that there be present at this service and in this procession the rectors, priests, vicars, and clergymen of the choir of Saint-Jehan, as well as the regular canons and chaplains of the church of Saint-Médéric," in other words, the clergymen of both churches (1606).[141]

However, the parochial movement of the Counter-Reformation did not, at least until the second half of the eighteenth century, eliminate the traditional attachment to religious communities, especially Dominicans and Carmelites, as we shall see presently.

Location in the Church

Once the church had been chosen for reasons of family and piety, it remained to decide where one wanted to be buried: in the church itself or in the cemetery, and above all, in what location.

Although some people left this choice up to their executor, the majority went to great lengths to describe easily recognizable landmarks in order to indicate more clearly the location they desired.

Usually it was a question of describing the location of the family grave beside which the testator wished to be buried. In most cases this grave was not apparent. The practice of marking the exact site of a grave by means of an inscription did not become widespread until the end of the eighteenth century. The custom of piling bodies on top of one another and moving them to other locations made it difficult to mark graves, and the practice was followed only in the case of a few monuments. There was no official diagram of the underground burial system. The obituaries in which the monks of the Middle Ages recorded the dates of burial of persons who had made endowments to the monastery referred only vaguely to their place of burial—for example, this reference to the anniversary of the burial of C. A., canon of Limoges, "who is buried in our cloister next to the wall or a pillar."[142]

The testator had to furnish the coordinates of a place that often was known only to himself: in the convent of the Dominicans, in the chapel where his wife, his sister, and his father's wife were buried, "which chapel is on the right when you walk from the nave to the choir" (1407); in the church of les Frères-Minimes-de-Saint-François, in Blois, "in the place which she says she showed her cousin, the clerk" (sixteenth century); "between the column by the altar of the Annunciation and the one below it, next to Pierre Feuillet's pew" (1608); "in the nave of their large church in Paris, on the right side . . . in the place I showed my brother"; "in Saint-Denis, in front of the statue of the Virgin"; "near the place where M. le doyen of Paris stands on Sunday morning for the ordinary procession" (August 10, 1612); "in the church of Saint-Nicolas-des-Champs . . . by the fifth column" (1669); "in the church of les Pères-Carmes in the place Maubert, in the tomb of his ancestors, which is in Saint-Joseph's chapel under a large tombstone, right below the steps that support the banisters of the altar of the chapel, on the right side" (1661). (We see that the presence of a "large tombstone," which certainly bore an inscription, was not enough to ensure identification of the grave.)[143]

One could not always be certain of being buried in the exact place thus designated, even if the priest and the churchwardens had given their

consent. The ground might be occupied by recent graves containing bodies
not yet decomposed. Consequently, it was sometimes a general vicinity
rather than a precise spot that was requested: "in the church of le Val-des-
Ecoliers, in the grave of his late wife, or next to it" (1401); "in les Innocents, near the place where his father and mother were buried, or some
other place nearby" (1407); "as near as possible to the tomb" (sixteenth
century); "in the grave of my father and mother, which is near the wall of
the church, on the left side as you enter" (1404).[144]

One finds from the pens of the testators or the clergymen who drew
up their wills expressions like "near the place where so-and-so is buried"
or "near the chapel." This approximation is customary, but there are
exceptions. A few leave no room for doubt: "in that place and location
where . . ." (1657); "in the same place where my mother is buried"
(1652).[145]

A fifteenth-century man went to considerable trouble to indicate
geometrically the place he wanted to be buried: "at the intersection obtained by drawing two lines, one from the crucifix to the statue of Our
Lady, the other from the altar of Saint Sébastien to the altar of Saint
Dominique" (1416).[146]

The choicest and most expensive location was the choir, near the altar
where Mass was said, in the place where the priest recited the *Confiteor*.
(The reader will recall that the underlying reason for burial *apud ecclesiam*
was the sacrifice of the Mass, rather than the protection of the saints.) "He
wishes his body to lie in the church of la Terne, which is of the order of
the Celestines, in the diocese of Limoges, and to be in the choir of this
church, quite close to [that is, right by] the high altar on the side next to
the wall" (1400). A physician to Charles VI wished to be buried *"in choro
dictae ecclesiae ante magnum altare"* (1410). Or again: "in the choir of the
church of les Frères-Minimes-de-Saint-François, in Blois, near the high
altar" (sixteenth century); "in the choir of the Hôtel-Dieu of the city of
Paris" (1662). A recording magistrate asked "to be taken to the church of
le Boulay and buried in the choir of said church" (1669).[147]

The parochial Mass was not always said at the high altar. One testator asked to be buried "in the church of Saint-Merry in the chapel where
Mass is said for the parish" (1413). In the seventeenth century the parochial Mass was said at the altar of the Blessed Sacrament: "Beneath this
tombstone lies the body of Messire Claude d'Aubray, knight," who died
on May 31, 1609, at the age of eighty-three. "Having had on this earth
a wholehearted and singular devotion to the precious body of Our Savior,
[he] desired that on the day of his decease he be laid to rest and buried
next to the Blessed Sacrament, that he might obtain mercy through the
prayers of the faithful who prostrate themselves before this very holy and

venerable sacrament and be born again with them in glory."[148]

After the choir, the next most sought-after location was the chapel of the Virgin or her "image." The family of the widow of Guillaume des Bordes, chamberlain, killed at Nicopolis, were buried "in the church of the priory of Saint-Didier and Brugères, in the chapel of Our Lady" (1416). One could be buried in front of the chapel but not inside it, like a widow by her first husband, a bourgeois Parisian, "now the wife of a surgeon to the king" who "desires her body to be buried in Saint-Jacques-de-la-Boucherie, her parish church, in front of the chapel of the Blessed Virgin, in the place where her deceased mother is buried" (a case where the parents were preferred over the husband; 1661). And another: "in the abbey of Saint-Sernin, near the chapel of Our Lady" (1600).[149]

Some, like this vine grower, asked to be buried in front of the statue of Our Lady "in the church at Montreuil in the same place where his dear wife was buried, which is in front of the statue of the Virgin" (1628). Again: "facing the statue of Our Lady that is in said church." A secretary to the king: "I wish my body to be buried in Saint-Jehan-en-Grève, my parish church, where I was second churchwarden at the time when his lordship the marquis d'Estrées was first [a fine position!], in front of the statue of the Virgin, in the part of the chapel . . . where my late wife, Mlle. Damond, is buried" (1661).[150]

There were also statues of Our Lady in cemeteries. At les Innocents "there is a small tower in place of a tomb with a statue of Our Lady carved out of stone, very well done, which tower a man had built because he had boasted when he was alive that the dogs would never piss on his grave." In the sixteenth century, people chose to be buried at les Innocents "in front of the statue of Our Lady," or "beside the statue of Our Lady." In 1621: "in the cemetery of les Saints-Innocents, in front of the altar of the Virgin Mary"; "in the cemetery of les Saints-Innocents, in front of the chapel of the Virgin Mary, which is in the middle of the cemetery."[151]

The other saints were mentioned much less frequently, yet they were still venerated, no doubt, as the patron saints of the confraternities to whom the chapels were dedicated. The wife of a gardener: "in the church of Saint-Gervais, opposite the chapel of Saint-Eutrope" (1604).[152] A procurator at Châtelet chose to be buried in the chapel of Saint-Joseph. This was in 1661, a time when Saint Joseph was becoming popular as the patron saint of the good death. In 1647 the Chapel of the Resurrection was chosen for the same reason.

Beginning in the fifteenth century and continuing into the seventeenth, after the choir and the chapel or statue of the Virgin, one finds the crucifix as the chosen place of burial. In 1402 a priest asked to be buried both *"ante crucifixum et ymaginem beate Marie."* There was always the fortunate possibility that the crucifix would be in the choir: "under the crucifix in the choir" (1690). But usually the crucifix hung in the nave. A Parisian bourgeois of 1660 "desires his body to be buried in Saint-Germain-l'Auxerrois, his parish church, at the foot of the crucifix." The crucifix could also be next to the churchwardens' pew. Some of the faithful, no doubt former churchwardens, chose this spot for their final resting-place. A baker and his wife: "in the church of la Madeleine, in front of the churchwardens' pew" (1560). Another: "in Saint-Médéric, my parish church, in front of the founders' pulpit, where my fathers and mothers are" (1649).[153]

We have seen that crosses served as landmarks in the cemeteries. Testators often use them as topographical reference points in describing the location of their graves. A Paris shopkeeper and his wife asked to be buried "between the cross and the elm tree in the cemetery of the church of Saint-Gervais" (1602).[154]

Finally, one of the popular locations in the seventeenth century was the family pew. People asked to be laid to rest near the place where they had attended Mass when they were alive: "in the nave near his pew, which is located in the back of the church against one of the columns of the tower, on the far side" (1622). A court attendant at Châtelet and his wife: "in Saint-Nicolas-des-Champs, their parish church, in front of their pew" (1669). In 1607 the father of a family signed an agreement with the church council to "have a tomb made in front of said pew in which to bury himself, his wife, and his children." Another: "in Saint-Jehan-en-Grève, his parish church, beside his pew" (1628).[155]

Curiously enough, Parisian Protestants under the regime of the Edict of Nantes showed the same devotion to the place where they had followed the liturgy during their lifetimes. Anne Gaignot, wife of Nicolas I of Rambouillet, who died in 1684, asked to be buried beside the temple of Charenton, in the old cemetery, near her fathers and mothers, "opposite the place where she had entered the temple."[156]

One finds in wills other choices that are more exceptional and less significant: "under the holy-water basin" (1404); *"prope piscinam"* (1660).[157]

Generally speaking, one finds that the places of burial most frequently chosen in the fifteenth through seventeenth centuries were primarily determined by devotion to the Mass and to the crucified Christ.

The locations thus designated by the authors of wills were subject to the approval of the clergy and the church council. It was almost always a matter of money, but the most farsighted testators arranged for alternate locations, which are interesting because they help us to understand the psychological relationship between burial in the church and burial in the cemetery: "in the church of Saint-Eustache, but if the churchwardens do not consent to this, then in the paupers' grave at les Innocents" (1641); "in the church of les Minimes . . . begging the priest of Saint-Médériq, his highly revered pastor, to approve of this arrangment" (1648); "in the parish church of the place where the aforesaid testator shall die, if convenient, otherwise, in the cemetery" (1590); "in the church of l'Hôtel-Dieu . . . if possible, if not, in such church or cemetery as Mme. Marj. Picard, my niece, shall choose" (1662); "in the church of the Capuchin monks. . . . begging their kind permission" (1669); "in the chapel of Notre-Dame-des-Suffrages-du-Taur [in Toulouse], if M. le recteur of said church agrees; if not, in the cemetery of said parish" (1678).[158]

In the above cases, burial in the cemetery is accepted only if burial in the church is impossible. However, some testators voluntarily chose the cemetery out of humility. Claude de l'Estoile, squire and lord of Soussy, "realizing himself to be a very great sinner, does not wish to be buried in the church, an honor of which he is unworthy, but only in the cemetery of his parish church" (1652). Being buried in the cemetery sometimes meant in the aristocratic part, the charnels: "Laure de Mahault wishes her body to be buried in the cemetery bordering on the charnel of Saint-Jehan, her parish church" (1660); "under the charnels of the parish church of Saint-Cosmas" (1667). It could also mean being buried in the common grave. In 1406 a lawyer at Châtelet asked to be buried "in the big paupers' grave." In 1539 Geneviève de Quatrelivres wanted to be "in the paupers' grave at the cemetery of les Saints-Innocents," like her father.[159] We shall see in part 3 of this book that the burial of people of quality in cemeteries, while still exceptional, became more common in the second half of the eighteenth century, indicating a change that foreshadows the abandonment of the practice of burial in churches.[160]

Church vs. Cemetery:
A French Example

The figures suggest that from the fifteenth to the seventeenth century the preferred place of burial was the church. Indeed, this is what Furetière says in his dictionary under the definition for *cimetière:* "Formerly people were never buried in churches, but always in cemeteries. Today hardly anyone is buried in cemeteries except the people."[161]

But who were the people? Let us take a closer look at the class distribution of burials. We are able to do this because the parochial registers gave the location of each grave, even when it was outside of the parish.

I have selected the registers of three parish churches in Toulouse at the very end of the seventeenth century. The first is Saint-Etienne, the cathedral church in the heart of the medieval town where nobles, officers, captains, and rich merchants still resided in greater numbers than elsewhere. Next, la Dalbade, in a neighborhood of artisans and shopkeepers, but also of officials of the court. Finally, less common than la Dalbade but not so aristocratic as Saint-Etienne, the abbey of la Daurade, which was isolated from the rest of the town.[162]

The registers allow us to distinguish between burials in churches and burials in cemeteries. We shall begin by considering the case of parishioners buried outside their parishes. Here we shall be concerned only with those buried in churches, for those buried in cemeteries were always members of the parish.

Table 1 shows the high percentage of burials outside the parish. I would not be surprised if this figure were higher for Toulouse than it is for Paris, based on my reading—by no means exhaustive—of Parisian wills of the period. In Paris at that time, permission to be buried outside the parish was difficult to obtain, except in the case of a family grave.

Substantial differences may be observed from one parish to the next. In la Dalbade, 62 percent of burials occurred within the parish (church and cloisters) as compared with 11 percent in la Daurade. In the parish with the highest proportion of common people, over half the burials took place in the parish church. In the more aristocratic parishes, people were more drawn by the prestige of other sanctuaries. The first phase of burial in church, a mark of social distinction, took place in one's own parish.

What churches did testators choose in preference to their own parish churches? A glance at table 1 tells us that essentially they were the monasteries of the mendicant orders: Franciscans, Dominicans, Carmelites, and Augustinians. Monasteries accounted for half the burials of the parishioners of Saint-Etienne and for 71 percent of the burials of the parishioners of la Daurade. At la Daurade, one-third of the burials went to the Dominicans, and another third to the Franciscans. The mendicant orders were the great specialists in death. They took part in the funeral services, and in the period after death, they presided over vigils, sought commissions for tombstones, and prayed for the souls of the departed. Starting at the end of the Middle Ages, the cordon of Saint Francis replaced the medallions of Saint Benedict, which were found in the tombs of the twelfth century. The phenomenon was widespread until the second half of the eighteenth century.

Let us now compare the number of burials in each parish in churches and in cemeteries.

1. Burial in Churches Other Than the Parish Church

Percentage for Each Church of Total Burials in Churches

	la Daurade, 1699	la Dalbade, 1705	St.-Etienne, 1692
Franciscans	33.5	17	11.0
Dominicans	33.5		12.0
Carmelites	4.0	13	15.5
Parish	11.5	62	27.7
Augustinians			12.0

2. Class Distribution of Burials in Churches and Cemeteries

	Percentage of Total Burials in Parish	Percentage of Burials within Churches and within Cemeteries		
		Nobility and Professions	Skilled Craftsmen and Merchants	Workmen and Unknown
St.-Etienne, 1692:				
church	64	38	51	10
cemetery of St.-Sauveur	36	0	33	66[b]
la Daurade, 1698:				
church	48	20	60	6
cemetery of les Comtes	21	0	60	30
cemetery of la Toussaint	31	0	34	50
la Daurade, 1699:				
church	37	20	68	12
cemetery of les Comtes	26	12[a]	60	17
cemetery of la Toussaint	37	0	26	72[c]
la Dalbade, 1705:				
church	49	9	68	13
cemetery	51	6[a]	48	46

[a]children [b]children, 20% [c]children, 18%

3. Burials of Children in Churches vs. Cemeteries

Percentage of Total Burials

	la Dalbade, 1705	la Daurade, 1699	St.-Etienne, 1692
Age 10 and up:			
Church	36.0	57.0	32
Cemeteries	67.0	62.5	48
Age 6 months and up:			
Church	10.0	18.0	4
Cemeteries	25.5	19.0	39

A cemetery is always associated with a parish church. But in some parishes, there are several categories of cemetery.

At la Dalbade we find the simple relationship between church and cemetery that we have analyzed in the preceding pages. But at Saint-Etienne and la Daurade the situation was more complex, because these two churches were the centers of communities of canons and monks and also because of their great antiquity and the changes undergone by their out-buildings and environs.

At Saint-Etienne the oldest cemetery was the cloister. In the seventeenth century it was still referred to as "the cemetery of the cloister," but more often simply "the cloister" or "the little courtyard." In fact, burial there was just as expensive and sought after as burial inside the church, so there was no difference in social status between the two populations of the dead. For this reason I have included them in the same category of burials in churches. Out of twenty-three burials in this category, only nine were in the nave; all the rest were in the cloister. The case is interesting because it shows that under certain circumstances, for instance, at Orléans, and no doubt in England, the atrium or cloister retained the function of an open-air cemetery that was both noble and venerable. For this to happen it had to be very old and not available to the poor.

The situation is similar in the ancient Benedictine abbey of la Daurade. In accordance with ancient customs preserved there and generally ignored elsewhere (except perhaps in the south of France), the dead were never buried in the nave or the choir. The 11.5 percent of the total burials that I have listed under parish burials were in reality *sub stillicidio* or *in porticu*, to borrow those old expressions, which still have their meaning here at the end of the seventeenth century: "in the porch of this church," "in front of the door of this church," "in the monastery of our church" (the cloister?), "in the gallery of this church," "in the cloister," "by the door of the church." It is remarkable that the priests who kept the registers never used the word *cimetière* to describe the location of these outdoor graves.

Now let us turn to the cemeteries proper of Saint-Etienne and la Daurade. The cemetery in which the parishioners of Saint-Etienne were buried in the seventeenth century was not contiguous with the church; it was separated from it by the whole thickness first of the wall and later of the boulevard that replaced it. It was called the cemetery of Saint-Sauveur, from the name of the small church or chapel that was built inside its walls and without which it could not have existed. There was no such thing as a cemetery without a church, or a cemetery that was physically separate from the church. Thus, the cemetery of les Champeaux was an extension of the little church of les Saints-Innocents. The difference is that Saint-Sauveur was not a parish church, like les Saints-Innocents, but a chapel or outbuilding of the cathedral. The cemetery of Saint-Sauveur dates from the period when the cemetery was beginning to detach itself from the church. We shall see other examples of this in Paris in chapter 6, "The Turning of the Tide." Saint-Sauveur was created to serve as a cemetery for the parish of Saint-Etienne.

The parish church of la Daurade had two cemeteries in addition to the cloister and the courtyard of the abbey: one very old and highly revered one that was called the cemetery of les Comtes, the other much more recent and intended for the poor, the cemetery of la Toussaint. The latter may have been contemporary with the cemetery of Saint-Sauveur. Both cemeteries were inside the walls of the abbey; the cemetery of les Comtes lay in front of the door of the church and to the side. It was a continuation of the cemeterial area of the courtyard and contained the graves of the counts of Toulouse. An early sixth-century sarcophagus now in the musée des Augustins, said to be that of Queen Pédauque, but probably the tomb of Ragnachilde, was once located, according to an old description, "in the outer part of the wall of the church of la Daurade, near the cemetery of les Comtes"—perhaps in a niche.

The other cemetery was located around the apse of la Daurade. Its name would lead us to believe that it was built after the first celebration of All Souls' Day, which was the day after All Saints' Day at the time when it became popular.

The existence of several cemeteries for the same parish church was not unusual in the sixteenth and seventeenth centuries. In Paris, Saint-Jean-en-Grève had a "new cemetery" and a "green cemetery." It was the new cemetery that was the more expensive. According to a contract signed in 1624 with the churchwardens, the gravedigger "shall charge for graves in the new cemetery no more than 20 francs, and for those in the green cemetery no more than 12 francs, this price to include both the digging of the graves and their construction and the lowering and burial of the bodies."[163] Let us compare this with the prices set in the same document for "those graves that shall be made in the church. Where there is no tombstone to lift, [the gravedigger] shall charge no more than 40 francs, and where there is a tombstone to lift, no more than 60 francs." So the price was twelve francs in the less desirable cemetery, twenty francs in the other cemetery, forty francs in the church when there was no tombstone, and sixty francs when there was a tombstone, that is, a monument.

At la Daurade, then, as at Saint-Jean-en-Grève, there was an intermediate category between the church and the commonest cemetery. This category did not exist at Saint-Etienne or la Dalbade.

Bearing this in mind, let us examine the figures in table 2, beginning with those in the first column, the percentages for each of the three parishes of burials in churches (meaning all kinds of churches, including monasteries) and burials in cemeteries.

One is immediately impressed by the substantial number of burials in churches, a fact that confirms the foregoing analyses. The proportion of those buried in churches is usually at least half, and never drops below a third of the total burials for a given parish. This high proportion indicates that at the end of the seventeenth century, close to half of the inhabitants of cities, and at least a third, were buried in churches. This means that the privilege was no longer reserved for the nobility and the clergy but had been extended to a considerable segment of the middle classes.

The aristocratic parish of Saint-Etienne reported more burials in churches (64 percent) than in cemeteries (36 percent). It is rather remarkable that the ratio we find here is very close to the one found by Antoinette Fleury in her study of the wills of rich sixteenth-century Parisians: 60 percent in churches and 40 percent in cemeteries. We may regard this ratio as a permanent characteristic of rich and noble parishes.

At la Dalbade, burials are evenly distributed between the churches and the cemeteries.

At la Daurade, the situation varied over two consecutive years. In 1698, the ratio was the same as that of la Dalbade for 1705. In 1699, it was exactly the opposite of that of Saint-Etienne for 1692: 63 percent in the cemeteries and 37 percent in the churches.

Now let us look at the last three columns of table 2, which give us an idea of how burials were distributed according to social position.

I have distinguished three very rough categories: first, nobles by birth or profession, captains, officials and members of the legal profession (in no particular order: councillors at Parliament, lawyers, captains, subdelegates, bailiffs, tax inspectors), clergymen, and doctors; next, merchants and skilled craftsmen; finally, unskilled workers, servants, maids, common people, and unidentified persons.

The intermediate category has no clear-cut boundaries. Some merchants had the life-style of law officers. Some craftsmen are difficult to distinguish from workers of the last category. But the classification, however imperfect, is adequate for our purposes.

One fact is immediately apparent. There are no people of quality, people in the first category, buried in the cemetery, with the exception of a few children. The 12 percent in the cemetery of les Comtes and the 6 percent in the cemetery of la Dalbade are all children. We shall return to this point later.

The percentage of people of quality buried in churches is highest at Saint-Etienne (38 percent of total burials), still substantial at la Daurade (20 percent), and small at la Dalbade (9 percent). If we included merchants in the first category, we would have 49 percent at Saint-Etienne and 18 percent at la Dalbade. The overall significance of the comparison would not be affected. The nobles, the people of quality, the rich were buried in churches; that much is clear. Those among them who in their wills may have chosen to be buried in the cemetery and the common grave out of piety and humility do not appear in the statistics for the years we have selected. We should not forget, however, that such cases continued to exist from the fifteenth to the eighteenth century.

But the most interesting aspect of these figures is the percentage of common people buried in churches. Such burials average around 10 percent, which is by no means negligible. Among the poor people buried in churches we find transporters and suppliers of stone, wives of laborers, watchmen, coachmen, journeyman bakers, and a few others whose trades the priest does not mention. The daughter of a cook from the parish of Saint-Etienne was buried in the Dominican monastery. Some children of textile workers and soldiers from la Dalbade were buried in the Franciscan monastery. Let us not forget what was said above about the popularity of the mendicant orders. Their churches included chapels for the trade brotherhoods. It was probably because of their membership in these trade organizations that these working-class men and their wives and children were buried in churches. (Of course, the fact that they were buried in churches did not necessarily mean that they had either visible tombstones or epitaphs.)

However, the majority of persons buried in churches (i.e., 51 percent in Saint-Etienne, 60 or 68 percent in la Daurade, and 68 percent in la Dalbade) belonged to the second category: merchants, tradesmen, skilled craftsmen, and their wives and children. The trades mentioned include master tailor, tapestry weaver, stained-glass painter, hosier, shoemaker, baker, weaver, apothecary, wigmaker, innkeeper, mason, dyer, brushman, cutler, carpenter, chandler, cloth shearer, serge maker, and spurrier. These people must often have belonged to trade brotherhoods, too, for one notices that the shoemakers tend to be buried at the Carmelites', the tailors at Saint-Etienne, and the merchants at the Franciscan monastery.

So we see that burials in churches seem to consist of almost all the nobles, members of the legal profession, and petty and high officials, as well as a large segment of the middle-class tradespeople.

Now let us consider the social composition of the cemeteries. The cemetery of Saint-Sauveur, in the parish of Saint-Etienne, contained 66 percent common people and poor people and 33 percent from the intermediate category. The common people were unknown transients, people who had died without name, address, or property; foundlings; watchmen; journeymen in all trades; lackeys; porters; and chair carriers.

Those belonging to the second category, the master craftsmen, are difficult to distinguish from other workmen buried in churches. At the cemetery of la Dalbade one finds as many craftsmen of the second category as common people, whereas at Saint-Sauveur, in the parish of the cathedral, there are twice as many common people as craftsmen.

It would seem that the more aristocratic the parish, the higher the percentage of lower-class people in the cemetery, and the more "common" the parish, the less apparent the distinction between church and cemetery, which are equally popular with middle-class tradespeople.

The case of the two cemeteries of la Daurade is interesting in this connection, because it clarifies the attitude of middle-class craftsmen. Of those buried in the cemetery of les Comtes, the more ancient and prestigious of the two, over half (60 percent) belong to the second category. The cemetery of la Toussaint, on the other hand, is populated primarily by the third category: 50 percent in 1698, 72 percent in 1699. The cemetery of les Comtes must have been an appendix of the church, with what in the eighteenth century would be called private graves, whereas the cemetery of la Toussaint consisted primarily of the large common graves for the poor.

The most conspicuous aspect of table 2 is the size and importance of the social group of middle-class professional people. The upper strata of this group were invading the churches; we find their graves beside those of nobles, clergymen, and members of the legal and mercantile professions. The humbler craftsmen, on the other hand, were difficult to distinguish from their workmen and from the common people who were buried in the cemeteries. The dividing line that separated those buried in churches from those buried in cemeteries was drawn neither between the nobility and the professional middle class nor between the latter and the common people, but rather within the middle class itself.

There was, however, another factor besides social position that affected the distribution of burials between the church and the cemetery, and that was age. The cemetery was not intended only for the poor, but also for the very young, as is apparent from table 3, which shows the percentage of children among total burials in churches and cemeteries.

Generally speaking, this percentage is enormous, which will be no surprise to demographers; the rate of infant mortality was very high at that time. This fact appears not only in total burials, but even in church burials of people of quality, where one would expect to find a lower rate of infant mortality. Of those buried in la Dalbade, 36 percent were under the age of ten as were 32 percent of those buried in Saint-Etienne and 57 percent of those buried in la Daurade. Children under ten represented a third of annual burials in churches, but over half of annual burials in cemeteries (except at Saint-Sauveur, where the figure was 48 percent). It will be noted that although the percentage of children under ten is higher in the cemeteries, it is nevertheless substantial in the churches.

On the other hand, infants under one year of age, curiously enough, are almost all buried in cemeteries. We have already seen that the only nobles or people of quality buried in cemeteries were small children: 12 percent in the cemetery of les Comtes, 6 percent in the cemetery of la Dalbade. It must have been the same for middle-class professionals, and in fact a large percentage of burials in cemeteries for this category were very small children. Thus, the infants of the best families also ended up in the cemetery. Between a quarter and a third of those buried in cemeteries were likely to be children under one year of age. Their destination was the cemetery, regardless of whether their noble, bourgeois, or petit bourgeois parents had chosen the church for themselves and their families. The cemetery was the domain of the poor and of small children.

Not all, however; at least not at the end of the seventeenth century, a time when we know that attitudes were changing. Of all burials at la Dalbade 10 percent were children buried in church, as were 18 percent of burials at la Daurade, doubtless beside their parents and siblings who died later and for whom there was no other space. The day would come, a century and a half later, when it was the small child who would be the favorite subject of the funerary art of the great urban cemeteries of Italy, France, and America.

An English Example

Generally speaking, we may assume that in the France of the *ancien régime*, between the sixteenth and eighteenth centuries, the majority of choices of burial mentioned in wills involved churches rather than cemeteries. In the small rural towns of the eighteenth century, middle-class graves seemed to be increasing, if one can judge by the growing number of tombs and epitaphs.

In rural parishes, however, it would appear that burial in church was always reserved for a smaller number of privileged persons: the families of lords, a few laborers and inhabitants living in a middle-class manner, and also priests, when they chose not to be buried at the foot of the Calvary cross, their customary burial place in the late eighteenth and nineteenth centuries.

We may assume that the situation was not very different in the other countries of western Europe, and that such minor differences as do emerge are highly significant.

An English book of wills from early sixteenth-century Lincolnshire, published in 1914, doubtless for genealogical purposes, enables us to make a superficial analysis of these similarities and differences.[164]

Out of the 224 wills, 34 contain no religious clauses; they are probably alterations of previous wills and are concerned only with the distribution of property. The remaining 190 wills all contain clauses regarding choice of burial.

The paragraph corresponding to the bequest *ad pias causas* (for pious causes) is sometimes in Latin. Allowing for certain special customs, such as a donation to the priest of a herd animal, known as a mortuary, the spirit and even the letter are the same as in France. Here are a few examples: "I wish to be buried in the churchyard of All Saints' Church in Multon. For my mortuary I bequeath whatever the law requires. For the high altar of this church, 20d. For our mother church in Lincoln, 4d. For the church in Multon, for new stalls, 3s. 4d. For the three lights of said church, 9d. For fuel for the lantern that is carried in front of the Blessed Sacrament when it is taken to the sick, 2d." (1513).[165]

"I wish to be buried in the churchyard of All Saints' Church in Fosdyke, my mortuary to be determined by custom. For the high altar of said church, to offset unpaid tithes and offerings, 12d. For the altar of Our Lady of said church, 4d. For the altar of Saint Nicholas, 4d. To the gylde of Our Lady of Fosdyke, 3s. 4d. To the gylde of the Holy Rode of Boston, 3s. 4d., so that the porters will do their duty at my funeral, or elles not. For our mother church in Lincoln, 4d. For Saint Catherine in Lincoln, 4d." A gift of a meadow, the income from which would provide for two candles to be replaced twice a year, "one made of a pound of wax in front of Our Lady of Mercy, the other half a pound for high mass, which shall be lighted every holiday in perpetuity."[166]

In other wills—some from Yorkshire, for example—we find the four mendicant orders mentioned in our French wills.

When the authors choose their place of burial, they name either the church or the cemetery. When they choose the church, they usually do not specify the exact location: "My body to be beried in the parish church of the appostilles petur and pall of W." But when they are more specific, the locations they choose are the same as in France, with the same order of preference, especially for the choir, the Blessed Sacrament, and the cross: in the choir or the high choir, in front of the Blessed Sacrament, in front of the *Corpus Christi,* in the Lady chapel, in front of the statue of Our Lady, in front of the crucifix, in the middle of the nave in front of the crucifix.

Finally, one does find expressions of detachment and humility in these English wills, but just as rarely as in France: "wherever it shall please Almighty God"; "in the church or the churchyard, at the discretion of my executor."

We see from this comparison that there are profound resemblances. One significant difference that emerges is in the distribution of social classes between church and cemetery. Forty-six percent of the authors of these English wills chose the cemetery, although their wills offered no evidence that they belonged to a different socioeconomic category from that of many who chose the church.

There is no mention of any particular location, except "in front of the porch of the church," the parvis.

In France the comparable percentage of those choosing the cemetery seems to be much lower. It seems clear that the English churchyard was not completely abandoned by people of quality during modern times as were the French atrium or charnels, which became the burial grounds of the poor. This may be the reason why the poetic image of the romantic churchyard originated in England, at the time of Thomas Gray.

Be that as it may, the percentage of burials in churches in Lincolnshire was 54 percent, exactly what it was on the Continent.

In this chapter we have watched certain burial practices spread to all of Latin Christendom and persist for at least a thousand years, with only slight regional differences. These practices are characterized by the accumulation of bodies in small spaces, particularly in churches, which served as cemeteries, in addition to outdoor cemeteries; by the constant relocation of the bones and their transfer from the ground to the charnels; and finally, by the daily presence of the living among the dead.

Part II

THE DEATH
OF THE SELF

3

The Hour of Death:
The Final Reckoning

The Importance of Eschatology

Until the age of scientific progress, human beings accepted the idea of a continued existence after death. One finds evidence of this belief in the first tombs of the Middle Paleolithic period with burial offerings; and even today, in the midst of an age of scientific disbelief, one meets watered-down versions of the idea of continued existence or obstinate denials of immediate destruction. Ideas of continuation form a foundation that is common to all the ancient religions and to Christianity.

Christianity adopted the traditional ideas of ordinary people and Stoic philosophers about the gradual deterioration of the human body from the moment of birth. The statement of Manlius' "When we are born, we start to die, and the end begins at the beginning" is a commonplace that we find in Saint Bernard and Pierre de Bérulle as well as in Montaigne. Christianity also adopted the ancient idea of survival in a gray and gloomy lower region, as well as the more recent, less popular, and more rigorous idea of moral judgment.[1]

Finally, it rekindled the hopes of the religions of salvation by making the salvation of man dependent upon the incarnation and redemption of Christ. In Pauline Christianity, life is a dying into a state of sin, and physical death is access to eternal life.

It would not be wrong to reduce Christian eschatology, with its legacy of older beliefs, to these few simple ideas. Yet within this very broad definition, there is room for numerous changes. The ideas that Christians have entertained about death and immortality have varied over the ages. How significant are these variations? They will seem minor to the philosophical theologian or to the simple and pious believer, each of whom tends to simplify his faith and reduce it to fundamentals. To the historian, however, they will seem highly significant, for he will recognize them as the outward signs of changes, all the more profound because unnoticed, in the idea that people in general, and not just Christians, have had of their destiny.

The historian must learn to decipher the hidden language of religions during those long ages bathed in the light of immortality. Beneath the statements of scholars and the legends of popular faith, he must rediscover the archetypes of civilization that both were translating into the only intelligible code. To do so he must rid himself of certain habits of thinking.

We tend to imagine medieval society as dominated by the Church or, what amounts to the same thing, as reacting against the Church by means of heresies or a primitive naturalism.

It is true that in the Middle Ages the world lived in the shadow of the Church, but this did not mean a total and unquestioning acceptance of Christian dogma. It meant rather the recognition of a common language, a single system of communication and understanding. The desires and fantasies that had risen from the depths of the human psyche were expressed in a system of symbols provided by the Christian lexicons. But— and this is what matters to us—the age spontaneously chose certain symbols in preference to others, because they better expressed the underlying tendencies of collective behavior.

If we limit ourselves to the lexicons and abstracts, we very soon find all the themes of traditional eschatology, and our historian's curiosity and appetite for change are quickly disappointed. The Gospel According to Saint Matthew, which shows the influence of pagan (especially Egyptian) traditions, already contained the whole medieval conception of the beyond, the Last Judgment, and hell. The very old Apocalypse of Saint Paul described a paradise, and a hell already rich in torments. Saint Augustine and the early church fathers developed a conception of salvation that was almost definitive. Consequently, the books of the historians of ideas give the reader who may be overly concerned with change a monotonous impression of stability.[2]

The abstracts of scholarly writers were soon complete. But in reality, only part of this material was utilized, and it is this part that was put into general practice that we shall try to define, despite the pitfalls and risks of error that attend this kind of research.

All the evidence indicates that the part of Christian doctrine that was chosen was the only part known, the only living part, the only part that had significance.

I shall begin by applying this method to representations of the Last Judgment.

The Second Coming

The earliest representation in the Western world of the end of time is not the Last Judgment.

Let us begin by recalling what was said in the first chapter of this book about the Christians of the first millennium. They believed that after their death they rested, like the Seven Sleepers of Ephesus, awaiting the day of Christ's return. Their image of the end of time was that of the glorified Christ as he rose to heaven on the day of Ascension, or as he is described by the visionary of the Book of Revelation (4:2): "and behold, a throne was set in heaven, and one sat on the throne," encircled in his majesty by an aureole—"and there was a rainbow round about the throne"—and surrounded by the four winged beasts, the four evangelists, and the four and twenty old men.

This extraordinary imagery recurs again and again in the Romanesque period; examples can be found over the main entrances of the cathedrals at Moissac and Chartres. It laid bare the mysteries of heaven and the divine personages or supernatural creatures who inhabited it. The people of the early Middle Ages awaited the return of Christ without fear of the Last Judgment. Their conception of the end of time was inspired by the Book of Revelation, and passed silently over the dramatic scene of the Resurrection and the Last Judgment recorded in Saint Matthew.

On those rare occasions when funerary art did represent the Last Judgment, it is apparent that the event inspired very little fear, since it was consistently seen from the point of view of the return of Christ and the awakening of the just, who emerge from their sleep to ascend into the light. In 680 Bishop Agilbert was buried in a sarcophagus in the chapel known as the Crypt of Jouarre.[3] On one of the short sides of this sarcophagus was carved the glorified Christ surrounded by the four evangelists. This is the traditional image that is repeated in Romanesque art. On one of the long sides we see the elect, their arms uplifted, acclaiming the returned Christ. We see only the elect; no damned are visible. There is no allusion to the curses and punishments predicted by Saint Matthew. Undoubtedly this was because they did not concern the "saints," who were considered to include all believers sleeping in the peace of the Church, entrusted to church soil. The Vulgate used the word *sancti* to refer to those whom modern translators designate by the name of *believers* or *faithful*.

The saints had nothing to fear from the severity of the Last Judgment. The Book of Revelation, in a passage that is fundamental to millenarianism, states explicitly of certain saints who had already risen from the dead once, "On such the second death hath no power" (20:5–6).

Perhaps the damned were not as visible as the elect because they had less reality, either because they did not rise from the dead or because they were not granted the glorified bodies of the elect. This would appear to be the correct interpretation of the rejected version of a passage from the Vulgate that reads, "We shall all be born again, but we shall not all be changed" (1 Cor. 15:51–2).[4]

The theme of the Last Judgment reappears in the eleventh century, this time no longer on a sarcophagus but on a baptismal font. The oldest font that is illustrated in this manner is at Neer Haspin, near Landen, in Belgium. Another, attributed, like the preceding one, to the studios of Teurnai, has been recovered at Châlons-sur-Marne;[5] it cannot be later than 1150.

The risen souls are emerging naked from their sarcophagi in pairs, husband and wife embracing. The angel is blowing a magnificent ivory trumpet. It is indeed the end of time but, as at Jouarre, there is no judgment. The relationship between baptism and resurrection without judgment is clear. Those who have been baptized were assured of resurrection and the eternal salvation it implied.

Further testimony confirms the evidence of iconography. In Christian epitaphs of the first century A.D. one finds fragments of a very old prayer that may have been inherited from the synagogue. If so, it goes back to at least the third century B.C. and has survived in religious practice down to our own time.[6] We found it on the lips of the dying Roland (see chapter 1). It was one of those prayers commending the soul of the deceased to God that the authors of French wills of the sixteenth and seventeenth centuries frequently referred to as *"Recommendaces"* (Commendations). Only yesterday it was to be found in the missals that were in use before the reforms of Pope Paul VI.[7]

Could the Jewish prayer for fast days have become the oldest Christian prayer for the dead, *Commendatio Animae?* Here it is:

Deliver, O Lord, the soul of thy servant, as you delivered Enoch and Elias from the common death, as you delivered Noah from the flood, as you delivered Abraham by leading him out of Ur of the Chaldea, as you delivered Job from his afflictions, Isaac from the hands of his father Abraham, Lot from the flames of Sodom, Moses from the hand of Pharaoh, king of Egypt, Daniel from the lions' den, the three young Hebrews from the fiery furnace, Susanna from a false accusation, David from the hands of Saul and Goliath, Saint Peter and Saint Paul from their prison, and the blessed virgin Saint Thecla from three horrible torments.

This prayer was so familiar that the first Christian stonecutters of Arles were inspired to use it in decorating sarcophagi.

But as Jean Lestocquoy has pointed out,[8] the precedents invoked to appeal to the mercy of the Lord do not involve sinners, but righteous men and women whom the Lord has tested: Abraham, Job, Daniel, and so on, ending with the holy apostles and a blessed martyr of sacred virginity, Thecla.

When the Christian of the early Middle Ages recited the *Commendatio Animae* at the hour of death, he was thinking, like Roland, of those occasions when God had intervened triumphantly to put an end to the trials of his saints. Roland had also confessed his sins, which may have marked the beginning of a new sensibility. But the *Commendatio Animae* did not awaken remorse for sins, it did not even call for forgiveness of the sinner; it was as if he had already been forgiven. It associated him with the saints, and likened the throes of the death agony with the trials of the martyrs.

The Last Judgment and the Book of Life

Starting in the twelfth century and continuing for about four centuries thereafter, Christian iconography projected on the historied portals of medieval churches the film of the end of the world, various readings of the great eschatological drama beneath whose religious language one can discern the new anxieties stirred in man by the discovery of his destiny.

The oldest Last Judgments, which date from the twelfth century, consist of two superimposed scenes, one very old, the other very new. The older one is the one we have just described: the Christ of the Apocalypse in his majesty. It is the end of the discontinuity in the Creation brought about by the Fall of Adam, the annihilation of the particularities of a temporary history in the unimaginable dimensions of transcendence. The brilliance of this light leaves no room for the history of humanity, still less for the personal biographies of individuals.

In the twelfth century the apocalyptic scene is there, but it covers only one portion of the portal, the upper part. At Beaulieu, at the beginning of the twelfth century, the angels who are playing the trumpet, the supernatural creatures, and the gigantic Christ with enormous arms outstretched still cover most of the surface and leave little room for other elements or symbols. A little later, at Sainte-Foy-de-Conques (1130–50), the Christ in his star-studded oval who floats over the clouds of space is still the Christ of the Apocalypse. But at Beaulieu, and even more so at Conques, below the traditional representation of the Second Coming, there appears a new iconography inspired by the Gospel According to Saint Matthew: the judgment of the Last Day and the separation of the just from the damned. This iconography represents, essentially, three operations: the resurrection of the bodies of the just, the acts of judgment, and the separation of the just, who go to heaven, from the damned, who are plunged into eternal fire.

The elements of the great drama were assembled slowly, as if the idea of the Last Judgment that was to become classical in the twelfth and thirteenth centuries encountered some resistance. At Beaulieu, the dead are indeed emerging from their tombs—perhaps for the first time, at least on this scale—but unobtrusively. There is nothing to suggest the act of judging, and (as on the sarcophagus of Jouarre and the baptismal font of Châlons-sur-Marne) as soon as the dead have risen, they belong to heaven, without undergoing any examination. Like the saints of the Vulgate, they are all destined for salvation. It is true that the damned are no longer altogether absent. If you look carefully, you can find them on one of the two bands of monsters that cover the lintel. Among these monsters, Emile Mâle has recognized the seven-headed beast of the Book of Revelation.[9] Some of them are devouring men who must be the damned. One cannot help being struck by the almost clandestine manner in which hell and its torments have been introduced. These infernal creatures are difficult to distinguish from the imaginary animals that Romanesque art borrowed from the Orient and produced in great numbers for reasons that were decorative as well as symbolic.

At the cathedral in Autun, which is later than the abbey in Conques, the Last Judgment is indeed represented, but the fate of the dead is still determined from the moment of their resurrection. Some go directly to paradise and others to hell, which makes one wonder about the purpose of the judicial operations that are taking place to one side. One has the impression here that two different conceptions have been juxtaposed.

At Sainte-Foy-de-Conques, there is no mistaking the meaning of the scene. It is preceded by inscriptions. On the cruciferous halo of Christ one reads the word *Judex*. The same word was inscribed by Suger at Saint-Denis. In another place the sculptor carved the words reported by Saint Matthew (25:34–41): "Come, ye blessed of my Father, inherit the kingdom prepared for you from the foundation of the world. . . . Depart from me, ye cursed, into everlasting fire, prepared for the devil and his angels." Hell and heaven each have their own epigraphic legend. We see the scene of judicial examination that precedes and prepares the sentence: the famous weighing of souls by the archangel Michael. The paradise inherited from the Book of Revelation now occupies no more space than that reserved for hell. Finally, in a remarkable detail, hell is also swallowing up some men of the Church: monks, identified by the *corona*, that is, the wide tonsure. Gone is the old idea that all believers are saints. No one among the people of God is assured of his salvation, not even those who have preferred the solitude of the cloisters to the profane world.

Thus, in the twelfth century an iconography was established that superimposed the Gospel According to Saint Matthew on the Revelation of Saint John, soon transformed both, and linked the Second Coming of Christ with the Last Judgment.

In the thirteenth century the apocalyptic inspiration disappeared, leaving only vestiges that were relegated to the splays surrounding the arches. The idea of judgment was now predominant. It is a court of justice that is represented. Christ, surrounded by angels bearing standards, is sitting on the judge's throne. The oval glory that had isolated him has disappeared. He is surrounded by his court, the twelve apostles, who are occasionally represented on either side of him, as at Laon, but more often lined up in the splays of the portal, on either side.

Two actions are now given considerable importance, the weighing of souls and the judgment. The first takes place in the center of the composition. It is a scene that gives rise to concern and anxiety. In the splays of the portal, the angels look on, leaning over the balconies of heaven. Each life ends in the pans of the scales; each act of weighing holds the attention of the celestial and infernal domains.

There is no question of avoiding an examination whose outcome is genuinely in the balance. Its importance is accentuated to the point where in some cases it seemed necessary to represent it twice. The elect and the damned are clearly indicated by the scales of Saint Michael, but as if this operation were not sufficient, they are separated a second time by the sword of the archangel Gabriel.

However, the judgment does not always follow the decision of the scales. Intercessors step forward and play a role not anticipated by the passage from Saint Matthew, the double role of advocate *(patronus)* and suppliant *(advocare Deum)* who appeal to the pity, that is, the mercy, of the sovereign judge. The judge is the one who pardons the guilty person as well as the one who condemns him, and it is the function of certain of his familiars to sway him to pardon. Here this role belongs to his mother and to the disciple who was also present with him at the foot of the cross, Saint John the Evangelist. We first see them appear unobtrusively on the main door at Autun, over the tympanum, on either side of the large aureole that surrounds the figure of Christ. By the thirteenth century they have become leading characters, and their importance is equal to that of the archangel who weighs the souls. They are kneeling with joined hands on either side of Christ, to whom they are addressing their supplication. The King is holding court, and since he is sitting, his primary function is to render judgment.

Public power was measured by the extent of the area over which one exercised the right of judgment. But here the judge and his court are no longer the spectators of a test, half magical and half religious, an ordeal in which the victor will be declared innocent. The sentence is preceded by an examination, and judgment is made on the basis of evidence. Among the actions of the people who are being measured in this way, the archangel takes into consideration the good and the evil. The devil's attorney claims his victim, for he almost always has rights over him, owing to the weakness of human nature. But the blessed advocates and patron saints intercede, and the sovereign judge delivers his verdict, whether he follows the law and damns the person or pardons him.

The apocalyptic descent from heaven to earth has become a court of justice, a transformation that, in the eyes of the people of that period, robbed it of none of its majesty. The court of justice was the model of the solemn ceremony par excellence, the image and symbol of grandeur, just as justice was the purest manifestation of power.

This deviation from eschatology in favor of judicial machinery, however stately, may be surprising to us today, with our increasing indifference and skepticism toward the law and those who administer it. The ordinary citizen of today avoids the legal world, unlike his ancestors, who were incorrigible legalists. The importance accorded to justice in daily life and in spontaneous morality is one of the psychological factors that distinguish and polarize ancient and modern mentalities.

This responsiveness to the idea and manifestations of justice really dates from the later Middle Ages, and continues throughout the *ancien régime*. Human life is seen as a long legal process in which every act is sanctioned by a legal transaction or at least by members of the legal profession. Government itself is conceived on the model of the court of justice, and every judicial department or treasury is organized like a court, with a president, councillors, prosecutor, and court clerk.

A fourteenth-century text shows that the appeal to the judge in legal terminology had become so natural as to be almost a reflex. The wife of the Castilian Count Alarcos has just learned that her husband is going to kill her so that he can marry the infanta of Castile. She says her prayer and her last farewell. Her soul is at peace, she does not seek vengeance, but she summons her murderers to appear before the divine judge. Justice must be restored, and curiously enough, the machinery will not be set in motion by the spontaneous intervention of the omniscient judge. It is up to the innocent victim to lay the matter before him and claim her right:

I forgive you, good count, out of the love that I bear you,
But I forgive neither the king nor the infanta,
And I summon them both to appear before the high tribunal of
God within thirty days.[10]

One cannot help admiring this woman who, though on the point of dying a Christian death, has the presence of mind to serve a summons in such good form.

There is a relationship between this judicial conception of the world and the new idea of life as a biography. Each moment of life will be weighed someday in a solemn hearing, before all the powers of heaven and hell. The creature responsible for this weighing, the standard-bearing archangel, became the popular patron saint of the dead. It was important to obtain his favor without delay. People prayed to him, just as they later took *"douceurs"* to judges, "that he might usher them into the blessed light."[11]

But how did the angelic examiner know about the acts that he had to evaluate? The answer is that they had been recorded in a book by another angel who was half court clerk, half accountant.

The symbol of the book is very ancient in Scripture. We find it in the vision of Daniel: "And at that time shall Michael stand up, the great prince which standeth for the children of thy people: and there shall be a time of trouble, such as never was since there was a nation even to that same time: and at that time thy people shall be delivered, every one that shall be found written in the book" (12:1). And again, in Revelation: "And I saw in the right hand of him that sat on the throne a book written within and on the backside, sealed with seven seals" (5:1). This book is the scroll that the Christ of Jouarre holds in his hand before the elect who are acclaiming him. It contained their names, and it was opened at the end of the world. But in the seventh century, the time of Jouarre, it served as a model for another *liber vitae* (book of lives), a real book this time, containing the names of the benefactors of the Church, which were read during the offertory prayers in the Gallican liturgy; a sort of census or inventory of the saints. The same book mentioned in Daniel and Revelation is represented on the main entrance at Conques. An angel is holding it open, and it bears the inscription: *"signatur liber vitae."* It contains the names of those who dwell *in terra viventium* (in the land of the living) in the words of the *Lauda Sion,* sung at the Feast of Corpus Christi—in other words, in paradise.

This is the original meaning of the *liber vitae,* but it was to change. By the thirteenth century, the book is no longer the *census* of the universal church; it has become the register in which the affairs of men are recorded. The word *registre,* which appears in French in the thirteenth century, is the sign of a new mentality. The actions of the individual are no longer lost in the limitless space of transcendence or, if you prefer, in the collective destiny of the species. From now on they are individualized. Life can no longer be reduced to a breath *(anima, spiritus)*, an energy *(virtus)*. It consists of the sum total of an individual's thoughts, words, and deeds: in the words of an eighth-century *Confiteor*—"*peccavi in cogitatione et in locutione et in opere.*"[12] Life is a body of facts that can be itemized and summarized in a book.

The book is therefore at once the history of an individual, his biography, and a book of accounts, or records, with two columns, one for the evil and the other for the good. The new bookkeeping spirit of businessmen who were beginning to discover their own world—which has become our own—was applied to the content of a life as well as to merchandise or money.

The book continued to figure among the symbols of morality until the middle of the eighteenth century, whereas the scales were represented less and less often, and Saint Joseph or the guardian angel took the place of the archangel who was *signifer* (a standard-bearer) or *psychopompos* (a conductor of souls).

A century after the execution of the main door of Sainte-Foy-de-Conques, where the meaning of the book was still that of the Revelation, in the Franciscan hymn *Dies Irae,* the book is carried in front of the judge in the terrifying din of the end of the world, and now it is a book of accounts:

> *Lo! The book exactly worded*
> *Wherein all hath been recorded*
> *Whence shall judgment be awarded.*

It is very curious and significant that what had originally been the book of the elect became the book of the damned.

A century after the *Dies Irae,* in the middle of the fourteenth century, a painting by J. Albergno shows Christ the judge sitting on his throne and holding on his knees an open book on which is written: *"Chiunque scrixi so questo libro sara danadi"* (He whose name is written in this book shall be damned). Although it is reserved for the damned, it is a record of the deeds of humanity. Even more remarkable are the souls that are pictured below the Christ figure in the form of skeletons. Each of these souls holds his own book in his hands and expresses by his gestures how much the reading frightens him.

In the large fresco of the Last Judgment on the apse of the cathedral in Albi, which dates from the late fifteenth or early sixteenth century, one finds the same individual booklets hanging like identification papers from the necks of the risen souls, who are otherwise naked.[13]

We shall presently see that in the *artes moriendi* (treatises on the art of dying well) of the fifteenth century the drama takes place in the bedroom of the dying person. God or the devil is consulting the book at the head of the deathbed. But it looks as if the devil is the one in possession of this book or public notice, which he brandishes vehemently to claim his due.[14]

The book appears in the baroque art of seventeenth- and eighteenth-century Provence. At Antibes, Time, pictured as an old man, is lifting the shroud that covers the body of a young man and simultaneously displaying a book. At Salon, in the church of Saint-Michel, a church dedicated to the patron saint of the dead, an eighteenth-century altarpiece pictures among the traditional symbols of death an open book on which one can read the words *liber scriptus. . . .* Is there a connection between this book and the book of the Vanities?[15]

At the end of the Middle Ages, in the fourteenth and fifteenth centuries, the accounts are kept by those who profit from them, the devils, who are confident that the evil will outweigh the good—a sinister conception of a hell that would be overpopulated but for the gracious intervention of divine mercy.

After the Tridentine reforms, as we shall see, the equilibrium that was threatened during the age of the macabre was once again restored. The way the bookkeeping had been left in the hands of the devil at the end of the Middle Ages no longer satisfied the devout person or moralist of the classical period. Treatises on the proper way to prepare oneself for death continued to appear. In one of them, a *Miroir de l'âme du pécheur et du juste pendant la vie et à l'heure de la mort* (1736), each man possesses two books, one for the good, which is kept by his guardian angel (who has taken over one of the roles of Saint Michael), and the other for the evil, which is kept by a demon.

In the picture of the bad death, "his guardian angel, distressed, abandons him [the dying man], dropping his book. All the good works that were recorded in it have been erased, because everything good he has done is without merit in the eyes of heaven. To the left, we see the devil presenting him with a book that contains the whole *history* of his evil life."[16]

I have stressed the word *history* because it is a significant indication of the biographical conception of life.

The picture of the good death shows the opposite situation: "His guardian angel joyously displays a book in which are written his virtues, good works, fasts, prayers, mortifications, etc. . . . The devil, confounded, retreats and throws himself into hell with his book in which nothing is written, because his sins have been erased by a sincere penitence."[17]

By the eighteenth century, the big collective book of the main entrance of Conques has become an individual booklet, a kind of passport or police record that must be presented at the gates of eternity.

While it is true that the book contains the entire history of a life, it is written to be used only once, at the moment when the accounts are settled, when the assets and liabilities are compared, when the balance sheet is closed.

After at least the twelfth century, it was believed that there was a critical moment. According to the traditional mentality, all individual biographies were combined and merged in the eternal present of daily life. At the time of the iconography of judgment, the individual biography no longer appears as part of a long, uniform development but as compressed into that moment, *dies illa,* when it is recapitulated and personalized. It is on the basis of this abridged account that it must be reconstructed and evaluated.

The entire life flashes into awareness in the space of an instant. It is remarkable that this instant was not the moment of death but was situated after death, and in the early Christian version, was postponed to the end of the world, an event that a millenarian age assumed to be imminent.

We find here the deeply rooted refusal to identify the end of existence with the dissolution of the physical body. There was imagined to be some sort of extended existence that did not always go so far as the immortality of the blessed but that at least provided an intermediate space between death and the definitive conclusion of life.

The Judgment of the Dying

The theme of the Last Judgment was not altogether abandoned after the fourteenth century. We find it in the fifteenth and sixteenth centuries in the paintings of Van Eyck and Hieronymus Bosch, and even occasionally in the seventeenth century, as at Assisi and Dijon. However, it had outlived itself, had lost its popularity, and was no longer really the way people imagined the final end of mankind. The idea of judgment had become separated from the idea of resurrection.

The resurrection of the flesh was not forgotten; iconography and funerary inscriptions continued to refer to it among Protestants and Catholics alike. But it had been detached from the great cosmic drama and shifted to the personal destiny of the individual. The Christian still sometimes declared on his tombstone that he would be born again one day; but whether that day was the day of the Second Coming or the end of the world was a question that no longer concerned him. What mattered now was the

Rapture

certainty of his own resurrection, the last event in his life, a life that obsessed him to the point where he was indifferent to the future of the Creation. This affirmation of individuality set the fourteenth and fifteenth centuries even further apart from traditional ideas than the twelfth and thirteenth centuries had been. The more peaceful afterlife, removed from the dramatic atmosphere of judgment in which the resurrection now took place, may seem like a return to the optimistic attitude of early Christianity. However, the comparison is superficial and misleading, for in spite of the affirmations of funerary epigraphs, fear of judgment continued to overshadow confidence in the resurrection.

The separation of resurrection and judgment had another, more obvious consequence. The traditional interval between judgment, the definitive conclusion of life, and physical death disappeared, and this was a great event.

As long as this interval existed, the person was not altogether dead, the balance sheet of his life was not closed, he continued to live a kind of half existence through his shade. Half alive and half dead, he still had the expedient of "coming back" to demand the help, sacrifices, or prayers that he needed from the living. A period of grace had been granted that the blessed intercessors or the pious faithful could turn to account. The remote effects of charitable works performed during the person's lifetime still had time to make themselves known.

But from now on, the fate of the immortal soul was decided from the very moment of physical death. There would be less and less room for those who return from the dead and their manifestations. On the other hand, the belief in purgatory as a place of waiting, hitherto long confined to scholars, theologians, or poets, would become truly popular, but not before the middle of the seventeenth century, when it replaced the old images of sleep and rest.

The drama no longer took place in the vast reaches of the beyond. It had come down to earth and was now enacted right in the bedroom of the sick person, around his bed.

Similarly, in the fifteenth century, the iconography of the Last Judgment was replaced by a new iconography that was popularized by the printing press in the form of books containing woodcuts, individual images that each person contemplated in his own home. These books were the treatises on the technique of dying well, the *artes moriendi.* Each page of text was illustrated with a picture so that not only the *literati* but also the *laici*, that is, those who could not read, could catch the meaning.[18]

This iconography, although new, is reminiscent of the ancient model of the recumbent figure on the sickbed in scenes of the Last Judgment; for bed, as we have seen, was the traditional place of death from time immemorial. It continues to be so but has ceased to be the symbol of love and rest and become, in modern times, part of the technological equipment of the hospital, reserved for the critically ill.

People always died in bed, whether of a "natural" death, that is, without illness or suffering, as was believed, or, as was more often the case, of accidents, such as "fever, abscess, or some other serious, painful, and protracted illness."[19] The sudden death, the *mors improvisa*, was exceptional and greatly dreaded. Even serious wounds or violent accidents allowed time for the ritual agony on the deathbed.

The bedroom, however, was to take on new meaning in the iconography of death. It was no longer the scene of an event that was almost commonplace, although more solemn than others. It became the arena of a drama in which the fate of the dying man was decided for the last time, in which his whole life and all his passions and attachments were called into question.

The sick man is about to die. At least this is what we learn from the texts, which say that he is crucified by suffering. We would not know it from the pictures, where his body is not particularly emaciated and he still has some strength left.

According to custom, the bedroom is full of people, for one always dies in public. But those assembled see none of what is going on, nor is the dying man aware of their presence. This is not because he has lost consciousness; his gaze is riveted with fierce attention upon an extraordinary spectacle visible to him alone. Supernatural beings have invaded the bedroom and are crowding around his bedside. On one side are the Trinity, the Virgin, the whole court of heaven, and the guardian angel; on the other side, Satan and his monstrous army of demons. The court of heaven no longer resembles a court of justice. Saint Michael no longer weighs the good and the evil in his scales. He has been replaced by the guardian angel, who is more spiritual attendant and confessor than advocate or court official.

However, the oldest representations of death in bed still retain the now classic drama of judgment treated in the style of the mystery plays. In an illustration for the prayer for the dead in a 1340 Psalter, the accused appeals to the intercessor: "Virgin Mary, Mother of God, I have placed my hope in you. Free my soul from care, and from hell, and bitter death." Satan, behind the bed, demands his soul: "I claim as my legal right the soul that is leaving this body, which is full of great corruption." The Virgin is baring her breast, Christ is showing his five wounds and transmitting Mary's prayer to the Father, and God is granting his forgiveness. "There are six reasons why your request should be fulfilled. I am moved by love that is honest, in all goodness I cannot deny you."[20]

In the *artes moriendi*, the Virgin and the crucified Christ are always present. However, when the dying man gives up his soul with the last breath, it is neither the sword nor the hand of the administrator of justice that the Father raises, but the merciful dart of death, which puts an end to physical torments and spiritual ordeals. In these cases God is less the judge in a court than the arbiter of a struggle between the forces of good and evil, a struggle in which the soul of the dying man is the stake.

In his analysis of the iconography of the *artes moriendi*, Alberto Tenenti suggests that the dying man attends his own drama as a witness rather than as an actor. It is "a battle between two supernatural societies in which the Christian has a slight possibility of choosing, but no way of hiding. Around his bed a relentless struggle is being waged between the hordes of hell on the one side and the legions of heaven on the other."[21]

This is obvious in certain pictures. For example, the pen-and-ink drawings illustrating the poem *"Le Miroir de la Mort"* in an Avignon manuscript from about 1460 may be interpreted in this way. One drawing represents the struggle between the devil and the dying man; others, the intervention of the good angel and the Crucifixion, the instrument of salvation; and the last one, the contest between the angel and Satan at the dying man's bedside.[22]

The idea certainly existed of a confrontation between the forces of good and evil, which may have been related to the doctrine of predestination. But this idea does not seem dominant in the *ars* published by Tenenti. On the contrary, it seems to me that here human freedom is respected, and that if God appears to have set aside the attributes of justice, it is because man has become his own judge. Heaven and hell do not do battle, as in the *"Miroir de la Mort"* of Avignon. They are present at this final ordeal that is being given to the dying man, an ordeal whose outcome will determine the meaning of his whole life. The supernatural beings are there simply as spectators and witnesses. But in that instant the dying man has the power to win or lose everything: "The salvation of man is determined at his death." It is no longer appropriate to examine the biography of the dying man, as was the custom at the tribunal of souls on the last day of the world. It is still too soon for this final reckoning, for the biography is not complete and is still subject to retroactive revision. There is no question of evaluating the life as a whole until after its conclusion, and this depends on the outcome of the final ordeal that he must undergo *in hora mortis* (in the hour of death), in the room in which he will give up the ghost. It is up to him to triumph with the help of his guardian angel and his intercessors and be saved, or to yield to the temptations of the devils and be lost.

The last ordeal has replaced the Last Judgment. It is a terrible game, and it is in terms of games and stakes that Savonarola speaks: "Man, the devil plays chess with you, and he does his utmost to capture and checkmate you at this point [death]. Hold yourself in readiness, therefore, and think well on this point, because if you win here, you will win all the rest, but if you lose, all that you have done before will be worthless."[23]

There is something terrifying about a risk of this magnitude, and we can understand how fear of the beyond could overtake populations that were still without the fear of death. It was, no doubt, this fear of the beyond that was expressed by the representation of the torments of hell. The merging of the point of death and the moment of final decision threatened to extend to death itself the fear aroused by an eternity of suffering.

The Macabre

Macabre subjects appear in literature and iconography at about the same time as the *artes moriendi*. The word *macabre* is often used, by extension of the term *danse macabre,* to refer to realistic representations of the human body in the process of decomposition. The medieval fascination with the macabre, which was so disturbing to historians from Michelet on, begins after death and stops at the skeleton. The dried-out skeleton, the *morte secca* so common in the seventeenth and even in the eighteenth century, does not belong to the iconography characteristic of the fourteenth to sixteenth centuries, which is dominated by repellent images of corruption: "O carrion who art no longer man."[24]

One receives the distinct impression, from the literature and art of the period, that a new feeling is emerging. The iconography of the macabre is contemporaneous with the *artes moriendi,* but it expresses a different message—although less different, perhaps, than historians, on the lookout for original trends, would like to think.

Of course, it is not difficult to find antecedents. The threat of death, the fragility of human life, had already inspired the Roman artist who chiseled a skeleton on a bronze bowl or drew another on the mosaic floor of a house to illustrate the pagan idea of *carpe diem.* Would Christians have been impervious to this feeling, since their religion was founded on the promise of salvation? We do find the figure of Death here and there, in the form of a horseman of the Apocalypse. On a capital of Notre-Dame in Paris, in the Last Judgment over the main entrance of the cathedral in Amiens, a blindfolded woman carries off a corpse on the back of her horse. Elsewhere, the horseman is holding the scales of judgment or the bow of death. But these illustrations are infrequent, unobtrusive, marginal; they simply comment, without undue emphasis, on the commonplaces of human mortality.

Is the early literature of Christianity any more explicit? The meditation on the vanity of earthly life, the *contemptus mundi,* is constant, and gives rise to images that will be adopted by the great poets of the macabre.

In the eleventh century, Odilon of Cluny unveils human physiology: "Consider that which is hidden in the nostrils, in the throat, in the bowels: filth everywhere." But here the point is not so much to prepare us for death as to dissuade us from all intercourse with women, for the moralist goes on, "We, who would be loath to touch vomit or dung even with our fingertip —how can we desire to clasp in our arms the bag of excrement itself?"[25]

Similarly, the Latin poets of the twelfth century were already celebrating the melancholy of former grandeur: "Where are they now, Babylon the triumphant, and Nebuchadnezzar the terrible, and the power of Darius? . . . They are rotting. . . . Where are those who were in this world before us? Go to the cemetery and look at them. They are no more than ashes and worms, their flesh has rotted."[26]

And later, Jacopone da Todi, author of the *Dies Irae:* "Tell me, where is Solomon, once so noble, where is Samson, the invincible warrior?"[27]

In the cloisters, monks who were too much tempted by the age were constantly being sermonized on the vanity of power, wealth, and beauty. Soon, shortly before the great flowering of the macabre, other monks, the mendicants, would leave the cloisters and use a vivid imagery to disseminate ideas that would make a profound impression on the urban masses. But the themes of these sermonists are the same as those of the poets of the macabre, and belong to the same culture.

We can afford to overlook these rare and unobtrusive predecessors of the great macabre voices of the fourteenth and fifteenth centuries. For the image of universal destruction that the Middle Ages present prior to the fourteenth century is of an altogether different order: it is dust, not decomposition, not worm-ridden corruption.

In the language of the Vulgate and the ancient liturgy of Lent, the notions of dust and ashes are confused. The meaning of the word *cinis* is ambiguous. It refers to the dust of travel with which penitents are covered as a sign of bereavement and humility, in the same way that they are dressed in sackcloth or horsehair: *in cinere et in cilicio, sacum et cinerem sternere.* It also refers to the dust of decomposition: "Dust thou art, to dust thou wilt return," the priest says when he applies the ashes on the first Wednesday of Lent.

But ashes are also understood to be the product of decomposition by fire, which is a purification. This cyclical process, in which dust and ashes go to make up nature or matter by the unceasing breaking down and building up of layers, suggests an image of destruction that is very close to the image of the traditional death epitomized by the phrase "we all die."

The new image of the pathetic and personal death of individual judgment of the *artes moriendi* was to have its counterpart in a new image of destruction.

The oldest representations of macabre subjects are interesting, because some of them still show the continuity with the Last Judgment or the individual moment of truth. In the great fresco in the Campo Santo in Pisa, which dates from approximately 1350, the whole upper or celestial half represents a battle between angels and devils over the souls of the deceased. The angels are carrying the elect off to heaven, while the devils are hurling the damned into hell. Accustomed as we are to the iconography of judgment, we feel perfectly at home. But in the lower half, we search in vain for the traditional images of resurrection. Instead, a woman shrouded in long veils with her hair unbound flies over the world, ignores a crowd of cripples begging her for deliverance, and cuts down with her scythe, when they are least expecting it, some young people in a crowd of suitors paying court to a lady. She is a strange creature, who partakes of the nature of angel (for she flies and her body is anthropomorphic) and also of the devil and bestiality (for she has the wings of a bat). There will often be a temptation to divest death of its neutrality and annex it to the territory of the devil. Ronsard calls it "old shadow of earth, ancient shade of hell."

But Death will also be regarded as the good servant, the faithful executor of the will of God. Pierre Michault has Death say, "I am commissioned to this by God."[28] Death still appears in this guise in Van Eyck's Last Judgment, where it covers the world with its body, as the merciful Virgin covers humanity with her mantle; the jaws of hell yawn beneath those giant legs. But here Death no longer has the form of a living woman, which it had at Pisa.[29]

At Pisa, the bodies of those cut down by her scythe are lying on the ground with their eyes closed, and angels and devils are coming to collect the souls that they exhale. The scene of the last breath has replaced the scene of the resurrection in which the reanimated bodies emerge from the ground. The transition from the Last Judgment to the decisive moment of personal death that we have already observed in the *artes moriendi* is still quite evident here.

But there is another scene to one side of the universal Death. A band of horsemen has come to a stop before the terrifying spectacle of three open coffins. The bodies lying in them are each in a different degree of decomposition, according to stages long familiar to the Chinese. The first still has his face intact, and he would look very much like those whom Death has struck down but whom she has not yet changed, except that his abdomen has already been distended by gas. The second is disfigured, rotting, and covered only with shreds of flesh. The third has been reduced to the state of a mummy.[30]

The half-decomposed corpse, or *transi,* will become the commonest type of representation of death. We find it as early as 1320 on the walls of the lower church in Assisi, the work of a disciple of Giotto. Wearing a crown, it is a figure of derision being pointed out by Saint Francis.

The *transi* is the most important minor character in the macabre iconography of the fourteenth to sixteenth centuries. We find it, of course, on the tombs dealt with in the admirable commentaries of Emile Mâle and Erwin Panofsky.[31] However, the tombs they analyze are the monuments of important personages, great works of art in which the *transi* fills one story of a monument that often consists of two: below, the recumbent figure, or the *transi* that replaces it, and above, the blessed soul in paradise. (We shall return to this iconography in chapter 5.) Examples of this treatment are the tombs of Cardinal Lagrange at the musée d'Avignon and of Canon Yver at Notre-Dame in Paris (see also the tomb of Pierre d'Ailly, bishop of Cambrai in the Gaignières Collection).[32] These works are so powerful that they may create the illusion of being representative. In reality, there are relatively few of them, and they do not in themselves express a main current of the sensibility of the age.

However, there exist more ordinary tombs where the signs of death are quite apparent, without taking the repellent form of decomposition. A recumbent figure may be wrapped in a shroud that leaves the head uncovered and one foot bare. (This treatment seems common at Dijon; see, for example, the tomb of Joseph Germain at the museum, 1424, and the tombs of the two donors of a chapel to Saint John.) We recognize a conspicuous cadaver where the flesh has rotted away to reveal the jawbone. The hair of the women is in wild disorder. The bare feet project from the shroud. It is the cadaver as it will be placed in the ground, and not a moment too soon. Even to us who have seen everything, on the floor of a church in Dijon, the sight is impressive.

Oddly enough, these *transis* do not always retain the realistic attitude of the recumbent figure. On another Dijon tombstone (Saint-Michel, 1521), the two *transis,* instead of lying side by side, are kneeling on either side of a Christ in majesty. They have replaced the praying figures in heaven rather than the recumbent figures on earth.

In the musée Lorrain, in Nancy, on a sixteenth-century tomb originally designed for the open space of a cemetery—it is a stele surmounted by a cross—a mummy is sitting with its head in its hand. However, the stone carver and his customer had some reservations about showing the signs of decomposition. Their *transi* is still unobtrusive.

Today we are struck when this discretion is violated and replaced by a grim expressionism; but we must not be taken in by a few rare cases. If one were to make a statistical study of the tombs of the fourteenth to sixteenth centuries, one would notice that the *transi* appears late in relation to the rest of macabre iconography and that it is rare and even almost completely absent from the great provinces of Christianity such as Italy (before the invasion of the skeleton in the seventeenth century), Spain, and Mediterranean France. It is found mainly in northern and western France, Flanders, Burgundy, Lorraine, Germany, and England. This geographic distribution coincides almost perfectly with the practice of covering the dead (see chapter 4). Macabre iconography exists in those places where the face was concealed; it does not exist in those places where the face was left uncovered.

The *transi* does not belong to the mainstream of funerary art in the late Middle Ages; it constitutes only a marginal and passing episode. Yet, in the fifteenth and sixteenth centuries the theme of the naked cadaver at various stages of decomposition was adopted by tomb makers in spite of their traditionalism, not only in eloquent works of great art but even on ordinary tombstones such as those in Dijon or in Dutch churches.

However, funerary art is the *least* macabre of the arts of the macabre period. Macabre subjects are more frequent and more frankly treated in other forms of expression, particularly in nonrealistic scenes such as allegories, which represent the invisible.

Thus, the *transi,* in the Franciscan fresco of 1320 at Assisi, invades the bedroom of the dying man, as the personification of death, unseen by anyone. It was generally absent from the *artes moriendi,* which we have discussed, where the drama was going on, unbeknownst to those present, between the forces of heaven, the forces of hell, and the free will of the dying man. But in Savonarola's *Arte del bene morire* (ca. 1497), we find it sitting at the foot of the bed. In another Italian *arte* of 1513, it is shown walking into the room.[33]

The *transi* is even less common in the *artes moriendi* than on tombs. Its favorite domain is the illustrations in books of hours for devout laymen, especially the illustrations of prayers for the Office of the Dead, an indication of the relationship between macabre iconography and preaching, especially the preaching of the mendicants.

The transition to the books of hours can be made without leaving the bedroom of the dying man. In a miniature from the *Hours of Rohan* (ca. 1420), Death enters the room with a coffin over its shoulder, to the great terror of the victim confronted with this unequivocal warning.

However, its favorite domain within the books of hours is the cemetery. Cemetery scenes now appear with great frequency and variety. Some of the finest of these represent a compromise between the deathbed scene of the *artes moriendi* and the burial of the corpse. Take, for example, the famous miniature from the *Hours of Rohan,* the so-called "Death of the Christian." Here the dying man is no longer in bed. By an act of surrealist anticipation, he has been transported to the cemetery, and is lying on the ground, where, as in all cemeteries, bones and skulls are scattered in the grass. He has been laid on the fine, blue, gold-brocaded shroud in which he will be buried; as will be seen, it was customary to bury certain persons in precious materials. The second feature that distinguishes this illustration from those in the *artes moriendi* is that instead of being hidden by the winding sheet, the body is completely naked; a transparent veil in no way conceals his abdomen. This nude is already a cadaver, but a cadaver before decomposition, like those on the tombs of Dijon.

In spite of these differences, we recognize the classic themes of the *artes moriendi* and Last Judgments. While the dying man is breathing his last, his soul is being disputed by Saint Michael and Satan. The archangel's role of cosmic combatant is combined with that of conductor of souls. God the Father, alone this time without his court, looks on and pardons him. In this composition one senses a desire to force the traditional iconography toward the more sensational aspects of death: the cadaver and the cemetery.

This death in the cemetery in the style of death in bed is probably not very common. We find it much later in a curious Gaignières reproduction of the tomb of the prior of Saint-Wandrille (d. 1542) at the monastery of the Celestines of Marcoussis.[34] The original was a painting in which the recumbent figure, in sacerdotal dress, his head on a cushion, is lying directly on the ground of the cemetery and Death, as a mummy, stands beside him, armed with the weapon with which it has struck him or is about to strike him. The cemetery has become the kingdom of Death, where it reigns in the form of a mummy armed with a scythe or spear. Here it is seated on a tomb as if on a throne. In one hand it holds its spear like a scepter, and in the other, a skull like the imperial globe. There, it rises with impatient haste over an open tomb; the tombstone is lifted back to reveal the face of a *transi.* But is it Death, ruler of the cemetery, or the corpse come out of its grave, this mummy with its skin intact except for the belly, open to reveal the entrails, and its grimacing head?

Here again, standing and triumphant, it brandishes its "dart" and threatens the cadaver, who lies at its feet on the lid of a sarcophagus in the final stages of decomposition. It is an extraordinary scene: the two superimposed cadavers are identical, but one is lying inanimate, the other standing up and alert. In cases where the two mummies are not juxtaposed, one cannot tell whether the figure is a ghost, the spiritual self or double that exists for each individual, the symbol of his underground destiny, or a personification of the force that destroys all living beings.[35]

The danses macabres are not miniatures from books of hours. They do not take us away from the cemetery where we have been brought by the Office of the Dead, because they are part of the cemetery decor, frescoes covering the walls of charnels or even the capitals of columns in the galleries.

There has been some disagreement about the meaning of the word *macabre*. It seems to me that it is the same as the word *macchabe* (corpse) in modern French slang, which is a conservatory of old expressions. It is not surprising that around the fourteenth century the dead body—the word *cadaver* was seldom used—was given the name of the holy Maccabees. The Maccabees had long been honored as patron saints of the dead because they were believed, rightly or wrongly, to be the originators of the prayers of intercession for the dead. Their feast day was probably replaced by the commemoration of November 2, All Souls' Day, but their memory was preserved for a long time afterward among the pious. At Nantes, for example, a painting by Rubens, intended for the altar of the dead, represents Judas Maccabaeus praying for the dead. In Venice, at the Scuola Grande dei Carmini, two paintings from the middle of the eighteenth century show in detail the sufferings of the Maccabees.

The danse macabre is an eternal round in which the dead alternate with the living. The dead lead the dance; indeed, they are the only ones dancing. Each couple consists of a naked mummy, rotting, sexless, and highly animated, and a man or woman, dressed according to his or her social condition and paralyzed by surprise. Death holds out its hand to the living person whom it will draw along with it, but who has not yet obeyed the summons. The art lies in the contrast between the rhythm of the dead and the rigidity of the living. The moral purpose was to remind the viewer both of the uncertainty of the hour of death and of the equality of all people in the face of death. People of all ages and ranks file by in an order which is that of the social hierarchy as it was beginning to be perceived at the time. This hierarchical symbolism has provided much information for the social historian of today.[36]

In danses macabres prior to the sixteenth century, which are the only ones we shall consider in this chapter, the encounter between man and Death is not violent. The gesture of Death is almost gentle: "My hand must fall on you." Death warns more often than it strikes:

> *Come here, I am waiting for you . . .*
> *You must die this very night . . .*
> *Tomorrow you must appear before the court . . .*

Death invites its future victim to look at it, and the sight serves as a warning:

> *Merchant, look this way . . .*
> *Usurer of manners free*
> *Come quickly and look at me.*

It delivers its summons ("You must come before the great judge") in a tone of mingled irony and pity:

> *For if God who is marvelous*
> *Has missed nothing, you lose everything.*

It says to the usurer. And to the doctor:

> *He is a good doctor who can cure himself.*

Emile Mâle thought that in the abbey at la Chaise-Dieu, Death was hiding its face so as not to frighten the little child it was about to carry away. It is true that when it speaks to the poor peasant, it is in the language of necessity and compassion:

> *You, laborer who in care and pain*
> *Have lived your whole life*
> *Must die, that is certain . . .*
> *You should be happy to die,*
> *For it frees you of great care . . .*

The living are not expecting this encounter. They start to make a gesture of retreat or denial, but they go no further than this. They betray neither profound anguish nor rebellion, only a regret softened by resignation: more regret among the rich, more resignation among the poor; it is only a matter of degree.

> *For God's sake go and get me*
> *The doctor and the apothecary*

demands the "pampered" wife whose husband is "such a fine businessman." On the other hand, the village woman accepts her fate:

> *I take death for better or for worse*
> *With patience and good grace . . .*

It is curious to find, beneath what were intended to be the hideous features of mortality, the old attitude of good-natured submission to destiny.

Other scenes seem to be developments of the simple encounters of the danse, because they also illustrate the idea of equality in the face of death and the *memento mori*. For example, the mummy or skeleton enters a room where princes and prelates are assembled, or approaches a joyous banquet —the banquet of life—and strikes one of the guests from behind, as in an engraving by Stradan. The emphasis here, more so than in the *artes* or the danses, is on suddenness. Death no longer grants a period of grace, it no longer gives a warning, it takes the person off guard. It is the *mors improvisa*, the death that was most feared, except by the new Erasmian humanists and the Protestant and Catholic reformers. But this sudden death is rarely pictured. In the rhythm, ultimately consoling, of the danses, which were so popular, first on the walls of charnels, then in the illustrations of wood-engravers, the terrible leader of the danse allows a brief respite.

Another theme that was contemporaneous with, if not older than, the *artes moriendi* and the danse macabre, and just as popular, was the Triumph of Death. The subject is different. It is no longer the personal confrontation between man and death, but the collective power of death. Death, in the form of a mummy or skeleton, stands with his symbolic weapon in his hand, driving a huge, slow chariot drawn by oxen. One recognizes this vehicle as the heavy cart used for holiday processions, inspired by mythology and intended for the grand entries of princes into their loyal towns. Here it is driven by a prince whose emblems are skulls and bones. It could also be the chariot from a royal funeral procession, and might carry either the waxen or wooden "representation" of a body decked out for the obsequies, or the coffin covered with the pall. In the fantastic universe of Bruegel the elder it became the incongruous little cart in which gravediggers piled the bones to transport them from one part of the church or cemetery to another.

But whatever its appearance, the chariot of Death is an engine of war, an implement of destruction that crushes beneath its wheels—and sometimes simply beneath its fatal shadow—a large number of people of all ages and conditions. As Pierre Michault describes it:

> *I am Death, the enemy of nature;*
> *I consume everything at last,*
> *I destroy the life of every human being*
> *Reducing every man to earth and ash.*
> *I am Death, nicknamed the cruel,*
> *Because I must bring all things to their end . . .*

> *On this ox which moves on, step by step*
> *I sit, nor do I spur him forward,*
> *But without haste I put to bitter death*
> *The gayest revellers with my cruel sword.*

Here Death is a symbol of blind fate, very different, apparently, from the individualism of the *artes* and the danses macabres. But let us make no mistake: The spirit of this allegory is even further than that of the danses from the primitive and traditional attitude of "we all die." In the traditional attitude toward death, a man knew that he was going to die and had time to resign himself to it, as custom decreed. The Death of the Triumphs comes without warning:

> *When I have taken aim, I prick and stab*
> *Without warning those who have lived enough . . .*[37]

The dead whose bodies he has strewn on the ground during his slow course suspected nothing; they were carried off in the sleep of unconsciousness.

Nor does one find in the language of the Triumphs the mingled irony and good-natured acceptance of the danses. The language of the Triumphs expresses an attitude that is undeniably different, one that was already apparent in the Campo Santo of Pisa but that was to be developed and accentuated later: the desire to express not so much the equality of conditions and the necessity of death as its absurdity and perversity. The Death of the Triumphs goes straight ahead, like a blind man. And in his hecatombs he spares the most miserable, the beggars and cripples who beg him to put an end to their suffering, as well as those desperate young people who run after him to expose themselves to his blows. He leaves the first alive by the side of the road and does not slow his pace to wait for the second. One has only to compare this allusion to despair with the condemnation of suicide in the *artes*, to sense the difference.

We have been working from iconographic sources, but we could just as well have used literary ones. Some of these, which we have already encountered, speak the same language as the images and may have served as commentaries on them: Pierre Michault on the Triumph of Death, or the anonymous versifier of the danses, or these lines by Pierre de Nesson:[38]

> *And when you pass away*
> *From that very day*

> *Your foul flesh will begin*
> *To have a loathsome stench . . .*

What will become of "carrion man," that "bag of dung," when

> *They bury you in the ground:*
> *And cover you with a big stone*
> *So you will never be seen again?*

No one will want to be with you anymore:

> *Who will keep you company then?*

We would find much the same thing from the writers of sermons, who were anxious to convert the living by frightening them, by showing them the vanity of life and inspiring them with the horror of death. But neither the sermonists nor the poets add very much to the lessons of iconography.

A few writers, poets like Nesson, saw a new relationship between the decomposition of the body after death and the habitual manifestations of life. The corruption that overtakes the dead body does not come from the ground:

> *Those worms that live in the earth*
> *Would not touch it, though they can.*

It comes from within the body:

> *For from the flesh itself do spring*
> *Those worms that are devouring.*

The corruption is there from the beginning. Man is born and dies in a state of "infection":

> *O most foul conception,*
> *O vile, fed on infection*
> *In the womb before your birth.*

The solids and liquids of corruption are concealed beneath the skin:

> *Job compares the flesh to raiment*
> *Which we put on like a garment*
> *That the body not be seen.*

If only we could see what lies beneath! And it is up to the poets and preachers, the moralists, to make us see it:

> *There is naught but filthiness,*
> *Mucus, spittle, rottenness,*
> *Stinking, rotten excrement.*
> *Consider the products of nature . . .*
> *You will see that each man brings*
> *Stinking matter, loathsome things*
> *From his body constantly.*

We recognize here Jankélévitch's idea of "death within life," the search for "death in the inmost recesses of life."

Henceforth, disease, old age, and death are merely eruptions out of the bodily envelope of the rottenness within. There is no need to look for outside elements like animal spirits in the air to explain disease; disease is always present. Conception, death, old age, and disease are combined in images that move and compel more than they frighten.

Eustache Deschamps's repulsive sexagenarian:[39]

> *I am growing stooped and bent,*
> *Almost deaf, my life declines . . .*

The decline allows the odors of corruption to permeate his body. Old age and death come when the fleshly envelope is no longer strong enough to contain them.

Villon's moribund "dies in pain":

> *His gall bursts in his breast*
> *Then he sweats, God knows how he sweats!*

Ronsard also felt and expressed how illness is a part of life, how suffering and death are inseparable from the self:[40]

> *I have varied my life by dividing the thread*
> *That Clotho spun me between sick and well,*
> *Just now good health within my soul did dwell,*
> *But soon disease, the great scourge of the soul.*

He knew this disease intimately; it was gout:

In old age gout did now torment my veins.

He died at sixty-one, the age of Deschamps's old man, but he felt the signs of illness and old age at thirty, and he dwelt on them complacently:

My eyes are darkly ringed, my face is ghastly,
My head gray-haired and bald, and I am only thirty.

He described his attacks of insomnia:

But that I cannot sleep, this is of all my woes
The greatest that vexes and afflicts my life . . .
Sixteen hours at least, I perish, open-eyed,
Turning, heaving myself this way and that
On one side and the other, I storm, I cry . . .
Have mercy, O my God! O cease to ravage me
For lack of sleep.

He took opium, but the drug dulled his mind without granting him sleep:

O blessed a hundredfold, you animals who sleep . . .
Without eating of the poppy that deadens every sense.
I have eaten and drunk of its forgetful juice,
Both cooked and raw, and yet sleep denies
Me the refreshment of her hand upon my eyes.

His infirmities condemned him to a state of emaciation that foreshadowed the end:

I am all bones, I am a skeleton
Stripped of flesh, of fat, of everything,
Struck down forever by the hand of death!

Exhausted, the sick man in the poem calls for death, but it is not the proverbial lament of the poor woodcutter:

In vain I call for morning, and I beg for death . . .
Give me (O death) your presence in these dark days,
The shortest of the year, or with your branch dipped
In the stream of oblivion, upon my aching brow
Close my poor eyes in sleep, dry my tears and rheum . . .
Bring me death, to drive away my pain.

Ah death! Our common port, the comfort of us all,
Come bury all my ills, I pray with joined hands.

But Death does not answer.

Then there is the temptation of suicide, one of the last temptations in the *artes moriendi:* "Go ahead and kill yourself" suggests the devil to the sick man who is already lifting his dagger.[41]

Old age and regrets for lost youth tempted Villon's La Belle Heaumière to follow the same example:

Ah! Old age, treacherous and proud,
Why have you brought me down so soon?
Who stays my hand, that I do not strike myself
This very moment and end my days?[42]

Death no longer brings comfort. Even for suffering invalids it is agony:

For when I hold them tightly in my hands
[it is Death Triumphant who speaks]
The final crossing with its cruel rigor
Gives them anguish and great languor [43]

But even when it does not go so far as suicide, this agony can cause despair and rebellion against God. The despair takes the form of a pact with the devil.

The Influence of the Missionaries and of the Plague

It is remarkable that these literary sources place as much emphasis on the decomposition during life as on that after death. One has the sense that a violent change has altered the traditional model of death in bed that was still present in the *artes moriendi*. An atmosphere of anxiety seems to have taken hold. People have come to desire the sudden death, once so greatly feared, in preference to the expected and ritual death.

How are we to interpret the themes of these documents? How are we to situate them in the long series that begins with the resurrection of the flesh and the Last Judgment? A preliminary answer is that describing the horrors of decomposition was a way for the mendicant friars to impress and convert the lay populations, especially in urban areas. We know that at this period the Church was not entirely satisfied with the ideal of perfection of the cloisters, and hoped to win over people whom it had previously more or less abandoned to a kind of half-pagan, half-Christian folklore as long as they avoided the more conspicuous doctrinal or moral heresies. The agents of this conquest, the mendicants, tried to impress people's imaginations with powerful images, such as images of death.

It was also necessary that this language be understood, that listeners respond to its stimulation. Today, we would reject it with disgust. Before the fourteenth century, as after the sixteenth, it would probably have been received with indifference by people who were too familiar with images of death to be much affected by them. The clergy have always tried to arouse fear, fear of hell more often than fear of death, but they have been only half successful. In the fourteenth to sixteenth centuries, it would seem that they were taken more seriously, if not literally. The preachers talked about death in order to remind their listeners of hell. The faithful may no longer have been thinking about hell, but they were impressed by the images of death.

From the fourteenth to the sixteenth century, the old familiarity with death may not have disappeared from the common forms of daily life, but it was partially repressed in places where representations of death were acquiring new vigor and appeal. Why this new appeal?

It is tempting to correlate the success of macabre subject matter with the high mortality rates caused by the plagues, the great demographic crises of the fourteenth and fifteenth centuries that are believed to have depopulated certain regions and brought about an agricultural recession and a general economic crisis. Most historians continue to recognize the catastrophic quality of the late Middle Ages. "No other epoch," writes Johan Huizinga, "has laid so much stress as the expiring Middle Ages on the thought of death."[44] The great epidemics must have left vivid images in the collective memory. Pierre Michault has Death enumerate all his "instruments": old age; war; illness, "my loyal servant"; famine; and mortality, "my excellent chambermaid."[45]

The Triumphs of Death of Pisa and Lorenzetti are contemporaneous with the great plagues of the middle of the century. The skeleton of Assisi may be earlier. However, the reaction to the shock of the epidemic does not always take the realistic form of the cadaver or the description of death. Millard Meiss has shown that in Florence in the late fourteenth century, the mendicants were instructed to idealize the traditional religious representations rather than to load them with realistic details, and they were also to exalt the role of the Church and of the Franciscan and Dominican orders by emphasizing the hieratic aspects of the sacred and of transcendence in an archaic, abstract style. Their work represented a return to Byzantine models and to the Romanesque spirit that bypassed the anecdotal tendencies of the thirteenth century.

Symbols were also used to suggest the plague in order to ward it off, for instance, the image of Saint Sebastian pierced by arrows as a symbol of humanity besieged by the epidemic. Later, however, in the sixteenth and seventeenth centuries, artists did not hesitate to show people dying in the streets, bodies piled in carts, the digging of the common graves.[46] But by this time the period of the macabre, properly speaking, was over, although the plagues continued to rage.

The correlation between the macabre and the plagues, however tempting, is not altogether convincing, particularly since the great crisis of the late Middle Ages is being called into doubt by the historians of today. Jacques Heers writes:

> It would seem that historians have erred in the direction of a pessimism that is often exaggerated and unjustified. . . . They have sought to verify the famous hypothesis of a catastrophe or at least a severe economic recession at the end of the Middle Ages, a compelling idea which since Henri Pirenne, at any rate, . . . has impressed all historians of medieval economics. This conception was so deeply rooted and was accepted so unquestioningly that it was impossible to write anything about this period without agreeing with it; any study of economic history had to start with this idea. For almost twenty years now, however, more cautious and better informed writers . . . have shown that this decline did not necessarily characterize the Western world as a whole. They speak more in terms of transformation than of catastrophe. . . . In the beginning, the idea of a catastrophic recession probably owed a great deal to certain tendencies which must now be rejected. For example, excessive faith in certain contemporary witnesses, men of the church often unaccustomed to handling figures, quite naturally inclined to magnify the losses and the problems, to present a distorted, fictionalized image, to lament the woes of a humanity whom they saw as struck down by the wrath of God, to lend credence to a kind of black legend of their time.[47]

We must now consider another source of information that supports a less pessimistic view than that of historical tradition: wills.

Antoinette Fleury devoted her unpublished thesis at the Ecole des Chartes, the School of Paleography and Librarianship in Paris, to a study of sixteenth-century Parisian wills. In the course of her research, she lived on intimate terms with these texts, and her spontaneous reactions, if not those of an expert, have value as evidence. Here is what she writes about the clauses concerning burial: "We have seen, from the funeral cortege, the long procession with lights, and the ceremonies in the churches, to which small children were invited, *the rather consoling idea of death that people had in those days* [emphasis added]. To give the ceremony a more *festive atmosphere,* it was customary to serve a meal or some refreshment to those who attended."[48]

A few years later Fleury, who is now librarian of the Minutier Central, a public repository for legal documents at the National Archives, would probably not have dared to express her first impressions with such simplicity. She would have expressed reservations and made apologies, and hesitated to associate the idea of death with a "festive atmosphere" in the middle of the age of the macabre.

It will be objected that Fleury is writing about the sixteenth century and that the peak of interest in the macabre had passed, that new demographic and economic advances had driven the grim apparitions away. In reality, representations of the macabre continue well into the sixteenth century, especially on tombs. "Death was a companion of the Renaissance," asserts Jean Delumeau.[49] It would have been surprising if the traumatized sensibilities of the fifteenth century had so quickly discovered a "festive atmosphere" in the sixteenth.

Moreover, there is no great difference in tone between the wills of the fifteenth and those of the sixteenth century. In the fifteenth century, one is a little more likely to find words like *carcass* or *cadaver* in place of *body.* On the other hand, allusions to funeral meals are more frequent in the fifteenth century, but this is usually to forbid them, in a spirit that anticipates the age of reform.

It must be acknowledged that the whole grim panoply evoked by artists, poets, and preachers was not used by ordinary people when they thought about their own death. This was not for lack of eloquence. Holograph wills are loquacious; they abound in digressions on the vicissitudes of the human condition, the dangers that threaten the soul, and the vanity of a body destined for the dust. Nothing but time-honored metaphors; no need for images that are too expressive. Fleury calls this idea of death "consoling"; without contradicting her, I would be more inclined to call it natural, or familiar.

The fact is that death in macabre art is not realistic death. Huizinga, victim of his own black vision, was wrong when he wrote, "Living emotion is paralyzed amid the realistic representation of skeletons and worms." This is not realism![50] However, it was an age that hungered for resemblances. In the next two chapters we shall have occasion to describe in some detail the desire, first apparent in the thirteenth century, to reproduce the features of the model. We shall see how this search for accuracy led to the use of the death mask. This is certainly the origin of those terra-cotta statues, dating from the early sixteenth century, that once stood around the choir of Saint-Sernin, in Toulouse, and that are today in the musée des Augustins. Historians long believed them to be sibyls, but the people used to call them the "mummies of the counts," and it is now agreed that they represent the counts of the family of Saint-Gilles, benefactors of the abbey.[51]

In all these cases the features of the cadaver were not reproduced in order to frighten, as in a *memento mori;* they were used much as an instantaneous and accurate photograph of the subject would be today. Those grimaces, which to the modern sensibility distort the features of the deceased and remind us of death, made no particular impression on contemporaries, who merely found them true to life. Thus, in the middle of the period of the macabre, artists sometimes made use of death to give the illusion of life, which was identified with the idea of resemblance. It was as if there were two very distinct realms: on the one hand, the realm of the macabre, in which death created alarm, and on the other hand, the realm of the portrait, in which death created illusion.

Not only is there no connection, there is even an antagonism between the art of the macabre and the immediate, physical sight of death.

In the following chapters we shall analyze a profound change in funerary practices that must have occurred in the twelfth and thirteenth centuries. Before this change, the body was laid out and transported from bed to grave with the face uncovered. Afterward, except in Mediterranean regions, the face was covered, and it would never again be exposed, even if the sight might awaken the very emotions that the art of the macabre was trying to arouse. The thirteenth century marks the onset of a reluctance to view the dead body that was unaffected by the period of the macabre. The body was hidden from view, not only by wrapping it from head to foot in a sewn shroud, but also by totally concealing its shape, by enclosing it in a wooden box and covering this box with a tapestried platform.[52]

In fact, macabre art almost never represents the moribund alive and disfigured, or the cadaver intact or almost intact. The rare exceptions—a few Burgundian tombs, mentioned above; a few victims of the Triumphs of Death; a few beautiful corpses—do not contradict the truth of this generalization.

The moribunds of the *artes moriendi* are not haggard. Neither the painter nor the sculptor was interested in showing the illness, the death clearly visible within life, that so fascinated the poet. It was acceptable to suggest these things with the symbolism of words; it was unacceptable to show them with the realism of facts.

What macabre art did show was precisely *what could not be seen,* what went on under the ground: the hidden work of decomposition, which was not the result of observation, but the product of imagination.

Thus, by gradual stages, we have been led to observe a discontinuity between macabre art and the miseries of life or the fear of death.

A Passionate Love of Life

Alberto Tenenti offers a subtler explanation that acknowledges the complexity we have glimpsed beneath the surface. He begins by observing that at the end of the Middle Ages death is no longer crossing or transition, but end and decomposition. The physical fact of death has replaced the images of judgment. "For centuries Christianity had not felt the need to represent the misery of the body." How are we to explain the appearance of this need? It "could only spring from a horror and regret that were incompatible with faith."[53] As Jankélévitch puts it, faith in eternal life ceases, but death goes on.

Macabre imagery is a sign that man is being confronted by a growing awareness of new needs: "Secular needs, the attachment to worldly goods [which are taking on more importance than before] would never have given men faith in themselves had not a profound inner experience already separated them from the religious orientation."[54] This profound inner experience is the "death in life" of which Jankélévitch speaks. The sense of the presence of death in the midst of life elicited two responses: on the one hand, Christian asceticism, and on the other hand, a humanism that was still Christian but that was already well on its way to secularization. At the beginning of the Renaissance, the collective consciousness was "violently polarized by the hallucinating reality of death. Some [mystics, such as Heinrich Suso, or preachers, such as Saint Vincent Ferrer] who were seemingly driven to immerse themselves in the contemplation of decay and physical destruction, drew conclusions that were altogether otherworldly. They were in that spiritual state most likely to leave them indifferent to the demands of modern culture [then in the process of being born] and of a secular sensibility. Others [such as Petrarch or Salviati] were led by the experience of pain and the resulting awareness of their organic destiny, their physical transformation, to affirm a love of life and to proclaim the preeminent value of worldly existence."[55]

Henceforth there appears in some thinkers "an imperious desire to make life an end in itself," a desire that sometimes went so far as the denial of the soul and its survival. In any case, "man claimed to possess in his own conduct sufficient basis for his eternal salvation. . . . Instead of a brief sojourn, life was seen as a period that was always sufficient to construct one's own salvation." There developed an ideal of a full life that was no longer threatened by fear of the beyond. The art of dying well "was fundamentally a new sense of time, of the value of the body as a living organism. It was based on an ideal of active life that no longer had its center of gravity outside earthly life."[56] "It no longer only expressed, as it once had, the impulse toward an otherworldly existence, but an attachment increasingly limited to a life that was merely human." By the end of this process, the macabre symbols had disappeared. "The bizarre aspects of the first contacts quickly disappeared; the face and the human sense of death re-mained."[57] The humanists of the fifteenth century had replaced the maca-bre symbols with an inner sense of the presence of death; they felt as if they were dying all the time.[58]

To summarize, Tenenti feels that the intense awareness of human mortality in the fourteenth and fifteenth centuries reflected "a violent disturbance of the Christian world view"[59] and the first stirrings of the secularization that characterizes the modern era. "Those who were for-merly Christians discovered their own mortality. They banished themselves from heaven because they no longer had the strength to believe in it in a coherent manner."[60]

Tenenti's analysis is very attractive, but I do not find it completely satisfactory. I cannot accept the polarity he establishes between a medieval Christianity turned toward the beyond in which earthly life is merely an antechamber to eternity, and a Renaissance turned toward the present in which death is no longer the beginning of a new life. If there is a real break, it is rather between the early and the late Middle Ages. If this Christianity existed, it was as a common language or system of reference; society was no more Christian in the Middle Ages than in the Renaissance, and probably less so than in the seventeenth century. If the Renaissance marks a change of sensibility, this change should not be interpreted as the begin-ning of a process of secularization, or at least no more so than other intellectual movements of the Middle Ages. I cannot follow Tenenti in this line of thinking, which is contrary to the whole conception of history that is defended in these pages.

On the other hand, I think that what he says about the full life, the value of earthly life, puts us on the right track, provided the love of life is not regarded as peculiar to the Renaissance, for it is also one of the distinguishing characteristics of the late Middle Ages.

To recapitulate, the macabre is not the expression of a particularly pro-found experience of death in an age of high mortality and great economic crisis. It is not merely a way for preachers to instill fear of damnation or contempt for the world and thus bring about conversion. The images of death and decomposition do not signify fear of death or of the beyond, although they have been utilized to that end. They are the sign of a passionate love for this world and a painful awareness of the failure to which each human life is condemned.

In order to understand this passionate love of life, let us return to the *artes moriendi* and to the last ordeal on which the eternal fate of the dying man depends and see what profound attachments it expresses.[61] The ordeal consists of two series of temptations. In the first series, the dying man is urged to interpret his life in terms of either despair or satisfaction. The devil shows him all his evil actions. "Look at your sins: You have killed, you have fornicated." He has also robbed the poor, refused to give charity, accumulated ill-gotten gains. But his sins are not recalled and presented in order to accuse him, to tip the scales of judgment toward hell. The guardian angel does not counterbalance this miserable biography with the good works he may have done; he merely exhorts him to have confidence in divine mercy, of which he cites examples: the good thief, Mary Magdalene, the denials of Saint Peter. Will the *bona inspiracio* of the angel enable the dying man to resist the morbid contemplation of his life and crimes? Or will he give way to the despair to which he is already inclined by his physical suffering and indulge in "indiscreet acts of penitence" that will lead to suicide? At his bedside a demon imitates him, striking himself with a dagger and saying, "You committed suicide."

On the other hand, the dying man may consider this same life with assurance; but the vainglory of the person who has too much confidence in man will be worth no more than despair. The devil will offer him all the crowns of self-satisfaction. In this first series of temptations, life is presented to the dying man no longer as an object of judgment but as a last chance to prove his faith.

In the second series, the devil holds before the dying man everything that death threatens to take away from him, everything that he has possessed or loved during his life, everything that he wants to hold on to and cannot bring himself to leave behind. *Omnia temporalia,* which he has accumulated with so much trouble, care, and affection, and which include both human beings—wife, child, dear friends—and possessions: "all the other things of this world that are desirable," objects of pleasure, sources of profit. The love of things is not distinguished from the love of human beings. Both belong under the heading of *avaritia,* which does not mean the desire to accumulate or the reluctance to spend, as does our word *avarice,* but the passionate and eager love of life, of persons as well as things, even persons whom we today consider worthy of unlimited attachment, such as wife or child. *Avaritia* is the "excessive attachment to *temporalia* or external things, to spouses or worldly friends or material wealth, or to other things that men have loved too much during their lives."

Two centuries earlier, Saint Bernard had compared two categories of men, the *vani* or *avari*, and the *simplices* or *devoti*. The *vani*, unlike the humble, sought vainglory; the *avari*, unlike those who devoted themselves to God, loved life and the world. Under the term *avaritia*, the Church condemned both the love of human beings and the love of things, for either one separated the self from God.

The ordinary Christian avoided such renunciations, but the sensualist shared the psychology of the ascetic or the moralist, and made no distinction between people and possessions. People were viewed as possessions that had to be preserved: "Be good to your friends." And things were loved like friends: "Take care of your treasure." The dying man rests his eyes on his large and beautiful house, his cellar full of wine, his stable of horses, which the devil's magic has caused to appear at the foot of his bed. He might also be moved by the sight of his family, who are gathered around his bed and whom he is about to leave, but it would seem that he puts less trust in them than in his fine things. Sometimes he even mistrusts their hypocritical tears, suspects them of being interested in an inheritance, and in a fit of rage and despair, he kicks them out of the room.

At the moment of death, one must leave houses and orchards and gardens; this was the temptation of *avaritia*. The man felt welling up in him a mad love of life, and he clung less to life itself, to the biological fact of remaining alive, than to the things he had accumulated during his lifetime. The knight of the early Middle Ages died in all simplicity, like Lazarus. The man of the later Middle Ages and of the beginning of modern times was tempted to die like Dives, the rich man in the parable.

He did not want to be separated from his possessions and wished he could take them with him. Of course, the Church warned him that unless he renounced them, he would go to hell. The threat was not without its consolations; for although damnation exposed him to torture, it did not deprive him of his treasure. Over the main entrance of the twelfth-century church at Moissac, Dives has kept his purse. It hangs around his neck, setting the style for all the misers who succeeded him in the hells of Last Judgments. In a painting by Hieronymus Bosch that could have served as an illustration for an *ars moriendi*, the devil is staggering under the weight of a huge bag of silver pieces, which he lays on the dying man's bed so that he will have it within reach at the moment of death.[62] There will be no chance of his forgetting it. How many of us today would feel the slightest inclination at death to take along a portfolio of stock certificates, a coveted automobile, a magnificent jewel? Medieval man could not bring himself to abandon his riches even at death. He sent for them; he wanted to touch them, to hold them.

The truth is that probably at no time has man so loved life as he did at the end of the Middle Ages. The history of art offers indirect proof. The love of life found expression in a passionate attachment to things, an attachment that resisted the annihilation of death and changed our vision of the world and of nature. This attachment inspired man to give a new value to the representation of these things; it invested them with a kind of life. A new art was born that was called *nature morte* in the Romance languages, and still life, or *still-leven,* in the languages of the North. Charles Sterling cautions us against "the facile poetry with which modern romanticism invests these terms by interpreting them as 'silent life.' " They mean only that the subject does not move. But the same author reports that in 1649 an artist was described by his contemporaries as "a very fine painter of the portrait and the quiet life." How else is one to translate this than as "silent life," and how is one to overlook the desire or instinct to create an image?[63]

Avaritia and Still Life

I believe that there is a relationship worth considering between *avaritia* and still life. The most casual observer is struck by the difference in the ways objects are represented in the period that precedes the thirteenth century and in the period that follows it, in the fourteenth and fifteenth centuries.

Before the thirteenth century the object is almost never regarded as a source of life, but rather as a sign, the symbolic representation of a movement. This is true of works that appear at first sight to contradict this thesis. For example, there is a large fresco of the Marriage at Cana in which the objects on the table are in the foreground and play an important role. From the standpoint of subject, this fresco is already a still life, but it is a still life by Cézanne or Picasso rather than a miniaturist of the fourteenth century, a painter of the seventeenth century, or even a Chardin.

I am talking about a large twelfth-century fresco in the church of Brinay.[64] On the tablecloth of the wedding feast seven terra-cotta bowls of a simple and beautiful design are lined up horizontally, one beside the other. Some of them contain large stiff fish that hang over their edges. They have no shadows, and are shown from both the side and the back at the same time. We also see the bottoms of the bowls, which would normally rest on the table; but we see these bottoms in a three-quarters view, as if the bowls had been raised and tipped slightly toward the back of the fresco. We know that the Carolingian and Romanesque artist employed a perspective that was different from that of the viewer: he showed the viewer what he could not see, as he ought to see it. The effect of the horizontality of the row of seven bowls is accentuated by the seven large parallel folds the tablecloth forms as it falls. These objects, these bowls, these fish, prefigure another table, that of the Last Supper. They have neither weight nor density, and although the series has its own rhythmic beauty, no single element holds our attention or distracts it from the composition as a whole.

Generally speaking, objects are often arranged in an order that bears no relation to their function but that is inspired by metaphysical hierarchies or other symbolic or mystical considerations. Take, for example, those curtains that were so common in Carolingian and Romanesque illuminations because of their role in the liturgy. In the Carolingian period, at least, they were part of the furniture of the sanctuary. They shielded the sacred objects from profane eyes, and they were opened and closed like the doors of the iconostasis in churches of the Eastern rite. In an eleventh-century miniature, the curtain is open to allow Saint Radegonde to approach the altar. The curtain has become inseparable from the sacred objects that have to be veiled or unveiled. It is made of a light material that falls in folds and stirs at the slightest breeze. The virtuosity of the illuminators does not suffer by comparison with the realistic skill of those later artists who painted drapery and linen in the annunciations and nativities of the fifteenth century. But the whole art of draping or folding the curtain was intended to make one forget the object as a thing in itself and to give it another function.

Sometimes the curtain is closed, as in a Carolingian sacramentary, where it divides Saint Gregory, who is being inspired by the Holy Spirit, from the rest of the world. A monk in the *scriptorium* is lifting it just high enough so that he can hear the saint's dictation. Often the curtain is pulled back, hanging from a portico and fastened to its columns, dividing the holy personages from the divine emblems that surmount them, like the hand of God. One is held back by large knots, and two figures who look like part of the architecture of the portico are holding out their arms to secure the ends. This drapery is not stationary; it is stirred by a breeze that is not of this world, a breeze strong enough to wrap around a column the curtain of the sanctuary where Saint Radegonde is praying.[65]

Beginning in the fourteenth century, objects are represented differently. It is not that they have ceased to be signs; the linen drapery and the book are no less symbolic then than they were in the Romanesque era, but the relationship between the sign and its meaning has changed. Purity is an attribute of the lily just as much as the lily is the symbol of purity. Things have invaded the abstract world of symbols. Each object has acquired new weight, proof of its autonomy. Henceforth, objects will be represented for

their own sake, not out of a desire for realism but out of love and contemplation. Realism, *trompe l'oeil,* illusionism may have been consequences of the
direct relationship that was established between the object and the per-
ceiver.

From now on, in every painting containing figures, it is almost as if
the artist has introduced one or more "still lifes." Two essential characteristics of still life appear by the end of the fourteenth century and are
developed in the fifteenth and sixteenth centuries: the density of the object
itself and the order in which the objects are arranged, usually inside an
enclosed space.

A good example is one of the annunciations of the Master of Flémalle,
from the first half of the fifteenth century. Here things have acquired a
solidity that they did not have in those rarefied spaces, filled with ara-
besques, of the early Middle Ages.[66] Take the long fringed towel: What
a difference between this motionless linen that hangs with all its weight and
the flimsy veils, stirred by otherworldly breezes, of the Romanesque painters. Still a symbol of purity, to be sure, it is first and foremost the fine,
expensive linen of an elegant home. But perhaps a piece of fine, well-cared-
for linen is associated with a certain idea of the moral virtue of the woman,
her household, her family. One could not say the same for the other objects:
the copper basin, the vase of flowers, the polygonal surface of the table. A
faint shading models them and places them in a three-dimensional space
where they have, if you will, a life of their own.

In the interior shown in this painting, the objects are organized in
subgroups, which one is tempted to consider apart from the composition
as a whole. This annunciation can be broken down into three small still
lifes. The first consists of a niche, the copper basin with a handle and a
spout used for ablutions that hangs from it, and finally the towel and its
carved and pivoting towel holder. The second includes the table on which
are lying a book of hours and its cloth cover, a copper candlestick whose
candle has just been snuffed—it is still smoking—and the Chinese vase
containing the emblematic lily. The third is composed of the large wooden
bench, the fireplace, the window and its shutters. Here the still life is ready
to detach itself from the subject, like those book-filled niches in the triptych
of the Annunciation of Aix.

These elements of still life that became so prominent in the fifteenth
century make their appearance timidly but deliberately in the French
miniature and in painting toward the end of the fourteenth century. In a
1336 manuscript of the trial of Robert d'Artois, the long wooden bench
that encloses the space reserved for the court in the foreground of the
drawing prefigures the benches of Flemish annunciations.[67] In a nativity
from *Les Petites Heures de Jean de Berry,* a jar of water has been placed

beside the recumbent Virgin, and Saint Joseph is sitting on a seat of braided straw. In the foreground of another nativity from the same period, we see a small low table, similar to a stool, on which there are a bowl, a spoon, a bottle—a group we shall see for a long time to come on inexpensive pottery—and a cup, all of terra-cotta.

What a museum of daily life one could construct with the help of these paintings, which overlooked no opportunity to represent objects in loving detail! Sometimes they were precious objects: in the fifteenth century, gold or silver goblets filled with gold pieces that the Wise Men offer to an infant Jesus, who is delighted by all these riches, or that the devil offers, this time in vain, to Christ in the desert. (This scene became less common, as if the iconography of the time preferred the displays of the Epiphany or the opulence of Magdalene to the indifference or contempt of the tempted Christ.) There were sumptuous objects adorning the tables of great lords, among which one recognizes one of the celebrated jewels of the collection of the Duc de Berry *(Très Riches Heures);* jewels in Flemish portraits of women and even of men, necklaces by Memling and Petrus Christus, rendered with a precision worthy of a silversmith's catalog; Oriental rugs, mirrors, chandeliers; and simpler objects, but sometimes quite fine, tableware decorating the Last Supper of Dierik Bouts, porridge bowls in representations of the Virgin and Child, bowls and basins in which newborn infants are being bathed in holy nativities; books piled up in the niches of prophets or in the hermitage of Saint Jerome; books of hours being read by the Virgin or by the subjects of portraits; bundles of papers and account books (Jan Gossaert); ordinary and rustic objects, flyswatters, and simple earthen dishes. The humblest objects enjoyed an attention that was henceforth focused on the richest ones. They emerged to become pleasing and beautiful shapes, regardless of the humbleness of their material or the simplicity of their design.

This art, which was "Gothic" and Flemish as well as Italian, celebrated in simple things the sign of a domestic affluence that even those who had made a commitment to evangelical poverty could not bring themselves to renounce. Like monks in their cells, the Holy Family in their destitute condition had the right to the company of a few objects. So the objects multiplied around the figures and filled the spaces of rooms, in which the artist also took his place, as if to arrange them better, rooms from the *Térence des Ducs* manuscript belonging to the duc de Berry, rooms too small for the people and things they contained, rooms that were the scenes of nativities. In the second half of the fifteenth century, it was as if the objects took up too much room in the scenes, had to be separated from them, and thus became the subjects of paintings on their own. Still life, in the true sense of the term, was born.

The first still life that was "independent and entirely devoid of any symbolic religious character ... the first to appear ... in Western painting since antiquity, that corresponds to the modern conception of the genre,"[68] is on the door of a medicine chest. It is painted in *trompe l'oeil* to depict another medicine chest, with books and bottles. On one of the bottles, Panofsky has deciphered a German inscription: *Für Zamme* (for toothache).

From now on, and for more than two centuries, not only things but also their pictorial representations will be part of the familiar decor of life. The love they inspired gave birth to an art that drew from them both subjects and inspiration.

It is difficult for us today to understand the intensity of the old relationship between people and things. It survives in the collector, who has a real passion for the objects in his collection and loves to contemplate them. Moreover, his passion is never completely disinterested; although the objects taken individually may be worthless, the fact of bringing them together in a unique series gives them value. By definition, therefore, the collector is a speculator. But contemplation and speculation, which characterize the psychology of the collector, are also the distinguishing traits of the protocapitalist, as he appears in the later Middle Ages and in the Renaissance. If we go back too far before capitalism, things do not yet deserve to be seen or held on to or desired; this is why the early Middle Ages were a time of indifference. Although commerce never deserted the West, and people always had fairs and markets, wealth was not seen as the possession of things; it was identified with power over men, just as poverty was identified with solitude. The moribund of the *chanson de geste,* unlike the dying man of the *artes,* does not think of his treasure, but of his lord, his peers, and his men.

In order for material possessions to become important to the dying man, they had to become both less rare and more sought after, they had to acquire a value of utility or exchange.

If we go too far forward in the capitalist evolution, the aptitude for speculation is preserved but the taste for contemplation disappears and there is no longer a sensual connection between man and his wealth. A good example is the car. In spite of its enormous hold on our imagination, the car, once it has been acquired, ceases to inspire contemplation. The object of present attention is no longer this car, but the more recent model that has already replaced it in the owner's desire. Or else one does not love this car as much as one loves the make, the brand to which it belongs and that wins all prizes for performance. Our industrial civilizations no longer believe that things possess a soul "which attaches itself to our soul and compels it to love." Things have become means of production, or objects to be consumed or devoured. They no longer constitute a "treasure."

Harpagon's love for his money box, in Molière, would today be regarded as a sign of underdevelopment, of economic immaturity. Possessions can no longer be designated by those dense Latin words *substantia, facultates.*

Can one describe a civilization that has emptied things in this way as materialistic? On the contrary, it is the late Middle Ages, up to the beginning of modern times, that were materialistic! The decline in religious belief, in idealistic and normative morality, did not lead to the discovery of a more material world. Scientists and philosophers may lay claim to an understanding of matter, but the ordinary man in his daily life no more believes in matter than he believes in God. The man of the Middle Ages believed in matter and in God, in life and in death, in the enjoyment of things and in their renunciation. Historians have erred in trying to polarize these ideas by assigning them to different periods, whereas in fact they were contemporaneous, and as much complementary as opposite.

The Sense of Failure

Huizinga clearly understood the relationship between the passionate love of life and the images of death. The macabre themes were no longer a pious invitation to conversion. "A thought which so strongly attaches to the earthly side of death can hardly be called truly pious. It would rather seem a kind of spasmodic reaction against an excessive sensuality."[69] But there is another motif that Huizinga has also perceived, "the sense of disillusionment and discouragement," and this brings us, I think, to the heart of the matter.

In order to understand thoroughly the meaning that this notion of disillusionment or failure had for the people of the end of the Middle Ages, we must leave aside for a moment the documents of the past and the debates of historians, and look into ourselves.

All men today, at some time in their lives, have experienced a feeling, whether weak or strong, admitted or repressed, of failure in their domestic or professional lives. The desire for promotion makes it impossible for any man ever to stop where he is, makes it necessary for him to press on toward newer and more difficult goals. The sense of failure is all the more persistent and profound the more longed for and inadequate the success, which is always pushed ahead into a more remote future. The day comes, however, when the individual can no longer keep pace with his progressive ambitions. He moves more slowly than his desire, he falls further and further behind, and he realizes that his model is becoming inaccessible. At this point he feels that he has wasted his life.

The crisis usually comes at about the age of forty, and it tends increasingly to resemble the problems of the adolescent in entering the adult world, problems that may lead to alcoholism, drugs, or suicide. However, in our industrial societies, the period of crisis always precedes the physical deterioration of old age and death. The individual discovers one day that he is a failure; he never sees himself as a corpse. He does not associate his bitterness with death. The man of the late Middle Ages did.

Is this sense of failure a permanent characteristic of the human condition? Perhaps in the form of a metaphysical inadequacy extended to a whole life, but not in the form of a specific and sudden perception of violent shock. Such a shock was alien to the cool and leisurely rhythm of the tame death. Every man was bound to a destiny that he had neither the power nor the desire to change. This situation prevailed for the long generations when wealth was a rarity. The life of the poor man has always been an ineluctable fate over which he has no control.

Beginning in the twelfth century, however, we see the rise among the rich, the well educated, and the powerful, of the idea that every man possesses a personal biography. At first this biography consisted solely of actions, good or bad, which were subjected to an overall judgment: what he was. Later, it came to include things, animals, or people who were passionately loved, and even reputation: what he had. At the end of the Middle Ages awareness of the self and its biography became associated with the love of life. Death was not only an end to being but a separation from having: One must leave behind houses and orchards and gardens.

In the midst of health and youth, the enjoyment of things was tainted by the sight of death. At this point death ceased to be a weighing, a final reckoning, judgment, or repose, and became carrion and corruption; it ceased to be the end of life, the last breath, and became physical death, suffering, and decomposition.

The mendicant preachers shared the natural sensibility of their contemporaries, even when they exploited it for religious purposes. This is why their religious image of death also changed at this time. Death was no longer the result of original sin, the death of Christ on the cross, the theological counterpart among the clergy of the resignation to destiny among the laity. Death became the bloody body of the descent from the cross, the Pietà, new and upsetting images that were the theological counterpart of the physical death, the painful separation, the universal decomposition that constitute the macabre.

In both religious representations and natural attitudes, then, we have moved by imperceptible stages from death as an awareness and summation of *a* life, to death as an awareness and desperate love of *this* life. The art of the macabre can only be understood as the final phase in the relationship between death and individualism, a gradual process that began in the twelfth century and that arrived in the fifteenth century at a summit never to be reached again.

4

Guarantees of Eternity

The Archaic Rites

In the first chapter, "The Tame Death," we saw how Roland and his companions died. Before they left for the Crusades without hope of return, they received absolution, which was given in the form of a benediction:

They were absolved and freed from their sins
And the archbishop of God made the sign of the cross over them.

The same ceremony would be repeated, perhaps more than once, after their death. When Charlemagne and his army arrived at Roncevaux "where the battle took place, . . . the French dismounted from their horses." It was time for the dead to be buried in graves or charnels. "All their friends whom they found dead they immediately took to a charnel."

This burial was conducted "with great honor." The essential feature of the ceremony was a new and more solemn absolution and benediction, which was accompanied by the burning of incense:

They were absolved and blessed in the name of God.

The words for "absolved" and "blessed"—*asols* and *seignez*—are the same ones that Archbishop Turpin used when he absolved and blessed his companions before they went to meet their death. For the poet, it was the same ceremony that was repeated over the living and the dead. Later usage reserved the sacramental term *absolution* for the benediction of the living and the scholarly term *absoute* for the benediction of the dead, in order to distinguish clearly between the two. The word *absoute* did not belong to the vernacular; it never appears in wills of the fifteenth to eighteenth centuries. I believe it did not enter the common language until the nineteenth century. "There are in the army numerous bishops and abbots, monks, canons, tonsured priests who give them absolution and benediction in the name of God. They burn myrrh and thyme and cense them with zeal and then bury them with great honor." Two of the gestures of the postmortem absolution are clearly described: the benediction, which is the gesture of absolution in the name of God, and the censing, with the same substances that were used to embalm bodies.

This account makes no mention of the recitation or chanting of certain passages; these were not yet an essential part of the ceremony.

This ancient scene recurs without major changes in two iconographic series of later date: the death of the Virgin and the entombments of saints. The first series corresponds to the ceremony for the living, the second to the ceremony for the dead. The death of the Virgin has been represented since the end of the Middle Ages. The Virgin is lying in bed, sick. She holds a candle in her hand, a later custom that is not mentioned in the early texts. Around the dying woman's bed is the usual crowd of spectators, with the apostles representing the clergy. One of them, sometimes wearing spectacles, reads or sings passages from a book, which is sometimes held by an acolyte. Another carries the holy-water basin and the aspergillum, and still another, the censer. The psalms and Commendations have been read, and the dying woman has been given absolution and sprinkled with holy water. This last gesture has been added to the benediction with the sign of the cross. Have the clergy censed her still-living body, or is the censer there so that the operation can be repeated after the last breath? Well before this later iconography, the Visigothic liturgy implies the presence of a large crowd of people in the house, who received the kiss of peace from the dying man and prayed around a portable cross during his agony.

The burial of the saint appears much earlier than the death of the Virgin: at Saint-Hilaire, in Poitiers, to name but one example out of an endless series. This series is uniform while the tomb is a sarcophagus, placed on the ground or half-buried in it. The body is laid on top of the open sarcophagus wrapped in a shroud, but with the face still uncovered. We recognize the same clergymen (the celebrant and his assistants who carry the book, the holy-water basin, the aspergillum, and the censer, sometimes a crossbearer and candlebearers). Once the ceremony is over, the body will be lowered into the sarcophagus and the sarcophagus closed.

Aspersion with holy water was not limited to the body; it was also extended to the grave. In the Visigothic liturgies there are special prayers for this purpose that are exorcisms designed to protect the grave from the attacks of the devil.[1]

If our hypothesis is correct, penitential absolution probably served as a model for the ceremony at the grave. Holy water and incense are still associated with the things of death. Even today, those who visit the dead are invited to honor them by sprinkling them with holy water. Although Christianity abolished the ancient practice of placing objects in tombs to appease the dead, in pre–thirteenth-century medieval tombs one sometimes finds prophylactic medals and ceramic censers containing coals. The liturgist Durandus of Mende recommends this practice: "In some places, after the body is placed in the tomb or grave, they add holy water and coals with incense."[2]

This very simple ceremony was the only one in which the clergy intervened to perform a religious ritual designed to wash away the sins of the deceased. The operation was repeated several times, as if repetition increased its chances of being effective. There was no other religious ceremony besides the absolution and the prayers that were said before, during, and after it. This statement may seem to contradict certain liturgical documents of the fifth through the seventh centuries that refer to a special Mass. Judging from the chivalric texts, this Mass was not the general rule, and at any rate it was not performed in the presence of the body, nor was it associated with the removal of the body from the place of death to the place of burial.

Another important manifestation was mourning. We have seen that the dying man regretted life no more than was appropriate; he retained his calm and composure right to the end. But if death itself was tame, the mourning of the survivors was wild—or had to appear so. As soon as death was determined, there broke out the most violent scenes of despair. When "Roland sees that his friend [Oliver] is dead and lying face down on the ground," he faints "against his breast, he clasps him tightly in his arms." He cannot bear to let him go. When Charlemagne discovers the battlefield at Roncevaux, "he cannot hold back his tears. . . . On the green grass he sees his nephew lying. Is it any wonder that he trembles with grief? He dismounts from his horse and runs over to him." He embraces the body, clutches it, "and falls senseless on it, so great is his anguish." A few moments later, he loses consciousness again. When he comes to, he abandons himself to the classical gestures of grief. In front of the whole army, in front of a hundred thousand Frenchmen, of whom "there is not one who does not weep violently" or "fall unconscious on the ground," the emperor pulls his white beard and tears his hair with both hands. A hysterical scene: all these strapping warriors weeping, rolling on the ground, passing out, pulling out their beards and hair, tearing their clothing!

When King Arthur finds the dead bodies of his barons, he behaves like Charlemagne at Roncevaux. "He falls off his horse in a swoon. . . . He claps

his palms together"—here we recognize the ritual gesture of mourners—
"exclaiming that he has lived long enough, since now he sees the best men
of his lineage slain. ["I wish no more to live," cried Charlemagne.] He
removes the dead man's helmet, and after gazing at his face for a long time,
he kisses his eyes and his ice-cold mouth." No doubt men kissed each other
on the mouth in those days. Then he runs to another body, "lying there
cold, . . . takes it in his arms, and clasps it so tightly that he would have
killed the man had he still been alive." There are cases of embraces so
violent that one of the parties is left for dead. "Then he fainted again and
remained unconscious longer than it takes to travel half a league on foot."
And while he was embracing and kissing the bloody body, the poet tells
us that "there was no man there who marveled at his mourning." When
Gawain recognized his dead brother, "his legs gave way, his heart failed,
and he fell as if dead. . . . For a long time he remained thus. Finally he
got up and ran to Gaheris, clasped him in his arms, and kissed him, but
the kiss caused him so much sorrow that he fell again, unconscious, on the
dead man's body."

It was customary, as we shall see, to suspend these excessive demonstrations of mourning for a while in order to express regret for the departed,
but the weeping and wailing sometimes resumed afterwards. This was the
case with Gawain, who, after saying the lament for the dead, "went to
them, and as he clasped them in his arms, he fainted so many times in rapid
succession that in the end the barons were alarmed, and feared that he
would expire before their eyes." It was possible to die of grief.

It was up to the entourage to check the transports of the chief
mourner: "Sire emperor," says Geoffroi d'Anjou to Charlemagne, "do not
abandon yourself so wholly to this grief." "Sire," the barons say to King
Arthur, "we think he should be taken from this place and laid in some room
away from people, until his brothers have been buried, for if he remains
near them, he will surely die of grief." In fact, this sort of isolation was
rarely necessary. The lament over the body, a demonstration that today
seems hysterical or morbid, was usually enough to release the friend's grief
and make the fact of separation bearable.

How long did this deep mourning last? A few hours, the length of the
vigil, or sometimes the length of the burial. A month at the most, in
extreme cases; when Gawain told King Arthur about the deaths of Ywain
and his companions, "the king began to weep bitterly and for a month he
was so sorely grieved that he almost lost his wits."

These gestures of grief were interrupted by the eulogy for the deceased, the second act in the drama of mourning. It was the responsibility
of the chief mourner to pronounce the farewell. "The emperor Charles
regained consciousness. . . . He looked on the ground and saw his nephew

lying there. Very quietly, he began the regret." The regret is also called the plaint, or *planctus:* "Charles said his plaint with loyalty and love." The beginning of the eulogy is difficult. The funeral orator keeps fainting, but then he gathers momentum and holds out for fifty verses: "Friend Roland, may God be merciful to you . . . who will lead my armies?" The lament ends, as it began, with a prayer "that your soul be sent to paradise."

Similarly, after King Arthur receives the dying breath of Lord Gawain, he faints several times on the body, tears his beard, and rakes his face with his fingernails, in accordance with custom. Then he delivers his great lament: "Ah! Arthur, miserable and wretched king, now you may truly say that you are stripped as bare of carnal friends as the tree is of leaves when the frost has come." The plaint is said for the survivor whom the deceased has left helpless and bereft.

As we see, the scenes of mourning, the gestures, and the laments have a certain sameness about them. They are repeated in the manner of customary obligations; yet they are not presented as rites, but as the expression of personal feelings. The emphasis is on the spontaneity of the behavior, which distinguishes it from the use of paid mourners in antiquity (a practice that continued into the Middle Ages and beyond in Mediterranean cultures). Here the friends, lords, and vassals of the deceased act as mourners.

Although mourning and the last farewell did not belong to the religious part of funerals, the Church accepted them. This was not always the case. The church fathers were opposed to the traditional lamentations. Saint John Chrysostom disapproved of Christians who "hired women, pagans, as mourners to make the mourning more intense, to fan the fires of grief, ignoring the words of Saint Paul."[3] He even went so far as to threaten those who recruited professional mourners with excommunication.

The practice was condemned less for its mercenary character than for the excesses to which it gave rise. Since it was a way of making others responsible for the expression of a grief that one did not really feel oneself, it was necessary at all costs to maintain a high level of intensity. It was a matter of principle that mourning exceed the bounds of propriety. The canons of the patriarchate of Alexandria also criticized this attitude: "Those who are in mourning must remain in the church, monastery, or house, silent, calm, and dignified, as befits those who believe in the truth of the resurrection." These practices were also condemned in the Sicily of Frederick II under the name of *reputationes,*[4] a term that Du Cange tersely defines as *"cantus et soni qui propter defunctos celebrantur"* (songs that are sung for the dead).[5] Fourteenth-century Spain seems to have accepted them, judging by a tomb on which groups of mourners are depicted in trance.

In the beginning and for a long time thereafter, the Church condemned the rites of *planctus* because they expressed the desire of the survivors to placate the dead. In chivalric poetry it is clear that the meaning has changed. The purpose of mourning—which was also assumed in pagan antiquity—was to release the grief of the survivors. How is one to go on living in the absence of someone so beloved, so precious? But the very act of asking the question marks the beginning of acceptance.

After the first absolution at the moment of death and the great demonstrations of grief, the body was taken away and brought to the place of burial. In the case of a great lord or venerable clergyman, it was first wrapped in a piece of precious fabric. Thus, King Arthur "had Lord Gawain wrapped in a silk shroud brocaded with gold and precious stones." Once wrapped in the shroud, the body was placed on a litter or bier hastily prepared for the occasion and transported to the place of burial. "Fifteen days before May, Lancelot felt his end coming. He asked his friends the bishop and the hermit [with whom he had been living in solitude for four years, praying, fasting, and watching] to carry his body to the Joyous Gard. . . . Then he died. The two good men made a bier, laid the body on it, and carried it very slowly to the castle." It was a simple procession consisting of two men carrying a bier.

Sometimes the body was escorted with greater ceremony: King Arthur had Lord Gawain placed "in a coffin very quickly. Then he ordered ten of his knights to take the body to Saint Stephen's, in Camelot, and to place it in the tomb of Gaheris. The good knight was escorted by the king and a multitude of lords and common people, all weeping and lamenting. . . . They proceeded in this manner until they were three leagues from town. Then the king and his attendants returned with the people, while the ten knights continued on their way." Ten knights, without a priest or monk: The cortege is composed of laymen, companions of the deceased.

If the body had to be transported farther, it was sometimes embalmed and wrapped in a leather sack. Charlemagne "had all three bodies [Roland, Oliver, and Turpin] cut open before his eyes. He collected their hearts in a pan. . . . Then the bodies of the three barons were taken and washed well with aromatics and wine and placed in deerskins."

Similarly, the giant Morholt, killed by Tristan in fair combat, was embalmed and "lay dead, sewn in a deerskin." This macabre package was sent to his daughter, the fair Isolde, who opened it and removed from the head the piece of the murderous sword that was still lodged in it.

At Roncevaux, Charlemagne summoned three knights and turned over to them the three bodies wrapped in skins and told them, "Put them in three carts." In this way they were carried, still without priests or monks, to Gironde and to Blaye, where Charlemagne had them placed in "white coffins."

Similarly, when Aude la Belle, mortally wounded by the disappearance of her fiancé, Roland, "reaches her end, Charlemagne, seeing that she is dead, immediately sends for four countesses. She is taken to a convent of nuns. All night long they sit with the body. At dawn, they bury her in a fine tomb beside an altar."

So in these remote times, the religious ceremony, properly speaking, was limited to absolution, once over the living body, once over the dead body at the place of death, and once again at the grave. No Masses were said, or if they were, they went unnoticed.

Other demonstrations, such as mourning and the funeral procession, were strictly secular, with no participation by ecclesiastics, unless the deceased was a clergyman. They were reserved for the family and friends of the deceased, who took this opportunity to regret his passing, praise him, and honor him.

The Prayer for the Dead

If the role of the Church in funeral rites was limited, what was the role of the dead in the Christian liturgy before the Carolingian unification? The question brings us to a very important and very difficult aspect of our history: the prayer for the dead.

The difficulty stems from the independence of the liturgy with respect to eschatological thought. Also, the liturgical texts themselves must not be taken literally, for the deterioration and vulgarization of meaning in these writings that is tacitly recognized by contemporary Christian writers is evident only by comparison with other sources, such as literature and iconography. It should also be noted that historians of the liturgy and the church fathers are inclined to be influenced by the later development of ideas that exist here only in their germinal state, and are inclined to assign them too much importance. Pardonable errors of perspective are apt to mislead the historian, who utilizes religious formulations not for their own sake but as clues to attitudes.

In the pagan tradition, offerings were brought to the dead in order to calm them and prevent them from returning among the living. The interventions of the living were not primarily intended to improve their stay in the shadowy realm of the underworld.

Jewish tradition was unaware of these practices. The earliest Jewish text, an account of the burial services for the Maccabees, which, as we have seen, the Church had regarded as the origin of the prayers for the dead, dates only from the first century B.C. Modern scholarship distinguishes two parts to this service. The first part is an old ceremony apparently designed to expiate the sin of idolatry committed by the dead; pagan amulets had been found on their bodies. The second part, believed to be a later addition, introduces the idea of resurrection: Only those who are delivered from their sins will rise again. This is why the survivors pray to the Lord.

But concern for the survival of the deceased and belief in the need to facilitate this survival by means of religious rites already existed in such religions of salvation as the Dionysian mysteries, Pythagoreanism, and the Hellenistic cults of Mithra and Isis.

We know that in the beginning the primitive Church forbade funerary practices tinged with paganism, such as the excessive lamentations of mourners, or offerings on the tombs, the *refrigerium,* a practice that was observed by Saint Monica before she learned of Saint Ambrose's prohibition. For the funerary meal, the Church substituted the Eucharist celebrated on altars located in the cemetery. In the Christian cemetery of Tebessa, we can still see examples of these altars, surrounded by tombs that we already know were *ad sanctos.*

Was this an early example of intercession for the dead? These Masses were regarded by conservative bishops more as expressions of gratitude to God on the occasion of the deaths of the just, the holy martyrs, or of Christians who had died in the Communion of the Church and were buried beside the martyrs. In the religion of the common people, which was a continuation of the ancient pagan tradition, the cemeterial Masses were associated both with the worship of martyrs and with the memory of less venerable dead. As a consequence, there was a long-standing confusion between the prayer in honor of the saints and the prayer of intercession for the salvation of the more ordinary dead, a confusion that we know about thanks to Saint Augustine's efforts to eliminate it.

Thus, there is no scriptural foundation, either in the Old Testament or in the New Testament (except in the disputed text of the Maccabees) for the intercession of the living for the dead. This Christian practice derives from pagan tradition, as J. Ntedika suggests. Its first form is a commemoration rather than an intercession. Indeed, why should there be any intercession, since the survivors had no reason to doubt the salvation of their dead?[6]

As we have already seen in chapter 1, these dead were saved. They did not, however, go straight to paradise; it was agreed that only the holy martyrs and confessors had the privilege of enjoying the beatific vision immediately after their death. Tertullian informs us that the bosom of Abraham was neither heaven nor hell *(sublimorem tamen inferis),* but the *refrigerium* of the Roman Canon: *interim refrigerium.* There the souls of the just awaited the resurrection at the end of the world, *consummatio rerum.*

I am quite aware that by the end of the fifth century, scholarly writers no longer accepted this notion, and believed that the soul was immediately welcomed into paradise (or thrown into hell). I would like to suggest, however, that the primitive idea of a place of waiting might be at the origin of the concept of purgatory, a time of waiting in a fire that was a means no longer of torment but of purification. There may have been a confusion in popular belief between the old idea of the *refrigerium,* the *requies,* the bosom of Abraham, and the new idea of purgatory.

For despite the disapproval of scholarly writers, the mass of the faithful remained attached to the traditional idea of waiting that continued to form the bedrock of the liturgy for funeral services until the reforms of Paul VI. The soul (or existence) of the deceased was not yet threatened by the devil, at least not in the liturgy. On the day of his death and on its anniversary, tradition required a religious ceremony, a Mass in which sinful man recognized his helplessness, but affirmed his faith, gave thanks to God, and celebrated the entrance of the deceased into the repose or sleep of blissful expectation.

The Ancient Liturgy:
The Reading of the Names

This conception, which may be called popular, of the continuity between paganism and Christianity, between this world and the next, without drama or interruption, is found not only in the prayers for the dead but also in the Sunday liturgy. Before Charlemagne, that is to say, before the introduction of the Roman liturgy, the Gallican Mass included, after the readings, a long ceremony which has since disappeared or of which there remain only indecipherable vestiges. Until the reforms of Paul VI, this ceremony occurred at the moment occupied by the secret prayers that the priest recited during the Offertory.

After the reading of the Gospel, which was not at that time followed by the *Credo,* there began a series of rites: the recitation of prayers that the new ordo of Paul VI has restored to the litany under the name of Prayers of the Faithful; then, after the dismissal of the catechumens (or rather, at this period, the penitents), there was the singing of psalms, *sonus,* and the triple Alleluia, which accompanied the procession of the offerings. The *offerentes* solemnly carried to one of the altars not only the oblation, the bread and wine for the Eucharist, but all kinds of cash gifts, which remained the property of the Church. This ceremony, to which the people must have been very much attached, may not have had the same appeal in Rome. It concluded with a Preface and a Collect.

Next came another ceremony more directly related to our discussion: the reading of the names, also referred to as the diptychs.[7] The diptychs were originally ivory tablets, carved and engraved, that were presented by the consuls as official notification on the day they took office. On identical tablets, or on old consular diptychs, Christians inscribed the list of names that was read after the procession of the offerings "from the top of the ambo." This list contained "the names of the benefactors, the most important magistrates, the highest-ranking clergymen of the same persuasion, the holy martyrs or confessors, and finally, the faithful who had died in the faith of the Church, in order to emphasize the close bond of communion and love that unites all the members of the Church Triumphant, the Church Suffering, and the Church Militant."

A more recent treatise, incorrectly attributed to Alcuin, has this to say about the diptychs: "The ancient custom was, as it still is today in the Roman church, an immediate recitation of the names of the dead [among others], which had been inscribed on the diptychs, that is, on tablets." The diptychs were placed on the altar, or else the lists were inscribed on the altar itself or copied in the margins of the sacramentaries.

The names were read aloud. We can form an idea of this long recitation from an excerpt from a Mozarabic liturgy.[8] The bishop is surrounded by priests, deacons, and other clergymen, and the people who have made the offerings are crowding around the altar or the chancel.

After the prayers for the Church, a priest *(presbyter)* says: "This sacrifice *(oblationem)* is offered to Our Lord God by our bishop *(sacerdos)*, the *Papa Romensis*, and others [the whole hierarchy], for themselves and for all the clergy and for the people *(plebibus)* who have been entrusted to this Church, and for the universal brotherhood." This idea of *universa fraternitas* was an important one. "This sacrifice is also offered by all the priests, deacons, clergymen, and by the people here gathered *(circumstantes)* in honor of the saints"—the tradition of the worship of the martyrs and confessors, a reference to the Church Triumphant— "for themselves and for their families." There follows a list of those laymen who had brought offerings. These are the benefactors of the Church, and each one must have been eager to have his name inscribed on this perpetual list, which was comparable to the Book of Life, in which God and his angel inscribed the names of the elect. After the priest has finished, the choir repeats, "They offer this sacrifice for themselves and for the universal brotherhood."

This first list is the *universa fraternitas* of the living, from the pope of Rome, bishops, kings, and lords, down to the benefactors and the anonymous people.

The second list, the list of the saints, being more venerable, is read not by the priest but by the bishop himself. The bishop says, "In memory of the blessed apostles and martyrs . . ." In some cases the list reached back through the Old Testament all the way to Adam. There follows the enumeration of the saints, as in the *Communicantes* of the Roman Canon, and the choir repeats, "And of all the martyrs . . ."

The third list, which is also read by the bishop, is the list of the dead. The dead are not mentioned after the living of the first list, but rather after the saints of the second list, in whose company they are. The bishop says, "And also for the souls of those who sleep (*spiritibus pausantium*), Hilary, Athanasius . . ." And the choir concludes, "And for all those who sleep."

These three lists—the living, the saints, and the dead—are read in succession, without interruption, except for three short responses by the choir. After this recitation, which, like the prayers for the Church that preceded it, has the repetitive quality of a litany, the bishop chants a solemn Collect, the *Oratio post nomina,* asking God to inscribe the names of the living and the dead among the elect: "From this time forward, inscribe us in your eternal company, that we be not confounded on the day you come to judge the world. Amen."

The names of the elect are inscribed on a waiting list, and thus they are assured of not being confounded on the Day of Judgment. It is still necessary to wait until that day.

The priest concludes, "Because you are the life of the living, the health of the sick [this for the living], and the repose of all the faithful who have gone before us [this for the dead], for ever and ever."

In the *Orationes post nomina,* the Gallican and Mozarabic liturgies constantly emphasize the solidarity of the living and the dead, the *universa fraternitas.* [9] In the same breath they request health of body and soul for the living and repose for the dead: "Granting by the mystery of this day health of soul and body for the living, and the joy of eternal renewal (*reparatio*) for the dead. . . . That by the prayers of this martyr forgiveness for sins be granted to the living and to the dead."

"That salvation be granted to the living and repose to the dead." Salvation, or the promise of eternal life, is requested for the living; repose for the dead while they await the end of time. In some of these versions, *salus* or *vita* is requested for the *offerentes,* and *requies* for the dead, clearly indicating belief in a zone of waiting. Other versions, however, make no distinction between *requies* and paradise: "Lead to the repose of the elect the souls of those who sleep, whose names have been commemorated."

Occasionally—although still rarely, at this period—the beyond appears in a less reassuring light: "That we may never be delivered to eternal torment. . . . That they may not endure the burning of the flames." Note that in their fear of hell, these *offerentes* think first of themselves and their own salvation.

Generally speaking, the dead are not regarded as separate from the living. They belong to the same unbroken family, and appeals to divine mercy are extended to the whole series of those whose names have been read. This list of names is the directory of the universal church, the earthly counterpart of the original, which is kept by God in paradise, the *liber vitae, pagina coeli,* or *litterae coelestiae:* "Inscribing also the names of the contributors in the book of life"; "Inscribe these names on the page of heaven"; "That they may be deemed worthy of the celestial archives."[10]

Here we recognize the scroll that is held before the elect on the sarcophagus of Jouarre. (Was this a memory of the *volumen* that the dead held in their hands on Roman sarcophagi?) Indeed, it is the iconography of Jouarre that is evoked by the Gallican or Mozarabic liturgy. It is not yet a question of the living praying in order to save the souls of certain of the dead. The procession of the people of God, the *universa fraternitas,* files by at the reading of the names in the Sunday liturgy, just as it files between heaven and earth on the Day of Judgment in the oldest images.

These pre-Carolingian liturgies bring us back to the model of the tame death: the affirmation of a collective destiny, symbolized by a long series of names, as in biblical genealogies, and the indifference to the idea of personal destiny.

The Fear of Damnation:
Purgatory and Waiting

Important changes were to occur in the liturgical versions of the tame death, changes that express, in the language of the Church, a new conception of destiny.

Even in early Visigothic texts, we sometimes find intimations of a belief in the risks of the future life that if not altogether new, was at least about to become more widespread and established. One senses that the age-old confidence has been undermined. The people of God are less assured of divine mercy, and there is a growing fear of being abandoned forever to the power of Satan.

Of course, the old sense of confidence did not rule out fear of the devil. The life of the saint was a struggle against the devil, but it was a victorious struggle. Henceforth, perhaps under the influence of Augustinian thought, even the saint—Saint Monica, for example—is in increasing danger of damnation; consequently, the living feel a growing fear for their own salvation. By the beginning of the seventh century, the time of Gregory the Great, the devil contends for the soul of the monk Theodore on his deathbed and drags the body of another monk out of the church where he had been buried in spite of his final impenitence.

The Day of Judgment, too, seems more formidable in certain Visigothic texts:[11] "Save the souls of those who rest from eternal torment. . . . May they be delivered from the chains of Tartarus. . . . May they be delivered from all the pains and torments of hell. . . . May she be saved from the prisons of hell. . . . May they escape the punishment of judgment. . . . May they escape the heat of the fire." Now we are beginning to encounter those terrible images that will pervade the liturgy of funerals until our own time. The Roman Mass for the Dead still belongs to the more ancient stratum of confidence and thanksgiving, along with the Requiem: *Requiem aeternam dona eis Domine.* Also from the same source come antiphons such as the *In Paradisum* and the *Subvenite.* On the other hand, the prayer of absolution, the *Libera,* which is, as we have seen, the only old religious ceremony performed in the presence of the body and over the body, belongs to this later stratum, already recognizable in Visigothic texts.

"Do not enter into judgment against your servant. . . . May he be worthy by your grace to escape the punishment of justice. . . . Deliver me, Lord, from eternal death. . . . I tremble and I am afraid before the final reckoning, when your anger will be made manifest. That day will be a day of wrath." This is the spirit of the first part of the *Dies Irae,* a poem by Jacopone da Todi that evokes the Day of Judgment, with none of the hope and confidence that the thirteenth-century Franciscan introduced in the second part: "Remember, sweet Jesus, that I am the reason for your coming." The Roman absolution seems to have retained the darkest and most desperate passages from the Visigothic prayers.

And when the absolution deviated from the original model, to which it was still faithful in the *Chanson de Roland,* it became an exorcism. If we go by the texts, this evolution seems to have started well in advance of the *Chanson de Roland,* but the liturgy inspired by the clergy was ahead of the customs of the laity, just as it was behind the thinking of theologians. There was a growing belief in the probability of damnation. The idea originated with clergymen and monks, and it resulted in a situation so intolerable as to demand remedy.

The more firmly people believed in the possibility of their own damnation, the more they thought about divine mercy, hoping to sway it even after death. It was the idea—if not altogether new, then at least hitherto neglected—of the intercession of the living for the dead. But in order to imagine that one might succeed in modifying the condition of the dead by prayer, it was necessary to find an alternative to the idea of uncertain salvation and probable damnation. This was no small matter, and probably required profound changes in attitudes. For a long time the Church hesitated between the impossibility of changing the judgment of God and the desire to alleviate the fate of the damned. Certain writers conceived of a *mitigatio* (softening) of the torments of hell. For example, these might be suspended on Sunday, without their eternity being called into question. Theologians abandoned these speculations, but they persisted in popular beliefs.

The idea of the intercession of the living could be accepted only if the dead were not immediately turned over to the torments of hell. It was agreed—and Gregory the Great seems to have played an important role in the development of this idea—that those who were *non valde mali* (not absolutely bad) and *non valde boni* (not absolutely good) were turned over after their death to a fire that was not the fire of eternal torment, but the fire of *purgatio*. This is the word for and idea of purgatory, but we must be careful not to assign it the same meaning in the time of Gregory the Great and Isidore of Seville that it had in the theology of the thirteenth and fourteenth centuries and in Dante. As late as the beginning of the seventeenth century, preambles to wills mention only the celestial court and hell; it was not until the middle of the seventeenth century that the word *purgatory* became common. Despite several centuries of theology, until the post-Tridentine reforms, people remained attached to the old alternatives of heaven and hell. And yet, for a very long time, as we shall see presently, Christians admitted the existence of an intermediary, probationary space, neither hell nor paradise, and believed that their prayers and good works, or the indulgences they earned, might intervene in favor of those who languished there. This space must have belonged as much to the old pagan beliefs as to the visions of the medieval monastic sensibility. It was at once a place where unsatisfied shades wandered (limbo), and a place where the sinner, by means of his expiation, could escape eternal death. The dead were not all concentrated in the guarded and organized enclosure of Dante or committed to the purifying and localized flames of eighteenth- and nineteenth-century altarpieces. They often remained at the scene of their sins or of their deaths, and appeared to the living, at least in dreams, to request Masses and prayers.

It is nonetheless true that the idea of an intermediate space between hell and paradise influenced the practice of Christianity in the West, although it was not until the seventeenth century that it succeeded in overthrowing the old image of the beyond.

This change must have been facilitated by the primitive belief in a happy period of waiting before entrance into paradise on the Day of Judgment. The idea of the *refrigerium, requies, dormitio sinus Abraham,* was probably soon abandoned by scholars, but persisted for quite some time among ordinary people. This space became the site of the future purgatory of theologians, the time of intercession and of pardon. The evolution was accelerated when the idea of possible redemption was reinforced by the similar but separate idea of payment.

If the destiny of the dead escaped the alternatives of all or nothing, paradise or hell, it was because each human life was no longer seen as a link in the common destiny but rather as a sum of graduated elements—good, less good, less bad, bad— capable of being evaluated on a fixed scale, and redeemable because capable of being assigned a price. It was no accident that intercession in favor of the dead appeared at the same time as the penitentials, manuals in which each sin was evaluated and its penalty determined accordingly. In the ninth century, indulgences, Masses, and prayers of intercession were to the dead what fixed penances were to the living, and both phenomena reflected the transition from the idea of a collective destiny to the idea of a personal one.

The Roman Mass: A Mass for the Dead

This growing desire to intercede for the dead is probably the principal reason for the major changes that took place in the ninth century in the structure of the Mass. Generally speaking, one may say that until Charlemagne, the Gallican, Visigothic Mass was the offering of all humanity since the creation and the incarnation of Christ, and that any distinction made between the living and the dead, between canonized saints and other deceased persons, was purely formal and theoretical. After Charlemagne, all Masses became either Masses for the Dead, said on behalf of certain of the dead, or votive Masses on behalf of certain of the living. In both cases, certain individuals were chosen to the exclusion of others. It is this situation that we must now examine.

The important event is the substitution of the Roman liturgy for the Gallican liturgy, a substitution that was imposed by Charlemagne and more or less accepted by the clergy despite occasional local resistance. The Roman liturgy, which survived until the ordo of Paul VI, was quite different from the one it replaced. It retained a vocabulary that showed the persistence of the very ancient notions of *refrigerium* and *requies.* It had not been invaded by the somber and anxious ideas of the Mozarabic versions (except in the *Libera,* but when?). The solemn procession of the offerings was not widespread, and the reading of names was not done in the same way. What took its place had been extracted from the rites for the offerings of the oblates and shifted to the middle of the Canon, breaking up a sequence that had a strong unity, from the Preface *(Immolatio)* to the Lord's Prayer.

What we now call the Roman Canon consists of the consecratory prayers, which commemorate, comment on, and re-create the Last Supper, together with some prayers that in the Mozarabic and Gallican liturgy (and perhaps also in the older Roman liturgy) were pronounced at the end of the procession of the offerings. The *Oratio super oblata,* the secret prayer of the Roman Mass, may be the vestige of a similar rite that has disappeared. When the prayers that accompanied the reading of the names became part of the Canon, they changed in character. They were not only moved, but dismembered, and each of the separate pieces treated in a way that makes it difficult for the uninformed reader or listener to tell that in other liturgies they once formed a whole. The list of saints, the list of benefactors, and the list of the dead, which were read in sequence in Gaul and Spain, have been separated. The list of saints has itself been divided into two parts, one located before the Consecration, the other after it, which shows the growing importance of the intercession of the saints. The list of benefactors was also divided in two, to distinguish more clearly between clergymen and laymen.

But the most important change is the fate reserved for the names of the dead. These have been separated from the names of the living, and no longer appear as part of the same genealogy. Death has put the souls of the deceased in a special situation, which has earned them this place apart. If the Roman liturgy remains faithful to the old notion of *requies,* the isolation of the Memento of the Dead expresses a new and different attitude that one does not find, or finds only traces of, in the Gallican and Mozarabic liturgies. The spontaneous solidarity of the living and the dead has been replaced by a solicitude on behalf of souls in danger. The earlier language has been retained, but it is utilized in another spirit and for another purpose. The commemoration of the dead has become a prayer of intercession.

It has also become a personal prayer. In the diptychs the long lists of names represented the entire community. In the Mementos, which replaced them—and this is true for the living as well as for the dead—the names are not the names of all church members whose memory is preserved, but only those of one or two dead, chosen for the occasion, specially recommended to the celebrant and accepted by him.

A Memento from the tenth century places this very personal prayer in the mouth of the priest: "Of X . . . and of all Christians who, because they fear God, have confessed their sins to me, and have given me their alms, of all my relatives, and of all those for whom I pray."[12] In the texts, the space reserved for the names is indicated by the words *illi* (m.) and *illae* (f.), which indicate the limited scope of the list and specify the personal nature of the choice better than the old *nomina*, which listed an indefinite number of names.

Finally, this personal prayer became a private prayer. The names of the persons who were the beneficiaries of the priest's prayer were no longer proclaimed in a kind of litany. In some cases they were not even pronounced quietly, like the rest of the Canon. When he came to the names in question, the priest would pause for a moment while he thought about the dead persons who had been recommended to him. In extreme cases the prayer was not only private but internal.

The Prayers from the Pulpit

We have come a long way from the endless lists, read out loud, of the Gallican liturgy. And yet this practice did not altogether disappear with the adoption of the Roman liturgy. The ceremonies that had been discontinued persisted on the margins of the Mass proper or on certain occasions, such as the offering for the Masses for the Dead, still observed in the southwest of France, or the distribution of the blessed bread (the procession of the offerings). The *nomina* were still read, no longer from the altar, but from the pulpit, and were known as the Prayers from the Pulpit. After the sermon, the announcements, and the notices concerning the life of the community, the priest would read in French or some other vernacular language, but not in Latin, the names of the benefactors of the Church, living and dead. I can still hear the voice of the priest reciting from the pulpit during the High Masses of yesterday: "Let us pray, my brothers," for such and such a family, etc. The congregation would say an Our Father. Then the priest would go on, "And now that we have prayed for the living, we shall also pray for the dead: So-and-so, so-and-so." The congregation would say a *De Profundis.* The lists were long, and the priest recited them at top speed, swallowing half the words. Under the *ancien régime,* donors had the priest say their names after the sermon on certain special days or feast days.

These recitations, which were sometimes interminable, give us an idea of what the reading of the diptychs—probably done in a monotone—must have been like, and how this differed from the personal quality of the Memento. To have a Mass said for someone was one thing, to have his name read from the pulpit after the sermon was another; the latter was a higher honor, and a more social one.

The new meaning given the Memento of the Dead in the Roman

liturgy turned all Masses into Masses for the Dead, which was not the case in the time of the diptychs. This is why, to begin with, the Memento was not general in Rome, and was omitted from Sunday and holiday Masses. It was not included in the sacramentary that Pope Adrian sent Charlemagne as a model of the Roman Mass. An eleventh-century Florentine sacramentary bore this rubric next to the Memento: "Not to be said on Sunday or on high holidays."

On these occasions the dead were simply removed from the genealogy of the faithful, as it was proclaimed in the diptychs, and later in the Prayers from the Pulpit, a genealogy that was no longer recognizable in the Memento of the Canon. They were removed, not out of indifference, but, on the contrary, because the special prayers for their benefit had taken on a new and greater significance. The numerous Masses said during the week in the early Middle Ages—they did not exist in the early Church—had become Masses for the Dead. The presence of the Memento was therefore capable of altering the festive quality of the Sunday ceremony. The Alleluia was dropped from the Mass for the Dead in ninth-century France. Were the dead beginning to sadden and alarm the living? We do not know, but we do know that from now on they are in a class by themselves and are no longer merged with the people of God as a whole. People became so conscious of the needs of their endangered souls that in the end the dead were readmitted into the Sunday Mass, where intercessory prayers are so important. In the tenth century, the practice of celebrating Mass for the Dead became so widespread that it was almost impossible to conceive of a religious ceremony from which it was excluded.

A Monastic Sensibility: The Treasury of the Church

It may well be that the laymen of the early Middle Ages, insofar as they were concerned at all, remained more attached to the concept of the diptychs than to the quiet or silent prayer of the priest during the Memento. This explains why the Prayers from the Pulpit continued in the margins of the Latin priestly Mass after the Gallican liturgy was abandoned. Indeed, these prayers did not lose their popularity until the twentieth century.

On the other hand, the impulse that isolated the Memento of the Dead and turned it into a prayer of intercession proceeds from the sensibility of an age when priests and monks had turned away from the world of laymen and organized themselves into a separate society.

The transformation of public prayers of offering into private prayers of intercession must be seen in connection with the importance of the private Mass in monastic life and worship.

We know that in the early Church there was only one Mass, the Mass of the bishop and the community. In the rural parishes that were founded later, the priest and his assistants celebrated the *Missa Solemnis* of the bishop without his presence. Except for a few nuances, matters of protocol, nothing had changed. This state of things has remained to the present time in Eastern churches. But in the Western rite, owing to circumstances whose highly obscure history is beyond our scope, it became customary for priests to say a spoken Mass during the week and with no one present, except perhaps one assistant. This Mass was, on the one hand, simplified and, on the other hand, overloaded with personal prayers, which were sometimes improvised for the occasion. According to Jungmann, these Masses were regarded as different from the *Missa Solemnis,* and were referred to as *Missae privatae, speciales,* or *peculiares.* [13]

Not only was Mass said every day, but each priest was tempted to celebrate several Masses a day in order to accumulate supererogatory merits and to increase his power of intercession. Pope Leo III (795–816) went so far as to celebrate nine Masses in a single day. Alcuin confined himself to three, perhaps in honor of the Trinity. In the twelfth century, Honorius of Autun still maintains that the celebration of one Mass a day is the rule, but that it is permissible to say three or four.[14] This proliferation of Masses made it possible to increase the treasury of the Church and to extend its benefice to a greater number of souls. The period from the ninth to the eleventh century was a period of the exploitation of indulgences, as was the period from the fourteenth to the sixteenth century. Between the two, there was a time of ecclesiastical reform. After the thirteenth century, the councils limited the number of Masses that could be celebrated to one a day, except at Christmas.

These Masses were Masses for the Dead. It is no accident that the name of Gregory the Great is associated on the one hand with the Roman Canon, to which he gave its definitive form (and in which he may be responsible for the present position of the Memento of the Dead), and on the other hand with the devotions especially intended to intercede for the dead. (A Gregorian is a series of thirty Masses for the Dead, celebrated one daily for thirty days, or formerly, sometimes, all in one day.) Pope Gregory's accounts of monks who were possessed or damned showed how powerful and how greatly feared the devil was in a regular community such as the one of which he was abbot, and what great need each monk had of prayers, both "antehumous" and posthumous, in order to escape him after death.

Since after this period monks usually became priests, Masses with Mementos of the Dead, that is, Masses for the Dead, were said continuously in a great many chapels or monastery churches after the ninth century. At Cluny, these Masses went on day and night. Raoul Glaber tells how a monk from Cluny, on his return from a pilgrimage to the Holy Land, at the beginning of the ninth century, was miraculously recognized by a Sicilian hermit. The hermit told him that he had learned by divine revelation how pleasing to God were the Masses for the Dead that were continually being celebrated at Cluny and how profitable to the souls that were redeemed in this way.[15] Cluny is also the source of a special feast day devoted to the redemption of the dead. It seems that various localities set aside one day a year for all the dead, that is, for those who, unlike clergymen and monks, were not assured of the help of their brothers—the forgotten people, the majority of laymen. These days for the dead fell on different dates according to the locality: January 26, December 17 (Saint Ignatius), the Monday of Pentecost, and especially the Feast of the Maccabees. As late as the seventeenth century, in the cathedral in Rouen, a chapel whose altar was decorated with an altarpiece by Rubens was dedicated to the Holy Maccabees. The date of November 2, chosen by Odilon of Cluny in 1048, was the preferred one and was eventually adopted by the entire Roman church, but not before the thirteenth century, an indication of the monastic origin of the sentiment and of the long indifference of the common people to this individualistic attitude toward the dead.

Because so many more Masses were being celebrated, it was necessary to increase the number of altars.[16] This tendency is to be observed everywhere after the eighth century. In the interior of Saint Peter's, in Rome, in the eighth and early ninth centuries, "more oratories appeared, a small chapel with an apse hollowed out of the thickness of a wall or pillar of the basilica, an altar protected by a chancel and a pergola." The oratory bore the name of the saint who was worshiped there. The pope who had built it "in order to earn a suitable place in heaven" was buried at the foot of the altar.[17]

Benoît d'Aniane endowed the church of Saint-Sauveur, which he built in 782, with four altars. The Abbey of Centula, finished in 798, had eleven. The plans for the reconstruction of the Abbey of Saint-Gall, drawn up in 820, had seventeen. These altars, which contained venerated relics, were placed against walls and very often against pillars, without altering the plan of the building. We can still picture this arrangement, which after the fourteenth century evolved into the lateral chapel, in the churches of the German Rhineland, where it was preserved until the seventeenth century: At Trèves, there are altars with altarpieces simply standing against pillars.

In Cluny, in Saint-Gall, in all the monasteries, these altars were occupied simultaneously or successively by celebrants softly singing their Masses. They had trouble reading *in secretum,* that is, in a low voice, as the customs of Cluny prescribed. The second Mass would begin before the first had ended, and so on, *ad infinitum.*

It was in these monastic and regular communities, then, during the eighth and ninth centuries, that there developed a sense, as yet unknown to most laymen, of uncertainty and anxiety in the face of death, or rather, of the beyond. It was in order to escape eternal damnation that one entered a monastery, and also—for this was not the original function of monks or hermits—that one celebrated Mass there; as many Masses as possible, for each one reinforced the next and contributed to the salvation of souls. In this way a network formed among the abbeys and churches for the mutual assistance of souls. Saint Boniface wrote to Abbé Optat, "so that a bond of brotherly charity may be established between us, so that a common prayer may be said for the living, and so that prayers and solemn Masses may be celebrated for the dead of this century, when we send one another the names of our dead."[18] Among the religious communities there were organizations that exchanged the names of the dead in order to form a common fund of prayers and Masses that everyone could draw upon as needed, to his own spiritual advantage. Gabriel Le Bras gives an excellent description of the situation. In the eighth century, "the theology of supernatural exchanges erased all administrative [and biological] boundaries. Romans and Celts described the kingdoms of the beyond and calculated the weight of sins [remember that this was also the time when the Penitentials were being written], and cooperated in the work of redemption by means of mutual prayers and private Masses. The dogma of the communion of the saints was embodied in the personalization of the holy sacrifice and of vicarious penance, in all this exploitation of supererogatory merits that was to culminate in indulgences and the theory of the treasury of the Church. . . . All of western Europe was covered with these monastic colonies of suppliants."[19] And Jungmann writes, "The bishops and abbots present at the Council of Attigny (762) agreed, among other commitments, to say one hundred Masses for each of the participants who happened to die. A confraternity established in 800 by Saint Gall and Reichenau stipulated, among other things, that each priest would say three Masses for a dead monk on the day that followed the announcement of his death and a fourth on the thirtieth day; that at the beginning of each month, after the conventual Mass for the Dead, each priest would say another Mass; and finally, that every year on November 14 [one of those local feasts for the dead mentioned above] there would be a commemoration for all the dead, with another three Masses to be said by the priests."[20]

For a long time to come, during the Middle Ages, certain abbeys that had joined together for the purpose circulated among themselves a document called the Scroll of the Dead, on which each community entered the names of its own dead, followed by a biographical notice, commending them in this way to the prayers of the other communities. Consequently, it was necessary to keep a record of the prayers promised not only to the confraternities but also to the lay benefactors, who soon aspired to the same benefits. Every day one had to know for whom Mass must be said; this was the function of the registers known as obituaries.

Between the eighth and tenth centuries, then, there developed an original cult of the dead which was limited to abbeys, cathedrals, collegiate churches, and the networks of affiliation they had formed: a society within society, with a sensibility all its own.

The New Rites:
The Role of the Clergy

By the eleventh century, at the end of the early Middle Ages, two distinct attitudes toward life after death have appeared. The traditional attitude, common to the great mass of laymen, remained faithful to the image of an unbroken family of living and dead, united on earth and in eternity. This image was evoked every Sunday by the Prayers from the Pulpit. The other attitude was peculiar to a closed society of monks and priests, and attested to a new, more individualistic psychology.

After the thirteenth century, it is as if the mentality that until then had been developed in the hothouse environment of the cloisters spread to the world at large. For a long time to come, death would be "clericalized." This was a great change, the greatest until the secularization of death in the twentieth century.

In the early Middle Ages, as we have seen, the rites of death were dominated by the mourning of survivors and the honors they rendered to the deceased: the eulogy and the funeral procession. These rites were secular, and the Church intervened only to perform absolution. Absolution both before and after death seem originally to have been almost indistinguishable. But beginning about the thirteenth century, certain changes occurred.

First, vigil and mourning. Some eighteenth-century observers were struck by certain practices that had always existed but that the funerary rituals of the monks had endowed with an aura of custom and solemnity. Such a practice was the *lavatio corporis,* described by the traveler Moléon: "In the middle of a very long and spacious chapel [at Cluny] through which one passes on the way from the cloister into the chapter house, is the lavatory, a room six or seven feet long with the floor hollowed out to a depth of seven or eight inches. There is a stone pillow carved out of the same piece as the trough and a hole at the other end through which the water ran out after the body had been washed. . . . In the cathedral churches of Lyons and Rouen one can still see the trough or lavatory stone where the canons were washed after they died."[21]

Moléon notes that the rite also existed among laymen, though not always with the same customary character: "The dead are still washed today, not only in the old monastic orders . . . but also by laymen generally in the Basque region, in the diocese of Bayonne, among others, and in Avranches, in lower Normandy. This old custom may be the origin of the superstitious ceremony in certain rural parishes of throwing out all the water in a house in which someone has just died. At one time it had to be thrown out, since it had been used to wash the body of the deceased. Throughout Vivarais it is the duty of the closest relatives and married children to carry the dead bodies of their fathers or relatives, dressed only in a shirt, to the river to bathe and wash them before they are buried."[22]

It is possible that the old pagan ceremony of the washing of the body and the discarding of the dirty water was revived in imitation of the rites of the monks. The monastic influence is unquestionable in the custom of exhibiting the dead on ashes or straw. "In the middle of this large infirmary [at Cluny]," Moléon goes on to say, "there is also a small groove about six feet long and two and a half or three inches wide. Here, on a bed of ashes, they placed monks who were about to die. This is still done today [around 1718], but not until after they are dead. . . . This seems to have been just as common among laymen, who had several ancient rituals. It is only the horror inspired by penitence and humiliation [already!] that caused this holy practice to disappear."[23]

We know that laymen were also sometimes laid out, if not on ashes then on straw. Some texts from 1742 speak of dead men coming back to life *in extremis*, one of them after he had been "on the straw for several hours. . . . Twelve or thirteen years ago, a woman of common extraction . . . was thought to be dead and laid on the straw with a candle at her feet, as is the custom."[24]

We have seen that in the *Chanson de Roland* and in the stories of the Round Table the tame death was associated with a wild mourning. In the later Middle Ages, it no longer seemed as legitimate or customary to lose control of oneself in order to mourn for the dead. In places where the traditional demonstrations of grief persisted, such as fourteenth- and fifteenth-century Spain, their appearance of spontaneity and their tendency to excess were toned down. In one of the *romanceros,* El Cid provides in his will for a departure from the customary rules governing obsequies:[25]

> *When I die, heed my advice:*
> *Hire no mourners to weep for me.*
> *There is no need of buying tears;*
> *Those of Jimena will suffice.*

The *romancero* assumes that spontaneity is unusual, that the custom is the ritual *planctus* with professional mourners. The illusion of spontaneity is no longer necessary, as it was in the *Chanson de Roland* or the Arthurian legends. It may well have been that those great declamations were in reality also ritual, and even left to mercenaries to perform, but in works of art and the imagination, a show of spontaneity was made.

El Cid makes only one exception, in favor of Jimena, wife and lover beyond compare. What had been common in the time of Charlemagne was becoming exceptional by the end of the Middle Ages. Jimena pronounces the eulogy rather calmly, with no great transports of emotion, although she does faint at the end of her long tirade:

> *This model of nobility*
> *Could not say another word.*
> *She fell upon the body*
> *In a swoon, as if dead.*

We have another example of the new way of reacting to death that is nearly contemporaneous with the *romancero* but that originates in the humanist milieu of Florence. Tenenti tells the story.[26] Salutati, the chancellor of Florence, was reflecting on death. Under the influence of the Stoic philosophers and the patristic tradition, he saw death as the end of all ills and as an access to a better world. He reproached himself for grieving over the death of a friend, because in so doing he was forgetting the laws of nature and the principles of philosophy, which instruct us not to mourn for either persons or things, since both are subject to corruption. In these remarks, so typical of the age, we detect both a scholarly rhetoric and the popular tendency to compare living persons with things, which were also highly valued: *omnia temporalia.* But there was still a great deal of the literary in his attitude.

Then one day in May 1400, Salutati loses his own son. Now it is no longer a question of literature. When a correspondent named Ugolino Caccini gives him back his own counsel, he realizes the vanity of the arguments that he formerly advanced in his letters of consolation. Caccini reproaches him for giving way to grief, and exhorts him to surrender to the divine will. Salutati justifies himself in terms that reveal the changed style of mourning. He replies that he now has a right to admit his distress, for at the time of his son's death, he did not give in to sorrow. He gave his son his last benediction without shedding a tear, watched resignedly as he died, and accompanied him to his grave without lamentation.

I think it would be a mistake to attribute this attitude to Stoicism, however influential that doctrine may have been in shaping humanist thought. Salutati's behavior was customary for people of his social class. He merely questions the rhetoric of consolation. He says that even if the soul does not die and the body is reborn, "that harmonious combination that made Pietro his son has been destroyed forever." There is nothing left for him but to turn to God, the source of consolation: *"Converti me igitur ad fontem consolationis."* But he does not question the legitimacy of self-control at the time of death and the funeral.

The social conventions no longer tended to express the violence of grief; henceforth they inclined toward dignity and restraint. What people did not want to say in words or gestures they signified by costume and color, according to a symbolism that was dear to the late Middle Ages. Was it at this time that black became the official color of mourning? In any case, the cloth in which the body was wrapped could be as conspicuous as gold. The author of a 1410 will asks that his body be covered with a piece of cloth of gold that later will be made into a chasuble.[27] In the fourteenth century the friends of the departed donated cloth of gold and candles to the funeral service, just as today we send flowers. People dressed in red, green, and blue; they put on their finest clothes to honor the departed. In the twelfth century Baudry, abbot of Bourgueil, pointed out as a curious novelty that the Spanish dressed in black when their relatives died. According to Louis Marie Quicherat, the first mention of deep mourning was at the court of England after the death of John the Good of France. When Anne of Brittany died, Louis XII dressed in black and required the court to do the same.

In Paris in 1400, a bailiff excused himself for not wearing the striped robe that was the badge of his office, but a "simple robe [that] he had put on because his wife's father had died, and he had to attend the funeral service."[28] A simple robe, undoubtedly black.

Although the wearing of black was customary in the sixteenth century, it was not yet required for kings or for princes of the Church. The custom has two meanings: the somber associations of death, which were to develop along with macabre iconography, and above all the traditional ritualization of mourning. The wearing of black expresses mourning and dispenses with more personal or dramatic demonstrations.

The New Funeral Procession

When someone has died, there is no longer room for the long and violent lamentations of old; nobody declaims the regrets and eulogies in a loud voice, as was once the custom. The family and friends of the departed, now calm and silent, have ceased to be the principal actors in a scene that has been divested of its drama. The leading roles are henceforth reserved for priests, especially mendicant friars, or certain monklike individuals, laymen with religious duties, members of the third, or lay, orders or confraternities, in other words, the new specialists in death. From the moment of his last breath, the dead man belongs no longer to his friends or family but to the Church.

The reading of the Office of the Dead has replaced the traditional lamentations. The vigil has become an ecclesiastical ceremony that begins in the home and sometimes continues at the church, where the clergy take up the recitation of the prayers for the dead, the prayers commending the soul to God.

After the vigil comes a ceremony that is to play an important role in the symbolism of the funeral, the procession. In early medieval poetry, as we have seen, the body had been escorted to the place of burial by the friends and relatives of the deceased. This was the last manifestation of a grief that had finally been assuaged, an unobtrusive and secular act in which the honoring of the deceased prevailed over the expression of regret.

In the late Middle Ages, particularly after the founding of the mendicant orders, the character of this ceremony changed. The small group of escorts became a solemn ecclesiastical procession. Relatives and friends were certainly not excluded; we know that they were invited to one of the services, and we are sure that they participated in funeral processions for royalty, where the protocol was known and the place of everyone carefully determined. But in ordinary processions, they are so unobtrusive that one is sometimes inclined to doubt their presence. They have made way for new officiants, who occupy all the space. First, there are the priests and monks, who often carry the body: priests of the parish, poor "unbeneficed priests," mendicant friars, members of the four mendicant orders—Carmelites, Augustinians, Franciscans, and Benedictines—whose presence was quasi-obligatory at all urban funerals. They were followed by a group, whose size varied according to the wealth and generosity of the deceased, made up of poor people and children from foundling homes. These people wore mourning robes similar to the cowl of southern penitents, with a hood that covered the face. They carried candles and torches, and, in addition to the robes, they were given alms in exchange for their attendance. They took

the place of both the friends of the dead man and the professional mourners. They were sometimes replaced by members of the confraternity to
which the deceased belonged or a confraternity that specialized in the
burial of the poor.

After the thirteenth century, the solemn procession of mourners became the symbolic image of death and funerals. Formerly this image was
the entombment, when the body was laid in the sarcophagus and the priests
pronounced the absolution, a scene frequently represented in Italy and
Spain before the Renaissance. In France, in Burgundy, the image of absolution was replaced by that of the procession, which was henceforth regarded
as the most significant moment in the whole ceremony. A procession of this
kind is depicted on the tomb of one of the sons of Saint Louis, which shows
that the custom was well established by the thirteenth century. The procession appears many times in funerary art before the Renaissance; I shall
mention only the famous tombs of Philippe Pot in the Louvre and of the
dukes of Burgundy at Dijon.

The order and composition of the procession were not left to custom
or to the clergy. They were decided upon by the deceased himself in his
will, and he often considered it an honor to be attended by the greatest
possible number of priests and poor people. A will dated 1202 provides for
"101 *presbyteri pauperes,*" the same poor "unbeneficed priests" of the
sixteenth and seventeenth centuries, a proletariat of priests without other
income who were supported by the works of death, that is, Masses and
endowments.

Sixteenth- and seventeenth-century wills attest to the importance that
the people of that time continued to attach to the composition of their
funeral processions. They discussed the subject with conviction and in
detail. In 1628 a vine grower from Montreuil asked that his body be carried
"on the day of his burial by six monks from the *Ave Maria.*" In 1647 a more
humble testator requests "that the procession take place with chimes, and
the usual decorations [funeral hangings in the home and the church], that
there be a dozen and a half torches weighing one pound apiece, a dozen
candles [carried by the poor], and that monks of the four mendicant orders
take part in the procession, as is the custom." In 1590: "In addition to the
unbeneficed priests of said parish, there shall also be invited ten members
of the four mendicant orders to carry said body, and each of the orders will
be given 20 sous after the service is over." Another "wishes the unbeneficed
priests to attend his burial and service . . . [and] that his body be carried
by four priests from the parish."[29]

The priests have obtained a monopoly on the carrying of the body, a
service for which they were remunerated. The number of poor people was
not always determined in advance. All those who were found in the vicinity

waiting for an opportunity of this sort were recruited for the procession. "Let a one-franc piece be given for the love of God on the day of his funeral to anyone whom God shall move to mourn for him." "At the time when his body is placed in the ground, let there be donated in charity to the poor in honor of and for the love of God and the seven works of mercy, seven francs."[30]

A century and a half later, the wording has hardly changed: "I desire that on the day of my burial one sou be given to all the poor people who are waiting by the gate after my burial" (1650). "I wish that on the day of my death the poor of the parish [not just any poor] be invited, and I request that they be given the sum of one hundred francs."[31]

It was customary to give alms to all the poor of the parish, but only a few were given robes. "Let robes be given to a dozen poor people who shall take part in said procession, and let each one be dressed in a robe and hood of the customary material" (1611).[32] This is still the traditional robe of mourning.

The Confraternity of Saint-Sacrement decided to take advantage of this gathering of the poor to teach them the catechism. "They resolved at that time to ask the priests not to permit the giving of alms at the time of burials until after a lesson in the catechism had been given to the poor who ordinarily gathered there to receive charity" (1633).[33]

A century later the number of the poor has not decreased, and it is still just as much an indication of the rank of the testator. A 1769 will specifies that the procession is to be preceded by "30 poor men and 30 poor women, each of whom shall be given four ells of cloth to clothe them [instead of the mourning robe, the alms consist of a simple habit]. Each one shall hold a rosary [a new form of devotion] and a candle on one side of the bier, and they shall proceed solemnly in the same manner to the place of my burial."[34]

In addition to the poor of the parish and the poor unbeneficed priests, there were also the little residents of orphanages and foundling homes. In Paris, these included the children of le Saint-Esprit, of la Trinité, and of les Enfants Rouges. These children, along with the four mendicant orders, had become specialists in death. No respectable funeral lacked a delegation from these establishments. Their presence was necessary in order to provide the asylums with an occasional source of income.

"To the hôpital de la Pitié in faubourg Saint-Victor, the sum of 300 pounds, provided 15 boys and the same number of girls attend his burial" (1652).[35]

The children summoned in this manner could also come from charity schools accompanied by their teachers. "To the poor children 30 pounds, provided the children take part in his procession." In a memorandum of the costs of a "service, procession, and burial" in 1697, one reads listed as an ordinary expense: "For the children of the school, 4 francs."[36]

From the thirteenth century until the eighteenth, the funeral procession was a procession of priests, monks, candlebearers, and paupers, stiff and solemn supernumeraries; an event of religious dignity in which the singing of psalms replaced the traditional cries and gestures of mourning. The size of this procession and the quantity of alms and contributions that it represented not only attested to the generosity and wealth of the deceased but also interceded in his favor before the court of heaven. The gathering of the poor at his funeral was his last act of charity.

The Concealment of the Body

Around the thirteenth century, at the same time that the vigil, mourning, and the funeral procession were becoming ceremonies of the Church, organized and directed by clergymen, something happened that may seem insignificant but that indicates a profound change in man's attitude toward death. The dead body, formerly a familiar object and an image of repose, came to possess such power that the sight of it became unbearable. Now, and for centuries to come, it was removed from view, hidden in a box, under a monument, where it was no longer visible. The concealment of the body is a major cultural event, for like all things related to death, it is also charged with a symbolism that was primarily ecclesiastical.

During the early Middle Ages, as we have seen, after death and after the expressions of mourning and regret, the body was laid out either on a piece of precious cloth, cloth of gold, or fabric dyed in rich colors—red, blue, green—or else simply on a shroud or winding sheet, generally made of linen.

The body and the shroud were then placed on a stretcher or bier and exhibited for a while in front of the door of the house. Later they were transported to the place of burial, after several stops usually dictated by custom. Finally, the bier was laid on the open sarcophagus. The priests chanted another *Libera,* with censing and aspersion with holy water; in other words, they performed a final absolution. Thus, the body, including the face, remained visible until the final closing of the sarcophagus, appearing on the bier, above the grave, just as it had appeared on the bed at the moment of death.

This is the custom that we have been able to reconstruct from old epics and also from images of fifteenth- and sixteenth-century Italy and Spain, which preserved the tradition of leaving the face uncovered and the associated practice of placing the dead in sarcophagi.

Many fifteenth-century paintings show the body lying on the bier during the funeral procession. At Santa Maria del Popolo in Rome, in the chapel of the Mellini, the late fifteenth-century tomb of P. Mellinus (d. 1483) depicts an open sarcophagus on which the body is lying. How does it remain balanced over the empty basin? If we look carefully, we see that the body is not lying directly on the sarcophagus, but on a wooden platform. The sculptor's concern for realism inspired him to show the heads of the three pegs that secured the two sides of the platform in each corner. What we have here is a piece of wooden furniture, independent of the stone sarcophagus and laid on top of it, a bier whose handles have been removed. We are fortunate that this detail is visible on this tomb. It is often hidden by the mattress of the bier and by the shroud, which hangs down and which after the final absolution will be folded back and held at each end by the attendants as they lower the body into the sarcophagus.

In the same church, another tomb from the early sixteenth century, that of Cardinal Bernard Lonati, shows a slightly different arrangement that was very common in Italy. The wooden bier does not rest on the open basin of the sarcophagus, but on the overturned lid. A wooden framework holds the rounded top of this lid in a horizontal position over the open basin. Although it is decorated, this wooden structure is not very attractive, and the artist had no reason to invent such a bizarre construction. This assemblage imitates the curious reality of funerals, the triple superimposition of the basin of the sarcophagus, the overturned lid, and finally the bier and the body. The traditional ceremony of entombment led to the elevation of the uncovered body onto a platform made up of the elements of the tomb, a tendency toward dramatic display that would be further developed with the catafalque, but that here still respects the visibility of the body.

But as we have seen, after the thirteenth century in Latin Christendom, except for Mediterranean countries, where the old practice has persisted to this day, the uncovered face of the dead man became unbearable. Shortly after death and right at the place of death, the body of the deceased was sewn into a shroud from head to foot, so as to be completely unrecognizable, and then often enclosed in a wooden chest or coffin.

In the fourteenth century, coffining was done in the house. As I have already mentioned, a miniature illustrating the Office of the Dead in a book of hours shows Death with a coffin over his shoulder walking into the sick man's bedroom. When the man leaves his room, he will be shut up in a nailed coffin, hidden from view.

People who were too poor to pay the carpenter were carried to the cemetery in a common coffin designed only for transport. The gravedigger removed the body from the coffin, buried it, and saved the coffin for further use. Some testators who were worried about the indifference of their heirs demanded to be buried in their own coffins. But rich and poor alike were always hidden in shrouds. There is a woodcut that shows the nuns in a city hospital busily sewing up their dead.

This disappearance of the body did not take place without resistance. The Mediterranean countries accepted the use of the wooden coffin, but refused to conceal the face, either by leaving the coffin open until the moment of burial, as was still done in Italy and Provence at the beginning of the twentieth century, or, less commonly, by constructing a coffin with a split cover and closing only the bottom half so that the top of the body and the face remained visible. A fifteenth-century fresco in San Pietro in Bologna shows the head and shoulders of the saint at the bottom of a wooden coffin that is only half closed, like a modern Californian casket (America has preserved vestiges, of Mediterranean origin, of the archaic aversion to covering the face).

The concealment of the body was not a simple decision. It does not express a desire for anonymity. Indeed, in the funerals of great temporal or spiritual lords, the body that was hidden in the coffin was immediately replaced by a wooden or wax image. This image sometimes lay in state, as in the case of the kings of France, and always lay on top of the coffin, like the recumbent figures on fifteenth-century Italian tombs. This statue of the dead man was known, curiously enough, as the representation. For this representation, the artists strove for the most exact resemblance, and they succeeded, at least in the fifteenth century, with the help of masks they took of the deceased immediately after death. The faces of the representations became death masks.

Exhibited on the coffin, at the house, during the funeral procession, and at the church, these images were modeled after the traditional recumbent figure, with the hands crossed on the chest. Sometimes they remained on display in the church after the funeral service pending the installation of the definitive recumbent figure on the tomb. At Westminster Abbey, these figures have been preserved, and one can still see them today, from the head of Edward III, who died in 1377, to the figure of Queen Elizabeth I. These "royal effigies" were considered venerable enough to be replaced. The one of Queen Elizabeth I was remade in 1760. These funerary statues made of wood, and later—in the seventeenth and eighteenth centuries—of wax, continued to be made even after they were no longer carried at funerals. The last effigies to be used at a funeral were those of the duke and duchess of Buckingham, who died in 1735 and 1743, respectively. (The effigy of the duchess was made during her lifetime.) The wax effigies of king William III and Queen Mary II, who died in 1702 and 1694, respectively, were placed in Westminster Abbey in 1725 and immediately attracted considerable attention. These statues were no longer recumbent figures but, like that of Queen Anne, they were majestic figures seated on their thrones.[37]

Representations have survived in another form that is more consistent with their origins. Even today in the Roman church, saints are exhibited for the veneration of the faithful in the form of wooden or wax effigies similar to the ones carried in royal funeral processions, from the fourteenth to the seventeenth century, that showed the deceased lying with joined hands in the ideal attitude of the recumbent figure. These effigies are intended to perpetuate the fleeting image of the saint immediately after death, at the moment when he is receiving the last honors and farewells of his disciples.

In the Vatican picture gallery, an anonymous painting from the late fifteenth or early sixteenth century shows the tomb of Saint Barbara. It would be an ordinary cubical monument were it not surmounted by what was called in France at the time a *représentation au vrai* of the saint, a statue in which the artist sought to create, by means of costume, color, and verisimilitude, the illusion of reality. An assemblage of oil lamps constitutes the third and final story of this monument. The design of the tomb was inspired by the ceremonies of royal funerals.[38]

At least by the sixteenth century, the devotion of pilgrims addressed itself not only to tombs and reliquaries where the remains of the saints were hidden or enshrined, but also to images that represented them on their deathbeds, as if life had just left them, giving the illusion of incorruptibility. The churches of Rome, in particular, are full of these lifelike representations of the dead; a French example is the shrine of Sainte-Thérèse-de-l'Enfant-Jésus at Lisieux.

Wooden or wax statues were reserved for the burials of temporal and spiritual princes; less important lords always did without them. But a few persistent practices betray the need to exhibit a portrait of the deceased on his coffin. In Spain, where there was an aversion to burying the dead, wooden coffins hung from the walls of churches had the recumbent figure of the deceased painted on the visible side, in the place where his representation would have been. Perhaps it was the same memory that inspired some Polish lords of the seventeenth and eighteenth centuries to reproduce their features on their coffins, portraits that were visible only during funeral services and were later buried in the ground.

But actually these examples of the persistence of the representation are rare. Generally speaking, there were no portraits on coffins, and when they did exist, they were part of a decor that was improvised for the occasion and immediately buried.[39]

The refusal to see the corpse was not a denial of physical individuality but a denial of physical death. A strange repugnance, coming in the middle of the age of the macabre, with its mania for images of decomposition, it demonstrates that art sometimes shows what man does not really want to see.

Curiously enough, the term *representation* survived the exhibition of effigies on coffins and persisted until the seventeenth century with the general meaning of what today we call the catafalque.

Later, the bare coffin inspired the same aversion as the uncovered body, and it, in its turn, had to be covered and concealed. During the procession, the coffin was covered, just as the body had once been, with a piece of cloth, the pallium or pall.[40] Sometimes this was a piece of precious material, brocaded in gold, that the testator asked to be used later as a chasuble by the priests at his chapel. Then it became a black ornament embroidered with macabre motifs and bearing the arms of the deceased or his confraternity, or else, the initials of the deceased.

During the late Middle Ages the rare but ancient practice of presenting the body at church for a Mass became more common, as we shall see. When this happened, the pall alone was no longer adequate to conceal the coffin, which now disappeared beneath a platform that was a replica of the one that had once supported the effigy or representation during royal funerals. This platform was also referred to by testators from the fifteenth to the seventeenth century as the representation, or the chapel, because it was surrounded by masses of candles, like the chapel of a saint. The use of our word *catafalque* in this sense seems to have come much later.

The monumental aspect of the catafalque would be retained. As early as the fourteenth century, its dimensions, although still modest, exceeded those of the coffin it surmounted. Illuminated by candles and torches and covered with brocaded fabrics, it was already an impressive sight. In the seventeenth century the Jesuits, those great impresarios of the baroque age, would turn it into an enormous theatrical prop, constructed around a theme and an action and animated with excited characters, commenting on ultimate ends: the *castrum doloris*, a veritable castle of grief. But the most impressive dimensions, the most exaggerated intentions, did not change the meaning of the ceremony. Let us not be deceived. The most remarkable phase of this history is not the one in the seventeenth century that loaded the catafalque with ornaments but the one in the thirteenth and fourteenth centuries that conceived the idea of hiding the naked face of death under the shroud, the shroud in the coffin, and the coffin under the catafalque. This was a major development in the rituals of death. The preachers of the macabre, the orators of the Counter-Reformation, may evoke the hideous realities of death in their funeral orations, but none of them will ever succeed in lifting the theatrical decor that now conceals the nakedness of the cadaver, once so familiar, from their listeners. It has become indecent to show the faces of the dead for too long, and yet their presence is still necessary, because they request it in their wills and because they help to bring about the conversion of the living. So they are henceforth represented by the symbolic apparatus of the catafalque, which eventually takes the place of the body, which has been, so to speak, eclipsed. It also takes the place of the body when the body is absent, as in anniversary ceremonies. The author of a 1559 will stipulates that his "end of the year" service take place, like his funeral service, "with no less ceremony, except that there will be only six torches weighing a pound and a half each and the four candles of the representation."[41]

The Revolution and the States General of the nineteenth and twentieth centuries secularized the catafalque, but they did not dispense with it. The Church was invisible; the *castrum doloris* remained in civilian or military public ceremonies. The ornamented and illuminated catafalque now replaced the older images of death: the absolution at the deathbed, the procession of mourners, the entombment, and the final absolution at the grave.

Burial Masses

The predominance of the catafalque over other images of death is due to the exorbitant importance now assumed by the High and Low Masses that took place in church. The old funeral rites, which consisted of accompanying the body from bed to grave without any form of ceremony other than the two absolutions at death and at burial, were submerged after the twelfth and thirteenth centuries by the fantastic quantities of Masses and services that the deceased prescribed in their wills. For half a millennium, from the twelfth to the eighteenth century, death was essentially an occasion for Masses. What would have struck a visitor to a church during this period was not so much the plowing of the ground by the gravediggers as the uninterrupted series of Masses said in the morning at all the altars by priests, for whom this was often the only source of income, and the frequent presence at both morning and evening services of the illuminated catafalque.

Usually the Masses of intercession began before death, from the onset of the death agony: "May it please them [the executors of the will] when he shall be *in agonia mortis,* to send, if possible, to the Augustinian monastery of the city of Paris and request five Masses *de quinque plagie* (for the five wounds of Christ), five *de Beata Maria* (for the Blessed Mary), and five *de cruce* (for the cross), and also to ask the monks of said monastery to pray to God for his poor soul" (1532).[42]

"She asked that when she was in the agony of death, her daughters and daughters-in-law send to Notre-Dame-de-la-Merci and have a Mass said at the high altar of said church" (1648).[43]

"Said testator desires . . . that at the time of her agony seven Masses be said in honor of the death and passion of Our Lord" (1655).[44]

Another "desires that when she shall be in the death agony there be said in her behalf 30 Masses at the Carmelite Fathers of Deschaulx, 30 at the Augustinian Fathers of Pont-Neuf, 30 at the Franciscans, and 30 at the Dominicans," that is, at each of the four mendicant orders. It sounds as if people were trying to steal a march on the sovereign judge before it was too late: "by the time God has disposed of my soul" (1650). But these deathbed Masses were only the beginning of a series: "A thousand Masses as soon as possible, and that they be begun while he is still in the death agony" (1660).[45]

In other cases, the celebration of this series of Masses started at the moment of death, and not before: "At the instant his soul is separated from his body, the testator begs his dear wife . . . to have said and celebrated three Masses in honor of the Holy Trinity [note the choice of the number three] at the high altars of Saint-Médéric, Sainte-Croix-de-la-Bretonnerie, and les Blancs-Manteaux, the first a Mass for the Holy Spirit, the second a *de Beata,* and the third a Requiem Mass for the remission of his sins and the salvation of his poor soul" (1646). In this case the number of Masses was limited to three per church, because they had to be said at the high altar. Generally speaking, testators sought a cumulative effect. Sometimes the number was not fixed in advance; the request was for the maximum number possible: "that on the day of his burial there be said and celebrated on his behalf at the church of Saint-Médéric as many Requiem Masses as there are present priests in the sacristy of the church" (1652). Starting on the day of his death, "as many Masses and prayers at said convent [les Minimes, where his brother was] as are available shall be said on behalf of and for the repose of the soul of said testator" (1641). Usually testators requested thirty, one hundred, or one thousand Masses. (Thirty or thirty-three Masses constituted a trental or Gregorian, in memory of its remote founder, the pope of death, Gregory the Great.) "As soon as my body shall be in the ground, let there be said 33 Low Masses [the age of Christ]," three a day: "3 for the Nativity, 3 for the Circumcision, 3 for the Passion, 3 for the Ascension, 3 for the Pentecost, 3 for the Trinity, etc. . . . as soon as possible," a precaution that is addressed both to the sovereign judge and to the clergy of the parish, who were suspected of negligence (1606).[46]

One testator asked for a hundred Masses "on the day of his death or the day after it in two churches," in other words, fifty Masses a day in each church (1667). "On the day of his death, if possible, or the day after it [because the churches were so overcrowded], a Gregorian of 33 Masses, and also one hundred Requiem Masses, as soon as possible" (1650).[47]

Sometimes the same testator would arrange for several series of 100 Masses each, one at the Capuchins, one at the Franciscans, and so on. Even as late as 1780, a testator requested 310 Masses to be concentrated on the day of his burial and the day after it.[48]

One thousand was a common number: "That on the day of my funeral and the following day there be said and celebrated one thousand Masses by poor chaplains [priests who lived on the income from chapels, that is, on pious endowments, mostly funerary] in the churches of Paris [five hundred Masses a day!], and that each chaplain be given II sous for his Mass."[49] This is 1394, but we find the same desire for quantity as we do in 1780.

On rare occasions the number of Masses reaches ten thousand, as, for example, in the case of Simon Colbert, ecclesiastical counselor at the Parliament of Paris in 1650.[50]

Finally, there is the annual, consisting of 360 Masses, whose distribution gives a good idea of the testator's two contradictory concerns: a concern for continuity, which led him to spread the masses out in time, and a concern for accumulation, which impelled him to concentrate as many Masses as possible in the shortest period. Some annuals did last for a calendar year; others were more concentrated in time: "by four priests every day, and that this annual be completed within the first three months after his death" ($4 \times 90 = 360$). This three-month period seems to have been quite common. A testator writing in 1661 requests three annuals of Masses "during the first three months, or twelve Masses a day in the two convents where his daughters are nuns." Another asks that Mass be sung "at the altar nearest my grave" (1418).[51]

Gregorians were also distributed in various ways, for instance: thirty-three a week (1628), three a day (1606), or according to a more complicated schedule: five Masses a day for four days (twenty) and thirteen on the fifth day, for a total of thirty-three (1582). The customary good measure was a Gregorian and a hundred Masses—and very often, an annual besides.[52]

The Church Service
on the Day of Burial

Every time a life came to its end, a regular series of Low Masses began, either at the onset of the agony or immediately following death, and lasted for days, weeks, months, even a year. These Masses succeeded one another without any relation to the funeral rites, which developed independently and were known as the service. The old liturgies provided for a solemn Mass that preceded burial, the Requiem Mass in the Roman liturgy, but this practice was probably reserved for clergymen and a few powerful laymen. Common usage required no ceremony at the church before the absolution at the grave. After the thirteenth century this situation changed. On the day of burial, which was almost always the day after death, it became customary to hold a service that ended with a final absolution at the grave. Until the sixteenth century this service did not require the presence of the body, which did not arrive until time for burial. However, it became more usual for testators to ask that the body be carried to the church on the day of burial. By the seventeenth century the presence of the body had become the rule. The importance acquired by the service, with or without the body, explains the role assumed by the representation in the ceremony of death from the late Middle Ages to our own time.

The solemn service at the high altar did not interfere with the celebration of those Masses being said in rapid succession for the same person at the other altars of the church. One testator requested one hundred Masses "immediately following my death, at all the chapels of Saint-Pierre-aux-Boeufs, during the service accompanying my burial and the rest on the following days, without interruption" (1658).[53]

This was a common practice that one still finds as late as 1812, in a will that was probably old-fashioned and unconventional: "I desire that on the morning of my burial six Masses be said every hour."[54]

The arrival of the body at the church was often accompanied by the singing of the *Salve Regina* or the *Vexilla Regis.* "That as soon as his body has entered the Church of la Madeleine, whether it is on the previous morning that the last Mass begins or whether it is on the previous afternoon that the Vespers for the Dead begin, the *Salve Regina* be sung devoutly with the customary verses and prayers."[55] If the burial takes place in the afternoon, there is no Mass, and the service consists merely of the Vigils for the dead.

In 1545 a testator ordered that his body arrive at Sainte-Chapelle, where he was to be buried, in a procession: first the crossbearer, flanked by two candlebearers, next the coffin, surrounded by four candlebearers, and finally a procession of twelve more candles. Upon arrival at the church, the twelve candles of the cortege were to be placed six on the altar and six in front of the relics, as was customary in Sainte-Chapelle. "And the 12 candles shall remain lighted in the aforesaid place during the Vigil, and at the end of this Vigil they shall be removed from these places and shall accompany the body until it is placed in its grave, and afterward the candles shall be returned to their places in front of the holy relics and on the high altar and shall remain lighted during the rest of the service, that is, the Lauds, the anthem *Salva Nos,* the Commendations, the procession [offering], and the Requiem Mass. Also, the testator desires and ordains that during the *Salva Nos* and the Requiem Mass, six wax candles be lighted in front of the holy relics, and as many on the altar on either side of the head of Saint Louis, and one to carry to the offering, the latter on a silver tray with a loaf of good bread and a jug of wine, as is customary at the service for the dead." Here the burial took place between Vespers and the rest of the service, which ended with a Requiem Mass.[56]

In this case, there was only one Mass. In fact, there was no fixed custom. Sometimes there was only one; sometimes—and for a long time this was the commonest case—there were several, usually three.

By the beginning of the seventeenth century, the usual order of the service had been established. In 1612 the will of a Parisian canon provides:

1. "That on the day of my death there be said a service, namely, Vespers, Vigils with 9 Lessons; after these Lessons, the entire *Libera,* then the Lauds for the Dead." This is the Office of the Dead, recited in the church. One notes that the service has moved from the home to the church (or is repeated in the church more solemnly, with a greater number of candles).

2. "On the following morning [still without the presence of the body] there shall be celebrated and sung two High Masses, one of the Holy Spirit and one of the Blessed Virgin [*de Beata*]."

3. The Commendations.

4. The arrival of the funeral procession at Notre-Dame. The pause before the image of the crucifix and the singing of "all of the *Creator Omnium Rerum.*" In this particular case, the ceremony will stop here, because the canon wishes to be buried in another nearby church, Saint-Denys-du-Pas.

5. "During the recitation of the *Libera* [as an absolution] my body shall be carried to Saint-Denys-du-Pas in order to be present during the last Mass," the Mass for the Dead. This Mass followed the other two High Masses mentioned above; the body was to arrive between the second *(de Beata)* and third (Requiem) Mass of the service.

6. Absolution and burial: "After said Mass is over, to the singing of the respond and verse of *Domine non secundum peccata nostra,* the psalm *Miserere mei Deus,* the *De Profundis,* and the usual prayers and orisons, my body shall be carried to my place of burial." Arrangements are also made in case the service cannot be held in the morning: "If my procession and burial cannot take place in the morning and if it is necessary to have them after Compline, my confreres at Saint-Denis shall say Vigils and Lauds an

hour after noon, then after Compline my procession and burial shall take place as indicated above."[57]

The ritual of 1614 was intended to simplify the liturgy of the funeral service.[58] The Office of the Dead declined in importance. The Mass of the Holy Spirit and the Mass of Our Lady were abandoned, and the service was limited to a single Mass, the Requiem. This sometimes happened as early as the sixteenth century, but throughout the first half of the seventeenth century a great many testators remained faithful to the traditional trio, as well as to the Vigils, Commendations, and Lauds.

By the end of the seventeenth century, usage had definitively established "that there be said one High Mass, in the presence of the body." Whatever the number of Masses, Commendations, or psalms, one must acknowledge the priority given to the service, that is, to the one Mass out of all the others that was said in the presence of the body and immediately preceding burial. When reading these wills, one is struck by the relative decline in importance of absolution and the ceremony of entombment. From now on, the main part of the funeral service takes place in church, where the High Masses of the service and the Low Masses of intercession are celebrated in front of the illuminated representation.

Services During the Days After Burial

The service for the day of burial was repeated several times in front of the representation after the body was no longer present, and then it included an absolution over the grave. The 1628 will of a vine grower from Montreuil provides for a service on the day of burial, with Lauds, Commendations, three High Masses, and a *Libera*. [59]

On the day after burial, the same service will be repeated with another *"Libera* and a *De Profundis* over the grave." A testator writing in 1644 stipulates, "On the three days following [his death], three services, and at each of them Vigils, three Masses . . . and another service on the octave." The service on the eighth day was customary, as was the service on the anniversary, the so-called end of the year. It included the Office of the Dead, High Masses, absolution with sprinkling of holy water over the grave, *De Profundis, Libera,* the "customary" prayers, *Salve Regina.* At the end of the year, as on the day of burial, alms were distributed to the poor. Some testators who were particularly impatient advanced the date of their anniversary: "I wish my end of the year to take place three days after my death" (1600). The end of the year and the annuals marked the end of the cycle of Masses ordered in advance and paid for in cash, "retail Masses," as Michel Vovelle calls them.[60]

Now a new cycle began, this one perpetual: endowment Masses. The testator bequeathed to the church council, monastery, hospital, or confraternity either a piece of property—land, house, field, vineyard—or a sum of money, or the income from an investment or business, such as a shop at the Palais-Royal, on the condition that the church or monastery or hospital community celebrate in perpetuity the services and Masses requested, precisely as indicated.

One of the types of endowment that is oldest, most significant, and richest in historical interpretations is the chantry, or chapel. This will, dated 1399, permits us to analyze the phenomenon: "I desire and ordain that the chapel I had started in Saint-Ypolite-de-Beauvais be completed and finished, well and suitably furnished with books, chalices, ornaments for holding services, and other things necessary to said chapel." The testator is referring, no doubt, to a lateral chapel built between the buttresses of the nave, such as were common in the fourteenth century, but not before, except in the ambulatory and the arm of the transept in the thirteenth century. The change is important. (Books bequeathed by certain testators were included in the chapel.)

The French word *chapelle* had two meanings, the one we have just encountered, of a physical edifice, and the meaning of an endowment for Masses: "Item, that said chapel be endowed with LX Parisian pounds of income . . . of which LX Parisian pounds there shall be L Parisian pounds for the chaplain who shall be ordained for said chapel to serve Mass. Which chaplain shall be obliged to say Mass every day in said chapel to pray for the souls of myself, my father, my mother, my brothers and sisters, and my other friends and benefactors. The other 10 Parisian pounds shall be to maintain the chapel [no doubt for candles, liturgical garments, and their upkeep]. . . . Item, I desire and ordain that said chapel belong by my presentation to my heirs, successors, and assigns."[61]

In another will dated 1416, the only meaning of *chapelle* is that of a perpetual endowment for Masses: "I desire and ordain that a chapel [or chantry] be founded in the parochial church and priory of Saint-Didier . . . of one hundred Parisian pounds annual income in perpetuity . . . on the condition that two monks of the abbey of Saint-Florent . . . shall say or have said [Masses] every day in perpetuity, that is, on Sunday the Mass of the Day, on Tuesday and Thursday, the Mass of the Holy Spirit, on Monday, Wednesday, and Friday, the Mass for the Dead, and on Saturday the Mass of the Annunciation, which Masses shall be said in this chapel for the salvation and restoration of the souls of my very revered lord and husband and of my dearly beloved son, together with a solemn anniversary each year . . . on the thirteenth day mentioned above, on which day my very revered lord . . . passed from life into death."[62]

Throughout the sixteenth century and the first half of the seventeenth, the authors of wills were always founding chapels or maintaining the chapels founded by their forebears. In 1612 Jean Sablez, lord of Noyers, *maître ordinaire* at the Chambre des Comptes, mentions in his will a chapel in the church in his seigniory of Noyers. His wife is already buried there, and he asks to be buried there too. So this chapel is not only a place consecrated to the celebration of Masses by endowment but also a place of burial. The testator hopes to transfer his mother's chantry, that is, the Masses by endowment for his mother, to the chapel of his seigniory of Noyers: "Item, I desire that the Mass by endowment that my late mother ordered in her will be celebrated at Saint-Gervais-et-Protais, in Gisors, in the chapel she has there, be celebrated there for thirty years after the day of her death, and after that, that this Mass be celebrated there or in Notre-Dame-de-Noyers, in my chapel, in perpetuity, according to the discretion of my heirs and to their greatest advantage and salvation and to be paid for by them every year if I have not made adequate provision during my lifetime." There must have been many testators and heirs who procrastinated in carrying out the promises made!

In addition to the usual morning Masses, the lord of Noyers requests an evening prayer: "Item, I establish for the salvation of my soul and that of my wife that a *Salve Regina* and prayer for the honor of God and of the Virgin Mary be said, celebrated, and sung in my low chapel [sic] in Notre-Dame-de-Noyers an hour before sunset, on the same days that they shall have died."[63]

In the fifteenth century, founding a chapel meant either building it physically or having Mass said there every day by an appointed priest. In the seventeenth century, the expression still referred to daily Masses, without necessarily specifying the nomination of the chaplain. But more and more often, it meant a place of burial.

But the chapel, which was equal to one Low Mass a day and one High Mass on the day of the anniversary of death, was not, of course, the commonest form of endowment. The minimum allowed was the anniversary service, the *obit*. A great many endowments fell between these two extremes, like that of our vine grower from Montreuil in 1628: six *Requiem* Masses per year, on All Saints' Day, Christmas, Candlemas, Easter, Pentecost, and the Day of Our Lady of Mercy. In addition, "that there be said in this church in perpetuity every day after Vespers the Passion of Our Lord before the image of Our Lady, said Passion to be accompanied by the ringing of bells. And to this end the testator has given and bequeathed to said church of Montreuil the sum of 400 pounds, which shall be invested by said churchwarden so as to provide an income for the works and council of said church."[64]

Charitable Endowments

Besides these endowments for Masses, of which there were a great many, there were also charitable endowments: a contribution to a hospital for a bed, or for the living expenses or dowry of a poor girl, in exchange for the celebration of an *obit.*[65] Donations to abbeys, monasteries, and schools were common and generous in the twelfth and thirteenth centuries. It is possible that after leveling off or even declining slightly, they rose again in the seventeenth century, which would explain the development of charitable establishments and hospitals during this period. Here are just two examples of endowments drawn from a large number.

The first, from the vicinity of Paris in 1667, concerns a small school for girls: "I give and bequeath in perpetuity every year to Saint-Martin an income of 100 pounds to be given to a woman or girl capable of teaching the girls of the village of Puteaux to read and to learn their catechism, said person to be chosen by my executor during his lifetime, and after his death, by the vicars, churchwardens, and leading inhabitants of the village."[66]

The second, from Toulouse in 1678, set up a kind of convent: "I desire that after the death of my heir, the curate of Taur have the use and enjoyment of my house during his lifetime, and after that, I desire that it be inhabited by 5 poor girls or widows in honor of the 5 wounds of Our Lord Jesus Christ . . . these girls to be chosen by the rectors of Taur successively in perpetuity, in the presence of the first bailiffs or officers of the confraternities of Saint-Sacrement, Notre-Dame-du-Suffrage, Sainte-Anne, and Charity."[67] This testator was farsighted, for the endowment of the convent had to wait for the death of the heir, then that of the curate of Taur. In those days no one hesitated to make a commitment involving a future that was imagined as unchanged, like an indefinite extension of the present.

From the thirteenth and fourteenth centuries until the eighteenth, the authors of wills were obsessed by the fear that the clergy, church councils, or recipients of their gifts would not carry out their obligations to the letter. Accordingly they posted publicly, in church, the terms of the contract, the gift that they had made, and a detailed list of the Masses, services, and prayers that were due them. "Item, he desires and ordains that a brass tablet be made and inscribed with his name, surname, and title, the day and year of his decease, and the Mass that shall be said in perpetuity for the souls of his late father and mother, friends, relatives, and the benefactors of said church" (1400). "I ordain that a bronze tablet bearing the endowment of the late M. St. Jehan, my first husband, be hung as near as possible to the place where he is buried and my own endowment, if it please the ladies of les Filles-Dieu to accept it according to the clause concerning the sum of IIICLL, which I have given them for a service in perpetuity every year on the anniversary of my decease" (1560).[68]

Endowment tablets are very common until the seventeenth century. Since they took the place of tombs, I shall examine them in greater detail in the next chapter, under the category "Tombs for Souls."

Besides the mural endowment tablet, there were two other ways of reminding survivors of the donors' intentions. One was to have an announcement made along with the other public notices, the so-called Prayers from the Pulpit, whose sentimental importance we observed at the beginning of this chapter. "When these 6 Masses shall be said, the churchwardens shall see that an announcement is made from the pulpit of the church" (1628).[69]

The other was to inscribe the endowment in a register similar to the obituaries kept by the curate to remind him of his commitments. This register bore the suggestive name *marteloyge,* an engraving on metal.

The museum at Cavaillon has a series of *donatifs,* or painted wooden (not stone or metal) tablets, dating from 1662 to the middle of the nineteenth century. They once hung in the old hospital in whose chapel the museum is located. Each *donatif* shows the name of the donor and the amount of the donation. In this collection there is also something that looks very much like a *marteloyge,* a calendar in the style of the eighteenth century consisting of two tablets of six months each; facing each day is the name of the benefactor to be remembered. The priests had to consult these tablets every day in the sacristy before saying Mass.

These endowments, as we have already seen, represented a considerable amount of capital that was diverted away from economic activities and toward the salvation of souls and the perpetuation of the memory of the dead, as well as toward charitable and social work. For good or for ill, they performed a service that today has devolved upon the state.

This practice is almost constant from the twelfth to the eighteenth century, except that the excesses of twelfth-century donors are no longer found among testators of the seventeenth century, who were more balanced, more reasonable, and above all more respectful of the rights of their heirs. But the basic desire or purpose remains the same.

However, a change does appear around the middle of the eighteenth century. Michel Vovelle has analyzed it with admirable perception: "Endowment Masses became increasingly rare, and were replaced by 'retail

Masses.' Even the richest testators preferred to convert into hundreds or even thousands of assured Masses the potential but illusory eternity of the perpetual services that their ancestors had founded." The religious communities were so overloaded with obligations that they sometimes obtained from the ecclesiastical authorities a "reduction" in Masses, which indicated a kind of "spiritual bankruptcy."[70] We shall not go into the underlying motivations for this very important phenomenon. Suffice it to say that it marks a final point in the long process that began in the twelfth and thirteenth centuries and that has brought us from the burial of the uncovered body to the accumulation of Masses and services and the concealment of the body inside the coffin and the catafalque.

The Confraternities

The result of all these changes was to relegate the family and friends of the deceased to a secondary position and to assign first place to ecclesiastics, priests, monks, or those representatives of God, the poor. The farewell of the living around the tomb was overlaid, if not replaced, by a large number of Masses and prayers at the altar, in what amounted to a clericalization of death. It was also at this time, after the fourteenth century, that associations of laymen were formed for the purpose of helping priests and monks in the service of the dead.

We have seen that affiliations of lay benefactors associated themselves with monasteries in order to take advantage of the prayers long reserved for monks. The persistence of this phenomenon is indicated by a will dated 1667: "[I ordain] that after my death, notification be given to the venerable Carthusian fathers of Paris, and that they be sent the letters of filiation and participation that I have obtained for our family from the Reverend Father General of the Grande Chartreuse [no doubt for a financial consideration], asking them to be good enough to say the customary prayers in their house and to notify the other houses for the salvation and repose of my soul [as in the days of the Scroll of the Dead], having great confidence in the prayers of persons so holy, and whom I have loved so fondly during my life."[71]

But the confraternities of the fourteenth to eighteenth centuries differed as much from the lay orders or monastic affiliations as they did from those trade brotherhoods or unions that Maurice Agulhon refers to as *confréries-institutions*. The fact is, however, that in the last centuries of the *ancien régime* every functional association had a sort of religious counterpart or double that was a confraternity.

The confraternities, which served as models for all the new forms of piety—devotion to the Blessed Sacrament, for example—were voluntary associations of laymen. Agulhon describes them as "societies that no one belonged to because of his position, age, or profession but only because he chose to do so."[72] Although a few ecclesiastics sometimes belonged to them in a personal capacity, these societies of laymen, presided over and administered by laymen, opposed the world of clergymen, and their importance in the area of death may seem to contradict what was said earlier about the ecclesiastical colonization of death. Was this a sort of laymen's revenge? Or was it rather a form of mimicry of clergymen by laymen under the penitent's hood? The confraternities were devoted to works of mercy, whence the name *charités*, which they were given in the north and west of France. Their activities are depicted in detail on altarpieces from the chapels they owned in or outside parochial churches, many examples of which are still in existence. The analysis of these works is very significant, not only because of the elements borrowed from scriptural tradition but also because of a new element that they added and that relates specifically to death.

The iconography of the works of mercy is based on the parable of the Last Judgment in Matthew (25:34–7), which, as we saw in chapter 3, is the main source of the eschatology of the late Middle Ages. When the Son of Man comes in majesty to sit upon his throne amid the gathering of the nations, he will separate the sheep from the goats. To the sheep placed at his right hand, the King will say, "Come, ye blessed of my Father, inherit the kingdom prepared for you from the foundation of the world: / For I was an hungred, and ye gave me meat: I was thirsty, and ye gave me drink: I was a stranger, and ye took me in: / Naked, and ye clothed me: I was sick, and ye visited me: I was in prison, and ye came unto me." Early representations of the Last Judgment had omitted these moving images, because the iconography was still dominated by the lofty inspiration of the end of time. The confraternities separated them from the vast eschatological fresco and moved them to another place, in a series of familiar scenes in which beggars receive bread, wine, and clothing, and wandering pilgrims are given shelter, cared for, and visited in asylums. Among the poor wretches who are given alms one recognizes the figure of Christ. The artist did not dare to place Christ behind the bars of the prisons or in the torture chambers. But although he is spared intimate association with convicts, he is always present, standing beside the good man who gives a coin to the torturer to make the interrogation easier or who gives food and drink to those sentenced to the pillory. These vivid and picturesque images were seen on altarpieces or the stained-glass windows of chapels. No iconography was more popular.[73]

In Matthew the works of mercy were six in number. But in the representations of the confraternities of the late Middle Ages, a new one was added that must have been dear to the hearts of men: *mortuus sepellitur* (burying the dead). This was placed in the same category as feeding the hungry, lodging pilgrims, clothing the naked, and visiting the sick and prisoners. And yet the Gospel is very reticent on the subject of funerary rites. When Jesus meets processions of mourners who are taking the dead outside the village to the accompaniment of flutes, he says nothing about it. He even makes an enigmatic remark that could well be interpreted as a condemnation of funeral rites: "Let the dead bury the dead." The evidence suggests that the late Middle Ages reintegrated the service for the dead into a Gospel whose silence on the subject had become uncomfortable. The *mortuus sepellitur* is still missing from the list of the works of mercy in the *Speculum Ecclesiae* of Honorius of Autun. It is mentioned in the *Rationale divinorum officiorum* of the liturgist and theologian Jean Beleth. Its appearance in iconography is contemporaneous with the confraternities; one finds it in the fourteenth century in Giotto's bas-reliefs in the Campanile in Florence. After the fifteenth century, its representation became commonplace.

Of all the works of mercy, the service for the dead became the main purpose of the confraternities. Their patron saints were often chosen from among the saints known as protectors against the plague and epidemics: Saint Sebastian, Saint Roch, and Saint Gond.

The confraternity filled three needs. In the first place, it provided assurance regarding the afterlife. The dead were assured of the prayers of their confreres. They were often buried in the crypt of the confraternity, beneath the floor of the chapel where the services for the repose of their souls took place. The pall of the confraternity covered the coffin, and the confreres marched in the funeral procession along with the clergy and the four mendicant orders, or in their place. After burial, the confraternity continued the services and prayers that the church council or monasteries were suspected of neglecting or forgetting.

Their second function was assistance to the poor, those whose poverty deprived them of any material means of winning spiritual intercessors. The sensibility of the age was relatively unaffected by the high mortality rates, but it refused to allow the dead to be abandoned without prayer. In rural communities, according to very ancient customs, even the poor were assured of the presence of neighbors and friends in their funeral processions. But in the towns, whose growth was so great in the late Middle Ages, the poor or isolated person no longer had access, in the liturgies of death, either to the old group solidarity that was preserved in the country or to the new assistance of those who dispensed indulgences and merits: priests, monks, and poor people of the parish (an "order" of poor people, which differed from the isolated pauper). The poor man was buried wherever he died, which before the sixteenth century, at any rate, was not always on church soil. So the confraternities took upon themselves the responsibility of burying him and praying for him. In Rome, the Confraternità della Orazione e della Morte was founded in 1560 for the purpose of burying in the cemetery of their chapel bodies that were found in the fields or dredged out of the Tiber. The confraternities took the place of the missing fortune of the deceased.

In France, in 1633, the Confraternity of Saint-Sacrement took charge not only of burying the poor but also of helping them at the time of death. "They hoped to be able to give them better care at the time of death than they were accustomed to receiving." This took place in the large towns, of course. Previously, the poor did receive the last sacrament, but "they [the confernity] felt this was not enough. They learned that after all the beggars had received Extreme Unction, no one bothered to help them face their death, and that they were left to die without the slightest word of consolation. The confraternity were moved to pity to see these poor people so abandoned at a time when they had such great need of spiritual assistance." No doubt they were not abandoned to solitude; they had carnal friends, but no spiritual friends. "So the confraternity appointed confreres to discuss the matter with the curates of the parishes that had the largest populations of beggars. But it does not appear that these good intentions were crowned with any great success."[74]

Finally, the third function of the confraternity was to provide funeral services for the parish. In many places the church councils left the organization of the obsequies, especially the funeral procession, up to them. Maurice Agulhon writes, "Under the *ancien régime,* the confraternities of the penitent order were entrusted, in fact if not by law, with an actual public service. . . . After [the disappearance of the penitent orders], people were sometimes at a loss to provide adequate funeral services. Indeed, this state of affairs was one of the main arguments advanced under the Consulate by those who advocated the restoration of the confraternities."[75] In modern Normandy, according to M. Bée, the charities continue to fulfill their traditional function, and the municipalities still give them exclusive authority over funeral services.

So the confraternities very early became, and very long remained, institutions of death. Their appearance in the fourteenth century is related to the changes that gave funerals and services for the dead the quality of religious ceremonies and ecclesiastical events. But the image of death that the paintings of confraternities have preserved is not the service at the church with the body present but concealed under the representation. On the contrary, it is the ancient scene of burial. The confreres carry the dead man, sometimes in a coffin, sometimes simply sewn into a shroud made of sacking cloth, along with the cross and the holy water, to the common grave of a cemetery.

This is no doubt because these paintings show charity funerals. The body of the poor man was not present at the church, and consequently, his burial was no longer covered over by all the religious ceremonies that masked it elsewhere. The funeral procession, as it was organized by the confraternities, was inseparable from burial.

Among the confraternities, the image of the grave and of burial retained an importance that they had lost among the clergymen and monks, even when it was not a question of a charity funeral. An altarpiece of a confraternity from the early sixteenth century preserved at the Rijksmuseum in Amsterdam shows a scene in the courtyard of a cemetery around a stone vault—a rarity at that time—whose lid the gravedigger is moving on a roller. This archaic image of death shows how attached the confraternity was to the gathering of the members of the funeral procession around the grave.

Was this because the confreres were laymen, a little behind the general tendency to clericalize funeral services? Or did they remain more attached to the traditional forms, which were still observed in rural regions? In this case we would emphasize the uprooting effect of the ecclesiastical reforms, and the persistence, even among pious laymen—before the Council of Trent—of a religion that was just as reticent in regard to priests as it was influenced by them and conservative of the past. However, we must not attach too much importance to this residual attraction of the grave in a funerary tradition in which it is more likely to be concealed.

The confraternities also took part in the solemn ceremonies that accompanied important funerals. In Michel Vovelle's south, they marched along with the four mendicant orders. In M. Bée's Normandy, they sometimes replaced them. The robe of the confreres, which in the south became the penitent's cowl, is the robe of mourning worn by members of the funeral procession as we see them on the tombs of Philippe Pot in the Louvre and the dukes of Burgundy in Dijon. It was a kind of clerical costume that, in spite of their avowed and independent secularity, transformed them into monks of a sort, like the members of a lay order. Moreover, a place was assigned to them in church, or outside it.

Under the pressure of these new devotions—new, at any rate, to the majority of laymen—the topography of churches changed in the fourteenth century, that pivotal period that keeps cropping up in our discussion. A specialized space was now devoted to the Masses and services of intercession. In the ancient Carolingian abbeys, supplementary altars were added in front of the pillars. (This was the case in Notre-Dame in Paris, before the great housecleaning of the canons in the eighteenth century.) It is possible, however, that this practice, far from being general, was limited to abbeys, cathedrals, and collegiate churches.

After the fourteenth century, it was necessary to set aside a space for all the chaplains and unbeneficed priests who owed their creditors enormous numbers of Masses, Lauds, Vigils, Commendations, and *Liberas*. Special chapels were constructed along the sides of the nave, either by families, as we have seen, or by confraternities, and soon there were very few churches without lateral chapels. These were very often funerary chapels, either family tombs or confraternity cemeteries.

The Function of the Will

The reader who has followed our history of funerary rites after the twelfth and thirteenth centuries will have been struck by a sense of *déjà vu*. It is almost as if the urban masses of the thirteenth to the seventeenth centuries were reproducing, after an interval of several centuries, the practices and ideas of the Carolingian monks—prayers for the dead, which are the origin of perpetual endowments, "retail Masses," perhaps funeral processions, affiliations for prayer, scrolls of the dead, and obituaries—all of which served as models or prefigurations for the confraternities.

A conception of death different from that of the early Church matured and developed among the monks of the Carolingian era. It was the expression of a scholarly religious thought, that of Saint Augustine and Saint Gregory the Great. It made no impression on the world of laymen, knights, or peasants, who remained faithful to the immemorial conception of the pagan-Christian tradition. After the twelfth and thirteenth centuries in the new towns, no doubt thanks to the influence of the mendicant friars, the laity was also won over by the ideas originating in the old abbeys concerning prayers of intercession, the treasury of the Church, the communion of saints, and the power of intercessors.

But if the laity was open to these ideas, it was because people were now ready to receive them. Previously there had been too great a gap between the mentality of the laity and that of the monastic societies, those islands of written culture and precursors of modernity. In the urban milieus of the thirteenth and fourteenth centuries, however, the two mentalities merged. We have just studied one of the means of this rapprochement: the confraternity. The other is the will. The will enabled each church member, even one apparently without family or confraternity, to obtain the advantages that the prayer societies assured their affiliates in the early Middle Ages.

When the will reappeared as a common practice in the twelfth century, it ceased to be what it had been in Roman antiquity and what it would become again at the end of the eighteenth century: simply a private legal document intended to regulate the transmission of property. It was primarily a religious document, required by the Church even of the poorest persons. It was regarded as a sacramental, like holy water; the Church enforced its use, making it obligatory under pain of excommunication. Anyone who died intestate could not, in principle, be buried in a church or cemetery. Wills were drafted and preserved by the curate as well as the notary. It was not until the sixteenth century that they became the exclusive responsibility of the notary, and for a long time cases involving wills continued to be referred to church courts.

At the end of his life, the church member confesses his faith, acknowledges his sins, and redeems them by a public document written *ad pias causas*. In exchange, the Church arranges for the reconciliation of the sinner and deducts from his inheritance a death tithe, which increases both her material wealth and its spiritual treasury.

This explains why until the middle of the eighteenth century, the will consists of two equally important parts: first, the pious clauses; and next, the distribution of the inheritance.

The pious clauses occur in an immutable order, which still follows the sequence of the gestures and words of Roland at the hour of his death. It is as if the will—or at any rate the religious part of it—had been oral long before it came to be written down.

In 1560 a Paris baker and his wife write: "Considering in their hearts that the life of every human creature is short and that they must die, but not knowing when or how, and not wishing to pass from this world into the next intestate, while sense and reason still govern their minds, [they] have made their testament in the name of the Father, the Son, and the Blessed Holy Spirit, in the form and manner that follows."[76] The notaries had a standard formula: "In view of the fact that nothing is more certain than death nor less certain than its hour, being at the end of his life, and not wishing to die intestate . . ."[77]

First comes the declaration of faith, which paraphrases the *Confiteor* and calls upon the celestial court as it gathers at the bedside of the dying man, in his bedroom, or in the cosmic heavens at the end of the world.

"And in the first place I commend my soul to God my creator, to the very mild and glorious Virgin Mary his mother, to Saint Michael the archangel, to Saint Peter and Saint Paul, and to all the blessed company of heaven" (1394).[78]

"And in the first place, as good and true Catholics [this is 1560, after the Reformation], they have commended and do commend their souls, when they shall leave their bodies, to God our Savior and Redeemer Jesus

Christ, to the Blessed Virgin Mary, to Saint Michael the angel and archangel, to Saint Peter and Saint Paul, to Saint John the Evangelist, to Saint Nicholas and Saint Mary Magdalene, and to all the company of heaven."[79]

(The John who interceded in Last Judgments was the Evangelist. This role was shifted to John the Baptist in the definitive text of the *Confiteor*, which has now been abandoned.)

Next come the redressing of wrongs and the forgiveness of injuries: "He wishes and desires that his debts be paid and that his wrongdoings, if any, be redressed and made good by his executor." This vine grower of Montreuil in 1628 uses the term *tortsfaits* (wrongdoings), written as a single word, just as Jean Régnier did in the middle of the fifteenth century:

> I wish my debts to be paid first
> And all my wrongdoings (tortsfaiz) to be redressed.

"I freely forgive all those who have done me some wrong or displeasure, praying God to pardon their offenses, just as I pray those who have received some injuries, injustices, or damages from me to forgive me for the love of God."[80]

Then comes the choice of burial, of which we have already given several examples. Finally, the instructions regarding the funeral procession, candles, and services, charitable endowments, the distribution of alms, and any obligations involving epitaphs or memorial plaques. This was also the place for the pious bequests that were the real *raison d'être* of the will from the Middle Ages to the eighteenth century.

We must remember what was said in the previous chapter about the intense love of life and the things of life that characterized the late Middle Ages and the Renaissance, and the power this love had over the dying man. He faced a dilemma that we have trouble understanding today and that the will helped him to overcome. This dilemma had to do with the fact that he was equally attached to the here and now and to the beyond. Modern commentators have a tendency to present these two feelings as if they were irreconcilable opposites, thus following the example of traditional Christian preaching. But in simple, spontaneous daily existence, the two feelings coexisted and even seemed to reinforce each other. In our own time, by contrast, we observe that both are losing their strength.

In the Middle Ages the dying man was faced with the following alternatives: either to go on enjoying people and things, and lose his soul, according to the men of the church and the whole Christian tradition, or else to renounce them and obtain his eternal salvation. This was the choice between *temporalia* and *aeterna*.

The will was the religious and quasi-sacramental means of obtaining the *aeterna* without altogether losing the *temporalia,* a way of combining wealth with the work of salvation. It was an insurance policy contracted between the mortal individual and God, through the intermediary of the Church, a policy that had a dual purpose. In the first place, it was, as Jacques Le Goff puts it, a "passport to heaven."[81] As such it guaranteed eternal wealth, but the premiums were paid in temporal currency, the pious bequests.

The will was also a *"laissez-passer,"* or permit, for use on earth. As such it legitimized and authorized the enjoyment—otherwise suspect—of property acquired during a lifetime, the *temporalia.* The premiums for this second guarantee were paid in spiritual currency, the spiritual counterpart of the pious bequests, masses, and charitable endowments.

So, on the one hand, the will provided an option on the *aeterna;* on the other, it rehabilitated the *temporalia.* The first sense is the best known. Historians have long emphasized the vast amount of property that changed hands during the Middle Ages and for a long time afterward.

In the oldest cases, the devolutions took place before death, when a baron or rich merchant would give away all his property and retire to a monastery to die, the monastery generally being the principal beneficiary of such a conversion. The practice of putting on the monastic habit before dying persisted for a long time. It was a privilege that was given by affiliation in a third lay order, along with the prayers of the monks and burial in the church.

Total renunciation of property and planned retirement were not exceptional in the twelfth and thirteenth centuries, but became less common after the fifteenth century. In a world that was already more urbanized and sedentary, the old man (of fifty!) was tempted to hold on to his economic activities and the management of his property. But transfers of property postmortem, by testament, remained numerous and substantial. Only a portion of the patrimony reached the heirs; the rest was set aside for the Church and pious endowments. Jacques Le Goff writes: "Unless we bear in mind the obsession with salvation and the fear of hell that motivated the people of the Middle Ages, we shall never understand their mentality, and we shall remain dumbfounded before this renunciation of power, of wealth, of the whole effort of a greedy life, which caused an extraordinary mobility of fortunes and revealed, albeit *in extremis,* how those most avid for earthly goods in the Middle Ages always ended by having contempt for the world; this mental trait, which prevented the accumulation of fortunes, helped to keep the people of the Middle Ages from acquiring the material and psychological conditions for capitalism."[82] In order to have contempt for the world, however, was it not first necessary to have loved it passionately, just as today the rejection of the affluent society necessarily comes from those who have enjoyed its advantages, and scandalizes those who are still waiting for them?

Jacques Heers regards the enormous size of the donations as one reason for the economic collapse of the nobility in the fourteenth century. The noble "impoverished his heirs by his pious and charitable endowments: bequests to the poor, to hospitals, to churches and religious orders, Masses for the repose of his soul that were counted by the hundreds and thousands." Heers sees this behavior less as a spiritual trait of the age than as a class characteristic. "The refusal to economize, to consider the future of one's family, are so many signs of a class mentality that seems retarded in this world of business."[83] But what of the merchants—did they not have the same habits? A frequently quoted passage by Sapori regarding the Bardi, merchants of Florence, emphasizes "the dramatic contrast between the daily lives of these bold and tenacious men, who amassed vast fortunes, and the terror they had of eternal punishment for having accumulated their wealth by doubtful means." In 1300 a merchant of Metz bequeathed over half his capital to churches.[84] Jean Lestocquoy has observed the same generosity among the merchants and bankers of Arras and Flanders in the thirteenth and fourteenth centuries.[85] Must we not recognize such a redistribution of income as an ongoing characteristic of highly developed preindustrial societies, in which wealth was hoarded? Only the forms change: liturgies or philanthropy in ancient societies; religious and charitable endowments in the Christian West of the thirteenth to the seventeenth century.

The matter has been clearly stated by Paul Veyne: "Preindustrial societies are characterized by disparities in the scale of personal incomes that are unimaginable to us, and by a total absence of opportunities to invest, except in the case of a few professionals who were specialists or willing to take risks. Until the last century, world capital consisted primarily of cultivated land and houses. The instruments of production, plows, ships, or looms, occupied only a minor place in this inventory. It is only since the Industrial Revolution that the annual surplus can be invested in productive capital, machines, railroads. . . . Previously, even in rather primitive civilizations, this surplus ordinarily took the form of public or religious buildings." It also took the form of fortunes, collections of gold or silver jewelry and works of art, and for the less wealthy, of beautiful objects, and finally for men of the church and lawyers, of education and belles-lettres. "Formerly, what the rich did not use up of their income, they hoarded; but every fortune must be redistributed someday, and on that day they would be less hesitant than ourselves to use it to build a temple or church [or to make a pious endowment], for this was always a good investment. Philanthropists and pious or charitable donors represented a type of *homo oeconomicus* that was very widespread before the Industrial Revolution and of which only a few representatives are left, the most conspicuous being emirs of Kuwait or American multimillionaires who found hospitals or museums of modern art."[86]

Veyne assumes that "the ancient city rested on this foundation [philanthropy] for a full five centuries." The same necessary function was filled in the Middle Ages by the redistribution of parts of fortunes in testamentary donations and even by the more modest donations, better proportioned to the inheritance, of the sixteenth and seventeenth centuries. In Arras, Lestocquoy has observed a decline in the generosity of testators in the sixteenth century and a return to the medieval situation in the seventeenth. It is only after the middle of the eighteenth century, according to Vovelle, that we observe a decline in bequests *ad pias causas*. In the seventeenth and even in the eighteenth century, in both Catholic and Protestant countries, all public assistance depended on charitable endowments. The directors and directresses of hospitals in the Netherlands deserved to have their portraits handed down to posterity.[87]

Wealth and Death

Nevertheless, there is a very important difference between ancient philanthropy and the medieval and modern versions. Although it may be true that "every fortune must be redistributed someday," the moment of redistribution is not a matter of indifference. During antiquity this moment depended on the hazards of the donor's career. In the Middle Ages and throughout the early modern era, it coincided with the moment of death, or with the conviction that this moment was imminent. Thus, a correlation was established that was unknown in antiquity, as in our industrial cultures, between attitudes toward wealth and attitudes toward death. This correlation is undoubtedly one of the distinguishing features of this society, which exhibited so much consistency from the middle of the medieval period to the last third of the seventeenth century.

Max Weber compares the precapitalist, who is eager for enjoyment, with the capitalist, who derives no immediate enjoyment from his wealth but regards the accumulation of profits as an end in itself. But in both cases he misinterprets the relationship that is established between wealth and death. He writes, "That a human being may choose as his task, as the single aim of his life, the idea of going to his grave loaded with gold and riches, can only be explained in this case [capitalist man] by the intervention of a perverse instinct."[88]

In fact, the truth is exactly the opposite: It is precapitalist man who wants to "go to his grave loaded with gold and riches" and to hold on to his fortune *in aeternum,* because he is hungry for it and cannot separate himself from it without a violent conversion. He accepted the idea of dying, but he could not bring himself to "leave houses and orchards and gardens."

On the other hand, since Père Goriot, who still exemplifies the traditional *avaritia,* there are few examples of a nineteenth- or twentieth-century businessman who shows at the hour of his death such an attachment to his businesses, his portfolio of stock certificates, his racehorses, his villas, or his yachts! The contemporary conception of wealth does not give death the position it was accorded from the Middle Ages until the eighteenth century, no doubt because this conception is less hedonistic, less visceral, more metaphysical and psychological.

For medieval man, *avaritia* was a devastating passion, not only because as a Christian it exposed him to the risk of eternal damnation, but also because the idea of losing his worldly riches at the hour of death tormented him. This is why he seized on the solution proferred him by the Church and why death was chosen as the occasion to carry out, by means of the will, an economic function that in other societies was filled by the gift or the priestly liturgies. In exchange for his bequests he obtained the assurance of eternal wealth, and at the same time—and this is the second aspect of wills—the *temporalia* were rehabilitated and *avaritia* retroactively justified.

André Vauchez has arrived at very similar conclusions: "The rich man, that is, the powerful man, is in a particularly good position to assure his own salvation." Other men can fast or make pilgrimages in his place. He has the advantage of a "penitential commutation," which is inaccessible to the poor. "By means of donations, pious endowments, and alms, he can constantly acquire new merits in the eyes of God. Far from being a malediction, wealth appears as a privileged means of access to sanctity. . . . The ascetic ideal that prevails in monastic settings exalts the capacity for renunciation as a tangible outward sign of conversion. But who is in a better position to renounce than he who possesses? The poor man, on the other hand, has no recourse but to pray for his benefactor. . . . This spirituality does not merely provide the generous rich man with a reward in the other world. *It guarantees him a reward in this world* [italics added]. A great many Tuscan wills whose beneficiaries were monasteries begin with the following words: 'He who gives to holy places . . . shall receive a hundredfold in this life.' The Crusaders were expected to receive victory and spoils, the signs of divine election. A collective letter from the bishops of the West on the subject of the Crusade contains this passage: 'Come, then, make haste to win the *double recompense* [italics added] that is your due, the land of the living and that other land in which milk and honey and all manner of nourishment are found in abundance."[89]

In the early fourteenth century, Baude Crespin, one of the richest bourgeois of Arras, ended his days in the abbey of Saint-Vaast, of which he was the benefactor. His epitaph, recorded in the necrology, stated that although he was a monk, he was not a monk like the others: "Never shall his like be seen again." Indeed, his humility was all the more praiseworthy and admirable because he had once been rich and powerful. "By his generosity there lived in great dignity more people than by one hundred others."[90]

At the abbey of Longpont, on a thirteenth-century tomb reproduced by Gaignières, there can be read this epitaph: "By miracle, he left children, friends, and possessions [the *omnia temporalia* of the *artes moriendi*] and lived steadfastly in this place, as a monk in the piety of the order, with great fervor and religion, and surrendered his spirit in sanctity and joyousness to God."[91]

Felix avaritia! The magnitude of the offense had made possible the magnitude of the atonement, since it had brought about conversions so exemplary and transfers of property so beneficial. How could the men of the church carry their ideas to their logical conclusion and irrevocably condemn things that ultimately found their way to their barns and cellars, and were transformed into a spiritual treasury of prayers and Masses? They condemned them, but only in the absence of atonement and redistribution. Even they, who lived at the very heart of the *contemptus mundi,* loved things, and the religious art of the late Middle Ages, with its Annunciations, Visitations, Births of the Virgin, Pietàs, and Crucifixions, was nourished by this love of things that was so closely associated with the love of God.

But let us beware of assuming, with Voltairean cynicism, that charitable donations to churches and hospitals were the only justification of earthly goods. An idea appears in testamentary literature that under certain circumstances erases misgivings and legitimizes the use of the goods of this world.

This idea is already well established in the wills of the fourteenth century: "Those goods that God my Creator has *sent and loaned* to me, I wish to organize and distribute by means of this last will and testament in the following manner" (1314). "We wish and desire to distribute and ordain concerning my body and my goods, which Jesus Christ has loaned me for the profit and salvation of my soul" (1399).

"To see to the salvation and restoration of his soul and to make arrangement and disposition for himself [his burial] and for those goods that God has given and administered unto him" (1413).[92]

The argument is found again, unchanged, in wills of the seventeenth century, with the addition of the new and important idea that this voluntary devolution is necessary to good understanding among the survivors: "Not wishing to depart from this world without putting my affairs in order or making disposition of those goods that it has pleased Almighty God to lend me" (1612).[93]

"Desiring to dispose for the profit of his children of those goods that it has pleased God to give him and in this manner to foster peace, amity, and harmony among his children" (1652)[94] This peace, amity, and harmony might otherwise have little chance of being maintained!

The Will as a Moral Duty

Thus, the disposition of one's property, not only *ad pias causas* but among one's heirs, became a duty, a matter of conscience. In the eighteenth century this moral obligation took precedence over charitable contributions and pious endowments, which were beginning to go out of fashion, or at least were no longer the main purpose of the will. The transition is important and worth remarking.

In 1736 the pious author of an eighteenth-century *artes moriendi* entitled *Méthode chrétienne pour finir saintement sa vie* wrote, "What does a sick man do when he sees that he is in danger of dying? He sends for a confessor and a notary." That the two are equally necessary seems quite extraordinary in a manual on the art of dying, which teaches detachment and contempt for the world. He explains: "A confessor, to put the affairs of his conscience in order, and a notary, to draw up his will." With the help of these two persons, the sick man must do three things: The first is to confess; the second, to take Communion. "The third thing that a dying man does to prepare himself to appear before the judgment of God is to settle his temporal affairs as best he can, to make sure that everything is in order, and to dispose of all his property." Note that it is not a question of a human precaution, an act of prudence and worldly wisdom, like the taking out of a life insurance policy, but of a religious, almost sacramental act, and that performing it is a prerequisite for eternal salvation. It was even an exercise of preparation for death in an age when the new pastorals of the Counter-Reformation instructed that a man should not wait for the hour of his death to convert, but should prepare himself for death throughout his life: "This must be done in good health by anyone who wishes to prepare himself to die properly. Although this is one of the most essential points of the preparation for death, nevertheless it is ordinarily the one most neglected."

By the middle of the eighteenth century, charitable contributions and endowments for Masses had ceased to be the essential religious purpose of the testament. They still existed, but their role was no longer as important as it had been. The spiritual author was content to advise the sick man not to forget his personal salvation through excessive concern for his relatives. "Take care, moreover, that in your testament, in thinking of others [that is, in making an effort to distribute your property among your heirs in an equitable manner], you do not forget yourself [that is, your salvation by redeeming your sins] even as you remember the poor and [do] other works of piety"—and this once again without going to excess, within reason, that is, "according to your faculties." In making pious bequests, it was also necessary to avoid ulterior motives of prestige that were alien to Christian humility and capable of endangering the legitimate rights of the family. One must not give indiscriminately: "Above all, observe the rules of justice without listening to the voice of flesh and blood [no favoritism] or of worldly reputation [no endowments for reasons of prestige]."[95]

Insofar as it is a religious document, the main purpose of the testament has shifted from philanthropy to family management. At the same time, it has become an act of foresight and caution that is performed in expectation of death, but of death as a distant possibility rather than an impending reality, not *in articulo mortis* (the grip of death).

This obligation is not reserved for the rich. Even people in modest circumstances, if not the poor, are obliged to arrange for the disposition of the few things they possess. Thus, in 1649 a "domestic servant . . . not wishing to be summoned [by death] before she had arranged for the disposition of her modest possessions [her bed, her dresses]."[96]

There is no question of rejecting things and possessions, of taking no interest in them. In these wills we encounter traces of the same ambivalent love of life and of the self that we encountered at the bedside of the sick man in the *artes moriendi* or in macabre art.

We have seen that the will was a religious, quasi-sacramental document. Could it be a personal document as well? Was it not obliged to imitate the fixity of the liturgy and respect the conventions of the genre? Michel Vovelle has studied this question for the seventeenth and eighteenth centuries: "[Was the will] a legal formula, a fixed and unyielding stereotype . . . or a sensitive index of changing ideas, those of the notary as well as of his clients?" After studying a great many wills, he found that there was certainly a lack of personal effusion, even in holograph wills; but this did not justify speaking of stereotypes. On the contrary, "there are almost as many formulas as there are notaries."[97] Although the seventeenth- and eighteenth-century will is not so intimate a confession as we moderns, with our contemporary passion for self-revelation and analysis,

might wish, the variety of formulas does imply a certain amount of freedom. This half-freedom permitted spontaneous impulses and feelings to
show through, in spite of the rigidity of convention. This is also true of
the record books kept by families or districts. Instead of personal impressions, like those found in journals from the eighteenth century to the
present, wills present a variety of little models, each of which is statistically
significant.

The Will as a Literary Genre

This variety of models enables the historian to utilize wills as the documentation of shifting attitudes. One can even go so far as to consider the
reappearance of the will and its development in the Middle Ages as a
cultural phenomenon significant in itself. The medieval will was more than
the religious document, at once voluntary and required by the Church, that
we have already analyzed.

In the fourteenth and fifteenth centuries, its already traditional forms
were a source of poetic inspiration; the will became a literary genre. No
matter how conventional it may have seemed in practice, it was chosen by
the poet to express his feelings about the brevity of life and the certainty
of death, just as in the eighteenth century, the novelist would choose the
letter. In each case, the writer selected from the forms of his age what was
most spontaneous, closest to an outpouring of personal feeling. The authors
of the Middle Ages retained the conventional form of the will and respected the style of the notaries, but this did not prevent them from making
these wills the most personal and immediate poems of their age. The will
is the first confession—half spontaneous, half forced—of man facing his
death and the image of his life that death holds before his eyes: a troubling
image, made up of desires and nostalgia, of primitive emotions, of regrets
and hopes.

The following poems exhibit all the elements that we have analyzed
in wills. Jean Régnier (1392–1468), writing from his prison, paraphrases the
will as follows:[98]

> *Every good Christian, they say*
> *When death is imminent*
> *Must give his goods away*
> *And make his testament.*

And François Villon, in a situation scarcely more comfortable, gives his
version of the traditional preamble:[99]

And since my time has come to part
And I know not when I come again
(For I am not devoid of fault,
A man of steel or of tin;
This life has no certainty
And after death my time is spent;
I travel to a far country)
I therefore make this testament.

The confession of faith, the appeal to the intercessors of the celestial court, the commendation of the soul, according to Régnier:

In the faith of God I wish to die
Who suffered passion for my sake . . .
To the saints I would complain
Male and female, one and all
That it please them to obtain
The salvation of my soul.

And according to Villon:

And this is how I shall begin:
In the name of God, eternal Father,
And of the Son of Virgin born,
God, coeternal with the Father
Together with the Holy Ghost
Who redeemed what Adam lost
And raised it up to deck the skies . . .

First I give my wretched soul
To the blessed Trinity
And commend it to Our Lady,
Vessel of divinity,
Praying for all the charity
Of the worthy hosts of heaven
That by them this gift may be
Carried before the precious Throne

The poet's last reference is to the ascension of his soul. Next come the admission of offenses, the atonement for wrongs, the forgiveness of injuries, again, according to Villon:

> *I beg everyone for mercy . . .*
> *That I may be pardoned for God's sake*
> *I wish my debts to be paid first*
> *And all my wrongs to be redressed.*

The choice of burial, according to Régnier:

> *At the Dominicans I choose the ground*
> *In which my coffin shall be laid.*

And Villon:

> *Item, my body I do bequeath*
> *To our great mother, the earth.*

My soul to God, my body to the earth: It was a classic formula. He also adds, according to the custom:

> *Item, I wish my grave to be*
> *At Sainte-Avoye and nowhere else.*

The funeral procession and the religious service, according to Villon:

> *Item, four laborers shall carry*
> *My body to the monastery . . .*
> *And as for the lighting of my bier*
> *I shall nothing say on it*
> *Let my executor decide*
> *And all dispose as he sees fit*
> *The singing of a single Mass*
> *of Requiem will suffice for me*
> *But my heart would the more rejoice*
> *If there might a descant be*
> *And also I wish fervently*
> *That all the singers who shall sing*
> *Be given gold or currency*
> *That their faces may be smiling.*

Perhaps the distant sequel to this literature must be sought in the sixteenth, seventeenth, and eighteenth centuries in what Vovelle calls, with a trace of irony, *"le beau testament,"* the bravura piece written in the evening of one's life for one's own edification and that of one's children.

Despite all the conventions he had to observe, the testator of the later Middle Ages expresses a feeling that is close to that of the *artes moriendi:* awareness of self; responsibility for one's destiny; the right and the duty to make arrangements for one's soul, body, and property; the importance of those last wishes.

The Persistence of the Tame Death

This, indeed, is the death of the self, the self alone before God, with one's lone biography, one's lone capital of works and prayers, that is, the actions and passions of one's life, one's shameful love of the things of this life and one's guarantees regarding the next: a complex network that man has woven around himself the better to live and the better to survive death.

An individualistic approach to this world and the next seems to separate man from the confident or weary resignation of time immemorial. It is true that we are moving in this direction, but a careful study of the will indicates that individualism does not go beyond a certain point, that it does not represent a complete break from the old habits. The will reproduces in writing the oral rites of the traditional death. By bringing them into the world of writing and of law, it divests them somewhat of their liturgical, collective, customary, almost folkloric quality. It personalizes them—but not completely. The old spirit of the oral rites has not disappeared. The will is alien to the sensibility of the macabre, to exaggerated expressions of love for life or regret for death.

It is remarkable that allusions to purgatory are slow to appear; there are hardly any before the middle of the seventeenth century. Although death as we perceive it through wills is particularized and personalized, although it is also the death of the self, it remains the immemorial, public death of the man lying in his bed.

5

Tombs and Epitaphs

Archaeological and epigraphic fragments of Roman graves dating from the early centuries A.D. abound in museums, at excavation sites, and on the walls of churches of Paleo-Christian origin. On these fragments we find the same formulas repeated over and over, until their very banality becomes instructive.

The first thing we notice is that in an ancient cemetery, whether pagan or Christian, the tomb is an object designed to mark the exact spot where the body has been laid. Either it is the container of the body or ashes, as in the case of the sarcophagus, or it is an edifice that covers a chamber in which bodies are kept. There were no tombs without bodies, and no bodies without tombs.

On the tomb a perfectly visible inscription of varying length indicates the name of the deceased, his position in the family, sometimes his rank or profession, his age, the date of his death, and his relationship to the relative responsible for burying him. These inscriptions are innumerable, and taken as a whole they constitute one of the sources of Roman history.

An inscription is often accompanied by a portrait: the husband and wife, sometimes with joined hands symbolizing marriage; the dead children; the man at work, in his studio or workshop; or simply the bust or head of the deceased in a scalloped frame or medallion *(imago clipeata).* In short, the visible tomb had to indicate where the body was and to whom the body belonged, and finally, it had to recall the physical appearance of the man, the symbol of his personality.

Besides designating precisely the site of funerary worship, the tomb was also intended to transmit the memory of the deceased to later generations. Hence its name of *monumentum* or *memoria.* The tomb was a memorial. The survival of the dead man had not only to be assured on the eschatological level by means of offerings and sacrifices, it was also dependent on a fame that was maintained on earth either by the tombs with their *signa* and inscriptions or by the eulogies of writers.[1]

Of course, there were a great many miserable graves with neither inscriptions nor portraits, which had nothing to transmit; the buried urns at the cemetery of the Isola Sacra, at the mouth of the Tiber, are anonymous. But in the history of the funerary colleges, the mystery cults, one senses the desire of the poorest persons, even slaves, to escape this anonymity that is true death, total and definitive annihilation. In the catacombs, the humble *loculi,* or cavities designed to receive the bodies, were covered with slabs that often contained brief inscriptions and a few symbols of immortality.[2]

The most casual observer who walks through the ruins of these cemeteries today has the sense that there is a single mental attitude underlying and uniting these three phenomena.

The Tomb Becomes Anonymous

Starting around the fifth century, this cultural unity was destroyed. The inscriptions disappeared, along with the portraits, and the tombs became anonymous. The first explanation that comes to mind is the decline of writing. Nothing was written, because there was no one to engrave and no one to read. But this lack of inscription was an accepted fact even on the tombs of illustrious personages, the only occasional exception being on those of saints. It is true that an oral civilization always allows more room for anonymity. It is nevertheless remarkable that this anonymity persisted in the cultures of the eleventh century A.D., when writing had already resumed a role that was by no means negligible. The phenomenon impressed erudite archaeologists of the eighteenth century such as Abbé Lebeuf, who remarked, in connection with the reconstruction of the cloister at the abbey of Sainte-Geneviève, in Paris, in 1746: "They dug up all the earth in the churchyard and found a large number of stone coffins with skeletons, but *not a single inscription* [italics added]."[3] Everything that once indicated the personality of the deceased, such as the professional symbols so common on the steles of Roman Gaul, has disappeared. Sometimes the name remained, painted in bright red letters, or later, engraved on a copper plate, but this was inside the sarcophagus. By the eighth and ninth centuries all that remains is floral or abstract decoration, or religious scenes or symbols. To borrow Panofsky's terminology, the eschatological tendency has prevailed over the commemorative impulse, at least in the main; for as we shall see, the old relationship between the two immortalities, the celestial and the terrestrial, persisted in the exceptional cases of kings or saints, persons who were the objects of public veneration.

Let us take as an example one of the many layers of sarcophagi discovered accidentally in the course of modern urban expansion. Under the porch of the abbey of Souillac, the tombs are stone coffins that have been piled one on top of the other to form a layer three stories high.[4] The oldest ones were buried beneath the present entrance to the porch of the tower and overflowed slightly into the interior of the nave. In photographs of the diggings one finds superimposed sarcophagi identical to those found in the Roman ruins of Africa, Spain, or Gaul; and yet this cemetery postdates them by more than seven centuries. The bottom layers are certainly very old, very anterior to the present construction. But others, apparently identical, which surmount or overlap them, are much more recent. They can be dated either by forms that characterize a later era, such as the trapezoid shape or the presence of a separate chamber for the head, or by objects found inside, such as vessels with holes in them containing coals (a kind of earthenware perfume brazier or censer); holy-water basins of terracotta, which were common in the late twelfth century, even more so in the thirteenth century; or pieces of clothing, such as the alms purse. With the help of such clues, archaeologists have been able to date the cemetery of Souillac between the thirteenth and fifteenth centuries. But what a striking resemblance these layers of monolithic coffins bear to those of the sixth to eighth centuries.

This uncertainty is due to the fact that apart from a few rare objects and morphological features, there is nothing to give these tombs a personality or a date. We do know, however, that they were not intended for the poor or the obscure. The "masonry" coffins, that is, those constructed of juxtaposed stone slabs, which have been found near the monolithic coffins, might be of humble origin. Burial *sub porticu* or *sub stillicidio* was just as sought after and prestigious as burial in the interior of the church, and yet there is nothing, absolutely nothing, to indicate the origin, name, rank, age, or dates of the deceased. Their anonymity remains complete. The use of the monolithic coffin, a remote descendant of Roman antiquity, persists, but it has been stripped of all distinguishing features and reduced to a stone basin devoid of history. The archaeologist author concludes, "To be buried by the door of the abbey was certainly a privilege that was sought after, and those who enjoyed this privilege must have possessed reputation and wealth, but they did not use this wealth for their tombs." Indeed, who is to say that some of them did not have erected in the abbey itself, far from the place of their burial, a monument that has since disappeared, a horizontal tombstone or mural tablet? The fact remains that the men of the late Middle Ages, from the thirteenth to the fifteenth century, seem to have

The Appian Way, Rome. In the foreground, the tomb of Sesto Pompeo Giusto (A.D. 14). "The cemeteries of antiquity were always outside the towns, along the roads" (page 30).

Christian necropolis around the basilica of Saint-Salsa, Tipasa, Algeria. These sarcophagi surrounding the walls indicate a profound shift in attitude toward the dead —from a pagan aversion to any proximity to a Christian acceptance of coexistence (page 30).

Saint-Bavon, Haarlem. It was common practice prior to the eighteenth century for the dead to be buried in church. Entire church floors would be paved with individual tombstones, so that the structure actually rises on top of cemeteries (p. 48).

OPPOSITE. *Les Innocents in the Time of François I*, sixteenth century. The cemetery was surrounded by charnel houses that contained the bones removed from older graves to make room for new ones. These charnels served as covered galleries, funerary chapels, and ossuaries (pages 54–5).

The Christ of the Book of Revelation, with the four winged beasts. Sculpture on the Royal Portal, Chartres, twelfth century. "The people of the early Middle Ages awaited the return of Christ without fear of the Last Judgment" (page 97).

The Last Judgment. Sculpture on the south portal, Chartres, thirteenth century. The apocalyptic inspiration disappeared, leaving the idea of judgment predominant. Christ's Second Coming became in the minds of Christians a court of justice, over which He would preside, on a judge's throne, surrounded by the twelve apostles, hearing intercessors plead for mercy and pardon for individual souls (page 101).

ABOVE LEFT. *Saint Sebastian Interceding for the Plague-Stricken*, 1497–9, Josse Lieferinxe. The last ordeal has replaced the Last Judgment. "The dying man attends his own drama as a witness," as heaven and hell struggle for his soul. Frequently, a saint intercedes with the Father to sway the contest (pages 109–10).

ABOVE RIGHT. *Death*, the shop of Hans Memling, late fifteenth century. A number of paintings of the period demonstrate a desire to force traditional iconography toward the more sensational aspects of death: the cadaver and the cemetery. The ambiguous figure may be Death, ruler of the cemetery, or a corpse from an opened grave, with grimacing head and skin intact except for its open belly (page 115).

BELOW. The tomb of Jean de Lagrange, 1402. The "transi," or half-decomposed corpse, one of the most significant representations of death in the macabre iconography of the fourteenth to the sixteenth centuries, reflects a new sensibility toward death and the threat of personal destruction (pages 112–14).

Danse Macabre, fifteenth century, la Chaise-Dieu. "The danse macabre is an eternal round in which the dead alternate with the living. The dead lead the dance; indeed, they are the only ones dancing. Each couple consists of a naked mummy, rotting, sexless, and highly animated, and a man or woman, dressed according to his or her social condition and paralyzed by surprise" (page 116).

The Triumph of Death, Florentine School, fifteenth century. "The subject . . . is no longer the personal confrontation between man and death, but the collective power of death. Death, in the form of a mummy or skeleton, stands with his symbolic weapon in his hand, driving a huge slow chariot drawn by oxen. One recognizes this vehicle as the heavy cart used for holiday processions, inspired by mythology and intended for the grand entries of princes into their loyal towns" (page 118).

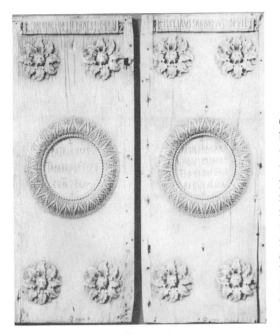

Consular diptych of Flavius Petrus Sabbaticus Justinianus, Byzantine, sixth century. "The diptychs were originally ivory tablets, carved and engraved, that were presented by the consuls as official notification on the day they took office. On identical tablets, or on old consular diptychs, Christians inscribed the list of names that was read aloud after the procession of the offerings." This three-part list (the living, the saints, and the dead) formed the company of the elect, whom God would not confound on the Day of Judgment (pages 149–50).

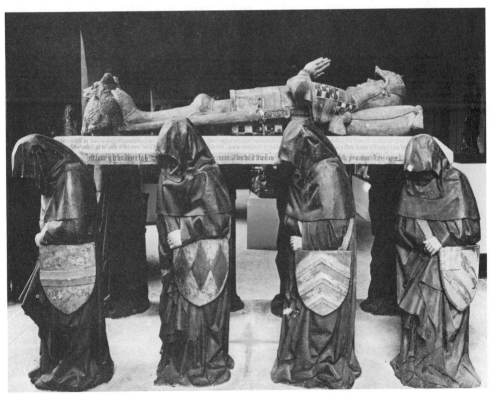

The tomb of Philippe Pot of Burgundy, fifteenth century. "After the thirteenth century, the solemn procession of mourners became the symbolic image of death and funerals." It "was henceforth regarded as the most significant moment in the whole ceremony" and appears in some of the most famous funerary sculpture in France (page 166).

ABOVE. Roman sarcophagus, with portrait of a physician seated in front of his cabinet of surgical instruments, fourth century. In ancient cemeteries, whether Roman or Christian, the tomb bore both an inscription summarizing the life of the dead person and, frequently, a portrait as symbol of his or her personality (page 202).

BELOW. Sarcophagus of Saint Theodechilde, seventh century, Crypt of Jouarre. Starting around the fifth century, both inscriptions and portraits on tombs begin to disappear, to be replaced by floral or abstract decoration in a shift in emphasis from commemoration to silence. An exception is this beautiful tomb, with its praise of Saint Theodechilde, first Abbess of the women's community (page 210).

Mural tomb of Guillaume Caucelme de Taillet, thirteenth century, Arles-sur-Tech. The earliest tombs, when they ceased to take the form of sarcophagi, were usually vertical and mural (pages 212, 239).

The earliest style of recumbent figures on tombs "do not represent dead people. ... They have their eyes wide open and the folds of their garments fall as if they were standing up instead of lying down" (page 241). The Abbot Isarnus (ABOVE) holds a crozier in his hands. Jean d'Alluye (BELOW LEFT) "stands" in the traditional posture with hands joined, as does the unknown lady (BELOW RIGHT), possibly Margaret of Gloucester.

Funerary monument of Louis XII and Anne de Bretagne, sixteenth century, Jean Juste, Abbey of Saint-Denis, Paris. By this period, "the model that was to dominate funerary iconography from the late Middle Ages to the beginning of modern times" —the superimposition of the recumbent and the praying figures—finds its most imposing expression in the massive, free-standing two-level tombs of the Valois. Here the sculpted body of the king lies stiffening in death. Above are the praying figures of Louis and Anne (pages 252–4).

LEFT. Funerary statue of Marie de Barbancon-Cany, attributed to Barthelemy Prieur (d. 1611), Palace of Versailles. By the seventeenth century, life-size praying figures were placed not just on top of the tomb, but almost anywhere in the church— a corner of the family chapel or near the choir as if attending services (pages 258–9).

RIGHT. The tomb of Nicolas Aubry, 1621, cemetery chapel, Saint-Hilaire, Marville. The mural tombs in this tiny church, almost all dating from the seventeenth century, are remarkable examples of the ordinary lower-class tomb of the *ancien régime*. Here, though badly damaged, one can still see the praying figures, the deceased kneeling with wife and family (page 274).

been as indifferent as ever to the container in which their body was placed and as free from any desire to identify it. In the case of Souillac, the monolithic coffin, the ancient sarcophagus, was used throughout the Middle Ages and perhaps as late as the fifteenth century. Its use is more common in Italy than in France, but not widespread in the Western world.

From the Sarcophagus to the Coffin or Bier

Another phenomenon that must be related to the disappearance of the funerary epigraph is the geographic separation between the funerary monument, when it does exist, and the actual container of the body, the exact place of burial. The abandonment of the stone coffin is one sign of this evolution.

In rare cases of important personages venerated in the manner of saints, the stone coffin was replaced after the thirteenth century by the lead coffin; lead is a substance as permanent as stone. We observe that the lead coffin was just as bare of ornamentation as the stone one, a fact that had nothing to do with the material of which it was made. (The eighteenth-century lead tombs of the Hapsburgs at the Capuchin monastery in Vienna are covered with ornaments and inscriptions.)

Generally speaking, after the thirteenth century, the new coffin is made of wood. This is an important change that has not been given the attention it deserves.

Two French words have been used to refer to the wooden sarcophagus: *cercueil* and *bière*. *Cercueil* comes from the same root as *sarceu*, or *sarcophagus*. Antoine Furetière defines it as "a lead coffin for transporting and burying the dead." We note the persistence of the idea of transport. But he adds, "When it is made of wood, it is called *bière*."[5]

But *bière* is none other than *civière*. *Cercueil* and *bière* were used indiscriminately to designate the litter used to transport the body to its place of burial. This primitive meaning of the word was to persist in charity burials, burials "without a box." In such cases the body, sewn into a crude winding sheet made of sacking, was carried to the cemetery on an ordinary *bière*, that is, a stretcher, then removed and thrown into the grave. The *bière* was then taken back to the church. This type of burial can still be seen today in small country churches in England.

Later, both *cercueil* and *bière* acquired their modern meaning of the box in which the body was definitively buried.

In Enguerrand de Monstrelet's *Chronique,* "the heart and horn of the good duke were each placed in a flat coffin (*pla sercus*) and covered with a bier of Irish wood."[6] But in the seventeenth century, Richelet defines *bière* as "a kind of chest made of wood or lead."[7]

Before we conclude this analysis of the words for sarcophagus, bier, and coffin, two observations should be made. First, the importance acquired by the *bière*, or *cercueil*, seems to have been contemporary with the importance invested in the actual conveying of the body; indeed it was then that the procession became an essential element of the funeral ceremony.

Second, the enclosing of the body in the coffin (see chapter 4) is a psychological consequence of the disappearance of the sarcophagus, a development that in its turn made the whole notion of the tomb less precise. In antiquity, there were only two types of tomb: the sarcophagus, or its poor imitation, and the humble cavity in the common cemetery. As long as the body was laid in a sarcophagus or chest of stone, it was simply wrapped in a sheet or shroud. When the use of the stone sarcophagus was abandoned, the body wrapped in its shroud could have been placed directly in the ground, without further protective covering—an ancient practice that persists to this day in Islamic countries. In the medieval West, however, there seems to have been an aversion to this bareness. It was then that the bier that served for transport was transformed into a closed wooden chest, the *sarceu*. This solution also satisfied the new need to conceal the body and face of the dead man from the eyes of the living. Hence, the coffin became a substitute for the tomb, a tomb that was just as anonymous as the stone one had been, and also corruptible. For, once placed in the ground, the wooden coffin underwent a rapid destruction that was considered desirable. Burial without a coffin became the equivalent of burial without a tomb, since the role of tomb had been filled by the sarcophagus and then transmitted to the coffin. Except in Islamic countries, burial without a coffin was ignominious, or at any rate, it was a pauper's burial.

The transition from the sarcophagus to the coffin further accentuated the anonymity of burial and the indifference regarding its exact location. This cultural trait that, as we have seen, characterizes the period from the end of Christian antiquity to the eleventh and twelfth centuries, seems to introduce a hiatus in the tradition—possibly several thousand years old— of the cult of the dead.

Commemoration and Burial

We shall now see that this attitude of anonymity steadily declined in Latin Christendom after the twelfth century, a decline that began first among the rich and powerful. However, anonymity persisted until the eighteenth century, at least among the poor, who first were deprived of coffins and later of memorial tombs. One of the major differences between the rich, or the less poor, and the real poor is that the first group tended increasingly to have individual tombs to preserve the memory of their bodies, while the second group had nothing.

The bodies of the poor and of the young children of the rich, who were treated like the poor, were sewn into shrouds made of cheap sacking and thrown into big, common graves. Charitable men of the fourteenth to seventeenth centuries, offended by the physical and spiritual abandonment of dead paupers in a society that was already relatively urbanized, sought to remedy what seemed to them the cruelest aspect of this dereliction, namely, the absence of help from the Church. They found it intolerable that those who drowned in the rivers or were the anonymous victims of disasters should be left to rot on the dump like animals, executed criminals, or the excommunicate. And so they formed the confraternities in order to provide these people with burial on church soil and the prayers of the clergy. But the pious confreres themselves did not mind the anonymity of these charity burials, something that would become intolerable two centuries later.

At the beginning of the early modern era, giving a public existence to one's own grave or to those of one's relatives was not experienced as a necessity. Burial on church soil was a charitable duty toward the poor, to whom circumstances had denied it. But the personalization and publicity of such burial was still a spiritual luxury. It was a luxury that was undoubtedly being extended to a larger stratum of the population, especially among the master artisans in the towns, but one whose absence was not yet regarded as an intolerable frustration. To bury the poor was acceptable; to give them individual and visible graves was not— or, at any rate, not yet.

Even among the rich and powerful, the need to perpetuate one's memory by means of a visible monument did not assert itself for a long time. As late as the sixteenth and seventeenth centuries there were numerous distinguished testators who differed from most of their contemporaries and peers in expressing no desire for a visible tomb. Even those who did request visible tombs did not insist that they coincide precisely with the places where their bodies were buried; mere proximity was enough. For them the tomb was not synonymous with the container of the body.

It was understood that this first resting-place for the body was temporary. Everyone was aware that sooner or later his dried-out bones would be
transferred to the charnels "all jumbled up together" *(ensemble en ung tas
pesle mesle)*, as Villon put it. When that happened, it would take "a strong
pair of glasses"—

> *At les Innocents to tell*
> *The decent people from the uncouth,*

or the rich from the poor, or the powerful from the destitute:

> *When I consider all the skills*
> *That piled up in those charnels be*
> *All could have been officials*
> *In the public treasury*
> *Or humble porters. Who can say*
> *Of the bishop or the bum*
> *Which of them is which today?*
> *To one favor all are come.*

Our modern idea of the "grant in perpetuity" was totally alien to the
mentality of this multisecular age.

Although the functions of commemoration of the personality and
containment of the body were not necessarily combined in the same place,
as in the ancient tomb or the modern cemetery, neither were they totally
separated; both were supposed to remain within the same ecclesiastical
enclosure. And it was always possible to have more than one tomb for a
single body, either because the body had been dismembered—there could
be separate tombs for the flesh, bowels, heart, or bones—or because the
aspect of commemoration prevailed completely over that of containment,
and monuments were built in several places, with no particular importance
accorded to the one that contained the physical body.

Viewed from the perspective of Sirius—or of today—such an evolution might seem like the beginning of a new attitude of detachment, a
liberation from old pagan superstitions regarding a mortal husk that was
no longer of any importance once it was devoid of life. But this attitude
was not quite that of the scientific agnostic or the Christian reformer in
our contemporary cultures. Moreover, after the eleventh century, we shall
witness a return to the individuality of the grave and its corollary, the
positive value attached to the dead body. It is a long and uneven evolution that may in certain respects resemble a return to Roman paganism,
but that will eventually culminate in the cult of the dead and of tombs of

the nineteenth and first half of the twentieth century.

I mention it here only to call attention to the tendency and to indicate the direction, as yet imperceptible, of the movement. But it would take centuries and cultural revolutions to arrive at this *terminus ad quem* in the nineteenth century. At the time we are writing about now, the heart of the Middle Ages, what strikes us is the reluctance with which the anonymity of the early Middle Ages was abandoned.

The Exceptions: Saints and Great Men

In fact, during the early Middle Ages, the identification of graves and the commemoration of the deceased had not disappeared so completely as we may have implied. There were a few illustrious exceptions in the case of saints and other great and venerable persons.

Saints were all thaumaturges (that is, miracle workers) and intercessors, and the faithful had to communicate directly with their relics, had to touch them in order to receive their magical emanations. Consequently, the tombs of saints necessarily coincided with their remains; indeed, there were as many tombs or reliquaries as there were fragments of their bodies. For example, the tomb of Saint Sernin, the martyred bishop of Toulouse, was in the confession of the abbey consecrated to him outside the town of Toulouse; but a fragment of his body was also exhibited in a twelfth-century-style sarcophagus modeled after those of antiquity at the abbey of Saint-Hilaire-de-l'Aude, where it can still be admired today. All the bodies of the confessors, martyrs, and evangelists of Christian Gaul have been the objects of a tactile worship that persists to this day. In 1944, at Saint-Etienne-du-Mont, in Paris, I saw with my own eyes the faithful file by to touch the reliquary of Sainte Geneviève.

These tombs were usually stone sarcophagi, with or without commemorative inscriptions. In the latter case the fame of the saint, or iconography, took the place of an inscription.

The so-called Crypt of Jouarre gives us an opportunity to analyze this mingled desire for commemoration and for silence. Dedicated in 630 to the founder of the abbey, Saint Adon, and to the blessed abbesses and bishops in his family, the crypt is all that remains of a cemeterial church in which the graves accumulated *ad sanctos* around the tombs of the revered founders. These were placed on a sort of platform, which has now disappeared but which once occupied one of the side aisles of the edifice. In the oldest part we can still see the oldest sarcophagi, which date from the Merovingian era. That of Saint Adon, brother of Saint Omer and disciple of the great Irish missionary Saint Columba, is quite bare of inscription or decoration. But that of his cousin Saint Theodechilde, first abbess of the women's community, is ornamented with a magnificent inscription in very beautiful handwriting: *"Hoc Membra Post Ultima Teguntur Fata Sepulchro Beatae"* (this tomb contains the last remains of the blessed Theodechilde). "Virgin without stain, of noble race, shining with merits." There is a biographical notice: "Mother of this monastery, she taught her daughters, virgins dedicated to the Lord, to run toward Christ." And the inscription concludes with the proclamation of celestial beatitude *"Haec Demu Exultat Paradisi Triumpho"* (now dead, she exults at last in the glory of paradise).[8]

The other two sarcophagi, those of her cousin Saint Aguilberte and her brother, Saint Agilbert, bishop of Dorchester, and later of Paris, are covered with carvings, but without inscriptions. That of Saint Agilbert is illustrated with the scene of the Second Coming which we discussed in chapter 3.

Thus, of the uppermost, visible sarcophagi, those of the founding saints, only one has an inscription, two are without inscriptions but are carved, and another is completely bare. Of course, one cannot be sure that inscriptions were not originally affixed to the wall over the anonymous sarcophagi. In any case, they have disappeared, and no one has thought to preserve or restore them. The graphic quality of Sainte Theodechilde's inscription and the formal beauty of the carvings is such that in the presence of these masterpieces, it is difficult to attribute the trend toward anonymity and bareness in sarcophagi to the inadequacy of scribes or artists. These sarcophagi were opened in 1627, in the presence of Maria de Medici. "When the coffins were opened, the two blessed abbesses appeared still intact and dressed as nuns, each in a sort of mantle of cloth of gold of which nothing remained but a few strands of gold thread and a clasp, also of gold, which Mme. Jeanne de Lorraine [the abbess] presented to Queen Maria de Medici. . . . The three holy bodies were placed in shrines and their heads in reliquaries of vermeil made for the purpose."[9]

Another example is provided by the graves of the popes of the third to the tenth century, which have been painstakingly studied by Jean Charles-Picard. These tombs *ad sanctos* consist of either a simple unburied sarcophagus *(sursum)* surmounted by an inscription, which has been preserved, or a chapel in a church, such as Saint Peter's. This chapel is composed of an apsidiole, an altar that contains the relics of the saint near whom the pope has chosen to be buried, and a sarcophagus, which Charles-Picard believes may have been buried three-quarters below the surface, so that only the lid was visible. There were two possibilities: Either the pope was a canonized saint, or else he was not regarded as a saint at the time of his death, but even in this case, he felt the need to have a visible and public tomb built during his lifetime. (Some of these tombs were moved because they were no longer visible enough in their original location.) Charles-Picard sees this choice of the location and form of the tomb as an affirmation of pontifical authority. The *memoria* of Mellebaude at the Hypogée des Dunes, in Poitiers, is not essentially different from this Roman pontifical model.[10]

One is struck by the desire for commemoration, particularly in the case of popes. Consider, for example, the funerary inscription of Gregory the Great, which has been reproduced, among many other places, in the article devoted to the great pope in the *Légende dorée:*[11]

A. *Suscipe, Terra, tuo Corpus de Corpore Sumptum*
    Receive, O Earth, this body taken from your body
B. *Reddere Quod Valeas, Vivificante Deo.*
    Which you must surrender when God shall bring it
    back to life.
C. *Spiritus Astra Petit, Leti Nil Supra Nocebunt,*
    His soul rises to the stars, death cannot harm him,
D. *Cui Vitae Alterius Mors Magis Ipsa Vita Est.*
    For whom the death of this body is the real life.
E. *Pontificis Summi Hoc Clauduntur Membra Sepulchro*
    In this tomb lies the body of the Sovereign Pontiff
F. *Qui Innumeris Semper Vivit Ubique Bonis.*
    Who by his innumerable benefits lives everywhere and
    forever.

Each line of this text expresses an interesting and significant idea.

In line A, there is the theme of *ubi sunt,* the return of the body to the earth, but this theme is only touched upon, not emphasized. The development of the idea actually takes the opposite direction. Indeed, the theme of the return to the earth is immediately corrected by that of the promised resurrection, *"Vivicante Deo,"* in line B. In line C, the theme of the migration of the soul toward heaven is contrasted with the temporary return of the body to the earth. This old idea occurs frequently in Christian inscriptions; for example, this one from the eleventh century: *"Clauditur hoc tumulo Bernardi corpus in atro ipsius* (This dark tomb contains the body of Bernard) *et anima deerat superna per astra* (while his soul is carried to the stars)."[12]

In line D, we have the Pauline theme of victory over death, the life that is more real than earthly life, which was a commonplace of traditional eschatology. But like the return to earth, this idea is also, if not attenuated, at least expanded by the glorious conclusion of the inscription, which occurs in line F, after the identification of the tomb in line E. A pious nineteenth-century translator recoiled from the *vivit* in line F, and obscured the meaning: "Whose universal benefits are proclaimed everywhere and forever." His benefits are not merely proclaimed; they cause the dead man to *live* on earth just as his soul enjoys life in heaven, *ad astra.*

"*Mens videt astra*" (the soul sees the stars) reads another inscription, perhaps contemporaneous with this one, which can be seen in Toulouse. The inscription concerns a certain Nymphius, a distinguished resident of his town. But this celestial immortality, obtained by the *sancta fides* (holy faith) that scatters darkness, is accompanied by an earthly immortality that is dependent on fame. "Just renown (*fama*) bore you to the stars (*ad astra*) and has given you a place in the highest ranks of heaven. You shall be immortal (*immortalis eris*) [it is difficult to tell which of the two kinds of immortality is meant], for praise shall keep your glory alive in future genera-tions (*per venturos populos*)."[13] This is the *gloriam quaerere* of classical antiquity that Sallust used as the epigraph of his *Bellum Catilinae.*

Finally, here is a later tomb, from the beginning of the twelfth cen-tury, which is also that of an important ecclesiastical figure, Begon, who was abbot of Conques from 1087 to 1107. This tomb is also accompanied by an inscription, which reads:

1. "*Hic est abbas situs . . . de nomine Bego vocatus*" (Here lies the abbot known as Begon): the identification of the grave. There is no date, and the omission is significant; we have not yet entered historical time.

2. Next comes the eulogy: a learned theologian *("divina lege peritus"),* a holy man *("vir Domino gratus"),* a benefactor of the abbey: He was responsible for the construction of the cloister.

3. "*Hic est laudandus per secula. Vir venerandus vivat in aeternum Regem laudando superum.*" The double consequence of his virtue and his power is fame in this world *(per secula)* and eternal life in heaven *(in aeternum).*

Here the inscription is an integral part of the tomb, and just as valuable. It is a mural tomb, a bas-relief framed by the inscription and located in a niche on the exterior of the church, against the south wall of the transept (the side that was most sought after by the first popes in the old church of Saint Peter's). The origin of this type of tomb, which is very ancient, is the sarcophagus under an arcosolium in a Roman catacomb. But here there is no longer a sarcophagus, which does not mean that there never was one. However, today one has the impression that what matters here is less the body itself in the sarcophagus than the commemorative slab, that is, the bas-relief beneath which the body may have been laid without this fact having any unusual importance.

This bas-relief, which was no doubt commissioned by Begon himself, represents the sacred conversation of the abbot with heaven, his assumption. The figure of Christ is in the center, flanked by Begon and a saint who must be Saint Foy, patron saint of the monastery. There are also two angels. One is crowning the saint, the other is holding his hands over the tonsured head of Begon. It will be noted that here the inscription is accompanied by a portrait, which is the image not of the human being but of a *beatus,* a saint, living henceforth for a blessed eternity in the celestial court, praising the Lord *(Regem laudando).* Begon is not a canonized saint but, like the noncanonized popes, he is nevertheless a real *beatus,* a predestinate, one who is assured of both eternal salvation and earthly fame. Because he was not a thaumaturge, it is no longer necessary to expose his body to the contact of the faithful. Also in cases like his there will not be the same concern for the exact location of the body, which will indeed be a matter of indifference. On the other hand, the personage is important and worthy of fame and veneration, whence the necessity of a commemorative tomb that will be maintained and even rebuilt when the opportunity arises if it starts to deteriorate with time. There are many examples of very old and venerable tombs that were rebuilt in the twelfth and thirteenth centuries.

Those tombs that survived until the early Middle Ages—with or without inscriptions, with or without effigies—express the concern to leave a memory behind. They express the conviction that there is a correspondence between heavenly eternity and earthly fame, a conviction that may then have been restricted to a few superior beings but that later became one of the distinguishing characteristics of the late Middle Ages and even of the nineteenth and twentieth centuries. The *Vie de Saint Alexis* recognizes the truth that the eternity of heaven is "the most lasting glory," which an intelligent self-interest invites one to prefer to a fame that is merely worldly but that is not qualitatively different.[14] In the heaven of the *Chanson de Roland,* the blessed are *glorieux,* saints in glory.

The saint is not always of clerical origin. We have seen that Roland became a model of the secular saint, which impressed itself on the world of clergymen and on Christian spirituality.[15] The feudal saint dominates the Arthurian cycle. A complex process of cross-fertilization between profane and ecclesiastical cultures culminated in the eleventh century in certain conceptions of piety and sanctity. These conceptions encompassed values that today are regarded as properly religious as well as others that seem to us rather of the earth and of this world. Until the sixteenth century, at least, the distinction is difficult to perceive. This is only another form of the ambiguity involving *aeterna* and *temporalia* that we found in wills, in the *artes moriendi*, and in the macabre. The myth of the Crusade revived and exalted the chivalric parallel between immortality and fame: "We shall now see who they are [the future Crusaders] who wish to earn the praises of the world and of God, for they shall win them both with honor."[16]

"Honor and service rendered to God" went hand in hand with "honor and glory won for eternity." The dead Crusaders "would win paradise . . . and would earn eternal fame, like Roland and the twelve peers who died at Roncevaux in the service of God."[17]

Ascetic disciples of the *contemptus mundi* did not escape the contagion of the chivalric cult of fame. The author of the *ubi sunt*, who might well have provided a model for Villon, agrees that nothing remains on earth of men who were once illustrious. But everything depends on the basis of their fame. The great Christian writers are spared this erosion of time, for they possess "lasting glory." For example, Gregory the Great, who "lives everywhere and forever," as his epitaph foretold, is still read, as Bernard of Cluny says, "far from worldly acclaim," in the solitude of retreats and cloisters. "His [earthly] fame shall endure throughout the ages, the world shall sing his praises, his fame shall endure now and forever. His pen of gold and fire shall never die, and the treasures contained in his pages shall be reaped by posterity."[18]

This relationship between the two forms of survival, the eschatological and the earthly, lasted a very long time. It survived the Renaissance and early modern times and was still perceptible in the positivist worship of the famous dead in the nineteenth century. In our industrial societies, the two forms of survival have been abandoned simultaneously, as if they were interdependent. And yet today we are inclined to regard them as contradictory. The secular and rationalist militants of the nineteenth century hoped to replace one with the other, and their opinion still influences us today. But the people of the Middle Ages and the Renaissance, like those of antiquity, believed them to be complementary.

Certain Renaissance authors whom we know thanks to Tenenti have theorized about this ambiguity, which was perfectly conscious. Porretane has the Dominican Giambattista speak about paradise. According to the monk, the happiness of those in paradise has two sources. The first is self-evident: the beatific vision, the face-to-face contact with God. The second is more surprising to us: the memory of good done on earth, that is, fame, for it was almost inconceivable that any good deed could remain altogether secret. This was a secondary cause *(praemium accidentale)*, but it counted. For the lay audience of the Dominican monk, things are even simpler. "Man must do everything he can in this world to obtain the honor, glory, and fame that make him worthy of heaven and that thus lead him to enjoy eternal peace." According to another humanist, Giovanni da Conversano, "The greatest felicity is, therefore, to be celebrated and honored in this world, and to enjoy eternal beatitude in the next."[19]

The motto of Duke Federigo da Montefeltro, which can still be read on the inlaid work in his *studiolo* in Urbino, summed up the same faith in the inevitable transition from terrestrial glory to celestial immortality: *"Virtutibus itur ad astra"* (by one's brilliant accomplishments, one goes to heaven). The formula is reminiscent of the epitaph of Gregory the Great. Even popes had to make themselves known by their virtues and prestige, as they wished their tombs to testify to future generations.

This difficulty in separating the idea of supernatural survival from the idea of fame acquired during earthly life stems from the lack of a clear-cut separation between this world and the next. Death was neither complete separation nor total annihilation. After the sixteenth century, rational and scientific thought, like Protestant and Catholic religious reform, tried to dissociate the two forms of survival. It did not immediately succeed; the Mediterranean baroque preserved something of the ancient communication across the barrier of death right in the midst of the Counter-Reformation. Similarly, in Puritanism, worldly success remained attached to the idea of predestination. In the celebrations of the French Revolution and in the debates over funerals and cemeteries of the Directory and the Consulate, something of this connection persisted; it would not really be dissolved until the middle of the twentieth century. In common practice, in the sixteenth and seventeenth centuries, and even in the eighteenth century, the commemoration of the living person was not separated from the salvation of his soul. Indeed, this is the fundamental meaning of the tomb.

The Situation
at the End of the Tenth Century

Thus, we see that by the end of the early Middle Ages—around the tenth and eleventh centuries—the visible tomb had lost its eschatological function in favor of burial *ad sanctos*. It was no longer necessary, either for the salvation of the deceased or for the peace of mind of the survivors, that the container of his body be exhibited publicly or even that its exact location be indicated. The only important condition was burial *ad sanctos*.

Public tombs identified by inscriptions had therefore disappeared, except in the case of saints, whose monuments had always to coincide with the body, and in the case of personages more or less comparable to saints —on sixth- and seventh-century mosaics, they wore the square halo instead of the round one—whose monuments no longer always coincided with the body. These two cases were exceptional.

There were, then, two categories of persons. The first category included almost all of the population, for whom an absolute faith in their survival prevailed over the memory of the body (which was entrusted to saints) and of earthly life: those who had little to say and had done nothing remarkable. The second category included those very rare individuals who had a message to communicate: those who possessed round or square halos. The first group had no tombs; they had confessed their faith and certitude by requesting burial *ad sanctos*. The second group had tombs that expressed the same eschatological belief but that also ensured the commemoration of their exceptional merits. In the latter case, the visible tomb represented both an eschatological act and a desire for commemoration.

The situation that we have just summarized might well have lasted at least as long as burial *ad sanctos* or in churches. The rise of rationalism, secularization, or agnosticism—whatever one wishes to call this aspect of modernity—in the nineteenth and twentieth centuries might well have replaced the old belief in survival and thus maintained the anonymity of the common graves, albeit for different reasons. In this case we would not have had the nineteenth-century cult of tombs and cemeteries, nor would we have twentieth-century administrative problems regarding the decomposition of bodies.

But things did not turn out this way. After the eleventh century, a new period began, a long and continuous period during which the use of the visible tomb—which was often separate from the body—became more frequent. The desire for commemoration spread from the great personages to include ordinary mortals, who very discreetly and gradually sought to emerge from their anonymity. However, they were still reluctant to go beyond a certain threshold of visibility or realistic presence that varies from one period to the next.

The Reappearance of the Inscription

The first important and highly significant phenomenon was the reappearance of the funerary inscription. Its return coincides approximately with the disappearance of the anonymous sarcophagus, which was replaced by the lead coffin, or simply by shrouding, that is, the burial of the body wrapped only in a shroud.

In the Parisian cemetery of Saint-Marcel one notes around the twelfth century the reappearance of inscriptions that had disappeared after the Paleo-Christian era.[20] Their reappearance has been attributed to a "revival of the ancient taste for epitaphs." But as we shall see, it was seldom until the fifteenth and especially the sixteenth century that epigraphic style deliberately imitated classical models. The earliest medieval epitaphs manifest quite spontaneously a new need to assert one's identity in death, a need that appeared at about the same time as the development of the iconography of the Last Judgment and the religious obligation to make one's will.

The use of the epitaph did not catch on immediately; there were resistances to be overcome. The twelfth-century tomb of a great ecclesiastical dignitary such as the abbot of la Bussière, in Burgundy, which was reproduced by Gaignières, is identified only by the sign of four croziers overcoming two dragons, an image more compelling than words.[21] And for a long time, even after the epitaph had become common and was starting to be positively garrulous, this archaic brevity continued to be found on tombs, especially those of monks and abbots. It is nevertheless true that in a few centuries the Western world moved from anonymous silence to a biographical rhetoric that, though precise, was also abundant, sometimes even redundant; from the brevity of the official death notice to the fullness of biography, from a discreet statement of identity to an expression of familial solidarity.

The Statement of Identity

The earliest epitaphs of ordinary people—those of popes and saints adhered longer to the style of Roman epigraphy—were confined to a brief statement of identity and sometimes a word of praise. Of course, they were reserved for important persons, such as the bishops of Châlons from the tenth to the twelfth century, who were buried in their cathedral: *"Hic jacet Gibuinis bonus epis"* (998), or *"Fridus I Epis"* (1247). Or an abbot of Citeaux, *"Hic jacet Bartholomeus quondam abbas loci istius"* (1083).[22]

In addition to the name, epitaphs soon started including the date of death—the year, and sometimes also the month and day, as on a slab preserved in the museum in Colmar, *"Anno Domini MCXX, XI Kalendas Martii Obiit bone memorie Burcard miles de Gebbiswill . . . Fundator loci istius,"*[23] or on a small stone embedded in the exterior wall of the church in Auvillar in Tarn-et-Garonne, *"N. Marcii incarnationis MCCXXXVI obiit Reverendus Pater Delesmus Capellanus hujus ecclesiae."*

The first tentative examples culminated in an epigraphic style that lasted into the fourteenth century and even beyond, despite the competition of more redundant formulas inspired by other motivations. In the twelfth and thirteenth centuries, the epitaph was almost always in Latin, *Hic jacet,* followed by the name of the deceased and his profession (*miles, rector, cappellanus, cantor, prior claustralis,* etc.), then *obiit,* and ending with a set phrase that had several variations: *Hic requiescit, Hic situs est, Hic est sepultura, Ista sepultura est, Hic sunt in fossa corporis ossa, In hoc tumulo,* and the rarer and more prestigious *Clauditur corpus.*

In the fourteenth century this formulation still persists, but more often in French, although Latin was to make a strong comeback in the late fifteenth and sixteenth centuries. There were all sorts of variations on the *ci-gît:* "Here lies the venerable and prudent so-and-so, who passed away in the year of grace such-and-such"; "Here lies a noble and wise knight"; "Here lies a bourgeois shoemaker of Paris"; "Here lies a bourgeois inn-keeper of Paris," concluding with a pious addition in French or Latin: "Who has gone to the Lord" (1352); "may his soul rejoice in Christ for all eternity" (1369); "may his soul rest in peace" (very common); "God has his soul. Amen"; "May God by his grace forgive his sins. Amen"; "Let us pray to God that he be remembered"; and so on.

The Appeal to the Passerby and the Prayer

Until the fourteenth century, the common epitaph consisted of two parts. The first, and older, part was a notice of identity giving the name, profession, sometimes a very brief word of praise, and the date of death. In the majority of cases, the epitaph did not include either the person's age or his date of birth. The second part, which became common in the fourteenth century, was a prayer to God for the soul of the deceased. The salvation of the soul of the Christian buried *ad sanctos* was no longer as certain as it had been during the preceding periods and the early Middle Ages. The prayer was inspired by a contemporary preoccupation with individual judgment and testamentary endowments.

At first sight, this prayer appears to be the anonymous prayer of the Church. But finding it reiterated constantly on stone and brass, on floors and walls, leads one to assume that it was intended to be said by someone; it invites a dialogue between the dead writer and the living reader. In reality a two-way communication was being established, a message to the deceased for the repose of his soul, and from the deceased for the edification of the living. In this way the inscription became both a lesson and an appeal. As early as the twelfth century, albeit still rarely, epitaphs on ecclesiastical tombs, written by clergymen—sometimes by the deceased himself—took the form of a pious invitation to survivors to better understand, by means of this visible example, the great Pauline lesson of death. This is the very ancient tradition of the *contemptus mundi* and the *memento mori,* which we are much too inclined to confine to the macabre periods of the late Middle Ages.

Sometimes the deceased writer confronts the survivor directly. A canon of Saint-Etienne, in Toulouse, who died in 1177 calls him *lector* and tells him: "If you wish to see what I was once and not what I am now, you deceive yourself, O reader who disdains to live in Christ. Death is a victory for you if, in dying, you enter into the happiness of eternal life."[24]

In the cloister of Saint-Victor, in Paris, there was once an inscription that expressed the same sentiment. It was that of a doctor to King Louis VI who died between 1130 and 1138. Addressing himself directly to the passerby, he confesses the vanity of medicine in comparison with God, while nevertheless hoping that God will be the medicine of his soul, and adds: "What we were, you are. What we are, you will become." The idea has become commonplace.[25]

In these two twelfth-century texts the deceased, or the author of his inscription, does not solicit the prayers of the passerby. The latter is merely invited to meditate on death and be converted.

This theme was persistent. We meet it again, among other places, in the cemetery of Saint-Sulpice on a 1545 tombstone cited by Sauval. It is the tomb of a twenty-three-year-old Frisian student who died in Paris, far from home. "What I was once, this effigy shows. What I am now, for all I know, my scattered dust will teach you." After a confession of faith that summarizes the doctrines of original sin, incarnation, and the resurrection of the body, he invites the passerby to be converted "and to mortify yourself, so that God will give you life."[26]

This appeal to conversion continues to appear in inscriptions in the seventeenth century, in less developed form.

In the fourteenth century another theme appears. The dead man no longer addresses the living person only to convert him, but also to obtain from him a prayer of intercession by which he may escape damnation or the torments of purgatory. For example, here is the mural epitaph of a Montmorency who died in 1387 and was buried in the church in Taverny:

> *Good people who pass this way,*
> *To God unceasingly please pray*
> *For the soul of the body that lies below.*

Care is taken to distinguish the soul from the body, a new development in this genre of literature in the thirteenth and fourteenth centuries. Next comes the notice of identity, accompanied by the brief traditional eulogy:

> *He was a man of great piety.*
> *Bouchard du Ru was his name.*
> *He died in 1387*
> *On the twenty-fifth day of October.*
> *Pray God he be remembered. Amen!*

This late fourteenth-century notice of identity still does not give the age of the deceased.

But who is this passerby? As men of the twentieth century, we must beware of making a serious misinterpretation. The passerby is not, as we would tend to assume on the basis of our own customs, a relative, friend, or familiar of the deceased, someone who knew him, who misses him and mourns him, and who comes to visit his grave. This sentiment is absolutely unknown until the end of the eighteenth century. The person who is being addressed by the deceased is literally a passerby, someone who happens to pass by the grave, a stranger who is walking through the cemetery or has come into the church either to say his prayers or because it is on his way, for, as we know, the church and the cemetery were public meeting places. Consequently the authors of wills no longer seek only the most sacred spots for their graves but also the most frequented; often the two qualities coincided. For example, this epitaph at Saint-André-des-Arts, in Paris, of a man of eighty-three who died in 1609: "Desired on the day of his death to be buried near the Blessed Sacrament [the Chapel of the Blessed Sacrament, the favorite devotion of the Counter-Reformation]." It was true that while he was alive, he had had, as he recalls, "a sincere and singular devotion to the precious body of Our Savior," but he had another reason for choosing this location: "in order to obtain mercy by the prayers of the faithful who prostrate themselves before this very holy and venerable sacrament, that I may be reborn with them in glory."[27]

In front of the crucifix at Saint-Jean-en-Grève, in Paris, Sauval found the following epitaph: "Pause here, stranger, for here rests a noble man [died in 1575]. Stranger, pray for him."[28]

Here the passerby is a devout person, but he may be simply a stroller or sightseer:

> *Thou stranger, who treadest on their ash*
> *Marvel not . . .*
> *But look, I pray, upon their noble graves.*

It is necessary to give this indifferent passerby some explanation of certain details of the tomb or the life of the deceased. The writers of inscriptions address themselves to him, not only to solicit his prayers but also to tell him a story, assuming that he will be interested in it and that he is capable of remembering it and passing it on to someone else. This is the first step in the process of fame.

In the thirteenth and fourteenth centuries, the epitaph no longer always has the extreme brevity it had in the heart of the Middle Ages. It is becoming longer and more explicit but without exaggeration, like that of Edouard de Fouilloy, bishop of Amiens, who died in 1222, and whose tomb in the cathedral in Amiens is one of the masterpieces of medieval funerary art:

> *He nourished his people. He laid the foundations of this edifice.*
> *The city was entrusted to his care.*
> *Here lies Edouard, whose fame is as fragrant as nard.*
> *He took pity on widows in distress. He was the protector of the*
> *   abandoned.*
> *He was a lamb with the gentle, a lion with the great, a unicorn with*
> *   the proud.*

Biographical Details

In this text, which is more expansive than usual, because the subject is a great and venerated personage, we encounter both the tradition of Paleo-Christian epigraphy and the use of standard forms of eulogy that would later become popular. It is this tendency toward eloquence and expansiveness that characterizes the most conspicuous epigraphy of the *ancien régime,* from the fifteenth to the eighteenth century. In Part 3 we shall examine the tendency toward simplicity that appeared at both ends of the social scale, among powerful persons eager for humility and among humble craftsmen or laborers who had ventured timidly into the cycle of recorded death. In the fourteenth century this eloquence takes the form of pious exhortation, a kind of paraphrase of the prayers for the dead. The Latin epitaphs are more repetitive and loquacious; the French ones are less common and, above all, more concise. Here is the inscription of a Montmorency at the church of Taverny:

"Here lies the knight Philippe who, as is well known, is renowned for his integrity. Open to him the gates of heaven, O judge who determines the preservation of all things, and to this pitiful creature deign to grant your mercy, O King and Father . . ." This is not the inscription either of a clergyman or of a famous personage but of a knight who is held up as an example because of his integrity. Indeed, the epitaph was usually expanded to include those virtues then considered to be the attributes of sanctity or nobility.

There is another change in funerary epigraphy that appears occasionally during the fourteenth century and almost always in the fifteenth. In addition to the date of death, we are now given the age of the deceased. After the sixteenth century, the practice became general, except on a few tombs of artisans who had too recently attained the status of the visible and speaking dead. It corresponds to a more statistical conception of human existence in which life is defined more by its length than by its content, a conception which is that of our bureaucratic and technological civilizations.

Finally, after the fifteenth century, a last trait is added to the notice of identity of the thirteenth and fourteenth centuries. This notice is no longer merely that of an individual. In the fifteenth and, above all, the sixteenth and seventeenth centuries, the funerary inscription becomes common to an entire family. It associates the first to die with his spouse and children or, if he is young, with his parents. It is a new and remarkable phenomenon: this need to state publicly on a visible tomb a familial relationship that was heretofore overlooked at this supreme moment of truth. Inscriptions became more and more often collective.

In Dijon, on a stone embedded in the exterior wall of Notre-Dame, an inscription is engraved, probably at the request of the mother, the last survivor of a family decimated by the plague. It mentions the head of the family, who passed away October 27, 1428, and his wife, who died June 28, 1439, and between these two dates, two children who died in September and October 1428, in the same epidemic that carried off the father, then another daughter in 1437, and "several of their children," whose names are not given. The list, which is without biographical comments, concludes with the standard invocation, "May God keep their souls. Amen."

All the formal elements of epigraphic literature have now been assembled: the notice of identity, the appeal to the passing stranger, the pious formula, the rhetorical development, and the inclusion of the family. These elements will be fully developed in the sixteenth and seventeenth centuries.

In the sixteenth century the pious exhortation, once limited to a few words or lines, becomes an edifying account of the life of the deceased. At the monastery of les Grands-Augustins in Paris, Anne de Marle sets the example of a good death at an early age: "Untimely death . . . announced her departure from life [it begins like a danse macabre]. Her age was scarcely eight and twenty [age appears as an important element of the account, which is becoming biographical]. Then, without consideration for the place from which she came, and setting at naught the glory to be had in this base world [albeit a legitimate glory, which justified the funeral ceremony], Anne requested that her body be placed among the poor [a remarkable act of humility worthy of being recorded on an imperishable substance] in this grave [she was not buried at the site of the epitaph, which was located in the chevet of the church, but in the common grave in the cemetery]." Here the pious, exemplary account ends, and the appeal to the passerby begins. It has the tone of a rather informal sermon: "Let us pray, dear friends, that her soul be among those blessed poor who are celebrated in this church." Anne de Marle died June 9, 1529.[29]

In the sixteenth and seventeenth centuries, as we see from this example, chosen from among many others, the epitaph becomes the account of a life, sometimes short, when the deceased is young, sometimes long, when he died old and famous.

In the sixteenth, seventeenth, and early eighteenth centuries, it very often happens that the epitaph is a true biographical account intended to glorify the deceased, something like the notice in a dictionary of celebrities, with special emphasis placed on military citations. The notices are no longer reserved for men of the church (indeed, the clergy are becoming more and more discreet in this age of the Counter-Reformation) but are very often devoted to the brilliant feats and outstanding services of men of war. The only clergymen who observe this secular style of funerary literature are themselves soldiers, the Knights of Malta.

The inscriptions that cover the floors and walls of churches and cemeteries are like the pages of a dictionary of famous people, a kind of *Who's Who* laid open for the perusal of passersby. These inscriptions are often pointed out as curiosities in the printed guides for tourists.

A few people whom life had mistreated used the epitaph as an opportunity to make a solemn protest against the injustices of fate. For example, the epitaph of Pierre Le Maistre (1562) in Saint-André-des-Arts, in Paris:[30]

> *Beneath the sacred shadow of this unyielding stone,*
> *Look, stranger, I pray you, upon the noble grave*
> *Of one who served God, Justice, and the Faith,*
> *Notary, secretary, and clerk to a great King . . .*

He met with nothing but ingratitude:

> *. . . And for all his labor earned alone*
> *Eternal oblivion for himself and for his own,*
> *Eternal oblivion, a hope that was vain,*
> *And finally death, the reward of all his pain.*

But the injustice of the great was unable to extinguish the brilliance of a reputation based only on his virtues, even if the latter were not given the recognition they deserved by his superiors. He retains for himself "the name of an honorable man." He remains forever:

> . . . Rich in that glory
> Which engraves in the heavens eternally his memory,
> Rich in that good name which overthrows the power
> Of Grave and Time and Death now and forever.

The deceased lays claim to a glory that men denied him during his lifetime but that his virtue and the reputation of this virtue assure him after his death, a glory of which his epitaph is public testimony. This resentful type of inscription is somewhat rare. On the other hand, the heroic epitaph is very common, especially in the seventeenth century, owing to the large number of casualties in the wars under Louis XIII and Louis XIV, and in the battles against the Turks. The floor of the church of Saint-Jean-de-la-Valette is covered with citations to the Order of the Crusade. Despite the vicissitudes of the Revolution and of archaeological and ecclesiastical restoration, the walls of French churches have managed to preserve a few of these. Collections of epitaphs are full of "the glory of the nobility and of the French nation," ideas that anticipate, on an individual level, our modern monuments to the war dead.

At the church of the monastery of les Celestines, in 1601, the Saint-Martin chapel had been granted to Marguerite Hurault, of the family of the Lords of Cheverny, so that she could have her parents buried there and "have made there all epitaphs and embellishments that she shall deem suitable." After her own death, her husband remarked that "in the Saint-Martin chapel there were no epitaphs, effigies, arms, or any other signs or marks of honor" of his family, and "desiring to remedy this situation and to bear visible testimony," he commissioned an inscription that summarized its history: "To the honor and memory of the family of the lords of Rostang, Alleyre, and Guienne, and of their marriages, mentioned in the oratory of this chapel, ancestors of the . . . ," and there follows a long list of marriages since the reign of Francis I, a sort of expanded genealogy with comments, which even so is incomplete: "there being also many other persons highly respected in this kingdom who are close relatives of said lord and lady of Rostang, Robertet, and Hurault."[31]

In the same monastery, in the Gesvres chapel, the epitaph of the tomb of Léon Potier, duc de Gesvres, peer of France, and founder of the chapel, who died December 9, 1704, consists of three parts. The first part is a statement of the identity of the deceased that is remarkably complete, since it includes the names of his ancestors, the third son of René, duc de Tresnes, and Mme. Marguerite de Luxembourg. The second part is an account of his brilliant exploits. We are told that in 1665, he had two horses killed under him at Nördlingen, that he was taken prisoner, and "managed to escape . . . and to rejoin his company and return to the charge." There is a list of his regiments and ranks: captain in the bodyguards, lieutenant, general: "He since served in every battle." Here is a thoroughness worthy of an obituary notice in an official newspaper. The third part is devoted to the founding of the family chapel at les Celestines; we shall return to it later.[32]

His children, the young men of the de Gesvres family who were killed in combat, were entitled to a tomb, whether or not their bodies were found, with an inscription to their glory: "To the praise of the god of armies [already!] and to the memory of the marquis de Gesvres. Stranger, you see before you the face of a gentleman whose life was so admirable that his death could only have been glorious." There follows a history of his military feats, the battles in which he took part: "For the quarrels of an offended heaven [the Huguenots] and for the vengeance of misprized royalty [the revolts] . . . this valiant man died with arms in hand . . . covered with the praise of his country and with the soil of her enemies [he was buried beneath the ruins of a bastion undermined at Thionville]. . . . Stranger, could a great soldier have a more honorable grave? If you are French . . ." (This appeal to French patriotism has an altogether contemporary ring; one would think this was the nineteenth or twentieth century.) ". . . If you are French shed a few tears for a noble warrior who shed his lifeblood for the honor of France and who died at 32, pierced with 32 wounds [a miraculous coincidence]. He asks only your piety, for he is content with his fate. . . . If your bosom thrills to noble deeds, you will pray for his soul." He died in 1643, but his epitaph must have been composed later, during the last half of the century, by his son, founder of the family chapel and mausoleum, who was also responsible for the epitaphs of his own two sons.

The first son, François, a knight of Malta, "went to Malta at the age of XVII to train his squadrons. . . . He was one of those who led the charge when the Christians took the town of Cairon, and it was at the siege of this important place that he met with a death that was glorious for his memory. . . . When his body was found among the dead, he was still holding his sword, which was in the body of a Turkish officer lying next to him. He had the reward, which he had always desired, of dying for the faith of Jesus Christ, which he did in the year 1685, at the age of XXI."

The other son, Louis, "following the example of his illustrious ancestors, spent the few years he had under arms, and finally gave his life cheerfully in the service of his king." The epitaph reports his campaigns, the engagements in which "he gave proof of heroic valor and consummate experience," and his death at the battle of Oberkirch. "He sustained two musket wounds and died on April 18, 1689, at the age of 28. Since he had always conducted himself with great wisdom and piety, he gave up his soul in the state of mind of a true Christian, with perfect resignation to the will of his Creator, but generally regretted by all."[33]

These great military exploits were probably the deeds most often celebrated by funerary epigraphy in the warlike France of the sixteenth and seventeenth centuries. But commemorative inscriptions also perpetuated, albeit more discreetly, more modest existences: diplomatic careers, skill in literature and science, erudition in both canonic and Roman law. The churches of Rome are full of such inscriptions dating from the fifteenth to the eighteenth century. Some, like those of the French gentlemen, are also very long, but many are more concise.

Sometimes, in a French church that has escaped the iconoclasts, one's eye falls upon some inscription that must have been ordinary in its time, such as this one of a law officer, proud of his career, on a pillar of the choir in the church of Saint-Nicolas, in Marville: "Here lies the honorable lord . . . of Goray, squire provost to their Most Serene Highnesses at Marville, who after faithfully serving the late emperor Charles V and Philippe, his son, the king of Spain, for 30 years in noble and honorable duties, on voyages to Africa as well as in wars with the Netherlands and elsewhere, chose this town [of Marville] for a place of retirement in his old age, and passed away on 11 Nov. 1609, after leaving to the Confraternity of the Holy Rosary the sum of One Thousand Francs. Pray to God for him."

And here is the posthumous eulogy, by his family and his fellow journeyman, of an artisan, sculptor, and cabinetmaker. It is found in Provins, in the church of Saint-Ayoul, against the wall: "Here lies an honorable man, Pierre Blosset, a native of the town of Amiens, during his lifetime master sculptor in wood, stone, and marble, who shortly before his death made all these beautiful works that you see [again, the words are addressed to the passing stranger, the sightseer, as much as to the worshiper] in this church and in other places. On 25 January 1663, at the age of 51 years, Our Lord called him, to reward him with the felicity of the blessed [what about purgatory?] for the care he had taken during his life in the decoration of his temples. Stranger [this time the sightseer is invited to say the prayer for the dead], as you gaze upon these fine works, he asks you to remember him in your prayers, and to say at least a *Requiescat in pace.*"

The loyalty of a humble law officer and the professional conscience and talent of a good craftsman were soon almost as worthy as were heroism and sanctity of being inscribed on the honor roll that consisted of the epitaphs on the floors and walls of churches.

Curiously enough, in the middle of the sixteenth century we also find a tribute to marital fidelity, a quality that, although traditionally required of wives, had seldom earned them posthumous glory. Conjugal happiness inspired this inscription to a happy couple in 1559 at Saint-André-des-Arts:

> *Here lies Master Mathieu Chartier*
> *A man whose heart was spotless and sincere . . .*
> *Jehane Brunon he took to be his bride*
> *Who spent her life chastely by his side,*
> *And fifty years true to one another,*
> *They shared their bed without strife or bother.*

And this epitaph, written by a husband in homage to his wife, buried during the same period in the Ave Maria:

> *This is the last dwelling place*
> *Of Mary de Tison*
> *Here her body sleeps in peace*
> *Till it wake and rise again.*

Finally, here is the biographical notice and the eulogy of domestic virtue:

> *From Augoumois, in Faiolle,*
> *She came to Bourbonnais to take a husband*
> *Who never in deed or word*
> *Found anything to reproach her for.*
> *Out of this union she brought forth*
> *An only son, handsome, healthy, and rich,*
> *Whom she left at a tender age*
> *To his father, Pierre de Chambrod.*

Emphatic references to only sons are still rather common in sixteenth-century inscriptions.

There are inscriptions that are not found on tombstones of stone or copper, or rather, there are "tombstones" that are not found in churches or cemeteries, tombstones made of a more spiritual substance that are no longer engraved but printed or simply handwritten for personal use. In the sixteenth century, composing one's epitaph was a way of meditating on death: "I put [the little tombstone that I composed for myself] in one of the drawers of the big desk in my study," writes Pierre de l'Estoile in his *Journal,* "along with my late father's paper and my own paper [What paper? Does he mean their wills?], and the revolutions of my planet." At that time people seriously believed in astrology.[34]

L'Estoile's epitaph is a religious exercise embellished by a play on the word *stella*, the Latin root of his name: *Anima ad coelum, stellarum domum* (spirit to heaven, home of the stars). He may have intended it to be engraved one day.

Other epitaphs were intended for publication, as one of the classic forms of the posthumous eulogy; these were known as literary tombstones. In 1619 the Jesuits of Pont-à-Mousson published a tombstone consisting of tributes in Latin and French to the memory of a young professed monk of the order who had died while he was a resident of their community. The book is entitled *Lachrymae convicti Mussipontani in obitu nobilissimi adulescentis F. Claudii Hureau.*

He was a good student; he won all the prizes. "As numerous as the prizes once received among the young disciples of Pallas, as numerous as the garlands reserved for your wise brow, O thou, triumphing among those on high in a holy death, are the eternal rewards of the unvanquished soul that you possess. Children (*pueri*) [which also includes adolescents], why limit your efforts to human honors [which are nonetheless legitimate and necessary]? Let your prizes be a foretaste of the vision of God."[35]

Eternal salvation is not incompatible with earthly fame. It is often, indeed normally, associated with it, but the two are no longer necessarily inseparable. The epigraphic literature of the sixteenth and seventeenth centuries shows both the persistence of the old correlation and the separation of the two domains, a separation that may have opened, or at least unlocked, the door to modern secularization. Fame is no longer the infallible path to immortality on earth and in heaven. It is well known that sometimes the trumpet of fame falls silent, or sounds at the wrong time. Nevertheless, there is still confidence in the authenticity of earthly glory, confidence that these errors on the part of the human vicars responsible for proclaiming virtue and honor do not condemn the victims of their unjust silence to oblivion. The reputation of an honest man spreads in spite of everything, and people are even beginning to doubt the judgment of those who have heretofore been accepted as its unchallenged arbiters. "Fame and renown" make their own way without the help of human eloquence—except in the case of epigraphy.

This brings us to what might be called the antiepitaph. Here is a tomb dated 1550, from Saint-André-des-Arts; it expresses clearly this pride in humiliation and humility:

> *Thou, stranger who treadest on their ash,*
> *Marvel not that here you see no vast*
> *Pillars of Parian marble rise aloft*
> *Richly wrought with Phrygian handicraft*

Or stately columns standing in solemn rows.
Such empty honors are suitable for those
Whose death erases all renown and fame
And vanquishes their glory with their name;
But not for those whose superior worth!
After death extols them to the earth.
Indeed, I would even venture to assume
That one need not build for them a tomb
By human art, since glory heaven-sent
Serves them as a living monument.[36]

Living monument: *tombe animée*—that is, a tomb with effigies.

At the same time that merits and distinctions were covering the walls of burial places as if they were so many pages in a book of gold, the idea that true glory has nothing to do with this display was beginning to make a discreet appearance. In the seventeenth century, the conviction became so strong that people avoided loquacious and indiscreet commentaries and preferred the silence of the name alone. It was not exactly the true humility of the paupers' grave; at least that was not how it was interpreted by survivors. A seventeenth-century Florentine had asked in his will that only his name appear on his tombstone, which was on the floor. But his heir, out of piety, and lacking the courage of the deceased, commissioned in his honor a fine bust, which still exists in San Salvatore del Monte. There is an inscription in which he admits his inability to follow the deceased all the way in a humility whose pointlessness the latter had naïvely failed to understand, unaware as he was of his own fame. "He did not realize that to obtain *fama et gloria,* either his name alone was enough or else nothing would suffice."

From the fifteenth to the seventeenth century, then, we see a growing desire on the part of the deceased or his heirs and relatives to use the tomb in order to perpetuate the memory of his life and deeds, whether glorious or modest. This is apparent in the long inscriptions that we have discussed. But it also appears in the brief and simple epitaphs, far more numerous than the preceding ones, from the sixteenth to the eighteenth century, that remained faithful to the bald medieval style. Almost all of them have disappeared, for they were of interest to neither genealogist nor historian nor artist. In those that have been preserved, one word keeps recurring, a very ordinary word, the word *memory:* "To the perpetual memory of . . ."; "To the eternal memory of. . . ." Granted the word is not new. Like *monumentum,* it belongs to the vocabulary of Roman funerary epigraphy. But when it was adopted by Christianity, it acquired a new, eschatological meaning. The *memoria* designated the tomb of a martyr, or else it evoked the pitiful soul. The epigraphs of the seventeenth century did not drop the mystical meaning, but they revived the Roman meaning. The expression *to the memory of* is an invitation not only to prayer but to literal memory, to the recollection of a life with its peculiar characteristics and actions, a biography.

This memory is not only desired by the deceased; it is also solicited by the survivors.

The Sense of Family

In the fifteenth, sixteenth, and early seventeenth centuries, the recording of those acts in the life worthy of being perpetuated was the responsibility of the testator himself. He had had ample time to think about it, and had sometimes written his own epitaph in the silence of his study. In the seventeenth century, this act of composition is more and more frequently a function of familial piety. This is particularly true, as we have seen, of all the young gentlemen who were victims of the wars of Louis XIII and Louis XIV.

Moreover, as we have also seen, the virtues of sanctity, military prowess, or simply of public office were no longer the only ones that guaranteed the right to the earthly immortality promised by epitaphs. It was no longer necessary to have performed heroic deeds in order to live on in the memory of men. The phenomenon is highly significant. The affection of the family —conjugal, parental, or filial love—was beginning to replace the noble official merits in the changed world of epigraph writers.

The custom of commemoration, which arose in the Middle Ages out of the religious duty to preserve holy deeds destined for terrestrial and celestial immortality and which was next extended to the heroic acts of public life, has now spread to include daily life, where it appears to be the expression of a new feeling, the sense of family. A correlation is established between the feeling for one's family and the desire to perpetuate their memory.

Often the inscriptions are devoted to the glorification of a given family. But in a more general and more significant way, the family has won a place in the epitaph, in accordance with an ancient custom rediscovered in the sixteenth century. Inscriptions of this type are composed of two parts, sometimes placed in different parts of the tomb, especially in the sixteenth and seventeenth centuries. The first is devoted to the eulogy, the biographical notice of the deceased, the second to the survivor who commissioned the epitaph and laid the monument. For example, the long accounts of the campaigns of the young Rostangs mentioned above are followed by this signature: "His father ordered this marble, which will provide for posterity an eternal monument to the virtue of so worthy a son and the grief of so generous a father." The tombstone of Mathieu Chartier and Jehane Brunon, devoted to a eulogy of conjugal virtue and happy marriage, was composed and laid by their children:

> *Their daughters and grandsons, full of bitter grief,*
> *Built them this tombstone with many a tear*
> *And honored them with this image here.*[37]

In the absence of natural descendants, the responsibility for transmitting the memory sometimes fell to a servant. I have already quoted the epitaph of a sculptor and cabinetmaker of Amiens who was buried in Provins. He had survived his children and must have been a widower when he died. Then, who had the job of arranging for the epitaph and the tombstone? The inscription tells us: "Made by Pierre Godot, his apprentice."

Finally, in a remarkable development that clearly indicates the invasion of the tombstone by the sense of family, even children and adolescents now become entitled to a eulogy and expression of regret by their parents, engraved on noble and enduring granite. Fathers and mothers are feeling the need to record on an imperishable substance their grief and their desire to perpetuate the memory of the dead child.

Here is an example taken from a collection of Parisian epitaphs: "To Anna Gastelleria, whom death stole as a little child from their sight but not from their memory, her grief-stricken parents, mindful of their sad duty, have raised this monument. *Vixit annos VI menses IV dies XIV. Obiit Kalendas Junii MDXCI.* Peace to the living. Rest to the dead."[38]

In Rome we can still read a great many epitaphs of the same kind and from the same period at their original sites, especially in the church of Ara Coeli. The epitaph of Michael Corniactus, a Polish nobleman and a young man of great promise who died in 1594 at the age of nineteen, concludes with the statement that his two brothers-german erected the monument. Also at Ara Coeli, a magnificent portrait is accompanied by a very beautiful inscription that gives an idea of prevailing attitudes toward age, for it is devoted to a young man of twenty-nine who was not married: "To Flaminius Capelletus, *juvenis,* very well educated in the fields of letters and sciences, admired and venerated by all for the beauty of his face [physical beauty has become one of the elements of the posthumous memory], his integrity, and the seriousness and elegance of his speech, who in the flower of his youth and fame, was torn away (*abripetur*) [snatched away by death, a familiar expression inherited from the macabre vocabulary of the fourteenth and fifteenth centuries] from his loving parents most cruelly, at the age of XXIX [a young man of twenty-nine had long been living the life of an adult, but Capelletus was not married, which is why, as we shall see, his obituary notice was not written by his wife, but by his parents], in the year of Our Lord 1604."

This is the first epitaph, the one devoted to the deceased. It is immediately followed by a second, which concerns the survivors, their situation, and their mourning: "His father, M. C., senator of the city, to his son once dearly beloved, henceforth deeply regretted (*desideratissimo*) [note the appearance of the very modern notion of "eternal regret"] and to P. P., his very pious wife, who survived her son by four years, deprived of the sight of their beloved faces, in mourning, dedicated this tomb." The author of the inscription was killing two birds with one stone, according to a procedure which was actually common in those days of low average longevity. His wife died four years after their son, but still before the arrangements for his tomb had been completed or the inscription engraved. This shows that although these matters sometimes proceeded slowly, still, in spite of long delays, they were not forgotten.

The same year, 1604, is also the year that Charlotte de Beaudoin died at the age of nineteen. Her father, who was master of the king's forests, wished to be buried beside his daughter, in the church of Saint-Sulpice-de-Favière in the Ile-de-France. He wrote her a sonnet, one of those poems that the French call a *tombeau* and the English an elegy and that are written on the occasion of notable deaths, and had it engraved on the tomb:

Receive, O my heart, this gift your father brings
Dedicated to you, O my purest love,
Since by bitter death Almighty God above
Has cut short the course of your delightful spring.

Receive, my sweetest love, this grief your mother sighs
Incessantly and utters night and day for you
Who was our consolation and our comfort too
By the very presence of our beloved prize.

Your soul is now with God, O pray to Him that He
Of us and of our woe so pitiful will be
That to a single tomb the three of us may go:

I vow to build one worthy of a love so rare
That after our death we may sojourn there
With you, our heart's delight, who once did love us so.[39]

As a general rule, the authors of epitaphs did not demonstrate the kind of originality we have found in the more personal or literary texts. Like wills, these inscriptions are a complex amalgam of individuality and convention. More often than not, they used a standard formula. In a little church in York on a tombstone that, like the church itself, was recently restored after the devastation of the last war, I found a Latin inscription, which, ordinary as it is, has the merit of recapitulating in a few lines the successive conventions of the thirteenth to the seventeenth century: "Dominus Gulielmus Sheffield, chevalier [he has placed himself at the beginning of the epitaph, but he is not the deceased, only the dedicator, who eventually became almost as important as the deceased], has arranged to have this tombstone erected at his own expense [the fact is worthy of being inscribed in granite], *non in vanam gloriam* [an affirmation of Christian humility and of that proud simplicity according to which the monument adds nothing to the glory due to the name itself; nevertheless, he did not think it irrelevant to have one's tombstone and one's statue], but as a reminder of our mortal condition and also to the memory of my beloved wife, Lady Elizabeth, daughter and heiress of John Darnley of Kikhurst, *in agro Thor.* She died July 31, 1633, at the age of fifty-five. *Requiescat in pace.*"

This epitaph from northern England will serve as a temporary conclusion. It summarizes the transition from the bald statement of the individual's civil status, definitively established at the moment of death, to the story of a life that was at first saintly or heroic and then more and more ordinary, and finally to the regret of the survivors, especially of the family. The death of epitaphs, after abandoning anonymity for the personal and biographical, has now become familial. But each of these stages was a very long one, and never completely replaced the earlier practices.

A Typology of Tombs: The Epitaph Tomb

For the purpose of this discussion we have separated the epitaph from its physical context, the tombstone, or its lack of such physical context when it took the place of the tombstone. But a procedure that is possible for the tombstone—admittedly, at the price of a certain artificiality—is not possible for the effigy, the representation or portrait of the deceased. Even more than the epitaph, the presence of the effigy—or its absence—is an integral feature of the tomb as a whole. Indeed, this is what makes the funerary statues in museums, which have been detached from their architectural context and their environment, so misleading.

The reappearance of the portrait in funerary decor is a cultural event just as important as the return of the epitaph, and must be seen in relation to the overall evolution of the tomb.

The forms of the medieval and modern tomb from the eleventh to the eighteenth century—the tomb inside or against the church—obey spatial requirements that are remarkably constant and remarkably simple, and we must be aware of them if we are to understand their attendant iconography. These forms can be reduced to three major types. The first, which might be called the epitaph tomb, is a small slab approximately 8 to 12 inches by 16 to 20 inches completely covered by the inscription to the exclusion of any other decoration. This type of tomb is very ancient; we have already observed it on the exterior wall of the church in Auvillar in the twelfth century. It is still common, and still visible today, on the interior and exterior walls of French Catalonian churches. Sometimes this slab is like the door of a safety deposit box; it seals off a small cavity carved out of the exterior wall of the church (in which case it is seen and read from the outside), a kind of *loculus* in which the dried-out bones of the deceased were deposited after being transferred from their first, temporary grave. These little *ci-gîts* were thus of very ancient origin. Engraved on stone or brass and fastened to the walls or pillars of churches, chapels, galleries, or charnels, they continued to be common until the end of the eighteenth century, with no significant changes other than the language, style, or length of the epitaph, and the character of the lettering. The history of the epitaph tomb is inseparable from the history of the inscription itself, as we have just seen in our attempt to trace its movement first toward the personalization of the individual and then toward the identification of the individual with his or her family.

The other two morphological types of tombs deserve even more careful attention, for it is here that we observe the reappearance of the portrait. The first type is vertical and mural; the second is horizontal and lies on the floor.

The Vertical and Mural Tomb, The Large Monument

The vertical and mural tomb is the direct descendant of the Paleo-Christian tombs of venerable persons such as the popes. It consisted of a sarcophagus without an inscription or portrait (the sarcophagus of the third and fourth centuries had both) placed against a wall (only three out of the four sides were decorated) with an inscription (not always preserved) above, the whole unit consisting of sarcophagus and inscription being placed under an arch, or in what was called an arcosolium. Sometimes the sarcophagus was located next to an altar, the oratory tomb, which probably served as a model for that of the eighth-century Mellebaude at the Hypogée des Dunes, in Poitiers, and for the sanctuaries of martyrs, in which the sarcophagus of the saint was contiguous with the altar. This latter arrangement was not imitated for long; the sarcophagi of martyrs were soon separated from the altar and taken down into the crypt of a confession, or else their relics were placed in reliquaries along the apse or ambulatory.

The arrangement under the arcosolium is, therefore, the most common. In the case of the abbess of Jouarre or the dukes of the first house of Burgundy at Cîteaux, the inscription, which was engraved on the sarcophagus (generally around the lid, like a long band), distinguished the tomb of a memorable and venerable figure from the tomb of an ordinary person, whose sarcophagus might be visible, half buried, or completely buried but still bare, anonymous, and devoid of history.

This custom of "ensarcophagusment," to use a neologism coined by Panofsky, was abandoned during the Middle Ages in the West, but has curiously persisted in certain regions, especially Spain and Italy. In Spain, the sarcophagus is sometimes suspended very high on the wall. When the sarcophagus was abandoned and replaced by the buried coffin, the tomb retained the shape of the sarcophagus, or the sarcophagus was represented in a bas-relief scene on the tomb. In Spain, sometimes the wooden coffin was painted, just as the sarcophagus had been carved, and also hoisted up onto the wall and exhibited to the general view, as the stone sarcophagus had been. We may assume that the bones it contained had been transferred from an earlier temporary location. In one whole area of the world, then, the sarcophagus remained the conventional image of the tomb and of death even after it had been abandoned as an actual method of burial.

As long as bodies were enclosed in this way in a container of incorruptible stone, it was felt to be enough that they had been entrusted to the Church. Their separate identities merged in the earthly bosom of the Church, just as the separate identities of their souls merged in the bosom of Abraham. When the stone coffin was abandoned and replaced by the wooden coffin or by simple burial in a shroud, it would seem that a need began to be felt, although these cases were still exceptional, to give them a separate and apparent personality. Throughout this history, we observe a constant tendency toward deeper burial. The early sarcophagi were placed on top of the ground; then they were half buried, some so that their lids still showed and others a little deeper so that still others could be placed on top of them, for they often accumulated in a small space around the holiest places. When the stone sarcophagus was finally replaced by the wooden coffin or the shroud, it became common to bury deep, without any visible sign appearing on the surface. (There were certain exceptions: the raised and painted coffins of fifteenth-century Spain or the exposed mummies of seventeenth- and eighteenth-century Italy.) It was at this time that survivors began leaving a visible mark, although not necessarily at the grave. The tomb was no longer always anonymous, like those of the early sarcophagi; it had an identity. This change coincides with the demographic and urban expansion of the high Middle Ages, which left little room for the cumbersome stone sarcophagi.

But let us return to the problem of forms. The sarcophagus under the Paleo-Christian arcosolium became the medieval tomb in the niche. The sarcophagus was replaced by a massive rectangular stone socle and above it, extending as far as the semicircular or broken relieving arch that formed the upper edge of the niche, there was empty space. Many of these tombs have been damaged, but one can still see the bare socle and the relieving arch on the interior or exterior of the wall of the church. In modern Bologna and Venice, they run along the wall that faces the street, and pedestrians walk by oblivious. In many of our country churches one notices the gaping space of an empty niche somewhere near the apse, in the place where the cemetery used to be.

This type of tomb had three bare spaces that invited decoration: the three lateral walls of the socle, the top of the socle (the position of the old sarcophagus lid), and the back of the niche. The history of the vertical type of medieval tomb is dominated by the different ways of filling these spaces: bas-relief or painting on the back of the niche, bas-relief on the lateral walls of the socle, three-dimensional sculpture on top of the socle.

As it developed, this mural tomb encroached on the wall to some extent in width and considerably more in height, until it attained great elevations and covered vast surfaces—sometimes the whole wall of a lateral chapel, as on the fourteenth-century tombs of the Angevin kings of Naples at Santa Chiara. It persisted in this ostentation and enormity in the fifteenth and sixteenth centuries and until the beginning of the seventeenth.

In the sixteenth century, its exuberant growth often forced it to break away completely from the wall that was limiting its expansion. It became an imposing and complex mass standing freely in space, but it continued to observe a vertical structure that divided it into superimposed levels, like the sixteenth-century double-decker royal tombs in Saint-Denis. After the seventeenth century this tendency to exaggerated monumentality was reversed, and the dimensions of the vertical tomb were reduced. During a period that historians usually accuse of baroque bombast and in which, indeed, lavish funeral ceremonies turned churches into operatic sets, the monumental Angevin, Valois, or Medici tomb shrank to more modest dimensions. It was the sign of a profound movement toward that "distancing" of death that will be the subject of the third part of this book.

Be that as it may, the vertical tomb lent itself to monumentality. It had a natural tendency to expand along wall surfaces and into interior space, in order to fill in the void. It was as appropriate for the burial of the great, memorable personages of the Church and of the new states as it was inspiring to the creativity of great artists, sculptors, and architects. On the other hand, the vertical tomb was also immediately miniaturized for more humble purposes. Indeed, the impulse toward modest proportions antedates that toward monumentality: There is already a slab several inches wide that serves as a tombstone for a thirteenth-century canon of the cathedral in Toulouse.[40] In its condensed form, reduced to a bas-relief in the back and an inscription, or an inscription and a bust, or a combination of the two, still maintaining its vertical orientation and fastened to a wall or pillar, the model served in the sixteenth, seventeenth, and early eighteenth centuries for the burial of large numbers of unimportant gentlemen, respectable bourgeois, officers of justice, men of the law and church, beneficed clergymen—in short, the members of what then corresponded to the upper middle class. The walls and pillars of the churches of the seventeenth and early eighteenth centuries must have been covered with these monuments that were about a foot wide. The reformist Catholic clergy of the eighteenth century—the Dutch Calvinists, after the first wave of iconoclasm, were more conservative—the revolutionaries of 1793, and the real-estate speculators of the early nineteenth century destroyed many of them in France. But in England, Holland, Germany, and Italy, especially in Rome, where they were better respected, we find them intact, and in their original locations.

The Horizontal Tomb

The other type of medieval and modern tomb is horizontal, low, and embedded in the ground. It consists of a single slab of flat, rectangular stone whose dimensions vary, but generally correspond to those of the human body. In rare cases it is larger; often it is smaller. New words were used to refer to it. *Tumulus, monumentum, memoria,* and even *sarceu,* in the sense of tomb, disappeared, to be replaced by *lame, fosse,* and *tombe* or *plate-tombe. Tumba,* in the sense of tumulus, had been borrowed from the Greek. In its Latin form, it seems to have been used for the first time by Prudentius in the fifth century, but it was very popular in the Middle Ages, for we find it in all the vernacular languages of the Western world: *tombe* in French, *tomb* in English, *tomba* in Italian.[41]

The French word *lame* designates both the stone that covers the tomb and the grave in which the body is laid. This type of tomb, therefore, primarily evokes the burial of the body underground, as distinguished from the placing of the body in a sarcophagus. Of course, the slab almost never coincided exactly with the grave where the body was actually placed in the ground, but that was immaterial. The slab was the visible sign of this invisible location, and this symbol was sufficient. It was part of the paving of the church, it blended into the floor, of which it was an integral part. It was, therefore, the hard boundary that separated the world above the ground from the world below.

The emphasis placed by this type of tomb on what is under the ground, in a Christian eschatology that virtually ignores that area—the medieval hell is not subterranean—strikes me as original. It also seems to me that, unlike the vertical tomb with its niche, this type of flat tomb has no direct prototype in pagan or Christian antiquity. One might point, by way of objection, to the funerary mosaics with inscriptions and portraits that covered the floors of the Christian basilicas of Africa. But we do not know whether there is a direct relationship between the mosaic tombs of the fifth century and the first slabs, decorated with a symbol or brief inscription, of the eleventh century, although Panofsky envisioned the possibility of a continuity running through the Spanish, Rhenish, and Flemish styles. The flat tomb seems to me rather to be directly related to the systematic burial of bodies henceforth deprived of the protection of the stone sarcophagus, and also to a greater consciousness of the idea of a return to the earth. Insofar as pagan and Christian antiquity constructed a visible edifice for the deceased, they tended to build a monument that was above the ground: simple stele, colossal mausoleum, sarcophagus, tomb house with rooms, etc. The Middle Ages continued this tradition with the vertical tomb, but it also created a new type of tomb that was more in keeping with its dream and that, although still visible, brings our attention down to the level of the ground from which we spring and to which we shall return. This is a feeling that could just as well have no relation to Christianity and that could have been inspired by a naturalism not overly concerned with hopes for the beyond. Are we not once again in the presence of those ambiguous elements of Christian culture that are seldom found in the religious societies of antiquity and that involve both a certain nihilism that is never carried to the limit and a firm belief in the beyond?

The appearance of the flat tomb is unquestionably an important cultural event. It bears witness to a calmer acceptance of, and more friendly cohabitation with, underground residents, who have ceased to inspire fear. There is no longer any reason not to combine their identification and even celebration with the recollection of their dissolution.

As we have seen, horizontal slabs were not the earliest form of tombs. The earliest tombs, when they were no longer sarcophagi, were more apt to be of the vertical and mural type, such as the rather astonishing example at Arles-sur-Tech in the Pyrenees. But horizontal slabs were undoubtedly the first that were intended to be both visible and humble. The first tombs were either invisible—anonymous or buried sarcophagi—or else when they were visible, they were mural, monumental, and ostentatious.

The flat tomb—almost bare, but identified by an engraving or sculpture—is, then, an original creation of the medieval genius and its ambivalent sensibility, the symbol of a compromise between the traditional abandonment to sanctified ground and the new need quietly to assert one's identity.

Just as the vertical tomb seemed destined by its morphology for monuments to the great—although it did occasionally serve as a model for commoner tombs—the flat tomb seems rather to have had a vocation of humility. It was part of the floor; it was deliberately exposed to being trodden underfoot. In the periods of great monumentality in funerary design in the fourteenth, fifteenth, and sixteenth centuries, it was the preferred choice of those who wished to demonstrate their humility. It was the only form of burial accepted by Catholic reformers such as Saint Carlo Borromeo, who stipulated that a tomb should not rise above the paving stones: *non excedens pavimentum*. It constituted the main part of the funerary decor of churches such as the church of Gesù, in Rome. In the seventeenth and eighteenth centuries, because of its discretion, it was adopted along with the epitaph tomb by artisans and laborers, those newcomers to the social privilege of the visible tomb.

It also lent itself to the embellishments of art and to the eloquence of the ambitious. Without rising above ground level, the marble mosaics of the sixteenth, seventeenth, and eighteenth centuries provided an opportunity for sumptuous and colorful heraldic decorations accompanied by elegant inscriptions. The finest of these are perhaps those at the church of Gesù, in Rome, and the church of the Knights of Malta, in Valletta. After the fourteenth century, sculpture in the round replaced the engraving or bas-relief of the preceding ages, giving rise to a statuary similar to that which surmounted the socle of the vertical mural tomb. Without losing its shape or its symbolism, the slab was raised above the floor, either on columns or on mourning figures, who carried it on their shoulders like the bier in the funeral procession.

Thus, in spite of certain structural predilections, both horizontal and vertical tombs lent themselves to a variety of manifestations of medieval funerary sentiment. They provided this sentiment with a context that was interesting and significant in itself, a context in which the portrait and the epitaph would take their place, reappear after a long absence, coexist, and then disappear again, each in its own direction.

An Imaginary Museum:
The Recumbent Figure

Let us imagine a museum that would bring together in sequence all known funerary monuments, classified according to age and region. In this way we would be able to trace the whole development of the collection at one continuous and rapid glance. Certain regional peculiarities would undoubtedly appear, such as the survival of the sarcophagus in the Mediterranean countries or the persistence of open-eyed recumbent figures in the so-called Gothic countries. But in the panoramic view, these differences would become negligible. What would strike us, rather, would be the genetic unity of forms from the eleventh to the eighteenth century, despite all the fluctuations of art and style. Before the eleventh century there is almost nothing but the vestiges of Paleo-Christian practices. After the eighteenth century there is something new, our contemporary cemeteries. But between the eleventh century and about the middle of the eighteenth century, the genetic continuity is unbroken. We pass from one form to another by imperceptible transitions that have more to do with details of style than with essential characteristics of structure.

However, the eye would quickly distinguish two different series of forms: one of recumbent figures and one of praying figures. The two series do not always coincide, nor do they succeed one another neatly; they overlap. These two figures, which persist for half a millennium, betray a secret and tenacious attachment to a popular conception of death that was profoundly felt but never openly expressed.

Let us look first at the series of recumbent figures and see what interpretation it suggests.

The unsophisticated and hurried visitor to our imaginary museum would see these recumbent figures as people who had just died and who were being displayed to the public before the funeral ceremony. He would certainly be struck by the resemblance between the recumbent figure of the Middle Ages and early modern era and the traditional exhibition of the dead until our own time, at least until the era of death in the hospital and the funeral home.

In fact, he would be only half wrong. The medieval recumbent figure is not a copy of a dead body, but the body may well have been laid out in imitation of the funerary recumbent figure.

The oldest recumbent figures do not represent dead people, and for a long time, particularly in the Gothic countries, they will not do so. They have their eyes wide open, and the folds of their garments fall as if they were standing up instead of lying down. In their hands they carry objects —a model of the church of Childebert (ca. 1160) in Saint-Denis, the crozier of Abbé Isarnus in Saint-Victor-de-Marseille at the end of the eleventh century—like the processionary donors in the mosaics of Rome or Ravenna. Everyone agrees on this point; neither the old historians, such as Emile Mâle and Erwin Panofsky, nor the new school of positivist and debunking archaeologists has yet challenged it. A recent author writes of the recumbent figures of the kings of the first dynasty in Saint-Denis, which were mass-produced by order of Saint Louis in the thirteenth century, "Their feet rest on a socle, as if the artist had momentarily considered raising them to a standing position. Their gestures are calm, and the expressions on their faces seem not of this world."[42]

These recumbent figures are neither dead men nor living men whose portraits were desired. They are identifiable, of course, but no longer as men of the earth. They are *beati*, blessed beings, glorified bodies, eternally young, "the age of the Christ of the Passion," according to Emile Mâle; "earthly members of the City of God," according to Panofsky; we would probably prefer to call them archetypes of the royal function.

This interpretation should not surprise readers who have followed me this far. They will recognize these living/nonliving forms, these dead who still see, as the subjects of the first and oldest liturgy of the funeral service, which is a liturgy of sleepers, persons at rest, like the Seven Sleepers of Ephesus. In fact, they are neither the carefree living, nor those dying in pain, nor the dead subject to corruption, nor yet those who have been reborn in glory, but the elect, who await in repose and peace the transfiguration of the Last Day, the resurrection.

To be sure, at the time when these blessed recumbent figures were carved and engraved, the liturgy had already overlaid the theme of rest with the themes of the migration of the soul and of judgment, which would henceforth dominate. But everything seems to suggest that this ancient model of repose, eliminated from the liturgy and from eschatological thought, survived in the image of the recumbent figure. It is a significant survival, for it reveals a profound and silent attachment to a belief abandoned by the elite.

Emile Mâle felt that this attitude was only peculiar to the early recumbent figures of the twelfth and thirteenth centuries. He observed, as no doubt the less experienced visitor to our imaginary museum would also do, that after the fourteenth century the eyes of the recumbent figures were closed (less often in France and Germany than in Italy and Spain) and the reclining posture was rendered more lifelike by the way the folds of the garments fell and by the position of the arms and legs. The head rested on a pillow. In short, according to Mâle, who regrets the metamorphosis, the blessed being has become an ordinary corpse, and soon a realistic corpse. The way is now open for the decomposed body, the *transi,* and the skeleton.[43]

Panofsky makes similar observations. He is less interested than Mâle is in whether the eyes are open or closed. On the other hand, he attributes considerable importance to aesthetic formalism. He assumes that after the fourteenth century, artists no longer tolerated the physical impossibility of the horizontal standing figure, which defies the realities of weight. This explains why the recumbent figure will either be set upright again (like the bishop of Saint-Nazaire, at Carcassone, who is giving the benediction), or else he will be lying in bed, sick or dead, or else—but this is a different subject, which we shall consider later on—he will be animated, seated, or kneeling.[44]

I agree with Mâle and Panofsky that a change in the attitude of the effigy occurs in the fourteenth and fifteenth centuries. But this change appears primarily in the monuments of great art commissioned from great artists for great personages. Tombs with effigies became more common in the fifteenth to seventeenth centuries. But let us leave aside great funerary art for the moment and turn our attention to more modest or even working-class tombs. The tomb that we will call ordinary in order to avoid calling it common, which would be inaccurate, adopts the two models of royal art, the recumbent figure and the praying figure. But in the case of the recumbent figure, this tomb remains faithful, until the first third of the seventeenth century (when the recumbent figure disappears), to the archaic type of the human being in a state of bliss. The woman with the hood or the man with the ruff of 1600 is represented on a horizontal slab, more often engraved than carved, which is mass-produced by a craftsman who leaves the head unfinished. The recumbent figures are represented as if they were standing with their hands joined or crossed on their breasts and their eyes wide open. A priest holds the chalice in his hand. The ordinary dead of the sixteenth and seventeenth centuries are standing up in a horizontal position, like the great personages of the eleventh to thirteenth centuries.

Perhaps by this time the correspondence between this attitude and the theme of repose had been forgotten. But artists continued to present the deceased lying on the ground as if he were alive, although in a position that would be unusual for a living person, even in prayer: a position of pious waiting, deferential immobility, uninterrupted calm, and peace. The traditional image conveys certain old ideas and hopes that, although no longer conscious, nevertheless continue to influence deep-seated feelings and buried memories.

The persistence until the beginning of the seventeenth century of the archaic type of recumbent figure in ordinary flat tombs eclipses the aesthetic changes in great funerary art observed by Mâle and Panofsky. The details of the forms of this great art are less significant than the productions of the craftsmen, which remained more faithful to the old models. What difference does it make, after all, whether the eyes are open or closed, whether the folds of the garments indicate a standing or lying position, if it is still apparent that the deceased is resting in peace? It is this feeling of peace that matters.

Two essential themes are combined here: on the one hand, the theme of the flat tomb, the closeness to the earth, the continuity with the ground; on the other hand, the theme of the recumbent figure, of repose in the beyond, a repose that is neither end nor void nor full consciousness, neither memory nor anticipation.

The early seventeenth-century flat tombs with recumbent figures of the educated elite, who were still the only people who had tombstones, are the last visible and unchanged vestiges of the ancient attitude of the tame death. They constitute a compromise between the new need for identification that appears around the eleventh and twelfth centuries and the millennial idea of repose: to go away, not forever, but only for a long sleep, a sleep that leaves the eyes open, that resembles life without altogether being either life or afterlife.

The Influence of the Recumbent Figure on the Exhibition of the Dead

The recumbent figure is a survival of an eschatological model that has been abandoned. In its ordinary, if not popular applications, it exhibits a surprising stability; but when adapted to the aristocratic uses of great funerary art, it shows unlimited variety. Sometimes it is the full-length portrait of the knight with sword in hand; more often it is a more realistic image of death. In fourteenth-century Germany and England, the recumbent figure is an armed man killed in combat. The English knight lies with his feet crossed on the rocky ground where he has fallen. With one hand he draws his sword from the sheath, which he holds in the other. His eyes are still open.

Panofsky describes a German recumbent figure from 1482 as "represented at the moment of transition between life and death. His head rests on a pillow and leans to one side. His eyes are not yet completely closed, but they are already invaded by death."[45]

Panofsky's description would just as well apply to a work that antedates this one by a century, the monument of Conrad Werner von Hattstadt, an attorney of Alsace. The recumbent figure, once placed in a niche in the Dominican church in Colmar, is now preserved in the museum that succeeded the monastery. His hands are joined; his head is turned to one side and rests on his helmet. His sword and gloves are lying beside him. The angle of the head breaks the hieratic attitude of the conventional *beatus*: This man has just died.

Even more pathetic is the recumbent figure of Guidarello Guidarelli, killed in 1501 in the service of Cesare Borgia. The sculptor, Tullo Lombardo, has captured all the sadness of the death of a young man. This work of 1520 is in the Accademia delle Belle Arte, in Ravenna.

In the cloister of Santa Maria della Pace, in Rome, a funerary bas-relief from the fifteenth century depicts a young man who has died a violent death. Seen in profile, the recumbent figure retains the memory of a supple body that has suddenly been deprived of life.

In the sixteenth century a new and scholarly model that is also limited to great funerary art without any wider influence illustrates this tendency to go beyond the sleeping figure. This model substitutes something more dramatic: the half-recumbent, or leaning, figure. Here the head and shoulders are erect, and the deceased is leaning on one arm; the other arm may be holding a book. It is an attitude inspired by Etrusco-Roman statuary and also by the symbolic gesture of the head resting on the hand, which, even in the frescoes of Giotto, already signified melancholy meditation. The artists of the sixteenth and seventeenth centuries were fond of this attitude, which lent itself to their fantasies: the moribund, half-raised, sustained on his deathbed by religion or awakened in his sarcophagus by the spirit of Fame or the angel of the resurrection. But this theme remained a noble one. It never left the realm of great art, and was unknown to common funerary iconography.

Another deviation from the theme of repose was the replacement of the recumbent figure, in the fifteenth and sixteenth centuries, by the *transi* or mummy. The traditional iconography of the recumbent figure was now exploited in another way, in order to express the bitterness of having to leave the exquisite things of this life. We know that the distribution of this model was limited both temporally and geographically (see chapter 4).

We may assume, then, that until the seventeenth century the peaceful recumbent figure was the dominant image of death on the tombs of ordinary people. Although the elite tried to deviate from this image, none of the resulting models achieved any lasting influence.

The foregoing analyses were inspired by evidence drawn primarily from so-called Gothic Europe: northern France, the countries of the house of Burgundy, and Germany. Aside from a few exceptional cases of great art, they have taken account neither of Mediterranean sources nor of the ordinary customs of that region. But it so happens that funerary themes that were commoner in these southern regions in the late Middle Ages were to have a determining influence on the actual presentation and exhibition of the dead body throughout the West until our own time. It is a rather complicated story of reciprocal influence between the dead and the living, between the statue or engraving of the recumbent figure and the preparation or exhibition of the dead body.

In order to understand this story, we must return to our imaginary museum. If we pay closer attention to the details of funerary data, we will find that a continuous evolution, without taking the recumbent figure too far from its original model, carries it toward an intermediary type. This intermediary type is not altogether the *beatus,* which looks more like a dead man, but it is nevertheless neither a moribund nor a *transi.* The type that appears at the end of this evolution is certainly a real corpse, but a corpse still presented as a *beatus,* a sleeping recumbent figure.

After the second half of the thirteenth century, not only in southern regions but throughout the West, the bas-reliefs covering the sides of the socle that supports the recumbent figure often represent the funeral procession, whose importance we have already seen in the funeral ceremonies of the later Middle Ages. At first a supernatural procession composed of angels and clergymen in alternating order, it becomes a real procession such as is described in wills, composed of monks, clergymen, and cowled mourners, who carry and accompany the bier. On the same lateral bas-reliefs, the scene of the final absolution follows that of the procession, especially in Italy and Spain from the fourteenth to the sixteenth century.

Thus, the body of the deceased—or its representation—appears several times on the same tomb: for example, twice in reduced form and in relief during the two ceremonies of procession and absolution, and another time life-size and in the round as a sleeping recumbent figure. But what is altogether remarkable is that the body—or its representation—which is transported on the bier during the procession or laid in the open tomb during the absolution, is shown in exactly the same attitude as the sleeping recumbent figure, dressed, with the hands joined or crossed. A physical parallel, a quasi-identity was established between the fleshly body, which is carried and exhibited, and the recumbent figure of stone or metal, which perpetuates on the tomb the memory of the deceased.

It became customary to dress the deceased after death. The thirteenth-century liturgist Durandus of Mende complained that people dressed their dead before burial instead of simply wrapping them in a shroud, as was practiced in antiquity and as he deemed suitable. He made an exception, however, in the case of priests, who were buried in their sacerdotal garments. And no doubt it was in imitation of the clergy that nobles wanted their bodies to be dressed in their ceremonial or official costumes, the coronation robe for kings, the suit of armor for knights.

This practice of preparing the deceased to resemble the sleeping recumbent figure of funerary art must date from the period when the stone sarcophagus was abandoned and the body, enclosed in the wooden coffin, was replaced by the representation, that is, first by the wooden or wax effigy and later, in a more ordinary and more durable form, by the catafalque.

During the brief interval between death and coffining, it became common practice to exhibit the body in the attitude of the recumbent figure on the tomb, or in the attitude of the representation, when it took the realistic form of an effigy. Survivors adopted the custom of laying the body on its back and joining the hands. This horizontal position, which was prescribed by Durandus of Mende (see chapter 1), seems to be a peculiarly Christian phenomenon. The Jews of the Old Testament died lying on one side with their faces turned to the wall, an attitude that the Spanish of the Renaissance regarded as the mark of the unconverted *marrano*. [46] In Islamic countries the narrowness of funerary monuments shows that the body was buried on its side. The horizontal position of the Christians eventually acquired a preventative power that protected the dead, body and soul, from the attacks of the devil. Jean-Claude Schmitt writes that "only in the vertical position can one enter hell."[47] This attitude acquired greater importance than the ancient preparations which consisted in washing the body, perfuming it, and cleansing it of impurities. One of its essential features is the joining or crossing of the hands, as in the marriage ceremony. If the hands are separated, the model is destroyed; it has lost its meaning. Thus, the sleeping recumbent figure of the twelfth and thirteenth centuries became the model for the actual dead. It did not seek to resemble the deceased, but vice versa.

In the fifteenth century, the deceased laid out and at rest reacted in turn upon the recumbent figure, its model. The Italian recumbent figure of the fifteenth and sixteenth centuries is indeed a dead body on display, and not a living soul in paradise. The subject has just died and is lying on a bier or a bed of state. But this is not a realistic corpse; the body, now empty of earthly life, shows none of the signs of dissolution. On the contrary, it assumes the attitude and expression of eternal rest, in peaceful expectation of the Last Day.

Let us return to our imaginary museum. Beside the recumbent figures, and later in their place, the most inexperienced observer will recognize another series of funerary effigies. Here the deceased is represented— usually kneeling, sometimes standing—before a member of the Trinity, or absorbed in the contemplation of some holy scene. We shall call these effigies praying figures. At first, they sometimes appear in conjunction with recumbent figures. Later, after the praying figure has replaced the recumbent figure in funerary convention, they are alone.

Our first impulse is to see this change of attitude in funerary art as a change in mentality. We would be both right and wrong to do so. There is indeed a change in mentality and in the conception of this life and of the transition to the next, but the old belief has not completely disappeared and persists beneath new appearances. The recumbent figure survives in the praying figure before the age-old idea of *requies* completely disappears.

The Migration of the Soul

The archaic recumbent figure is *homo totus,* like the Sleepers of Ephesus. It is both in body and in soul that he is dedicated first to repose and later to transfiguration, at the end of time. After the twelfth century, a different image of repose and of judgment appears, or rather, reappears; for the sarcophagi of pagan antiquity already showed the *imago clipeata,* the medallion framing the portrait of the deceased that two spirits carry *ad astra* in the manner of an apotheosis. We have already encountered this scene at Conques, on the tomb of Abbot Begon. The illustrious and venerated abbot has arrived in heaven and dwells there among the saints, in the attitude of sacred conversation. The elect is not waiting; he has already received his eternal reward; he is standing in an attitude of thanksgiving. In the case of Begon, it is still the *homo totus* who is carried to heaven, body and soul. In the thirteenth century, artists started showing the elect not only upon his arrival but also at his departure, thus combining the new idea of celestial translation with the old idea of repose. At Elne, angels stand at the head of the recumbent figure, ready to take him in their arms and carry him to the celestial Jerusalem.

Elsewhere, this translation takes the form of a supernatural absolution, in which angels have replaced the officiating clergymen and carry the candles and censers themselves, bringing to the deceased who has been carried off in this way the crown of the elect.

An old anthem from the Roman funeral liturgy, the *In Paradisum,* describes the scene as we can see it on many of the tombs in our imaginary museum. "May the angels take you to paradise, may the saints and martyrs come to meet you, welcome you, and lead you into the holy city, the heavenly Jerusalem, like poor Lazarus." The death of Lazarus, prototype of the death of the just man, was often represented. "May you have eternal peace." The idea of rest was associated with the idea of paradise and of the beatific vision, as if they were a single state. The recumbent figure of the tomb, carried away to heaven, is both the dead man who waits, like the Sleepers of Ephesus, and the dead man who contemplates, like Abbot Begon. Moreover, an architectural element covers his head, a sort of canopy similar to those on the statues on porches or the figures of prophets, apostles, and saints in the stained-glass windows of the fourteenth and fifteenth centuries. This canopy symbolizes the celestial Jerusalem, which the blessed individual has reached. The image of repose has not been profoundly altered by entry into paradise.

However, a new and more revolutionary theme appears, the theme of the migration of the soul. Another anthem from the Roman liturgy, the *Subvenite*, describes this scene. "Come, ye saints of God [this is the invocation to the celestial court, as in the *In Paradisum*, not for the purpose of intercession, as in the *Confiteor* or in the preambles of wills, but in a spirit of thanksgiving, in the enthusiasm of the glorious vision]. Hasten, ye angels of the Lord, take his soul, bear it before the Most High, may the angels guide it to the bosom of Abraham [represented in medieval iconography by an old man sitting and holding on his lap a number of little children, who are souls]."

One can argue today that the word *anima* referred to the whole being, including the body. But after the thirteenth century, iconography in general and funerary iconography in particular clearly indicate that death was seen as the separation of the soul and the body. The soul is depicted as a naked child, sometimes in swaddling clothes, as in Last Judgments, being exhaled by the recumbent figure; this is probably the origin of the French expression *rendre l'âme* (to give up the ghost), which is still in use today. As the soul comes out of the mouth, it is caught by angels in a piece of cloth, whose two ends they hold, and it is in this manner that it is conveyed to the heavenly Jerusalem. In this way the soul of poor Lazarus is escorted by the angels, whereas a horrible, greedy devil snatches the little symbolic child out of the mouth of the evil rich man even before it has been exhaled, as if he were extracting a tooth. In fifteenth- and sixteenth-century Crucifixions, it is not uncommon to find an angel coming to catch the soul of the good thief.

The most significant and famous example of this theme is found in the fifteenth-century *Hours of Rohan*, where the dying man is shown at the moment he gives up the ghost. The body is almost naked. It is neither at peace, like the body of the recumbent figure, nor decomposed, like that of the *transi,* but it is emaciated and pitiful, and a remarkable detail is that *rigor mortis* has already set in. The man is lying on a piece of rich fabric, which will serve as a shroud, according to the ancient custom that had probably been abandoned by then. No, this body is not a peaceful recumbent figure; it is a lifeless corpse. It has been abandoned to the earth, which will receive and consume it. But the body is only one element of the composition. There is also the child representing the soul, which has taken its flight *ad astra* under the protection of Saint Michael, who is wresting it from the devil (see chapter 3). The conspicuous separation between the body and the soul is also present on tombs with niches where the exhalation of the soul is associated with the scene of final absolution on the deathbed. Examples of this treatment are the German tombs of 1194 at Hildesheim; the tomb of Bernard Mege in Saint-Guilhem-du-Désert; the tomb of Saint Sernin in Saint-Hilaire, near Limoux; and the tomb of Bishop Randulph in Saint-Nazaire, in Carcassonne. The recumbent figure is not structurally altered by the loss of his soul. The two images are simply juxtaposed: the recumbent figure below, the soul above.

In Saint-Denis, the sculptor of the tomb of Dagobert, which was restored in the thirteenth century, devoted the whole back of the niche to a kind of comic-strip presentation, with dramatic details, of the perilous voyage of the soul of the king in a Celtic afterlife. But down below, on the socle, the body of the king rests in peace, like the *homo totus* of the traditional recumbent figure, seemingly unaffected by the loss of his soul.

A canon of Provins who died in 1273 is engraved on his tombstone in the attitude which had become conventional for the graves of priests. He is depicted horizontally as a standing figure, eyes open and holding a chalice in his hands. Above, the soul of the deceased is being borne away in a piece of cloth by two angels, who are taking it to the pavilions of the celestial Jerusalem.

Sometimes the migration of the soul is associated not with the recumbent figure but with a new type of glorious deceased, which we shall analyze presently, the figure kneeling in prayer. A tombstone dated 1379, painted on a pillar of the nave of the cathedral in Metz, is composed of two levels —three, including the inscription. Above, we see the voyage of the soul, as on the tomb of Dagobert, a soul that Saint Michael has just saved from the dragon. Below, the deceased kneels before the scene of the Annunciation.

The role of the migration of the soul in the funerary iconography of the fourteenth and fifteenth centuries is a little like that of the *transi.* Neither is exceptional, each is significant, but each rapidly disappears without ever becoming one of the perennial or structural elements of the tomb.

Artists of the later Middle Ages hesitated to represent the recumbent figure and his soul on the same level. There was some sort of profound aversion or resistance to the implications of the doctrine of the immortality of the soul, whether the outcome was happy or unhappy.

Sometimes, in the southern countries, the recumbent figure was sacrificed to the soul. Panofsky describes a Spanish sarcophagus dated 1100 at the monastery of Santa Cruz, in Jaca, on which the scene of the migration of the soul occupies the whole center of the long side.[48] This scene is flanked by two scenes of absolution, one with the bishop and the clergy celebrating, the other with a group of seated mourners. (Mourners are often represented on Spanish tombs, but very rarely elsewhere. In other countries, they have been replaced by the procession, consisting of the clergy, the four mendicant orders, the confraternities, and the poor in penitential costume.) Two centuries later, at les Augustins in Toulouse, the translation of the soul is still alone on the deliberately archaic sarcophagus of a great fourteenth-century prior of Malta. Here the mandorla, or almond-shaped panel containing the soul, is flanked no longer by scenes of absolution but by two coats of arms, a good example of the role played by heraldry both in decoration and in the process of individualization.

But these cases are rare. In general it is the soul that disappears, and the recumbent or praying figure that remains in its traditional attitude.

The exhalation of the soul will disappear from iconography in general, with the single exception of the death of the Virgin, whose soul is received by Christ himself. The scene of deathbed absolution, which disappeared from common usage after it was replaced by the Commendations and the Office of the Dead, survived until the seventeenth century in the Dormition of the Virgin. The very word *dormition* brings us back once again to the idea of repose, although in the fifteenth and sixteenth centuries the body of the Virgin, before her total assumption, was marked by the colors and signs of agony, suffering, and dissolution.

The Recumbent Figure and the Praying Figure: Tombs with Two Levels

The migration of the soul, like those macabre signs of decomposition that are nearly contemporaneous with it, however ephemeral they may have been, marks a period of crisis in the traditional concept of the individual at rest.

A tendency appears at this time that will culminate in the sixteenth century in some great masterpieces of funerary art, without, however, establishing a durable type: a tendency to subdivide the human being. This resulted in the formation of a model in which effigies of the deceased recur in different attitudes on several levels of the same monument. Art historians have assumed that this model was reserved for royal burial chambers, where church doctrine and artistic innovations carried more influence. In reality, this model appears after the thirteenth century even on ordinary tombs.

As evidence I offer the small (14½ × 17½ inches) mural tomb of a canon of the cathedral in Toulouse in the late thirteenth century. It is one of those miniature tombs that have appeared before and that will be seen in great quantity but that were neglected because they were so common and were destroyed remorselessly over the ages.

This tomb betrays no artistic pretensions or desire to be conspicuous. It reflects the ideas about death and the beyond that a distinguished but not illustrious clergyman valued sufficiently to combine without any concern for aesthetics. The limited surface of the tombstone is filled right to the edge. The space where it was customary to have only a short inscription had to accommodate a whole eschatology. The inscription is therefore relegated to the periphery. It runs in two lines around all four sides of the tombstone like a border: *Anno Domini MCCLXXXII XVI Kalendas Augusti, illustrissimo Philippo Rege Francorum, Reverendissimo et valentissimo Bertrando Episcopo Tolosano, obiit magister Aymericus canonicus, cancellarius et operarius Ecclesiae Tolosanae* [official notification of death with the date of death and the rank of the deceased; the age is missing], *ejus anima requiescat in pace."*

The identity of the canon given in the inscription is also confirmed by his coat of arms, which appears twice. All of the space framed by the inscription is occupied by scenes in bas-relief. This carved section is divided into two levels. Below, we recognize the recumbent figure: The canon, wearing the amice on his head, is lying in the traditional attitude, with his hands crossed on his breast and his feet treading on an animal of indeterminate species, according to the passage from Scripture *"Conculcabis leonem et draconem"* (you will tread on the lion and the serpent). He has vanquished evil. He is resting in peace, as he is invited to do in the inscription.

The upper level is subdivided into two scenes, which are juxtaposed horizontally. To the left is the migration of the soul, pictured as a child being conducted by an angel; to the right is the beatific vision, *In Paradisum.* God the Father appears in the center of an oval glory supported by two angels, like the Christ of the Apocalypse in a twelfth-century tympanum. With his raised right hand he is giving the blessing. (At that time the sacramental gesture of benediction had very profound meaning.

The bishop imitated it on earth, and it was in the attitude of benediction that he was represented on his tomb.)

In his left hand God the Father, like the emperor, holds the globe of the world. Canon Aymeric is kneeling before him with joined hands, in the attitude that art historians refer to as that of the donor and that we recognize as the second great type of funerary effigy, the praying figure.

This icon from 1282 contains in concentrated form several of the themes to which Canon Aymeric and some of his contemporaries were devoted. These themes had existed for a long time in doctrinal literature, but not until now did they emerge in funerary iconography or in the unconscious feelings that this iconography expressed. These themes are derived from the subdivision of the individual into the body that life has abandoned, the soul during its migration, and the blessed being in paradise. One senses the need in the person who inspired the tomb to represent these different moments simultaneously. The plurality of the individual and the simultaneity of these representations are the two new characteristics that dominate iconography during a short period of crisis. One senses a hesitation between the traditional concept of the individual at rest and the new concept of the plurality of the individual that will eventually prevail. This hesitation is visible only in tombs commissioned by a political and intellectual elite to which Canon Aymeric presumably belonged. Others belonging to this same elite or slightly below it who were less advanced in their ideas remained faithful to the old model symbolized by the recumbent figure.

We may therefore regard the tombstone of Canon Aymeric as a kind of program announcing a whole new line of development. One part of this program, the migration of the soul, had already been abandoned by 1285. But the rest, that is, the superimposition of the recumbent figure and the praying figure, was to be of longer duration.

However, the superimposition was not to be adopted without hesitation. Other forms of superimposition preceded this one, and they cannot be ignored, not only because of their intrinsic qualities but also because they inspired great sculptors.

The evidence suggests that artists tried several types of superimposition before they arrived at the combination of the recumbent and praying figures. One of these types is the superimposition of two recumbent figures of the same personage, an arrangement probably suggested by the funeral ceremonies of the great. On the tomb of a son of Saint Louis, who died in 1260, on one side of the base we see the dead body being carried on a litter during the funeral procession; above the socle, a statue of the deceased lies in the traditional attitude of the recumbent figure.[49]

Later one finds another type of superimposition involving two recumbent figures, both representing the same person, one showing the signs of death, the other with the attributes of life. Jean-Pierre Babelon sees this arrangement as an imitation on the tomb of the actual superimposition of the coffin and the wooden or wax representation during the funeral service.[50]

The wish to juxtapose these two states of being inspired the iconography of both the tomb and the funeral ceremony to assume the same expressive form. The logical conclusion of this model was that one of the two recumbent figures, the one representing the dead body, would show visible signs of decomposition, in other words, would become a *transi*. An example is the fourteenth- or fifteenth-century tomb of Canon Yver in Notre-Dame, in Paris, where the *transi* and the recumbent figure are superimposed.

On the tomb of Louis XII, in Saint-Denis, the *transi* has been replaced by a figure at the point of death: "It is no longer the dead body being devoured by worms, but rather the transition from life to death that is shown here. Louis XII is stiffening in a kind of spasm . . . his eyes are closing, his lips are exhaling a last gasp."[51]

Artists soon abandoned this superimposition of two recumbent representations of the same person without, however, abandoning the principle of superimposition on this type of tomb, to which they were very attached. They tried to place other figures on the two levels. For example, they superimposed the figures of two different people, such as man and wife, as on the fourteenth-century tomb of Ulrich and Philippe de Verd, in Strasbourg. They also superimposed two ages in the earthly life of the same personage, as on the tomb of Jean de Montmirail in the abbey of Longpont. Below we see the knight with his hands joined on his breast in the classic pose of the recumbent figure. Above, we see the same man lying, but here he is dressed in the monk's habit, which he adopted late in life, and his hands are hidden in his sleeves.[52]

One has the impression of a conflict between the old common belief, which was expressed by the single recumbent figure, still very widespread, and a new idea of plurality, which was expressed by the structural symbolism of dual representation. This conflict was gradually resolved, not only by the superimposition of the recumbent figure and the praying figure but also by the replacement of the first by the second.

The model that was to dominate funerary iconography from the late Middle Ages to the beginning of modern times is characterized by the superimposition of the recumbent and the praying figures that is anticipated in the tomb of Canon Aymeric. Another monumental tomb, also from the late thirteenth century, in Neuvillette-en-Charnie has the recumbent figure below. His sword is at his side, his hands are joined, his eyes are open, and two angels are sprinkling him with incense. At the back of the niche, the praying figure is kneeling before the Virgin and Child.

On the tomb of Enguerrand de Marigny at Ecouis, the recumbent figure in knight's armor is lying on a bed of state with hands joined. On the wall in the back of the niche, Enguerrand and his wife, together with the two great intercessors, the Virgin and Saint John, are kneeling on either side of Christ.[53]

The oldest forms of this type of representation in mural tombs with niches seem to have combined sculpture for the recumbent figure with painting for the upper scene. The painting was later replaced by bas-relief.

It is often maintained that the juxtaposition of the recumbent figure and the praying figure, which was a relatively common and stable arrangement for almost a century, was invented for the huge two-level tombs of the Valois in Saint-Denis. These tombs, which have become famous as masterpieces of funerary art and, indeed, of art in general, have the recumbent figure below and the praying figure above. Philip II was to imitate them at the Escorial, except that there only the praying figures are visible in the upper church. The recumbent figures of the lower level were replaced by the actual bodies, which were enclosed in the niches of the crypt. These great works illustrate the tendency to monumentality and grandiosity that characterizes the tombs of the late Middle Ages and the beginning of early modern times. Because they are so impressive, art historians have accorded them an importance that may be misleading. We must ask ourselves whether they are truly representative or whether, on the contrary, they have not given a false prominence in art, and later in history, to a conception that never really took root, namely the exceptional and somewhat scandalous association of the living and the dead.

The Praying Figure

Because of the importance assigned to these tombs, they have been recognized as the source of the praying figure. The praying figure as it appears at the summit of the tomb is thought to have been a new version of the upper recumbent figure, which was now in danger of being invisible from below. But praying figures existed well before this, not only on the tombs with painted backgrounds of the thirteenth and fourteenth centuries (for example, the tomb of Durandus of Mende at Minerva), but also on sculpture, bas-reliefs, paintings, and stained-glass windows. They are the famous "donors" that one finds almost everywhere after the end of the thirteenth century.

Because of the ubiquitousness of these figures art historians have assumed that they did not necessarily have a funerary role. I believe, however, that their presence is related, if not to the tomb properly speaking, at least to an expanded conception of the tomb, which was not then limited to the fact of burial, still less to the place of burial. The tomb's dual role of commemoration and confession extended beyond the grave and the symbolic monument on which the identifying inscription was engraved to include the immediate surroundings, the chapel where the tomb was located with its stained-glass windows and the altarpiece on its altar, where Masses were spoken or sung for the deceased. In the case of important personages, the role of the tomb extended to the entire church, which then became a funerary chapel, a family burial vault. The donor, that is, the future deceased, or the heir of the deceased, sometimes had himself represented on the main door as a praying figure, like the duke of Burgundy in the Carthusian monastery in Champmol. It is as if there were two tombs, one inside the other, one compact and the other diffuse. Indeed, praying figures appear inside the church when the donor wishes to represent his future in the next world.

For the praying figure is a supernatural personage. During the first phase of its long existence, from the fourteenth to the beginning of the seventeenth century, the praying figure, whether it is on a tomb or elsewhere, is never represented alone. It is always a member of the celestial court as it is described in the *Confiteor* or in the preambles of wills. It appears among the saints, he is associated with a holy conversation, without being presented as one of the celestial personages. Iconographic convention separated the canonized blessed from the ordinary blessed, the other inhabitants of heaven, or those who were still inhabitants of earth but who were already assured of heaven by their virtues. In the Byzantine tradition, at Ravenna and Rome, popes and emperors appeared on the mosaics along with apostles and saints, from whom they were distinguished only by the fact that their halos were square instead of round.

The praying figures of the end of the Middle Ages are the successors to the personages with the square halos in the celestial antechamber. They kneel with joined hands, whereas the established members of the celestial court are standing up. The privilege of being represented in paradise, formerly reserved for a few popes and emperors, was extended to virtually all those notables of the fifteenth to seventeenth centuries whose standing in their communities entitled them to the privilege of a visible tomb.

The essential point here is that the praying figure, even if it is still living, is not a man of this earth. It is a figure of eternity, kneeling before the majesty of God the Father (like Canon Aymeric) or before the Virgin and Child (like Chancellor Rollin) or before a row of great saints. It has been transported not only to paradise but into the midst of those divine events that are reported by Scripture and commemorated in the liturgies of earth and heaven. It is at the foot of the cross, in the garden of the Mount of Olives, or before the empty tomb of the Resurrection.

Its attitude expresses the anticipation of salvation, just as the attitude of the recumbent figure expressed the enjoyment of eternal repose. Eternity in either case, but here the accent is on the drama of salvation, whereas there it was on the passivity of repose. Like the saints, but with its own peculiar attributes that set it apart, it has entered the world of the supernatural. It will be a conspicuous presence in this world until the Protestant and Catholic reforms render such confidence presumptuous and inspire the living with more humility and fear. As long as the praying figure is kneeling there with hands joined, there is no visible boundary between this world and the next.

It is possible to reconstruct the genesis of these forms. The praying figure, as we have just described it, was first represented in heaven, before God or Christ or the Virgin, or the Crucifix, or the Resurrection, on the upper level of the tomb. It corresponds to one phase in the life of the individual, the other being depicted by the recumbent figure.

Then the recumbent figure disappeared, as if despite the pressure of more elevated theologies and spiritualities, a stubborn belief in the integrity of the individual had triumphed, as if there could not be two different representations of the same person on the same tomb. It had to be either one or the other. The choice of the praying figure is, therefore, significant; it was a choice in favor of the soul.

In the course of this history, the tomb—which was almost always mural—eliminated all but the group consisting of the praying figure in heaven in the midst of a religious scene. Often this group was separated from the tomb proper and shifted to an altarpiece or to some other important spot in the church.

Finally, the religious scene disappeared, and the praying figure remained alone, as if it had emerged from the corner of the group to which it had once belonged to become the principal subject of the tomb. Although it symbolized the deceased, its attitude was associated with death itself, whether already past or whether still awaited and anticipated.

From then on, that is, from the sixteenth to the eighteenth century, the sculptured tomb almost always featured a praying figure. This tomb took two forms, one miniature and the other monumental. The miniature form was the mural tomb, or tablet, consisting of an inscription surmounted by a praying figure before a religious scene (bas-relief or engraving). The monumental form was the huge tomb with a socle and a statue of the praying figure, generally alone, and often elevated to the top of a sarcophagus.

The praying figure with its flexibility and adaptability—qualities that the recumbent figure lacked and that explain its success over a long period of time—lent itself to the new needs of familial and religious sensibility. In the sixteenth and seventeenth centuries it was no longer always alone but was associated with the whole family, who also entered into the supernatural world in an order that soon became conventional: to the left of the celestial personages, the wife with all her daughters, and to the right (that is, in the place of honor), the husband, with all his sons lined up behind him.

This was the first visible image of the family. It provided the model for family portraits, which for a long time were groups of praying figures before a religious scene, in other words, pieces of funerary iconography detached from their original function. It was in the attitude of prayer that one had one's portrait painted for oneself and one's friends. Such a portrait was at once a *memento mori*, a souvenir of parents or friends, living or dead, and a pious image.

The praying figure was accompanied not only by his family but also by his holy patron, the advocate and intercessor by whom he was introduced to the celestial court, especially in the fifteenth and sixteenth centuries. The latter stands behind the praying figure, sometimes with one hand on his shoulder, and presents him. There are many examples of this scene. For example, there is a sixteenth-century fresco tomb on a pillar of the cathedral in Metz. The tomb is approximately 4½ by 6 feet, and consists of an inscription below and a Pietà above. Opposite the Pietà we see the deceased as an armed knight kneeling before a prie-dieu on which a book of hours has been placed. Behind the praying figure his holy patron, a Franciscan monk, is waving a banderole bearing the invocation *"O Mater Dei, Memento Mei."* The patron speaks for the deceased in the first person, like a lawyer making his speech for the defense. (The phrase *memento mei* was a pious invocation to the saints before becoming, in the nineteenth century, a symbol of remembrance for the living.)

The role of the intercessor corresponds to the importance assigned to the family. Each family had a baptismal name that was carefully transmitted from father to son and from mother to daughter. The patron ceased to be merely the patron of the deceased or of an individual and became the patron of all male or female descendants, according to his or her sex.

The intervention of the saint on the tomb occurs two or three centuries after the appearance of the Virgin and Saint John on the Last Judgments of the great tympana. This was the interval required for uncertainty about salvation to become completely familiar and spontaneous and for postmortem help to become necessary. Representations of heaven underwent a similar change. In the beginning they evoked the beatific vision directly: God the Father, or his hand emerging from the clouds, the Trinity, Christ, the Virgin and Child. Later this type of representation became less common, as if it presumed to know the result of the judgment, which had come to preoccupy people's minds. In the sixteenth and seventeenth centuries it was replaced by a pious scene from the Passion and Resurrection of Christ; or by one that had an eschatological meaning, such as the resurrection of Lazarus, or that bore witness to divine mercy, such as Our Lady of Mercy surrounding with her mantle a human race carefully segregated according to sex, the men on her right, the women on her left; or by the Annunciation, the first step in the redemption of sinners. Scenes from the life of Christ were not situated outside of paradise. Fifteenth-century altarpieces often showed canonized saints—Saint Augustine, Saint Anthony, or one of the blessed Apostles—in heaven, yet contemplating a scene from the Gospel.

During the seventeenth century the model of the praying figure in conjunction with a religious image became the convention and lasted until the middle of the eighteenth century, with very few changes other than in style and decor. It is a period comparable to the reign of the recumbent figure, which proves in each case how closely the model corresponded to a profound and enduring psychological necessity.

Like the flat tomb, the tomb with praying figure lends itself to modest and commercial uses, to mass production by craftsmen. One could buy ready-made mural slabs measuring a yard by half a yard in which the space for the inscription, as well as the faces of the figures, was left blank. For example, there would be a Pietà flanked by a knight in armor with a Saint Nicholas or a Saint Peter on one side and a hooded matron with a Saint Catherine or a Saint Madeleine on the other. This was the commonest type of visible tomb in the seventeenth and early eighteenth centuries. A great many of these have disappeared.

Although in the seventeenth century the most ostentatious, and for this reason better preserved, tombs were inclined to abandon the pious scene that persisted on the tombs of lesser dignitaries, this was not for lack of belief but in a spirit of asceticism and humility. In such cases the sarcophagus, or rather the catafalque that represented it, or the massive element that had replaced them both and that had completely disappeared from the mural tomb with praying figure and pious scene, reappeared to become one of the principal elements of the structure. The other, equally important, element was the praying figure. Once a miniaturized donor, it now became life-size and sometimes even larger than life. Sometimes the praying figure was on top of the pseudosarcophagus, like the old recumbent figure. But it could be almost anywhere—an opening in the choir screen (Saint-Etienne, in Toulouse), a corner of the family chapel, or near the choir where it could follow the Mass. These praying figures were scattered all over the church as if they were attending the service: great lords, officials of sovereign courts, prelates. In seventeenth- and early eighteenth-century France, they have the austere and meditative attitude of the Gallican reform, which was averse to excessive manifestations of spirituality.

In the Rome of Bernini and Borromini, on the other hand, they move around in an uninhibited manner, giving free rein to gestures that openly express their mystical emotion. They kneel life-size in the churches where they were the generous churchwardens, in the balconies where they once attended Mass. They lean over to get a better view, as in the loges of a theater. They communicate their feelings to one another with all sorts of lifelike gestures. Their exaltation is both terrestrial and celestial. In these cases the praying figure has abandoned his traditional hieraticism, but within the new baroque mobility he has retained his supernatural character. With his human eyes of stone he follows the Mass of the parish church, which the post-Tridentine reforms have invested with new solemnity. But this Mass is also the eternal Mass celebrated on the celestial altar in that paradise to which he has already been transported.

An old lady of seventy was buried in the Roman church of San Pantaleone, next to the main door—a very desirable location, judging from the evidence of wills—facing the high altar and the miraculous icon of the Virgin, an object that she venerated during her lifetime. The praying figure has its hands crossed at its throat in a gesture that is no longer the traditional one of offering or prayer but one of ecstasy. It is both mystical transport and beatific vision.

In places such as the Protestant countries, where this anticipation of paradise was not accepted, people remained faithful to the old models, either the medieval model of the flat tomb with recumbent or praying figure, or the early modern model of the mural tablet with donor and religious scene, or the austere praying figure of the Gallican type.

There is no doubt that in the course of this evolution, whose details are complex but whose general direction is simple, the praying figure became so common as almost to be called popular. After the recumbent figure, the praying figure became the conventional image of death.

The Reappearance of the Portrait,
the Death Mask,
and the Commemorative Statue

The principal merit of praying figures for us today is that they are excellent portraits. They hold our attention because of their realism. For this reason we have a tendency to confuse individualization with resemblance, whereas in reality the two notions are quite distinct. We have just seen that individualization of the grave first appears among the great in the late eleventh century. But it is not until the end of the thirteenth or the middle of the fourteenth century that funerary effigies truly become portraits. Modern archaeology tends to set the date even later. Albert Erlande-Brandenburg says of the effigy of Charles V (d. 1380) in Saint-Denis: "For the first time, or at least one of the first times, a sculptor executed the recumbent figure of a living person. He did not hesitate to make his work a portrait. Until then there had only been idealized images."[54]

An interval of five to six centuries had elapsed between the disappearance of the old tomb with effigy and inscription and its reappearance around the eleventh century, but three centuries had to pass before the individualized effigy became a likeness. Until then, it was enough to identify the personage by showing the attributes of his position in the ideal order of the world. But these attributes included more than the scepter of the king, or the gesture of benediction, crozier, and sacerdotal garments of the bishop. Facial expression was also part of the panoply. One had to have the face for the part, and if one did not have it by birth, the artist was expected to create one that was more appropriate for posterity. The function of the effigy was to convey a complete sense of the person's role, whereas the purpose of the inscription was simply to furnish the official information.

After the middle of the fourteenth century our imaginary museum becomes a portrait gallery. The process begins with royal and episcopal art and gradually extends to the categories of powerful lords and educated dignitaries. For a long time it bypasses the world of petty legal officials and craftsmen, who were content to have the artist indicate the sartorial and decorative attributes of their rank.

This desire for resemblance is not inevitable. There are highly developed civilizations in which it is unknown. The tendency toward realism in the portrait that characterizes the late Middle Ages—as well as Roman art —is an original and remarkable cultural phenomenon that must be related to what we have said in connection with the will and macabre imagery about the love of life and the desire to survive. There is a direct relationship between the portrait and death, just as there is a direct relationship between the macabre awareness of decomposition and the desire for an afterlife.

I once believed I had found an indication, if not a proof, of this relationship between the portrait and death in the monument of Isabel of Aragon for the tomb containing her flesh at Cosenza. After the death of Saint Louis in Tunis in 1270, she was returning to France by way of Italy with the whole court and the Crusaders. It was an extraordinary funeral procession (indeed, it must have been the first such expedition in history), for they were carrying the bodies of the king and several other princes. She died in Calabria in 1271 during the journey, when a horseback-riding accident brought on a miscarriage. On the site of her death her husband, Philip the Bold, erected a monument of the mural type with a praying figure that is undoubtedly one of the first of its kind. She is kneeling—the image is carved rather than painted—before the Virgin and Child.

There is a plaster cast of this monument in the Trocadero. The visitor is struck by this swollen face, with a scar across it and the eyes closed. It is not surprising that the sculptor is believed to have copied a mask that was made immediately after death. We know that the practice of making death masks was widespread in the fifteenth and sixteenth centuries; it is conceivable that it was already known in 1271. I was tempted by the hypothesis that the artist gave the young woman the face of a dead person, not in order to frighten, as in macabre imagery, but in order to achieve a good likeness.

Today this hypothesis has been abandoned. "There is no evidence for the death mask in this period. Indeed, we must await its appearance until the fifteenth century. The explanation of this face is found in the stone. The presence of a vein of clay in the marble explains the sculptor's mistake."[55]

Perhaps, but what about the closed eyes? Praying figures never have their eyes closed. Even if there was no mask of wax or plaster taken directly from the dead woman's face, is it not conceivable that the face of the monument was still an imitation of reality?

If the use of the death mask was not known, people had long known how to manipulate dead bodies, particularly when they had to be transported. The oldest method was to sew them into a leather sack, as in the romance of Tristan. But before this was done, the heart and bowels were removed, aromatics were added, and the body embalmed. There was an unstated relationship between the preservation of the body and that of the soul; the bodies of certain saints had been miraculously preserved. This practice made it possible to increase the number of burial places and of the visible tombs that marked them. William the Conqueror had his bowels buried in Châlus; his body in the abbey of les Dames, in Caen; and his heart in the cathedral in Rouen. Much later King Charles V had three tombs, one for the heart, one for the bowels, and one for the body. His high constable, Bernard Du Guesclin, had four, one for the flesh, one for the heart, one for the bowels, and one for the bones; the bones had the honor of being buried in Saint-Denis.

In the later Middle Ages, when it was necessary to transport the body, it was no longer sewn into a leather bag. Instead, it was boiled in order to separate flesh from bone. The flesh was buried at the place of death, which provided an excuse for an initial tomb. The bones were saved for the most desirable burial place and the most impressive of the monuments, for the dry bones were regarded as the noblest part of the body, no doubt because they were the most durable. There is a curious parallel between the division of the body into flesh, heart, bowels, and bones and the division of the individual into body and soul.

In the fourteenth century this practice was so widespread that Pope Boniface was moved to forbid it. But during the Hundred Years War there were departures from the prohibition. This sort of manipulation of cadavers and the practice of having a separate tomb for each part of the body bear witness to a new concern for the body as the seat of the personality. The making of a death mask, at whatever date the practice arose, seems to me to belong to the same series of operations and to be inspired by the same motives. There is an impulse to save from destruction a few things that express an incorruptible individuality, particularly the face, which contains the secret of the personality. The use of the death mask has persisted until this century. The death mask of Beethoven was part of the decor of the middle-class drawing room. We have already seen that the mummies of the counts of Toulouse in the musée des Augustins, which are terra-cotta statues from the sixteenth century, were executed from death masks. In the seventeenth century admirers no longer waited for a person to die to capture an unmistakable resemblance. Samuel Pepys describes the trouble he was put to by someone taking an impression of his face when he was in perfect health and had no thought of death. Reproducing the features of death was the best way to imitate life.

In the last analysis, it is irrelevant to my demonstration whether or not the face of Isabel of Aragon at Cosenza is the copy of a death mask. We may assume that the sculptor was inspired by the dead woman's face. We have already observed the reluctance of medieval sculptors to represent the recumbent figure as someone who is dying or has just died. On the other hand, sculptors and creators of wax or wooden representations sometimes used a resemblance of the dead person in order to create an authentic likeness of a living one.

What matters is the contemporaneity of these different phenomena: the relationship between the face of the deceased and the portrait of the living person, great processions and solemn obsequies, the first monumental tombs elevated vertically in the manner of catafalques and their representations.

A close relationship was established between death and resemblance, which corresponds to the close relationship between the recumbent or praying figure on the tomb and the realistic portrait.

A growing interest in resemblance was added to the desire to transmit the biography of a man that was expressed by the epitaph. It would not have been surprising if the commemorative function of the tomb had now developed at the expense of the eschatological—or, as Panofsky calls it, the "anticipatory"—function. And yet until the eighteenth century, despite certain appearances that are misleading today, the two immortalities, the terrestrial and the celestial, were too closely related and interconnected for one to prevail over the other and replace it. The separation is often said to have occurred in the Renaissance; the tombs of the Valois are attributed with a commemorative impulse free of any underlying religious motivation. But according to this thesis, the same would apply to those biographical bas-reliefs, full of pomp and heraldry, that decorate the tombs of the popes of the Counter-Reformation. In reality, the long epitaphs of the sixteenth and seventeenth centuries, which proclaim the merits of the deceased and which are comparable on their own level to the stone chronicles of the popes and kings, confirm rather than deny the certainty or presumption of salvation in the next world.

It was not until the eighteenth century that this situation changed, first among those who may be called the great public servants of their countries, those who were entitled to the recognition of the people and the recollection of history. These are no longer only kings, but great military leaders as well. At Westminster Abbey it is possible to follow without a break the gradual transition from the complete tomb—the tomb that is both eschatological and commemorative—to the tomb that is merely commemorative, official, and civic, to the public monument of today.

We shall analyze this development first by comparing two Dutch tombs, the commemorative tomb of William the Silent, under construction from 1614 to 1622, in the Nieuwe Kirk in Delft, and the tomb of a national hero, a kind of Dutch Nelson who was killed in combat in 1665, in the Grote Kirk in The Hague. The tomb of William the Silent still corresponds to the princely double-decker style of the late Middle Ages, except that the upper part has been brought down to the same level as the lower part, while still remaining distinct from it. The stadtholder is represented in front of the monument rather than on top of it and no longer kneeling, but sitting triumphantly, as if on a throne. This attitude was traditional for sovereigns, from the tombs of Henry VII in Pisa and the Angevins in Naples to the popes of Bernini, by way of the Medicis of Michelangelo. Their majesty was likened to that of God. This stance proclaims their role as *pater patriae,* to use Panofsky's term.

The solemnity of the effect is somewhat diminished, however, by the familiarity of the recumbent figure. But does the term still apply to this reclining man? He is dressed informally in indoor clothes and a soft cap. His jerkin is half buttoned, his eyes closed, his expression peaceful. He looks as if he were asleep. His hands are neither joined nor crossed in the traditional attitude of prayer; his arms are at his sides and his hands are lying flat, as often happens when one sleeps on one's back. Only the straw mat on which he is lying indicates that he has just died and that he has been laid out, according to the custom, "on the straw." There is no question here that in abandoning the gesture of prayer, the recumbent figure has lost its traditional meaning. This is simply a dead man with a handsome face.

The tomb of Admiral J. Van Wassenaer was executed some fifty years later. Its creator was certainly familiar with the then famous monument of William the Silent, so the ways he chose to depart from it are significant. He retained the winged spirit of Fame sounding the trumpet, which may well be a secularized version of the angel of the Last Judgment, and gave it an important place in the composition, which contains no recumbent figure (in other monuments of the sixteenth and eighteenth centuries, this role is filled more discreetly by the Egyptian theme of the pyramid). Thus, it is not the mortality of the great man—or even his eschatological immortality—that the artist wished to proclaim, but his fame. The statue of the admiral fills the whole volume of the tomb.

The same evolution from the medieval recumbent figure to the large commemorative statue is also found on Catholic soil, in Venice, during an earlier period. In the fourteenth and fifteenth centuries, the earliest tombs of the doges are very often large mural compositions in the same monumental spirit that inspired the Angevins of Naples and later the Valois of France. But the recumbent figure still occupies the center of the composition. As on the tomb of the doge Marosini, in Santi Giovanni e Paolo, the doge appears as a praying figure only when he is part of a religious scene of transcendent importance—for example, at the foot of Calvary, where he is presented by his holy patron.

Otherwise, from the fifteenth to the eighteenth century, unlike the Valois of Saint-Denis or the Hapsburgs of the Escorial, he never kneels when he is alone. He is always either seated in majesty, like other princes, or else, more often, he is standing.

It was then that the idea arose, perhaps here in this Italian province, of representing the great men of state standing up and the great men of war preferably on horseback. Inside the Venetian church of the Frari, Lorenzo Bregno, 1500, is standing; Paolo Savelli, 1405, is on horseback. In the earliest examples, in Venice as in the Netherlands, the tomb is combined with the commemorative monument to a famous national figure. The association persisted for a long time in Westminster Abbey and Saint Paul's in London, or in the case of the marshal of Saxony standing on his tomb in Strasbourg. But by now the statue has only a tenuous connection with the tomb and is about to become detached from it altogether, as the commemorative function prevails over the eschatological and individualizing one. The process began in Venice at the end of the fourteenth century with Verrocchio's statue of Colleoni, which is out of doors, in the center of a public square; but the case of Colleoni remains exceptional and somewhat ahead of its time. And the stubborn tradition of burial *ad sanctos*, the reluctance to separate the commemorative and eschatological functions of the individual tomb, gave rise in Venice to some rather surprising compromises that were not imitated. At the end of the seventeenth century, the statues or busts of the visible tomb were erected outdoors, where they were exposed to the view of passersby; however, they were not yet separated from the church, but elevated onto its grand facade over the main entrance. At Santa Maria del Giglio, the facade is entirely covered with statues of the Barbaro family. Above is the eminent sea captain, who died in 1679, with all the attributes of his power, and below, also standing, are the civilian members of the family, wearing wigs and robes.

In seventeenth-century France, the statue was separated from the tomb and became an element of urban architecture dedicated to the glory of the prince. Examples are the statue of Henry IV at the Pont Neuf, the statue of Louis XIII in the place Royale, today the place des Vosges, and the statues of Louis XIV in the place des Victoires and at Versailles. From then on, the statue was designed not so much for tombs in churches as for public squares or the facades of public buildings. It is curious to note that in Washington, D.C., twentieth-century American patriotism has remained more faithful to the traditional association of the memorial, or empty tomb, and the civic monument.

One of the dominant features of the commemorative monument is the lifelike portrait of the great man. The monument has become a statue. During the same period, that is, from the sixteenth to the eighteenth century, the portrait also became the most important element, along with the inscription, of the ordinary tomb. Not the full-length statue, which was a privilege reserved for the elite, but the bust or even simply the head. The fundamental characteristics of the personality were more and more concentrated in the face, with the result that other parts of the body became less interesting and were overlooked. It was no longer necessary to represent them. Thus, the praying figure was reduced to the head alone.

This tomb is mural, approximately 3 by 1½ feet. It consists of the head inside a niche, with an inscription underneath, the whole enclosed in an ornate frame with an architectural decor. This type of tomb, which is almost ubiquitous, is particularly widespread—and well preserved—in Rome. It gives the churches of the Holy City the charm and animation of a museum full of wonderful portraits.

When twilight fills the church, all the heads, arranged in no particular order along the walls or against the pillars, seem to lean out of their niches as if out of windows. The flickering flames of the candles cast patches of yellow light on their faces, and the fleeting contrasts of dark and light bring out the expressions of the features, giving them a kind of motionless and concentrated life.

Elsewhere in the same period, in Catholic Spain or Calvinist Holland, the face is replaced by a more abstract symbol of identity, the coat of arms. In this case the tombstone, whether on the wall or on the floor, consists of a coat of arms and an epitaph.

The Eschatology of Recumbent and Praying Figures

Before proceeding further in our imaginary museum, let us pause for a moment to compare the recumbent figure and the praying figure.

The praying figure has seemed closer to the immortal soul, while the recumbent figure has eventually come to be identified with the corruptible body. The opposition of soul and body was undoubtedly the essential reason for the duality expressed by the two models. We have seen, however, that the artistic expression of this duality, however consistent with theological teaching, met with a silent but stubborn resistance. Eventually, after the disappearance of the recumbent figure, the praying figure took its place as *homo totus,* spirit and matter, in spite of its exclusively spiritual origin.

Has the praying figure always seemed more individualized than the recumbent figure? If so, the attitude of the praying figure would express a desire to reveal its biographical originality, whereas that of the recumbent figure would remain faithful to a more anonymous and fatalistic conception. In fact, the type of the praying figure became widespread at the same time as the realistic portrait, with its interest in the face; indeed, the praying figure is the origin of the portrait, whether individual or familial. The recumbent figure also sought and achieved resemblance, but only at the end of its long career. In the ordinary tombs of early modern times, the two are equally unconcerned with resemblance, and content to indicate the rank of the deceased.

Is the praying figure more animated than the recumbent figure? Its kneeling posture would lead one to believe that it is. To the casual observer, the praying figure seems closer to life, the instantaneous life of a good portrait. The recumbent figure, on the other hand, is closer to death. Indeed, it eventually came to represent death, whether the solemn death of liturgical exhibition or the subterranean death of decomposition. However, the appearance of life in the praying figure is misleading. This seemingly living person is in reality immobilized in a hieratic and fixed attitude. It does exist in the supernatural world, but it does not react to the celestial visions that ought to transport it, as they do in fact transport the personages of Bernini or Borromini. As we know, it was sometimes said of the recumbent figure that it lives without living. One might say of the praying figure that it is in heaven without being there.

The truth is that both the recumbent figure and the praying figure are close to a neutral condition, from which they sometimes deviate in the direction either of life or of death or of beatitude. These hesitations are fascinating, and reflect pressures of scholarly thought and written culture, which have made them better known. But even more interesting and impressive is this central neutrality where the two come together. In this primordial neutrality we must recognize a vestige of the immemorial attitude toward death that I have called the tame death and that is best expressed by the idea of *requies*.

This interpretation is not obvious and may well meet with disbelief on the part of scholars. One must read it in the silent language of images and of their implicit logic, on the margins of written culture.

The belief in a neutral state, which is gloomier in certain cultures (the gray world of Hades) and happier in others (the Sleepers of Ephesus) has survived, despite the reticence or hostility of the clergy. It has persisted in forms that are elementary, obscure, and never quite conscious. It has given rise to deeply rooted and obstinate attitudes that express themselves in a series of denials: a denial of the duality of human existence, a denial of the opposition between the dead and the living, a denial that life after death for human beings is identical to the ineffable glory of celestial creatures. This belief seems to have disappeared in the eleventh century and to have been replaced by a more orthodox eschatology. But in reality it only went underground, and it reappeared with the first visible tombs and the model of the recumbent figure, which translates it perfectly into the world of forms. It was still alive at the end of the Middle Ages, and it was this belief that altered the original inspiration of the praying figure and oriented it toward the tradition of immobility and repose.

Thus, for half a millennium a profoundly unconscious tendency was imposed on funerary iconography—and on the collective sensibility—a massive consistency that written culture cannot explain and of which it was unaware, a representation of the beyond that does not exactly coincide with the teachings of the Church. This tradition, which was no less important for being subterranean, began to disappear in the seventeenth and eighteenth centuries. Part 3 of this book will deal with the changes in sensibility that would put an end to a continuity that had lasted for close to a thousand years. The recumbent figure disappeared at the beginning of the seventeenth century; the praying figure disappeared at the end of the eighteenth. In the new conceptions, of scholarly origin, that came to dominate oral cultures and the collective sensibility, the ancient and durable idea of a neutral, intermediary state beyond death, between life and heaven, disappeared, to be replaced by beliefs in which we rediscover the idea, now accepted on an intuitive level, of the separation of the soul and the body. Nothingness was the fate of the body. On the destiny of the soul there were various opinions: survival in a fully conceptualized beyond, the terrestrial survival of commemoration, or again nothingness. We are now in the altogether new world of the eighteenth to twentieth centuries.

In the Cemetery: Crosses on Tombs

Almost all of the tombs that we have analyzed so far were originally located in churches, and one must stand in the interiors of churches if one is to follow the continuity and grasp the meaning of the iconographic series. But what was going on on the other side of the church wall, in the cemetery? Were there visible tombs there? Fewer than inside the churches, certainly, and different in appearance, but they were not altogether absent.

One part of the cemetery, the periphery, was like a continuation of the church, and the funerary decor there was the same and just as abundant. The outside walls of the church were occupied by tombs with niches. The low galleries of the charnels were divided into chapels that were analogous to the lateral chapels of churches built after the fourteenth century, and these chapels had the same funerary function. They were covered with epitaphs and mural tombs.

But even in the central area of the atrium, which was constantly harrowed by gravediggers, between the large common graves that swallowed up the anonymous masses of the dead, there were a few monuments scattered here and there. Nothing, of course, that resembled the density and regularity of our modern cemeteries. To be convinced of this, one need only go to the musée Carnavalet and look at the precious painting of the cemetery of les Innocents at the end of the sixteenth century. Among the sparse monuments that dot the ground, a few were intended for collective and public use: an outdoor pulpit, a chapel reminiscent of the *lanternes des morts* of central and western France, a Calvary cross that provided a stopping place for the Palm Sunday procession. Like the interior walls of the church, these external niches could be put to funerary purposes: Tablets with epitaphs were sometimes fastened to their bases. In the space between these niches and the large common graves, we can make out a few tombs: slabs raised on short pillars or covering a massive substructure, such as were also found in cloisters, or crosses mounted on steles whose sides are carved or engraved and planted directly in the ground.

Here is a description of les Innocents by Berthold: "In the churchyard . . . the location of the grave was marked simply [but not always, which explains the open spaces without signs or monuments] by a cross of stone or wood [often protected by a little two-sided roof such as can still be seen today in the cemeteries of central Europe] bearing [at the base] a painted or engraved epitaph, by simple slabs [flat tombs, sometimes raised] or by inscriptions fastened to the walls of the charnels [mural tablets with epitaphs]." And in Vauvert: "In the cemetery there are several crosses of stone as well as of wood."[56]

The new form that catches our attention in all these descriptions of cemeteries is the cross. These crosses marked the gravesites of individuals or groups. Antoinette Fleury writes: "Some sixteenth-century testators had a cross erected in the cemetery of les Saints-Innocents, and the graves of members of the family were grouped around it."[57] In 1557, for example, Marie Valet chose "to be buried in the place where her late husband was buried, which is next to a cross belonging to them and commissioned by them in the aforesaid cemetery [les Innocents]."[58] In 1558, Henriette Gabelin asked to be buried in les Innocents, "near a cross that she had placed and established there."

Thus, there were several graves, sometimes apparently unrelated, around one cross; there might also be a family group of crosses. In 1411, an important personage, procurer general at the Parliament of Paris, describes the tomb that he wants built for his children, who were too young to deserve the honor of church burial, and his parents, who had chosen to be buried in the Coulommiers cemetery. (For his wife and himself he preferred the interior of the church.) He writes: "Inasmuch as my father in his will ordered that there be built over the graves of himself and his father in the Coulommiers cemetery two high tombs of plaster [there was a tradition of plaster sarcophagi in the Ile-de-France in the early Middle Ages] with fine plaster crosses, since which I have buried three or four of my children [three or four! he can't remember exactly how many]." Apparently he had not yet arranged for the construction of the crosses requested by his father, for he goes on to request "that my executors or heirs . . . shall have made 5 tombs, all of the same length, with fine plaster crosses, and that the cross in the middle be the tallest and the two on either side of the cross in the middle a little shorter, and the other two at the ends still shorter." The point seems to be not to give everyone a tomb but to create an architectural group of symmetrical and graduated crosses. "I desire that they be of adequate height, for instance, from two and one-half to three feet, and that they be constructed in such wise that the water will run off them when it rains, so that they will last longer."

But this set of five crosses is not sufficient. It must be dominated by a still larger cross, a public cross such as was seen in the cemeteries at the time. Not only this, but it had to be ordered from Paris: "I desire that there be commissioned in Paris a fine wooden cross painted and constructed like the ones in the cemetery of les Saints-Innocents and that it be modeled after those of medium size, not the largest nor the smallest." This is a pedestal cross, and on the pedestal is a tombstone of the mural type: "And that on one of the sides [of the stele] there be the Crucifixion and on the other side, the Virgin Mary holding her Child. And below the Crucifixion two praying figures or representations of two bourgeois people [these representations did not have to look like anyone in particular; a few indications of social status were sufficient], and below Our Lady a man, a woman, and some children [how many?] and that it be fastened with stout iron clamps to the top of the tallest of the five tombs and set well into the ground so that it will last as long as possible."[59]

Whatever their original function may have been, crosses served as topographical landmarks. In 1404 the author of a will chose to be buried "in the cemetery of the Carthusians in Paris between the two stone crosses that are there."[60] In the cemetery in Vauvert in the seventeenth century, the crosses were numbered like the slabs on the floors of some churches and bore epitaphs. The tenth cross bore on its front face the epitaph of Jacques Bourgeois, a lawyer who died in 1612, and on its back face an interminable inscription relating the history of the de Fenes family for the past three hundred years. "Jean de Fenes, once secretary and financial adviser to the king, house, and crown of France, who survived his father and mother, had this inscription placed at the foot of this cross as an eternal mark of his love and respect for their memory. Pray to God for their souls."[61]

At first collective, then gradually individual, the cross became the essential element of a new prototype of tomb created in the seventeenth and eighteenth centuries. Let us try to trace the formation of this model.

In the musée Lorrain, in Nancy, there is a sixteenth-century tomb that must originally have been in a cemetery and that is a good example of the first stage of the individual tomb with cross. It is based on the model of the public pedestal cross, but it has reduced this model to the height of a man. The cross itself has become quite small, occupying only the top of the stele, which has become much longer to compensate for the space once occupied by the cross of the cemeterial model. In other words, the stele consists of three superimposed parts, the top with its carved cross, the middle section with a macabre bas-relief (a *transi* sitting with his head in his hand), and the bottom, a broader base or socle on which is inscribed the name of the deceased and the invocation *"Ave Maria,* Mother of God." The tomb is from a cemetery, not from a church, but it is a fine stone tomb, the tomb of a rich man. In this case the tomb is like a pillar, without a flat horizontal member.

There is another type that combined the flat tomb and the cross. It is described in the seventeenth-century will of a canon of Paris who chose to be buried not in the Cité but in the cemetery of Saint-Cloud, an open-air cemetery "where his late father and mother are buried, and that there be laid a tombstone raised on four low pillars [a flat tomb] with a cross at the head, all this as simple as possible." This is still the tomb of a rich man, despite the expressed desire for humility.

The type of the tomb with cross was therefore invented for important persons. It was to become the tomb of ordinary people, the tomb of the poor man, when he had one at all. The evolution is related to changes in the population of the outdoor cemetery.

Until the sixteenth century, in spite of a clear preference for churches, the cemetery had not yet been completely abandoned by persons of quality. It never was in England (see chapters 2 and 11). In the beginning the walls of the church and the galleries of the charnels were only slightly less sought after and expensive than the interior of the church. Each cemetery was surrounded by a girdle of highly respectable mural monuments. These rich tombs sometimes migrated from the edges of the cemetery toward the central space.

When, in 1569, the general council of the Knights of Malta decided to rebuild the conventual church of Valletta, in Malta, they ordered that "there be reserved a space large enough to serve as an enclosed cemetery." It was known as *il cimeterio del cortile.* The Knights of Malta were buried there until 1603. Only then was it abandoned in favor of the church.

On its site there was constructed a private chapel reserved for the spiritual practices of the Knights, and it was in this chapel and in its crypt that the Knights were henceforth buried. The text of 1631 makes no further mention of the enclosed cemetery of 1569: "That none of our brothers may be buried in any church other than our major conventual church or in the crypt of its funerary chapel."[62]

So it was in the seventeenth century that the cemeteries were virtually abandoned by the upper classes, except for the galleries, and were left to the poor, to those without visible tombs. But this desertion was compensated for by an opposite movement from the church toward the cemetery. Certain important persons chose to be buried in the cemetery not out of respect for tradition, as might have been the case previously, but in a defiant gesture of humility. We do not know what type of tombs they preferred, for they expressed no interest in how they were buried and left everything to the discretion of their heirs or executors. We may assume, however, that their outdoor tombs, when they had them, adopted either the impressive classical forms of the obelisk, pyramid, or column or the simpler form of a cross of stone or painted wood.

And in the eighteenth century a new population was to erect visible tombs in the cemetery. Persons of humble rank—petty officials, craftsmen, and laborers—were no longer content simply to sleep in sanctified ground with no thought of the memory they left behind them. Now they, too, aspired to a visible tomb. The hierarchical conception of society probably did not permit them to use the same models as the upper classes. A few, however—shoemakers, tailors, middle-class Parisians—did not hesitate to copy the mural tablets with inscriptions that were found in churches. (The musée de Cluny, in Paris, has some rather ornate examples dating from the end of the Middle Ages.) It is true that these master craftsmen constituted a true middle class, a petite bourgeoisie that occasionally bordered on affluence. Like the peasant elite, they were inclined to decorate their tombs with the proud symbols of their profession, the tools of their trade. In the musée des Augustins, in Toulouse, a little stone cemetery cross from the sixteenth or seventeenth century has a weaver's shuttle on one side (on the other side is the shell of a pilgrim to Saint-Jacques). In the musée Lorrain, in Nancy, a plow and harrow are pictured on the tomb of a laborer who wanted to show his true wealth. In the cloister of the Dominicans in Toulouse, one can find slabs from the eighteenth century on which the name of the deceased is followed by the name of his trade: This is the grave of X, Master Chandler (or Master Cooper), and his family. Candles or tools are the only decoration.

However, this indication of the trade is very rare, even if one allows for the number of these humble monuments that were probably destroyed. The impulse was stifled, and we have almost nothing that resembles the numerous professional symbols of Gallo-Roman tombs.

The new category of ordinary people who invaded the cemeteries, especially after the end of the seventeenth century, naturally adopted the simplest of the already existing types of tombs: brief inscriptions consisting of the name and a pious invocation in the vernacular of northern or southern France. But from the beginning these people showed a preference for the cross, which could be either a three-dimensional cross set in the ground or a design engraved or carved on the surface of a stele. After the middle of the seventeenth century, these very simple tombs became more numerous. At first they were bare slabs with only the name, an invocation, and very often a small cross. A few of these have been accidentally preserved and are still to be found in churches, like the one in Poissy from the middle of the seventeenth century with a clumsy drawing of an "intendant de Mons. le président de Maisons," or the one in Santa Maria dei Miracoli, in Venice, dated 1734, engraved superficially, like a graffito, on a small square ceramic tile of the floor. Others have been preserved in the cloisters of monasteries. But many of those that were once in cemeteries have disappeared. In this first type of tomb, the cross is merely a symbol, the only ornament on the slab.

The other type is the stele in the shape of a cross, a small cross, which may be made of stone but which would more often be made of wood. There are some stone examples of this type in the musée des Augustins, in Toulouse: not the tall, slender cross resting on a pedestal, but a short, low cross with thick arms of equal length. The very brief inscription is engraved in the center.

In Avioth, in Ardennes, there are still a few vestiges of an old cemetery next to the church. These include a *lanterne des morts* called *la Recevresse* and a low wall dating from the late eighteenth century. The wall was probably built to comply with the injunctions of the bishops, who complained about the poor maintenance of the cemeteries and demanded that they be enclosed. Some funerary steles have been built into the wall and form a part of it. They are simple and beautiful, and consist of two parts: above, a cross in bas-relief and below, an oval cartouche containing a very short epitaph.

These steles in the shape of crosses or, more often, with crosses carved on them as a decoration, are found in the old cemeteries of England and the grand duchy of Luxembourg. In the grand duchy a small eighteenth-century cemetery near the church still has neat rows of steles on which the moss has not erased all the dates. The form of the stele is vertical and massive, and the cross carved in bas-relief on one side is framed by palm trees suggesting paradise: a reminder of the *refrigerium* in the midst of the Age of Enlightenment!

In the south of France, under the porch of the little village church of Montferrand, in Aude, there are some eighteenth-century steles that were in the cemetery before its reorganization around 1850. These narrow vertical steles end with a cross that is carved and inscribed inside a circle. It is possible that the famous Basque steles are simply a variant of this type, which has been preserved intact until our time.

Between the fifteenth and eighteenth centuries, then, an original model of outdoor tomb developed, a model that bears no resemblance to the tombs found inside churches and that combines a cross and a short inscription on a vertical stele. But this model was not the only one used in the cemeteries of the seventeenth and eighteenth centuries. There were others that did not have the same originality and were mere imitations of the flat tomb or the mural tablet with epitaph found inside churches.

The Cemetery of Marville

Examples of this type may be seen in their original places in the poetic setting of a cemetery that may not have changed very much since the end of the Middle Ages. Marville is a little town in Ardennes that has grown up around a château that belonged to the comte de Bar in the late Middle Ages. It is a new town built next to the site of a much older town where there is still a chapel devoted to Saint-Hilaire. The site was abandoned, but Saint-Hilaire continued to be the parish church of Marville until the construction of the church of Saint-Nicolas in the fourteenth century, and its cemetery continued to be the town cemetery. Because it was already separate from the town, an exceptional circumstance in those days when the dead slept among the living, this old medieval atrium satisfied contemporary legal requirements, and Marville did not have to move its cemetery, which explains why it is so well preserved. Marville has another curious feature. Halfway between the cemetery of Saint-Hilaire and the fortified site of the present town there is a Gothic aedicula representing the Crucifixion. This aedicula resembles the "Montjoie," the stone monuments that served as stopping places for royal funeral processions between Paris and Saint-Denis.

The Saint-Hilaire church is very small, and could not have contained many tombs. Most of the graves were made outside the church, in the cemetery itself. Some inscriptions have been engraved directly on the exterior wall. A great many steles were planted in the ground of the cemetery. There are still some left, too badly damaged to have been moved.

In 1870, the finest and best preserved, almost all dating from the seventeenth century, were removed and placed for safekeeping in the nave of the little church. Saint-Hilaire has become a veritable museum of the ordinary lower-class tomb under the *ancien régime,* a museum that is probably like no other in existence.

In these tombs we find an exact replica of the mural epitaph tablet that we also found inside the churches or in the galleries of charnels. Above is the religious scene: Crucifixion with the Virgin and Saint John, Pietà, entombment, Resurrection, angel slaying the dragon, Immaculate Conception, or representations of saints—Saint John the Baptist and especially Saint Nicholas, patron saint of the new church of Marville. Opposite the religious scene, on the same level, are the praying figures, the deceased kneeling with his wife and family. Below is the inscription. Although the style is clumsy and naïve, these are people of a certain rank; officials of the bailiff's court appear on these outdoor tombstones.

The effect is curious. It is as if pictures have been removed from the walls where they once hung, and stuck in the ground. The practice was still common in the early nineteenth century. It is found everywhere where burial in cemeteries has been common, that is, rarely in France, very often in England, colonial America, and even central Europe, as for example in the famous Jewish cemetery in Prague.

Next to these vertical steles, in Saint-Hilaire, in Marville, one also finds cruciform steles with oval cartouches for the inscription similar to those in the wall of Avioth, which happens to be nearby. There is also another type that merits our attention. It consists of a vertical stele derived from the mural tablet and a horizontal slab derived from the flat tomb. It is as if a mural tablet had been planted at the head of a flat tomb. The inscription is on the vertical stele. The only decoration on the horizontal slab is a cross engraved between two candles. The candles symbolize light and refer to the candle that was placed in the hand of the dying or at the bedside of the dead. This combination of a vertical and a horizontal element prefigures the ordinary tomb of the nineteenth and twentieth centuries in France and Italy. We need only replace the stele by the cutout cross—here the cross was merely engraved or carved on the slab—and transfer the inscription from the stele to the slab in order to arrive at the model that is most commonly found on the Continent today.

But if we wish to re-create the cemetery of the seventeenth, eighteenth, and early nineteenth centuries from what is left of it today, we need one more element, the wooden cross. We know that at least as early as the fifteenth century the crosses in cemeteries, even those next to important graves, were made of wood.

A painting dated 1859, Jules Breton's *Plantation d'un Calvaire,* provides a realistic picture of a cemetery in the middle of the nineteenth century. However, there are many indications that this was an old cemetery. For one thing, it is around the church, whose appearance at the end of the eighteenth and beginning of the nineteenth centuries must not have been very different.

The exterior walls of the church and of the cemetery are covered with mural plaques of a type that is no longer seen today but that was common after the seventeenth century in Holland and Germany. These plaques are in the shape of a lozenge that contains the inscription, and are surmounted by a small cross. These monuments of notables remained true to an old tradition and did not attempt to coincide with the exact site of the grave, which explains why they were abandoned. The central part of the cemetery is occupied, no longer by the common graves, which had long been prohibited, but by simple wooden crosses surmounted by two-sided roofs. This type of cross existed in les Innocents in the sixteenth century, to be replaced either by more ambitious monuments or by the simplest type of wooden cross, the cross used for soldiers and the poor. But the form of the cross is unimportant; what matters is that the model of the simple common tomb has now been determined: the wooden cross at the head of a mound of earth.[63]

Thus, from the fifteenth to the early nineteenth century we have observed the formation of a model for common tombs in cemeteries in which the symbol of the cross occupied all the room left for decoration and iconography. Definitively established by the end of the eighteenth and the beginning of the nineteenth centuries, the period when cemeteries were beginning to be populated by the visible tombs of a class of people who had never had them before, the model later spread and was standardized, and it has been carefully preserved, even in regions that are regarded as de-Christianized. Even today, not to put a cross on one's grave or on the graves of one's relatives is an exceptional act of defiance. Societies that are the least apparently religious are still attached to the presence of the cross. This is first of all because in the last two centuries the cross has become the symbol of death. A cross in front of a name means that the person is deceased. Next, even among nonbelievers, the cross, more or less detached from its historical Christian meaning, is vaguely recognized as a symbol of hope and protection. People are attached to it without knowing why, but they are attached to it all the same. It evokes not the next world but something else, something mysterious, profound, and inexpressible, of which we are only dimly aware.

Endowment Tablets

In the preceding pages, in speaking of mural tombs with praying figures in churches as well as in cemeteries, we have often used the word *tablet.* We must return to this word, for it refers to the form of tomb that was most popular, most ordinary, and that also most frequently signified the new mentality that triumphed at the end of the Middle Ages.

The funerary inscriptions and monuments that we have just analyzed reveal a double desire: a desire to anticipate the beyond by representing oneself in an attitude of transcendent repose or immobility, and a desire to live on in the memory of others. This is nothing very new in the religious history of Western civilization; Panofsky has clearly understood this continuity. I have merely tried to emphasize and even to contrast two forms of transcendence: one of literate origin, in which the soul and the body are quite separate in the beyond, and the other of oral and popular origin, in which the *homo totus* waits in peace.

The tablet of the late Middle Ages shows that the dualistic model followed by educated people had captured the popular imagination. In it we shall once again encounter the individualistic conception we found in wills, their way of treating matters pertaining to salvation and the beyond with the legal and financial precision and cautious circumspection required by the affairs of this earth.

Sometimes the words *tablet* and *epitaph* were used interchangeably to mean "tombstone," because the epitaph filled most of the space of the tablet, although, as we shall see, the nature of the inscription in the two cases was not always the same.

But the language of the time—the end of the Middle Ages and the beginning of the modern era—did distinguish the tablet from the tomb. A tablet might be one of several tombs belonging to the same personage. It might also be his only tomb. Take, for example, the 1400 will of Guillaume de Chamborand, equerry to the king. First we find the choice of burial: "He wishes his body to lie in the church of la Terne, which is of the order of the Celestines, in the diocese of Limoges, in the choir of the church near the main altar on the side next to the wall."[64]

Next the author talks about his tomb proper: "Over his body there shall be erected and established a tomb [a slab] raised a foot and a half above the ground. [It will be] of stone on which shall be his representation decorated with his arms [that is, a recumbent figure]. And there shall be inscribed on and around said tomb his name and title, and the day and year of his death."

The recumbent figure lying on a socle was to constitute the lower level of a tomb with a niche placed against the wall. "And above this tomb there shall be a picture of Our Lady holding Our Lord her Child in her arms, which shall be painted on the wall and which shall be beautiful and well done. And in front of this picture there shall be a representation of his person painted on the wall over his tomb in which he shall be kneeling, in his armor, with joined hands. And he shall be preceded by two pictures, one of Saint John the Baptist, the other of Saint William."[65] We recognize the two-level tomb with the recumbent figure below, surmounted by the praying figure with a religious scene and the holy patrons.

A fine tomb, no doubt, and quite complete, but it was not enough for the testator. He arranged for a second funerary monument, which he refers to not as a tomb but as a tablet: "Item, he desires and ordains that there be made a *copper tablet* on which shall be written his name, surname, and title, the day and year of his death [but neither his age nor his date of birth] and the Mass that shall be said in perpetuity for the souls of himself, his late father and mother, friends, relatives [friends and relatives are placed in the same category], and benefactors of the church." The cost of this perpetual service will be covered by the income from a sum of money bequeathed to the church council: "And this tablet shall be placed on the wall over his tomb, under the picture of Our Lady and his representation [his portrait as a praying figure], which shall be painted on the wall over his tomb, as has heretofore been described." The tablet is separate from the tomb, and it is usually in another place altogether. But here the testator has put them in the same place.

A testator of the same period, a priest who was canon of Reims and secretary to the king, asks for "a fine and dignified tomb . . . and a copper tablet fastened to the wall, on which shall be written what his executors shall ordain," that is, the details of the endowment.

Another will, dated 1409, also calls for a tomb and a tablet: "She wishes and ordains a brass tablet to be made and fastened to a pillar or the wall of the church, near the tomb mentioned above [the same desire for the proximity of tablet and tomb], which tablet shall make mention of the anniversary Mass for herself, her son-in-law, and her daughter." Forty Parisian sous were provided for its execution. The tomb is described next: "Over said grave there shall be made and established a tomb of stone on which there shall be engraved three figures or representations, one of herself, another of her son-in-law, and the other of her daughter."[66] The author is describing a tomb with praying figures, also mural, but quite distinct from the endowment tablet.

Two centuries later, in 1622, we find the same desires and customs unchanged. For example, this "permission granted by the churchwardens of the church of Saint-Jean-en-Grève" to the widow of a "surgeon ordinary to the king" to "have an epitaph placed against the pillar that stands against the widow's pew [where she attended Mass], or in front of the grave where the deceased was buried, and to have engraved on it whatever she shall choose, to the memory of the deceased," and in addition, "to have placed over the grave a tomb. On this tomb, she may have engraved the figures of a man and woman and around these she may also have engraved another inscription."[67] From the description, it sounds like another flat tomb with engraved recumbent figures. The same deceased was therefore entitled to a mural tablet and a flat tomb, in the same church.

Some testators cared more about their tablets than they did about their tombs. "And he wishes that this endowment be inscribed on a tablet which is to be attached to the chapel by an iron chain" (1411).[68]

This type of monument was not intended to reach posterity in general, like the biographical inscriptions that we analyzed above. The tablet was addressed to the small but self-renewing group of persons on whom the religious services depended and who were suspected of neglecting them. Some shrewd testators made it worthwhile for their heirs to keep an eye on the directors, churchwardens, and priests of the charitable institutions and churches they endowed by arranging to have them recover possession of the legacy in the event the conditions were no longer fulfilled.

The endowment tablet was, therefore, an extension of the will, a means of publicity to ensure its execution. This is why testators were not always satisfied with a single tablet near their grave. They preferred to have several, one in each place to which they had made a substantial endowment. This practice was common in the sixteenth and seventeenth centuries.

A seventeenth-century will clearly illustrates how the publicizing of endowments via the mural tablet outweighed the transcendental and commemorative values of the tomb with recumbent figure, praying figure, and eulogistic epitaph. In 1611 Claude Evrard, a nobleman of Moustier, in Brie, left no instructions regarding his burial except that it be in "the Saint-Jean church, where his late father is buried." He does not specify any particular location or type of tomb. "He leaves everything up to the goodwill and discretion of his executor," a formula that at that time indicated indifference. However, he goes into considerable detail about his pious legacies and the obligations they imposed on the beneficiaries. The first substantial legacy was to the Saint-Louis hospital: "They [the manager and the director of the hospital] shall be obliged in perpetuity to have said, chanted, and celebrated in the chapel of said place every week of the year in whatever suitable place can be found, a Low Requiem Mass followed by a *De Profundis* and the customary prayers . . . that there be celebrated aloud every year after the day the testator shall die in this chapel a High Requiem

Mass with Lauds, Vigils, and Commendations, and that there be provided by the manager and director such ornaments, candles, bread, and other things as are necessary to the celebration of High Mass."

In exchange for the legacy he further required the director of the hospital, in order "to perpetuate the memory of said endowment," to place "at the expense of his heirs a marble epitaph in the chapel in the most suitable place that can be found." Similarly, at Neuf-Moustier-en-Brie, the recipient of the other legacy, "he wishes also that in memory of said endowment there be placed by the [churchwardens] of said church a marble epitaph."[69] The memory that is being perpetuated here is not the memory of a man or his life, but the memory of the endowment.

Most endowments are to hospitals, but others to schools are not unusual. Bequests were made for catechism classes or small schools, and also for scholarships, as we can see from this tablet dated 1556, which is still hanging in Saint-Maclou, in Pontoise: "The wise and venerable Maître Renault Barbier, during his lifetime priest, prior, curate of Auvers, and apostolic notary in Pontoise, has bequeathed to the school of this house 32 pounds 10 sous 5 deniers annual income on the condition that the directors of the school shall admit 4 children from the parish of Auvers and pay the regents for them by the month, and shall have celebrated every year at this school a High Requiem Mass in his behalf on the 16th of April, and also in his behalf shall have sung on the day before the feast days of the Virgin Mary by the children of this school under the direction of a regent at 11 o'clock in the morning a service with *De Profundis* in the chapel of the confraternity of scholars, as specified in the will of the aforementioned Barbier, drawn up in the presence of notary . . . in Pontoise on the 18th day of March, 1596. *Requiescat in pace.*"

Some people, for reasons of economy or humility, do not go to the expense of having a brass or marble tablet. In this case they use another, more precarious form of publicity. For example, in 1628 our vine grower from Montreuil left four hundred pounds to his parish church "on the condition . . . that the testator be included in the prayers that are said in the church [the Prayers from the Pulpit during High Mass on Sunday], and also, on the condition that when the six Masses shall be said [on All Saints' Day, Christmas, Candlemas, Easter, Pentecost, and the Day of Our Lady of Mercy], the churchwardens see that an announcement is made from the pulpit of the church."[70]

The posting of the tablet, like the laying of a tombstone, was the subject of a contract signed by the testator, or his executor, and the churchwardens in the presence of a notary. Here is an example dated 1616: "Permission granted by the churchwardens of Saint-Jean-en-Grève to Pierre Vieillard, councillor to the king, president and treasurer general of

France in the Department of Finances at Soissons, and general legatee of Nicolas Vieillard, his uncle, who during his lifetime was president and treasurer general of France at Soissons, to have placed in perpetual memory of the deceased [and not merely of the endowment; here the two ideas of commemoration and redemption are combined] in the chapel of Saint-Claude in the Saint-Jehan church, on the south side [always the most sought after] in front of and opposite the altar of said chapel [a tablet], which shall contain an inscription describing the endowment made by the deceased to the catechism class of the Saint-Jehan church [like the scholastic endowment, an endowment of the Counter-Reformation for the purpose of religious education] and their successors in accordance with the contract signed by the predecessors of the churchwardens, on the one hand, and by M. Vieillard, on the other hand, concerning this endowment in the presence of Maître . . . [the name of the notary is left blank]."[71]

Tombs for Souls

The importance accorded to the endowment tablet from the sixteenth to the eighteenth century was such that it often replaced the tomb. This gave rise to a very popular type of mural tombstone that combined in a single small monument the characteristics of the epitaph with praying figures and religious scene and the endowment tablet. It begins with a narrow band of engraving in which the praying figures kneel before a religious scene, executed in a somewhat schematic style, since this composition is no longer the essential element. Below, the inscription occupies almost the whole surface of the tombstone. It consists of two parts. The first, which is very brief, is the epitaph, the bald statement of the identity of the personage, without biographical or hagiographical details. The second, which is very long and precise, describes the endowment, its amount, and the services required, and often gives the name of the notary.

These monuments must have been extremely common in France from the sixteenth to the middle of the eighteenth century. In spite of all the vicissitudes our churches have suffered from the eighteenth century to the present, in spite of the indifference of priests, architects, archaeologists, and even historians, there are enough of them left for us to imagine how the walls and pillars looked covered with these plaques. They must have been a little like the walls of those modern sanctuaries that are covered with the votive offerings of twentieth-century pilgrims.[72]

Sometimes the epitaph is dominant, sometimes the endowment. Here the row of praying figures is well represented; there it is neglected. But the general appearance remains the same, revealing a continuing desire to perpetuate the precautions taken for the salvation of the soul. With these tablets we enter into a mentality that is as different from the archaic one of the recumbent and praying figures as it is from ours today. It is the same mentality as the one expressed in wills. The tablet constitutes a new type of tomb, which I call the tomb of the soul.

Here is an example taken from Gaignières; it is dated 1392. "Under this marble tomb lies the late Maistre Nicholas de Plancy, during his lifetime lord of . . ., who passed away in the year 1392 [a very expeditious epitaph] and who, together with his wife, has ordained and established this chapel of CIIX pounds income, to be converted and distributed in the form of bread to the canons and chaplains, provided they say a Mass every day immediately after the elevation of the body of Jesus Christ during High Mass in this church [an indication of the quasi-magical devotion to the sight of the *Corpus Christi* at the moment of the elevation of the host] and say the solemn Masses that are said every year, the Mass of the Annunciation, the Masses of Saint Nicolas and Sainte Catherine, and the Mass of the Conception of Our Lady."[73]

At Cergy-sur-Oise there is a mural plaque dated 1404. At the top, in the narrow section devoted to the praying figure, are Saint Christopher, patron saint of the church, and the deceased kneeling before him in armor. All the rest of the space is taken up by the inscription: "Here lies a nobleman, Pierre Cossart, during his lifetime squire and lord of Dammartin, who left to the priests and churchwardens of Saint-Christophe-de-Cergy the sum of 60 Parisian sous income per year from a business belonging to Roger de Quos, located in Pontoise at the corner of rue de Martre bordering on one side on Robin the turner, leading to the heirs of Richard de Quos, and on the other side on the Pavement du Roi. [This fifteenth-century address has all the precision and clarity of an address in modern London!] In consideration of which the priest of this church shall every year, on the anniversary of the day the deceased passed from this life, say and celebrate a High Mass with Vigils with IX psalms and IX Lessons [penitential psalms], with deacons and subdeacons, and in addition the priest shall every Wednesday of the IIII times a year say and celebrate a High Mass with deacons and subdeacons and Vigils for the dead with IX psalms and IX Lessons. And in order to maintain this service, the priest shall have the sum of XL sous per year, paid by the hands of the churchwardens. The remaining XX sous the deceased has left to the church council for books, ornaments, and candles to be used for this service and to collect said LX sous per year income [the cost of collection]. Which lord passed away 9 April 1404, two days after Easter. Pray for his soul." The legal precision of the text is admirable.

Another tablet, dated 1458, also from Saint-Maclou, in Pontoise, has a Pietà flanked by the kneeling figures of the deceased man and wife, being presented by their holy patrons.

"Here lie the late Pierre de Moulins, deputy from Pontoise to the king, and Martine Lataille, his wife, who have endowed this church of Saint-Maclou, in Pontoise, so that there will be said and celebrated two Low Masses each week of the year in perpetuity at the altar of Our Lady, at about . . . o'clock for the help of their souls, one of these Masses to be on Tuesday and the other on Thursday, with Vigils, IX psalms, and Lessons. Once a year each of these Vigils the first Sunday of the XII months. All of which Vigils and Masses the council of this church is obliged . . ."

In the same church in Pontoise, there is another epitaph, dated 1550: Nicolas Lefebre and his wife have donated a meadow to the church council provided there be "said, chanted, and celebrated in this church each Friday of the IIII times a year in perpetuity for the souls of the deceased and of their deceased friends [that is, close or distant relatives] Vigils, and High Requiem Masses." The church was obliged to provide whatever was necessary and to "place the pall over the graves" during the services. The epitaph also mentions the distribution of money to the clergy and contains instructions regarding chimes and a prohibition against transferring the endowment.

Artisans did not lack the impulse toward generosity or publicity. The archives of Parisian epitaphs include this tablet, dated 1564: "Here lies an honorable man, Jacques de La Barre, during his lifetime a tailor and bourgeois of Paris, who passed away on the XXIInd day of October MDLXIV, and who left to the Confraternity of the Blessed Sacrament of the Altar in the church of Saint-Benoît-le-Bien-Tourné, in Paris, 5 pounds income, to be paid every year by a business at the sign of the Golden Rattrap in the city of Paris, provided the priests shall have said and celebrated on the day that the deceased shall die, or on other suitable days, a High Requiem Mass with deacons, subdeacons, and cantors, with Vigils and Commendations, a *Libera*, and a *De Profundis*."[74]

In the seventeenth century nothing changes. Here is a mural cartouche dated 1674, still from Saint-Maclou, in Pontoise: "The honorable Antoine, bourgeois lord of Pontoise, whose body lies in this chapel, out of the devotion he always had for the Very Blessed Sacrament, has founded in perpetuity in the church of Saint-Maclou, in Pontoise, XII evening services of the Blessed Sacrament, to be said the first Thursday of each month with exhibition of the Blessed Sacrament [a devotion of the Counter-Reformation] with 10 candles of white wax on the altar. The service shall include the chanting of the *O Salutaris Hostia*, the Vespers of the Blessed Sacrament, the prayer *Exaudiat*, the verse *Fiat manus tua*, the prayers for the king, *Ecce Panis*, *Bone Pastor*, *Qui Cuncta*, and *Ave Verum*

Corpus [no *Tantum Ergo?*], while the priest gives the benediction, and *Libera* and *De Profundis* over the grave, over which shall be placed the representation of the dead [a catafalque covered with the pall], together with four burning candles of white wax. Each service shall be announced from the pulpit on the preceding Sunday, the big bells and chimes shall be rung, and the services shall be celebrated with all the fine red ornaments, all this for a consideration of 2,000 pounds, according to the contract signed in the presence of J. F. and H. D., notaries, in Pontoise on 13 March 1674."

Another tablet, also in Pontoise, begins with the names of the notaries, as if they were actually more important than anyone else. "According to a contract signed in the presence of C. L. and B. F., notaries, in Pontoise on 4 January 1681, there shall be held in said church for the repose of the soul of the deceased, by Messire Pierre du Monthiers, knight, lord of Saint-Martin, president of the bailiff's court of Pontoise, on behalf of Lady Marie Seigneur, his wife, and by Martin Seigneur, squire, councillor secretary to the king, son of the deceased, a complete service of three High Masses. . . . All necessary items shall be provided by the curates and churchwardens in consideration of the sum of 360 pounds, as provided by the aforementioned contract. Pray to God for his soul."

A tablet dated 1722 from the cathedral in Toulouse omits any allusion to the place of burial. It is difficult not to see this silence, which was common at that time, as a sign of indifference. Here the philanthropic purpose tends to prevail over the goal of redemption: "Messire Jean de Cabrerolle de Villespan, councillor at Parliament and provost of the church of Toulouse, has founded in perpetuity a Mass for the Dead [it used to be called a Requiem Mass, because there was more than one Mass for the Dead] to be celebrated by the gentlemen of the chapter of the church on 31 March, the day of his death, for the repose of his soul, with an honorarium of 20 sous for each of the gentlemen of the chapter and 10 sous for each of the gentlemen of the lower choir, payable only to those actually present by the Hôtel-Dieu Saint-Jacques, his beneficiary. In addition, he has endowed the hospital with 24 beds for destitute incurables, with a chaplain who is to say 2 Masses per week at the altar of this chapel, dedicated to Saint Stephen, for the repose of his soul and those of his parents." There follow some instructions on the choice of chaplains. I shall have occasion to return to this document in connection with the founding of chapels.

To recapitulate: In the fifteenth century, the tablet was often found near the tomb without actually being part of it. Sometimes it was in a separate place. Between the sixteenth and eighteenth centuries the tablet became the commonest form of tombstone. Either it separated itself completely from the tombstone and was transferred to the site of each endowment or else it merged with the tombstone, becoming its essential element. In the eighteenth century it was no longer called a tablet, but was referred to simply as the epitaph, which had become synonymous with tombstone.

These documents have led us to isolate a fourth type of tomb after the recumbent figure, the praying figure, and the cruciform steles found in cemeteries, a type whose meaning we must now attempt to discover. Praying figures, recumbent figures, and crosses all bore witness to the belief in an intermediate state between earth and heaven. Epitaphs commented on the merits of the deceased in this world and the next. With the endowment tablet, there is a complete change in attitude. We have noticed that on the tablet the biographical account, so well developed in other inscriptions, is usually limited to a brief notice of the official data. The religious scenes and pious invocations are also treated in the most elliptical manner and are reduced to a few symbols. These elements are no longer essential —and yet we are in the middle of the baroque period. The main purpose of the endowment tablet is to oblige the priests to celebrate the Masses prescribed and paid for in advance for "the salvation of his [the donor's] soul." At this point the tombstone ceases to be "anticipatory" and commemorative. Together with the will, it constitutes one element of an insurance policy for the soul in the beyond. It is written in the same style as the will, from which it even quotes passages, and the notary is one of the main characters in the drama, together with the deceased, the clergy, and the saints. What must be perpetuated is neither the rank nor the honors nor the merits of the deceased, nor even the generosity of his legacies, but that which the Church gives in exchange for his donations, that is, the religious services.

Of course, the belief expressed here in the communion of the saints and the treasury of the Church is very old. We have seen it give rise to the fraternities of Carolingian abbeys and the pseudosacramental wills of the later Middle Ages (see chapter 4). But it was not until the end of the fifteenth and, above all, the sixteenth and seventeenth centuries that this belief overcame the secret resistances of older beliefs drawn from the ancient reservoir of oral cultures. These archaic beliefs avoided the separation of soul and body and overly active representations of the beyond. The endowment tablet marks the triumph of another conception, which had probably long been taught by the scholarly orthodoxy of the churches; but the churches would not have succeeded in imposing the new conception had not the traditional defenses given way and the collective sensibility been ready to accept it.

The most popular tomb, no doubt, the endowment tablet is no longer the tomb of the body, but the tomb of the soul. The *homo totus* and the body have retreated into indifference, while the soul has invaded every dimension of the individual; the soul has become the whole man. It is a soul that is in danger of being lost, yet capable of being saved by means of a precise and methodical program of prayer. Long after the Last Judgments of the cathedrals and the individual judgments of the *artes moriendi*, and thanks to the individualistic practice of writing wills, the soul has penetrated that profound and well-defended part of the collective unconscious that finds expression in the morphology of tombstones. The soul is that incorruptible and ethereal element that death has released from the heavy uncertainties of this life and that can now assume, in full consciousness, a destiny that was formerly murky and confused. In a world that is now transparent, the soul is clearly destined for the best or the worst. The great medieval acts of charity have become powerless to change the laws of Providence. However, man's free will enables him to prepare while he is still on earth, where he is half blind, for the journey of his immortal soul. The fate of his soul tomorrow depends on his works today, on his consciousness, self-control, and foresight, and on the arrangements he is wise enough to make here and now. The soul has become the advance guard of the self.

Ex-votos

The late sixteenth and early seventeenth centuries also saw the rise of a new genre, born out of popular piety, that bore an interesting relationship to the funerary iconography that we have been studying. I am referring to the *ex-voto,* an offering in fulfillment of a religious vow.

I do not mean, of course, the facsimile of an object offered to God as a token of gratitude: the healed eye, leg, breast, or stomach; the shipwrecked vessel from which one has been miraculously saved; the chains of the freed prisoner or galley slave. These customs are very ancient, dating from well before the Christian era, and are still observed today. No, what appeared at this time was a painting placed in the sanctuary of the saint who was invoked in time of danger, by way of thanks for his or her protection.

The oldest examples of these paintings are divided into two parts. To the left is the donor on his knees, to the right a celestial scene, showing the blessed intercessor appearing in the clouds. Later a third element was added to the first two: the scene of the miracle, the description of the danger the donor had escaped. In the eighteenth century this new element took up more and more space, until by the beginning of the nineteenth century it had reduced the donors and saints to the status of bystanders.

The miracle has retained its supernatural character—it would be ridiculous to attribute this evolution to the development of some sort of rationalism —but the supernatural has descended to earth, and its primary manifestation is the miracle rather than the apparition.

This arrangement is reminiscent of the popular small mural tablets with praying figures, the "tombs for souls." Indeed, the spiritual distance between the tablet and the *ex-voto* is not great. The first represents the ascent to heaven of the deceased after his death; the second represents a descent from heaven on behalf of one living but in danger, on the occasion of a miracle. The donor of an *ex-voto* is at least temporarily involved in the supernatural world in which the deceased permanently resides.

In some cases the *ex-voto* came to resemble the tombstone so closely that it replaced it, producing something the German historian Lenz Kriss-Rettenbeck calls a *Totentafel.* A plate from his book shows a 1767 *Totentafel* representing two cradles in which four children are lying, two in each. But only one child is alive; the other three hold small red crosses in their hands, signifying that they are dead. The father and mother, also in bed, have survived, and are represented again in a corner in the attitude of praying figures.[75]

It seems likely that an epidemic struck this family and that only the parents and one child escaped death. Hence this *ex-voto,* which fills the two functions of gratitude for the living and prayer for the dead.

Another painting, dated 1799, represents a family gathering in front of a religious scene: three men, three women, and four children wrapped in swaddling clothes. The children are all dead, as are two of the men and two of the women. The only ones alive are the man and woman who are the donors.[76]

In these canvases, the dead take their places alongside the living in the row of praying figures. This is in no way surprising, for in that antechamber of the supernatural world that is the domain of the praying figure, the differences between life and death no longer matter. However, the two groups are distinguished by a symbol: a small red cross, almost imperceptible to anyone who is not looking for it, which the dead hold in their hands or which is suspended over their heads.

This symbol is by no means restricted to the *ex-voto* or to popular art. In the museum in Brussels, one finds it in sixteenth-century Flemish altarpieces over the heads of certain donors. And in the sacristy of the cathedral in Frankfurt am Main, one finds it over several members of a family kneeling at the foot of a fine copy of Vandyke's Crucifixion, a painting that is probably funerary in origin and associated with a tombstone, chapel, or endowment.

These *ex-votos* showing a family stricken by misfortune, with the dead and the living side by side, disappear in the nineteenth century. The sensibility of the age no longer tolerated the combining of gratitude for the survivors with regret for the deceased. However, it produced another type of funerary *ex-voto* of a completely different inspiration, but which also illustrates the persistence of the praying figure and the spirit of the endowment tablet.

This new type of *ex-voto* is, in effect, the tomb of those who have no tomb: drowned woodcutters carried away by the logs they were hauling, or soldiers killed in battle. Three soldiers who died during the Russian campaign of Napoleon I are shown kneeling before Saint Martin, their patron saint.[77]

In the eighteenth century an extraordinary document represents the conjunction of three related iconographies: the endowment tablet with praying figure, the *ex-voto* offered in gratitude, and the altarpiece depicting souls in purgatory. A soldier kneels before the Immaculate Conception, and a new image appears at his feet. It is the image of purgatory. The presence of purgatory gives the *ex-voto* a sense of supplication rather than of thanksgiving, but it is a supplication in a context of hope, a prayer that one may assume will be answered.[78]

In the eighteenth and nineteenth centuries, at least in the central part of Europe studied by the historian, those who died in combat or as the result of an accident were no longer permitted to go without some sort of monument. The tombstones given to such persons were copied from the *ex-voto suscepto,* which in turn retained the design of the old tombs with praying figures. Consequently the tomb of the unburied dead of the nineteenth century was still a tablet with praying figures, in an age when this model had not been used for over a century. Kriss-Rettenbeck publishes reproductions of two wooden tablets, dated 1843 and 1845 respectively, each 5½ by 1¼ feet, in which the donor is shown below the holy patron along with an inscription and a death's-head. The *ex-voto* provided the occasion for an extraordinary persistence of a late-medieval funerary decor in the middle of the nineteenth century.[79]

Chapels and Family Vaults

In these examples from the late Middle Ages or early modern times the reader will not have failed to remark a constant ambiguity regarding the distance between the location of the tombstone and the actual resting-place of the body (see chapter 2). This ambiguity appears with the abandonment of the sarcophagus.

However, instructions concerning burial are often given as if the two places had to coincide. In 1400, for example, a testator stipulates that his body "be taken to the church of la Terre and laid under the aforesaid tombstone."[80] Some seventeenth-century testators talk about having stone monuments placed over their graves. But we know that this conjunction was not required and could not be respected in the case of mural tombs or of memorial tombstones without graves.

Indeed, along with the expressions indicating conjunction, there are a great many others that only indicate proximity: "near the tomb," "as close as possible," etc. In certain rare cases, the inscription actually refers to the site of the grave. A late sixteenth-century epitaph at the Ara Coeli in Rome indicates that the body of Brother Mathias of San Eustachio has been buried elsewhere, "between the monument of Saint Helena and the door of the old sacristy"; but here the deceased was a high dignitary of the Franciscan family.

At the end of the *ancien régime,* however, one observes a desire to reunite the dead of the same family in the same chapel, a modern impulse that led to the contemporary custom of requiring, in principle, an exact correspondence between the body and the tomb. This will be the last stage in this lengthy history.

In our study of wills, we have already encountered two meanings of the word *chapel:* "the altar where Masses were to be said" and "the endowment provided for the priest who would celebrate these Masses." Later there appeared a third meaning, that of "burial place."

In the beginning there was no thought of combining the religious purpose of the chapel with burial. But when the donor made his requests concerning services, the arrangement of the place, and permission to lay tombstones and epitaphs, he began to ask for the right to be buried under the chapel, no longer directly in the ground but in a burial vault.

The great feudal and princely houses were undoubtedly the first to move away from the traditional site of the tombs *ad sanctos.* In preference to the noble parts of the church, like the choir, they chose the reserved space of a lateral chapel. In the sixteenth century, sovereigns wanted to give these chapels a different and more grandiose appearance, like those of the Borghese in Santa Maria Maggiore, in Rome. Sometimes they went so far as to separate their chapels from the church, although still maintaining the necessary access for distribution of the sacrament. Examples are the chapels of the Valois in Saint-Denis, the Medici in Florence, and later, the house of Lorraine in Nancy.

This personalization no doubt inspired the funerary use of chapels in châteaux, like that of the La Trémoille family in Niort. However, these cases were limited to the very great families with royal pretensions. The dominant practice remained what it was in the fourteenth century: the appropriation by a family for funerary purposes of a lateral chapel in the conventual or parish church. This practice became common in the seventeenth and early eighteenth centuries among well-to-do families.

This is how matters were handled in those circles: "Permission granted [on May 8, 1603][81] by the churchwardens of Saint-Gervais for the construction in the cemetery of said church [that is, in the part of the cemetery situated next to the church, an example of the erosion of old cemeteries by chapels and oratories in the sixteenth and seventeenth centuries] of a chapel and oratory, to be built against the outside wall of the church, measuring 12 feet long by 12 feet wide by 8 feet high, below and adjoining the chapel and oratory previously built by M. Etienne Puget, councillor to the king and treasurer of his savings." This permission had to be given "for the purpose of burial," that is, in order to "make a vault [as opposed to a grave made directly in the ground] the same width [as the chapel], whenever he shall see fit, in order to bury the bodies of himself, his wife, and his children."

The chapel must open onto the church to make it possible to hear divine service. The chapel will be enclosed on the side toward the church by "a wooden railing with a door that opens into the chapel. And this door shall be kept locked, and the key kept in the possession of [the donor and his heirs] so that they may go there to attend divine service."

Another document, dated 1603, by the same church council also mentions "having a chapel and oratory built at her expense [that is, at the expense of the donor], making an opening in the outside wall of the church" and building "a wooden railing . . . for Mme. Niceron and her children, grandchildren, and assigns in perpetuity . . . where they may hear divine service [this is the primary purpose of the chapel; in exchange, Mme. Niceron gives up the pew that she previously had in the church] and where she may make a vault the same width as the chapel whenever she shall see fit to do so in which to bury the bodies of her family." Burial is therefore the second purpose of the chapel, which nevertheless remains a place of worship. These two functions were regarded as equally important.

Some of the records mention only arrangements for hearing divine service, no doubt because the family had a tomb elsewhere. In 1617, for example, the churchwardens of Saint-Gervais granted permission to "the noble man Jehan de Daurs, councillor to the king and general inspector of his buildings, to have enclosed with a wooden railing in the aforesaid church a pew in the shape of an oratory next to the altar of the chapel of Saint Nicholas, which pew shall be bounded on one side by the aforesaid altar, on the other side and on one end by the outside wall of the church, and on the other end by the chapel of M. Texier, master of the accounts, said oratory to be about 5 feet wide by 6½ feet long."[82]

In the same chapel the donor received permission to build two other pews, which are described just as precisely: "which three pews he desires to have arranged in such wise that he can retire to the aforesaid church and hear divine service."

Only rarely, however, is the purpose of worship not combined with the chapel's other, funerary purpose. What is remarkable and unprecedented is the combining of the tomb, which is already familial, with the private chapel to which the family comes to make their devotions and to attend Mass.

Even when they did not have a real chapel enclosed by walls and a railing, people wanted to have their pew over the grave of a parent or relative. In 1622 a parishioner asks permission "to have a limestone slab [a flat tomb] laid over the grave where the deceased was buried, in the nave, near his pew, which is located at the back of the church against one of the pillars of the tower next to the font." He also asks permission to place on this same pillar, over the pew, "a stone epitaph . . . to be inscribed with a *ci-gît* to the memory of the deceased." It is a kind of miniature chapel consisting of a pew, a tombstone, and an epitaph, all brought together in a small space around a pillar.[83]

The practice persists, although it may have become less common, in the second half of the eighteenth century. In 1745 Pierre Bucherie, squire, gendarme in the garde ordinaire of the King, and captain in his troops, requested "that after my death my body be buried in the church of the parish of Muzac, to which church I give and bequeath the sum of 1,000 francs to be paid in one installment, to be used to build a chapel in honor of the Blessed Virgin, which chapel shall be placed on the south, the noble side, of the church."[84]

It was not unknown for several families to share the same chapel under the supervision of the churchwardens—for in spite of these concessions, the church council remained the owners of the property—and the records are always emphasizing the permanence of their right. In 1617, in one of the chapels described above, the churchwardens authorized the donor to place one of his three pews over a tomb belonging to a family who already had their pew next to it, "provided [the newcomers] had the small pew detached and removed whenever Mlle. de L., her daughter, their relatives or heirs required access to the tomb over which the small pew is placed."

The expression *require access* is significant. From now on, descendants require access to the tombs of their ancestors. This access is necessary for new burials and anniversary services, of course; but one also finds a new attitude quietly making its appearance in these texts. Gradually it is becoming customary among persons of quality for the living and dead members of the same family to gather together in an enclosed part of the church to which they have the key and that only they have permission to enter, as if they were the owners. This chapel often has a stained-glass window that they have donated and in which one of them is represented as a praying figure. The floor is covered with slabs and the walls with paintings, carvings, and epitaphs that describe and illustrate in words and portraits the history of their family. They are still in the church, and it is here that they gather to attend Mass, but at the same time they are also at home and in the presence of their dead.

Moreover, these dead have not been buried in the ground, in a grave that was either freshly dug or reopened. They have been laid in a *cave* (an old word for *caveau*). The *cave* was a vaulted recess in which the coffin was protected from contact with the earth. The word *voûte* (vault) was sometimes used as a synonym for *cave,* as in this 1606 text: "to make under this chapel built in Saint-Gervais a *voulte* in which to bury the bodies" of the donor, his wife, and children. *Vault* was used almost synonymously with *chapel:* "Desires his dead body to be buried in the Dodonville church in the vault that he had built there" (1650).[85]

So the first burial vaults were built by the founders of chapels to the dimensions of the chapel, a practice very different from medieval custom and closer to ours today.

In the course of the eighteenth century it would seem that the notion of the burial vault took on more and more importance, without replacing the idea of the chapel, whose symbolism remained very strong. The increasing importance of the burial vault corresponded to a growing concern on the part of survivors for the physical preservation of the body. Priests responded to this sentiment by dividing the underground area of their churches into cemented and numbered stone vaults. A parishioner of Saint-Jean-en-Grève obtained permission to have the body of his father, a councillor of state who died in the country, transported "to one of the vaults under the communion chapel, which is the fourth and last near the door leading to the charnels, to be *lodged there in perpetuity,*" with the right to place an epitaph in the chapel.

Thus, the dead have also obtained a space of their own, a vaulted cavern where they will remain—this is promised—forever, exempt from the traditional disruption of having their dried-out bones transported to the charnels. This space for the dead is the subterranean counterpart of the space for the living, the chapel in which the latter gather to attend services. We are now in the presence of a new type of burial and a new attitude toward the dead, which in the nineteenth century will overtake all of society.

An attentive visit to our imaginary museum of tombstones and graves would probably tell us more about collective attitudes toward death and the beyond than a library full of scholarly works on theology and religion. To be sure, the dominant ideas of this literature, especially the dualism of the body "awaiting the resurrection" and the soul destined for the joys of heaven or the pains of hell, made a profound impression on funerary decor. But in this decor we also find evidence of certain beliefs that are rarely expressed elsewhere and that we would have no other way of knowing, about, beliefs that were thought lost but that had merely gone underground. Finally, we see signs of altogether new attitudes that foreshadow the romanticism of the eighteenth and nineteenth centuries.

Three major tendencies may be isolated from the whole of this vast corpus. The first is no surprise, as it has already been suggested by our previous analyses of the iconography of the Last Judgment, the economics of wills, and the liturgy of funerals: the discovery of the individual, the discovery, at the hour or thought of death, of one's own identity, one's personal biography, in this world as in the next. The desire to be oneself forced tombstones to emerge from their anonymity and to become commemorative monuments.

At the same time this desire made the soul the essential element of the personality. Liberated from the weight of the species, the soul became the crystallization of the being, the individuality itself, an individuality whose characteristics, whether good or bad, nothing could now alter. The tomb of the soul is the expression of this sentiment, which was first restricted to a clerical elite but which by the end of the Middle Ages and the beginning of modern times was being extended to include a large category of the nobility and middle class.

The second general tendency that stands out in our imaginary museum is the persistent belief in a neutral state of repose that lies somewhere between the agitation of earth and the contemplativeness of heaven. This belief inspired the hieratic position of the recumbent and praying figures in churches, and today it finds expression in the crosses in cemeteries, which continue to symbolize a vague and ill-defined hope. We recognize here the age-old conception of the tame death and of the peaceful and subdued afterlife.

The third tendency is seen in the chapels, where the living and dead members of a single family were brought together in the same specially designed space. This tendency indicates a desire, hitherto unknown, for a physical proximity between the living and the dead.

Part III

REMOTE AND IMMINENT DEATH

6

The Turning of the Tide

We have traced the development in the Middle Ages of a sensibility that assigned an increasingly high value and an increasingly important role to physical death. This tendency, which dates back to the monastic anxieties of the Carolingian period, first appeared among the literati and grew with the rise of literacy. It developed steadily for several centuries until by the end of the Middle Ages it had reached an intensity that found expression in the startling images of the macabre. It culminated in a concentration of the mind and senses on the actual moment of physical death. Having reached this degree of intensity, it subsided and seemed to recede.

It is this backward movement, this ebbing of the tide, that we must now consider. It coincides approximately with the Renaissance and continues into the seventeenth century. It is difficult to isolate this tendency from the complexity of events; one must sense it under an appearance of stability and respect its discretion and ambiguity.

For on the surface, things will remain very much as they were in the medieval past: the same literary genre of the *artes moriendi*, the same danses macabres,[1] more skulls and bones than ever in the churches, the same obligation to make one's will, and the same sacred character attributed to the will. One is tempted to believe that nothing has interrupted the age-old continuity, but the lack of visible change is deceptive. Beneath this illusion of permanence a new attitude is beginning to appear, or, if not a new attitude, an unconscious devaluation of the old attitudes.

For the distance that is now taken with respect to death does not coincide with the great schism that has dazzled generations of historians and that is by nature theological and ecclesiastical, and therefore more or less elitist. I am referring to the schism that occurred between the two Christian reformations and, according to some, between the religious orientation of the past and the free thought of the future.

We shall draw freely on both Catholic and Protestant sources of documentation. Their differences, when they exist, are not on the level of collective psychology, which was almost the same on both sides.

In order to understand this change, we must begin with the moment of death. In actual experience, of course, death was neither more nor less frightening during the later Middle Ages; the literati were as true to tradition as the people. However, if death was not yet causing fear, it was causing uncertainty. Moralists, the religious, and mendicant friars exploited the new anxiety for purposes of conversion. A literature of edification, distributed by means of the new printing techniques, enlarged on the pain and delirium of the death agony, presenting the moment of death as a struggle of spiritual powers in which the individual was in a position to gain or lose everything.

After the sixteenth century, the actual moment of death, in the bedroom and in the bed, will be more or less abandoned by pious writers, at least by scholarly ones, who in so doing are actually anticipating a tendency of the collective unconscious.[2]

Devaluation
of the Hour of Death

The all-important role of the warning is diminished and even disappears: The person who is about to die is no longer given notice.

In Erasmus illness takes over the role of the warning. He had more than his share of illness, that great *maladif* who somehow managed to fall off his horse at a time when he was already suffering from kidney stones. Poor health is an invitation to withdraw from the world. "I keep turning over in my mind how I might devote the time I have left to live (I don't know how long it will be) [he was not yet forty when he wrote those words in 1506] entirely to piety and to Christ." This desire to withdraw from the world—the retreat into the desert of Molière's Misanthrope—may seem consistent with tradition, and no doubt it is. But Erasmus is not talking about the asceticism of the monastery. He will remain in the world but devote himself to meditation, and all meditation leads to death. Indeed, if we are to believe Plato, philosophy is always such a meditation. But how one must have suffered to be receptive to this philosophy! This is what happened to Erasmus when the pain of the kidney stone made him long for death. The kidney stone is the great teacher *(Monitor calculus);* that is our philosophy, that is the true meditation on death.[3]

And Robert Bellarmine observes rather unkindly that old age alone does not incline a man to repentance or the thought of salvation; old age is no longer regarded as a warning. There is none so deaf as he who will not hear, and the old do not wish to know anything. "They think only of living, and although death is near, it is the furthest thing from their minds," observes the author of a *Miroir de l'âme pécheresse*, which was reissued in the eighteenth century.[4]

We are no longer in the age of those old men with flowing white beards who sliced their enemies in two, led great battles, and presided wisely over their courts. This is the period of the Ages of Man, a popular subject for the new printing techniques, in which the final stages were occupied by drowsy, senile, and unappetizing invalids.

The sick man is lying in bed. Soon he will die, and yet nothing extraordinary is going on, nothing resembling the great dramas that invaded the bedrooms of the *artes moriendi* of the fifteenth century.

Even his suffering has become suspect. In 1561 the English Puritan Thomas Becon, author of *The Mannes Salve*, writes that the pangs of death have been lingered over too lovingly by medieval rhetoric. The "bitter agony" is really "a little and short pain" compared with the torments of the martyrs and prophets. Dying is a natural phenomenon that should not be dramatized. "It is naturall to dye, why then labour we to degenerate and growe out of kind?" The Stoic idea of death as a voyage was revived, if indeed it had ever disappeared from popular consciousness.[5]

A century later, also in England, Jeremy Taylor, author of *The Rule and Exercises of Holy Dying* (1651), a nonsectarian who was not ashamed to take his inspiration from the Catholic literature that started with Saint Ignatius, bluntly dismissed deathbed visions as "phantasms" of Satan, "abused fancies" of depressed and neurasthenic invalids.

Bellarmine is amazed that men devote so much time to their lawsuits, their property, and their business, and so little to their salvation, or more precisely, that they put off thinking about eternity to a time when they will be weak and almost unconscious, no longer the masters of themselves. Insofar as he deigns to consider the pangs of the death agony, he sees only their negative aspect, the destruction of the will and of consciousness, and he has no tenderness or natural reverence for these remains that real life has already abandoned. Medieval imagery granted more longevity to man's freedom, his capacity to give and receive in this body that was turning into a corpse. Bellarmine is just as hard on the dying as he is on the aged.

Spiritual writers are unanimous in recognizing that death is not the hideous caricature they inherited from the last days of the Middle Ages. The Catholics say it more cautiously; the Protestants lack their timidity. Calvin writes, "We are afraid [of death] because we apprehend it not as it is in itself, but as grim, haggard, and hideous, as the painters [of the danses macabres] were pleased to represent it on walls. We flee from death, but because we are preoccupied by such vain fantasies, we do not take the time to look at it. If we will but pause, stand our ground, and look death squarely in the eyes, we shall find it quite different from the way it has been depicted to us, and with a very different aspect from that of our miserable lives."[6]

But if death is no longer the person lying in the sickbed, sweating, suffering, and praying, then what is it? It has become something metaphysical that is expressed by a metaphor: the separation of the soul and the body, which is like the separation of man and wife or of two dear old friends. In an age when survivors erected monuments to the soul, and when dualism was beginning to penetrate the collective psychology, the thought of death is associated with the breakdown of the combination that makes us human. The pain of death is seen not as the real suffering of the death agony but as something comparable to the sorrow of a broken friendship.

The New Arts of Dying

It is not, therefore, at the moment of death or in the presence of death that one must think about death; it is throughout one's life. For the Lyonnais Jean de Vauzelles, who in 1538 published the text for a danse macabre of Holbein the Younger, which Nathalie Z. Davis has studied, earthly life is a preparation for eternal life, just as the nine months of gestation are a preparation for this life.[7] The art of dying was replaced by an art of living. From now on, no crucial scene occurs in the bedroom of the dying man. Everything is spread out over the whole span of a lifetime and affects every day of that life.

But what life? Not just any life, but a life dominated by the thought of death, a death that is not the physical or psychological horror of the death agony but the opposite of life, the absence of life, a death that invites man's reason not to become attached to life; this is why there is such a close relationship between living well and dying well.

> To be blessed in death, one must learn to live.
> To be blessed in life, one must learn to die.

These Jesuitical verses were written by the Calvinist Duplessis-Mornay. The person who has trusted in God all his life, as Erasmus hoped to do, is ready to die and needs no further preparation:

He who in God has always placed his trust
Lives in Faith and so at one with life
That death frees him to live among the blessed.[8]

Moreover, it is not possible to live in the world, that is, outside the protective wall of the monastery, unless one can convince oneself of the vanity of the things among which one must live, which one moves and manipulates, and from which one derives profit. This is why the meditation on death is central to the proper conduct of life. "The images of death," wrote Jean de Vauzelles, "are the true and proper mirror by which one must correct the deformities of sin and embellish the soul."[9] In the spiritual treatises of the sixteenth and seventeenth centuries the main purpose is no longer to prepare the dying for death but to teach the living to meditate on death.

There are techniques for this, a way of educating the mind and imagination whose master is Saint Ignatius with his *Spiritual Exercises.* These techniques are well known. All we need note here is that in this new economy, death has become the pretext for a metaphysical meditation on the fragility of life that is intended to keep us from giving in to life's illusions. Death is no more than a means to living well. It could be the invitation to pleasure of the Epicureans; actually, it is the rejection of this pleasure; yet the skeleton on the goblets of the pleasure-seeking Epicureans of Pompeii is the same as the one in the engravings of the *Spiritual Exercises.*

The French Protestant and the Anglican theologian speak like the Roman cardinal. On this point, there is unanimity among the Christian elite. From now on, there is a conviction, even among traditionalist and conservative Catholics, for whom the testimony of the medieval monks is still valid, that barring the intervention—which can never be ruled out in advance—of an exceptional act of grace, it is not the moment of death that will give the individual's past life its true worth or determine his fate in the other world. By then it will be too late, or in any case the risk is not worth running. The illumination of the last moment is not going to save from damnation a life completely given over to evil. One cannot count on it. "It is neither reasonable nor just that we should commit so many sins all our lives and then allow only a day or an hour to repent of them."[10] We must at every moment in our lives be in the state the medieval *artes moriendi* recommended for the dying: *"in hora mortis nostrae,"* as it says in the *Ave Maria,* which in fact became popular in the sixteenth century.

This doctrine is illustrated by two anecdotes. The first belongs to the Counter-Reformation; Jesuit tradition assigns it to Saint Louis of Gonzaga. One day when the young saint was playing ball, he was asked what he would

do if he knew that he was about to die. We can imagine what a monk of
the tenth to fifteenth centuries would have answered: that he would cease
all his worldly activities, devote himself entirely to prayer and penitence,
and go into a solitary retreat where nothing could distract him from the
thought of his salvation. A layman would have answered that he would take
refuge in a cloister. But the young saint of the Counter-Reformation replied
simply that he would keep on playing ball.

The other anecdote, dated 1534, is from the work of an English
humanist who had been won over by the ideas of the Reformation. Inspired
by Stoicism, he borrowed Seneca's account of the death of Canius to offer
as an example. The philosopher Canius had been sentenced to death by
Caligula. When the executioner came to take him to his death, he found
the philosopher playing chess. He was even winning.[11]

For a man who is ready to die, every moment is like the moment of
departure. "Even in the best of health," Calvin tells us, "we should have
death always before our eyes," so that "we will not expect to remain on this
earth forever, but will have *one foot in the air,* so to speak."[12]

In one of his *Colloquia* Erasmus describes an example of the effect
of this state of mind in everyday life.[13] It was during a shipwreck. The
sailors and passengers fell into a panic; but while most of them called upon
the saints and sang hymns, taking refuge in prayer and awaiting a supernatural intervention, according to the practices of the time, a courageous and
reasonable young woman, instead of losing her head, conducted herself
without fear or bravado, but with common sense. "Of all of us . . . the one
who remained most composed was a young woman who was holding a baby
whom she was nursing. . . . She was the only one who did not shout, weep,
or bargain with heaven. She did nothing but pray quietly to herself while
clasping the baby tightly on her lap." A prayer that was merely a continuation of her regular prayer, a prayer that did not ask any exceptional favor
related to the event. Her composure and simplicity stood her in good stead,
for she was the first to reach the shore. "We placed her on a bent plank
and gave her a spar to use as an oar. Then, with a fervent prayer, we
entrusted her to the waves . . . and this woman, holding her baby in one
arm, rowed with the other." "What does Christ do," Erasmus remarks,
"but invite us to live watchfully, as if we were about to die any moment,
and to adhere to the practice of virtue, as if we were destined to live
forever?"

But Erasmus believes that this exemplary attitude of the shipwrecked
woman was exceptional for his time. This is because the fear of death and
the quasi-magical formulas for outwitting death had become all too common, thanks to the scandalous propaganda of the mendicant friars. "How
many Christians have I not seen make a miserable end! Some place their

confidence in things that do not deserve it; others, conscious of their wickedness and racked with doubts, are at their last breath so tormented by ignorant fools [Gerson's "spiritual friends"] that they give up the ghost almost in despair. [And yet despair was one of the classical temptations of the death agony, one whose danger the spiritual friends well understood and which they were trying to avoid, if we are to believe the old *artes moriendi.*] I blame those criminals and the superstitious or, to temper my language, those naïve ignoramuses who teach the faithful to rely upon such ceremonies and to neglect the very things that transform us into true Christians."

Erasmus finds this belief in the virtues of the last rites superstitious for the same reasons as Jean de Vauzelles, whom I quoted above, and many other seventeenth-century writers: because they seemed designed to permit a dissolute life to be saved *in extremis.* "When the last hour finally comes, certain ceremonies for the occasion are already prepared. The dying man makes his general confession. He is given Extreme Unction and the last sacrament. The candles and the holy water are there. No chance of forgetting the indulgences! A papal bull is unrolled before the dying man's eyes; if necessary, it is even sold to him. Then arrangements are made for the elaborate funeral service. A last solemn promise is extracted from the dying man. Someone shouts in his ear and hastens his end, as often happens, either by excessive noise, or by a breath that reeks of wine."

This is a caricature of the traditional scene of the last rites, which was given a more dramatic and clerical form—one that Erasmus found intolerable—by the *artes moriendi.* The Church of the Counter-Reformation would retain the essential elements, reducing the parasitical devotions and concentrating on the *Viaticum* and Extreme Unction. But popular piety would remain faithful to the penitential psalms and Commendations.

And even Erasmus admits that not everything about these customs is bad. "I concede that these things are good, especially the ones handed down to us by Church tradition [essentially, the sacraments]. But I maintain that there are other, more discreet ones [inspired no doubt by a personal relationship between God and man] that can help us leave this world with a light heart and with Christian confidence."

The reformist elite of the Catholic and Protestant churches, following the example of the humanists, continued to mistrust last-minute repentances extracted by the fear of dying. In the Catholic church of the nineteenth century there was undoubtedly a return to the situation before the Counter-Reformation under the influence of popular customs that had persisted. After the sixteenth century, the reflections provoked by the subtle transformation of the *artes moriendi* constituted a new genre that retained the old labels. The *artes* were no longer manuals for dying; they became a new category of pious literature for the devotions of everyday life.

Of course, they still had a section devoted to the visiting of the sick, the attentions to be given to the dying, the last rites and sacraments; the Roman church recognized the power of these traditions. But an Anglican author no more radical than Taylor accepts them only as social usages. Although he gives a few words of advice for the last moments, he frankly admits that for him the death scene no longer has any of the intensity that it still has in Catholic writers like Bellarmine. The traditional ceremony has become a polite formality with neither religious nor moral value. "A death-bed repentance is like the washing and dressing of the corpse: It is cleanly and civil, but it changes nothing beneath the skin."[14]

The popular pious literature written in French in the middle of the eighteenth century was not very different from what we found in the humanists, Taylor, or Bellarmine. A title like *Le Miroir de l'âme du pécheur et du juste pendant la vie et à l'heure de la mort* (The mirror of the soul of the sinner and the righteous man during life and in the hour of death) tells us clearly that the book is concerned as much, or more, with the art of living as with the art of dying. The *Miroir* makes a dramatic contrast between the fate of the sinner and that of the righteous man. It is a flat and mediocre book of piety, which borrows the ideas of Ignatius and recommends that one imagine one's own death: "It is certain that I must die in two hours. . . . My body will be nothing but a horrible cadaver that will be abhorrent to everyone. [Bellarmine dispensed with these descriptions, perhaps because they belonged to the classical methods of meditation.] I will be thrown into a grave and covered with earth. My body will be eaten by worms and will rot." Once again these images presented for meditation are offered as tested methods for obtaining a good death well in advance because of the good resolutions they inspire. They are not intended to prepare one immediately for a natural death.

On the other hand, the author vigorously opposes the error denounced by Jean de Vauzelles in the sixteenth century and still widespread in his own time—namely, that one can count on a good death to make up for a bad life. "You are no doubt persuaded that to die a Christian death it would be enough before you die to receive the sacraments, kiss the crucifix, be attended by a priest, and repeat after him the acts of religion that are ordinarily administered to the sick. If that were enough, your imprudence would be less reprehensible, but in fact it is far from enough. Hell is full of people who died after doing all those things. To die like that is to die a death that may indeed be consoling to the relatives but is ordinarily disastrous for the dying man when he has made no other preparations. . . . Sinners, at their death, call upon the Lord, which means that they will receive the sacraments, if you will [curious form of concession], but it does not mean that they will therefore go to heaven. For if in order to deserve heaven one need only perform a few Christian acts at the moment of death, it would follow that Jesus Christ had spoken falsely. No, one must set about it from the beginning, which means that it takes no less than a lifetime to prepare oneself for the state that is required for a good death, the state that certain presumptuous persons hope to attain instantaneously the moment death announces its arrival."[15]

Popular Devotions Relating to the Good Death

The same Protestant moralists never tired of denouncing certain superstitious practices that promised a miraculous knowledge of things hidden, a knowledge that could be exploited in order to save one's soul at the last moment, as if by a throw of the dice that one could predict in advance. "In some prayer books," wrote Père Doré, a Jesuit, in 1554, "there are prayers to Our Lady and the saints that are preceded by various apocryphal statements such as 'Whoever says this prayer will know the hour of his death [an ancient preoccupation that sometimes inspired the divination of magicians in the Middle Ages], for Our Lady will appear to him fifteen days before.' . . . The prayers are good, but one must put no faith in such inauthentic instructions."[16]

But in practice the Roman church did not really proscribe all the devotions centered on the good death that were condemned by its elite. In fact, devotions of this kind filled the churches and attracted the people, who remained stubbornly faithful to them. They were particularly attached to the scapular and the rosary. The scapular gave the person who wore it the assurance of a good death, or at the very least, a reduction of his time in purgatory. Gaby and Michel Vovelle have clearly demonstrated the connection between the scapular of Saint Simon Stock or the rosary, which was then attributed to Saint Dominic, and the devotion, very popular in the late eighteenth and nineteenth centuries, to souls in purgatory.[17] The rosary and the scapular were attributes often represented in the altarpieces that adorned the chapels reserved for souls in purgatory. In a painting in the church in Pertuis, a soul whom an angel is saving from the flames and carrying off to heaven carries the scapular clasped in his hands. In the church in Pelissane, the soul being saved has a rosary wound around his wrist.

It was no doubt at this time, when the post-Tridentine devotion to the rosary became widespread, that the hands of the deceased—which, like those of the soul in purgatory, were already joined in the traditional attitude of the medieval recumbent figure—were entwined in a rosary, a practice that has come down to our own time.

Certain tenacious beliefs regarding the virtues of the scapular persisted in the nineteenth century. There is an unusual and pathetic proof of this in a place where one would least expect it, a youthful work of Charles Maurras that he later repudiated. It is a story entitled *"La Bonne Mort"* that was included in the first edition of the *Chemin de Paradis,* a somewhat scandalous book published in 1891, but withdrawn from the edition of 1924. It is an account of the suicide of a young student at a religious school who resembles Maurras like a brother. The boy, who was barely adolescent, hanged himself because he was tempted by the sin of the flesh and was afraid that if he gave in to it, he would die and go to hell. However, he was convinced that as long as he wore the scapular he would be saved by the Virgin, no matter how serious his offenses. But if tomorrow, carried away by some madness, he should neglect to wear the scapular, he would go to eternal destruction. It was therefore better to take advantage of his present security, kill himself while he was wearing the miraculous amulet, and in this way win eternity. A strange story, but one whose essential elements were provided by the actual memories of an adolescent who was tempted by suicide and whose religious teachers or mother had taught him the supernatural virtues of the scapular.[18]

Apparently a compromise was established between certain beliefs, which were flatly rejected as superstitious but persisted anyway, and the rigor of the reformers. One observes this in altarpieces representing souls in purgatory, where certain popular beliefs are combined with a dogma that was long limited to a small elite of theologians such as Saint Thomas Aquinas or philosophical writers such as Dante: the dogma of purgatory. Purgatory rarely appears in popular writing before the middle of the seventeenth century; one seldom finds references to it in Parisian wills before 1640. But then it became popular, at the same time as the tomb of the soul and the endowment tablet. There is both an acceptance of the radical ideas of the reformers and a tempering of these ideas by the continuation of old practices.

One senses the same compromise in wills. The dominant doctrines do not quite succeed in eliminating the anxiety about the Last Day and the deeply rooted belief in all the extraordinary possibilities of that moment that is like no other. In 1652, "a girl enjoying all her rights and in good health" decides to make her will. But it may be a long time before she dies, and one can feel that this distance, which is recommended by reformist moralists, worries her. She asks, "May God grant that at the end of my life I may make a good confession and penance for all my sins, and that I die like a good and true Christian, and that I renounce from this day forward [in the presence of a notary!] all the temptations that might befall me."[19] One senses that despite all the precautions, her mind is not completely at rest.

And in 1690, a priest writes, "My advanced age and the grave illnesses that frequently befall me warn me that death is near [the traditional warning] and that I may die at any time [he has waited for the warning, instead of adopting the new practice followed by the young girl of 1652]. So as not to be taken unawares, I have made it my responsibility [the will is still an essential obligation, in Protestant as well as Catholic treatises] to do as soon as possible all those things that I would like to have done in the last moment of my life [perhaps it is better to do them then, but we now know that this is very risky], when perhaps I shall no longer be capable of doing anything, owing to the state of weakness to which my mind and heart shall be reduced."[20]

It is evident that in daily life, death is still a dominant theme. But the men who shaped Christian doctrine from the sixteenth to the eighteenth century are reluctant to admit this, and try to soften its intensity.[21] This attitude on the part of the humanists and reformers was to weigh more and more heavily on the customs of the people. Modern historians are inclined to identify this attitude with modernity, and no doubt they are right. We must now try to discover for ourselves the effects and the underlying meaning of this attitude.

The Nonnatural Death and the Beautiful and Edifying Death

The first effect of the dethronement and desanctification of death is that death loses its almost magical and certainly irrational powers, once charged with a primitive savagery. Both the sudden death and the violent death have now become commonplace. Neither Salutati nor Erasmus nor Bellarmine sees any particular danger in the *mors improvisa*. Indeed, Salutati and Erasmus prefer it to long illnesses, which cause deterioration and suffering. Erasmus's kidney stone drove him to long for death, and he remembered the *graves auctores* of antiquity who "not without reason wrote that a sudden death was the greatest blessing that life could bring. . . . Indeed, the soul that has entrusted itself once and for all to the divine will is ready to endure a thousand deaths."[22]

The attitude of the reformers toward the execution of criminals condemned to death is also surprising. For them—though not, of course, in actual practice—the death penalty had lost its character of a solemn compensatory sacrifice. In their eyes the victim was no longer the dreadful personification of evil, struck down by all the human and divine forces he had defied. It made no difference to them that in important cases the execution was performed in public like a religious ritual. For a large part of the Middle Ages it was commonly believed that the criminal about to be executed was a diabolical creature who had already gone to hell. Under the circumstances, all spiritual consolation was seen as useless and forbidden, if not sacrilegious. The Church had never accepted this belief, and had required the presence of a confessor next to the executioner.

For Bellarmine and the writers who came after him, the condemned man was actually rehabilitated by his suffering and his repentance. His piety transformed his execution into an expiation, and his death became a good death, better than many others. "When they have begun to depart from mortal life," Bellarmine wrote almost admiringly of condemned criminals, "they begin to live in immortal bliss."[23]

May we interpret the devaluation of the moment of death as a reevaluation of life, as Tenenti ingeniously suggests? If I understand him correctly, Tenenti sees this devaluation as the second stage in a much older movement whose first manifestation was the reaction of the macabre. While I admit that macabre imagery actually expressed a vast love of things and creatures, I believe that the turning away from death that is the subject of our present analysis is not a second phase of the same impulse; on the contrary, it expresses a different conception of life that is more ascetic, if not more somber.

The attitude of the later Middle Ages toward the world and the things of the world was ambivalent. On the one hand, there was that reprehensible love that the writers of the sixteenth century blamed for being immoderate and that was called *avaritia*. On the other hand, there was the definitive break with the world, the total renunciation: distribution of one's property to the poor and retirement to a monastery. It was all or nothing, and the only recognized way of balancing these two extremes was a complex system of reassurance in which material riches were guaranteed by the spiritual riches they supported.

Beginning in the Renaissance, when death was separated from the final moment and integrated into the total life, other attitudes appear that find expression in a different evaluation of virtues and vices. It is now generally accepted that man must live in the world, although he is not of it. Retirement to a monastery is no longer presented as the Christian attitude in its most perfect form. It is normal and acceptable to make use of material things, as Abraham and Solomon did, as long as man realizes that he does not possess wealth, he is only its usufructuary. This moral consideration is not a peculiarity of pious writers but is often found in the letters and wills of ordinary people of the sixteenth and seventeenth centuries, as we have already seen. Bellarmine has a very fixed opinion on this subject: In his relations with other people, every man is the master of his own property; there is no question of doubting the legitimacy of ownership. But in his relation to God, which is essential, he is only an administrator.

This notion of usufruct gave rise to a new virtue whose name is very old, but whose meaning and tone are altogether new: sobriety. "This virtue," writes Bellarmine, in his *De arte bene moriendi*, "is not merely the opposite of intoxication"; just as in the fifteenth century, *avaritia* was not merely the fear of going without and the reluctance to spend. Sobriety is synonymous with moderation and temperance, whereas *avaritia* is denounced as *amor immoderatus*. Sobriety means that "man decides according to reason, and not according to his own pleasure, what things are necessary for the care and preservation of his body." Bellarmine adds that this virtue is very rare.[24]

In a world in which the Christian must live and evolve spiritually, moderation is not merely sensible behavior, it becomes a cardinal virtue that governs one's whole way of life. This explains its importance in sexual morality in general, and marriage in particular. It involves a consciousness and forethought that were not previously customary.

From this it follows that *avaritia* becomes the deadliest of the sins. Let us not forget that *avaritia* still includes that love of one's fellow creatures that seems to us entirely legitimate. Marguerite de Navarre writes about the good death and the devout and joyous deceased:

> *Without regret for father, mother, sister,*
> *Or any memory of this world below,*
> *My soul in joy embraces her redeemer.*[25]

Avaritia is the immoderate love of the world. It is not so much a sin for which one feels shame and remorse as it is the hatred of God, *odium Dei*, which leads to callousness, defiance, and alliances with the devil. Those who practice it are self-willed and self-assured.

In Bellarmine's treatise the *odium Dei*, which accounts for a substantial number of the temptations that assail man in the sixteenth and seventeenth centuries, has two aspects, two sides of the same vice. The first is sorcery. Bellarmine is not talking about the pact with the devil; he is analyzing the rational psychology of those who are convinced, rightly or wrongly, that they will enjoy in the next world, and probably even in this one, the immense powers of the devil. This is why they demonstrate such assurance in the face of tortures and ordeals. For it is well known to Inquisitors that the devil provides them with an insensibility to pain that guarantees that they will not repent.

The second aspect of *odium Dei* is *avaritia*. It is very significant that *avaritia* and sorcery came under the same heading. Indeed, they share the assumption, clear or confused, explicit or implicit, that the devil, or the non-God, has powers over the world. In order to exercise these powers in this world or the next, man has no need of God. Indeed, God would deny him these powers in the name of his Providence.

Thus, a world in which moderation must reign is gradually replacing a world of excess in which man oscillates between a love of life and a renunciation of it that are equally exaggerated. In this new world, death no longer has the same power to call everything into question when its shadow falls upon a life. Death, too, is subject to the law of moderation.

The final effect of the phenomenon we are analyzing here is a model of the good death, the beautiful and edifying death, which replaces the death of the medieval *artes* in the bedroom invaded by the powers of heaven and hell, the memories of life, and the feverish fantasies of the devil. This is the death of the righteous man who thinks little about his own physical death when it comes, but who has thought about it all his life. This death has neither the excitement nor the intensity of the death of the *artes moriendi* of the late Middle Ages. It is not exactly the death of Roland, La Fontaine's laborer, or Tolstoi's peasants, but it is not so unlike it either. It has their serenity and their public quality, whereas the death of the *artes moriendi* was dramatic and internalized. Everything happened out of sight of the circle of friends.

This new model appears at the end of the fourteenth century and lasts until the eighteenth. Tenenti gives a few early examples. The first, which was suggested by Salutati in 1379, is the death of Hermes Trismegistus. Like Socrates, Hermes Trismegistus died in public, surrounded by his friends. "Heretofore an exiled pilgrim, I am now returning to my homeland. Do not weep for me as if I were dead. I shall wait for you with the Sovereign Creator of the world."[26]

More touching and closer to the sensibility that prevailed until the end of the eighteenth century is this eyewitness account of a good death from a letter from Francesco Barbara to his daughter. The dying person is a holy woman "in the flower of her youth." She has been stricken with a horrible disease, which has covered her with ulcers and racked her with pain. She offers her suffering to God, "who strikes in order to save and kills us that we may not die."

She knows she is about to die (the traditional warning). After receiving the sacrament, she gets up and kneels on the bare floor. This is a position for the dying person that I believe was unknown in the Middle Ages. In those days, the dying man lay on his bed in the attitude of the recumbent figure. But here the moribund assumes the position of the praying figure which, as we know, came later: a surprising imitation by the living of the dead, but the happy dead. It could not have been easy for a woman on her deathbed to rise and go down on her knees. Bellarmine seldom gives details of this sort. Though he recommends this position, he feels obliged to provide some justification: God, he writes, often gives the dying the extraordinary strength to make this last gesture of faith and submission. It is worth noting that those representations of the death of the Virgin, which were so common from the end of the Middle Ages onward, sometimes show the Virgin kneeling.

Luchina, the young woman in this example, was "so exhausted that although she was still alive, she seemed already invaded by death. She who in her time had been so beautiful and stately was incredibly disfigured. But after she had gone to sleep in the Lord, the pallor and rigidity were erased from her face. Her features lost their repellent aspect, and a noble beauty and a majestic dignity pervaded her countenance. Seeing her so beautiful and no longer disfigured, those present did not believe that she was dead, but thought that she was asleep." Here, in this milieu of humanists—erudite and rational, but sensitive and inclined to mysticism—we rediscover the traditional model of the recumbent figure sleeping the sleep of peace. But a new emphasis has been placed on beauty, the ineffable beauty that appears after the last horrors of the death agony. This beauty is here included among other quasi-supernatural manifestations that have been observed in the bodies of saints and have served to prove their sanctity in inquests to determine beatification: preservation of the body and sweetness of its odor. The body of the saint is not subject to the universal corruption or its physical horrors: "Then, without any medical assistance, all the sores with which her body was covered were instantly healed, their stench was replaced by a delightful fragrance, and everyone inside and outside the room was struck with admiration."

The author of the letter explains the phenomenon as the triumph of a pure soul over an afflicted body. Luchina had lived in faith. Consequently her body, although covered with ulcers and foul-smelling, appeared after death as healed, glowing, and fragrant, because of the beauty of her soul, "as if the *nobilitas* of her soul had clothed her in a garment of beauty."

Such cases of the miraculous transformation of the body after death will seem less and less miraculous as we move forward in time. What is here still an exceptional characteristic of the death of the righteous person will in the nineteenth century become a commonplace but consoling aspect of the death of the loved one. How many times, even today, do visitors, when they are still permitted to view the dead body, murmur admiringly, "He looks as if he's asleep"?[27]

The beautiful and edifying death of the pious models of the sixteenth and seventeenth centuries dimly foreshadows the romantic death, but we must not force the comparison. The death we are examining is still closer to the traditional death, the tame death.

Another example of the simple and familiar death is the real death of the English Jesuit Robert Parsons as reported by his confreres. Parsons was the author of a rather complicated *ars moriendi;* but he himself, as his biographer points out, died "in typically Jesuit fashion . . . quietly, undramatically, while he was at work." However, he made the request, which seems strange to us, that during the recitation of the Commendations, that is, during the death agony, the rope that had been used to hang the Jesuit martyr Edmund Campion be placed around his neck.[28]

Parsons's death confirms the impression left by Luchina's story. The beautiful and edifying death that marks the end of a righteous and godly life spent in the world is similar to the traditional death, the familiar and confident (or resigned) death, with the addition of a bit of drama—or melodrama—which connoisseurs will recognize as the mark of the baroque. This dramatic element will remain discreet until the end of the eighteenth century, and will find full expression in the overblown rhetoric of neobaroque romanticism.

The Death of the Libertine

This model of death based on a calm acceptance of mortality is very different from the medieval model of a life haunted by the idea of an eleventh-hour conversion. But the disappearance of this obsession might have had another result less favorable for piety. To turn away from the agony of physical death was to run the risk of succeeding too well and forgetting altogether the metaphysical meaning of mortality; it was to expose oneself to the danger of indifference and even of disbelief. And indeed, this is what actually happened. Such cases are no longer exceptional or abnormal, although they need not necessarily be seen as the beginning of an irreversible evolution toward atheism or the scientific denial of immortality and the beyond.

When Erasmus fell sick, he recognized his kidney stone and his horseback-riding accident as a sign from Providence inviting him to think about death and salvation. But Giovanni Battista Gelli, whose thought Tenenti has analyzed, had a different reaction to illness.[29] He did not believe in the warning, and boasted about his disbelief. "I remember that

I had an illness that brought me to the threshold of the next world, but not for a moment did I think that I was going to die. I laughed when they wanted me to confess. [We are not far from Bellarmine's *odium Dei.*] If I had died then, I would have left without so much as a thought and without the slightest pain."

To leave without being aware of it, to forget that death exists—this is the best thing that could happen! This is the great advantage that animals have over men. Gelli says that on the island of Circe, Ulysses asks one of his men why he does not want to be turned back into a man. The animal he has become replies that the great affliction of mankind is the knowledge of death, the fear that results from this knowledge, and the sense of the passage of time. Animals have neither this knowledge nor this sense. The best moments in a man's life are those during which his awareness of duration is suspended, as in sleep.

Elsewhere Gelli reports the conversation of two friends who were talking about what happens after death. One said, "I entrust myself to whoever is more powerful in the next world, God or the devil." The other, believing that the soul might well be mortal, exclaimed before he died, *"Presto sarò fuori d'un gran fosso"* (Soon I shall be out of a great pit). In Gelli, as Tenenti has noted, there appears a profound skepticism with regard to the beyond and salvation. For him the only idea that matters is "that love of one's neighbor that is the sum total of the Christian religion." A man of the Enlightenment, so soon?

Ideas of this kind might seem exceptional, anachronistic, and unrepresentative were they not supported and confirmed by the testimony of Bellarmine. Bellarmine was no casual reporter and would have avoided giving a dangerous importance to cases too rare to cause alarm. According to Baroccius, he tells how a college professor was overtaken by death at a time when he no longer believed in the Trinity. He appeared enveloped in flames to one of his colleagues in order to warn him.

But the most interesting case is one that Bellarmine witnessed personally. He was called to the bedside of a dying man, who told him with perfect composure, " 'Your Eminence, I wanted to talk to you, not for my own sake, but for my wife and children; for I am going straight to hell, and there is nothing you can do for me.' And he said this calmly, as if he were talking about going to his villa or his château." Bellarmine confesses his astonishment in the face of this cold assurance. He places this greedy and unjust lawyer among the sorcerers, because he shares their trait of obstinacy.[30]

Death at a Discreet Distance

All the foregoing observations were inspired by one little fact of religious, and especially of pastoral, significance: that clergymen stopped urging deathbed conversion and started insisting that the consideration of death be part of one's daily religious practice.

Are we to interpret this little fact as a phenomenon of religious history, the work of an elite of humanists and reformist clergymen? In this case it would be primarily a change in religious philosophy, the deliberate transition from a medieval religion in which the supernatural reigned to a modern religion in which morality was dominant. Or does this fact belong rather to cultural history as a whole, and is it the translation into the code of churchmen of an elementary reaction to life and death on the part of the collective unconscious? I prefer the second interpretation, convinced as I am that in most cases spiritual writers exploit, rather than create, the tendencies of their times.

In the later Middle Ages, writers focused their attention on the moment of death because it was surrounded by uncertainty and aroused the passionate interest of their contemporaries. After the Renaissance they abandoned the subject, because it aroused less uncertainty and perhaps even the beginnings of real anxiety. But it was an anxiety so visceral and mysterious that the churchmen were afraid of it and preferred to ignore it in favor of a bittersweet meditation on the fragility of life and the passage of time.

In so doing, they created their own distortion of the medieval attitude toward death and life, a distortion that must be deciphered if the new attitude is to be understood. When this is done, we discover that modern man began to experience a feeling of constraint regarding the moment of his death, a constraint that was never expressed and probably never clearly conceived. This constraint created a tendency to keep this once-privileged moment at a distance. The separation was obtained through the intermediary of the Church, by means of the books of piety that were being produced in large numbers by the printing press. It was a discreet separation that did not go so far as a deliberate denial, neglect, or indifference; the familiar attitudes toward death and all the traditions and experiences they involved were still too powerful for that.

The idea of death was now replaced by the idea of mortality in general. In other words, the sense of death that had formerly been concentrated on the historical reality of the moment itself was henceforth diluted and distributed over the whole of the life, and in this way lost all its intensity.

Life also underwent a subtle change. Where once it had been divided into short segments by pseudodeaths, actual death putting an end to the last segment,[31] from now on it was full, dense, and continuous. Death, although always present, had no place in it except at an end that was remote and easily forgotten, despite the realism of the *Spiritual Exercises.* It was a life without interruption. The tunic had to be seamless; but this did not make it the garment of happiness and pleasure. On the contrary, it was a work garment, cut out of rough cloth, designed for laborious jobs of long duration. This life in which death was removed to a prudent distance seems less loving of things and people than the life in which death was the center.

A Debate
over Public Cemeteries

The prudent distance that we have just discovered in the new *artes moriendi* may also be found in the cemeteries. There, too, something new happens in the sixteenth and seventeenth centuries, something very subtle that demands interpretation.

In a short defamatory article of the late sixteenth century entitled *"Plaintes des Eglises réformées,"* the French Protestants, whose public existence was now recognized, complained of the obstacles that the Catholics were placing in the way of their right to freely choose their place of burial. The Catholics "interfered with their use of those [cemeteries] that had been given to them previously by the law or that they might have acquired for their own private use." In reality privacy was not the most serious issue. They were protesting primarily against "being denied access to the sacred cemeteries of the Catholics."[32] This is what really bothered them.

The Protestants were not content with the cemeteries authorized by the regime of the Edict of Nantes, and may have believed that there they were on "unhallowed ground." "In most of the towns where you are in the majority, not content with the public cemeteries, you also want to be buried in those churches in which you cannot prevent the Catholics from holding their services." It was in opposition to this claim that Bishop Henri de Sponde wrote a little book entitled *Les Cimetières sacrez,* which was published in 1598 in Bordeaux.

Despite his penchant for polemic, the bishop cannot conceal a slight confusion. He does not dare challenge directly the right of the Protestants to burial in a public cemetery. The expression, which seems new, indicates how closely a public character was now attributed to the cemetery, not only by unconscious habit but by conscious desire. Like certain other places, the cemetery symbolized membership in the community, a membership that the Protestants wanted and that outweighed their aversion to cohabiting with papists.

Being on shaky ground, Sponde resorts to arguments of practicality. If Catholics and Protestants were buried side by side, "we would risk provoking sedition and quarrels." The two groups should be separated, in death as in life. Let each side have its own cemeteries. The Catholics might just as well take the initiative and do what Sponde will ultimately ask the Protestants to do. "At the end of each field, let us make a new cemetery, have it consecrated, and transfer there the bodies of any of our dead who may be in the cemeteries you have occupied." They seem to be saying— if I may speak for these sixteenth-century Catholics—that they have no objection to the idea, in principle. They are not so attached to these sites that they believe to be traditional but that really are not, as we shall see. They would turn them over to the others without hesitation. Only, "what would we accomplish thereby? For you would immediately want a place there in the new ones, and if it were not given to you, you would accuse us of barbarity, inhumanity, and vengefulness."

But why do the Protestants care so much about being buried in public places? "Why are you not satisfied with your own cemeteries? Why do you want to be buried in the cemeteries of the Catholics?" How can you contemplate such promiscuity without disgust? "Do you want to be seen on the day of resurrection emerging from the same cemeteries, from the same graves, as the Catholics? . . . You have a horror of entering their churches and cemeteries while you are alive; yet you have no fear of being buried in these same cemeteries and churches after you are dead." The Protestants must have had a very good reason, to have led them to such a contradiction.

They did indeed, and Sponde tells us what it is: "These are the graves and cemeteries of our fathers"; they do not want to be separated from them. It is a serious and impressive answer, and one wonders whether it would have been stated as precisely a century earlier. Is it not rather the expression of a new attachment, that sense of family that was promoting the creation of family chapels in the churches and under the charnels?

It was a sentiment that had already become widespread, and Sponde is careful not to question it. He even agrees with it. But he tells the Protestants that they are defeating their own purpose, and this is very interesting. You are really the victims of an illusion, he says. You believe that these public cemeteries of today are the cemeteries of your fathers. But they no longer are, and through your own fault: "You have dug up the ground where your fathers lay and rooted among their tombs with your impure snouts. You have gorged on their flesh and bones, burned them, and played with them with all the mockery and license in the world." You have profaned the traditional cemeteries. That is why these cemeteries were moved during the religious wars. "These graves and cemeteries that remain today and that you claim have been usurped are no longer the old ones that you imagine them to be. You have destroyed the old ones and we have built these new ones. . . . You do not belong here anymore."

And for that matter, why are you so anxious to be "buried together," since the cemeteries of your fathers have been destroyed forever? "Where in the Gospel [since the Gospel is all you believe in] does it say that a person cannot be buried privately in his woods, or his field, or his house, as was Abraham . . . and as was done almost universally by the ancients, both Jew and Gentile alike? . . . Therefore, search, if you will, in other cemeteries than these, to which you no longer have any right, either by nature [they are no longer the cemeteries of your fathers] or by humanity [one can bury the dead anywhere] or by religion."

We may draw two conclusions from this passage. The first is ambiguous. A certain sentiment impels members of the same family or community to assemble their dead in the same place, whose public character, which was once merged with its religious and ecclesiastical character, is becoming more conscious. This public character is no doubt an added reason why the place remains sacred, as it had always been. However, what is sacred for Sponde is less the community of graves, although he cares enough about it to exclude the Protestants, than the single, "private" grave that he recommends to his adversaries. One senses a hesitation between two currents of opinion as yet ill defined.

The second conclusion to be drawn from the passage is very clear. At least in the towns, and in those places where there was conflict between Catholics and Protestants, the cemeteries have been moved. Sponde is sure of the fact, and we have no reason to doubt his testimony. He attributes these changes in location to the damage caused by the religious wars. His observation is correct, but his interpretation is open to debate.

Relocation of the Parisian Cemeteries

We have good reason to believe that the religious wars were not responsible for this. If we confine ourselves to Paris, the relocation of the cemeteries must have begun by the end of the sixteenth century, since it had already caught the attention of Sponde, but it does not really become apparent until the seventeenth century, and continues into the eighteenth. This relocation was a result of the enlargement of church buildings, which was in turn necessitated by the new devotional and pastoral practices that appeared after the Council of Trent. This transformation of space, and above all the detachment and negligence with regard to the dead that attended it, has a psychological significance.

In 1763, in order to prepare for the transfer of the cemeteries outside of town, and as part of an overall program of public sanitation, the procurator general of Parliament asked the inspectors of Châtelet to conduct an investigation into the condition of Parisian cemeteries. We possess the official records of their visits and the reports submitted to them by the priests and churchwardens. In each case, the inspector made an effort to determine the date of the founding of the cemetery. These documents are the basis of the observations that follow.[33]

In the first place, as we might have expected, a great many churches had no cemeteries of their own and sent their dead to les Innocents. But by the end of the eighteenth century, the church councils maintained veritable underground cemeteries under the churches. These burial vaults had first been granted along with family chapels, but later became a customary form of burial for the rich.

Apparently all the churches, even those that sent their dead to les Innocents, had their own cemeteries or charnels. A few of these had survived and were still in use in 1763; examples are Saint-Severin, Saint-André-des-Arts, Saint-Gervais, and Saint-Nicolas-des-Champs. The last one had been consecrated in 1223 because the monks refused to allow parishioners to be buried in their cemetery, as had been customary until then. "The dead have been buried there from time immemorial," the priests and churchwardens declared, not without pride.

But remarkably enough, a large number of these early cemeteries have disappeared. They have been destroyed and replaced, at dates that are known and not so long past, by others that are no longer "adjacent." Except for les Innocents, most of the large cemeteries of eighteenth-century Paris date only from the seventeenth century. In 1763 they were no more than a century old: Saint-Eustache (the cemetery of Saint-Joseph), 1643; Saint-Sulpice (the Old Cemetery), 1664; Saint-Benoît, 1615; Saint-Jacques-du-Haut-Pas, 1629; Saint-Hilaire, 1587; Saint-Etienne-du-Mont, 1637; Saint-Martin, 1645; Saint-Côme and Saint-Damien, 1555; Saint-Laurent, 1622; Saint-Jean-en-Grève, around 1500; Sainte-Marguerite, 1634; Saint-Roch, 1708; la-Ville-l'Evêque, 1690.

These constitute, so to speak, the first generation of the modern cemetery, as distinct from the medieval cemetery. The second generation was founded in the eighteenth century. The cemeteries of the first generation are not "adjacent" to the church, but they are not far from it either. Those of the second generation, however, are frankly eccentric; their locations were determined by the availability of cheap land. In 1760 Saint-Eustache added another cemetery to the one built in 1643; the new one was located in rue Cadet. The second cemetery of Saint-Sulpice, which was consecrated in 1746, was near Vaugirard, on the outskirts of Paris. The priests complained about the inconvenience of the distance.

The question naturally arises as to what became of the earlier cemeteries. We know that some, such as Saint-Jean and la-Ville-l'Evêque, became markets. Such a transformation was in keeping with the traditional model, and the market did not always drop the old name, as in the Saint-Jean cemetery. But in the majority of cases, the cemetery was absorbed by additions to the church. Some of these additions were necessitated by the building of lateral chapels, and in such cases they may date from the sixteenth century, as in Saint-Germain-le-Vieil. "About three hundred years ago, they had [a cemetery] adjoining their church, which was destroyed when the church was enlarged. The land is part of the church today."

At Saint-Gervais, the cemetery had not been destroyed but merely reduced until it became inadequate for the needs of the parish: "The eight lateral chapels, the charnels, and the Communion chapel were built on top of it." The reference to a Communion chapel should be noted. In most cases, the construction projects that ate into the space of the cemetery were either chapels or oratories for new devotions like the Blessed Sacrament or for the more regular observance of communion or confession, or they were rooms provided for church business: churchwardens' offices, sacristies (previously nonexistent), presbyteries, residences for priests active in the secular community, rooms used for catechism classes, convent schools, retreats, etc.

At Saint-Jean-en-Grève, "next to the church and near the town hall," there was a small cemetery "that, in view of the small size of the church, had been destroyed about forty years ago [early eighteenth century] in order to build a Communion chapel."

In 1708 Saint-Roch opened a new cemetery. On the site of the old one the church council built a Calvary chapel—a new form of worship of Franciscan origin inspired by the Stations of the Cross—"to be used for religious education, catechism classes, retreats, and for most of the confessionals."

We know that before the Council of Trent, the pastoral functions of the clergy were very limited except for preaching, which was restricted to monks. When the Counter-Reformation increased their activities, it was necessary to make space for their new functions, and this space was unhesitatingly appropriated from the cemetery. This explains the creation of the cemeteries of the seventeenth century.

The cemeteries of the eighteenth century were created for demographic reasons. In response to population growth, the parishes had, or wanted to have, two cemeteries, an adjacent or at least nearby cemetery for the rich, whose bodies were taken through the church, where a service was held in the presence of the body, and another, more distant cemetery for the poor, whose bodies did not pass through the church but went directly from the place of decease to the common grave. The topographical separation of the rich and the poor in death was very clear-cut: for the rich, churches and adjacent or nearby cemeteries; for the poor, remote and suburban cemeteries. It was a segregation that foreshadowed the situation today.[34]

The Weakening Link
Between Church and Cemetery

The last two centuries of the *ancien régime* saw the destruction of the old cemeteries for reasons of ecclesiastical policy and the creation of new ones that were increasingly remote.

The first thing that strikes us is the divorce between the church and the cemetery, a divorce that was already almost consummated in the mind of Sponde. There was no hesitation about building a cemetery that was physically separate from the church, and in the towns this situation became the most usual one. The only disadvantages to the separation were practical ones: fatigue and loss of time for the clergy who performed the funeral services. The situation would change at the end of the century, when there was a movement to abolish parochial cemeteries in favor of one large cemetery for all churches. The sensibility that we are analyzing here is that of the period of relocation in the seventeenth and early eighteenth centuries. The psychological climate of the end of the eighteenth century is different, and will be discussed in chapter 11.

Actually, the relocations were organized by the church councils themselves. They had the result, however, of making the cemetery a specialized space for burial, something it had not been for a thousand years. Without mentioning it or even being aware of it, people stopped burying *ad sanctos,* except for the rich, and then not all of them. It is likely that the number of "private" burials in outdoor cemeteries increased in the second half of the eighteenth century without the number of burials in churches necessarily decreasing. Requests of this kind became more frequent, and the priests mention them in their reports of 1763 as perfectly ordinary cases. As early as the seventeenth century small outdoor cemeteries were created as extensions of family chapels, such as that of Chancellor Séguier at Saint-Eustache, "his own private cemetery."

There is no doubt that during the seventeenth century the umbilical cord that connected the church and the cemetery was loosened, without yet being cut. It was a silent event that might have gone completely unnoticed and that might be interpreted as a mark of secularization, whereas actually it was the work of the spiritual elite, from which the Parisian clergymen and churchwardens of the seventeenth and eighteenth centuries were recruited.

But the silent and as yet very incomplete separation of the church and the cemetery is not the only aspect of this phenomenon. One can only imagine all the unearthing, jumbling, and crushing of human remains that was involved in the destruction of the cemeteries. No one took the trouble to remove the bones to a safe place. The workmen piled up the earth that contained pieces of human bodies and laid on top the foundations of the structures required by the new forms of worship. At Valletta in the sixteenth century the Knights of Malta built their private chapel right over the cemetery of their forerunners. Clergymen and townspeople alike were indifferent to the treatment accorded to the remains of their fathers. This indifference was not like the previous familiarity of the living and the dead, the fraternization in the charnels among the bones that lay on the surface of the ground. There was no longer the inclination to pick up a skull, like Hamlet, as one wandered through this macabre garden. The skull would have been tossed aside or used as fill, unless it was enlisted for some unmentionable and esoteric purpose.

7

The Vanities

This chapter is a continuation of the previous one. It provides a different set of illustrations for the same phenomenon: the subtle distancing of a death that is nevertheless still close. In it we propose to trace the rise, in the late seventeenth and eighteenth centuries, especially in the second half of the eighteenth century, of a desire for simplicity in the things connected with death. At first this desire expresses, but with more conviction than in the past, the traditional belief in the fragility of life and the corruption of the body. Later, it reveals an anxious sense of nothingness, which finds no solace in hope of the beyond, although this hope continues to be expressed. Eventually, it culminates in a kind of indifference to death and the dead, which may signify an abandonment to a benevolent nature among the literate elite or an unconscious negligence among the urban masses. Throughout the seventeenth and eighteenth centuries there is a kind of inexorable downward movement on all levels of society toward the yawning gulf of nothingness.

The Desire for Simplicity in Funerals and Wills

This desire for simplicity is expressed in wills. Indeed, it had never been absent from them; we have already seen that there had always been a category of people who renounced, with a humility that was sometimes a trifle ostentatious, the customary display of the burial service. But after the end of the seventeenth century, this type of will becomes commonplace, and even more significant than the number of references to simplicity is their banality. In the beginning—in the sixteenth and seventeenth centuries—the request for simplicity is more of an affectation and is accompanied by instructions that contradict it. In the seventeenth and eighteenth centuries, simplicity is frequently mentioned, until finally, in the eighteenth century, it is taken for granted.

The great are no exceptions, and indeed they sometimes anticipated the trend. In her will dated 1684, Elisabeth d'Orléans, one of the daughters of Gaston d'Orléans (she died in 1696), requested that there be no vigil after her death, except by the two priests in charge of reading the prayers, and only because this reading was part of the funeral liturgy. "Let me be laid on a straw mattress on the bed in which I shall die, with a sheet over me [instead of being exhibited like a representation]; let my curtains be drawn [so she will be concealed from sight]; on a table at the foot of my bed let there be a crucifix and two candlesticks with two yellow candles [not much for such a great lady, a princess of the royal blood], no funeral hangings [the reduction of mourning will be discussed later], two priests from my parish church [and no representatives of the four mendicant orders] to say the prayers, and no women to watch over my body, since I do not deserve more elaborate treatment. I beg my sisters not to oppose my wishes, and I ask them for this proof of their friendship, since having renounced the world and its vanities at my baptism [no last-minute conversion, but a stoical acceptance of a way of life], I would like to be buried as I should have lived. I therefore request that I be buried in my parish church, Saint-Sulpice, in the vault under my chapel, without any ceremony."[1]

In 1690 Françoise Amat, marquise de Solliers, who requested two thousand Masses, of which one thousand were to be said on the day of her death, also asked to have only one priest watch over her body. "I ask the almshouse [which took charge of burying the poor] of the parish in which I shall die to assign a priest to watch over my body during said Masses" and to bury it "in the cemetery of the almshouse in their usual manner," that is, without stopping at the church, early in the morning or late in the afternoon.[2]

In 1708 a canon of Paris wrote, "I would like to request explicitly that everything connected with my funeral service take place with great simplicity and even poverty. . . . During this ceremony and service, let there be more candles on the Blessed altar than there are around my miserable body [the emphasis is on the misery of the corruptible body]. . . . In this ceremony let no bells be tolled, and let the priests omit any other expenses that are not absolutely necessary, as long as there is a precedent for such omission in the funeral of some dignitary or canon of the church of Paris." The humility of the canon's service must not detract from the dignity of the chapter or the benefice.[3]

Toward the middle of the eighteenth century, the reference to simplicity became a standard formula that allows for little variation. In the late seventeenth century, people were still writing that they wanted to be buried "with as little ceremony as possible." By the eighteenth century, they were saying, "I want to be buried with the utmost simplicity at seven o'clock in the morning," or, "I want to be buried as simply as possible." In English wills the expression was a "decent funeral."

Holograph wills, Michel Vovelle's "beautiful wills," do not have much more to say. In 1723 Jean Molé, a councillor at the Parliament of Paris, wrote, "I desire and wish that after my death the funeral procession and the transport and burial of my body be done without ceremony and at very little expense."[4] Even Saint-Simon, who was incapable of saying anything simply, instructed in his will of 1754, which is a solemn testimony to conjugal love, that the tombstone to be placed near his vault be executed "without magnificence or anything that is not modest." If he indulges himself to the point of dictating a fuller inscription, it is only because this one is intended for his coffin, which will be under the ground, so that no one will be able to read it.[5]

It was also at the end of the seventeenth and especially in the eighteenth century that the authors of wills stopped making the arrangements for their funerals and left things in the hands of their executors. This confidence in the executor is ambiguous; it probably had two meanings. The first is disinterestedness. In some cases the context clearly indicates that the author has left no instructions other than those recorded in the document, and that he simply refuses to pay any further attention to the fate of his earthly remains. In 1660, for example, a bourgeois of Paris asks to be buried in Saint-Germain-l'Auxerrois, his parish church, at the foot of the crucifix, for this point is too important to be left to anyone else's discretion. On the other hand, "the arrangements for his procession and funeral service he leaves to his executors . . . humbly beseeching that they be simple and in keeping with Christian modesty."[6]

In 1657, a respectable bourgeois of Paris asks to be buried in les Innocents (a proof of humility), where his parents have already been laid to rest. He adds, "I wish my funeral procession and service to be in accordance with the wishes of the executors of the present will . . . entrusting myself entirely to them."[7]

The practice of leaving everything to the discretion of the executor acquires new meaning at the end of the eighteenth century, although this is not apparent simply from a reading of the texts. The meaning shifts from a desire to let go of earthly things to a proof of affectionate confidence in the executor—but from which the desire for simplicity is not necessarily excluded.

The Impersonality of Mourning

Finally, a certain restraint in the outward signs of mourning must be seen in connection with this tendency toward simplicity. Restraint in mourning —can such language be applied to the age of the great baroque funeral services? But these were actually theatrical events that amplified the effects of a much older ceremony, involving the representation and the catafalque, that lent itself to spiritual exercises and satisfied a taste for spectacle. However, as soon as one moves away from the court or the high offices of the kingdom, it is not so rare for testators humbly to request that ostentatious displays of mourning be eliminated in the home and at the church; this goes along with their request for simplicity. "As for her funeral procession and burial, she desires that it be as inexpensive as possible, excluding armorial bearings and anything that is not necessary" (1648).[8] "I forbid the use of black hangings for my funeral procession, service, and burial" (1708).[9] Or testators may excuse their heirs, when they are poor, from wearing costly mourning costumes, like this Parisian widow in 1652: ". . . gives and bequeaths to her maid and her manservant 500 pounds, and she does not wish them to wear mourning."[10]

However, the importance of these cases should not be exaggerated. They did not invalidate the general use of mourning at the time of death, during the ceremony, or during the period following death. The conventions involving mourning were scrupulously respected, especially when they involved the person's social status, because they served to confirm it or because their neglect would have placed it in doubt. This was true at court, where a detail of costume, whether or not one wore black, indicated one's place in the hierarchy.

What strikes us today is the social or ritual character, the obligatory quality, of demonstrations that originally purported to express the pain of loss, the agony of separation. Of course this tendency to ritualization is very old, dating from well before the seventeenth century. It arose in the heart of the Middle Ages, when the priests and the mendicant friars, and later the confreres and the poor, took the place of the weeping family and friends in the home, the funeral procession, and the church. We have seen that this transformation did not affect the Mediterranean South, Spain, parts of southern France, or southern Italy. We know from the *romancero* that there may have been mourners at the funeral of Jimena. On fifteenth-century Spanish tombstones, bas-reliefs representing scenes of absolution show very clearly the dramatic gestures of the entourage, particularly the women. These gestures simulated spontaneity. The use of hired mourners still existed in the eighteenth century. A doctor wrote in 1740, "I observed that the custom of lamentation has by no means died out in France. At least it is still observed in Picardie, not in the towns, except among the common people, but only in the country. Just before they take away the coffin, all the women throw themselves on top of it with the most dreadful howls and call upon the dead man by name without shedding a tear or even feeling so inclined. They would do the same for a total stranger if they happened to find themselves in the home of someone who had died at the time the body was taken away. . . . A young maid who was asked about this howling answered that she had always seen it done under these circumstances."[11]

These traditions, which are particularly powerful in the Mediterranean South, have persisted to our own time in Sicily, Sardinia, and Greece.[12] However, they have become more and more like ritual exercises, totally devoid of spontaneity. This is how they are described by the eighteenth-century doctor, and this is how they appear to Coraly de Gaïx in the rustic country towns of the nineteenth century.[13] This ritualization had already taken place by the end of the Middle Ages. The seventeenth century saw a further increase in impersonality and ritualism, after a temporary abatement in the sixteenth century.

That mourning expenses were sometimes regarded as a social necessity rather than a personal expression of grief is shown by a lawsuit recorded in Toulouse in 1757. A dispute arose between the marquise de Noë and her sister-in-law after the death of her husband. The marquise requested eight thousand pounds from her husband's estate to reimburse her for her mourning costume. But in the opinion of her sister-in-law, "the offer of 3,000 pounds that I made her for mourning clothes is sufficient for everything she has a right to claim in this connection." The widow develops her arguments in a written memorandum. "Since social propriety demands that wives wear mourning for their husbands, it is fair that they be reimbursed for their mourning clothes as well as for the funeral expenses. . . . The mourning clothes that are provided for the widow are neither an advantage nor a profit to her. Since she is legally required to wear mourning but not to pay for its cost, it is the responsibility of the husband's heir to provide her with mourning."[14]

This does not mean that there is no regret for the deceased, although in the seventeenth century, when people fainted so readily, news of death was received quite coolly. Someone who lost a husband or wife tried to replace him or her as soon as possible, except in the case of unmarriageable women or when the survivor retired from the world to await his own end. This impassivity, bordering on indifference, was perfectly acceptable, but it was not the general rule. There were a great many exceptions. There were many people who grieved and who wanted to show their grief, but their emotion was channeled into certain rituals from which it was not permitted to depart. The expression of sorrow at the deathbed was not allowed; or at any rate it was a silent expression, at least in the northern countries, in good society, and among true Christians. On the other hand, grief was acceptable after the sixteenth century and until the middle of the nineteenth century in funerary inscriptions and elegies. After the period of mourning, no further personal demonstrations of grief were tolerated. The man who was too afflicted to return to a normal life after the short period of time allowed by custom had no alternative than to retire to a monastery, or to the country, outside the world where he was known. At least among the upper classes and in the towns, mourning had become too highly ritualized and socialized to play the role it had once filled, that of emotional release. It had become impersonal and cold. Instead of allowing people to express what they felt about death, it prevented them from doing so. Mourning acted as a screen between man and death.

The desire to simplify the rites of death, to reduce the sentimental importance of burial and mourning, was actually inspired by a religious motivation, by the practice of Christian humility. But this Christian humility soon became confused with a more ambiguous sentiment, which Gomberville, like the devout writers, calls a "proper contempt for life."[15] This sentiment is still Christian, but it is just as "natural" as it is Christian. The empty space that death has created in the heart of life, the love of life, and the things and creatures of life, is as much the result of a natural feeling as it is the result of the direct influence of religion.

An Invitation to Melancholy: The Vanities

This sentiment is not limited to the time when a man writes his will, or to those critical moments when he thinks about death; it pervades all of his daily life. Men of the sixteenth century liked to surround themselves, in their bedrooms and studies, with pictures and objects that evoked the swift passage of time, the illusions of this world, and even the tedium of life. These pictures and objects were referred to—by a moralist's term that clearly expresses their flavor of renunciation—as vanities.

The vanities of the sixteenth and seventeenth centuries—they become rarer in the eighteenth—combine two elements, an anecdotal one that provides the subject or theme (portrait, still life, etc.), and a symbolic one, an image of time and death.

Originally confined to religious settings like the walls of churches and charnels, tombstones, or books of hours, macabre images soon overflowed these boundaries and found their way into domestic interiors. From then on, a secularized version of the macabre was part of the decor of private life in the homes of those sufficiently prosperous to be able to afford both private life and decor. But a few prints also found their way into the crowded, all-purpose living rooms of the common people.

The transition from church and cemetery to home altered the form and meaning of the macabre. The purpose of the macabre was no longer to reveal the subterranean work of corruption. The horrible *transi*, the naked cadaver being eaten by worms and bitten by snakes and toads, was replaced by the beautiful skeleton, clean and gleaming, the *morte secca* with which children still play today on All Souls' Day in Italy, and all year around in Mexico. That skeleton is neither so frightening nor so wicked. He no longer appears as the assistant and ally of the demon who recruits residents for hell.

In the sixteenth and seventeenth centuries the skeleton is the end of life, a simple agent of Providence today and of nature tomorrow. In his allegorical roles, he is also replaced by Father Time, a kindly and venerable old man without questionable ulterior motives. On a sixteenth-century Brussels altarpiece, he takes the place of the patron saint; he stands behind the donor, in the same protective attitude. On eighteenth-century tombstones, he carries the portrait of the deceased to heaven, taking the place of the angels, who are usually entrusted with this mission of apotheosis. In the church of Gesù e Maria di Corsica, in Rome, the symmetrical tombs of two brothers flank the main entrance. The principal difference between them is that in one the figure of Time occupies the place that the skeleton occupies in the other. It was the dark, disembodied shadow or the shrouded ghost, rather than the skeleton, that inspired fear after the seventeenth century.

The skeleton need not be whole in order to play its role. It may be dismantled and divided into small pieces; each of its bones possesses the same symbolic value. These little pieces of bone are easier to fasten to the surface of a small painting or some object. Their small size and inertness make them suitable for the role of objects within objects. They do not disturb the equilibrium of the small world of the bedroom or the study, an equilibrium that might be destroyed by the extravagant size and animation of the whole skeleton. So the skull and crossbones were separated from the rest and multiplied in a kind of algebra or heraldry, or combined with other symbols such as the hourglass, the church clock, the scythe, or the gravedigger's shovel. These symbols invaded not only funerary art but also those familiar objects that were the vanities.

A vanity may also be a portrait. Now that the subject is no longer represented in the hieratic attitude of the kneeling praying figure, he is often painted, sculpted, or engraved looking at a skull or holding a skull in his hand. The skull has taken the place of the religious scene that was once associated with the donor. Perhaps this arrangement was copied from desert scenes with Saint Mary Magdalene or Saint Jerome. In any event, this type of portrait is very common. Perhaps I am mistaken, but it seems to me that the skull is more often found in the hands of a man than a woman. One finds the same theme on sixteenth-century mural tombstones, which are composed like paintings, especially the tombstones of humanists. On the tombstone of J. Zener, in Berlin, there is a half-length portrait of the deceased. In his left hand is a death's-head and in his right hand a watch, which, like the hourglass, was a symbol of the passage of time.

The subject does not hold the death's-head only when he is alone; it also appears in group portraits. A portrait by Jan Molenaer dated 1635 shows a family group consisting of three couples and four generations: an old couple, with the woman holding a book and the man a death's-head; a middle-aged couple (today they would be in their forties, then they were probably in their thirties) playing the lute and the harpsichord; a pair of lovers (the boy is offering the girl flowers); and finally, a group of children playing with fruit and animals.[16]

The group portrait is sometimes presented as an allegory of the Ages of Man in which the skull and skeleton are the attributes of old age. The death's-head has a place of honor in the studio or study. The sedentary occupations of reading, meditation, and prayer are reserved for the middle and later years, whereas the physical activities of war, commerce, or farming define the prime of life, and love belongs to youth. In the very popular engravings of the Ages of Man, the skeleton is the last stage in the life of man, or else it crouches under the pyramid of the ages as if at the back of a cave at the heart of the world.

The presence of the skull turns the vanity portrait into an intermediary stage between allegory and genre painting. Genre paintings were also inspired by the contrast between youth and old age, or life and death. In the Kunsthistorisches Museum, in Vienna, an early sixteenth-century painting by Gregor Erhart shows a pair of lovers, beautiful and naked, and next to them, not yet the dried-out skeleton, but an ugly, toothless, withered old hag—a medieval tradition that will be found three centuries later in Goya.

In the Flemish and Dutch manner, Gerard Dou creates the interior of a surgeon's home, or perhaps it is the home of his patient. On a shelf, among the plates and pewter pots, is a death's-head.[17]

In Italian painting, the discovery of a solitary tomb in the countryside is inspired by the same preoccupations. In its oldest form—we find it in the Dream of Polyphilus—the subject is treated as a *memento mori*. It is the theme of the shepherds of Arcadia, which was used by Guercino. A group of carefree young men are standing around a sarcophagus: *"Et in Arcadia ego."* But these words, as Panofsky has shown, are spoken by Death: They issue from the skull that is placed on the tomb. In Poussin's version of the same scene the feeling has shifted from the traditional *memento mori* toward the vanities. In an early version, Poussin kept the skull. In a later one, which is in the Louvre, it is eliminated. The shepherds are deciphering the epitaph on the sarcophagus. This time it is no longer the symbolic and impersonal personification of death but the man buried in the sarcophagus who is delivering the message and telling them: I too, like you, was once in Arcadia. "The thought of death enriches the sense of the precariousness and preciousness of life."[18]

Finally—and this is the sense in which the term is usually understood —a vanity may be a still life in which the objects, either because of their function or because of their worn look, evoke the passage of time and the inevitable end. Examples of this type of vanity are numerous and well known. I shall mention only one particularly significant one from the middle of the seventeenth century. In a painting by Leonard Bramer in the Kunsthistorisches Museum a rusty suit of armor, some old torn books, and some broken dishes are laid out on a table. Beside the table a Rembrandt-esque old man looks on, and finally, at the back of a cellar, one can make out two skeletons. There could be no better expression of the parallel between the death of man and the deterioration of things.

Symbols of the end of life and things are not merely the subjects, sometimes secondary, of paintings or engravings; they also come down from the walls and mingle with furniture or clothing.

Savonarola recommended that everyone carry about with him a small death's-head made out of bone and look at it often. In a Holbein portrait in the National Gallery, in London, Jean de Dinteville wears one on his hat. In England in the sixteenth and early seventeenth centuries, rings were also decorated with macabre motifs. In 1554 an Englishwoman left her daughter a ring "with the weeping eye" and her son another ring "with the dead manes head." "Sell some of your clothing and buy yourself a death's-head and wear it on your middle finger," advises the Elizabethan author, Philip Massinger.[19]

There are jewels of this kind in museum collections. In the musée de Cluny in Paris, at Yale, and in the Walters Gallery in Baltimore, there are seventeenth-century rings bearing the skull and crossbones. These mourning rings were distributed along with gloves to those who attended burial services in New England.[20] In the museum in Amiens there is a watch from the same period with a death's-head engraved on it. The Victoria and Albert Museum, in London, has brooches in the shape of coffins. In the home, familiar objects and articles of furniture were intended to inspire the same reflections. On the cabinet in one's study one could place a small skeleton such as the sixteenth-century example in the Walters Gallery, in Baltimore. In the shop of a Parisian antique dealer I saw a late eighteenth-century writing desk in the Scandinavian or Germanic style, a wedding gift, inlaid with initials and a skeleton. As late as the mid-nineteenth century, the skeleton was still a favorite subject for earthenware dishes.

It was customary to engrave maxims recalling the brevity and uncertainty of life on the mantels of fireplaces. Emile Mâle quotes several of these.[21] In the musée Calvet, in Avignon, there is one with the inscription, *"Sortes meae in manu Dei sunt"* (My fate is in the hands of God). One could have in one's home or on one's person the same themes and mottoes that met the eye in the street, on the walls of churches, or around the sundial: *"Respice finem"* or *"Dubia omnibus [hora] ultima multis."*

All these objects were an invitation to conversion, but they also expressed a melancholy awareness of the uncertainty of life. They combined the two ideas, just as landscape painting started by combining nature with a genre scene that was its excuse for being. Like landscape painting, the vanities eventually won their independence. They dispensed with the appearance of moralizing; and the essential melancholy was enjoyed for its own sake. The bittersweet, overripe fruit of the end of the season, this melancholy expressed a permanent sense of the constant though diffuse presence of death at the heart of things, a presence that cast a veil of emotion over every life. Death was no longer a sudden emergence from a subterranean world of monsters, cadavers, and worms. The death of this later era of the macabre was both present and remote. It was no longer represented as a decomposed body but in a form that was no longer human: a creature as fantastic as the intelligent and animated skeleton or, still more often, an abstract symbol. And even after death has been given such reassuring features, it is elusive: It comes and goes, it rises to the surface and then returns to the depths, leaving nothing but its reflected image. In a painting in the Kunsthistorisches Museum, in Vienna, the German painter Furtenagel has shown a husband and wife looking at themselves in a mirror. But in the back of the mirror, as if at the bottom of a pool, one can see a death's-head.

It is a presence never obvious, never clearly visible, thanks to the appearances that close over it without ever concealing it altogether. From now on, the presence of death can be visible only in the intermittent reflections of a magic mirror. Holbein the Younger concealed the death's-head in his anamorphoses. It appears only if one looks at it from a certain angle. As soon as one moves away, it disappears.

Death is now an intrinsic part of the fragile and empty existence of things, whereas in the Middle Ages death came from the outside.

Death at the Heart of Things

The sense of life and death in the sixteenth and seventeenth centuries was fundamentally different from that of the later Middle Ages, although nothing, or very little, had changed in the customs or rituals of death.

It is remarkable that the vanity of the seventeenth century is the reverse of the still life of medieval origin as it persists in this same period, against the current we are tracing here. Still life, as we saw in chapter 3, expressed a passionate and, according to religious moralists, immoderate love of life and the things of this world: *avaritia*.

In the vanities, as in the later versions of the *artes moriendi*, the situation is reversed. This world, so pleasant and beautiful, is rotten and precarious. Death, which hides in its recesses and shadows, is, on the contrary, the blessed haven, safe from the troubled seas and the quaking earth. Life and the world have taken the place of the negative pole that the people of the late Middle Ages and early Renaissance had identified with death. Death and life have switched roles.

The vanities have helped us to discover a new idea, not of death, but of mortal life, an idea that I shall refer to as a common idea, just as there are commonplaces. A culture, especially a written culture like ours, is characterized by a number of these common ideas, which are offered to, if not imposed on, society as a whole like a kind of bible. Such ideas are a powerful part of the conditioning that gives the society its cohesion. In order to be effective, these ideas need not be recognized or admitted or even unanimously accepted. They need only be present as truisms or commonplaces in the air of the time.

Since World War II we have known some of these common ideas, which are disseminated by the press, the mass media, and word of mouth. For example, the idea of the lack of communication between people, the "lonely crowd." This idea has distinguished and personal origins, philosophical ancestors such as Sartre and Camus, among others. But it quickly took on a life of its own, and the intellectuals who invented or revived it would no longer recognize it in the condensed and depersonalized form that inevitably results from vulgarization. The success of these common ideas is due to the fact that they fluently express certain simple and profound feelings that now motivate masses of people after once affecting large and influential segments of the population. The concept of the vanity of life is one such idea. It came out of the writings of churchmen and passed into the collective unconscious, where it inspired a new attitude toward wealth and pleasure. One must ferret it out, as we have done, in the hidden recesses of art and of devout literature; one must surprise it in all its naked simplicity. Certainly its origins are religious, but not its real roots.

Beneath the veil of melancholy that covers them, riches are no longer desirable for themselves, for the pure pleasure they afford. Enjoyment is disturbing, whether it is mystical or sensual. The world is permeated with the tincture of death; it has become suspect from one end to the other.

Of course, this common idea was not the only element in that civilization in search of complexity that was the Western world in the seventeenth century; but it had a profound influence on the culture. Capitalism would not have prevailed if the pursuit of pleasure and the immediate enjoyment of things had continued to be as powerful as they were in the Middle Ages. The capitalist entrepreneur had to agree to postpone his enjoyment in order to accumulate his profits. The acquired wealth immediately became the source of other investments, which in turn created further wealth.

Such a system of accumulation over a period of time was dependent upon certain socioeconomic and cultural conditions. But at least one of the conditions was psychological: the end of *avaritia* and its replacement by a more ascetic attitude toward life and the things of life. It is a curious and seemingly paradoxical fact that life ceased to be so desirable at the same time that death ceased to seem so punctual or so powerful.

Simplicity in Tombs: Kings and Private Individuals

The bittersweet melancholy of the vanities that permeated the seventeenth century had its counterpart in a change in tombs and cemeteries, a change so subtle and gradual that it was hardly noticed by either contemporaries or historians. The death of tombs and cemeteries, like the death of the *artes moriendi* and the vanities, would become in its turn silent and unobtrusive, summoned to its own "extinction," as Vovelle suggests.[22]

There is one aspect of this change that would not fail to impress a Frenchman. The kings of the most powerful dynasty in Europe, those proudest of their rank and fame and at the height of their power, have no tombs and did not really desire them. The Valois had a chapel; the Bourbons did not, and in fact they allowed the chapel of their ancestors to be destroyed and their tombs transported to Saint-Denis. Of course, it was not decided all at once that the Bourbons would have no great funerary monuments. On the contrary, the question of building a chapel for their graves arose more than once. Bernini was consulted, among others. But all these plans came to nothing. So great a builder as Louis XIV had no interest in them. One may argue that a royal palace like Versailles, with the park radiating around the statue of the sovereign, played the part of the great memorial tomb in the seventeenth century. Nevertheless, there is something arresting and disquieting about the disappearance of the royal coffins into the vaults of Saint-Denis, with nothing showing above the ground.

Where dynastic funerary chapels do exist—Nancy, the Escorial, and Vienna—they have acquired an original character that helps us to understand the radical attitude of the Bourbons. The Escorial is particularly interesting, because it seems to represent a transition between the chapel of the Valois and the underground burial chamber of the Bourbons. It might be described as a Valois chapel on top of a Saint-Denis vault, although in fact the vault at the Escorial is a massive underground structure such as was never attempted at Saint-Denis.

The part of the tomb-chapel that is visible is actually a part of the church. On either side of the high altar are assembled the families of Charles V and Philip. They are in the traditional attitudes of praying figures, like the upper half of a two-level tomb. They are attending Mass. But they will remain alone, like illustrious and inimitable heroes. None of their successors will come to kneel beside them. Although they will be buried here, their resting-place will be in the vault beneath the church, according to a subtle protocol that persists until the twentieth century. This burial vault, which was called the Pantheon, fascinated the seventeenth-century visitor. It was the Pantheon that Saint-Simon wanted to see when he came to Spain in 1721. He wrote: "As we were walking down to the Pantheon, I saw a door on our left halfway down the staircase. The fat monk who went with us told us that this was the Pourrissoir." There they buried the coffins inside the walls. Perhaps they abandoned certain princes of no great reputation in the Pourrissoir, as Saint-Simon spitefully implies. Kings, and queens who had issue, were taken to "the drawers of the Pantheon." Infantes and queens who died without issue were taken to a vault adjacent to the Pourrissoir, which looks like a library. "The end opposite the door and the two long sides of this [windowless] room, which has no door except the one one enters by, look exactly like the walls of a library, except that whereas the shelves of a library are built to accommodate the books for which they are designed, these shelves are constructed to the size of the coffins. The latter are lined up side by side, with the heads against the wall and the feet toward the outside edge of the shelves, each of which bears an inscription with the name of the person who is inside. These coffins are covered, some with velvet and others with brocade. . . . Then we went down to the Pantheon."

The Pantheon is an octagon. One side is occupied by the door and four others by four rows of superimposed niches. Each sarcophagus contains a black marble cippus designed to receive the bones from the Pourrissoir. To the left are the kings, to the right are those queens who left progeny. "My guides did me the singular favor," Saint-Simon goes on, "of lighting about two-thirds of the enormous and admirable chandelier that hangs from the middle of the vault, and whose dazzling light enabled us to distinguish not only the tiniest strokes of the smallest writing but the most intricate details in every part of the Pantheon."[23] One thinks of this gigantic columbarium when one sees the superimposed niches in the cemeteries of the Mediterranean countries or of South America, which are no longer underground but in the open air.

In Vienna, in the Capuchin church where the Hapsburgs of Austria chose to be buried, the visible portion of the Escorial has disappeared. All the monuments are in the burial vault, the Kaisergruft, a simple structure that has none of the architectural splendor of the Pantheon. But neither have the coffins been abandoned in some out-of-the-way corner, like those of the Bourbons in Saint-Denis, which might as well be underground. The burial vault in Vienna can be visited, and is well worth the time. The monuments are coffins, or at least they seem to be. The visitor of today knows immediately that he is not in a chapel or a cemetery, looking at the visible and sterilized aspect of death. He is inside a tomb, surrounded by bodies. The coffins are lined up next to each other in rows. The oldest and the most recent are unadorned, but those of Maria Theresa and her relatives are lost in a mass of rococo ornamentation. They are surrounded by portraits, insignia, gesticulating angels, weeping women, allegorical figures sounding the trumpet of fame, and all kinds of macabre symbols. Only one coffin, that of Maria Theresa and her husband, has on the lid two recumbent figures leaning on one elbow, as on an Etruscan tomb. But however ornate they may be, these tombs are still coffins, lead coffins like many others, and the intricate carvings that writhe in every direction are made of the same material as the sculpture on the ornamental lakes of Versailles.

In all three cases, almost everything happens underground, and in Saint-Denis there is nothing left to see that one cannot see in the burial vault of an ordinary family chapel. The kings agreed with what Bossuet said when he preached on Holy Saturday from the pulpit of the College of Navarre: "When I consider the splendid tombs in which the great of this earth seem to be trying to hide the shame of their corruption, I never cease to wonder at the extreme folly of men, who erect such magnificent memorials to a handful of ashes and a few old bones."[24]

The kings set the example; they started the fashion. There will continue to be sumptuous and ornate tombs, those of the popes most of all: funerary chapels in which gesticulating angels carry portraits off to heaven or life-size allegorical figures surround a pyramid or obelisk and act out some story. Examples are the Sangro chapel in Naples, the tomb of the comte d'Harcourt in Paris, and the tomb of the marshal of Saxony in Strasbourg. Saint Paul's in London is full of tombs of this kind. They may recall the monumental works of the late Middle Ages and anticipate the theatrical scenes of romanticism, but they are no longer typical of the mentality of the seventeenth and eighteenth centuries. Any tombs that are still grand and ambitious are unique products, the isolated creation of an artist with an original bent. Out of the whole series of these masterpieces one cannot distinguish sufficient common characteristics to constitute a model such as the medieval ones we studied in chapter 5.

In place of the medieval models, there are only two types of ordinary tombs: the lead coffin in the burial vault and the very modest horizontal slab, the simplified descendant of the flat tomb that was part of the paving of the floor.

The bishops of the Counter-Reformation had tried to revive the old custom of burial in cemeteries, but they had to be content with requiring that the grave be no higher than the floor of the church. Indeed, this arrangement was in keeping with the tendency toward simplicity in funeral services. And those who remained attached to the tradition of display were not without resources. Just because their tombs were low, they did not have to be humble. The requirement that the tomb be flush with the ground must have been a great boon to mosaic workers, who carpeted the floors of churches with their marble designs. The churches of Gesù, in Rome, and of the Knights of Malta, in Valletta, are full of these marvelous multicolored patterns, many of them based on the themes of heraldry, which represent the final flowering of the art of mosaic before the bathrooms of the twentieth century.

But these magnificent flat patterns of multicolored marble on the tombs of princes and cardinals were rare. The floor of San Giovanni dei Fiorentini, in Rome, is composed of drab circles and rectangles alternating in a monochromatic pattern. The rectangles are all individual tombs with very simple inscriptions. In front of the high altar there is a large circle that covers the burial vault of the Confraternity of the Nation of Florentines. These simple slabs found their way outside the church and into cloisters and cemeteries, such as the cloister of Santa Annunziata, in Florence. Extreme simplicity continued to characterize the funerary slab in Italy until the middle of the nineteenth century, which was the age of those grandiose tombs with statues, portraits, and theatrical scenes at the Campo Santo in Genoa.

The same was true elsewhere, but as a result of the relentless alterations of the nineteenth and twentieth centuries, these humble slabs without artistic character have disappeared. A few have been left intact in poor and remote regions. In Bozouls, in France, in the little Romanesque church, the floor is still almost completely composed of eighteenth-century funerary slabs whose extreme simplicity may be due to the proximity of Protestants. They bear the name alone, or the name and a date, or, more infrequently, the name, a date, and the profession. Sometimes there is the image of the cross on Calvary. The tombs of priests are identified by the letters PRT and an open book. The overall effect of these simple slabs is a profound impression of austerity and renunciation.

The Revival
of the Outdoor Cemetery

But the most striking innovation of this period with respect to burial is the return to the cemetery. A greater number of people of quality who, in the sixteenth and early seventeenth centuries, would have been buried in churches are, in the late seventeenth and eighteenth centuries, buried out of doors, in cemeteries.

In France, some people chose the cemetery for the same reason that others who preferred the church chose the slab flush with the pavement, for the sake of humility. At least this was the reason they gave for a choice that had never been completely abandoned.

The 1763 investigation of the procurator general of Parliament that we referred to in the preceding chapter gives some precise information on the subject. Burials in the cemetery were common enough for the priests to use them as an argument for moving the cemeteries outside Paris. At Sainte-Marie-Madeleine-de-la-Cité, "their parish church has no other cemetery except les Innocents to bury [not the poor, but] those parishioners who, in a spirit of humility, did not wish to be placed in the burial vault of their church."[25]

The priest and churchwardens of Saint-Sulpice were worried about the plans for moving the cemeteries outside the city, and insisted that it was necessary to keep their cemetery in the rue de Bagneux: "It cannot be an inconvenience to anyone in the vicinity . . . but there are other reasons peculiar to the parish of Saint-Sulpice that make them [the cemeteries] necessary. The most important is that the parish of Saint-Sulpice contains within its vast area a number of citizens of the highest reputation who, out of piety and humility, have asked to be buried in cemeteries."

At Saint-Louis-en-l'Ile the church council feared "the relocation of the cemetery" for the same reason. They "would more frequently advise the families of deceased persons to request burial in the vaults of the church [instead of the cemetery], since it was impossible to accede to the last wishes of many highly esteemed persons whose piety and humility would impel them to be buried in the cemetery among the poorest people, of which persons there are many examples in the parish of Saint-Louis." One example was Lieutenant General of Police La Reynie.

In his portrait of La Reynie, Orest Ranum writes that he "was inspired by his sincere religious devotion to an extraordinary act of humility. He asked in his will to be buried anonymously, without a tombstone, in a little cemetery near Saint-Eustache."[26]

Some of these parishioners from the Parisian area also chose the cemetery for civic reasons, from a sense of the collective welfare, rather than out of humility; at least that is the reason they gave. An example is the chancellor of Aguesseau. The obelisk opposite the church of Auteuil, in Paris, is a remnant of his outdoor tomb.

In rural areas in the eighteenth century there may have been a new feeling on the part of the community in favor of the cemetery and against the priest, who gave too much consideration to the dead buried in the church. Yves Castan cites a case that was tried in September 1735, involving the priest of Viviers, near Mirepoix, and one of his parishioners and her husband. The court clerk reports that "the day after the local feast (September 9), she protested about the omission of the *Libera* in the church. She took the book away from the cantor, pushed the people outside, and told them, 'Come to the cemetery.' Her husband said that she had spoken 'on behalf of the women' and that she wanted to restore the custom of saying prayers in the cemetery."[27]

It must be admitted, however, that the rebirth of the cemetery in France, although well documented, was slow, and it is difficult to trace or to imagine, because hardly any visible tombs from these cemeteries are left today.

In England the situation is quite different. As in France, of course, there remain very few outdoor tombs from the end of the Middle Ages and the beginning of modern times. The ones there are are often in the form of a narrow vertical stele ending in a disc carved with a cross, a type similar to the ones we have found in the sixteenth century on the Continent. On the other hand, there are many tombs left inside churches, with carved or engraved recumbent figures, which indicates that in England, as in France, nobles, merchants, and important people were buried in church. However, there are indications that by the end of the Middle Ages the cemetery was less deserted in England than it was in France.

But it is after the Restoration, in the second half of the seventeenth century, that the evidence begins to accumulate. In 1682 John Evelyn noted in his *Diary* that his father-in-law wanted to be buried in the church-yard, not in the church, "being much offended by the novel custom [novel in relation to the early Church and canon law] of burying everyone within the body of the church."[28]

A great many vertical steles from this period still exist today, if not always in their original places, then lined up against the wall of a church or cloister. Their quantity gives us an idea of what a churchyard must have been like at the end of the seventeenth and beginning of the eighteenth century: a kind of meadow in which the minister's animals grazed and which bristled with headstones, many of them richly decorated. It may be that a few of the more primitive examples were inspired by wooden models. But the majority are derived from the most common type of mural tablet, removed from its traditional context inside the church building and planted in the ground. They have retained the inscription, the ornate frame, and in some cases even the religious scene: the Creation and the Fall, the resurrection of the flesh, or the ascension of the soul in the form of an angel. So it is not the form of the tombs that makes the English outdoor cemetery unique, but their quantity and antiquity. It is curious to discover headstones of the English type in Jewish cemeteries of Central Europe such as that in Prague.

What caused English people of quality to be buried in cemeteries? Something a little different from the radical and ostentatious humility in the Jansenist manner that was professed in France; something midway between the absolute indifference of the Puritans and the traditional desire to maintain a posthumous rank and leave behind a memory; something that is implied in this inscription of 1684: "In this church porch lyeth ye body of William Tosker, who chose rather to be a doorkeeper to the house of his God than to dwell in the tent of wickedness."[29]

This psychological tendency was so widespread that the English immigrants imported it to America as a fundamental trait of their culture. In the English colonies of America, the customary place of burial was the cemetery, a fact whose originality, novelty, and precocity American histori-ans do not seem fully to realize. In Puritan New England, tombs in churches were unheard of, and the cemetery was always the scene of solemn and memorable funeral services.[30]

In Virginia, after the middle of the seventeenth century, the impor-tant people in the colony chose to be buried outdoors, in nature, either on their plantations, or in the churchyard. They were also buried in the churches, but not exclusively, and with decreasing frequency. Flat tombs or mural tablets appear in 1627 and disappear in the mid-eighteenth cen-tury, when burial in church was discontinued. There is a large collection of these outdoor monuments, inventoried and studied by Patrick Henry

Butler. Without attempting to go into all the details, we will note three categories of tombs, for in this case morphology is significant.

First there is the box tomb, which is derived from the medieval tomb with recumbent figure. The figure has been omitted, and there is nothing left but the socle, or base. There were examples of this type at les Innocents in the sixteenth century, as we can see from the painting in the Carnavalet museum. They also existed in England, of course; there are examples in the little cemetery of the Royal Hospital in Chelsea. In Virginia, these tombs were reserved for important personages. The sides were decorated, first in the baroque style and later in the classical style. In the second half of the eighteenth century there were more rustic models built of bricks. Butler has photographed examples dated 1675, 1692, 1699, and 1700.

More numerous and more ordinary, although also decorated and sometimes imported from England, are the flat tombs, or slabs, and the steles, or headstones, which re-create on the other side of the Atlantic the English churchyard of the late seventeenth century. The oldest headstone discovered in connection with Butler's research is dated 1622. There was also an abundance of headstones in New England, which even exported them to Virginia in the eighteenth century.

The only difference between the Anglican tombs of Virginia and the Puritan tombs of New England is their iconography. In Virginia, as in England, two subjects are found at this time on the tops of the steles, that is, the space reserved for the religious scene and the effigy of the deceased in the mural tablets found in churches. The first is the angel, or angel's head with wings, symbol of the immortal soul and its ascension to heaven. The second is the skull and crossbones, symbol of the decay of the body. This macabre theme was very popular in New England.

The use of the cherub seems to make more sense than the macabre algebra that had become so commonplace at this time throughout the West. The winged cherub is seldom found in France. In Italy it is lost among other decorative elements. In America it has a flavor and intensity all its own; people had not forgotten that it represented the immortal soul. This explains why in eighteenth-century New England, where the meaning of death was changing and the Puritans were belatedly ceasing to cultivate the fear of death, the winged death's-head was transformed into a winged angel's head by an almost cinematic process in which the face gradually became fuller and gentler.[31]

So in the seventeenth and eighteenth centuries, in England and her American colonies, a space grew up around the church that was no longer the cemetery of anonymous graves, the burial place of the poor and the humble. This area was dotted with simple but often quite elegant monuments on which it was easy to trace the influence of the great artistic movements and on which the baroque gave way to Palladian classicism before the advent of romanticism, expressing, perhaps, a general desire for less display and more simplicity.

This image of the cemetery is not totally unknown outside England. Even today, tombs of this kind crop up where one would least expect to find them. In the little cemetery of a Catalonian village right next to the Spanish border, I was surprised to find some old tombs simply marked by an engraved stele at the head and a bare stone at the foot. In England and America the site of the grave was actually defined by the headstone and the footstone. This practice bears witness to a new concern for indicating the location of the grave on the surface of the ground, but it does not seem to go back very far into the eighteenth century. In the early years of the nineteenth century it was the customary model, even for the rich.

In *Wuthering Heights*, Emily Brontë describes a little country cemetery. Two important families live in the same parish in two houses of equally noble appearance. One family, that of the squire, has its tombs in the church, the other in the churchyard. The squire's wife, on her deathbed, asks to be buried in the cemetery instead of the church. So her husband renounces the grave of his ancestors in order to lie beside his wife in a corner of the cemetery near the wall. They will have a single headstone and "a plain grey block at their feet, to mark their grave."

The country churchyard with its stones lying flat or planted upright, surrounded by nature, bears witness to a serene and somewhat distant attitude in which hopes and fears are equally remote. It was this cemetery that Thomas Gray contemplated in the middle of the eighteenth century. It was this cemetery that inspired the romantics when they discovered another way of being and feeling in the presence of death.

The Temptation of Nothingness

We might expect to arrive, by the beginning of the eighteenth century, at a certain equilibrium of melancholy simplicity, an equilibrium that would be symbolized by the English and American cemetery. But already the bittersweet sentiment in which this culture was steeped was turning sour, and there was a shift from the vanities to the void. Not always, not necessarily, but often enough to characterize the style of an era. What took place was a sort of dramatic return of a melancholy life to its empty center. The moment of this return was no doubt the time of retirement, the retreat "in the desert."

In his *Vie de Rancé*, Chateaubriand talks about Mme. de Rambouillet, who died in 1655 at the age of eighty-two. "For a long time now she had ceased to exist, unless you count days of tedium. She had written her epitaph: 'Stranger, if you would count the number of her woes,/You need only count the moments of her life.' "

At that age, it was appropriate to withdraw from the world and think about death, for there was nothing else left for an old person to do. But this isolation was no longer so total as that of the medieval cloister. One of the usual "exercises" was to write one's memoirs. Max Fumaroli "sees the memoirs of the seventeenth century [which were so numerous, and generally written when the author was retiring from active and secular life] as spiritual exercises" in the manner of Saint Ignatius. These memoirists are "in search of past time, and in their work, time is perceived as a foundation of vanity, as emptiness, nothingness."[32]

This trend toward nothingness must be seen in connection with the growing belief, which we have already noted, in the duality of human nature. Of course, people still believed in the resurrection of the flesh; it was sometimes mentioned in epitaphs, and the deceased expected it; but this belief was no longer central to spirituality, it no longer allayed the prevailing anxieties of the age. The opposition between the body and the soul culminated in the destruction of the body.

"As long as we are at home in the body," Increase Mather, who was descended from a family of great New England preachers, wrote in 1721, "we are absent from the Lord. . . . We are willing rather to be absent from the body and at home with the Lord."

The body that remains after death is of no interest to the English Puritan. "Thy body, when the soule is gone, will be a horrour to all that behold it, a most loothsome and abhorred spectacle. Those that loved it most cannot now finde in their hearts to look on it, by reason of the griefly deformedness which death will put upon it. Down it must into a pit of carions and confusion; covered with wormes, not able to wag so much as a little finger, to remove the vermine that feed and gnaw upon its flesch." Not so the soul: "When the soule departs this life, it carries nothing away with it but grace, God's favour, and good conscience."[33]

Bossuet comes very close to the English nonconformist when he asks in his "Sermon sur la mort," "Will I be permitted today to open a tomb in the presence of the court, and will not those delicate eyes be offended by such a dismal sight?"

Bossuet had started this meditation on death when he was twenty years old. In his "Méditation sur la brièveté de la vie," he writes, "My life will consist of eighty years at most. . . . How little space I occupy in the great abyss of time!" He repeats the idea almost word for word in his "Sermon sur la mort": "If I cast my eyes before me, what an infinite space in which I do not exist! And if I look behind me, what a terrible procession of years in which I do not exist, and how little space I occupy in this vast abyss of time!"

We recognize here the idea of vanity, the brevity of life, the flight of time, the insignificance of man in the vastness of time and space; a Pascalian idea. As early as 1648, in his *"Méditation sur la brièveté de la vie,"* Bossuet made the transition from this little space to nothing at all: "I am nothing. This little interval is incapable of distinguishing me from the void into which I must go. I am a nonentity; the world had no need of me." This passage is also repeated word for word in the *"Sermon sur la mort."*

"I am nothing . . . the world had no need of me." This, from a man who was so important that the treasury of the Church was mobilized for his personal salvation, his successes and failures were of vital concern to the entire community, and there were holidays celebrating the great events of his life. This life was now regarded as "a candle that had consumed its substance" by Bossuet, a puff of smoke in the breeze by the German Cryphius (1640), "a drop of dew that has fallen on a lily" by Binet *(Essay des merveilles)*, a drop of dew or a soap bubble by the Englishman Richard Crashaw:

> *Sphere not of glass*
> *And yet more luminous*
> *And yet more delicate,*

As delicate as life, and as marvelous as life's illusions:

> *I am a tincture made*
> *Of snow and roses,*
> *Of water, air, and fire*
> *Painted, jeweled, gilt.*

But this whole luminous edifice, like a baroque ceiling, is nothing, according to the untranslatable ending of this poem:

> *O sum, scilicet, O nihil.*

Figures of speech, you will say; the images of a poet. But these same words will be used by Bossuet, not from the pulpit, but in an informal letter to the abbot of Rancé. Bossuet is sending him the funeral orations of the queen of England and of Madame (the king's sister-in-law): "I have given instructions to send you two funeral orations that, because they emphasize the nothingness of the world, may have a place among the books of a recluse and that in any case may be regarded as two rather touching reminders of the vanity of this world."[34]

Whether intimate or lofty, these variations on the theme of nothingness are now buried in books that are seldom read. This nothingness has lost some of its impact. We can pass by without noticing it and pretend that we have forgotten it. At most, it could be an exercise in erudition. But even today nothingness can compel our attention with the same force as in the seventeenth and eighteenth centuries. In the churches it remains beneath the surface; but tombs and epitaphs hurl it in our faces like a dirty word, and anyone who has seen this word can never forget it. The power of expression of funerary art can be extraordinary.

The best illustration of what I mean is the tomb of the Altieri, a husband and wife, in a lateral chapel of Santa Maria in Campitelli, in Rome. It is a particularly beautiful and moving monument. The tombs— for there are two separate ones—date from 1709. They are similar and symmetrical, and are placed on either side of the altar.

The lower part of each tomb consists of an enormous sarcophagus of red marble. On the lid of the sarcophagus two sorrowful angels carry an overturned torch and hold an inscription on which is written a single word, in huge gold letters that stand out like the letters on an advertising bill-board. This word is *nihil* (nothing) on the tomb of the husband and *umbra* (shadow) on that of the wife.

Nihil and *umbra*: the last confession of people who no longer believe in anything, one might think, if one kept one's eyes on the lower story of the tomb—as if Bossuet's remark had been taken literally, apart from its context. But if we look further up, above the terrible word, everything changes, and we recognize some familiar and reassuring forms. The two dead persons are kneeling in the traditional attitude of the praying figure in heaven. The man has his hands crossed on his breast, and his prayer is close to ecstasy. He is gazing at the altar, which is both that of his earthly parish and that of the celestial abode. His wife is looking the other way, toward the door of the chapel. She is holding her prayer book half closed over one finger. She has a melancholy expression, as if she were waiting.

Two ideas appear in this magnificent work. On the one hand, there is the melancholy of a shadowy realm that is neither the black of night nor the emptiness of the void; on the other hand, in a world that is altogether separate, there is the beatitude of the beyond. The contrast is violent and apparent.

The same contrast is found on the tomb of Gisleni in Santa Maria del Popolo, in Rome, although here it is attenuated by a more traditional inspiration and a more expansive rhetoric. The idea of nothingness is held in check by doctrine, but it pours out of the images.[35]

The tomb, which is dated 1672, is very tall and vertical. At the top is a painted portrait of the deceased in a round frame with the legend *"Neque hic vivus"* (not alive here). At the bottom—and this is the most impressive part of the work—a skeleton looks out at us from behind bars: *"Neque illic mortuus"* (not dead there). Between the portrait and the skeleton are epitaphs, inscriptions, and symbols of immortality, such as the phoenix and the butterfly emerging from the chrysalis. These quite orthodox inscriptions undoubtedly repeat the Pauline theme that only the dead are really alive and that the living are really dead. But the passerby to whom the tomb is addressed overlooks the details of these little symbolic scenes and their reassuring commentaries. All he sees, all he hears, is the skeleton behind his bars.

More simple and ordinary, and hence less expressive, but perhaps more representative of the average attitude, is a late sixteenth-century slab in San Onofrio, still in Rome; baroque Rome is the city of nothingness. As in the two previous tombs, the idea of nothingness is juxtaposed with the idea of blessed immortality. The inscription begins by stating boldly that to live is nothing: *"Nil vixisse juvat."* The brutality of the statement is then corrected. It is *"stabile et bonum"* (everlasting and good) to live in heaven. But thanks to the spirit of the Latin, the whole weight of the statement falls on the initial *Nil,* and the rest of the sentence loses its force. In addition, the epitaph is surmounted, as by a title on the top of a page, by another word, *Nemo. Nihil* and *Nemo:* nothing and nobody. Many other funerary inscriptions of the same period dispense with theological subtleties and make no attempt to balance contradictory truths. They state bleakly that the world is nothing, with no allusion to salvation, Christ, or any celestial comforter to act as a counterbalance. For example, this Neapolitan epitaph at San Lorenzo Maggiore:

> *What is the world?*
> *What is it? Nothing.*
> *If it is nothing, why is it?*
> *The world is as nothing.*

Or this other epitaph, also Neapolitan, at San Domenico: *"Terra tegit terram"* (Earth covers earth). Cardinal Antonio Barberini, who died in 1671, can hardly be suspected of atheism; yet he chose for his Roman epitaph the same idea, which strikes our ears with the accent of despair: "Here lie ashes and dust [these are the traditional symbols of penitence, but the last word falls like an executioner's blade] and nothing."[36]

Even among these Christians of the seventeenth and early eighteenth centuries, who were certainly full of faith, the temptation of nothingness was very strong. No doubt they managed to keep it within bounds, but the balance became precarious when the two realms, the realm of nothingness and the realm of immortality, became too widely separated, without communication. It required only a decline in faith or rather, as I believe, a decline in eschatological concern within the Christian faith, for the balance to be destroyed and for nothingness to take over. The way was now open for all the fascinations of nothingness, nature, and matter.

Comfort and Terror: The Two Faces of Nature

This is what happened in the eighteenth century, but then nothingness was not seen in its pure form—a privilege reserved for the twentieth century, no doubt—but was immediately identified with, and corrected, or attenuated by, the idea of nature. This was certainly true of the second half of the eighteenth century, but it was already perceptible in Gomberville in 1646. In his *Doctrine des moeurs,* Gomberville talks about death and rejects the macabre disguise it has worn since the Middle Ages. "The wise man" ignores these images. "In his mind [he gives death] the true face that it ought to have, he looks upon death in the same way that he considers his origin."[37] Indeed, the notion of origin is fundamental: "We shall all return to the state we were in before we were born," writes the priest Meslier in his *Testament,* more than a century after Gomberville. It is remarkable that today the prenatal world provides us with more realistic and more repellent monsters than the old infernal bestiary. When the painters of the 1950s wish to express the horrors of war, genocide, and torture, they replace the skeleton and the mummy with the fetus, that incomplete and monstrous image of origin.

For Gomberville, of course, man's origin is not the repellent fetus but a metaphysical origin that is serene and reassuring. It is an origin that is both end and beginning, it is nature: "We must give back to Nature what she has lent us. We must return from whence we came."

This nature where everything ends has two aspects. One we already know. It is the cemetery, the country churchyard of Thomas Gray and the English elegiac poets of the eighteenth century. That is the positive aspect. The other is the darkness of night and the underground burial vault, the concrete image of nothingness.

At the end of the second volume of Gomberville's *Doctrine des moeurs*, there is an illustration representing the cemetery as an allegory of the *finis vitae*. It is not a real cemetery of Gomberville's day. Instead it anticipates, in 1646, the imaginative flights of Piranesi, Boullée, and the cold visionaries of the late eighteenth century; the cemeteries of those urbanists were cities of the dead sealed off from the world of light. Gomberville's cemetery is an elongated burial vault, a cryptoporticus such as were discovered in Rome and imitated in Italian villas, but without windows. The walls are lined with funerary urns. Sarcophagi stand open, skeletons lie on the ground, and the only movement is provided by passing shadows.

The seventeenth and eighteenth centuries presented another image of death: the subterranean vault, a large enclosed space that was not, like hell, another world; it was of the earth, but devoid of light, a *camera obscura*. Under the circumstances one can understand how the tombs of seventeenth- and eighteenth-century kings, instead of rising vertically like those of the fourteenth to sixteenth centuries, descended under the earth and disappeared. This is why the burial vault—along with the country cemetery —became the dominant image of death in the eighteenth and early nineteenth centuries, especially in preromantic England. In the mid-eighteenth century two poems were published, among many others, one on the outdoor cemetery, Thomas Gray's "Elegy Written in a Country Churchyard" (1751), and the other on a burial vault, Robert Blair's "The Grave" (1743). The "dread thing" is a dark, deep vault, "where nought but silence reigns, and night, dark night." Under its arches dripping with moss, the flickering light of the torches makes the night even more sinister, and "lets fall a supernumerary horror." The theme of the burial vault has been employed by the Gothic novels of Ann Radcliffe and Matthew Gregory Lewis to intensify situations more or less erotic and sadistic in nature.

The image of the burial vault was also appropriated by funerary art, where it was combined with more traditional symbols of immortality, such as the apotheosis of the deceased, whose portrait is carried off to heaven by angels, or with newer symbols from an imaginary Egypt, such as the pyramid and the obelisk.

Some countries—especially England and America—where the image of the cemetery in nature was definitively established, ultimately rejected the model of the subterranean vault. Hence, the symbolism of the burial vault is by no means universal. In those places where it does exist it is impressive. We find it in Canova's tomb of the archduchess Maria Christina (d. 1805), in the Capuchin church in Vienna. Here death is a solemn descent under the ground. The door, a symbol borrowed from Roman funerary iconography, is open, not to heaven but to a world of darkness. The soul as portrait may continue to ascend to heaven in many other more traditional tombs; but the new creative imagination is drawn no longer upward but downward. The deceased descends. An angel who is no longer the cherub of baroque apotheoses but a naked ephebus, the symbol of youth and love, guards the entrance to the black door. But here, as in Gomberville, nothingness is associated with nature. The cold night of the burial vault is mitigated by the almost pastoral appearance of the procession that accompanies the dead woman, who is decked with flowers as in some distant memory of Dionysiac rites. The tomb may open onto nothingness; however, although the tomb is still inside a church, it is a nothingness located in nature. In front of the door of the vault the artist has depicted the countryside. The day would come when nature would no longer be imitated around the tomb, when the tomb itself would be transported into real nature.

The Neglect of the Cemeteries

Let us now turn to the relationship between what has been said here about the vanities and nothingness and a new phenomenon that appeared throughout the Western world in the second half of the eighteenth century. I am referring to the growing realization of the poor condition of the cemeteries and the threat they posed to public health. This phenomenon, which will be studied in Part 4 of this book, is introduced here only in passing, because it contributes to our understanding of people's attitudes toward vanity, nothingness, and nature.

The phenomenon has two broad aspects, which are not always related. One is the legal and sanitary aspect, the threat of epidemic. The other is the moral and religious aspect, the idea that it is shameful to bury human beings like animals.

It is in England in the second half of the seventeenth century that we find the first complete and reasoned denunciations of an intolerable state of affairs: "We saw several graves open and the bones thick on the top" (1685).[38] This was an altogether normal situation that had existed until then in all cemeteries without giving rise to complaints. What is new and significant is the connection made by the English and Protestant writers of the time between the state of neglect of the cemeteries and the lack of dignity of funeral services.

In *Cérémonies funèbres de toutes les nations* (Paris, 1679), a book translated into English in 1683 as *Rites of Funerals,* Pierre Muret is highly critical of the English manner of burying the dead. He recalls that at one time people honored the memory of the dead every year. Today the dead are not even mentioned; that would smack of popery. If one should happen upon a funeral procession, those who are escorting the body behave with such impropriety, joking and making idle chatter all along the way, that you would think they were going to the theater instead of to a funeral. In the old days the tombs were decorated with flowers, but nowadays that is unheard of. "There is nothing more distressing than a cemetery, and to see these tombs, one would think that they had served to bury the carcasses of a pig or an ass."[39] (In his *Colloquia* Erasmus remarks, "I saw the tomb of Saint Thomas [of Canterbury] covered with precious gems. I am sure that this great saint would have preferred to see his tomb decorated with leaves and flowers."[40] A fresco in Bologna shows the bodies of the martyrs crowned with flowers. These are rare indications of a custom that may have been introduced belatedly in imitation of antiquity.)

Contemporaries attributed the state of the cemeteries to the influence of the nonconformists and the ravages of the Puritan iconoclasts. As usual, they tended to explain in terms of a particular cause a general phenomenon that they did not perceive as a whole. But the reasons they advanced do not really concern us. What is remarkable is that they were the first to denounce the condition of the cemeteries as an intolerable situation that was offensive to the dignity of man.

In France the first observations also date from the early seventeenth century, but they are only concerned with public health, and bear witness to the ever-present fear of epidemics: "those dreadful calamities [infection and pestilence] that must be prevented and warded off with diligence and appropriate regulations, by having those bodies that are really dead [!] buried promptly in very deep graves, even when there are a great many, as occurs in war and other events giving rise to mass mortalities, or if there is reason to believe they died of leprosy or poisoning." This passage is from the *Grande et Nécessaire Police* of 1619.[41] We know that plagues were frequent and devastating at that time, especially in France.

It is toward the middle of the eighteenth century that complaints and investigations become numerous. Voices are raised against the impropriety of turning the churches into cemeteries, and badly maintained cemeteries at that. The dignity of the sanctuary is being violated, and people are starting to be concerned about it. However, it is the sanctuary, and not the dead, that excites their compassion and solicitude. The moral and social aspect is overlooked, either because Catholic ceremonies were more decent than nonconformist funerals or because the French were less concerned about that aspect of things, which would explain why it took them so long to adopt the outdoor cemetery.

In the American colonies, which are interesting sociological laboratories, the laxity of funeral services and the poor maintenance of cemeteries were denounced as going hand in hand. The situation aroused all the more indignation because the American rural cemetery was relatively new and free of that contamination which in Europe sprang from age-old use, because the cemetery was the preferred burial place of important persons, and finally because, especially in New England, it played a vital unifying role in the community. In response to these protests, laws were passed requiring that bodies be buried at a minimum depth and setting standards for the decency of funeral services, at the same time as sumptuary laws were being designed to curb the extravagance of funeral ceremonies. In New York at the end of the seventeenth century, measures were taken to compel the neighbors of the deceased to follow the funeral procession to make sure that the gravediggers did not dispose of the coffin along the way instead of taking it to the cemetery.

In England and France other, less scandalous phenomena were observed that show both the lack of respect for the dead and the resentment it aroused. For example, priests came under attack for using cemeteries as meadows where they had right of pasture. In 1758 in Montpalach, near Saint-Antonin, in the south of France, there was a case involving a priest who was charged with having, "with contempt for religion and for the respect due the remains of the faithful, . . . undertaken to construct a barn in the cemetery of said parish." Actually only one grave had been cited as evidence, that of the sister of a brewer who, according to the court clerk, had refused to go to the site and assess the situation "to avoid the possibility of aggravating his grief."[42] One notes in this late eighteenth-century anecdote a mixture of indifference and positivism on the part of the priest and sentimentality on the part of the townspeople.[43]

In England in 1550 a parson was prosecuted for penning his sheep in the church, or at least under the porch. In 1603, however, a vicar had no trouble building a barn in his cemetery, like the eighteenth-century French priest. In the eighteenth century, French bishops issued numerous prohibitions against letting animals graze in the cemeteries and instructions to keep them penned in. This was the time when private graves were often surrounded by little railings to protect them from the depredations of the animals.

In France the bishops were sometimes obeyed, and the cemetery was kept fenced in and forbidden to animals, as it was to be in the nineteenth century. But sometimes it remained what it had been since the Middle Ages, a thoroughfare for man and beast. In eighteenth-century England, however, right of pasture was granted to the parson, and the presence of the sheep no longer bothered people, not because they were indifferent but because it corresponded to a new pastoral image of romanticism.

Another interesting case is that of the French Protestants in the eighteenth century, after the revocation of the Edict of Nantes. Having lost the right the edict had given them to have cemeteries of their own, such as the one in Charenton, they had no other legal recourse—since they now had no legal existence—but to bury their dead in the public cemeteries, which were Catholic. We have seen that by the end of the sixteenth century they were demanding this as a right. Some of them must have submitted, but in the eighteenth century many others refused, choosing to renounce the public character of the grave, which had still been sought after at the time of Sponde.

In 1737 the abbot of Saint-Maximin, vicar general of Alais, wrote a thesis opposing "false converts," who went to church when they had no alternative, but did not bother to conceal their derision. "As soon as they think they can avoid paying the fines [penalties for absence from church services], they do not bother to come, and we do not see them again until there is a wedding in their family." They baptized their children so that they would have civil status, but "they have such an aversion to coming to church that many fathers refuse to accompany them." They might also have come back one last time to bury their dead, like Gabriel Le Bras's "seasonal" Catholics, but they rejected this privilege. "The sick man always dies full of confidence [without benefit of a priest] and is buried clandestinely [without funeral procession or ceremony], without his death being marked by any public monument, which does not prevent his property from being divided, his will from being drawn up, or his widow from remarrying."[44]

A last case, which is both utopian for the eighteenth century and anachronistic for the year 1806, is the will composed in all seriousness and with genuine conviction by the Divine Marquis. It reveals a complete merging of two attitudes hitherto close but distinct, the contempt for the body and the radical rejection of immortality. Sade asked that immediately after his death "an express message be sent to M. Le Normand, wood seller, . . . asking him to come himself, followed by a cart, to get my body and convey it under his escort in said cart to the woods of my estate, Malmaison, . . . near Epernon, where I want it to be laid without any ceremony in the first copse on the right when you enter the woods from the side of the old château by the wide path that divides it in two [the same precision that was once used to specify place of burial in a church]. The grave will be dug by the tenant farmer of Malmaison under the supervision of M. Le Normand, who will not leave my body until it has been laid in the grave. In this ceremony he may be accompanied, if he so desires, by those of my relatives or friends who, without any sort of display, may wish to give me this mark of their affection. Once the grave has been filled in, it will be planted with acorns so that in time to come the site being covered over and the copse being once again as thickly wooded as it was before, the traces of my grave will disappear from the surface of the earth, just as I am pleased to think that my memory will be erased from the minds of men, except, perhaps, for that handful of persons who were good enough to love me to the end and of whom I carry a very fond memory to my grave."[45]

A character in a novel from the same period (1804–1805) said on his deathbed: "Nothing will be left of me. I die utterly, as unknown as if I had never been born. Nothingness, receive your prey."[46]

This is the return to nature and to imperishable matter. Few, if any, chose to be buried as Sade requested. Some, no doubt, in the crowded towns of the late eighteenth century, were buried without ceremony against their wishes because of a general indifference, but these perfunctory services, held in overcrowded and badly maintained urban cemeteries, lacked the elegiac or savage poetry of the return to nature. The utopian will of the Marquis de Sade indicates a tendency of the age that was never carried to its logical conclusion, but that attracted even Christians and opened to some levels of society the vertigo of the abyss.

8

The Dead Body

In the two preceding chapters we have seen how death—that is, the moment of death—became diffused over the whole length of a life and diluted into a melancholy sense of the brevity of this same life. Death seems to have become more remote, to have lost the vigorous presence that it had among the literati of the late Middle Ages. We shall now see how in the seventeenth and eighteenth centuries, that is, during the same period, death will return in another form, that of the dead body, macabre eroticism, and natural violence.

We shall begin with two medical works that reveal the state of affairs at the end of the seventeenth century. We should note in passing that from now on, doctors will be the best spokesmen for popular beliefs, replacing clergymen, who had more or less monopolized this role in the Middle Ages and the Renaissance. They are not always real scientists, if that term has any meaning; they are credulous, because the boundaries of medicine and the science of life are unclear, and because the data are transmitted by means of oral accounts in which it is difficult to separate fact from fable. Consequently they are just as open as the churchmen were to the prevailing ideas of their times.

The first of these works is Paul Zacchia's *Totius Ecclesiatici protomedici generalis, quaestionum medicolegalium libri tres.* My source is a Lyonnais edition published in 1674. The book is a treatise on forensic medicine (*médecine légale,* a term already in use then). The genre was not new; it began in 1596 with the treatise of Fidelis. It actually goes back to the use of doctors as experts in certain judicial cases (supervision of torture, criminal cases, homocide investigations) in which it was necessary to examine the body. Doctors were also consulted in criminal and civil cases involving the mechanisms of reproduction: birth and miscarriage, cases of sterility and impotence, conditions of fertility, investigations of paternity or consanguinity (which led to the study of resemblances), and the determination of sex. They were asked to distinguish between natural occurrences and miracles, and they made examinations in cases of inquisitorial torture, to determine whether illness was being simulated in order to avoid such torture, and how long it could be used in specific cases. They were consulted on matters of public health, such as diagnosing epidemics and prescribing hygienic measures involving water, air, sanitary conditions, and so forth.

This treatise reserves a special place for the cadaver. This is not only to aid in the preliminary investigation by the courts of cases of violent death, but also because the cadaver contains the secrets of life and health.

The second medical treatise I have consulted is devoted to the cadaver and to death. It is the work of Christian Friedrich Garmann, a German Lutheran doctor from Dresden who lived from 1640 to 1708. It was published posthumously by his son, also a doctor, under the curious title *De miraculis mortuorum* (Concerning the miracles of the dead). Did cadavers perform miracles? In any case they performed prodigies that could be neither understood nor explained, and it was the responsibility of doctors to distinguish the natural phenomena from the rest.[1]

Death and the dead body themselves constitute objects of scientific investigation, quite apart from the causes of death; men studied death before they knew its causes; their motive was not solely to discover these. They looked at the dead body just as later they looked at the live body of the sick man in his bed. It is an attitude alien to modern medicine, in which death is inseparable from the disease of which it is one of two possible outcomes, the other being recovery. We now study the disease and no longer the death, except in very special and now rather marginal cases of forensic medicine.[2]

So these two books will tell us about death as it was seen by the doctors of the seventeenth century. Garmann is immediately impressed by the resemblance between death and sleep, an idea that was a commonplace of pious literature. Sleep gives man a knowledge of and communication with God that is not available to him in the waking state. In both sleep and death there is a concentration of the soul outside the body, whereas ordinarily the soul is diffused throughout the body. The resemblance between sleep and death leads one to wonder about the powers of death and the degree of separation between soul and body. This question, which is at the heart of the medical interest in death, is also one of the central preoccupations of the age.

Death is regarded as a complex phenomenon that is not very well understood. Garmann compares two theses concerning the nature of life. There is still some life in the *Mummia,* from which the embalming preparations have removed the elements of corruption. Life ends when the virtue of the balms disappears, when corrupting nature recovers her dominion. *Life is therefore an exception to nature:* a very important idea that was to secretly determine a new attitude toward death.

The second thesis, which is consistent with scholastic philosophy, is that life is neither matter nor substance, but form: *ipsissima rei forma.* Life is light and beginning *(initium formale),* a beginning that is always given anew by the Creator, as fire is given by the flint.

These two theses are compared in the study of the cadaver. The first thesis, which is close to that of Paracelsus, is attributed to Jewish medicine and the rabbis. The cadaver is still the body and already the corpse; death has not robbed it of a certain sensibility. It retains a *vis vegetans,* a *vestigium vitae,* a remnant of life. This opinion is based on numerous observations reported from Pliny to the present, and on the testimony of funerary epigraphy: Some Latin epitaphs ask that the earth rest lightly on the dead. Another authority is invoked to support the same thesis. In a curious example of bad faith, Tertullian's arguments in favor of the immortality of the soul and life after death are interpreted as if they concerned the body instead, and are used to prove the existence of sensibility in the cadaver.

Among the observations reported are the *cruentatio* of the cadaver, that is, the prodigious bleeding of the corpse of a murder victim when placed in the presence of the murderer, and other phenomena of sympathy and antipathy. Garmann also reports the contemporary case of a widowed nobleman who told the gravediggers to carry his wife gently for fear of hurting her. Popular superstition is convinced that the body still hears and remembers after death. This is why it is considered unwise to speak in its presence any more than is necessary to honor the dead man and to certify the fact of his death. To this latter end, survivors called to him several times by name.

The second thesis, which denies the survival of the cadaver, cites the authority of Seneca and others. "The soul of man can do nothing outside the body." The body without the soul is nothing.

Here, then, are two opposite opinions. On the one hand there are those who believe in the continuation of a certain kind of life and sensibility in the cadaver, at least as long as the flesh is preserved and the body not reduced to the state of the dried-out skeleton. These people implicitly recognize that human beings cannot be reduced to the union of body and soul. Indeed, for a long time ordinary people were reluctant to believe that the loss of the soul deprived the body of all life.

On the other hand there are both the orthodox Christian elite—the heirs of medieval science and scholasticism, for whom the union and separation of soul and body account for Creation and death, respectively

—and certain minds that seem to us today more rational, because their critical sense has triumphed in modern science.

This opposition not only divides two communities of scholars, it also represents two conceptions of life that are themselves related to two existential attitudes. It is unclear whether our doctors have made a choice, and if so, which of the two theses they accept. This ambiguity explains why Garmann was dismissed by the authors of medical biographies of the late eighteenth century—men almost modern in their thinking—as a credulous writer who believed the most absurd stories. It is true that he hesitates, not daring to make up his mind. Belief in the sensibility of the cadaver has the support of the people, and what we would call folklore, but scientists distrust the popular penchant for superstition. Garmann notes that there are a great many reliable observations in favor of this opinion, but he is cautious. When he tells an extraordinary story, he immediately adds a skeptical and rational commentary, but his reservations do not prevent him from giving all the details. This kind of prudence was a standard device for advancing controversial ideas while taking a minimum of risks.

In fact, Garmann accepts the thesis of the sensibility of the cadaver, for it enables him to explain certain closely observed phenomena. Besides the bleeding of the cadaver in the presence of the murderer, which is questionable, there were definite, well-documented cases of movement in the dead body. Indeed, it is this movement that makes it so difficult to determine death, for although a dead body moves differently from a living body, it does move. Hair, nails, and teeth continue to grow after death (a belief that is still widespread today), perspiration continues to flow. Death does not prevent the erection of the penis, commonly observed in hanged men, whence the belief in the sexual excitement produced by hanging. In the eighteenth century, stories were told about certain aesthetes who pursued the pleasures of the initial phase of hanging, on the assumption that they could recover their balance *in extremis,* which was sometimes too late. When survivors undressed soldiers who had died on the battlefield, they found them, according to Garmann, in the state they would have been in if the engagement had taken place in the bedroom. Furthermore, erection may be produced in dead men artificially, simply by injecting a certain solution into the arteries.

Speculations about the cadaver are related to the question of the indivisibility of the body. Does life belong to the whole body or to its elements, which are capable of separation? It is obvious that the doctrine of the sensibility of the cadaver implies that of the indivisibility of the body. Garmann reports cases of grafting that were well known in his day, with full particulars and dates. For example, a gentleman had lost his nose in the war and had had another nose grafted onto his face. The operation had been successful, and the nose had remained in place up to a point, when it had started to rot. It was later discovered that the rotting started at the time of the death of the donor, who had somehow carried his absent and distant nose to his own death.

These are natural phenomena; but there are others that are certainly miraculous, like those dead who walk or whose bodies are fragrant, sure indications of saintliness. Other phenomena are ambiguous, and it is uncertain whether they should be ascribed to nature, popular credulity, misinterpretation, or an actual miracle or diabolical prodigy: for example, some of the movements of parts of the body after death. When a nun presses the hand of another now dead, the hand of the dead nun responds and squeezes the hand of the living nun three times.

Also doubtful, but serious and worthy of thorough study, are the cases of cadavers that emit sounds like the squealing of pigs from the depths of their graves. When one opens the graves, one finds that the dead have devoured their shrouds or their clothing. This is a terrible omen of plague. Garmann devotes a long chapter of his book to these noisy and hungry corpses. These phenomena were regarded as half natural, half diabolical. The matter is open to debate.[3] What we should keep in mind here is not only the lack of a clear-cut boundary between the natural and the supernatural—the difficulty in distinguishing the natural, the often diabolical preternatural, and the authentic miraculous or supernatural—but above all, the verisimilitude of the phenomena, however extraordinary, that prove the existence of some sort of sensibility in the cadaver. The phenomena are discussed, not without reservations or regrets, but in the end they are accepted.

The sensibility of the cadaver has practical consequences for daily life that cannot be overlooked. In the first place, it is the basis of a whole pharmacopoeia. Cadavers provide raw materials for some very effective remedies of a nonmagical character. For example, the perspiration of corpses is good for hemorrhoids and tumors, and the hand of a cadaver applied to a diseased area can heal, as in the case of a woman suffering from dropsy who rubbed her abdomen with the still-warm hand of a corpse. Indeed, this explains why anatomists always have healthy hands. There was a whole series of remedies designed to heal the living member by the same part of a dead body: the arm by the arm, the leg by the leg, and so on. The desiccated skull relieves the epileptic; the bones are ingested in the form of decoctions made from their powder. The priapus of the stag is useful in treating hysterics and is also effective in cases of impotence, an indication of a relationship between hysteria and love.

These remedies are determined by applying to the cadaver a general principle of sympathy and antipathy that implies a remnant of life in dead bodies. According to this principle, if one is so unfortunate as to make a drum out of the skin of a wolf and the skin of a lamb, the skin of the lamb will break the first time the drum is played for fear of the wolf.

Pliny reported that a wounded man could be cured if he ate the flesh of an animal killed with the weapon that had injured him. Similarly, a wound made by an arrow should be treated by a dressing made from the ashes of arrows. The sword that had killed a man possessed therapeutic qualities.

Bones also have the power to prevent disease. It is recommended that they be worn around the neck or sewn into one's clothing, not as a *memento mori*, but for their intrinsic virtues. The *memento mori*, the rosary made of vertebrae, has become the prophylactic amulet. Soldiers who carry with them the finger of a dead comrade are protected from harm.

The soil of graves, especially the graves of hanged men (still the same obsession!), is also rich in therapeutic properties beneficial to human beings as well as animals. The proximity of a dead body accelerates the growth of a plant, land full of bones being the most fertile. The use of cadavers as fertilizer, which has been justified by modern science, is not separated from other medical uses. Corruption is fertile; the soil of the dead, like death itself, is a source of life. It is an idea that will become common in the eighteenth and early nineteenth centuries, until the Pasteurian revolution.

The list of the beneficial properties of the cadaver includes an aphrodisiac potion made from the ashes of the bones of happily married couples and lovers. Even a fragment of the clothing of the dead cures headache and hemorrhoids, at least so the Belgians believed.

Garmann even gives a recipe for "divine water," so called because of its miraculous powers, according to Thomas Bartholin and Jerome Hirnhaim. You take the whole body of a man who had been in good health but had died a violent death, cut it into very small pieces—flesh, bones, and viscera—mix everything thoroughly, and reduce it to liquid in an alembic. The resulting liquid, among many other medical uses, enables one to determine accurately the chances for recovery of someone who is seriously ill. To a certain quantity of this liquid you add three to nine drops of the blood of the sick man and agitate gently over a flame. If the water and the blood mix well, it is a sign of life; if they remain separate, it is a sign of death. (In place of blood, one may use urine, perspiration, or other secretions.)

These remedies made from cadavers were sought and used primarily by illustrious patients, for they must have been expensive and difficult to prepare. During his last illness, Charles II of England drank a potion containing forty-two drops of extract of human skull.

There are cases, however, when contact with the dead body is harmful.

A mixture of bones in beer makes those who drink it cruel. The touch of a cadaver may stop a woman's menstrual periods. A nail from a coffin laid against a plant will make it incapable of bearing fruit. Indeed, plants have been destroyed by the vapors from cemeteries—an observation that will later serve as an argument in the campaign to relocate the cemeteries. Here, however, the dangers are treated as a particular case of a much more general phenomenon: the effects of the cadaver on man and other living things.

The useful effects of cadavers undoubtedly outweigh the harmful ones. Both are regarded as natural; cases of magical use are rare. However, people did make use of the right hand of a premature, aborted, or unbaptized child, or a parchment made from its skin, and remember the role played by children in Goya's scenes of sorcery. It was also said that by the light of a candle made of the fat of human bodies one could rediscover hidden treasure.

Zacchia devotes a long chapter to miracles, that is, supernatural phenomena that the doctor is asked to authenticate: miraculous cures, plagues, epidemics sent by God. Among the events considered miraculous are bodies that fail to decompose. But in keeping with the customary ambiguity of this school of medicine, there are cases of incorruptibility that are natural and others that are miraculous. There is a whole treatise on the decomposition of bodies in which we see what enormous importance the subject has for the author. It has a practical importance in criminal trials and public health; a scientific importance, for the body's resistance to decay implies a remnant of life and sensibility; and finally, a sentimental and almost sensual importance, for the cadaver has an interest and fascination of its own that almost amounts to an obsession.

Among the cases of normal incorruptibility are those involving art: evisceration with or without embalming, that is, the introduction of aromatics, is very effective. There are also amazing cases that support the thesis of the "sensibility" of the cadaver, of the body of a hanged man that remained where it was for two years without rotting. There is also a series of cases in which the preservation of the body occurred naturally, without intervention of artifice, and was explained by various factors such as the type of disease, the season, or the age of the deceased. Incorruptibility may be accompanied by phenomena such as bleeding or perspiring, which were mentioned above in connection with the movement of the cadaver.

The factor that receives the most attention is place of burial. There are types of soil that consume, and others that preserve, the body. The same is true of minerals. Lead coffins preserve, which is why the great men of the world preferred them to other materials.

Depth of burial also plays a role. Bodies that are buried very deeply become shriveled and dried out and are preserved like "smoked meat." It is also said that bodies exposed to the rays of the moon rot quickly, at least that is what Galen says, and Zacchia reports it, without believing it for a moment.

Certain cemeteries were well known for the rapidity with which they consumed bodies. At les Innocents, nicknamed the "flesh eater," it was said that a body was reduced to its bones after twenty-four hours. Other cemeteries preserved the bodies and transformed them into mummies. Zacchia mentions les Cordeliers, the Franciscan church in Toulouse, and a campo santo in Rome, the Capuchin church of the Immaculate Conception near the Piazza Barberini. In the early nineteenth century, Emily Brontë writes that in the little cemetery in *Wuthering Heights,* "the dampness of the peat was said to have the same effects as embalming on the few bodies buried there." It was a soil of this kind that explained the preservation of a *Mummia Danica* observed by Thomas Bartholin in the seventeenth century. After fifty years the flesh was still firm, the skin dry, the red and sparse hair still intact. The people, who were fascinated by these cases of preservation, believed the mummy to be accursed, either because during her lifetime she had been executed by royal command or because she had lived on bad terms with her husband. In this case preservation of the body was seen as a punishment. In general, consumption of the body was sought after as an advantage. Authors of fifteenth-century wills who could not be buried in les Innocents asked that a little of the soil of this cemetery be placed in their graves. The popularity of les Innocents is an indication of the success of the ideas of nothingness and contempt for the body analyzed in the two previous chapters in connection with the vanities.

Zacchia cites the case of a hand that was found intact in a tomb from which the rest of the body had disappeared. Rumor had it that this hand had been raised against a father or mother. For this reason it remained as a sign of infamy. But Zacchia decides that "these reasons are supernatural," like Bede's story that children born on certain days at the end of January escaped corruption.

This has been a very brief summary, for the literature is abundant and garrulous. Such works attributed to the dead body a kind of personality; they implied that it retained a remnant of life that on occasion was manifested.

Nineteenth-century medicine was to abandon this belief and adopt the thesis that death does not exist in itself but is merely the separation of the soul and the body, the distortion or absence of life. Death became pure negativity. It would no longer have any meaning beyond the disease —identified, named, and classified—of which it was the final stage. However, there is still something of the old school of medicine in an article that appeared in the *Revue française de médecine militaire* in 1860. The article was devoted to the expressions on the faces of soldiers killed on the field of battle, and it was a very serious physiognomic study of cadavers.

Dissection and Embalming

Thus, doctors replaced or rivaled clergymen in translating the unexpressed, in revealing the inner workings of human perception. Their ideas circulated well beyond scientific circles and were discussed everywhere. Knowledge of the body extended to a vast audience of literati.

In order to arrive at this knowledge, some people resorted to dissection, a procedure already traditional in the faculties of medicine. They did so not only in the interests of scientific observation but also for practical reasons, such as the preservation of bodies by skilled nonmedical practitioners.

As early as the fourteenth century, the bodies of important personages had been treated so that they could be transported to a distant place of burial or else divided and disseminated among several tombs. One began by dismembering the body like a large game animal. Then the result was parboiled in order to remove the flesh and extract the noble portion, the dried-out bones.

These techniques did not correspond to a desire for total preservation, but rather for reduction of the body. They betrayed a curious mixture of respect toward this concentrated version of the body and indifference to the body as a whole.

In the fifteenth century, these methods were replaced by embalming for the purpose of preservation. Embalming became widespread during the period when royal funerals were great ceremonies exalting monarchical feelings and dynastic fidelity. The king did not die. As soon as he had breathed his last, he was exhibited as if he were still alive in a room where a banquet was prepared, with all the attributes of the power he had wielded during his lifetime. The preservation of the appearance of life was necessary to the verisimilitude of this fiction, just as the arresting of decomposition was physically required by the length of the ceremonies. The body thus preserved played the role that was later assumed by the wax or wooden representation.[4]

The embalming of kings was imitated by princes of the royal blood and by the great nobility. Lawrence Stone has observed that it was very common among the English aristocracy of the late sixteenth and early seventeenth centuries. He attributes this to the solemnity and complexity of funerals, the numerous steps required for their preparation, and the long interval that separated the moment of death from the moment of burial.

In the second half of the seventeenth century Stone observes a decline in embalming that coincided with quicker and simpler funeral services. This observation should not surprise us; it corresponds to the general trend toward simplicity, if not poverty, which we analyzed in the preceding chapter. An example given by Stone brings out the importance of the time factor in the refusal to be embalmed. A woman asked in her will that her body not be opened, and that after her death she be placed "in brann" and in the coffin *before her body was cold.*[5]

Among the French nobility of the seventeenth century embalming was also practiced as an established tradition. If there are few allusions to embalming in Parisian wills, this is because the authors regarded it as a routine procedure that went without saying. It was taken for granted in every case where there was a separate tomb for the heart, and consequently evisceration. It was sometimes explicitly mentioned in cases where the testator asked that the body be taken to another location, necessitating a prolonged interval before burial. Take, for example, this holograph will of 1652: "I wish and ordain that twenty-four hours after my decease my body be opened, embalmed, placed in a lead coffin, and carried, in the event that I die in this town, to the Dominican monastery . . . and there placed for safekeeping near the tomb containing the heart of my dearly beloved former wife [who had been embalmed], both to be kept there for two or three weeks or less if possible, and from there taken together to my church in Courson, where they shall be placed in the vault of my chapel."[6]

Unlike the Englishwoman quoted by Stone, the French testator does not ask to be placed in the lead coffin before he is cold but, on the contrary, after twenty-four hours. The difference is significant, and is one of the earliest indications of the fear of being buried alive, a fear that was to become obsessive and that would henceforth always be a factor in decisions regarding the opening of the body. In the eighteenth century, when a testator specifies that the body is to be opened, unless he offers some other reason, we may assume that the decision is inspired by the fear of being buried alive. The opening of the body was as good a method as any of verifying death; for did not Abbé Prévost, who was left for dead, come back to life under the anatomist's scalpel?

In her will dated 1771, the comtesse de Sauvigny wrote, "I wish my body to be opened [first precaution] 48 hours after my death [second precaution], and during the interval I wish to be left in my bed [third precaution]."[7]

Jean-Antoine Chaptal tells how he became disgusted with medicine. "One day Fressine came and told me that he had just had a cadaver brought to his private amphitheater. We went there at once. I found the cadaver of a man who had been dead . . . for 4 or 5 hours. I prepared to dissect the body, but at the first thrust of the scalpel into the cartilage that connects the ribs to the sternum, the cadaver lifted his right hand to his heart and feebly moved his head. The scalpel dropped from my hands, and I fled in terror."[8]

Most of the allusions to dissection are negative. It was not pleasant to wake up under the anatomist's knife, and there were other ways of verifying death. People often mention dissection in order to forbid it. In 1669 a testator specified, "I desire that my body be guarded as long as possible before burial, but without any opening being made to embalm it." And Elisabeth d' Orléans, daughter of Gaston and a princess of the royal blood, certainly destined by her rank to be embalmed, demands that her burial be very simple: "I do not wish my body to be opened, and I wish to be buried after 24 hours." The refusal to be opened was combined with an interval of time for the sake of security and with various tests to verify death. Françoise Amat, marquise de Solliers, wrote in 1690, "I wish that my body not be opened, and that I be left twice twenty-four hours in the same bed."[9]

In addition to these reasons there appears a concern, which I believe to be new, that the body be left intact. In the will that he composed in 1597, two years before his death in Madrid, the duke of Terranova chose to be buried in Sicily, although he had left there two years before, "in the church of San Domenico de Castelaetrana [a monastery founded by his ancestors in 1440, with a family chapel], in the tomb in front of the altar in which the duchess, my beloved wife, is buried."[10] In spite of the long journey required, he explicitly instructs that his body "not be opened in order to insert aromatics or anything else, but be left as is and buried that way." A century or two earlier, what manipulations and preparations the noble body would have had to undergo before its bones arrived at the Sicilian sanctuary! Here we get a sense of the idea, already encountered in the doctors, of the total cadaver, possessor of a unity and existence of its own.

By the end of the seventeenth century a third reason is invoked to justify opening or the refusal to be opened. The purpose of dissection is now less preservation than scientific knowledge, as well as a certain existential anxiety and curiosity.

In his will dated 1754, the duc de Saint-Simon is quite explicit. After taking the customary precautions to avoid a false death, "I wish that my body . . . after this period of time [thirty hours without being touched] be opened in two places [partial dissection], namely, at the top of the nose and at the throat, to reveal for the general benefit the causes of this congestion, which amounted to a disease, and these strange fits of breathlessness from which I have always suffered." His body was then to be transported to his country church. There is considerable likelihood that it was eviscerated and embalmed, but this is not mentioned.[11]

It may well be that dissection for pseudoscientific reasons prevailed at the beginning of the eighteenth century. In Thomas Green's *The Art of Embalming,* which appeared in 1705, the author deplores the fact that "today dissection is the principal occupation of the anatomist. And yet I shall describe another practice which is older and more widespread, which is the preservation of the human body as a whole . . . , a practice which has [wrongly] fallen into disuse and which would nowadays be regarded as the cause of useless expense and inconvenience."[12] The publication of this book would tend to indicate a renewed interest in the preservation of the dead body, although there were other ways of obtaining this besides embalming, such as choice of burial where the soil had the property of mummifying the body. We shall return to this point presently. For the moment, let us remain in the realm of "anatomical preparations" and scientific curiosity.

Some testators refused to be opened in spite of the scientific arguments that were invoked all around them. Here is a will dated 1712: "In the first place [immediately after the profession of faith and the commendation of the soul, among the most important wishes], I forbid that my body be opened for any reason whatsoever, persuaded as I am that this would not provide any information for the use and benefit of my dear children, whom I love enough to overcome my reluctance if I thought that it would do them the slightest good."[13]

We find the same arguments in the will of Jean Molé, councillor at the Parliament of Paris, in 1723: "I desire and wish that my body not be opened for any reason whatsoever, even with a view to preventing certain temporal accidents in others."[14]

Anatomy for Everyone

In the absence of instructions to the contrary, the family surgeon often performed a discreet dissection in a private anatomy room. Indeed, the value of anatomy was not restricted to doctors and surgeons. Anatomy was also important to the philosopher, according to the author of the article on the subject in the great eighteenth-century *Encyclopédie:* "Knowledge of the self presupposes knowledge of the body, and knowledge of the body presupposes knowledge of a network of causes and effects so prodigious that there is not one that does not lead directly to the notion of an all-knowing and all-powerful intelligence. Anatomy is, so to speak, the foundation of natural theology." It was also important to magistrates, who were otherwise "obliged to adhere blindly to the reports of doctors and surgeons," that is, experts. It was also necessary to painters and sculptors, of course, but in fact, it was useful to everyone: Anatomy was part of the indispensable equipment of every well-educated man. "It is in everyone's interest to know his own body." Anatomy is a path toward the knowledge of God, at any rate the God of the eighteenth century: "There is no one whose belief in an all-powerful Being cannot be confirmed by the structure and appearance [of the parts of the body]. In addition to this all-important motive, there is an interest that cannot be overlooked in being informed on the means of keeping fit, prolonging one's life, explaining more clearly the locations and symptoms of one's malady when one is unwell, recognizing charlatans, and judging, at least in a general way, the remedies prescribed. . . . *The knowledge of anatomy is important to every man* [italics added]."[15]

In the journal of a *Bourgeois de Paris sous la Révolution*, Célestin Guittard de Floriban observes the functioning of his body every day and takes careful notes on his findings.[16]

So it was important to be well versed in anatomy. It was necessary, therefore, that the subject be taught in a way that was perfectly accessible, and "that there be in the different hospitals anatomists sufficiently experienced to be able to prepare all the parts together and separately on different cadavers, and that all those who are obliged by profession or whom curiosity might move to educate themselves be permitted to go to these places. . . . This would suffice for those not interested in making a thorough study, and I believe that they could dispense with taking part in these dissections themselves."[17]

The popularity of the subject rapidly caused the word to enter the vernacular. According to Furetière's dictionary, "It is said proverbially that someone is 'a real anatomy' when he has become so wasted as the result of a long illness that he could be mistaken for a skeleton."[18]

The word was used in baroque poetry.[19] Agrippa d'Aubigné writes:

> *In an anatomy my adoring eye perceives*
> *Diana's portrait in between the bones.*

And Chassignet:

> *Like an anatomy, in me now you see*
> *A heart without a beat, a mouth without a smile,*
> *A head without hair, bones that lifeless be.*

Thomas Diafoirus, a rather stupid suitor who was only conforming to certain customs of his day that Molière and a few others were beginning to find ridiculous, presented his fiancée with an anatomical drawing and invited her to a dissection. The anatomy lesson that was so often depicted in the engravings and paintings of the seventeenth century was, like the defense of a thesis or a college play, a great social event that the whole town attended, with masks, refreshments, and diversions.

Moreover, collections of anatomical plates, far from being technical works of interest only to specialists, were among the fine books sought after by bibliophiles. As André Chastel has pointed out, "these plates were often inspired in their composition by famous paintings or sculptures. The skeletons and the flayed bodies adopted the attitudes of figures in works by Raphael, Michelangelo, or the artists of antiquity." They were also vanities of the same type that we analyzed in the previous chapter: sermons on death, meditations on nothingness or the flight of time. "They appear in a moralistic context, with explicit inscriptions, . . . for example . . . the skeleton meditating upon the skull of his fellow, . . . or the skeleton as a gravedigger leaning on his spade." Finally, the anatomy lesson provided a pretext for a group portrait in place of the religious scene with donors, a further indication of the substitution of the things of the body for those of the soul. Chastel writes, "The group portrait is perfectly unified by its setting and, one might add, by the force of the feeling that seems to cast everyone present into a meditation on the strangeness of the organism and the mystery of life."[20]

In the eighteenth century some people complained that young surgeons could not find enough bodies because of the competition of private dissections, dissections performed outside medical classes, whether these were given in the public amphitheaters of universities or in the private lecture rooms that proliferated at the time.

Private Dissections and the Stealing of Cadavers

Dissection had become a fashionable art. A rich man who was interested in nature might have his own private dissecting room, just as he might have his own chemical laboratory. But this room had to be supplied with bodies. This explains a remark in the article on the cadaver in the *Encyclopédie:* "Each family wants their deceased member to enjoy his burial service, as it were, and rarely, if ever, allows him to be sacrificed to the cause of public education. At most, they may allow a body to be used for their own instruction or to satisfy their own curiosity." This is the meaning of certain clauses in wills.

We have some idea of these private dissections thanks to a very chaste novel by the marquis de Sade, *La Marquise de Gange* (1813). Sade borrowed the theme from a famous incident. The marquise de Gange was abducted by friends of her husband and held prisoner in one room of an old castle. This is the Gothic novel complete with keep, secret dungeons, burial vaults, and tombs. "In a cruel state of apprehension, she was running up and down this large room . . . when she thought she saw a little door standing ajar. It was still night [there were only "a few feeble rays cast by a pale moon"]. She flew to this door. . . . By the light of a lamp that was about to go out she made out a room and walked inside. . . . But what a hideous object offered itself to her sight! On a table lay a gaping cadaver, horribly mutilated, on which the surgeon of the castle, whose laboratory this was," had just been working, and which he had left in order to go to bed, postponing the rest of the dissection until the morrow.[21]

It was an anatomy room such as might be found in the home of a rich and well-educated amateur anatomist. The practice dates from the sixteenth century, in Italy at least, as we can see from this passage from 1550 that is placed in the mouth of Death: "More than once I have been tempted . . . to walk into the rooms of these people who cut up cadavers and fasten the bones together to decorate their homes. I would put on those bones, wake them up in the middle of the night, and so terrify them that they would lose forever the habit of taking home the spoils of the cemeteries, these trophies of my victories."[22]

We can imagine what one of these places was like from what is left of eighteenth-century Naples—for example, the one in the palace of Prince Raimondo di Sangro (1710–71). According to his epitaph, the prince had distinguished himself in all his enterprises, especially military science, the training of infantry, mathematics, medicine, and something we might call biology, but a biology of a mysterious and exciting kind: *in perscrutandis reconditis naturae arcanis*. Once again, we meet this notion of secrets that must be unlocked, as if Nature could and did defend herself against invasions of her privacy. The anatomy room communicated with the chapel, and it is in the sacristy of the chapel containing the family tombs and a few works of art of a strange and "morbid" character that the vestiges of the famous room, some men flayed to reveal the veins or muscles, are still preserved today. There is no doubt that dissections were performed there, and that mutilated cadavers lay about, as in the castle where Mme. de Gange was held prisoner.

These laboratories of death had a profound impact on the imagination of the time. If they seemed mysterious and disquieting, it was not because of the rarity of the experiments that took place in them, for dissection was widely practiced—a doctor of Aix who later became physician to Louis XVI boasted that he had dissected twelve hundred cadavers—but rather because of the vertigo that people experienced in the presence of the sources of life.

The marquis de Sade invented the decor of an anatomy room for the fantastic gallery of the grand duke of Tuscany: "A bizarre idea had been executed in this room: a sepulcher filled with cadavers in which one could observe all the different stages of decomposition from the moment of death until the total destruction of individuality. This grim work of art was made of wax that was colored so naturally that Nature herself could not have been more expressive or more real."[23] There exist wax figures of this kind representing victims of the plague. In the eighteenth century the anatomical model or flayed body replaced the *transi* of the fifteenth and sixteenth centuries, which had disappeared in the intervening hundred years. However, the anatomical model acquired another meaning. It was less and less a *memento mori*, and more and more a confused and uneasy interrogation about the nature of life (as, for example, the flayed body that rises on the facade of the Duomo, in Milan).

It took a great many cadavers to meet the demand created by such a "passion for anatomy," to borrow Sébastien Mercier's phrase. Cadavers were fought over, and the literature is full of stories about cadavers being stolen from cemeteries. These stories were told and retold for reasons that went beyond the pressures of supply and demand.

But these tales were not pure imagination. In the late eighteenth century the reports of Joly de Fleury's investigations speak very seriously about actual cases of the theft of cadavers. Cemeteries had to be guarded "to prevent the abuse of the sale of cadavers." All that is holy "cries out for the protection of the authority of your office to stop a theft that is as scandalous as it is distressing to men of feeling. In the course of this winter [1785–86] there took place in this cemetery [Saint-Jean], whose closing the petitioners urgently demand, various abductions involving several bodies at a time; these were turned over to students of surgery in this capital for dissection. The whole neighborhood has protested against this crime, which offends humanity and violates religion. The people have lodged a complaint with the church council of Saint-Eustache, who replied that the responsibility lay not with them but with the civil authorities. The gardeners who work on the property adjacent to the cemetery [which was accessible because the walls had partly collapsed] went to the chief of police to inform him of these thefts and of the damage done to their plants, but the thefts did not stop. On the contrary, on the night of Thursday 12th to Friday 13th, January 1786, 7 bodies of adults and 3 of children were removed from the grave now open, which bodies were carried by 6 men in two places through these same gardens."[24]

Sébastien Mercier describes these thefts. "They [the young surgeons] set out in groups of four, take a carriage, and scale the walls of a cemetery. One deals with the dog who guards the dead, the next goes down into the grave with a ladder, the third straddles the wall and throws over the cadaver, and the fourth picks it up and puts it in the carriage." The cadaver is taken to a garret. "There it is dissected by the hands of apprentices. And to conceal the remains from the eyes of their neighbors, the young anatomists burn the bones. They heat their garrets with the fat of the dead."[25]

The same thing happened in London. In 1793 a young French emigré named René de Chateaubriand lived in a garret whose dormer window looked onto a cemetery. "Every night the watchman's rattle announced that more cadavers had just been stolen."[26]

Sometimes public opinion was aroused by discoveries that were regarded as sinister. In 1734, Barbier reports, "The other day 15 or 16 bodies of small children were taken to the morgue in Châtelet. . . . This spectacle attracted a large crowd and frightened the people. . . . How could all these children have been found together, and at the same time? . . . They say that it was the doctor who is in charge of the Jardin Royal who had picked up all these dead children at the surgeon's [a doctor did not perform dissections himself] to make skeletons. When the neighbors heard about this, they lodged a complaint. The authorities took the children away, and the situation was explained by the doctor."[27]

Eros and Thanatos in the Baroque Age

The almost fashionable success of anatomy cannot be attributed solely to scientific curiosity. It is not hard to understand; it corresponds to an attraction to certain ill-defined things at the outer limits of life and death, sexuality and pain. These things have always been suspect to the clear-cut moralities of the nineteenth and twentieth centuries, which placed them in a new category of disturbing and morbid phenomena. This category, which was born in the nineteenth century of the union of Eros and Thanatos, was conceived in the late fifteenth and early sixteenth centuries and developed during the first half of the seventeenth. At that point we leave the world of real facts exemplified by the dissections in the anatomist's laboratory and enter the mysterious and convoluted world of the imagination.

If the danses macabres of the fourteenth and fifteenth centuries were chaste, those that were created in the sixteenth century are both violent and erotic. Dürer's Fourth Horseman of the Apocalypse is mounted on an emaciated animal who is all skin and bones, but his leanness emphasizes the size of the genital organs in a contrast that is certainly deliberate. In Nicolas Manuel, Death no longer merely points out a woman, his victim, by approaching her and drawing her away by an act of the will; he violates her, he plunges his hand into her vagina. Death is no longer the instrument of necessity but is driven by a desire for pleasure; death has become sensuality.

Another series of images is the Garden of Torments. Here the eroticism is less flagrant. The inspiration is innocent and spiritual, but the manner of execution, the style, and the gestures betray the unconscious emotions provoked by that blend of love and death, pleasure and pain that will later be called sadism. From the sixteenth to the nineteenth century one observes a rise in sadism: unconscious in the sixteenth and seventeenth centuries, admitted and deliberate in the eighteenth and nineteenth.

It is interesting to see how the images change in the sixteenth century and become charged with a sensuality previously unknown. Let us compare two versions of the same subject, the martyrdom of Saint Erasmus, from the fifteenth and the seventeenth centuries.

In the Flemish painting by Dierik Bouts, which has the serenity of the miniature, a conscientious torturer is winding the saint's intestines around a winch before the emperor and his court. The atmosphere is peaceful. Everyone is doing his job without haste, violence, or passion, with a kind of indifference. Even the saint observes his martyrdom like a stranger, as the dying man in an early *ars moriendi* observed his own death. There is nothing to disturb the tranquillity of the scene.[28]

In a painting by Oragio Fidani in the Pitti Palace in Florence, which treats the same subject in the seventeenth century, the saint is lying perpendicular to the picture plane. He is therefore seen in perspective, as is often true of the cadaver in an anatomy lesson or the body of Christ in a Descent from the Cross. There is a connection between the depth of the perspective and the violence of the scene. A torturer is opening the lower abdomen of the martyr and removing the viscera. This is not the placid winding of a Dierik Bouts; it is the first step in a dissection performed on a living body. The torturers are great naked giants with powerful muscles; their backs are arched with the effort of their task. It is the same characters and the same scene, but a different sensibility, one in which the excitement represented and aroused is not always of a religious nature and inspires other feelings besides devotion.

Another comparison, this time a literary one, was suggested by Jean Rousset. He contrasts two descriptions of the same scene, the execution of the Maccabees, one prebaroque, the other baroque.[29] The first is from Robert Garnier's tragedy *Les Juives*. Rousset comments, "In Garnier, the murder is related in a few restrained and polished verses":

> *No sooner had these words been said*
> *Than from his neck they did remove his head.*
> *The warm blood gushed, staining the place around*
> *And the trunk fell motionless upon the ground.*

"The whole scene is as calm and linear as a martyrdom by Fra Angelico." Whereas Virey de Gravier uses the same facts to construct a whole drama of torture:

> *And now on the wheel the victim must be stretched*
> *. . . and to each foot must be attached*
> *Two heavy irons . . .*
> *Thus tearing out his bowels by force. . . .*
> *And they must cut his tongue out with a knife*
> *And flay him afterwards, like a calf.*

A painting by Menescordi (1751–76) on the walls of a confraternity chapel in the Scuola Grande dei Carmini, in Venice, also represents the martyrdom of the Maccabees. In these scenes of torture, one of the Maccabees is being scalped—his hair is being pulled out by means of a winch—while a torturer is preparing to finish the job with a scalpel. Another is observing the body he is about to flay with the precise attention of the technician.

Flaying, the technique of the anatomist, was the favorite form of torture in the seventeenth century. Victims included not only Saint Bartholomew, patron saint of shoemakers precisely because of the skin that was removed from him, but also his pagan counterpart, Marsyas, who was flayed by Apollo, and the unjust judge, a subject borrowed from Herodotus and painted by Dierik Bouts.

From one torment to the next, it is the whole catalog of martyrs that one is invited to contemplate, as it is represented in screams and gestures on baroque walls or described in the lives of saints. For example, there is Saint Lawrence on his gridiron; in a *Flos sanctorum* published in Spain in 1603, Rousset comments, "The torturers are busy preparing the gridiron, lighting the fire, tearing off the saint's clothes, stripping his flayed body, and throwing him on the glowing coals. The tyrant, with bloodshot eyes, grinning face, and foaming mouth, howls with sadistic joy as servants fan the flames."[30]

A Saint Agatha by Cavallino (1622–54) is plunged into an ecstasy that is both amorous and mystical. Swooning with pleasure, she holds her hands over a bleeding bosom from which her breasts have been severed: round, full breasts that are being presented on a plate. Then there is Saint Sebastian, protector from the plague and model of masculine beauty. From the seventeenth century to Delacroix, in the nineteenth century, his beauty and his agony stir the emotions of holy women, whose tender hands pluck the arrows from his soft body with gestures that are more like caresses.

R. Gadenne has drawn our attention to the work of the good Bishop Camus. One of the titles is suggestive: *"Les Spectacles d'horreurs."* Published in 1630, this was a collection of horror stories that, but for their lack of perversity, anticipate those of the late eighteenth century. They are full of tortures and executions: "These two wretches who were hanged by their feet by order of the court served for a long time as horrible examples to those who saw them. In the end [when they had rotted], they had no other grave than the one given to asses." One of the tales is entitled *"Les Morts entassés."* Gadenne has made an inventory of the deaths in Camus: thirty-eight by murder, thirty-three under torture, nine by suicide, twenty-four by accident, and nineteen by various means (eight of fear, six of pain, one of hunger, four by animals). Only three died natural deaths.

In Camus one finds stories worthy of the fables reported by Garmann in *De miraculis mortuorum.* For example, there is the story about the three calves' heads that a butcher sold to a murderer. The calves' heads turned into human ones and accused the murderer. They did not recover their original form until justice had been done and the criminal had been hanged.

This series of catastrophes and dramas made Gadenne decide that Camus could "rightly be regarded as the forerunner of Prévost and Sade."[31]

Death is no longer a peaceful event. As we have seen, only three out of all the deaths in Camus were from natural causes. Nor is death any longer a moment of moral and psychological concentration, as it was in the *artes moriendi.* Death has become inseparable from violence and pain. It is no longer *finis vitae,* but, in Rousset's words, "a rending away from life, a long gasping cry, an agony hacked into many fragments."[32] These violent scenes excited spectators and aroused primitive forces whose sexual nature seems obvious today.

For a long time historians, with the exception of Mario Praz and André Chastel, refused to see what was only too obvious to Paulina, Pierre-Jean Jouve's heroine of 1880, and it is she who provides the best commentary on the tortures of baroque art: "As a young girl, Paulina loved above all else, in the churches, the martyrdoms of the saints. She went to church to watch them suffer. . . . In many little [Italian] churches tucked away in crowded neighborhoods, there was nothing but the sound of sobbing, the dripping of blood, the agony and the final beatitude on the face of the saint. Paulina knew nothing about painting and never read poetry, but she adored a picture she had by Il Sodoma, of the ecstasy of Saint Catherine of Siena, with a love that was obscure, vertiginous, and totally unconcious. Saint Catherine is kneeling and about to swoon. Her hand has been wounded by the stigmata; it lies chastely in the hollow between her thighs. How female she is, the pure image of woman, this nun, with those wide hips, that soft bosom beneath the veil, those shoulders. . . . The hollow between the thighs signifies love. . . . It is an idea of the devil."

The Saint Catherine of Il Sodoma recalls the swooning holy women of Bernini in Rome, the famous Saint Theresa of Santa Maria del la Vittoria, or the Saint Ludovica Albertoni of San Francesco, in Ripa. Other women, such as Aurora Bertiperusino at San Pantaleone, in Rome, wanted to resemble them and to appear in the same attitude on their tombs. It is the attitude of sensual swooning after the highest peak of pleasure that pierces like the arrow of an angel.

These mystical ecstasies are ecstasies of love and death. These holy virgins are dying of love, and the little death of sexual pleasure is confounded with the final death of the body:

Sweet is death, who comes like a lover.[33]

The confusion between death and pleasure is so total that the first does not stop the second, but on the contrary, heightens it. The dead body becomes in its turn an object of desire.

By comparing two versions of the same subject, as we did in the case of Saint Erasmus and the Maccabees, we may be able to determine when this macabre eroticism first appeared. The earlier sensibility is illustrated by a Latin poem of Politian inspired by the death of the beautiful Simonetta, the mistress of Giuliano de' Medici.[34] She died young. Love sees her lying on her bier with her face uncovered, as was the custom in Italian funerals. Her lifeless face is still desirable and beautiful: *"Blandus et exanimi spirat in ore lepos."* So beautiful that Love believes that death could not take her from him. She will still be his, although devoid of life. But alas! He cannot deceive himself; he realizes in the same instant that it is hopeless. No sooner has he said the words than he is already weeping. Love has understood that the moment of death could not be a moment of triumph, but only a moment of tears.

In the seventeenth century, however, the illusion will be cultivated. Love persists, but it is not exactly the beauty of the living body that one continues to love. It is a new beauty, adorned with other attractions: the beauty of death.

Among the attributes of death, the great macabre period of the fifteenth century had focused on decomposition, the breakdown of the tissues, the subterranean swarming of worms, snakes, and toads. Beginning in the sixteenth century, all the attention and emotions surrounding death were brought to bear on the first signs of death. Painters took pleasure in seeking out the colors that distinguish the body touched by death from the body of a living man, colors that betray the still-subtle signs of decomposition, greens unknown to fifteenth-century painting. A Le Sueur in the musée de Rennes shows Agar in the desert looking at his son, whom the angel is about to raise from the dead. There is no doubt that the resurrection will have all the characteristics of authenticity required by Zacchia, for the child's body is still green.

The same livid and fungic hues were sought by Rubens for a Medusa or a Descent from the Cross (Kunsthistoriches Museum, in Vienna), not in order to express horror, but one would almost say for the pleasure and sumptuousness of the color itself. A Bolognese painting by Donato Creti (1671–1749) shows Achilles, naked, dragging the body of Hector behind his chariot. The contrast between the living and the dead flesh is striking.[35]

Necrophilia
in the Eighteenth Century

From now on, the first signs of death will no longer inspire horror and flight, but love and desire, as can already be clearly seen in Poussin's *Adonis*. A whole repertoire of forms and attitudes and a whole palette of colors were elaborated and would continue to be refined until the beginning of the nineteenth century.

Here again, the best commentary on this "morbid" school of painting is provided not by intimidated historians, but by the author of a Gothic novel, this time from the early nineteenth century. In *Melmoth the Wanderer* (1820), Charles Robert Maturin tells the story of a handsome young man who sells his blood in order to save his family from poverty. But alas! The vein is ligated improperly, and he bleeds to death. The author describes the appearance of the beautiful corpse, which reminds him of all the beautiful corpses of recent painting: "This corpselike beauty which the light of the moon rendered worthy of the brush of a Murillo, a Rosa, or another of those painters who, inspired by the muse of suffering, took delight in representing the most exquisite human forms in the height of agony: a Saint Bartholomew flayed, his skin hanging over his arm like an elegant drapery, or a Saint Lawrence roasting on his gridiron, exposing his beautiful anatomy, surrounded by naked slaves fanning the flames." None of these works "could rival this body lying in the moonlight which half-veiled and half-revealed it." Further on, the same author waxes ecstatic over the beauty of a young monk being tortured: "No human form was ever so beautiful."[36]

Certain painters of the late eighteenth and early nineteenth centuries do not hesitate to emphasize an erotic dimension that their predecessors of the seventeenth century expressed more discreetly, or simply more unconsciously.

In a painting by William Etty in the museum in York, Hero throws herself passionately upon the body of the drowned Leander, which the sea is washing up on the shore, and whose ivory pallor contrasts with the rosy freshness of the skin of the living woman. A Brunhilde by Fuseli, wearing a transparent dress that accentuates her nakedness, is lying on a bed and looking at the man whom she has turned over to be tortured. Gunther is naked, his hands and feet bound together, his muscles taut. The works of Fuseli and Etty are only a few examples among many others of the emotions aroused by the dead body and the beautiful victim. In the world of the imagination, death and violence have merged with desire.

In seventeenth-century England and France, the theater also reveals a penchant for scenes set in tombs and for the theme of premature burial.[37]

This was probably not a complete innovation. Since the Middle Ages, graves and cemeteries had been too familiar, too much a part of daily life, for storytellers not to use them, naïvely and without any disturbing ulterior motives, whenever they were so inspired. Medieval bawdy literature was full of tombs and cadavers; but we must understand how these subjects were used. In Boccaccio's fourteenth century, a lascivious monk who was half sorcerer gets rid of a jealous husband for a while by giving him a potion that produces the appearance of death. The husband is buried "with the customary ceremonies." When the woman becomes pregnant and things must come to an end, the "dead" man comes back to life and emerges from his tomb. Another time, also in the *Decameron*, a girl with an incredibly inventive imagination decides to test her two lovers. She orders one to lie in a grave in place of a body that has just been buried, and the other to steal the false corpse under cover of night. But in these cases the tomb is not a source of emotion, but simply a familiar instrument of subterfuge.

Sometimes, however, we find the stirrings of a desire sufficiently powerful to attract a living person to a corpse. A girl kills herself while clasping to her bosom the heart of her recently killed lover, which her father has brought to her in a golden cup. Another girl learns in a dream that her lover has just been killed and where he has been buried. She goes to his grave, cuts off the head of the corpse (in those days people were not squeamish about such dismemberments), and places it in the bottom of a large vase in her garden. In the vase she plants a basil plant, which she waters with her tears and which grows into a magnificent tree. However, these pieces of cadavers are more like holy relics that perpetuate a carnal memory than objects intended to arouse and heighten desire.

Stranger at first sight, and closer to modern eroticism, is this other tale of love and death. A woman is believed dead following an apparent miscarriage. She is buried. A knight who loved her in his youth and whom she rejected decides that this would be a good opportunity to steal a few kisses. He opens the tomb and kisses her face, wetting it with his tears. "The idea came into his mind not to stop there. Why not touch her bosom, he said to himself, as long as I am here? It will be for the first and last time." But suddenly he realizes that she is alive. He cuts short his caresses as if all desire had abandoned him. He respectfully lifts the woman out of the tomb and carries her to his mother, where she gives birth. Then he takes her and the child to the husband, and becomes the friend of the family. Here one senses an almost imperceptible transition from familiarity with the dead to macabre eroticism, but one also sees how this eroticism dries up at its source.

In seventeenth-century theater, however, it dares to go further. Lovers lie in the bottoms of graves, in cemeteries, which from now on are places conducive to desire. But they still do not go so far as making love to a corpse. Not that they would be loath to do so themselves, but just when things threaten to get out of hand, the corpse wakes up. It is a false corpse, a living corpse, or, as Georges de Scudéry puts it, "a corpse that moves." Or else a welcome metamorphosis tips the scene at the last minute toward the fantastic. For example, in a play by the German playwright Andreas Gryphius a cadaver is disinterred, and Cordenio thinks he recognizes the mistress who abandoned him. He follows her, catches up with her . . . and finds a skeleton. "Under the body of the living and beloved woman," comments Rousset, "it is death itself that the lover embraces. Life is nothing but a mask for death."

Things are always disguised in this transvestite world. Actual possession of the dead body is indicated only by the presence of the tomb as a bed of love.[38] The reality of the union of Eros and Thanatos is still hidden. This is the great difference between the first half of the seventeenth century and the end of the eighteenth century. Of course, the underlying motivations and subjects differed very little in the two periods: the same delicious torments, the same graveyard decor, the same pale, greenish flesh, the same emphasis on the beauty of the dead body, the same temptation to place love in the midst of death; but in the seventeenth century all this still takes place in the realm of the unconscious and unadmitted rather than in that of the inadmissible. Nobody yet knows the names of the demons that stir up these dreams. No doubt the torturers, the spectators, and the victims themselves derive from this fatal violence a pleasure that it is easy for us to recognize and to call sadistic. But their contemporaries suspected neither the perversity nor the sexual basis of their taste for horror. Neither the pious Bernini nor his ecclesiastical patrons nor the excellent Bishop Camus suspected what was seething inside them and exciting their imaginations. They believed they were doing a pious and edifying work as they piled up punishments and tortures, and to them the nudity of the torturers was merely a pardonable concession to the taste of the times.

In baroque theater there was also a tendency to intensify love by placing it as near as possible to death, but the rapprochement never went so far as to cross the forbidden threshold. A last-minute morality brought the action back either toward the fantastic or toward the idea of vanity and the *memento mori*. Nevertheless, the reader and the spectator must have been profoundly aroused in spite of themselves, on an unconscious level; this can be felt in a vertiginous quality that we sense today in baroque art and literature.

In the eighteenth century, everything changes. The president of Brosses was not mistaken about Bernini's Theresa. He saw in the sculpture what the artist had unwittingly put into it, and understood what his contemporaries had unconsciously felt. There was no merit in his perspicacity, for the mask had been torn off. A powerful current of sensibility had taken hold of art, especially literature, a literature that in the nineteenth century would soon become popular. Eighteenth-century texts are already full of stories about love with the dead, some of which were "true" stories.

One of the best of these is told by the surgeon Antoine Louis in a book about premature burial.[39] As we shall see, this was not simply a case of apparent death, but of love; serious works on death are never completely free of ambiguity. A young gentleman was forced to take religious orders without vocation. While traveling he stopped at an inn. The owners were in mourning for their daughter, who had just died. "Since the girl was not to be buried until the next day, they asked the monk to watch over her body during the night. All that he had heard about her beauty having aroused his curiosity, he uncovered the face of the would-be corpse, and far from finding her disfigured by the horrors of death, he found there certain lively graces that, causing him to forget the sanctity of his vows and stifling the lugubrious thoughts that death naturally inspires, incited him to take with the dead girl the same liberties that the sacrament would have authorized had she been alive." The monk made love to a corpse.

But in reality, the corpse was not a corpse. In baroque theater, this discovery was made before the fact; in the late eighteenth century, it was not made until afterward. "The dead girl came back to life" after the monk's departure, and "nine months later, to the great astonishment of her parents and herself, gave birth to a child. The monk happened to stop at the inn at the time [a happy accident, worthy of a novel] and, feigning surprise upon finding alive one whom he had pretended to believe dead, acknowledged that he was the father of the child, after having been released from his vows."

In the second half of the nineteenth century the doctors who still refer to this story find that "the extraordinary fact . . . does not present quite the degree of authenticity that one would desire." Louis had quoted it from *Causes célèbres.* In the eighteenth century it still seemed possible, and was quoted as altogether credible. At that time, however, one point seemed questionable, and that was how an inanimate woman had been able to conceive. It was believed that pleasure—or at least movement—was necessary to fertility. "Citizen Louis thought that this girl had actually been excited by the movements that must have preceded the act, as well as by the act itself."[40]

These themes we have been discussing are often associated with macabre eroticism in the eighteenth and nineteenth centuries. The reluctant monk or nun (the theme of Diderot's *La Religieuse*) and the incestuous lover are stock characters of the Gothic novel.

Intercourse with the dead occurs frequently, of course, in the work of Sade. After Justine is struck by lightning, she is sodomized by the accursed abbot and his companions. If certain cases of necrophilia are extravagant, others are merely spiced-up versions of anecdotes that were popular at the time. The theme runs something like this: A character spends the night in a church in order to open a tomb, either in despair over a dead lover or out of sexual perversion or simply to rob the cadaver of jewelry.

La Durand and Juliette, Sade's heroines, remain in church after it is closed for the day. "How I love this lugubrious silence. . . . It is the image of the serenity of coffins, and . . . I lust for death." A young girl has just been buried. Her father, who has had the same idea as the two women, arrives with the gravedigger. "Bring her up again. My grief is so great that I want to embrace her again before I must take leave of her forever. . . . The coffin reappears, the body is taken out and laid on the steps of the altar." Up to this point there is nothing that is particularly abnormal for the world of the Gothic novel. Now Sade introduces incest, which in fact was not exceptional. The father, left alone with his daughter, takes off her clothes and makes love to her as if she were alive. Juliette and her friend join him, and the orgy continues at the bottom of the vault where the body and the coffin have been replaced. Juliette even allows herself to be shut inside the vault for the father's pleasure. The story leaves the framework of the Gothic novel and plunges into the fantastic world of Sade.[41]

But here is another story from the same folklore, this one more ordinary and no doubt more significant. It is from Potocki's *Manuscrit trouvé à Saragosse* (1804–1805). Trivulce had killed the woman he loved and her fiancé in church just as the priest was marrying them. They were buried together then and there. Later the murderer, overcome with remorse, returned to the scene of his crime. "Trivulce walked over, trembling. When he reached the tomb, he kissed her and shed a torrent of tears. . . . He gave his purse to the sexton and received permission to enter the church whenever he wished. And indeed, he began coming there every evening." One evening when he was inside the church, "he decided to spend the night there because he liked to sustain his grief and nourish his melancholy. At midnight he saw the tombs open and the dead, wrapped in their shrouds, chanted the litany."[42]

Still in the same vein is a story told in Toulouse that begins like those of the marquis de Sade and Potocki but ends more realistically. A certain M. de Grille "fell in love with a beautiful young woman, who died of smallpox. He loved her so deeply that he could not console himself for her loss. In despair, he hid in the Dominican church where she was buried. In the evening, the monk who was in charge of putting oil in the lamps was very much surprised to find M. de Grille. With one hand the man offered him a purse containing 400 francs, provided he would open his mistress's tomb, and with the other he brandished a dagger with which he threatened to kill him if he refused." The monk managed to alert the police, who seized the unhappy lover and took him home, where he killed himself.[43]

A variation on the theme of the reopened tomb is the story in which a living person passes for dead, changes his identity, and starts life over again. A nun from Toulouse who was in love with a gentleman "decided to jump over the wall of the convent to follow him. . . . Another nun had been buried that day. Since the tomb had not yet been sealed, she went inside when the whole convent was asleep and carried the dead nun to her cell. [In these stories people carry heavy cadavers with no apparent difficulty!] She laid her on her bed and set fire to the body. . . . Everyone believed that it was she who had burned."[44]

Toulouse seems to have specialized in such cases, for here is another, dated 1706: M. de Saint-Alban, a councillor in the Parliament of Toulouse, had lost his young wife. This wife had before her marriage been engaged to a gentleman named de Sézanne, who was believed to have been killed in the Americas. But this was not the case, for M. de Sézanne married and returned to Toulouse. M. de Saint-Alban was struck by the resemblance between Mme. de Sézanne and his dead wife. (You will recall the problem of resemblances discussed by Zacchia.) To set his mind at rest, he obtained permission to have her body exhumed. The coffin was empty. (The nun in the other story had been more clever.) M. de Sézanne explained that on his return to France, he learned of the marriage and death of his fiancée and decided to kill himself. "But before ending my life, I wanted to pay a last visit to the one whom I had loved so much. . . . In vain I told myself that in violating this tomb, I would be guilty of an act of profanation . . . and of a crime. . . . It seemed to me that I was drawn along by some fatality."

This was the voice of Providence, "which had chosen me to repair a dreadful error on the part of men." He persuaded the gravedigger to open the coffin. (These clandestine exhumations must have been a boon to the guards and caretakers of those days!) "The next moment, the loose boards afforded me a glimpse of a white shroud, under which I could make out the vague outline of a human form. I knelt down and gently separated the folds of the funereal drapery. To my tear-dimmed eyes appeared a head crowned with abundant hair." This is not the marquis de Sade; here people weep and pray instead of blaspheming and defying, but the underlying sensuality remains the same: "I leaned down to place a last kiss on her brow. As my face came closer to hers, I thought I felt or heard a last sigh. . . . She was alive!"[45]

Were these fantasies inspired by actual events? Sade tells us, "In Paris I often saw a man who bought the cadavers of young girls and boys who had died violent deaths and had been recently placed in the ground. He paid their weight in gold. He had them brought to his home, where he committed an infinity of abominations on these fresh bodies." The marquis is not a reliable witness. However, his remark is strangely confirmed by a memorandum on the indecency of burials addressed to the procurator general of Paris in 1781. "The bodies lowered into this common pit are every day exposed to the most infamous violations. On the pretext of study, certain persons, not content with the bodies that are given to the hospitals, also steal dead bodies from cemeteries and commit on them everything that impiety and debauchery might inspire."[46] Whether or not this was true, people believed it, and amateur anatomists were suspected of engaging in "libertinage" with cadavers. In Naples, Raimondo di Sangro had an evil reputation because of his experiments on the human body. We may believe these accusations to be groundless, but even today one has a strange feeling in the chapel of his palace, which contains the family tombs. It is decorated with some statues that would be surprising under ordinary circumstances, but are even more so when one realizes that they are right next to an anatomist's laboratory. They look like fresh cadavers covered with fine, damp shrouds that hang in folds. According to the most respectable hypothesis, they seem to be awaiting the anatomist's scalpel. But they could just as well be offering themselves to the macabre perversions of some rich amateur.

The Cemetery of Mummies

Let us not look too hard for the reality that lies beneath these fanciful tales. Even if there is some truth to them, and there must have been, the real is only a passing effect of the imaginary. What is essential here takes place in the imagination. The most important events, those heaviest with consequences, do not belong to real life but to the world of fantasies. Like the writings of the doctors, these fantasies assume that the cadaver has a kind of existence of its own that arouses desire and excites the senses.

Were these the beliefs of scientists impressed by observations of the residual sensibility of the cadaver, or of perverse men, bored idlers in pursuit of violent sensations, unknown pleasures? Both, no doubt; but they were also part of the climate of the age and were widely accepted, even in popular circles. The common denominator of these ideas is the assumption that the cadaver should not disappear, that it retains some vestige of life, that it should be preserved, and that it is good to exhibit it and to see it. In the seventeenth century—not everywhere, but in certain places, especially the Mediterranean regions and Latin America—a conviction of this sort succeeded in altering the physical appearance of cemeteries. It is the source of what, for lack of a better term, we shall call the cemeteries of mummies, which disappeared in Europe at the end of the nineteenth century but lasted longer in Latin America.

We will recall that the doctors of the seventeenth century, even Zacchia, were preoccupied with the preservation or nonpreservation of buried cadavers. This interest in preservation was not unknown, as we have seen, to anatomists, painters of cadavers, and manipulators of bodies, whether scientific or libertine. But it was also related, on a more popular level, to a belief regarding the future of the body after burial. We now observe the rise of the idea that the body should not be abandoned definitively, that physical contact with it should be maintained. There was a desire to follow the body in its various stages, to intervene in its transformations, to remove it from the ground and display it in its final state as mummy or skeleton.

There is a new element here. The idea of the ritual transfer of the body that exists in certain cultures was unknown in the pagan and Christian West. In the West, the body was buried once and for all. It is true that in the Christian Middle Ages the bones were dug up long after burial and piled in the galleries of charnels, sheds, or chapels. There were no cemeteries without these storage places. But the transfer to the charnel had no symbolic meaning; its only purpose was to make room for other graves. The bones remained close to the church and to the saints under whose protection they had been placed. The charnels were no more anonymous than the graves of the early Middle Ages. We have seen how much time and psychological innovation it required to abandon this anonymity.

There are only two exceptions to this widespread and ancient rule: the transfer of saints' relics, and a very local and unusual custom already noted in chapter 2. In the Middle Ages, cavities were made in the walls of the Romanesque churches of Catalonia to receive the dismantled bones of the deceased. However, these cases in no way invalidate the general rule.

But in the seventeenth century, burial in two stages, although rare, is no longer unknown. There are even illustrious examples in which a single body receives two successive burials, which are separated by the period required for the body to be consumed. The final tomb is the one containing the bones or the dried-out body.

This practice seems originally to have been reserved for famous persons, without necessarily being extended to every member of royal families. In Malta, it was provided for the great masters of the order. Whereas Ordinary Knights were laid in coffins covered with quicklime at the bottom of a vault, with a visible mosaic tomb on the floor of the church, the Great Masters were buried in the crypt, in a temporary monument, where they remained at least a year, and later transferred to a large tomb in a chapel of the church. The ceremony of the Order determined the requirements of a solemn rite in which the coffin was opened, the remains were identified by a doctor who specialized in cadavers, the coffin was reclosed, the absolution was chanted, and the coffin was laid in its final resting-place.[47]

A transfer of the same kind was provided in the Escorial for the royal family of Spain. The bodies were first laid in what Saint-Simon called the Pourrissoir: "For every body that is laid there a niche is hollowed out in the wall and the body is placed there to rot. The niche is resealed in such a way that no sign of it can be seen on the wall, which is of a dazzling and uniform whiteness, and indeed the place is full of light." This surprises Saint-Simon, who is accustomed to associating death with the darkness of the underground vault. "After a certain interval [the bodies] are removed and carried without ceremony [either] to the drawers of the Pantheon," or to another vault adjoining the Pourrissoir. There they "remain forever."[48]

The function of this temporary storage place seems to have been to save the final resting place for bodies that will no longer move, either because they have been reduced to dry bones or because they have been preserved with their flesh, that is, mummified. Either way, the stages of decomposition were bypassed and the body was maintained in a state of desiccation that was perfectly presentable.

This technique was not limited to royal personages. One finds it here and there, in southern regions (the same ones that exhibited their dead with faces uncovered), although I can discover no apparent reason for this localization. "I went to the church of the Franciscans [in Toulouse]," writes a correspondent of the early eighteenth century, "and saw the charnel that I had heard so much about." Beware, for here the word *charnel* means something different from the old medieval charnel as it still existed at les Innocents, and as we have often encountered it in the course of our investigation. This is a charnel of mummies, "where the bodies are preserved intact for centuries. The body of the beautiful Paula still retains vestiges of her beauty. I asked the good fathers by what means they could protect these bodies from corruption. [The techniques of the Franciscans were famous, and earned them a large "clientele."] They told me that they buried them first in a certain soil that consumed their flesh, and later exposed them to the air [no doubt in a room of the bell tower, as we shall see presently]. When they were sufficiently desiccated, they were placed in charnels [with inscriptions on the walls; they were lined up in rows, either upright or lying down]. While this monk was talking to me, I saw other monks come down from the bell tower with bodies over their shoulders, bodies from which the fresh air had completely removed everything they might have had in the way of foul odors, and from this I judged that the good Franciscan had spoken correctly." The dead were deposited in three successive locations, of which only the first was underground. They were treated somewhat as American morticians treat their clients, except that in this case the experts were monks and the treatment required more time, the various stages lasting at least a year. In the end, the bodies were placed in a charnel, where visitors—for people went there as if to a spectacle— were presented with a mixture of bones and mummies.[49]

There are a few cemeteries of this kind still in existence. There is one in Rome in the vault of a Capuchin church, near the palace of the Barberini, who were buried there. Here one finds vertical mummies similar to the ones that lined the charnel of the Franciscans in Toulouse. They are said to be monks who died in the fragrance of sanctity. They may also have been laymen, Franciscan tertiaries, who had the privilege of being buried in the habit and cord. At Palermo, there is another famous cemetery of mummies, also connected with a Capuchin church. These mummies are laymen in street clothes, whom their families came to visit. This form of ostentation lasted until 1881, and could not have started much before the fifteenth century.

In Rome, in the Capuchin church, and in the cemetery of the Confraternità della Orazione e della Morte (unfortunately rebuilt after the construction of the quays on the Tiber), the walls and ceilings are covered with a decorative ossuary in which bones replaced pebbles or shells. A few skeletons, such as those of three small Barberini children, have been reconstructed with remarkable success. Elsewhere, each bone is used according to its shape: Pelvic bones are arranged in rosettes, skulls are stacked in columns, tibias or limbs support the arches of niches, vertebrae form garlands or serve as candlesticks. The work is attributed to an eighteenth-century monk. Here the charnel is no longer merely a repository; it is a stage set in which the human bone lends itself to all the convulsions of baroque or rococo art. The skeleton is exhibited as a theatrical prop and itself becomes a spectacle. Of course, it does not have the vegetative life that seems to persist in the mummy; it has lost its individuality. It is a collective life that animates this decor through the grinning mouths of hundreds of heads, the gestures of thousands of limbs.

At the same time that kings were going underground and renouncing visible monuments, and the nocturnal kingdom of death was taking the form of arched vaults such as the ones churchwardens were building and Gothic novelists or fantastical engravers imagining, another impulse was bringing the bodies back to the surface, where they were preserved and exhibited to the people as in a parade. It was important to see them and to be able to talk to them.

It is interesting to compare these real cemeteries with the older paintings of Carpaccio. In a painting in the Dahlem Museum, Berlin, the body of Christ is laid out before burial. The cemetery (which is really a dump, for there are even animals there) is strewn with bones, which was normal for a cemetery of that time. But these bones are no longer scattered here and there like stones. Mummies and skeletons of men and animals are protruding from the ground still intact, with faces that are almost animated. This cemetery is one of those whose soil preserves: It produces good mummies.

In another painting in the Frick Collection, in New York, Carpaccio has represented the meeting of the hermits in the desert. Hanging on the wall over the head of Saint Anthony is his rosary, which is made of little vertebrae, like the candlesticks in the cemetery of the Confraternità della Orazione e della Morte, in Rome.

Spiritual writers, including Bossuet, claimed that they would have liked to open up the tombs in order to make an impression on the living and remind them that they were going to die. But they did not really dare; the horror would have been unbearable. And yet, not very far away from them bodies were already being brought out and exhibited, albeit in an acceptable form that had preserved some semblance of life.

Mummies in the Home

Mummies are found not only in cemeteries but also on altars. The bodies of saints are no longer merely bones piled in a reliquary but real mummies wearing clothes and exhibited like representations. Wax or wooden effigies were substituted for mummies when there was no alternative. The churches of Rome have preserved some of these holy mummies in transparent reliquaries with glass sides. For example, the mummified body of Saint Frances of Rome lies in the church in the Forum, of which she is the patron saint. In San Francesco, in Ripa, another mummy is exhibited in the attitude of the recumbent, or rather the leaning, figure. The mummy is wearing a long robe with a slit through which one can see the body through a veil. All of the visible part of the skeleton is wrapped in a net that keeps the bones in place. Also in Rome, the Doria family had the privilege of possessing a mummy of their own, in the little private chapel of their palace. I am not sure that many people today would agree to sleep under the same roof as a mummy, let alone in the next room.

But there is no reason why people should not have extended this taste for mummies to their immediate surroundings. We shall see in chapter 10 how a new sensibility made the death of loved ones more cruel for survivors and led to an almost fanatical cult of remembrance. At this point we shall merely indicate how this sentiment took advantage of the taste for mummies, of which we have found considerable evidence in the eighteenth century.

The fascination is very old. We find traces of it as early as the beginning of the seventeenth century, not in real life but in the theater. In a tragedy by the Elizabethan author Christopher Marlowe, the protagonist, Tamburlaine, keeps with him the embalmed body of his beloved Zenocrate.[50] The Roman Confraternità della Orazione e della Morte (the confraternity of gravediggers who had an underground burial vault decorated with bones), on their annual feast day, put on *tableaux vivants* which were later recorded in the form of engravings. One of these that represented purgatory made use of real cadavers.

In the eighteenth century the practice spread from the theater to the town. It was rare, but not absolutely exceptional, to keep in one's home the body of a beloved one from whom one could not bear to be separated by burial. In 1775 Martin van Butchell kept his wife's body in his home until his second wife had had enough of this spectacle. The mummy was then turned over to the Royal College of Surgeons, in London, where it remained until the bombings of World War II.

Another case is that of Jacques Necker, minister under Louis XVI, and his wife, Suzanne Curchod, the parents of Mme. de Staël. Mme. Necker was afraid of being buried alive and had written a treatise on the subject, *Des Inhumations précipitées* (see chapter 9). She hoped to maintain communication with her husband after death, a desire that became widespread in the late eighteenth and especially the nineteenth centuries and that we shall analyze in chapter 11. "Do exactly as I have said," she wrote him. "Perhaps my soul will wander around you. . . . Perhaps I shall be able to benefit delightfully from your exactitude in fulfilling the desires of the one who loves you so much." She left instructions that a mausoleum be built for herself and her husband at Coppet, their estate on the shore of Lake Geneva. Both bodies were to be preserved in a tank of alcohol. After she died, Jacques Necker kept her body at home for three months. The French spy who was watching the family reported that Mme. Necker had "ordered her body to be preserved in alcohol, like an embryo." And Germaine de Staël wrote, "Perhaps you do not know that my mother gave orders so singular and extraordinary concerning the various ways of embalming her, preserving her, and placing her under glass in alcohol that if, as she believed, the features of her face had been perfectly preserved, my poor father would have spent the rest of his life looking at her."

The mausoleum was reopened on July 28, 1804, in order to deposit the coffin of Mme. de Staël. "In the black marble basin, still half filled with alcohol, beneath a large red mantle, lay Necker and his wife. Necker's face was perfectly intact. Mme. Necker's head had fallen and was concealed by the mantle."[51]

An issue of *Paris-Soir* in October 1947 contains the following story: "On May 21, 1927, the Marquis Maurice d'Urre of Aubais died in Paris. A man of seventy, without children, he left his immense fortune to the French government under the following strange conditions: 'After my death,' he stated firmly in his will, 'I wish to be seated in an armchair under a glass dome. This dome must be placed facing the sea, in a public place, near a lighthouse and a radio station, and must be perpetually illuminated.' " In fact his coffin—and not his visible mummy—was installed in one room of his castle, which was transformed into a kind of permanently illuminated chapel.

Jeremy Bentham, who died in 1832, asked that his embalmed body be kept at the University of London, which he founded, where it could be seen and examined from time to time.

We shall have occasion to return to this phenomenon, and the custom of preserving a body in the home will be less surprising now that we know the role played by the mummy in the imagery of the time.

It is likely that the Freemasons were no more squeamish about using embalmed cadavers in their initiation ceremonies. We know from Michel Vovelle's study of Joseph Sec that the body of Anicet Martel, who murdered M. d'Albertes in 1791, had been stolen by medical students from the Pénitents Bleus (who were to have buried it) and prepared for use in the initiation ordeals of a Masonic lodge in Aix. And at the musée Arbaud, in Aix-en-Provence, there is a plaster cast by the provincial sculptor J.-P. Chastel that represents, with all the realism of the death mask, the moment of death of a carpenter following a workmen's brawl at the construction site belonging to this same Joseph Sec, a real-estate dealer and Freemason of whom Vovelle has given us a curious portrait. As late as 1873 in a former summer house of this man, there was a walnut seat that was "a kind of bizarre compromise between a sofa and a sarcophagus." If you lifted the seat and opened one of the long sides of the base, you found Chastel's statue, realistically painted, no doubt a polychrome copy of the white original in the musée Arbaud. Vovelle believes it to be "an accessory of the meditation room of a Masonic lodge, an object used in initiation ceremonies."[52] In short, the equivalent of a mummy, a representation like those of saints in baroque churches.

When it was not possible to preserve the whole body, survivors had to be content with one part of it. For a long time the part most sought after, the noblest part, was the heart, the seat of life and emotion. There is a symbolism of the heart whose first example in our culture is the tombs we have already discussed. When the body was eviscerated, the heart was separated from the bowels, which were also assigned their own burial place. These tombs of separate parts of the body have existed for centuries. The latest example I know of is the tomb of Charles Maurras, who wanted his heart to be kept in his mother's sewing basket! A bizarre wish, worthy of a testator—who may have been a Mason—of the late eighteenth or early nineteenth century.

For a long time the heart was represented in an idealized form: the heart pierced by Cupid's arrow, or the Sacred Heart of Jesus. But in Mexico in the seventeenth and eighteenth centuries, the same period when the dead body was provoking strange temptations in Europe, the Sacred Heart was no longer represented in its stylized form, but rather as dripping blood, with the veins and arteries severed as in an anatomical colorplate. The obsession with the heart is also found in Mexico in the treatment of purgatory. Whereas in southern Europe souls burn and angels come to deliver them, in Mexico the same image is reinforced by a second scene, which takes place in heaven: the child Jesus placing in a wicker basket a heart that represents the delivered soul.

The revolutionary cults also adopted the theme of the heart. After the death of Marat, during a celebration given in his honor in the Luxembourg gardens on Sunday, July 28, 1793, his heart was presented on a *reposoir* in "a precious pyx from the furniture repository." It should not surprise us that the heart did not remain in the tomb, any more than did the mummy, but that it became a domestic and transportable object. The marquis de Tauras (the husband of Mlle. de Bernis) who was fatally wounded in Flanders in the campaign of the marshal of Luxembourg, "ordered that as soon as he died, his heart be removed and taken to his wife."

In 1792, during the burial in exile of Mirabeau-Tonneau, brother of the great Mirabeau, an unusual ceremony was added to the traditional rites. "The embalmed heart of the viscount, which had been placed in a lead box, was attached to the flagstaff of the volunteer battalion" (the Mirabeau Legion, which he had trained). We have gone beyond the tomb of the heart in a church. The heart has now become an object, a souvenir that one carries about and passes on to one's heirs. The hearts of the the La Tour d'Auvergnes and the Turrennes have been preserved to this day in the family.

In the nineteenth century—and even in the eighteenth—the heart was frequently replaced by the hair: another part of the body, but this one dry and incorruptible, like bone. At the Victoria and Albert Museum, in London, there is a whole series of jewels that are either designed to contain hair or partly made of hair: brooches with cameo portraits on a background of hair—the oldest ones date from 1697, 1700, and 1703—and numerous bracelets made of hair from the nineteenth century. In the museum of the Archaeological Society of Provins, there is a souvenir of Hégésippe Moreau representing her tomb surrounded by weeping willows, which are made from the hair of the deceased.

There were sometimes humorous sidelights to the pious manipulation of the body. In 1723 there was much ado about an incident that would not have troubled the preparers of royal bodies in the fifteenth and sixteenth centuries. After the duke of Orléans died, "the body was opened in the usual way before embalming it and placing the heart in a box to take it to Val-de-Grâce. During the evisceration there was a Great Dane belonging to the prince in the room. Before anyone could stop him, the dog pounced on the heart and ate a good quarter of it."[53]

A Modern Prometheus

It is time to end our exploration of this confused world where the subterranean springs of the imagination meet the currents of science. There is a popular version of this material that is found almost everywhere and that constitutes a common background of knowledge and belief. It is true that one also finds these preoccupations in the doctors of the eighteenth century, in scholarly ideas about nature; but just as one can best measure the influence of psychoanalysis on the culture by studying women's magazines, similarly it is preferable for our purposes to study the phenomena of death in the bastard forms of vulgarization.

One stormy evening in 1816 on the shores of Lake Leman, Shelley, Byron, the physician Polidori, and the English writer Matthew Gregory Lewis, author of *The Monk,* whiled away the time by making up horror stories. This was the origin of Mary Shelley's *Frankenstein, or the Modern Prometheus,* which was published in 1818. The author confesses how greatly preoccupied they all were by the problem of the origins of life. "They say that he [Darwin] had kept under glass a piece of vermicle which, after a certain interval, by some extraordinary means, had started to move. [Worms, vermin, everything that swarms in the dark depths of burial vaults and tombs, is a source of life. There is an undeniable correlation between corruption and life.] Perhaps someone would succeed in bringing a cadaver back to life [the unadmitted dream of the old school of medicine, which was obsessed with the question of the residual life of the cadaver]. Galvanism was already giving indications of this possibility." Electricity, along with corruption, is at the origin of life.[54]

Jan Potocki discusses the same two phenomena in *Manuscrit trouvé à Saragosse.* "As for man and the animals, . . . they owe their existence to a generating acid that caused matter to ferment, giving it certain constant forms. . . . He regarded the fungous substances produced by damp wood as the link that connects the crystallization of fossils to the reproduction of vegetables and animals." "We recognize here," adds the author in a note, "the primary acid of Paracelsus." So much for corruption. As for electricity, "Hervas knew that thunder had been observed to sour wines and cause them to ferment. . . . He believed that lightning might have furnished the original impulse to the generating acid."[55] Hervas had the same ideas as Frankenstein.

Frankenstein was tempted to apply these ideas to an extraordinary project involving the reconstruction of a human being. "Perhaps one might succeed in determining the elements of the human being, assembling them, and communicating to them the vital warmth," with the help of fermentation and electricity. This research required a thorough knowledge of the human body. "One of the phenomena which had peculiarly attracted my attention was the structure of the human frame, and, indeed, any animal endowed with life. Whence, I often asked myself, did the principle of life proceed?" Frankenstein rediscovers the correlation the old doctors made between the body, life, and the cadaver. "To examine the causes of life," he writes, "we must first have recourse to death." And death meant the cadaver, the cadaver from which life had not completely disappeared. "I became acquainted with the science of anatomy, but this was not sufficient; I must also observe the natural decay and corruption of the human body. . . . I was forced to spend days and nights in vaults and charnel houses. I beheld the corruption of death succeed to the blooming cheek of life; I saw how the worm inherited the wonders of the eye and the brain." Was this an evolution capable of being reversed?

From the wonders of cadavers Frankenstein will wrest the secret of life. In the cadaver there was knowledge, and in the cadaver there also remained a vital element. "After days and nights of incredible labor and fatigue, I succeeded in discovering the cause of generation and life; nay, more, I became myself capable of bestowing animation upon lifeless matter."

It was then that he decided to reconstruct a human body and bring it to life. "I collected bones from charnel houses, and disturbed, with profane fingers, the tremendous secrets of the human frame. In a solitary chamber, or rather cell, at the top of the house, and separated from all the other apartments by a gallery and staircase, I kept my workshop of filthy creation. [Filthy for two reasons: because it was made of decomposed flesh, but also, as we shall see, because the vital force, in its crude and natural state, is unclean.] The dissecting room and the slaughterhouse [Carpaccio's cemetery of mummies was also a dump for animals] furnished many of my materials; and often did my human nature turn with loathing from my occupation."

One day the inert thing that was reconstructed in this manner was brought to life by an electric spark. Out of the separate pieces that had been put together, a living creature was born. Was it a man or a devil? An evil being, no doubt; but that is another story. Here we are only interested in the miracle on the dissection table: a *miraculum cadaveris*. It was possible to make the leap from inanimate matter to life because there is a continuity in nature, or matter; the two words are almost synonymous. Potocki's atheistic scientist, Hervas, talks like Mary Shelley's modern Prometheus: "He believes in the forces of nature, attributing to matter an energy that seemed to him to be capable of explaining everything without recourse to Creation."

Sade's View of Man and Nature

Nature is generally recognized as the contrary or negation of man's social power, the power that regulates society and produces order and work. Nature is always destructive and violent, and may be harmful. The degree of its harmfulness depends on man's preconceived attitude toward it.

The most radical attitude, the one that laid the greatest emphasis on the evil of nature is, of course, that of the Divine Marquis. His very excesses help us to understand the popular attitude toward nature, whether it was regarded as malefic or benevolent.

Sade criticized Montesquieu for assuming justice to be an eternal and immutable principle of all times and all places. "Justice is wholly dependent upon human conditions, upon the character, temperament, and psychological climate of a country." The world of man is alien to that of nature, at least, and to Sade, the two worlds are at war. Justice is one of man's attempts to oppose nature. "I regard unjust things as indispensable to the operation of the universe, which is disturbed by an equitable order of things." "All the laws we have made, either to encourage the growth of the population or to punish destruction, necessarily oppose all her laws . . . but on the contrary, every time we obstinately refuse to participate in this propagation that she abhors [by means of a sterile eroticism], every time we cooperate in these murders that delight and serve her [eroticism and torture, or violent death, are the two ways in which the world of man and the world of nature can communicate], we are sure of pleasing her, and certain that we are acting in harmony with her views." Nature desires "the total annihilation of the creatures she produces, so that she may enjoy her faculty of producing new ones." Nature destroys in order to create; this has become a commonplace. There are several ways of participating in this universal destruction; the one recommended by Sade is crime. "The most abominable murderer . . . is therefore merely the instrument of her laws." Murder is the disorderly and passionate breaking of prohibitions, it is pure violence. "Everything that is violent in nature is always somehow interesting and sublime." This is why the child, who is closer to the state of nature, spontaneously manifests a ferocity that society has not yet overcome. "Does not the child himself offer an example of this ferocity that surrounds us? He proves to us that it exists in nature. We see him cruelly strangle his bird and take pleasure in the poor animal's convulsions."

Destructive violence is one of the characteristics of Nature, and ensures her continuity. Although the excessive violence recommended by Sade may not be unanimously accepted, almost everyone more or less accepts the idea of this continuity that theoretically eludes death. Death is a notion cultivated by man that disappears in the overall plan of nature. Death is pure "imagination." Sade also says that "there is no death. . . . Death exists only figuratively; it has no reality. Matter, once deprived of the sublime portion of itself that gave it movement, is not thereby destroyed; it merely changes its form, it is corrupted." Therefore, movement is never completely eliminated in the cadaver, thanks to corruption. Sade was never tempted to work backward, from corruption to humanity, to play Prometheus; he was not sufficiently interested in the human, and preferred, as we know from his will, the transformation of the human into other forms of life: "She [death] provides nourishment for the earth, she fertilizes it and serves the regeneration of other kingdoms [i.e., animal and vegetable]."[56]

Many eighteenth-century thinkers would refuse to go as far as Sade and to recognize "the singular correspondences between physical excitement and moral deviation." On the contrary, they were to develop other aspects, which they found more tranquilizing, of the continuity of nature and the infinite work of destruction and re-creation. They would see the possibility for man of dominating this destructive force and making it beneficent by studying its laws and adapting himself to them. This is the "nature" of the philanthropists as opposed to the nature of the Sadeians. However, both have the same foundation, and the transition from one to the other is easily made.

The Sadeian tendency has certainly been more widespread than has long been believed, but in forms more socially acceptable and less aggressive. We find it in the new forms of satanism. The new Satan is the man who has espoused nature, like the monstrous creature of Frankenstein. The modern temptation tends rather toward the superman, the successor of Satan. For certain types of strong men who have understood the Sadean system of nature, there is no more "legal order"; everything is permitted. As Potocki puts it, "The satisfaction of his own desires must be his natural goal." They know that the virtues of the philanthropists are pure hypocrisy: "Religious piety, filial devotion, passionate and tender love, the clemency of kings, are so many affectations of egoism." Here man's encounter with nature takes place not on the level of virtue but on the level of blind and immoral omnipotence.

Love and Death

The omnipotence of nature asserts itself in two areas: sex and death. In our Western cultures, these two realms were alien to one another until the end of the Middle Ages. This incompatability is not a Christian phenomenon; sexual allusions are very rare in Greek and Roman funerary art, with the exception of the Etruscans. But after the sixteenth century love and death came closer together, until by the end of the eighteenth century they formed a veritable corpus of macabre eroticism. Almost everything else connected with death remained unchanged. The solemnity or simplicity of funeral services continued, amplifying traditions that were born in the heart of the Middle Ages. The change in the art of dying well through meditation on the melancholy of life, though real, was discreet and unobtrusive. The relocation of the cemeteries where the excommunicate and criminals were now accepted took place silently, without scandal or sensation.

It was in the depths of the unconscious, in the seventeenth and eighteenth centuries, that the disturbing changes occurred. It was in the world of the imagination that love and death came together until their appearances merged. This union took place, as we have seen, in two stages. At the end of the sixteenth century and in the first half of the seventeenth, the baroque era, a whole undiscovered world of emotions and fantasies began to stir. But the undercurrents that were created barely reached the surface of things; contemporaries did not even notice them. However, the distance between love and death had already diminished, and artists unconsciously tended to suggest resemblances between the two that had previously been unknown.

In the middle of the eighteenth century it was a whole dangerous and savage continent that emerged, bringing to the collective consciousness things that until then had been carefully repressed and that found expression in violent and destructive conceptions of nature. The breadth of this movement has been clearly perceived and analyzed by Georges Bataille, in a climate of surrealism favorable to its understanding.[57] Let us try, by way of conclusion, to interpret this great phenomenon of the imagination.

For thousands of years, *homo sapiens* owed his progress to the defense system he erected against nature. Nature is not some well-regulated and beneficent Providence, but a world of annihilation and violence that, although it may be judged more or less good or evil according to the tendencies of philosophers, always remains external, if not hostile, to man. Man has therefore set the society that he has constructed against the nature that he has controlled. The violence of nature had to be maintained outside the domain reserved by man for society. The defense system was achieved and maintained by the creation of a morality and a religion, the establishment of government and law, and the founding of an economy by means of the organization of work, collective discipline, and even technology.

This bulwark erected against nature had two weak spots, love and death, through which a little of the savage violence always leaked. Human society took great pains to reinforce these weak spots. It did everything it could to tone down the violence of love and the aggressiveness of death.

It confined sexuality by means of taboos, which varied from one society to the next but which have always tried to curb its expression, reduce its power, and prevent deviation. It even divested death of its brutality, incongruity, and contagious effects by weakening its personal quality in favor of the permanence of society, by ritualizing it and making it only one more transition in every life, only slightly more dramatic than the others. Death had been tamed, and it was in this primitive form that we found it at the beginning of this book.

There was now a certain symmetry between the two worlds of human society and nature. Both worlds were continuous; the continuity of society was ensured by the traditional institutions and codes of morality. They followed the same rhythm, and although they communicated with each other, their exchanges were limited by custom, and the traditional boundaries were seldom violated.

It was the role of holidays to open the floodgates periodically and allow the violence to enter for a while. Sexuality was another domain where, with great discretion, space was allowed for instinct, desire, and pleasure. In certain civilizations—among the Malagasy, for example—death was the occasion for a temporary suspension of the taboos. In our Western and Christian civilizations the supervision was more rigorous, the ritualization more constraining; death was better guarded.

Against this ceremonial background the first change appeared in the Christian West, or at least among its elites, in the middle of the medieval period. A new model appeared, the model of the death of the self. The traditional continuity was broken. Tradition had taken the edge off of death, so that there would be no break in this continuity. But in the Middle Ages, death was redefined as the end and curtailment of an individual life. The old continuity was replaced by a sum of discontinuities. It was then that the duality of the body and the soul began to replace the idea of the *homo totus.* The survival of the soul, beginning at the moment of death, eliminated the intermediary phase of sleep, to which popular opinion had long been attached. Once deprived of the soul, the body was nothing but a handful of dust, which was returned to nature. This idea had no great impact as long as nature was not attributed with a demiurgic personality rivaling God.

However, the substitution of a series of biographical discontinuities for the primitive continuity was not yet universal, and the ancient model of the tame death persisted. Consequently, the relationship between the order of society and the disorder of nature was not really disturbed until the seventeenth century. The defense system was still intact. It began to crack at the time of the great Catholic and Protestant religious reforms, the great purifications of feeling, reason, and morality.

The order of reason, work, and discipline gave way before the assault of love and death, agony and orgasm, corruption and fertility. The first breaches were made in the realm of the imaginary, which in turn opened the passage to the real. Through these two gates, in the nineteenth century, the savagery of nature invaded the city of man just as the latter was preparing to colonize nature by expanding the frontiers of technological advancement and rational organization. It is almost as if society, in its effort to conquer nature and the environment, abandoned the old defense system that had surrounded sex and death, and nature, which had apparently been conquered, surged back *inside* man, crept in through the abandoned fortifications and made him savage again.

All this was far from being actually accomplished by the beginning of the nineteenth century, but the distress signals were flashing. The fantasies of the marquis de Sade appear as portents of apocalypse. Very unobtrusively, but very effectively, an irreparable change had taken place in the ancient relationship between man and death.

9

The Living Dead

In the last chapter we saw how unclear the boundary between life and death was in the art, literature, and medicine of the seventeenth and eighteenth centuries. The living corpse became a constant theme, from baroque theater to the Gothic novel. But this strange theme did not remain confined to the world of the imagination. It invaded everyday life, and we meet it again in the form of the apparent death. In 1876 a doctor wrote that a "universal panic" had taken hold of people's minds at the idea of being buried alive, of waking up in the bottom of a grave. He was not exaggerating.[1]

Of course one must not confuse apparent death with dormition, the sleep of Barbarossa or Sleeping Beauty. When the girl in a French song is abducted by three captains, who intend to violate her,

> *The beauty fell dead,*
> *Never to wake again.*

But the three captains do not pounce on her inanimate body. Instead they complain, "Alas, my darling is dead, what shall we do?" The only solution is to carry her to her father's castle and bury her under the white rosebush:

> *But after three days*
> *The beauty rose again:*
> *Open the door, my father,*
> *Open now to me.*
> *Three days have I lain here*
> *To guard my purity.*

Nobody expresses the slightest fear about those three days under the white rosebush. But fear is the essential characteristic of the feeling aroused by the apparent death. This particular anxiety appears for the first time in wills around the middle of the seventeenth century. We can get some idea of the date of its appearance from this anecdote: In the middle of the sixteenth century a Frisian student had been buried in the Saint-Sulpice cemetery. The recumbent figure that adorned his tomb, no doubt a reclining one, had lost an arm. In the seventeenth century, people had forgotten that this arm had been broken, and believed that the mutilation of the visible tomb corresponded to some underground catastrophe. Sauval reports that the boy's tutor, who had been away at the time of his death, had the body exhumed upon his return, and that it was then discovered that the cadaver had eaten its own arm. The case is a classic of medical literature, but in Sauval's time it was believed that the young man had been buried alive.[2]

However, it was not until around 1740 that doctors seized upon the issue and began denouncing one of the serious dangers of the age.

The Rising Fear of Apparent Death

An abundant specialized literature took a new look at the old stories about the miracles of cadavers, hungry cadavers, and cries heard from tombs, and reinterpreted them in the light of what was known about apparent death. For a long time people had feared premature burial, and ancient wisdom cautioned prudence. The traditional rites of burial were really only so many precautions for avoiding premature burial. These precautions included not only the *conclamatio*—calling three times in a loud voice the name of the person presumed to be dead—but the customs regarding toilet, exhibition of the body, lamentation (the noise of which could also awaken the living corpse), the exposure of the face, the waiting period before cremation, and so on.

Some of these customs were still in existence at the time Jacques-Bénigne Winslow and his French translator Bruhier were writing. They observed that funerals were always accompanied by the demonstrations of mourners, and not only in the Mediterranean South; they had also seen them in Picardy. I might add that the *conclamatio* was still in use in the time of Tolstoi; the doctor called his name three times in the railway station where he lay dying. Even today, church protocol dictates that when the pope is on his deathbed, he must be called three times by his Christian name.

These ancient practices must have been abandoned under pressure from the Church, and this may have been the first time that the Church had to face the accusation, which was common by the end of the century, of lack of respect for dead bodies. "By what turn of fate did precautions as wise as those of the Romans come to be entirely neglected in Christianity?"[3] Winslow, who is the author of these lines, knew whereof he spoke. Hadn't he himself had two narrow escapes, once as a child and once as a young man, from the hands of impatient doctors and gravediggers?

The imprudence and negligence of those in charge of burial—the clergy—resulted in some well-known incidents, some of them contemporary, which the authors report, as Garmann had once reported the miracles of cadavers.

There are several kinds of cases. The least serious are those in which the "resurrection" takes place while the body is being transported to its place of burial. The daughter of an artisan, "after being taken to the hospital and judged dead, . . . happily gave signs of life while lying on the stretcher that was being used to carry her to her grave." "A porter who lived in the rue des Lavandiers fell sick and was taken to the hospital. He was believed to be dead and was taken to Clamart along with the other dead from the same hospital, where he was thrown into the same grave with them. He regained consciousness about 11 o'clock at night, tore off his shroud, knocked at the porter's hut, got him to unlock the gate, and went home."[4]

Sometimes humor was not forgotten, even in situations just as serious: "Ledran reported to Louis [a doctor interested in the same problem] that the late M. Chevalier, a Paris surgeon, contracted a sleeping sickness, in which he gave no sign of sensibility. He had been moved and shaken quite violently in every way without success. He had been called by name in a loud voice [the *conclamatio*] with no result, when someone who knew him to be a great piquet player had the idea of calling out the words *quint, fourteen, point!*, whereupon the sick man immediately came out of his lethargy."[5]

How many times did survivors notice nothing and unknowingly bury someone who was still alive? Sometimes a fortunate accident happened just in time to save the poor wretch trapped inside his coffin. The following story is not the observation of a doctor, but an incident related by a sort of gossip columnist who relished the scandalous, the unsavory, and the macabre. In Toulouse, a pilgrim from Saint-Sernin died "in a cabaret where he had stopped," and was taken to la Dalbade. "The body was left in the church until time for it to be buried. The next day a devout woman who was saying her prayers in the chapel [of the confraternity in charge of burial] thought she heard something moving inside the coffin. Terrified, she ran to summon the priests. At first they thought she was imagining things, but when she insisted that she had heard a noise, they opened the coffin and found the man presumed dead still alive. He made a gesture that they understood to be a plea for help. But everything they did for him was useless, and he expired shortly afterward. I saw this with my own eyes not a fortnight ago, and I tremble every time I think of it. For I fancied that they often bury persons who are still alive, and I confess that I would not like to have the same fate."[6]

Here is another doctor's story: "P. Le Cler, former president of the college of Louis-le-Grand, . . . told the following story to anyone who would listen. The sister of his father's first wife had been buried with a ring on her finger in the public cemetery in Orléans. That night a servant, attracted by the hope of gain, found the coffin, opened it, and, unable to slip off the ring, decided to cut off the finger. The violent shock that the wound caused to the nerves revived the woman, and her cry of pain struck terror into the thief, who took to his heels. But the woman struggled out of her shroud . . ., returned home, and outlived her husband," after first giving him an heir.

These stories made the rounds of town and court. "We must not be astonished, therefore," remark our doctors in 1740, "at the precautions that some people took in their wills when they instructed that they not be placed in their coffins for at least 48 hours, or until various tests had been performed on them with fire and knife to make absolutely certain of their death."[7]

Testators' Precautions

Beginning in the 1660s, as we have seen, such precautions become frequent in wills and testify even better than the observations of doctors to an anxiety that was widespread, at least among educated elites.

The earliest will in my sampling that reveals this preoccupation is dated 1662. "Let my body be buried 36 hours after my decease, but not before." And in 1669: "Let the bodies of the dead be watched until the day after decease."[8]

The first, and more usual precaution, was to provide a certain interval before burial. This interval was generally one or two days, but sometimes it was longer. In 1768 a noblewoman instructed "that after my decease, my body be guarded for three days before it is buried." Three days without any means of preservation could have been a long time.[9]

The second precaution was to be left just as one was, without being touched—dressed, undressed, bathed, or, of course, cut open—for a certain period of time, or even forever. In 1690 a testator requested "that I be left twice twenty-four hours in the same bed in which I shall die, and buried in the same clothes without being touched or handled in any way." And in 1743 another, "that upon her decease she be left 12 hours in her bed in the same clothes she is wearing and twenty-four hours after that on the straw." And in 1771: "I wish to be buried 48 hours after my decease, and during that time I wish to be left in my bed."[10]

The last precaution was scarification. This was less common, but became more frequent at the end of the eighteenth century. In 1696 Elisabeth d'Orléans instructed: "Let me first be scratched twice with a razor on the soles of the feet." And in 1790 a middle-class woman from Saint-Germain-en-Laye stipulated: "I wish my body to remain in my bed in the same state it shall be in at the moment of my death for 48 hours, after which I wish to be scratched on the heels with a lancet."[11]

Indications of anxiety continued to appear throughout the first half of the nineteenth century, although the references became less common in the more discreet wills. The 1855 will of Mathieu Molé, composed in the old style of the "beautiful will," states: "I wish my survivors, before burying me, to assure themselves of my decease by scarification and all the methods utilized in such cases."[12]

One realizes the persistence of this two-century-old obsession when one reads a speech delivered before the Senate of the French Empire on February 28, 1866, by Cardinal Donnet, archbishop of Bordeaux, a prelate who riddled his diocese with so many neo-Gothic steeples that he was jokingly accused of making it look like a hedgehog. "In a village that I served at the beginning of my pastoral career, I personally prevented two premature burials. The first victim lived for another twelve hours; the second returned to life completely. . . . Later, in Bordeaux, a young woman was thought to be dead. When I arrived at her side, the nurse was about to cover her face [the gesture denounced by all adversaries of premature burial]. . . . She became a wife and mother."

But what follows is more personal and more impressive. One can imagine the shudder that passed through the assembly; people in Bordeaux long preserved the memory of this extraordinary event. My mother, who grew up there, told me the story long ago: "In 1826, in a cathedral full of listeners, a young priest suddenly collapsed in the pulpit. . . . A doctor verified the death, and permission was given to bury the body the next day. The bishop was already reciting the De Profundis at the foot of the funereal bed, and dimensions had been taken for the coffin. Night was drawing near, and one can imagine the terror of the young priest, whose ear registered the sound of all these preparations. Finally, he heard the voice of one of his childhood friends, and this voice inspired him to make a superhuman effort, and brought about a miraculous result." The return to life was rapid and complete, and "by the next day he was able to mount the pulpit. He is among you today." It was the cardinal himself to whom this adventure had occurred when he was a young priest. My mother added that his hair had now turned white.

This powerful obsession was the source of the measures taken starting in the late eighteenth century regarding the supervision of burials. Today we would be inclined to attribute these measures to a concern for law and order, the desire to solve murders; but actually they were motivated primarily by the fear of premature burial. Even in the eighteenth century the bishops had imposed an interval of twenty-four hours, which was the interval generally requested in wills. There was no longer a risk of being disposed of a few hours after one's death, by nightfall, as happened formerly. In 1740 Bruhier proposed the post of inspector of the dead. In 1792 the decease had to be verified by two witnesses. A decree of the twenty-first of Vendémiaire, Year IX, advised, "Persons who shall find themselves near a sick man at the time of his presumed decease shall in future refrain from covering him and wrapping his face, removing him from his bed, and laying him on a straw or horsehair mattress, thereby exposing him to too cold an air."

Apparently it was necessary to overcome a certain reluctance on the part of doctors to get them to verify death. In 1818 the author of a sixty-volume dictionary of the medical sciences that still devoted a substantial amount of space to death wrote, "Doctors are rarely called in to certify death. This important responsibility is left to mercenaries or individuals who have no knowledge whatsoever of the human anatomy. When a doctor cannot save a man's life, he avoids being in his home after he has died, and all practitioners seem totally convinced of the axiom of the great philosopher that it is not seemly for a doctor to visit the dead."[13]

At the end of the eighteenth century there was a movement to establish "repositories" where bodies could be kept under observation until the onset of decomposition in order to be absolutely certain of decease. The plan was not carried out in France, but it was in Germany. These first "funeral homes" were called *vitae dubiae azilia* (shelters for doubtful life). There were examples in Weimar in 1791, in Berlin in 1797, in Mainz in 1803, and in Munich in 1818. One such establishment provided the setting for a novel by Mark Twain, who was fond of macabre tales. The arms of the bodies were attached to small bells, which rang at any unexpected movement.

Late-Nineteenth-Century Doctors

By the time legal steps were taken, the anxiety about premature burial was already beginning to subside. The case of Cardinal Donnet was already regarded as outdated; no one had listened to his heart. The doctors of his day contested the reality of apparent death and the danger of premature burial with as much authority and assurance as their predecessors of a century before had sounded the alarm and spread terror. In both cases the reaction took place in the name of positivist science against the superstitions of another age.

The article entitled *"Mort"* in an encyclopedic dictionary of medical sciences published in 1876 gives a historical survey of the question. The fabulous stories of the miracles of cadavers were still taken seriously by the generation of doctors of 1740, although they were interpreted as cases of apparent death. In 1876, however, they were regarded as idle chatter not worth considering. Although there had always been cases of reanimation, "it was primarily to the impetus provided by Winslow in 1740 . . . that the question of apparent death owed its popularity." The doctor-historians of 1876 recognize two great peaks in the prevalence of the obsession, one around 1740 and the other in the 1770s. The second peak coincided with the campaign to move the cemeteries out of the towns, and the same personalities took part in both movements. But none of this is serious in the eyes of late nineteenth-century doctors. "No chapter in medical literature is richer than the one regarding apparent death; but this wealth is often sterile." The eighteenth-century doctors are now accused of being garrulous and gullible: "Their science is encumbered with data accumulated uncritically and with tales inspired by imagination or fear." This was obviously true of the stories of Bruhier and his contemporaries. "A love of miracles is often associated with a vain desire to stir the emotions of the people. There is a great deal of mystification in the history of apparent death."[14] This amounts to saying that apparent death is not a real problem.

In a book published in 1883, a doctor named Bouchot criticizes Bruhier, Vicq d'Azyr, and other eighteenth-century doctors for claiming that the burial customs of ancient peoples were inspired by "the fear of being buried alive." Superstition denouncing superstition! The enlightened physicians of 1883 know perfectly well that these customs were "born of mysticism and superstition, and perpetuated by pride." They "attest more to the form of religious belief and the level of civilization of these people than to their fear of being buried alive." To be sure, "this fear prevailed for a long time in the world and in science," a science infected with philosophy and superstition: "for the doctrine of the uncertainty of death and the belief in stories about burial have always had a hold over certain minds," even scientific ones. "It is a rather widespread fear, and one that must be taken into account," but only in order to exorcise it. "I maintain that simply by paying careful attention, the physician will always be able to recognize death the instant it occurs." The author brings to this book the fruits of thirty-five years of study: "a guarantee of security in matters of burial."[15]

As a matter of fact, stories about apparent death did become increasingly rare, and even today when a corpse "comes to life" in the morgue of a hospital, the incident no longer causes a sensation. By the end of the nineteenth century, apparent death has lost its obsessive power, its fascination. People no longer believe in this form of living death.

Doctors and Death

In the seventeenth and eighteenth centuries, then, the calm surface of people's outward attitudes toward death was broken by a sort of upheaval. A formidable threat arose and then, after two centuries, subsided and disappeared. This monstrous anomaly is undoubtedly the first manifestation of the great modern fear of death. It was not widely exploited by the arts of evasion and illusion, as usually happens when a vast anxiety takes hold of the collective consciousness. When a threshold has been passed, one tends to remain silent. Society banished apparent death from the mirror in which it caressed its fantasies.

Consequently, our primary access to this obsession is through the eyes of doctors. Doctors are the new mediums, the decoders of the psychological mysteries of their time. As we have seen, there were three periods during which doctors were concerned with apparent death: the sixteenth and seventeenth centuries, the eighteenth century, and the late nineteenth century.

The doctors of the late nineteenth century, who spoke the language of today, rejected the idea that apparent death represented a real danger, seeing it as a superstition without experimental foundation or scientific validity. They did so with a passion that surprises us. This is because the debate over apparent death raised the possibility that death could be, at least for a time, an ambiguous condition. They did not accept the idea that there could be a state that partook of both life and death; it had to be one or the other. It was no more possible for death to have duration than it was for a geometric point to have density or thickness. *Death* was a vague popular expression that must be eliminated from the precise language of science in order to designate accurately the arrest of the machine, a concept of pure negativity. The concept of death as a state was intolerable.

For the doctors of the two earlier periods, the time of death was indeed a state that partook simultaneously of life and death. Death was not actual or absolute until later, at the onset of decomposition. By delaying decomposition, one delayed absolute death. Embalming and preservation of the body made it possible to extend this time of death as a state in which some characteristics of life continued to exist.

The difference between the doctors of the two earlier periods lies in the relative predominance of life or of death before actual decomposition. For the doctors of the sixteenth and seventeenth centuries, the period of uncertainty began at the time of apparent death and continued in the cadaver or mummy. Except in cases of accident, feigned death, ingestion of a sleeping potion, or magical dormition, it was unusual for death to encroach on life. On the contrary, it was life that encroached on death. Whence cadavers that bled, bit, or perspired, and on which hair, nails, and teeth continued to grow.

For the doctors of the eighteenth century, such phenomena are not necessarily absurd; it is the old interpretation that is foolish. In their opinion the encroachment takes place in the opposite direction: It is death that encroaches on life. The appearance of death sets in while the person is still alive. In the literature the signs of apparent death replace the miracles of the dead.

Apparent death was charged with the same existential anxiety that was aroused by the miracles of cadavers. The two forms of anxiety, the old and the new, meet in the eroticism of the macabre: the graveyard scenes and the kissing of mummies in French or Elizabethan baroque theater, not to mention the necrophilia of tales of medical and/or pornographic inspiration. The theme of apparent death also has a sexual aspect. Quite apart from what has been said here and in the last chapter, one cannot help being struck by the parallels between eighteenth-century medical views on apparent death and on masturbation. We are aware of the role of masturbation in medical literature, which saw it as the root of all kinds of physical, psychological, and social ills. Similarly, apparent death had become for other doctors the *raison d'être* of whole religions and the cause of considerable commotion. In both cases we recognize the same pretense of scientific objectivity and the same passionate desire for demythification. Neither is like an ordinary malady, or even a serious one like the plague, which can be discussed coldly, with the detachment of a man of science. In both cases we are in the presence of something else, something that arouses fear and that must be exorcised.

Sources of the Great Fear of Death

The doctors lose their composure as they approach the floodgates through which the chaos of nature threatens to invade the rational city of man. In the solitary vice and the "comatose" state, they discover sex and death in unusual and untamed forms, which they denounce with the conviction and authority of guardians of civilization. In both cases one senses in these men of science and enlightenment a rising fear: the fear of sex, which is beyond the scope of our discussion, and a more basic fear, which is the fear of death.

For until now, incredible as it may seem, human beings as we are able to perceive them in the pages of history have never really known the fear of death. Of course, they were afraid to die; they felt sad about it, and they said so calmly. But this is precisely the point: Their anxiety never crossed the threshold into the unspeakable, the inexpressible. It was translated into soothing words and channeled into familiar rites. People paid attention to death. Death was a serious matter, not to be taken lightly, a dramatic moment in life, grave and formidable, but not so formidable that they were tempted to push it out of sight, run away from it, act as if it did not exist, or falsify its appearances.

An even better proof of the calmness of the traditional attitude toward death and the improbability of its degenerating into panic is the alacrity with which clergymen exploited the germ of anxiety that was there in order to magnify it and transform it into a source of terror. They did everything possible to inspire fear, short of leading the faithful to despair, which was the most serious of temptations. It is obvious that no society could have resisted this pathetic appeal to terror, this threat of apocalypse, if they had really accepted and assimilated it. But Western society took what it needed and left the rest; the most rigorous moralists knew this, and took it into account when they increased the doses. From among the terrible images people took those that corresponded to their collective and secret vision of death, which the clergymen also felt spontaneously and expressed in their own way. In this literature on man's ultimate ends, which was actually popular and not merely imposed on them, people liked the consolation offered by the Church. They also liked the sense that everyone found there of his own identity, his own history, and the melancholy brevity of that history. On the other hand, they rejected the terror, or at any rate they disarmed it. This terror, was more of a didactic spectacle that brought about a few conversions and inspired proselytes and vocations among certain militant elites. It also deceived some people who took it literally, the most recent examples being the men of enlightenment and progress of the eighteenth and nineteenth centuries—and the historians of today.

When people started fearing death in earnest, they stopped talking about it, starting with clergymen and doctors; death was becoming too serious. We have already discovered this silent fear in the rhetoric of the doctors that succeeded the apocalypses of the clergymen, and in the discreet confessions it extracted from testators.

When a man or woman of Louis XIV's day instructed that his or her body not be touched, that it be left where it was for a specified period of time, that the sheet be pulled over the body after certain verifications by knife, one senses behind all these precautions the fear that lurked in a secret corner of the self. Man had been manipulating cadavers for thousands of years. Only the poor were sent to their graves more or less intact. To oppose these traditional preparations, there had to be very powerful reasons. Who knows whether the vogue of cemeteries of mummies, in which these bodies were exhibited to the public, did not reflect the same anxiety to escape the suffocating earth, the same fear of waking up some day buried under its weight?

It was a mad fear that the doctors of the nineteenth century denounced as irrational because it was abating but that, in contrast, the doctors of the eighteenth century had placed at the center of their nascent science because they felt it themselves.

It is curious that this fear appeared in an age when something seems to have changed in the traditional intimacy that had existed between man and death. The sense of the dignity of death, which had coexisted with its familiarity, was also affected: People play perverse games with death, even going so far as to sleep with her. A connection has been made between death and sex; the one has become as fascinating and obsessive as the other. These are the signs of a fundamental anxiety that does not yet have a name. Death remains restricted to the more or less forbidden world of dreams and fantasies, and the new attitude does not succeed in shaking the ancient and solid world of actual rites and customs. When the fear of death appeared, it was first confined to the realm where love had so long been kept under cover and at a distance, the world from which only poets, novelists, and artists dared to lead it forth: the world of the imagination.

The pressure must have been too great, and in the seventeenth and eighteenth centuries, the mad fear burst the confines of the imaginary and invaded the real world in feelings that were conscious and expressed.

But it did so in a limited and manageable form that did not extend to the entire myth, in the form of apparent death, the danger of becoming a living corpse.

Part IV

THE DEATH
OF THE OTHER

10

The Age of the Beautiful Death

"We live in an age of beautiful deaths," wrote Coraly de Gaïx in her journal in 1825; "the death of Mme. de Villeneuve was sublime."[1] *Sublime*—the word came naturally to Chateaubriand: "The paternal features had taken on, in the coffin, something of the sublime."[2] And the prevailing mythology liked to think of death as a desirable and long-awaited refuge "where one could eat and sleep and take one's ease." The traditional idea of repose was combined with other, more recent ideas of eternity and fraternal reunion.

"Rejoice, my child: You are going to die." Thus spoke the priest of a little village near Castres to a poor, sick man "lying on his bed of straw." And Coraly de Gaïx, who was with the priest, adds, "These words, which would have made a rich man shudder, almost brought a smile to his lips."[3]

Was this the momentary triumph of a Catholic reaction, an abnormal and morbid devotion? On the contrary, the *Encyclopédie* had blamed the clergy and the Church for concealing beneath its strange and frightening machinery the "narcotic sweetness" of death, and for changing its nature, a nature that romanticism would redeem and exalt.[4] "I would like to arm decent people against the specters of pain and agony of this final period of life, a widespread prejudice that has been so well attacked by the eloquent and profound author of the *Histoire naturelle de l'homme* [Buffon]. . . . One has only to ask doctors and ministers, who are accustomed to observe the actions of the dying and to hear their last thoughts. They will agree that with the exception of a small number of acute illnesses in which the agitation caused by certain convulsive movements seems to indicate that the patient is suffering, death is quiet and painless. And even these terrible agonies are more frightening to the spectators than they are painful to the patient. [Contrary to medieval and even modern tradition, the author tends to minimize not only the reality of the great suffering of the death agony but also the preparation for the moment of death, both of which might weaken his case for the sweetness of death.] . . . One would expect that in military camps the pangs of death would be terrible. However, those who have seen thousands of soldiers die in army hospitals report that their lives are extinguished peacefully. It is as if death slips a noose around their necks that does not so much strangle as spread a narcotic sweetness. Painful deaths are very rare, and almost all deaths are unconscious."

Unconscious, but not yet happy. Before death can be happy, it must be divested of the prejudices that distort it: "Did we not awaken these fears by means of these gloomy attentions and lugubrious ceremonies that in society [but not in nature, and more often in the town than in the country] precede death, we would not see it coming. [This is not yet the romantic dramatization, but it anticipates it.] . . . The fear of death is largely a result of habit, education, and prejudice. But profound terror is found primarily among persons raised luxuriously in towns whose education has made them more sensitive than the rest; for the common run of men, especially in the country, look upon death without fear. For the poor, death means the end of their troubles and calamities."

It is an important observation. Thanks to the Rousseauean myth of the corrupt town as opposed to the innocent country, close to nature, the man of the Enlightenment had his own way of expressing a physically observable fact: the striking contrast between a tradition of familiarity with death that was preserved in the country and among the poor, and a new attitude, more common in the towns and among the rich and well educated, which tended to magnify the significance and possibilities of death. We recognize here the two attitudes that I have called the tame death and the death of the self. But curiously enough, the man of the Enlightenment disliked, or pretended to dislike, an attitude that had, at least initially, been a phenomenon of the literati. And yet the preparations for death of the seventeenth and eighteenth centuries were intended to draw attention away from the final end and toward the life as a whole. The man of the Enlightenment was not interested in this belated and unobtrusive change; indeed, he did not notice it. In the urban way of death he saw the influence of priests and the triumph of their superstitions. He expressed the desire to recover the old familiarity with death that characterized the country. "Men are afraid of death the way children are afraid of the dark, only because their imaginations have been filled with phantoms as empty as they are terrible. The elaborate ritual of the last farewells, the weeping, the mourning, the funeral ceremony, the last convulsions of the machine that is breaking down: These are the things that tend to frighten us."

Of course, things did not take the turn that the author of the *Encyclopédie* seems to have desired. He would have been horrified if he could have foreseen the deep mourning and dramatic productions of the nineteenth century. Perhaps he would have been less violently opposed to the altogether modern prohibitions surrounding death. There are two tendencies in his thought: a nostalgia for the simple and familiar death of yesterday and a desire to taste the "narcotic sweetness" and the wonderful peace. This last idea was a product of the seventeenth- and eighteenth-century imagination, and would, in the romantic era, lead to a kind of baroque apotheosis that no baroque author would have dared to invent. In the beginning, and for quite some time, the romantic neobaroque did not present itself as a manifestation of Christian eschatology but, on the contrary, as a victory over Christian preaching and propaganda about man's final end. Thus, the Lamartine of 1820, the poet of "La Mort d'Elvire" who described with emotion the pious vigils and the kissing of the crucifix, made a distinction between the immortality of enlightened deism and that of clerical superstition:

> *Hail to thee, O death! Liberator divine,*
> *On me thou dost not turn that countenance malign*
> *With which fear and error have long invested thee . . . :*
> *Thy brow is not cruel, thine eye not treacherous;*
> *A merciful God sends thee to rescue us;*
> *Thou dost not destroy, thou deliver'st: Thy hand,*
> *Celestial messenger, bears an angelic brand. . . .*

And the next two lines might well describe some tomb by Jean Antoine Houdon or Antonio Canova on which the spirit of Hope and the allegorical figure of Grief accompany the deceased to a door that may open onto either a peaceful pastoral scene or a luminous beyond:

> *And the hope I feel musing on a sepulcher,*
> *Resting on Faith, discloses a world more pure.*

Here we are moving gradually away from the rejection of the medieval superstitions and rites of preparation for death toward the great liturgies of the romantic death:

> *What pious throng now welcomes me with tears?*[5]

The La Ferronays Family

Evidence of the romantic attitude toward death is abundant. Some of it is very well known, because it belongs to literature; some is not so well known. It is one of the lesser-known documents that I shall now examine at length: the correspondence and intimate journals of the La Ferronays family, which were published in 1866 by Pauline de La Ferronays, Mrs. Augustus Craven, under the title *Récit d'une soeur.* [6]

First a word about the family. The Compte Auguste Marie de La Ferronays was born in 1772 in Saint-Malo, like Chateaubriand, who called him "my noble friend." Thus, he was twenty years old in 1792. He emigrated with his father, a lieutenant general, and served in the army of Condé and at Klagenfurt, in the Austrian province of Carinthia, where the army was billeted. In 1802 he married the daughter of an officer, the comte de Montsoreau. (A sister of the new comtesse de La Ferronays had married the duc de Blacas.) He was a friend of the duc de Berry. He belonged, then, to a very royalist milieu, hostile to the Revolution. After the Restoration, the comte de La Ferronays embarked on a diplomatic career. He was made a peer of France in 1815, became minister to Copenhagen in 1817, and ambassador to Saint Petersburg in 1819. He won the confidence and friendship of Alexander I, who guaranteed him a pension (which was later paid to his widow), then became minister of foreign affairs in the cabinet of Martignac. The Revolution of 1830 found him ambassador to Rome. He did not return immediately to the France of Louis Philippe, but remained in exile as a point of honor, without, however, pursuing his political activities, except for one mission to Charles X in exile, to reconcile him with the duchesse de Berry after the unfortunate Vendée episode.

However, in this family so closely connected to the Bourbons, one observes no royalist enthusiasm. Among themselves they almost never speak of politics, except in 1848, at the end of the *Récit d'une soeur.* The count even regrets that his elder son, Charles, thought it necessary to leave the army after the Revolution of 1830 and the change of regime that it brought about. His other son, Albert, one of the heroes of the *Récit,* was, on the contrary, very well connected in liberal Catholic circles. He knew Montalembert, Lacordaire, Abbés Dupanloup and Gerbet, and the Italian Vincenzo Gioberti, which does not strike one as very suitable company for the son of the aide-de-camp of the duc de Berry and the brother of the future confidential agent of the comte de Chambord.

In their Russian and Italian exile the La Ferronays were converted to an exalted, baroque, ultramontanist form of Catholicism, or, as the Comtesse Fernand, wife of one of the sons, put it, Catholicism in "the Italian style." In 1899 this countess published a book of memoirs full of spicy details about her husband's family, whom she detested.[7] Not only did she have to endure the contempt of these nobles for an old family of lawyers that had long since bought its way into titled respectability, but she was also divided from them over the question of religious beliefs. One day, in a conversation in which they must have been discussing exceptional cases, she asked what was meant by a stigmatic. "A glacial silence greeted this imprudent question, which everyone pretended not to have heard."

The Comtesse Fernand was not a nonbeliever; she was a good French Catholic in the eighteenth-century manner. She called Mary Tudor the Bloody Queen, admired Elizabeth I, and regarded "Gregory VII and Innocent IV as the scourges of the human race. This is the way history was taught, and with a few modifications, I have not yet [around 1890] entirely recovered from this way of thinking. . . . I had been brought up by a father whose ideas were still influenced by the age of Voltaire, a fact of which he was totally unaware, and a mother whose sincere piety had an almost Gallican severity and did not allow her to approach the sacraments without careful preparation. In my husband's family things were quite different. By adopting the religious practices of Italy [in other words, romantic Catholicism], they had anticipated what has now become customary in France. Everything has changed in our country, even the form of religious worship."

We can imagine that the Comtesse Fernand was ill at ease in the exalted world of her husband's family. But it was not simply a matter of religious differences, as she believed; there were also profound differences in sensibility. Thus, when Pauline (one of the daughters of the comte de La Ferronays) who had inherited the journals and letters of numerous family members who had died, felt the need to collect and publish them, this publication struck the Gallican Comtesse Fernand as the height of indiscretion, if not indecency. "It is a book that has always irritated me profoundly. It seems to me that in baring to the public the intimate feelings of those whose name I bear, Mrs. Craven had done the psychological equivalent of forcing someone to stand on top of the column in the place Vendôme in his nightgown."

But Pauline did not share the modesty of the countess. She was erecting a "literary tombstone" to those she loved, whose memory she wished to perpetuate, and with whom she remained in communication. "Recollection of the happy days we spent together has remained for me a joy rather than a sorrow, and far from desiring oblivion, I ask heaven that I may always retain a vivid and faithful memory of the days that have vanished. . . . To think about them and speak of them has been a pleasure to me now that they are no more."

The *Récit d'une soeur* is the history, based on original documents, of an early nineteenth-century family that belonged to an aristocracy that was not only French but international. It happens that this history is a succession of illnesses and deaths, for the family was decimated by tuberculosis.

The curtain rises in Rome, in 1830. The comte de La Ferronays is forty-eight; he has been married for twenty-eight years and has had eleven children. Four have already died at an early age; their mother has piously guarded their memory, evoking it regularly long after their deaths. Of the seven surviving children, the last two are daughters who were born in Saint Petersburg when their father was ambassador there.

The first part of the *Récit d'une soeur* consists of the letters and journal of one of the sons, Albert, and his fiancée, Alexandrine, who soon became his wife. It is the story of their love, their marriage, and Albert's illness and death. Albert is a very intelligent and sensitive young man, without a trace of that aristocratic hauteur that was denounced by his future sister-in-law, the Comtesse Fernand. He does not espouse the political quarrels of his spiritual family. He feels none of the legitimist passions of his milieu, in spite of his loyalty to the elder branch. "Try as I may, I simply cannot get excited about these little party disputes. And should my relatives be forced to disown me for keeping such company [Belgian liberals], I am afraid that on that point I should have to resign myself to displeasing them." Imbued with the spirit of brotherhood and a touch of Saint-Simon, he believes that the railroads will "destroy national prejudices and hatreds" and spread "new ideas of unity. . . . The spirit of nationalism and patriotism, which is fine in itself but in which, from the highest point of view, one still finds egoism, will gradually give way to that spirit of union that, I am convinced, must one day reign over the Christian world." This gentle utopian dreams of an "association of [Christian] nations." He barely feels regret for these nationalities condemned to "disappear . . . in the society that is about to begin and within which everything will be united, simplified, and equalized." The vehicle of this transformation will be religion. "Religion, I believe, is the soul of our future, the final transformation of society. When our perfectibility reaches the end of its flight, we shall be restored to our first destiny: the dazzling purity, the white light of heaven."[8]

His fiancée, Alexandrine, was born in 1808. She is the daughter of the count of Alopoeus, a Swede by birth and Russian ambassador to Berlin, and a German woman. At twenty-two, she is a friend of the young La Ferronays ladies, especially Pauline, the narrator. Long afterward, in 1867, Pauline writes of Alexandrine, "Our friendship was one of those that nothing in life can ever change and that death itself cannot sever." We shall see that these words were not said lightly.

In 1831 the whole family is gathered in Naples, at the Acton Palace. "We spoke often of God and the other world," a subject that recurs constantly in their conversations over the years. In the same year the count of Alopoeus dies; it is the first in a long series of deaths. Alexandrine is now fatherless. She is very much affected. As a Lutheran, she must have some doubts about the salvation of her father, who has not, perhaps, led a blameless life. She prays to God that "she not have another moment's happiness on this earth, but that he be happy eternally." With every pleasure that she feels, this girl of twenty-three (born in 1808) exclaims, "My God, let me suffer in my father's stead." We shall see that her prayers were answered.

On February 9, 1832, Albert notes, "I spat a little blood. My throat was still sensitive following an illness I had recently in Berlin." The illness is not named, although it was already well known. A few days later, Albert meets Alexandrine, a friend of his sister. It is love at first sight. They stroll through the gardens of the Villa Doria-Pamphili, in Rome. "We talked for an hour, I think, about religion, immortality, and death. We agreed that it would be sweet to die in these beautiful gardens."

Since Alexandrine collects calling cards, Albert gives her his with an inscription: "How sweet is that immortality that begins in this world in the hearts of those who miss you." And Albert comments in his journal, "Singular and melancholy words, to be found in an album of frivolities." Since the inscription inspires ridicule, Albert removes the card and replaces it with a blank one.

One day Alexandrine opens a notebook of Albert's and comes upon this line of Victor Hugo: "I shall leave soon, in the middle of the ball." Then this remark of Jean Baptiste Massillon: "One fears death less when one's mind is at rest about what comes after." And finally, "I die young, as I have always wanted. I die young, and I have lived long."[9]

In June 1832, Albert writes to Alexandrine, "I swear to you that when I am with you, what I feel seems to be a portent of another life. How could such feelings not survive the grave?"

What is surprising is not the religious and mystical flavor but the concentration of religious feeling on death and the beyond, and the combining of this feeling with love. Alexandrine confides to her journal, "Oh! Death is always mingled with poetry and love, because it leads to the realization of both."

Death is now revealing an aspect of itself that we have not yet encountered in a conversation, however exalted: the infinite. The two friends are walking at Castellammare at sunset: "Oh, if only we could go where the sun is going! We long to follow the sun, to see another land. I am sure," writes Alexandrine, "that at that moment he would have been happy to die."

A year or so later, in 1834, he has the same inspiration, and writes: "Went riding. Overcome with joy while galloping on the beach. I often feel the desire to immerse myself in the sea in order to be surrounded by something immense." The need to lose oneself in an immensity: the immensity of death.

Their parents are a little worried about their friendship and decide to separate them to test its seriousness. They spend their last evening in the San Carlo theater. Alexandrine is so sad. "The room, the light, the stage . . . suddenly I felt as if I were in an illuminated tomb."[10]

Around them people are constantly dying, "carried away by a swift malady" whose name is never mentioned, and Alexandrine admits, "Until the last months of his life, I was in a strange state of blindness about his health." There is not the slightest medical curiosity, not the slightest confidence in medical intervention. The doctor looks after the patient but does not cure him; he changes nothing.

Albert has a new attack of fever, which his family attributes to the grief of separation. In fact it is leading up to a great crisis that overwhelms him in Civitavecchia, whence he was to have accompanied his mother to France. He sends her on alone to give him time to be bled. "This habit of being bled," Alexandrine writes much later, "which was so common and so fatal in Italy, was adopted all too eagerly by Albert. He often felt the blood going to his head or chest and resorted to this remedy without anyone's knowledge and without orders from his doctor." Pauline comments, "There was a rapid and violent inflammation, and the doctor announced that his life was in danger, and that the case was almost hopeless." It is his father and his two younger sisters who nurse this highly contagious invalid in the middle of an attack. "The fever was violent, the tongue dry, the cough agonizing. . . . Sauvan [the doctor] had performed extensive bloodletting (10 ounces of blood)." Mustard plasters are applied to his feet. "Dear friend," the comte de La Ferronays writes to his wife in France, "I cannot tell you what I felt when I saw our poor child being tortured this way."

At eight o'clock in the morning, the patient is bled again. "As I write, I am looking at this poor boy, who is so horribly altered. His emaciation is frightening to behold. His eyes are large and staring; they seem to be in the back of his head." Once again the fever rises; once again the patient is bled. At last comes the perspiration that indicates remission: "That blessed perspiration . . . became prodigious. . . . I really believe I could have drunk it, that healing sweat that saved our child." Confidence is restored:

"The doctors say that this terrible attack, at the age of twenty-one, will restore his health, and that if he takes care of himself, he will be better than ever and live longer."[11]

But Alexandrine has a premonitory dream in which Albert invites her to walk with his mother to a cemetery in the bottom of a deserted valley. All this is discussed in the home of the countess of Alopoeus, who finds Albert's health "rather alarming" but is much more concerned about his lack of fortune or career, not to mention his Catholic proselytism. It does not occur to any of them that Albert has not long to live. Their only fear is that his health may be delicate. It is after this terrible attack that the parents of Albert and Alexandrine realize how much they love each other and stop delaying their marriage. It takes place April 17, 1834.

Ten days after the wedding, Albert spits blood. Alexandrine appears unconcerned, but the seeds of anxiety have been planted. She is afraid whenever she sees a funeral procession go by, especially if the deceased is a young man.

On August 28, 1834, Pauline, the narrator, is married to an Englishman, Augustus Craven.

Albert has moments of lassitude when he feels nervous and irritable. "But who would not, after two years of treatments, sleepless nights, pain, bloodletting, and visits from doctors?"

As for the doctors, they think it will do him good to travel, and they send him from Pisa to Odessa. He coughs incessantly. He becomes a chronic invalid, without imagining—he who is so familiar with the idea of death—that he is doomed. His only fear is that he will never completely recover, that he will be sickly all his life, incapable of resuming his activities. As for Alexandrine, she is convinced that they must be patient for another five years, when Albert "will have reached the blessed age of thirty. . . . I think that then he will be handsome and strong, . . . and I shall be old, aged more by cares than by the years, and my health destroyed by worrying about him."[12]

For the first time she realizes the seriousness of the case; yet she still has no interest in identifying the disease, in naming it in order to know it better. There is nothing here that resembles our desire to know, or our fear of knowing, the diagnosis. She is indifferent, as if the science of the doctors were of no use to her. But in Venice the attacks become more frequent. "He speaks to me with effort, and tells me that we must send for a priest. 'Have we reached that point? Have we really reached that point?' I exclaimed." Only now does she want to know: "I asked the name of this horrible malady, I had to know. Pulmonary consumption, Fernand told me at last. Then I felt all hope abandon me." Fernand, her brother-in-law, knew, the doctors knew, but no one has said anything to her. She goes back into the sickroom. "I was in a kind of stupor, but I showed nothing. For several days I had been struggling to conceal my fears."

As for Albert, he is exhausted by suffering and longs for the final rest. "If in the tomb one feels that one is asleep, that one awaits the judgment of God [a curious reversion to the belief in a period of waiting between death and judgment], from which, even if one has committed great crimes, one has nothing to fear; then this repose mingled with vague ideas that are no longer the confusing ideas of earth, this sensation of having fulfilled one's destiny is, perhaps, preferable to anything that earth can offer. . . . The clue to the riddle is that I long for rest, and if old age or even death will give me that, then I shall bless them."[13]

He is afraid that he is going to die far from France although he has not lived there for a long time: "Oh, France, France, let me see you again, and I will lay down my head and die."

Alexandrine gives up all illusion. Her only wish is "that this dear angel may cease to suffer, he who has already suffered so much, and that all the joys of heaven may surround him and give him eternal bliss."[14] However, she is afraid of being alone with him when he dies.

She writes that sometimes "the expression on his face is so sad, it almost breaks my heart. But I must force myself to seem cheerful. . . . Ah! I cannot bear this secret between us, and I often think that I should prefer to speak openly with him about his death so that we could try to console each other with faith, love, and hope." This wish is to be granted. That very day he calls her to him and asks her to remarry after his death. Then he adds, "If I die, remain French; do not leave my family, do not go back to your mother." Having obtained her conversion to Catholicism, he is afraid that after his death her mother's influence might bring her back to Protestantism! It is true that he had offered his life to God for the conversion of Alexandrine!

He wants to die in France; so now a long voyage begins in which the dying man is moved in slow stages. On April 10, 1836, they leave Venice; on April 13, he is in Verona; on April 22, in Genoa; on May 13, in Paris. There, for the first time, a doctor warns Alexandrine "that it was mortally dangerous for me to sleep in the same room with Albert." It is about time! Everyone believes he is at the point of death. He holds out a few weeks longer.

"One day Albert suddenly threw his arms around me and exclaimed, 'I am dying, and we have been happy.' " Mass is said in the dying man's bedroom, and the Host is divided between husband and wife.

On June 27, Albert is given Extreme Unction by Abbé Dupanloup. The room is full. After the sacrament, he makes the sign of the cross on the foreheads of the priest, his wife, his brothers, his parents, and his great friend, Montalembert. "When he came to him, Albert burst into tears, which broke my heart. But he recovered himself at once . . . and motioned to the nun who was taking care of him to come forward, not wishing to exclude her from this tender and general farewell." On June 28, he receives the last absolution. We can imagine the length of this death agony. Alexandrine breaks down. "Unable to bear it any longer that we could not pour out our souls to each other, and wishing to take advantage of the few minutes I had left, I said to him, 'Montal has brought me your letters; they are such a joy to me.' He stopped me. 'Enough, please; don't excite me,' he said. . . . 'Oh, Albert, I adore you!' That was the cry that rose from my heart. I ached to talk to him, but for fear of upsetting him I had to remain silent. My lips closed over the last word of love they had uttered, but he heard it, as he had once wished, as he was dying."

During the night of the twenty-eighth, the patient is moved and placed so that he is facing the rising sun. "At six o'clock [he was now seated in an armchair near the open window] I understood that the time had come." The sister recites the prayers for the dying. "His eyes, already fixed, were turned toward me . . . and I, his wife!, felt something I would never have imagined: I felt that death was happiness."

Eugénie, Albert's younger sister, describes the rest in a letter to Pauline. "On the twenty-ninth, the day before yesterday, he was laid out on his bed. His face was calm. He seemed to be asleep, resting at last after all his trials." The beauty of the dead. "Yesterday he was laid in his coffin and placed in the middle of the room. We covered him with flowers. The room was fragrant." This custom of placing flowers on the coffin, or inside it, is mentioned occasionally in the sixteenth and seventeenth centuries. Sometimes flowers were also thrown into the grave. But before the end of the eighteenth century the references are too infrequent for us to attribute any ritual meaning to the gesture. After the beginning of the nineteenth century, however, the offering of flowers occurs repeatedly. Flowers are becoming an important element of the ritual.

"On the morning [of July 1] he was taken away. Alex and I [Eugénie] continued to pray by his coffin outside the door. Then both of us attended his service, concealed in a corner of Saint-Sulpice." They were concealed because, at least among the nobility, women were not allowed to follow the funeral procession or attend the service or the final absolution. The traditional proprieties decreed that they be confined to the house. By the early nineteenth century this practice was no longer limited to the aristocracy. The widow's name was also omitted from the notification of death, a survival among the nobility of a custom that had once been much more general. In Sicily, even today, the women of the house do not attend funerals.

In Paris in 1836, the La Ferronays women refuse to obey this law, which seems to them too cruel. Not wishing to create a scandal or even to appear to violate a respectable custom, Alexandrine makes a sort of compromise with the proprieties by attending her husband's service without being seen. After she returns home, she confides to her journal, "Hidden in the church, I saw and heard everything." And she writes this last farewell: "My dear friend! My two arms have supported you, one in your last sleep on this earth [just before his death in the early morning], the other in this sleep whose length I do not know." One is struck by the reappearance of the old image of sleep among these exalted Christians who hunger for heavenly reunions. We have already encountered this image in Albert, when he longed for his own death as a release from great suffering. Here sleep seems to signify a kind of peaceful purgatory, a period of waiting before the great reunions. "May God grant that after my death, these same two arms may open to you at our immortal meeting in the bosom of God, in the bliss of eternal reunion." This attitude of welcome appears commonly in statues of the dead on ordinary tombs of the nineteenth century.

She bares her soul at last in a long letter to her great friend and sister-in-law, Pauline Craven, who could not be there at the end. "I was able to see Albert's eyes go dim, I was able to feel his hand grow cold forever. . . . He died resting on my arm, my hand holding his, and I was not troubled for a moment when I saw that he was taking his last breaths, that he was in the death agony. I asked the sister whether he was still suffering, and she said no. So I let him go without regret, or so it seemed. [We must not take her too literally. This is not the serene resignation of the traditional attitude. It is neither rebellion nor resignation, but a deep mourning that has been so completely assimilated as to become second nature.] Very calmly, I closed those eyes, which were still sad, though devoid of sight and perhaps of sensation. Then, bending very close to his ear, I called the name I love so much: Albert . . . so that in that last obscurity, in that last dark passage leading to the light, he might hear my voice coming from further and further away, my voice, like myself, obliged to remain within these confines. . . . Perhaps he heard me, like a sound gradually dying away; perhaps he saw me, like an object gradually disappearing into eternity."

During the Mass, during the elevation of the Host, she has a kind of vision: "I closed my eyes, and my soul was filled with a sweetness equal to what I was hearing [the music of the organ; she was a very good musician, and music always accompanied her great moments of emotional and religious exaltation], and I saw (deliberately, you understand, there was nothing at all extraordinary about it) my own death. There was a moment of complete darkness, and in this darkness, I felt the presence of an angel. I dimly saw a kind of white glow, and this angel led me to Albert. . . . And our bodies were transparent and shone like gold." They were disembodied spirits.[15]

Returning to her journal again, trying to clarify her feelings, Alexandrine writes on July 4, "I wish I knew what is happening in me. It really seems as if I want to die." She who was so fond of life, conversation, music, theater, art, and nature feels "indifference for all the things of the earth. Cleanliness and water are the only things I still love." Cleanliness! That great virtue of the Victorian age, so deeply rooted that it has survived the general devaluation, along with God and love. The water of physical intimacy, the unlimited love of those who are dear to us, which demands everything of them and wants to give everything in return, death, which takes away but which also restores.

And yet, how great is the pain of his absence! "Sometimes," Alexandrine writes Pauline, "I feel a painful desire to get away from myself, to break out, to try somehow to recapture one moment of the happiness I have lost: his voice, his smile, his eyes." She retires to Albert's room. "There, I am at peace. Oh! how I wish I could die there!" And little Eugénie worries about what people will think of this deep, passionate mourning: "I hope God is not offended by this excessive grief," provided, of course, she remains a Christian! "To feed her is a consolation." The others cannot resign themselves "to seeing her sad for the rest of her life," but Eugénie believes that sorrow is henceforth the vocation of this young widow: "We can allow her a grief that will become more and more her nature."

However, there is still no peace for the remains of poor Albert. They are waiting in the Montparnasse cemetery to be transported to Boury, in Normandy, to the family château. The comte de La Ferronays is in charge of the operation: "We are now engaged in preparing the cemetery where, God willing, we shall all lie some day." Alexandrine will be buried there too. "Today this is our main preoccupation, the thing we talk about, the future for which we long. [Evidently the classical virtue of moderation was not a highly cultivated one among the La Ferronays!] For many people all this would be sad, but not for us. . . . Dear, good child [Pauline], when your mother and I are lying beside your blessed brother, you will come and visit us and give us your good prayers. And then one day—ah, yes! my child— one day, let us hope, your delightful dream will be realized in all its fullness." What delightful dream? Pauline explains it in a note. It was a dream about her own death: "One day I had written a sort of reverie [the La Ferronays were prolific writers: letters, intimate journals, etc.] about the other world, in which I described the infinite joy of being reunited with those one has loved on earth."[16]

At last the cemetery at Boury is ready. The carriage containing the body arrives one day in October with Alexandrine and probably M. de La Ferronays too. Eugénie writes Pauline, "At the cross that stands at the entrance to the village my mother and sisters were waiting. They fell to their knees at the sight of the carriage." The Abbé Gerbet, a great friend of Albert's, was also there "with the procession, followed by the whole village. The carriage was open. He blessed the coffin. Mama and Alexandrine kissed it." The kissing of the coffin takes us back to the fantasies of the late eighteenth century, the imagery of macabre eroticism. These kisses of a mother and a wife are devoid of apparent sensuality, but they do express a sense of physical proximity and, in the wife, a sense of the profound union of body and soul, of the whole being.

There follows a service at the church and the burial at the cemetery that has been prepared with so much care. Alexandrine "looked almost joyously at this empty grave" that was destined also for her. A single slab was to cover the two tombs, "for inside the grave, the two coffins would be touching, as our poor little sister had requested."

A few days later there was an extraordinary scene that would be incomprehensible if we did not recall all the stories, incidents from Gothic novels, and tales of apparent death and love in burial chambers. Here is the macabre eroticism of the eighteenth century, but real, sublime, purified, an eroticism from which the sexuality is either absent or repressed: "After the translation of the remains, the grave had been temporarily covered over with boards. Yesterday these boards were removed, and Alexandrine was able to carry out a plan she had conceived. I am telling you this in the strictest confidence [Olga, the next to the last of the La Ferronays children, to Pauline], for she has not told anyone for fear it will seem extraordinary. Well, yesterday, accompanied only by Julien, with the help of a little ladder, she went down into the grave, which is not very deep [this could still be some Ignatian spiritual exercise, like a meditation on a coffin or an open tomb; but what follows shows clearly that the act belongs to another sensibility, another religion], so that she could touch and kiss, one last time, the coffin that contains everything she has ever loved. As she did this, she was kneeling in her own grave."

Albert's tomb becomes, as the comte de La Ferronays puts it, "the object of a daily pilgrimage, in which we pray for him and ask him to pray for us." He is sixty, and the countess is fifty-four.

On the third anniversary of Albert's death, June 29, 1839, Olga writes in her journal, "Albert! Pray that I may die well. This tomb covered with roses made me think of heaven."

The account of Albert's death is finished, but he is not the only one to die. His great liturgical death is surrounded by a constellation of other deaths of friends, which are reported in some detail. We shall pass over them, except to note that they made it possible for Olga to write with a kind of satisfaction, "Everyone is dying young these days."

But life goes on. In 1840 Mme. de La Ferronays and Olga go to Gorizia to see "the king" (the compte de Chambord). Then the family returns to Rome, except for Alexandrine, who has remained in Paris to be with Eugénie, who is very ill, and her husband Adrien de Mun. But now it is M. de La Ferronays who dies. It is no ordinary death, of course, but one surrounded by miracles.

On Sunday, January 16, 1841, M. de La Ferronays dines at the home of the Borghese with Abbé Dupanloup. M. de Bussière talks of the presence in Rome of a man named Ratisbonne, Sainte-Beuve's executor, author of stories for children, and a Jew whom he hopes will be converted to Catholicism. The case of Ratisbonne makes a deep impression on the comte de La Ferronays. The next day, Monday, the weather is magnificent, and the count makes a pilgrimage to Santa Maria Maggiore, where in the Borghese chapel he says his regular daily prayers in preparation for death. In the evening he complains that he is "having his pain" (no doubt cardiac; this account is taken from a letter from Mme. de La Ferronays to Pauline). First the family sends for the surgeon for a bloodletting. Next come the doctor and the priest, Abbé Gerbet. The patient's condition grows worse, and Abbé Gerbet gives him absolution. The doctor announces that there is no hope, and everything happens quickly, although there is time for the farewells. "Farewell, my children, farewell, my wife." Then "he seized the crucifix that was hanging over his bed and kissed it passionately. . . . Soon the weakness came. I spoke to him, but he no longer heard me. I begged him to press my hand, but that dear hand did not move. . . . A few hours later, Adrien de Mun found me on my knees holding that dear hand tightly in mine. He must have thought me mad when I told him, 'I am fine, I feel so close to him, I feel as if we have never been so close!' " She spent the whole day "still holding his hand, which I warmed in mine so that it seemed almost alive."

It was a death that might have been like many others of this period were it not for an extraordinary event, a "veritable thunderbolt of grace," as one of the La Ferronays described it with the family's characteristic simplicity.

The Jew Ratisbonne, whose conversion the comte de La Ferronays had asked of God in his last prayer, had a spiritual revelation in Sant' Andrea della Fratte, at the altar beside which the tomb of his intercessor was being prepared. After his supernatural vision the neophyte's first words were, "This man must have prayed very hard for me." "What a tribute, dear child, to your good father, whose body was about to be brought into this church!" The dead comte de La Ferronays had thus been the instrument of Ratisbonne's conversion. We can imagine the transports of emotion this event inspired in the family. Even these indefatigable letter writers are at a loss for words. Eugénie writes to Pauline, "God has visited us. I am too overcome to tell you about it, but you shall know everything, all the details of what has happened and the glorious things that have surrounded us. Oh! Pauline, if only you were here to receive such consolation!"

But the family does not have long to rejoice over this extraordinary event. Another drama is about to begin: the death of Eugénie.

In February 1838, Eugénie had married Adrien de Mun. She was to be the mother of Albert de Mun (the great Catholic and royalist leader was named Albert in memory of his uncle, Albert de La Ferronays).

Eugénie kept a journal as a young girl and during Albert's illness. In it we see her obsession with death, her religious feeling, and her passionate love for her family. "I want to die," she wrote, "because I want to see you, my God! . . . To die is a reward, because to die is to see heaven. . . . If only I am not afraid at the last minute. My God! Send me trials, but not that one. All my life death has been my favorite idea, death has always made me smile. Oh, no, you will not let this constant thought of going to you abandon me at the last moment. . . . Nothing has ever been able to make the word *death* lugubrious for me. It is always there before me, light and shining. For me, nothing can separate that word from those two charming words, *love* and *hope*. . . . Shakespeare said that happiness was not to be born! But that cannot be, for one must be born in order to know and love God. No, happiness is to die." Such are the spiritual exercises of a girl not yet twenty. And yet she is not afraid of the world, and foresees that she might well play her part with passion: "If I were to become a nun who understood nothing of the world, I would never miss it. But also, who knows? Thrust into the middle of this same world . . . I might feel for it an attraction equal to my present aversion."[17]

Before her father's death, Eugénie gave birth to a second son. Tubercular as she was, she never recovered. Pauline begins to worry about her in far-off Brussels: "The shadow of a specific terror took the place of the vague uneasiness I had felt until then."

As usual, the doctors prescribe travel, and she is sent to Italy with her son and husband, where she witnesses the "miraculous" death of her father.

She suffers a relapse, and has a moment of rebellion that alarms the ever-vigilant Pauline in her Belgian observatory; but this temporary phase is soon followed by the return of a peace that is "unbroken by either the dejection of her soul or the suffering of her body."

On April 2, 1842, she leaves Rome for Sicily; the doctors have prescribed another "change of air." The family accompanies her as far as Albano. "After she had said good-bye to all the others, her baby was brought inside the carriage. Mme. de Bussière . . . heard her murmur as she gave the infant a last kiss, 'You'll never see your mother again!' "

On April 5 she leaves Naples for Palermo, a voyage that must have hastened her end. She tries to write to Pauline, but can go no further than the words "Dear sister of my life. . . ." Her death is swift and quiet; she is too weak to take part in the usual production. The marquis de Raigecourt, one of the witnesses—for there were always people present, even when the spectacle was short and improvised—wrote Abbé Gerbet, "This morning between seven and eight o'clock, I witnessed the death, or rather the glorification, of an angel. . . . She slipped away smoothly, effortlessly, in short, as quietly as she had lived."

And Mme. de La Ferronays, who in a few months has lost her husband and her daughter, concludes this new episode in the family history in a letter to Pauline: "I weep with you for all of us, for as for Eugénie, we need only look at her, glorious in heaven with her good father, and Albert, and the four little angels who have been waiting for all of us for so long."[18]

A year would not pass without another member of the family succumbing to tuberculosis. Albert and Eugénie had been the first victims; now it was the turn of Olga, the second to last of the La Ferronays children. After Eugénie's death, Olga had gone to live with Pauline in Belgium. The two sisters spent a few days at the seashore near Ostend. "It was there, on that dismal shore, on a day that I shall never forget, that, looking at Olga by the light of an ominous sky, I suddenly realized how much she had changed and was struck by the certainty that she, too, was going to die." The pallor of the face, the redness of the lips: Pauline is certainly becoming familiar with the signs; but in comparison with our clinical attitude of today, she is very slow to make the diagnosis or even suspect it. That very night Olga has her first attack, a violent pain in the chest. The sisters return immediately to Brussels, to the home of the Cravens. Olga takes to her bed and never leaves it again. She holds out for five months, "during which we lived through all the fluctuations of that horrible illness that, more than any other, tortures the heart with hopes and fears." One observes greater precision in Pauline in 1843 than in Alexandrine in 1835.

Like Albert, like Eugénie, Olga too has her moments of discouragement and despair. "At the beginning of her illness, she sometimes wept, but after the beginning of January [1843], that is, from the time when her condition became desperate, she never had a moment of depression or self-pity."[19]

On January 2, 1843, Olga writes Alexandrine, who has remained in Paris, to wish her a happy New Year: "I am weak, I cough, I have a pain in my chest, I am tired, I am nervous. . . . My dear little sister, pray that I may be patient and endure as long as God wills it. I have resolved to act as if I knew that I was going to die of this illness." No one has told her that there is no hope, and indeed, "the doctor says that I shall be well by spring."

Whereas in her journal Olga was always talking about death, the deaths of others and her own, when the time comes for her to die (it is true that she is scarcely twenty), she fails to realize it for some time. "One day when she was in the drawing room, when she was still able to walk downstairs . . . , she had been thoughtful for a long time. I had been sitting silently beside her, listening anxiously to her too-rapid breathing and looking at her face, which was becoming more haggard every day. Suddenly she said calmly, 'You know, I am really in a good position! Yes, it's true. For if I get well . . . I shall enjoy the spring, and the pleasure of feeling my strength return . . . and of seeing my dear Narishkins [her great friends] again. But if I die, this whole year we have spent [the deaths of her father and her sister Eugénie] and this illness of mine, and the plenary indulgences that I hope to earn at my death [Very important: It was to have time to earn them that the comte de La Ferronays, as soon as he realized that he was about to die, looked around for his crucifix and "tore" it off the wall], all this makes me think that I shall go straight to heaven.' After a moment's reflection, she went on with the same serenity: 'But after all, if I did get well, some day I'd have to suffer all over again. So that, since I've suffered so much already, since I've come this far. . . .' She broke off, and then went on, 'In any case, I hope that if someone told you, or if you noticed, that I were worse, you would not be so foolish as not to tell me so right away.'"

Olga composes pious verses. On February 3, she is given Extreme Unction. After that, Mass is said every day in the room next to hers, and she is given Communion.

On February 10 at ten o'clock, the agony begins, with the whole traditional liturgy. Here it is, as described by Pauline in her journal: "After the first moments of faintness and suffocation, she asked for a priest. Then she looked anxiously toward the door to see if my brothers were coming. After a few moments, M. Slevin (a good Irish priest who happened to be living with us at the time) began reciting the prayer for the dying. Olga crossed her arms on her breast and said in a low, fervent voice, 'I believe, I love, I hope, I repent.' Then, 'I forgive everyone, may God bless everyone.'" It is the traditional scene of the farewells and benedictions. Here the dying person is a young girl, almost a child; yet it is she who presides, with an authority and assurance born of long familiarity with these ceremonies. A moment later she says, " 'I leave my Virgin to Adrien,' looking up at the Virgin of Sassa Ferrata hanging by her bed. Then, seeing my brothers, she called Charles over first and kissed him, saying, 'Love God, be good, please.' She said more or less the same thing to Fernand, but more emphatically, adding a few words of farewell for the Narishkins." After the family, she takes leave of the servants. "She kissed Marie and Emma, and whispered a few words to them. Then she said, 'Thank you, poor Justine' [the chambermaid who had borne the burden of nursing her]. She kissed me [Pauline]. Then at last she turned to my mother, for whom she seemed to be saving her last kiss. Once again she repeated, 'I believe, I love, I hope, I repent. I commend my soul to you.' And then some inarticulate words of which the last—and the only one I understood—was the name of Eugénie. Père Pilat had arrived in great haste, and he pronounced the great indulgences associated with the scapular. Olga lifted her eyes to heaven and died. Her last gesture had been to kiss her little crucifix, which had never left her hand and which she had kissed at least ten times during this brief agony." She was still beautiful: "A radiant expression triumphed over the terrifying alteration of her features. She panted, but like someone who is winning a race." A few hours after her death, she was even more beautiful: "The most consoling transformation had taken place. All traces of the malady had disappeared. The room had become a chapel in which our angel lay sleeping, surrounded by flowers, dressed in white, and once again beautiful, more beautiful than I had ever seen her in life." She was buried in Boury.

A few years pass quickly for lack of sufficient deaths, for Pauline is interested only in death. Births and marriages are barely mentioned, as landmarks. But around 1847 her interest picks up, and we sense that new liturgies are being prepared: one pathetic and romantic, that of Alexandrine; the other more discreet and classical, that of Mme. de La Ferronays. The last event concludes this long series of six major deaths and several minor ones that have occurred in a period of a little over ten years.

Since the death of her husband, Alexandrine has been absorbed by pious works and devotions. She occupies a room in the convent where she lives. Soon, in 1847, she grows thin, she coughs, she chokes, she has attacks of fever. There is nothing surprising about the fact that she, too, has become tubercular.

In February 1848 she takes to her bed. Mme. de La Ferronays moves into the convent to take care of her. She writes to Pauline, "She speaks quite simply of her death. Yesterday she said, 'Mother, let us talk about it openly.' "[20] During the night of the eighth or ninth of February, one of the sisters awakens Mme. de La Ferronays: " 'The end is near.'. . . When she saw us, Alexandrine said, 'Do you think I am worse?' The sister said yes. A moment later Alexandrine went on, 'But what makes you think I am going to die? I don't feel any worse than usual.' The sister replied that she was growing weaker. I pressed her hand, unable to speak. She was calm. She spoke with difficulty, but she pronounced her words very clearly."

Today when the dying are suffering from thirst, their discomfort is relieved by intravenous injections of serum, but at that time one could only moisten their mouths. Alexandrine thinks they are trying to prolong her life and is worried, but they reassure her that they are only trying to make her more comfortable.

The moment for the public ceremony of death has come. "Albertine [the last of the La Ferronays daughters], Adrien, Charles, and Fernand had arrived one after the other. The prayers for the dying were said. She made the responses in a very clear, firm voice. . . . After we thought she had lost consciousness, she motioned that she wanted to kiss the crucifix. She stopped breathing at eight thirty. What an angel! She was reunited forever with her Albert, with all our dear saints, and it was for ourselves that we wept"—we who could no longer live without their presence.

The day before she died, Alexandrine had written two letters to those who were closest to her heart and who had been unable to come. The one that she still had the strength to write herself was addressed to Pauline. "I have longed to see you with all my heart, but what does it matter? We are never really apart, and soon I shall be in that place where we know the admirable unity that binds us all in God, and I hope I shall be able to look at you. But pray for me often when I am in purgatory [for there she will be cut off from communication with her loved ones, and will not have the power to look at Pauline]. . . . In heaven [where she hopes to go quite soon, thanks to so many good works, indulgences, etc.], where all is love, I shall love you even better, and we shall talk together, my dear ones and I. But, my God! I have not even mentioned what it will be like to see God and the Blessed Virgin." Indeed, it was time she remembered that, and this rather belated reference to the beatific vision shows clearly how secondary it was to her, and indeed to all of them, despite their strenuous piety. The true happiness to be found in paradise is the reunion of "loved ones."

The other letter, which she had to dictate, is for her mother. We will recall that Albert, on his deathbed, had made her promise not to go back to her Lutheran mother. Here we see the aggressive and fanatical aspect of nineteenth-century Catholicism. Both Catholics and Protestants were convinced that a conversion to the other side would deprive them of each other's company in paradise. The family does not dare openly condemn Alexandrine's mother to hell, but they are sure that Alexandrine has little hope of finding her in heaven. It is as if there were a clearly separated paradise for each confession, according to the best—and least likely—hypothesis. In this moving and cruel last letter from Alexandrine to her mother there is an underlying uneasiness about the difference in their religions and its effects in the beyond. "I hope that nothing will shake your faith in God. . . . We shall see each other again, we shall never be separated.

A row of Hapsburg sarcophagi in the Kaisergruft, the Church of the Capuchins, Vienna. "The visitor of today knows immediately that he is not in a chapel or a cemetery, looking at the visible and sterilized aspect of death. He is inside a tomb, surrounded by bodies. The coffins are lined up next to each other in rows" (page 335).

The Pantheon in the Monastery of San Lorenzo, the Escorial. Engraving by P. de Villafranca, 1654. This rendering of the domed burial vault shows three of the eight walls with their neat tiers of sarcophagi, each containing the bones of a king or a queen who had issue (page 334).

New England burial ground, Wakefield, Massachusetts. By the end of the seventeenth and beginning of the eighteenth centuries, the churchyard had become a "kind of meadow in which the minister's animals grazed and which bristled with headstones, many of them richly decorated" (page 339).

New England headstones. In America the winged cherub had "a flavor and intensity all its own; people had not forgotten that it represented the immortal soul. This explains why in eighteenth-century New England, where the meaning of death was changing, and the Puritans were belatedly ceasing to cultivate the fear of death, the winged death's-head was transformed into a winged angel's head by an almost cinematic process in which the face gradually became fuller and gentler" (page 340).

Brunhilde Watching Gunther Suspended from the Ceiling, 1807, Henry Fuseli. The attraction to certain ill-defined things at the outer limits of life and death, sexuality and pain, manifests itself more clearly in certain painters of the late eighteenth and early nineteenth centuries. Brunhilde, here, exemplifies this new emotion aroused by the dead body and the beautiful victim. "In the world of the imagination, death and violence have merged with desire" (page 369).

OPPOSITE ABOVE. The Ecstasy of the Blessed Ludovica Albertoni, 1671–4, Gianlorenzo Bernini, Church of San Francisco, Ripa. This statue, which recalls Bernini's famous Saint Theresa of Santa Maria del la Vittoria, exemplifies the mystical ecstasies of love and death (page 373).

OPPOSITE BELOW. The Martyrdom of Saint Daniel, 1592, Tiziano Aspetti. From the sixteenth to the nineteenth century, one observes a trend toward sadism as death expresses itself in a new form, macabre eroticism (page 353).

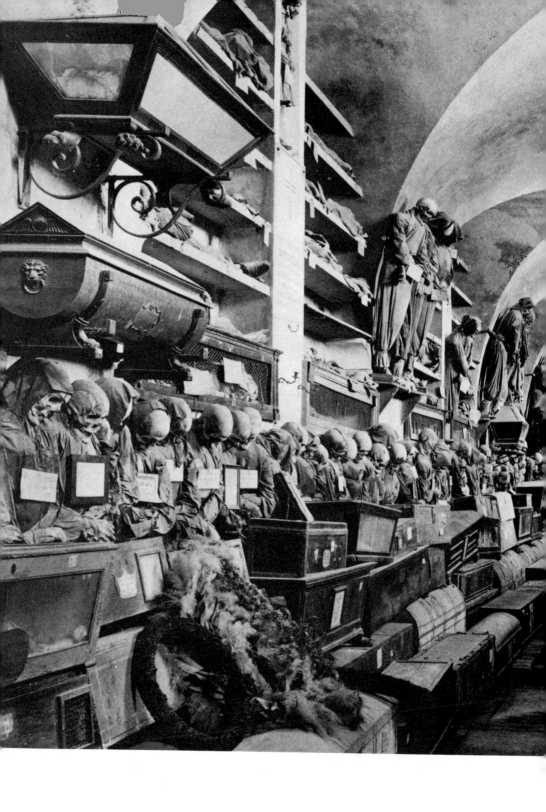

Catacombs of the Capuchin Convent, Palermo. There are certain cemeteries still in existence—in Rome, in Toulouse, and this one in Sicily—where the mummified bodies of the monks and laymen were placed in a charnel different from the medieval charnel of bones. Here the bodies were preserved intact for centuries, as a spectacle for visitors (page 383).

OPPOSITE. *The Tomb of Spurzheim, Mount Auburn Cemetery.* Engraving after a drawing by James Smillie, 1847. ABOVE. Alley, Père-Lachaise, Paris. The new cemeteries were places where relatives and friends liked to gather around the graves of their dead. Two models that were originally rather similar later diverged until they characterized two vast cultural domains. The idea was to create a new Elysian Fields, a rolling garden in which beautiful monuments were dominated by greenery. The cemetery should become a school of religion and philosophy, providing a sense of continuity, of perpetual home. In Mount Auburn, as in America and England generally, Nature retained its emotional power, and its connections with death are real and profound. In France, however, Nature gradually lost its impact and all emotion was completely absorbed by the monument. The park gave way to a "built-up" invasion of stone (pages 532–4).

Diederich M. Havemeyer monument, Greenwood Cemetery, Brooklyn, New York. As the cemetery becomes a museum of the fine arts, funerary monuments take on a social role. They are to be appreciated publicly, and one begins to observe structures with an embarrassment of classical and neo-classical motifs—urns, obelisks, wreaths, whole or broken columns (page 535).

BELOW LEFT. *The Little Margaret*, funerary portrait sculpted after a photograph, ca. 1900, Green Mount Cemetery, Montpelier, Vermont. BELOW RIGHT. *Pierrette*, Woodlawn Cemetery, The Bronx, New York. The tomb has turned into the scene of a physical presence, a place to remember and mourn. By the second half of the nineteenth century, portrait statues are becoming more and more common (page 526).

The Tomb of Raffaele Pienovi, 1879, Genoa. Some tombs are organized into actual genre scenes, with a woman saying farewell to her husband on his deathbed, an image almost unknown before the end of the eighteenth century (page 536).

Jane My Wife, Griffith family monument, Greenwood Cemetery, Brooklyn, New York. "The dead may reappear anywhere, but especially in the houses they have lived in and loved." This awareness of the presence of the dead among the living is translated into stone in nineteenth-century cemeteries. To one mourning father, the Reverend Cuyler, whose son was buried there, Greenwood was "simply a vast and exquisitely beautiful dormitory" (page 526).

But in return, you must very sincerely surrender your whole will to God. [Today we would call this spiritual blackmail.] I beg you . . . to pray every day to the Blessed Virgin. . . . Farewell, I feel a sweet assurance, and so, without any more pain, and above all, with the infinite happiness of no longer offending God. . . ." It is clear that the real motivation of their behavior is the possibility or impossibility of a reunion beyond the grave. Alexandrine dictated the letter in French, but with her dying hand she added, in German, "dear sweet Mama."

She was buried in Boury, and Mme. de La Ferronays writes, "The confraternity [a Norman charity] would allow no one to help them carry the coffin, and they did not leave her until they had laid her beside her Albert."

A few months later, it is the Revolution. The family fears a return of '89, and once again the former emigrés take the paths of exile. Albertine is sent to Baden "in the part of Germany . . . that the revolutionary tide had not yet invaded." Mme. de La Ferronays takes refuge with her daughter Pauline in Brussels. It is there that she will die on November 15.

Her case is interesting, because although she shares the sentiments of her husband and children, she has never completely assimilated them. The Comtesse Fernand, who detests her husband's family, sees clearly that her mother-in-law is not of their kind. "Sincerely pious all her life, she was far from having the intransigance of the recent convert that was so pronounced in my father-in-law." She even had a slight sense of humor, which was absolutely alien to her husband and his children, and which actually survived their life together. In the letter in which she tells Pauline the circumstances of Alexandrine's death, she reports that Alexandrine declared to her one day, " 'Tell Pauline how sweet it is to die!' Then another time, to me, 'And you, my mother, are you not also impatient to see God?' " Good Christian that she is, Mme. de La Ferronays is not so impatient: "And I, coward that I am, was seized with fear, thinking that she might perhaps take me with her, as she had tried to lure me to the catechumenate, and then on her retreats, and now here [the convent]. . . . I told her that I was not brave enough to pray for death, and that I was content to place myself in the hands of God and accept whatever he wanted of me." A pretty answer with an Erasmian ring, a breath of the seventeenth century amid this torrent of romanticism.

When she becomes ill, Mme. de La Ferronays takes to her bed. At first her condition is not considered serious. But after she has been sick for four days the doctor suddenly announces that her condition is dangerous, and "an hour later, desperate." Pauline is at a loss. "When she came from her bath . . . while I was wondering how to tell her what the doctor had said, she said to me suddenly, 'But I can't see anything anymore, I think

I am going to die, I think that this is death.'" This is natural; the traditional, matter-of-fact manner. She begins to pray: "My God, I give you my heart, my soul, my will, my life." Pauline is relieved. She has not reacted with panic as her brothers and sisters had, as reported in the letters and journals with both anxiety and discretion. Things proceed in the traditional way, with respect for custom.

"I knelt down and asked her to make a little cross on my forehead (that was her way of blessing us). She blessed me and Albertine [back from Baden] and told us, 'And the same for all the others, too.' Then she made the same sign on Augustus's forehead. I asked her to pardon me. . . . She added after a moment, 'I assure you that it is with great joy that I think of dying; but why, my children, haven't you sent for a priest?' We had already sent for her confessor, a frail old man who could not come until the next morning. 'Tomorrow may be too late,' said my mother." They decide to send a message to the vicar of the parish. "While waiting for the vicar, my mother explained a few little details regarding the disposition of her property [details that were once part of the will but that are now simply confided to the entourage]. Then she remembered that the vicar spoke nothing but German, a language she barely knew! 'But after all, I made my confession a few days ago!'" If we compare this serene, matter-of-fact manner with the exaltation of her husband and children, we realize the magnitude of the change that has taken place in one or two generations.

The priest arrives. He gives Extreme Unction. The sick woman is propped up in an armchair. "I saw on her face a great and solemn change, one of those changes that precede death. But this change was very beautiful. . . . After she was back on her pillows again, she said to me as distinctly and calmly as possible, 'Give me your father's crucifix.' She meant the one my father had held in his hands when he died." Oh, the crucifixes of the dead!

Thou whom I caught at her expiring lips
With her last breath and her last farewell,
Symbol twice blessed, gift of a dying hand,
        Image of my God . . .
One arm hung down from the funereal couch;
The other, laid languidly across her breast,
Still sought, it seemed, to offer to her mouth
        The image of our Lord . . .
Her lips half parted to press it once again,
But her soul had vanished in that heavenly kiss,
Like some faint essence that the flame consumes
Before the fire can burn. [21]

"My mother took it [the crucifix], and only then did her hand let go of a little case containing a portrait of my father that she carried with her always [the romantic love of the family historians]. She used to put it under her pillow at night, and had held it in her hands until this last moment. Now she took the crucifix and kissed it tenderly. [The moment no longer belongs to the *temporalia,* however legitimate, but to God. This is the old tradition of the *artes moriendi,* neglected by romantic Catholics.] Then she recited some prayers that she had admired at Olga's death: 'I would like to say what she said when she died.' " But death is slow in coming, and they begin all over again, starting with the scene of the farewells: "She turned to us and made the sign of the cross on our foreheads again, all three of us. She placed her hand on our heads and said, 'I bless you all, absent, present, old, and young.' Then she took the crucifix again, looked at it, and said, 'Soon.' " They repeat some ejaculatory prayers, the *Pater* and the *Ave.* But she is inexhaustible. "She said the *Credo* with me. Then she began it alone and said it all the way through to the end. . . . After this she dozed off, then woke up, a little agitated, saying, 'My God, my God,' as if in pain. We began praying for her again; she soon calmed down and listened to what we were saying. During the litanies of the Blessed Virgin she stopped speaking, but her hand continued to press Augustus's at each response until her dear life was extinguished peacefully in my arms." The *Récit d'une soeur* ends with the death of the mother.[22]

In these documents, which were not intended for publication but were written by individuals for themselves or for their brothers, sisters, parents, or children, one is impressed not only by the facts themselves but by the care taken in reporting them, the precision of the details. For the woman who brought them together, they are a treasury of memories. For was it not Alexandrine herself who said, "I make my home in the chamber of memory"?

Alexandrine de Gaïx

However original the La Ferronays family may have been, their attitude toward death was in no way exceptional. Here is another document almost contemporary with the *Récit d'une soeur,* but no longer from the cosmopolitan and ultramontanist milieu of the great nobility. This time we are near Castres, in 1824, with the Gaïx family. In her correspondence Coraly, who is twenty-four, talks about her little sister, who is ill, perhaps tubercular. We find the same indifference to doctors, but stated more bluntly: "We haven't much faith in the doctors." She does not mention the disease itself, except to say that little Alexandrine is suffering. The family address themselves to

God as often as to the doctors; there are Novenas and Masses in the local sanctuaries. In October: "We have written on her behalf to the prince of Hohenlohe in Germany [a Jesuit healer]. The newspapers are full of miraculous cures obtained through his prayers. I also have great faith in the Blessed Virgin. . . . But I am afraid my poor sister can only be cured by a miracle, and we are not good enough to obtain one."

Little Alexandrine knows that she is very ill. She is not in a panic; she even makes jokes about her condition. "Once when she was in the bath she had all her weight on her arms; her body was not touching anything. 'Look,' she said to me, laughing, 'I'm hanging on to the earth by a hair.' " She received Extreme Unction on the night of the sixteenth of November, 1824. " 'My child, it is a sacrament that heals the sick. Tell the good Lord to make you well.' When she heard these words, she turned to me with a serene face. 'I am not afraid of death,' she replied. 'If not for yourself, ask for your father, your mother, for us.'

"After the ceremony, 'Well,' I said, 'Did you deliver my message to the good Lord?' 'Yes,' she replied, 'I mentioned it.' Then, after a moment of silence, 'Father, let this cup pass from me, but if not, let thy will be done, not mine.' "

Coraly does not speak at once of tombstones or burial. She returns to the subject more than ten years later in some notes on the crucifix: the crucifix of clandestine Masses during the Reign of Terror, the crucifix of the dead of her family. "A few lines of a charming simplicity, written the day of her [Alexandrine's] first communion, told us her secret: 'I love the saints who died young,' she said. 'Dear God, let me die young like them.'

"She was fifteen years old when a long and painful illness, which she endured without a word [and without anyone noticing], took her from our love. . . . Yes, she was happy, there was always a smile on her lips, and when she was told that she would have to die, her face became radiant. . . . The next day, the body of our Alexandrine was carried to Saint-Junien by all the young girls of the parish. She was buried at the foot of the stone cross. A bare stone was placed over her grave. But this name that is not on earth is written in heaven."[23]

The Brontë Family

Ultramontanist reveries, you will say; the morbid elucubrations of women dominated by priests in the exalted atmosphere of the Holy Alliance. And yet we are about to encounter the same sentiments—just as exalted, despite differences of expression—in social, economic, and cultural conditions that are altogether different: a large family, like the La Ferronays, but poor, Protestant, even Methodist, very antipapist (and anti-French); a family of Protestant ministers living in a country vicarage buried in the moors of Yorkshire and seeing no one but priests and servants. Like the La Ferronays, the Brontës read and wrote a great deal, but whereas the countless journals and letters of the La Ferronays left no mark on literary history, *Wuthering Heights* is a masterpiece, and *Jane Eyre* a fascinating document. The parallel between the Brontës and the La Ferronays is suggestive. It would have been easy to use the letters of the Brontës to create a picture similar to the one I just painted with the documents of the La Ferronays. As a matter of fact, this has been done, although unfortunately not in permanent form. In May 1974 Raymond and Hélène Bellour did a remarkable series of radio broadcasts for France-Culture based on the youthful journals and letters of the Brontës; they were variations on the theme of death. I heard the broadcasts and was struck by the resemblances to the La Ferronays, even though the Brontës—at least Emily—also had genius. The comparison suggests the existence of an underlying cultural tendency, here deeply felt and spontaneous, which is about to become a commonplace.

The imaginative work of the Brontës takes us further than their family history toward the submerged part of the iceberg. You will recall that the life of the Brontës, like the life of the La Ferronays, was a series of deaths, of losing battles with tuberculosis. The mother dies, leaving six children. The eldest, Maria, takes the place of the mother, in spite of her youth; she is eight years old when Mrs. Brontë dies. In 1824 she goes to school with her sister Elizabeth. She contracts tuberculosis and has to be sent home, where she dies immediately. Little Elizabeth follows her the same year to the grave. This first series of deaths does not prevent Mr. Brontë from sending his other two daughters, Emily and Charlotte, to boarding school in 1825. They have to be sent home the following winter because of their health. Emily dies in 1848; she is followed five months later by her sister Anne. One finds the same series of dramatic scenes involving tuberculosis in the Brontës as in the La Ferronays.

All the Brontë children retained an extraordinary impression of their eldest sister, Maria. It is she, no doubt, whom they hear tapping at Emily's window on winter nights, like Catherine in *Wuthering Heights,* the pale ghost whom the terrified visitor seizes by the hand and cuts on the wrists. Twenty years after the death of Maria and three years before her own death, Emily evokes her memory:

> *Cold in the earth, and the deep snow piled above thee!*
> *Far, far removed, cold in the dreary grave!*

All my life's bliss from thy dear life was given—
All my life's bliss is in the grave with thee.[24]

And Charlotte Brontë is thinking of her sister Maria when she imagines the death of Helen Burns in *Jane Eyre*. Helen Burns is suffering from consumption. The headmistress of the boarding school where she is a student observes anxiously, but helplessly, the slow progress of the disease. No one thinks of placing her under a doctor's care; doctors were only called in the event of a crisis. One day the boarding school is struck by an epidemic of typhus. The author contrasts the swift epidemic with the slow consumption. Helen's condition grows worse. She is isolated both from the typhous and from the healthy, in the headmistress's room. Jane Eyre, Helen's schoolmate and friend (they are fourteen), is not worried: "By consumption I, in my ignorance, understood something mild which time and care would be sure to alleviate."

One day Jane Eyre questions the nurse who is taking care of Helen just after the doctor has been to see her. The nurse replies, without the diplomacy that we would expect today and that had already been used by the La Ferronays, "He says she'll not be here long." Jane Eyre realizes then that her friend is going to die. She wants to say good-bye to her before she goes: "I must embrace her before she dies." Time is short, and the students are not permitted in the sick girl's room. Jane waits until everyone is in bed, gets up, puts her dress on over her nightgown, leaves the dormitory, and slips into the room where the dying child is resting. The nurse is asleep. The scene is altogether comparable to the deaths of the La Ferronays.

> "I came to see you, Helen. I heard you were very ill, and I could not sleep till I had spoken to you."
>
> "You came to bid me good-bye, then: you are just in time probably."
>
> "Are you going somewhere, Helen? Are you going home?"
>
> "Yes; to my long home—my last home."
>
> "No, no, Helen!" [A fit of coughing interrupts the conversation. It resumes a few moments later. Helen guesses that Jane is cold.]
>
> "Jane, your little feet are bare; lie down and cover yourself with my quilt."
>
> I did so: she put her arm over me, and I nestled close to her. After a long silence, she resumed; still whispering:
>
> "I am very happy, Jane; and when you hear that I am dead, you must be sure and not grieve: there is nothing to grieve about. We all must die one day, and the illness which is removing me is

not painful; it is gentle and gradual: my mind is at rest. I leave no one to regret me much. [This is a real consolation; for if death is painful here, it is not because it deprives us of the pleasures and riches of life, as in the Middle Ages, but because it separates us from those we love.] I have only a father; and he is lately married, and will not miss me. By dying young, I shall escape great sufferings. I had not qualities or talents to make my way very well in the world: I should have been continually at fault."

"But where are you going to, Helen? Can you see? Do you know?"

"I believe; I have faith: I am going to God."

"Where is God? What is God?"

"My Maker and yours, who will never destroy what he created. [Like the La Ferronays, she has faith in salvation, and this belief, which allows no place for hell, is very far from that of the Puritans.] I rely implicitly on his power and confide wholly in his goodness: I count the hours till that eventful one arrives which shall restore me to him, reveal him to me."

"You are sure, then, Helen, that there is such a place as heaven; and that our souls can get to it when we die?"

"I am sure there is a future state; I believe God is good; I can resign my immortal part to him without any misgiving. God is my friend: I love him; I believe he loves me."

"And shall I see you again, Helen, when I die?" [That is the most important question for this age, for death has become an intolerable separation.]

"You will come to the same region of happiness: be received by the same mighty, universal Parent, no doubt, dear Jane." [She replies with a pious commonplace that evades Jane's question somewhat, I think. But Helen does not want to stray too far from the orthodox formulations. The La Ferronays were more naïve and answered more openly. But in spite of her reserve, Helen's underlying thought is certainly that heaven is a place of reunion.]

I clasped my arms closer round Helen; she seemed dearer to me than ever; I felt as if I could not let her go; I lay with my face hidden on her neck. Presently she said in the sweetest tone:

"How comfortable I am! That last fit of coughing has tired me a little; I feel as if I could sleep: but don't leave me, Jane; I like to have you near me."

"I'll stay with you, dear Helen: no one shall take me away."

"Are you warm, darling?"

"Yes."

"Good-night, Jane."
"Good-night, Helen."
She kissed me, and I her; and we both soon slumbered.

A few hours later, when the headmistress returns to her room, she finds Jane in Helen's bed, "my face against Helen Burns's shoulder, my arms round her neck. I was asleep, and Helen was—dead."[25]

This is not the great public liturgy of the La Ferronays. This scene is rare among the Brontës, those wild spirits. This is almost a clandestine death, but not a solitary one. A great friendship has replaced the crowd of friends, relatives, and priests; the last words come from the heart.

The death of Edgar Linton in *Wuthering Heights* is closer to the French romantic type, although it, too, is more discreet. The Brontës do not clutter the rooms of their dying; they prefer the intimacy of great exclusive loves. Edgar Linton has known for a long time that he is going to die, and everyone in the house knows it and accepts it. His daughter, Catherine (the second Catherine), is at last able to escape from the neighboring country house where she is held prisoner by her husband, so that she can be with her father at the end. This presence is a great joy to Edgar. "He gazed at his daughter passionately, he fixed on her features his raised eyes, that seemed dilating with ecstasy. He died blissfully, Mr. Lockwood: he died so. Kissing her cheek, he murmured, 'I am going to her [his wife, the first Catherine, who died giving birth to his daughter, the second Catherine]; and you, darling child, shall come to us!' "[26] An extraordinary statement in which a dying father anticipates the death of his daughter and looks forward to their complete reunion in the beyond. In this short description of a deathbed scene one finds the two essential elements of the romantic death: happiness and the family reunion. The first is the release, the deliverance, the flight into the immensity of the beyond; the second is the intolerable separation that must be compensated for by a restoration in the beyond of what has been temporarily removed.

Emily's poems, composed within the context of that family drama, contain both of those elements.

She was not yet twenty when she began to write verses that sound more like the work of an embittered old man:

> *We were not once so few;*
> *But Death has stolen our company*
> *As sunshine steals the dew:*
> *He took them one by one, and we*
> *Are left, the only two . . .*

This young girl is already surrounded by the tombs of her friends and relatives:

> *For lone, among the mountains cold*
> *Lie those that I have loved of old,*
> *And my heart aches in speechless pain,*
> *Exhausted with repinings vain*
> *That I shall see them ne'er again!*

And the memory of the dead keeps her awake at night:

> *Sleep brings no joy to me,*
> *Remembrance never dies;*
> *My soul is given to misery*
> *And lives in sighs.*
>
> *Sleep brings no rest to me;*
> *The shadows of the dead*
> *My waking eyes may never see*
> *Surround my bed.*

Memories too bitter to be a source of joy: They poison each day with regret and make life unbearable. The desire for death expressed by these doomed young invalids is not a literary affectation but a deep wound; not a personal wound but the accident of an age and a culture. I believe these witnesses who will die young and who know it:

> *Sleep brings no wish to knit*
> *My harassed heart beneath;*
> *My only wish is to forget*
> *In sleep of death.*

Death is therefore a joy:

> *Dead, dead is my joy,*
> *I long to be at rest;*
> *I wish the damp earth covered*
> *This desolate breast.*

And yet the joy of death is tainted by the pain it inflicts on those who remain:

> *But the glad eyes around me*
> *Must weep as mine have done,*
> *And I must see the same gloom*
> *Eclipse their mourning sun.*

But what happens to the dead? Are they abandoned in their graves? Do they live again, together, in a better world?

The faith of the La Ferronays never wavers. Emily Brontë does not share their disturbing certainty; she falters at the edge of the abyss. When she muses by the tomb of her eldest sister, the maternal sister,

> *Cold in the earth, and fifteen wild Decembers*
> *From those brown hills have melted into spring—*

"The world's tide" pulls her, tries to make her forget. But she does not forget. On the contrary, she has to struggle against the temptation of suicide:

> *Sternly denied its burning wish to hasten*
> *Down to that tomb already more than mine!*
> *And even yet, I dare not let it languish,*
> *Dare not indulge in Memory's rapturous pain;*
> *Once drinking deep of that divinest anguish,*
> *How could I seek the empty world again?*

Here "Memory's rapturous pain" is associated with the darkness of the grave. Elsewhere, however, she proclaims in a major mode her belief in survival far from that underground silence:

> *Oh, not for them should we despair,*
> *The grave is drear, but they are not there;*
> *Their dust is mingled with the sod,*
> *Their happy souls are gone to God!*

It is the classic image of Christian eschatology:

> *But I'll not fear, I will not weep*
> *For those whose bodies rest in sleep,—*
> *I know there is a blessed shore,*
> *   Opening its ports for me and mine;*
> *And, gazing Time's wide waters o'er,*
> *   I weary for that land divine.*

For this shore will be not only divine, but the scene of an eternal reunion:

> *Where we were born, where you and I*
> *Shall meet our dearest, when we die;*
> *From suffering and corruption free;*
> *Restored into the Deity.*

Alexandrine de La Ferronays, the year after her marriage, had copied into her journal these lines from Lamartine's *Harmonies:*

> *Let us pray for them, we whom they loved so well . . .*
> *Have they lost the sweet names of this world?*[27]

This question preoccupied these Catholic or Protestant Christians, and the traditional eschatology of their religion failed to provide the answer. This eschatology dated from a time when people did not feel the need to prolong beyond death the affections of life, which seemed too human for that state. By the time of the Brontës, however, people were afraid these affections would be lost in the infinite immensity of God.

Will the dead be deaf to our appeals?

> *Oh, no, my God! If the celestial glory*
> *Had destroyed all memory of this human plane*
> *You would have erased our memory too;*
> *If our tears for them be shed in vain*
> *Then let their souls be drowned in your breast.*

We concede that to theology, but for us that is not the essential:

> *But preserve our places in their hearts.*
> *They who once partook of earthly joy,*
> *Can we be happy without their happiness?*

Very ordinary sentiments, which Lamartine also summed up in this Racinian line:

> *Of all who once loved you, is there no one left to love?*

Lamartine, the La Ferronays, and countless other anonymous romantics who left nothing in writing found satisfaction in the assurance of a paradise of reunited friends. But Emily Brontë is uneasy on one point: In passing into a beyond, even one so "homelike," would those friendships lose the somber yet irreplaceable colors of the earth?

A very fine poem of hers expresses this hesitation, this visceral attachment to the loyalties of earth in this good Christian who believes in eternal life. The first image is a meditation on a cemetery:

> I see around me tombstones grey
> Stretching their shadows far away.
> Beneath the turf my footsteps tread
> Lie low and lone the silent dead;
> Beneath the turf, beneath the mould—
> Forever dark, forever cold.

The other image is the abode of the blessed, where there is a danger that the attachments of this world may be dissolved:

> Sweet land of light! thy children fair
> Know nought akin to our despair;
> Nor have they felt, nor can they tell
> What tenants haunt each mortal cell.

Then let each remain where he belongs:

> Well, may they live in extasy
> Their long eternity of joy;
> At least we would not bring them down
> With us to weep, with us to groan.

We, the living and the dead, continue to be connected to our mother, the earth, long after our death. How long? Perhaps until an event that is not named but that may well be the end of the world, the Parousia of traditional eschatology:

> We would not leave our native home
> For any world beyond the tomb.
> No—rather on thy kindly breast
> Let us be laid in lasting rest;
> Or waken but to share with thee
> A mutual immortality.

The archaic idea of sleep, the *requies* during an intermediary period of waiting, reappears here, reinterpreted, perhaps, in the light of seventeenth- and eighteenth-century speculations on living cadavers. But in Emily, this idea is in conflict with another idea that was more accepted, more popular in her time: death as an infinite abyss. It is an idea that was probably related to the idea of death as happiness, of losing oneself in the infinite abyss—of God? of Nature? It does not matter. What is important here is the almost physical notion of the infinite.

This notion was starting to become commonplace during the romantic era. It existed in the minds of the La Ferronays; we have already noted how Albert de La Ferronays was drawn by the immensity of the sea, which was a symbol of death, God, and happiness. In Emily Brontë we find the image of the sea with the same meaning.

The past is "an autumn evening," which the romantic poets also saw as the image of death. The present is "a green bough laden with flowers." Will the future be summer? No, the analogy of the seasons breaks down here:

> *And what is the future, happy one?*
> *"A sea beneath a cloudless sun;*
> *A mighty glorious, dazzling sea*
> *Stretching into infinity."*

There are other images of infinity besides the sea: the wind, the stormy heath, the fog, the night:

> *I'm happiest when most away,*
> *I can bear my soul from its home of clay*
> *On a windy night when the moon is bright*
> *And the eye can wander through worlds of light—*
> *When I am not and none beside—*
> *Nor earth nor sea nor cloudless sky—*
> *But only spirit wandering wide*
> *Through infinite immensity.*
>
> *I will be an ocean rover,*
> *I will sail the desert sea.*

Not in order to know them;

> *Nor ever let my spirit tire,*
> *With looking for what is to be!*

But to plunge into eternity:

> *There cast my anchor of Desire*
> *Deep in unknown Eternity;*

Then she will be able to—

> *. . . brave*
> *Unawed the darkness of the grave.*
> *Nay, smile to hear Death's billows rave.*

It is no longer a question of the dear departed ones. Individual deaths lose their meaning and become links in the great chain of being, an idea from eighteenth-century naturalism and biology that has been totally assimilated by this young recluse in her solitary world of moors, fog, illness, and death.

> *Strike it [time] down, that other boughs may flourish*
> *Where that perished sapling used to be;*
> *Thus, at least, its mouldering corpse will nourish*
> *That from which it sprung—Eternity.*

This brief comparison of the Brontës and the La Ferronays shows that the two series of deaths are very similar. In both we find the same intolerance of the death of loved ones, the same sadness of a life deprived of its affections, the same desire for and certainty of reunion with the deceased after death, and, indeed, the same admiration for the phenomenon of death, for its intrinsic beauty. We have also observed some differences: less interest on the part of the Brontës in the public aspects of death—the ritual at the bedside, the farewells, burial—and a special emphasis in Emily on the symbols and images of the infinite.

But the differences in details are minor. It is quite evident that we have arrived at a turning point in people's attitudes toward death. For centuries these attitudes had remained almost fixed, only slightly disturbed by minor changes that did not alter their general stability. And suddenly, at the beginning of the nineteenth century, within one or two generations, there is a new sensibility that is different from everything that has preceded it. It is the first time in the course of this inquiry that we have seen opinions and attitudes change so quickly. Such a rapid transformation in a psychological field so durable, a history so gradual, is a remarkable phenomenon that requires some explanation. Emily Brontë's *Wuthering Heights* provides the missing transition.

This extraordinary book belongs to two worlds at the same time. It is a demonic Gothic novel similar to those studied by Mario Praz in *The*

Romantic Agony,[28] but it is also a novel of the Victorian, romantic nineteenth century in which the most violent passions and sentiments do not seem to oppose conventional morality, but on the contrary conform to it, or pretend to do so. The difference between the immorality of the eighteenth century and the morality of the nineteenth century is not great, and perhaps it would require little effort to rewrite *Wuthering Heights* in the manner of Diderot or Lewis. But this little effort represents the fragile boundary between two sensibilities. Let us try to see how the transition from one to the other was made.

The hero of *Wuthering Heights* is a man of the late eighteenth century, a man of demonic romanticism, a rebel. He reminds me of the freethinking lawyer in Bellarmine's *De arte bene moriendi,* who dies as if he were leaving for his villa in the country. Heathcliff is picked up in the streets of Liverpool. He comes from out of nowhere; he has no name. One day he leaves, no one knows for where; he returns rich and powerful, no one knows how. He is dark-skinned, like the accursed children of Egypt or Bohemia. He lives among huge fires, like the damned, surrounded by ferocious dogs. He is cruel to human beings as well as to animals, without ceasing to look like a gentleman: "one with the flux of nature, child of rock and earth and storm."[29] The main theme of the book is the passion of Heathcliff, a character out of Satanic literature, for Catherine, also a creature of earth and wind, with whom he was raised as brother and sister.

Everything that has to do with sex is unstated without being absent. The word *incest* is never mentioned, and actually there is no real incest, but something that is alien to human morality, closer to the animal kingdom. One day there is a terrible scene provoked by Heathcliff in which Catherine collapses. Nobody has informed us that she is pregnant, nobody has noticed the fact that she is about to deliver, although it must have been obvious. But such things are not said, not even seen. She dies the day after giving birth to Catherine, her daughter by her husband, Edgar Linton, the village squire, a man of civilization as opposed to these creatures of the earth, Heathcliff and Catherine. When Heathcliff marries Isabella, nothing is said about their sexual relationship, but everything is arranged so that we can deduce it if we want to take the trouble. They sleep in separate rooms, but a child is conceived immediately after the marriage. The sexual aspect is clearly present, although very carefully concealed and never mentioned.

Everything that in an earlier novel would have been erotic, macabre, and diabolical becomes here passionate, moral, and funereal. The book is a symphony on the intertwined themes of love and death. In one episode we move imperceptibly from the macabre eroticism of the seventeenth and eighteenth centuries to the beautiful death of the nineteenth century. Catherine is buried not in the church but in the churchyard. Heathcliff is wild with grief. "The day she was buried there came a fall of snow. In the evening I went to the churchyard . . . all round was solitary. . . . Being alone, and conscious [that] two yards of loose earth was the sole barrier between us, I said to myself—'I'll have her in my arms again! If she be cold, I'll think it is this north wind that chills me; and if she be motionless, it is sleep.' I got a spade from the tool-house, and began to delve with all my might —it scraped the coffin; I fell to work with my hands; the wood commenced crackling about the screws." We recognize the scene: It is straight out of Gothic and Sadeian literature. We did not expect to find it in all its ambiguity issuing from the pen of this chaste daughter of a Methodist minister who had scarcely ever left her country vicarage. But the resemblance stops with this abortive exhumation, for Heathcliff goes no further, at least not this time: "I was on the point of attaining my object, when it seemed that I heard a sigh from someone above, close at the edge of the grave. . . . There was another sigh, close at my ear. I appeared to feel the warm breath of it displacing the sleet-laden wind. I knew no living thing in flesh and blood was by; but, as certainly as you perceive the approach to some substantial body in the dark, though it cannot be discerned, so certainly I felt that Cathy was there: not under me, but on the earth." This is the communication of a spirit: a new phenomenon, different from the appearance of a ghost. Formerly the return of a soul was a sign of misfortune or distress that had to be prevented by satisfying its demands by means of black or white magic. But here it is the spirit of the deceased returning to the one she loved, who is calling her.

"A sudden sense of relief flowed from my heart through every limb. I relinquished my labour of agony, and turned consoled at once: unspeakably consoled. Her presence was with me: it remained while I refilled the grave, and led me home. You may laugh, if you will; but I was sure I should see her there. . . . I looked round impatiently—I felt her by me—I could *almost* see her, and yet I *could not!*"

This marks the beginning of a period of torment for Heathcliff. He sleeps in the bedroom Catherine had occupied as a child, in the panel bed whose sides she had covered with graffiti. He follows her footsteps around the house. He believes that she is about to appear to him, he feels her presence, but just when he thinks he is going to catch her, she eludes him. He closes his eyes and expects to see her. He opens them again: nothing. Nobody.

Heathcliff is assured of the survival of the one he loves in the form of a spirit or disincarnate being. He has a sense of this presence, which he never succeeds in realizing, whence the ordeal of a futile chase after a phantom that is at once near and inaccessible. One has the impression of an authentic experience, a personal confession on the part of the author, who is remembering futile attempts to make contact with dead relatives. We have seen that her poems express an agonizing alternation between the silence of the tomb and the reunion or return of souls. Her hesitation is important to an understanding of the nineteenth-century mentality. The deceased is both in the tomb, where he has no longer really been contained since the early Middle Ages (when he was entrusted to the Church, to do with him what it would), and also at large, either in the heavenly abode, or hovering around the living, an elusive presence.

Heathcliff feels the same double attraction. On the day of Catherine's burial he closes the coffin again in order to follow her airy spirit, but in vain. Later he will return to the cemetery and reopen the tomb. An opportunity presents itself when Catherine's husband, Edgar Linton, dies. He is not buried in the church beside his ancestors but in the churchyard next to his wife. "I got the sexton, who was digging Linton's grave, to remove the earth off her coffin-lid, and I opened it." This time we find ourselves in the circumstances of erotic and macabre literature. Does he kiss her? The author does not tell us, of course, but it is quite likely that he does. And yet she has been buried for seventeen years. Amazingly, miraculously, she is intact. This is implied rather than stated. "I thought, once, I would have stayed there: when I saw her face again—it is hers yet!—he had hard work to stir me; but he said it would change if the air blew on it." So Heathcliff closes the coffin again and moves it away from her husband's coffin. He bribes the sexton to place his own coffin next to it on the day of his burial, which, he knows, will not be far off, so that "by the time [Linton] gets to us he'll not know which is which!" The dead return: Heathcliff, who believes in nothing, least of all in God, never doubts this. "Were you not ashamed to disturb the dead?" asks Nelly Dean, his servant and childhood companion, to whom he confides all this. "I disturbed nobody, Nelly; and I gave some ease to myself. I shall be a great deal more comfortable now; and you'll have a better chance of keeping me underground, when I get there." Indeed, if his demand is not met, he will no longer be the spirit who returns to be near those who miss him, but the accursed phantom who must be exorcised. Seeing Catherine's body again and having a moment of physical proximity with her restores his peace of mind. "Now, since I've seen her, I'm pacified." When Heathcliff dies, the two diabolical lovers will be reunited, not in the paradise of God and his angels, where they do not belong and have no wish to be, but under the ground, "dissolving" together. For there is a *miraculum mortuorum* here: After seventeen years underground, the body of Catherine is preserved. The village cemetery has the reputation of "embalming" corpses. It is a cemetery of mummies. Thanks to the peculiar qualities of this soil, Heathcliff was able to find the features of his beloved unchanged.

Things might have turned out differently. He could not have been sure of such a preservation when he opened the coffin. The servant asks him, "And if she had been dissolved into earth, or worse, what would you have dreamt of then?" "Of dissolving with her, and being more happy still [since that would be complete union; the eternal embrace]. . . . I expected such a transformation on raising the lid: but I'm better pleased that it should not commence till I share it." Catherine waited for him to join her in the ultimate rendezvous of mutual dissolution. While waiting for this last moment, Heathcliff goes into an ecstasy similar to that of the saints, a state that goes on for days. He has lost the reflexes of life: "I have to remind myself to breathe—almost to remind my heart to beat!" And finally, that, too, comes to an end.[30]

In the work of this young girl isolated in her vicarage on the Yorkshire moors but brought up on the literature of the eighteenth century as well as on folk tales and legends, we find a number of different attitudes toward death: There is the traditional image of rest and waiting; the temporary survival of the buried cadaver; the physical beauty of death; the vertigo that the plunge into death produces in the living; the lure of the infinite (another form of this vertigo); the idea of mutual dissolution in the endless cycle of nature; and finally, in the face of those desires that draw people no longer toward the motionless abode of God but into a perpetual flux, the only fixed point in this world adrift, the reunion, in a beyond that is not necessarily paradise, of all those who loved each other on earth, so that they may prolong their earthly affections for eternity.

The Letters of American Settlers

American historians have started to study attitudes toward death in their country, and their enterprise is of great interest. They have at their disposal an abundant documentation that in Europe either never existed at all or has disappeared: letters written to relatives to give news of the family and to inform them of births, marriages, and deaths. These letters are the work of the frontier settlers, often displaced persons who are poor and of humble origins but who know how to write, although the style may be clumsy, the spelling incorrect, and the punctuation nonexistent.

What attitude toward death do these letters reveal? Lewis O. Saum, who has analyzed them, has been struck by the frequency of accounts of deaths (much as historians of the late Middle Ages were impressed by macabre themes).[31] He has concluded that during the first half of the nineteenth century the American sensibility was dominated by death. While it is probably true that death was as important as he says, we know this from other sources; these letters do not provide the proof. On the contrary, they amply demonstrate the persistence, in the mobile American population of the time, of the ancient attitude of familiarity with death that was common to pagans and Christians, Catholics and Protestants, throughout the Latin West.

If there is a new element here, new enough to obscure the nature of the phenomenon, it is that in America the record of death is written rather than oral. This shift from the oral to the written must be the consequence of the mobility of the American population during the westward movement and the methods of long-distance communication that it imposed. Either the children had left or the husband had left the wife and children at home; brothers and sisters were separated for life and knew that they would never see each other again. Letter writing kept alive family ties that would otherwise have broken down. Most of the letters and journals are handwritten by their authors, not dictated to a public letter writer. But except for the use of handwriting, there is almost nothing about these letters that is not ancient and traditional, nothing that can be attributed to the innovating influences of the nineteenth century.

Saum cites the anonymity of small children as an example of the obsession with mortality. Lists of family names in order of age end with the youngest children. When these children are under a year old, they are designated as "anonymous," "not named," or "unnamed." But the anonymity of, or indifference to, small children is characteristic of all traditional societies, and these documents simply show that the attitude persists among the poor people of America. Here it is made even more apparent by the Protestant custom of not baptizing children at birth. But postponing baptism is one thing, not naming a child is another.

A similar effect is created by rhetorical references to the longevity of persons, including, of course, children. For example, when parents who have already lost a child announce the birth of a baby, they temper their joy with a conventional reservation calculated to ward off the worst: "But how long we shal be allowed to keep him is inknown to us." The author of an intimate journal begins, "Tomorrow I'm twenty-three, if I live." "If God grants me life," they used to say in old France. It is a way of acknowledging the certainty of death and the uncertainty of the time of its coming, of recognizing the familiarity of death, that old companion.

Saum remarks that in his documents the powerful moments, the ones shared by the most people, take place at the deathbed rather than at the grave. He is inclined to see this as a sign of thanatophilia. But these deathbed scenes are like the sickroom scenes of our wills, the crowded rooms of peasants that the hygienically minded doctors of the eighteenth century could not succeed in clearing, the rooms of the dying in the *artes moriendi*, which were gathering places for worldly friends. It was in the nineteenth century that the tomb and the cemetery came to play a new role in the ritual spectacle of death, a role that was added to the more traditional one of the bed. Under the circumstances is it any wonder that the solitary death, the *mors repentina*, was just as dreaded as ever? It was one of the great fears of the pioneers who left for the West. To die surrounded by friends and relatives was a satisfaction. But to be one of those surrounding the dying man, to be present at his death, was also a "privilege." The word is common currency. It was the duty of one of these privileged persons to be the indispensable herald of death, and sometimes he had to warn the unfortunate person in plain language. If the dying man understood the warning and accepted it, he was "sensible"; but if not, he was "very stupid."

Indeed, the dying man was expected to die well ("to expire mild-eyed"). Death was still a spectacle of which the dying man was the director, and performances varied in quality.

A son writes his mother, in an English full of mistakes, asking for details on the death of "dear old pappy." Not having had the privilege of being present himself, he wants to know how it went, what the old gentleman said, whether he played his part well (that is, accepted the situation), and what were his last words, for himself and for his family.

This death is traditional. And yet here, at the deathbed of the humble settler, there appears a little of the romantic dramatization we observed in the La Ferronays and the Brontës. It is interesting to follow in these accounts the transition from the traditional death of the man lying in his sickbed to the triumphant death that is a distinguishing characteristic of the romantic era. Sometimes the phrase *triumphant death* is used with the same apparent meaning as the *welcome death* of the seventeenth century. But the underlying meaning is not the same; it is the one we have come to know in this chapter.

An Ohio man writing back to Connecticut describes the death of his grandmother. The old lady showed "pleasing evidence of interest" in Jesus Christ, but it seems that she lacked enthusiasm; the "privileged" were not completely satisfied. "This is all we could have expected and nearly all we could have wished. We should indeed have been glad if her departure had been of the more extatic and triumphant cast." Here, naïvely expressed, is the difference between the traditional and the triumphant death.

M. Banassis, Balzac's country doctor from the same period, makes a similar remark. He shows his visitor into the house of a peasant who has just died. The body is laid out. There are a few tears, a few regrets, a few laudatory remarks, but not enough for Balzac, who was expecting more pathetic demonstrations. "Here, you see," he says, "death is an expected accident that does not interfere with family life." The exalted death requires that the routines of daily life be suspended out of feeling rather than for the sake of form.

Thus, we find triumphant deaths among the settlers of the 1830s and 1840s as well as among the romantic nobility and bourgeoisie. The romantic model is beginning to spread, perhaps with the rise of education and the art of writing letters.

In 1838 a couple from Indiana inform a brother of the death of their mother. It is a beautiful death. "I feel gratified to inform you that she left the wourld in the triumfs of faith, in her dying moments Jesse and myself Sung a Cupple of favorite hyms and She slapt her hands and shouted give glory to god and retained her senses while she had breath. [This last feature is beginning to be regarded as a privilege.] Which gave us all a great deel of Satisfaction to See her happy." Here is an American and popular but very faithful version of death in the manner of the La Ferronays.

And what of the hereafter? What was the view of these humble letter writers? The question is important, for we know the realism and exactitude of ideas about survival in the romantic sensibility.

Lewis Saum was struck by "the almost total absence [in his documents] of explicit references to otherworldly rewards or even to the assurance that, whatever they were, a particular person would enjoy them." People died "happy," "in the triumph of the faith," but they said little about the place where they were going, and sometimes even failed to mention that they were going anywhere. This may astonish the Christian of today or the observer who identifies Christianity with what it became after the Protestant and Catholic reforms of the sixteenth and seventeenth centuries, but it will not surprise us. In the traditional attitude nothing could be more natural or ordinary than the indefiniteness of the state that follows death, the vagueness of the abode of the dead. "Pore John," writes his sister in 1844, "could not talk to nun of us if he could he would have told us he was agowing home whare Christians are at rest." The "better world" is the one where the restlessness of the earth shall cease, where one is at peace. It is the very old idea of *requies*, reappearing in a very young country.

The new phenomenon of the eighteenth and nineteenth centuries will be the replacement of the ancient ideas about the beyond (the idea of repose, so general and so popular, and the later idea of the beatific vision, which was slow to gain acceptance and in fact never completely won over the masses) by a new and anthropomorphic image, a transference of the emotional demands of earthly life.

This image has both noble and bourgeois origins. The deaths of peasants in the French rural regions of 1830, if we had been able to record them, would have shown the same discretion, the same reserve with regard to the beyond as those of American letter writers. But in the educated American middle class, people who wrote and who read books, although without literary pretensions, we shall find the same sentiments that moved the La Ferronays and the Brontës and that Lamartine and Victor Hugo expressed as the common denominator of their age.

Consolation Literature in America

So we must turn to a different source. In the same anthology in which Saum's study appeared, another American historian, Ann Douglas, has analyzed the books of consolation published in America in the nineteenth century. Her contribution has the appealing title "Heaven Our Home."[32]

Most of these books were written on the occasion of the death of someone near and dear, usually a child. The authors were either clergymen or women who were the wives or daughters of clergymen. We shall be particularly concerned with the role of women, for it is an important characteristic of the age. Alexandrine, Pauline, Eugénie, and Olga de La Ferronays, Coraly de Gaïx, Emily and Charlotte Brontë: The sensibility of the nineteenth century may well have been molded by women, at a time when women had lost much of their legal power and economic influence.

The letter of condolence is a classical genre that was cultivated as much in antiquity as in the Renaissance and the seventeenth century and was related to the elegy, the literary tombstone, and the epitaph. In nineteenth-century America the genre, once intimate, became public, and the nature of the arguments, the tone, and the style changed completely. The titles are suggestive: *Agnes and the Key of Her Little Coffin* (1837), *Stepping Heaven-ward* (1869), *Our Children in Heaven* (1870), *The Empty Crib* (1873), *The Memorial of Little Georgie*. The authors of these books are obviously obsessed with the idea and images of death.

Ann Douglas quotes Oliver Peabody, author of a biography, or rather a hagiography, of his brother, the Reverend William Peabody, the minister, writer, and poet who died in 1849. Here is a specimen of his poetry:

> *Behold the western evening light!*
> *It melts in deepening gloom;*
> *So calmly Christians sink away*
> *Descending to the tomb.*

The death of the minister is beautiful in the romantic manner; he had a reputation for sanctity. In the last years of his life, he seemed already to be "standing on the confines of the eternal world, as one ready to be offered; permitted just before entering its gates to point out to those he loved, with the failing accents of a dying voice, the way to reach its blessedness." Here sanctity is related to an attitude toward death, and to its degree of exaltation.

In Lydia Howard Sigourney's *Margaret and Henrietta, Two Lovely Sisters* (1832), the author describes the death of Margaret, whose last words were "I love everybody." Curiously, as Ann Douglas points out, these same words of banal piety, uttered by this fictional character, will also be the last words of Mrs. Sigourney herself, on her deathbed. She had rehearsed her own death; she talked about it constantly. As a schoolmistress of twenty she urged her pupils not to miss future reunions even if "the voice that now addresses you should be silent, the lip that has uttered prayers for your welfare should be sealed in the dust of death." So much for the tone. She combined the idea of death with revelations about the beyond. In 1823 she confided to her listeners that during an illness she had reached the boundary of the spirit world, and had brought back solemn words of wisdom.

Sigourney and her heroines are reminiscent of another young girl from the same period and cut out of the same cloth, whom Mark Twain describes in *Huckleberry Finn.* [33] Destined to die at the age of fifteen, Miss Grangerford also thinks only of death. She has a talent for art and poetry. One of her paintings represents a veiled woman all in black "leaning pensive on a tombstone on her right elbow, under a weeping willow, and her other hand . . . holding a white handkerchief." Beneath the picture is the inscription "Shall I never see thee more Alas." This is a mourning picture such as existed in great numbers at the time. Painted, engraved, or embroidered, they were intended neither for the church nor for the cemetery but for the home, where they preserved the memory of those who had died.

Our young artist also paints genre scenes, provided the subject is death. In one of these a young woman at a window looks at the moon; she is weeping. In one hand she holds a locket that she presses to her lips and in the other (Miss Grangerford's figures always have their hands full) an open letter sealed with black wax.

After her death Huck Finn comments: "Everybody was sorry she died, because she had laid out a lot more of these pictures to do, and a body could see by what she had done what they had lost. But I reckoned that with her disposition, she was having a better time in the graveyard. She was at work on what they said was her greatest picture when she took sick, and every day and every night it was her prayer to be allowed to live till she got it done, but she never got the chance. It was a picture of a young woman in a long white gown, . . . with the tears running down her face, and she had two arms folded across her breast, and two arms stretched out in front, and two more reaching up towards the moon—and the idea was, to see which pair would look best and then scratch out all the other arms." Alas, she did not have time to make her choice.

Miss Grangerford has also been a poet since the age of fourteen. "This young girl kept a scrap-book when she was alive, and used to paste obituaries and accidents and cases of patient suffering in it out of the *Presbyterian Observer,* and write poetry after them out of her own head." She writes one poem about the death of a boy who died—not of whooping cough or measles or stomach trouble. No, such was not the fate of young Stephen:

> *His soul did from this cold world fly,*
> *By falling down a well.*
> *They got him out and emptied him;*
> *Alas it was too late.*

Indeed, "she could write about anything you choose to give her to write about, just so it was sadful. Every time a man died, or a woman died, or a child died, she would be on hand with her 'tribute' before he was cold."

After the death of this little prodigy, her room remains as it was at her death (like the red room of Mr. Reed in *Jane Eyre*). Her mother takes care of the room herself, and comes there to sew and read the Bible.

Although a fictional character, Colonel Grangerford's daughter is more real than life, in spite of (or perhaps because of) a touch of good-natured ridicule.

If death was simple and its triumph discreet in popular emigrant circles, it was pompous and rhetorical, but just as sincerely felt in bourgeois society.

The fascination of death was one of the wings of the diptych. The other was the heavenly home. According to a strange logic, death was cultivated and desired because it was a step toward the reunions of eternity. In heaven people found everything that made them happy on earth—that is, love, affection, family—without what made them sad—that is, separation.

After the death of his son, Georgie, the Reverend Theodore Cuyler published a book devoted to the memory of the dead child. He received thousands of sympathetic letters from grateful mourners, some of which he published in later editions. Ann Douglas quotes this one: "My dear sir, If it ever falls in your way to visit Allegheny Cemetery, you will see there a flower on *three* little graves: Anna, aged 7 years, Sadie, aged 5 years, Lillie, aged 3 years; All died within six days, and all of scarlet fever! It sometimes may reconcile us to our own affliction to hear of one still greater elsewhere."

Consolation literature proliferated, especially in the second half of the century, producing true stories and novels in which the authors, often women, try to convince their readers that death has not really taken away those dear to them, that they will see them again, either after their own deaths, or even here and now. Eunice Hale Cobb devoted a literary memorial to her dead child entitled *Memoir of James Arthur Cobb*. A little prodigy of piety, goodness, filial love, and macabre imagination, "Little James" hoped that his mother and he would die in each other's arms. However, he died alone, and his mother survived him but was haunted by his memory. She reports the marvelous circumstances of his death: He "enjoyed extended communications with the spirit world: he watched angels dancing in anticipation of his speedy arrival, saw various deceased members of his own family and relayed their messages back to the living. He was quite literally a medium and after his death he continued to appear to his relatives."

In this passage, as in a great many other similar ones, there are two remarkable ideas: the re-creation in heaven of the friendship of earth and communication with spirits. The first is quite familiar to us. A pastoral treatise of 1853 already describes the two aspects of heaven: the first, traditional in Christianity, the beatific vision; the second, altogether new, "our father's home, with . . . familiar homelike scenes."

In the 1860s and 1870s there was a desire to go further, an attempt to form a detailed picture of life in heaven. "The authors of consolation literature increasingly felt the need of 'some great spiritual telescope [this is 1870, a time of great technological advance] to bring [the dead] near to us in all their beautiful reality'; the need of a clear, consistent, philosophical authorized revelation of the life after death" (William Halcombe, quoted by Ann Douglas). Heaven now becomes the "home beyond the skies" sung about in hymns. (Meanwhile, in the Catholic churches of France the faithful were singing, "In heaven, in heaven, in heaven, we shall meet again.")

Elizabeth Stuart Phelps, a well-known popular writer who wrote *Between the Gates* and *The Gates Ajar*, describes in her books the daily life of the inhabitants of heaven: their eating habits, occupations, life-styles, methods of child care and courtship. She knows everything that goes on in heaven, thanks to the revelations of a doctor (or the spirit of a doctor) who visits her in a mysterious manner. In *The Gates Ajar*, an old lady sees heaven as a place where the soldiers killed during the Civil War chat with Lincoln, where some poor young girls have a piano of their own, and where her hair is no longer gray.

All this is not very different from the popular beliefs of Catholic Italy and France, which were rarely written down. However, perhaps because expression is freer without ecclesiastical censorship, the style in America is more naïve and crude, without nuance or nicety. The writers give free rein to their fantasies and do not hesitate to relate them as they see them, as they believe them to be.

The Rise of Spiritualism

A second idea appears very clearly in the account of the death of Little James: Little James is a medium. He serves as an intermediary between the living and the spirits of the dead, and after his own death he comes back to speak with his parents. This is out-and-out spiritualism, and it is no accident that spiritualism was born in America. There is no doubt that the desire to communicate with the dead manifested itself there earlier and with greater determination.

In the Catholic mentality of the time—in the writings of the La Ferronays or Lamartine—the survivor is content to cultivate the memory of the deceased. He does not go so far as to demand an actual apparition. Sometimes, however, the intensity of the memory succeeds in creating the illusion of reality. For the young Lamartine of the *Méditations,* is the appearance of Elvira a reality or a waking dream?

> *I dream of those who are no more,*
> *Sweet light, are you their soul?*
> *Perhaps these happy shades*
> *May glide among the groves.*
> *Surrounded by their faces,*
> *I seem to feel them near.*
> *If it be you, beloved ghosts,*
> *Far from the crowd and far from the din,*
> *You must return to me each night*
> *And mingle with my reverie.*

Doubt persists, but the apparition recurs. Lamartine goes further than the La Ferronays. Those orthodox Catholics resisted temptation and accepted the need to wait for death in order to be reunited with the departed.

> *But I hear footsteps on the mossy floor!*
> *A light breeze murmuring. . . .*

A breeze is one sign of the presence of a spirit.

> *Yes, it is you, it is not a dream,*
> *Angels of heaven! I see her again. . . .*
> *Your soul has crossed the boundary*
> *That divides the two worlds.*
> *His grace has permitted me to see*
> *What my eyes were seeking still.*

For Elizabeth Stuart Phelps, the dividing line no longer exists:

> *I lean above you as before,*
> *Faithful, my arms enfold . . .*
>
> *There is no vacant chair. The loving meet—*
> *A group unbroken—smitten, who knows how?*

These lines come from beyond the grave; they were dictated to Elizabeth by the spirits of the dead. She collected and published them in 1885 under the title *Songs of the Silent World*. Like all the works of Elizabeth Stuart Phelps, this anthology was a great commercial success. By the middle of the century the bourgeois beliefs that her books expressed had penetrated those popular circles already noted for their conservatism.

Saum reports nothing of this sort in his letters, with one interesting exception. The date is 1852. Ginnie dies in childbirth; she had lost another child the year before. She is not afraid to die; she is smiling sweetly. In short, the "mild-eyed death." But toward the end she hears children singing and recognizes the voice of little Willie, her dead child. Her husband, who has not read Mrs. Sigourney, thinks she is delirious. He tries to tell her that what she hears is only the voices of children playing in the yard. Husband and wife embody the total difference in attitude.

Disembodied Spirits

Jane Eyre, Charlotte Brontë's heroine, stands midway between the La Ferronays and the American para- or prespiritualists. She is more reserved and discreet than the Americans, but she does not conceal the fact that she believes in communication with spirits, living or dead, who are separated from their bodies. She calls them "disembodied souls."

Jane Eyre discovers one day that she cannot marry Mr. Rochester because he is already married and his wife is mad. When Mr. Rochester asks her to live with him in the south of France, she is tempted to become his mistress. She thinks it over one evening while gazing at the moon, that star of the dead and of ghosts that appears in all the paintings of Miss Grangerford. That night the moon presents an extraordinary spectacle, for it is swept by clouds, and suddenly "a white human form shone in the azure, inclining a glorious brow earthward. It gazed and gazed on me. It spoke to my spirit: Immeasurably distant was the tone, yet so near, it whispered in my heart, 'My daughter, flee temptation!' 'Mother, I will.'" This cannot be a memory, for Jane scarcely knew her mother; she never speaks of her. From the beyond her mother protects her. Just at the moment when this young Victorian daughter is in danger of losing her virtue, her mother intervenes like a *deus ex machina* and miraculously saves the situation.[34]

In the same novel there is another case of communication with spirits, but this time it is between the spirits of two living people who love one another and are separated by absence. Jane receives a proposal of marriage from a minister, a missionary who wants to take her to India. She is about to give in to his entreaties out of inertia, although she does not love him. It is midnight. Suddenly, she starts as if she has had an electric shock: "I saw nothing: but I heard a voice somewhere cry 'Jane! Jane! Jane!' nothing more . . . It did not come from out of the air—nor from under the earth —nor from overhead . . . It was the voice of a human being—a known, loved, well-remembered voice—that of Edward Fairfax Rochester. 'I am coming!' I cried, 'wait for me! Oh, I will come!'" She ran outside, but no one was there. "'Where are you?'" And at the same moment, a long way away, Rochester, who is now almost blind, alone, and in despair, is leaning out the window and calling, "Jane! Jane! Jane!" He hears the answer "I am coming, wait for me, I am coming," and a moment later, "Where are you?" It is a clear case of telepathy.[35]

There will be a great many more such cases in time to come. Indeed, by the beginning of the twentieth century there will scarcely be a family that does not have some legend of this sort: a terrible dream that comes at a certain time of night, when, it is later learned, a loved one died or almost died, and so on.

In order for death to appear as an absolute rupture, in order for belief in communication with spirits to spread, it was necessary for popular ideas about the nature of existence to incorporate the new conceptions. It took a long time for the popular idea of *homo totus* to give way to the idea of the soul as separate from the body. The soul then became the essential principle of the individual, his immortal part.

When Heathcliff hesitates between the opening of the coffin and communication with the spirit, his dilemma clearly expresses the ambiguity of this attitude. And in the next chapter we shall see the importance that was now attributed to the cemetery and the tomb. Alexandrine de La Ferronays does not open her husband's coffin, but she does go down into the burial vault. It is in the cemetery that the ancestors of the spiritualists, the first American authors of consolation literature, will most easily evoke the deceased. It is as if the dead were sleeping there and would awaken to answer the calls of the living. The site of the body would be a favorite haunt of the spirit. It is a conception that will be abandoned by the spiritualism of the twentieth century. Today those most convinced of the survival of spirits and the possibility of communicating with them usually feel nothing but disgust for the cemetery. As a place of meditation and recollection, they prefer the room of the departed, left just as it was. It is the end of the long episode that began in the seventeenth and eighteenth centuries with the partial survival of the body and the miracles of the dead.

But in spite of this important interlude, there was in the seventeenth to nineteenth centuries a rising belief in the autonomy of the spirit, a conviction that the spirit was the only immortal part of the human being. In rural France this belief was probably spread by the great Catholic missions of the early nineteenth century, which helped the priests teach the peasants the tenets of the catechism, including the existence of the immortal soul. The soul of the catechism was the forerunner of the "disembodied spirit."

These disembodied spirits are not bodies of flesh and blood; they do not obey the law of gravity; but neither are they pure spirits, unheard and unseen. Someday they will even leave impressions on photographic plates. They are imagined, even before they have been seen, as shapes clad in a luminous glow, gliding through the air. They have their own physical reality, although it is not yet known to scientists. Their features are recognizable, without being exactly those of the body abandoned to the earth. During earthly life they were inside the body; after death they survive it. They provide each individual with a visible identity that during earthly life is camouflaged by the flesh but that is changeless in eternity.

In *Jane Eyre*, Charlotte Brontë puts this ideology into the mouth of Helen Burns.[36] Helen has very decided ideas about religion and the future life that do not seem to coincide with orthodox Protestantism, and do not even refer to Christ or the Gospels. Helen is convinced of the unworthiness of the flesh. Sin is born of the flesh and will disappear with it. There will remain only "the spark of the spirit" (she says *spirit* rather than *soul*). The soul is indeed opposed, more or less, to the body, a constituent element of the individual along with the body and coinciding with it. Life requires the union of body and soul. The soul has some connection with the old conception of *homo totus*. The spirit, on the other hand, has expanded to include the whole being. It has filled the empty space left by the body. It corresponds both to the soul of Christian eschatology and to an aura around the body that is not completely immaterial.

For Helen, the spirit is "the impalpable principle of life and thought." It is as pure as it was at the moment of its creation by God, before original sin united it with flesh. The spirit is the noble part of the individual, the only part that will survive death. After death, the spirit will return to its source. In Helen Burns, and no doubt in Charlotte Brontë, there is no more fear of hell than there was in the La Ferronays (a suprising attitude to find both in Puritan England and in the France and Italy of the Counter-Reformation). Eternity is "a rest, a mighty home, not a terror and an abyss."

Helen professes absolute confidence in the blissful beyond, which she awaits, and this enables her to endure injustice and persecution on earth with tranquillity. Never has resignation been so active, as it were; never has Christianity so insistently emphasized the duty of passivity. In the Middle Ages, in the early modern era, the Church tried to reward the resignation of the unfortunate by the establishment of charitable institutions. But Charlotte Brontë, insofar as she coincides with Helen Burns, conceives of no alleviation of suffering on earth. These ideas are not exceptional; they were sufficiently widespread to provoke numerous protests and denunciations.

The paradise of Helen Burns resembles that of American consolation literature, but it is less naïve and more realistic. It is "an invisible world," "a kingdom of spirits: that world is round us, for it is everywhere." God is less important than the spirits themselves, "and those spirits watch us, for they are commissioned to guard us."

These French, English, and American texts provide an understanding of the ways in which all conditions conspired to promote the development of spiritualism.

The Roman church held out as long as it could against this invasion from the beyond. It did not even try to channel it into the new devotions, whose orthodoxy was now established. Of course, many Catholics died like the La Ferronays, with the conviction that they would be reunited in heaven with those whom they had loved and venerated on earth. Saint Thérèse of Lisieux hoped to find in paradise an exact replica of les Buissonnets with its inhabitants, its memories, and all the exquisite colors of her childhood. But the clergy generally remained very discreet and did nothing to encourage these ideas. They concentrated on the prayers for souls in purgatory, which were becoming a very widespread and popular devotion.

Neither these devotions nor the example of the mystics was enough to alleviate all the anxiety of separation. Many turned away from classical eschatology and undertook to construct, sometimes within the Church but more often outside it, and sometimes in opposition to it, an elaborate theory of survival and a technique for communication with the beyond: in short, spiritualism.

Maurice Lanoire has summarized the development of these ideas during the second half of the nineteenth century: "In 1848, the first séances were held at the Fox farm in the state of New York. The manifestations that occurred there are generally regarded as the birth of modern spiritualism. Comte Agenor de Gasparin, a former minister to Louis-Philippe and a Protestant, published a well-documented work certifying the reality of these prodigious phenomena. In 1852 Victor Hugo was initiated in Jersey by Mme. de Girardin and became a fervent adept of spiritualism when Léopoldine [his drowned daughter] manifested her presence."

It was also in the midnineteenth century in France that Léon Deni-zart-Rivail took the Celtic-sounding name of Allan Kardec when he became a spiritualist. "Theorist of the new revelation, to which he gave a religious character," Allan Kardec received the secret communications of everyone who was anyone in the other world. Camille Flammarion spoke at his funeral in 1868. Even today his tomb, which was recently restored, is the object of a cult. It is always covered with flowers. Pilgrims go there to pray, with one hand resting on the monument in order to receive the sacred emanation, as on the reliquary of a saint. One afternoon when I was visiting Père-Lachaise just as the cemetery was closing, a young woman dashed up, breathless, and demanded to be let in despite the lateness of the hour. She only wanted to go to the grave of Allan Kardec; it was obvious that this visit could not wait.

The religious aspect that was dominant in the beginning did not disappear, as is clear from the interest Gabriel Marcel took in these phenomena, but it declined in favor of a would-be scientific approach. Spiritualism, which was originally a religion of survival, the offshoot of a religion of salvation like Christianity, now started to become more secular. "In 1852," continues Lanoire, "Edward White Benson, who later became Anglican archbishop of Westminster, founded the Ghost Society in Cambridge. Its purpose was to study supranormal phenomena in an ambience devoid of any religious or spiritual assumptions and according to rigorously scientific methods. Then, in 1882, this Ghost Society adopted the definitive name by which it is now known throughout the world, the Society for Psychical Research, or SPR. . . . After that the line was clearly drawn between spiritualism proper and the new science that Charles Richet [a famous French physician] some twenty years later was to baptize psychics and that today is more often known as parapsychology." An agnostic science of so-called supranormal phenomena that was moving away from eschatological questions was no longer interested in the exploration of paradise.

In spite of this secularization, the idea of the transcendence of death and the expectation of the happy reunions that will follow it have remained a fertile subject of research. In his work on premonition, Richet cites a case very similar to those encountered earlier in American consolation literature. The subject is a little girl of three. "A month after the death of an aunt who adored her, she went to the window and looked out fixedly, saying, 'Mama, there is Aunt Lili calling me.' The incident recurred several times. Three months later, the child fell sick. She told her mother, 'Don't cry, mama, my Aunt Lili is calling me. How pretty it is! There are angels with her!' The poor child died four and a half months after her aunt." And upon reflection, the psychic physician is brought back to the miracles of the dead: "In vain do I call upon all my rationalism; it seems impossible to deny the presence, at the moment of death or before it, of supernatural beings, phantoms possessing some objective reality. It is true that these phantoms are seen only by a child and not by the other persons present. [In the American documents collected by Ann Douglas, the subjects are almost always children. In middle-class circles in the nineteenth century, the death of the child has become the least tolerable of all deaths.] But there is nothing absurd in the assumption that children who are about to die and are in a sort of mediumistic coma are able to perceive beings whom the other persons present do not see."[37]

In the beautiful death of the nineteenth and twentieth centuries, the room of the dying man is filled with disembodied friends and relatives who have come from the other world to assist and guide him in this first migration. If we compare this image with the engravings in the *artes moriendi* of the fifteenth century or even in the *Miroir de l'âme pécheresse* of the eighteenth century, we can assess the sentimental and psychological revolution that has occurred in the interval.

Commemorative Jewelry

Not everyone was a medium. Not everyone went so far in their representations of survival as the American and English spiritualists or paraspiritualists; not everyone shared the exaltation of the La Ferronays. However, there was probably almost no one in the nineteenth century who was not sooner or later somehow affected by the new feeling of intolerance for the death of another, and who did not show it.

In the Victoria and Albert Museum, in London, there is a remarkable collection of jewelry. One whole display case is devoted to funerary or commemorative jewels. This series, which includes objects from the late sixteenth century to the late nineteenth century, allows us to trace an evolution that starts with the *memento mori* and ends with the souvenir. The oldest object, dating from the Elizabethan era, is a small gold coffin the size of a snuffbox and containing a silver skeleton. It is a portable *memento mori*, but a rather unwieldly one. The sight of it was supposed to inspire meditation. It is altogether in keeping with the tradition of the treatises on preparation for death.

The next example, like all the other items of the series, is not a bulky portable object, but a real jewel. It is a pendant in the shape of a tiny gold coffin filled with hair. On its lid in microscopic letters is engraved the inscription *"P. B. obiit ye 1703 Aged 54 ye."*

Within a century the coffin acquired a new function simply by becoming smaller. The first contained a skeleton and served as a reminder of our mortal condition; the second contained the hair of a dead loved one and served to guard his memory as well as to preserve a fragment of his body. The *memento mori* has become a *memento illius,* a request to remember the deceased in one's prayers.

Another miniature from the same period has the same double function. It represents a tomb with two levels. Below is a stone slab on which a skeleton is lying in the attitude of the recumbent figure; above, two angels are carrying to heaven a medallion on which, for lack of space, the portrait has been replaced by initials. The background is made of woven human hair. The skeleton belongs to the *memento mori,* all the rest to the *memento illius.*

These two jewels, which date from the very beginning of the eighteenth century, are unique in their genre. But a large number of other eighteenth-century jewels offer variations on another model. The subject is also a miniature tomb—not, this time, an interior monument calculated to inspire *contemptus mundi,* but a tomb in nature: a stele or funerary urn in the classical style. Beside it sits a weeping woman accompanied by a child or a small dog; above, a branch of weeping willow. We recognize the mourning picture reduced to the dimensions of a miniature. The background and certain elements of the landscape are made of hair.

The theme is still the tomb, but a tomb with a different appearance and function. It is a commemorative monument, to be visited as one visits a friend living in the country. The memory of the deceased has completely replaced the fear of death and the invitation to conversion. One of these jewels, dated 1780, bears the inscription "May Saints embrace thee with a love like mine."

In the nineteenth century, after more than a hundred years, the image of the tomb disappears. The jewel becomes a simple locket, often containing a portrait and always one or two locks of hair. When there is only one lock, it is that of a loved one, living or dead. When there are two, it is a symbol of the bond that unites two lovers in life and beyond the grave. Hair is also used to make bracelets and rings. The hair itself is a vehicle of memory.

At the end of this evolution the subject is no longer death or the death of the loved one. Death itself has been erased, as it were, and all that remains is a substitute for the body, an incorruptible fragment.

Souls in Purgatory

Attachment to the other beyond the grave is revealed in another series of documents, the altarpieces depicting souls in purgatory that were one of the new forms of devotion to the souls in purgatory adopted at the end of the seventeenth century. It is a Catholic rite, for as we know, the rejection of this devotion was central to Luther's break with Rome. Protestant orthodoxies refused to grant the living the right to intervene in favor of the dead, whose fates were entirely in the hands of God. It is true that the reason for the human intervention was not the same in the late Middle Ages as it was in the romantic nineteenth century. In the late Middle Ages the emphasis was on the self. The idea was to force God's hand and ensure one's salvation by an accumulation of prayers, good works, indulgences. Later, the intervention was more and more often for others. In the eighteenth and especially in the nineteenth century, it became an opportunity to prolong beyond death the solicitude and affections of earthly life.

Although Protestants were forbidden to pray for their dead, after the eighteenth century there was a new reluctance to abandon them to an unknown and fearful destiny. Since there was no question of challenging the opinions of the reformers and returning to the superstitions of papism, people tended to avoid the theological obstacle altogether and behave as if there were no such thing as predestination, judgment, or damnation. There was no reason to pray, since there were no risks. But perhaps people also came to believe that there were no risks because they could not intervene. The death of Helen Burns in *Jane Eyre* is a simple passing to a better world, the happy home in which we shall one day be reunited with our dead and from which they come to visit us.

The absence of purgatory and the impossibility of interceding in favor of the dead accelerated the psychological movement that tended to reduce the irrevocability of death and to bridge the gap between the living and the dead. The dead became pseudoliving, disembodied spirits. This may be one reason why Protestant countries provided more fertile soil than Catholic ones for the development of spiritualism and communication between the living and the dead.

The Catholic church, because it had long organized an exchange of spiritual goods between earth, heaven, and purgatory, was inclined to keep relations between the two worlds within the limits of this authorized pattern. It opposed any other form of communication except the cult of the souvenir and the tomb, which we shall examine in the next chapter. And so it was within the traditional devotions on behalf of souls in purgatory that the new solicitude for the departed found expression.

Belief in a place of purgatory reaches back among the church fathers to medieval theologians such as Saint Thomas Aquinas and literati such as Dante. However, the religion of the people was slow to accept the idea. There are two almost contradictory aspects to this attitude.

The first is the rarity of allusions or references to purgatory. Purgatory is not mentioned until the seventeenth century; it does not belong to familiar piety. The authors of wills do not mention it until the middle of the seventeenth century; they know only the celestial court, or hell. The testator borrows the language of the *Subvenite* or the *In Paradisum* to express his hope that the celestial court will welcome him after his death. The word *purgatory* does not occur in the *Credo,* the *Confiteor,* or the Liturgy for the Dead.

When the word and the idea of purgatory appear in wills, it is simply as an antechamber of heaven. Thus, in 1657 a testator prays to God "to grant me after my death admission to purgatory that I may wash away in the fire all those stains that I have not erased in this sinful life by my tears and the sacred indulgences of the Church, and to let me enter paradise."[38]

The second aspect is more consistent with official doctrine. At the moment of death, the die is not yet cast; there is an intermediary period between death and the final decision during which all may yet be saved. It was long believed that this period was one of rest and waiting. But in some cases rest was not granted. Those who were not permitted to rest came back to ask the help of the living in the form of prayers and Masses that would enable them to escape the fires of hell. In short, two states were conceived of: rest and damnation. In certain cases God suspended damnation, and it was up to the reprieved sinner to solicit prayers in his own behalf and to expiate his sins either by his accursed wanderings or by more precise punishments. This conception is related both to the old pagan ideas of restless ghosts and to the official church doctrine of expiation. Thus, purgatory has the character of an exception reserved for doubtful cases. But after the Counter-Reformation it will become a normal and necessary stage in the migration of the soul. The intermediary period of repose disappears, and one passes directly from earth to heaven only in cases of exceptional and unpredictable sanctity.

However, even long after this ecclesiastical conception of purgatory became widespread, traces of the old popular images persisted. Gilbert Grimaud explains that purgatory was usually considered a place of suffering coexisting with hell and paradise and, like them, a permanent and constituent element of "the order God has established to rule the world. . . . Nevertheless, sometimes, for the greater good of mankind . . . he does extraordinary things. Thus, in the case of purgatory God does not adhere so strictly to this specific place that he may not choose other places for the same purpose when he deems it suitable." These extraordinary cases were the old pseudopurgatories of the Middle Ages. "There are some whom God assigns to various places on the earth as he thinks best."

Here is an example reported, according to Grimaud, by Thomas de Champré, "which he affirms he learned from a bishop who was a very great personage. . . . He says that there was in the Alps a gentleman given to all sorts of vices, including robbery. One day he was hunting with some friends in the mountains. While chasing a stag, he found himself alone in a very wild spot. He ran to and fro listening for a while. At last he heard two of his dogs barking on the top of the mountain. He climbed up as best he could. When he arrived, he found himself in a lovely meadow. He saw in front of his dog a man, handsome but covered with wounds, lying on the ground, and next to him, two large iron sledgehammers, one on either side. This spectacle filled him with amazement and fear; but plucking up his courage, he asked the man whether he was there by order of God, and conjured him to say who he was and what he was doing in this place. The man answered that he was there by divine decree to do penance for his sins, and added, 'I was a gendarme at the time of the wars between Philip of France and Richard of England. When the English invaded Poitou and Gascony, I took up arms and abandoned myself to all manner of violence, murders, theft, and indecency, without restraint. In the meantime I fell sick of a high fever, and since my strength was failing, I was asked to confess and to receive the sacraments, but I refused. . . . At last after the power of speech suddenly failed me, by a stroke of the infinite goodness of God, I felt my heart melt. [We recognize the conversion *in extremis* of the earliest *artes moriendi,* which had become so suspect to the moralists of the seventeenth century.] I was plunged into [the] grief and distress [of penitence]. With these sentiments, I gave up the ghost, and was immediately delivered over to these two demons that you see at my sides, to be tormented by them until the Day of Judgment. [Here the period of repose is replaced by one of torment.] They roll me over precipices and through thickets by beating me with their sledgehammers. My only consolation is that one day these torments will cease.' "39

Little by little the idea of purgatory as a fixed and organized place will completely replace these exceptional punishments inflicted on ghosts in a few accursed corners of the earth. At the same time, the authorized relationships between the living and the souls of the dead will undergo certain subtle changes that foreshadow the romantic era. The "every man for himself" attitude of the medieval and Renaissance will is broadened by a sense of social duty toward the unknown masses of suffering souls. In wills, impersonal and collective charity toward the souls of the dead as well as toward the "uncomplaining poor" becomes habitual: "I wish and ordain that upon my decease . . . there be said and celebrated 100 Low Masses, eighty for the remission of my sins and [the proportion is substantial and the language classic] twenty for the deliverance of the souls of those in purgatory" (1657).40

But the most significant change is revealed by iconography, according to the work of Michel and Gaby Vovelle.41 From the seventeenth to the early twentieth century, prayers for souls in purgatory become the most widespread and popular devotion of the Catholic church. In all churches large enough to have more than one altar, a chapel is set aside for this devotion and is often maintained by a specialized confraternity. Over the altar is a painting that almost always represents the same scene; we find it in Vienna, Paris, Provence, Rome, and Mexico. Below, the souls are burning in the flames, their eyes raised toward paradise, from which deliverance will come. Above, heaven lies open, with Christ or the Virgin and Child on one side and on the other, one or two holy intercessors chosen from among the most popular. These include Saint Agatha, with her breasts cut off, but especially the mendicant saints who were believed to be the founders of the great devotions and fruitful indulgences: Saint Dominic and his rosary, Saint Simon Stock and his scapular, and Saint Francis, whose cord is used to rescue some trusting monk or layman who took the precaution of joining a third order. Finally, a group of angels sprinkles consolation, symbolized by fresh water from a watering can, on those whose time of deliverance has not yet come and raises to paradise those whose time of trial is over.

This same iconography is still found in many stained-glass windows from the late nineteenth century. The most interesting change involves the group of burning souls. In the beginning—in Vienna, for example—these souls resemble those in Last Judgments: naked, symbolic, and without individuality; an anonymous mass. But soon they become portraits, or would-be portraits. As early as 1643 in Aix-en-Provence, the painter Daret placed his son in this group of souls, thereby indicating his confidence in his salvation and offering him to the prayers of the faithful. In the early nineteenth century, the burning souls are magnificent bearded gentlemen with long sideburns, of the sort who frequented racetrack bars, and ladies with corkscrew curls such as one saw at the opera. Everyone could pick out a relative, husband, or child. In the eighteenth and nineteenth centuries the group of souls does not illustrate a catechism lesson or reinforce a threat. Instead it represents the departed whom the affection of the survivors has not abandoned, whom they console with their prayers, and whom they hope to rejoin in heaven. This solicitude is accepted and even encouraged by the Church. If the spiritualistic pleasures of the future reunion do not receive the same official sanction, they are not absent. Thus, the celestial fatherland of Fénelon already foreshadows that of the La Ferronays and resembles it: "There is a fatherland that we come closer to every day and where we shall all be reunited. . . . Those who die are merely . . . absent for a few years or perhaps a few months. . . . Their loss [is only] apparent."[42]

However, in certain popular traditions in southern Europe, from the seventeenth century to the present, the souls in purgatory have retained the anonymity of medieval Last Judgments and the scrupulous reciprocity of the exchanges of services between this world and the next that is characteristic of old wills. In Santa Maria delle Anime del Purgatorio in Naples, which dates from the middle of the seventeenth century, anyone can choose a skull at random in the charnel and take it into a crypt transformed into a mortuary chapel. One visits one's skull periodically to keep the candles lit and recite prayers. One hopes that the unknown soul thus favored will be promptly delivered from purgatory. And he in turn, from his new celestial abode, may one day repay his benefactor in kind. Here the modern devotion to souls in purgatory is adapted to a medieval and Renaissance individualism that was generally replaced in the nineteenth century by the love of a very dear person in this world and the next.

As early as the seventeenth century, solicitude for the departed was associated with another popular devotion, that of the good death, depicted in a painting in the same or a neighboring chapel. The good death was that of Saint Joseph, or the Virgin, or Saint Anne, sometimes even of the last two at once, which allowed the baroque painter to assemble an impressive throng at the bedsides of the famous saints with exalted faces and already cadaverous bodies. The death of Saint Joseph was quieter.

By the end of the nineteenth century the iconography of souls in purgatory began to show the effects of the invasion of spiritualism. In certain great academic paintings, as in the cathedral in Toulouse, the soul has become a disembodied spirit whose astral body floats through the air. These cases may be more arresting than exemplary. In general, though, iconography, although otherwise unchanged, lost the impulse to personalize the damned. In neo-Gothic stained-glass windows of the nineteenth century, there was a return to the simplified symbolism of old, the simple catechism lesson.

The explanation is that the personalization of the deceased had found other, more refined means of expression. Among the French bourgeoisie of the early twentieth century, it became customary to distribute to the family and friends of the deceased printed leaflets consisting of a photograph, a biographical notice, and pious quotations in the style of funerary inscriptions, in short, a "tombstone." This leaflet was known as a *memento*. In the nineteenth century *memento* no longer means *memento mori*, but *memento illius*.

With the theme of souls in purgatory we have seen how a devotion that was originally individualistic became altruistic. The change is a consequence of the development of affectivity.

In interpreting medieval sorcery, Jules Michelet instinctively gives it a similar emotional orientation. He transforms a technique for gaining power, wealth, and knowledge into a way of bringing back dead persons whose loss is intolerable.

In ancient times when sorcerers called forth the dead, it was to wrest from them the secrets of the future. When they abducted cadavers, it was to extract from them certain virtues. But Michelet attributes to sorcery a purpose that did not exist in the days of real sorcerers, that was alien to the world of traditional sorcery, and that is really the goal of the American spiritualists of the nineteenth century. The ingenuous anachronism is obvious to the modern reader.

Michelet imagines that medieval man asks the sorceress to give him back "for one hour, for one moment . . . those beloved dead whom we have loaned [to you, Nature]."[43]

He also attributes to medieval man his own intolerance for the forgetfulness of the dead: "Our dead must indeed be prisoners, not to give me some sort of sign. What shall I do to make them hear me? How is it that my father, who loved me so violently—me, his only son—how is it that he does not come to me?" Fear of hell? But to save them from hell one need only resort to the treasury of the Church, the indulgences and intercessions. Here is the difference between Catholic piety for the deceased, or devotion to the souls in purgatory, and the practices of the nineteenth-century spiritualists. The latter, like the men of Michelet's neo–Middle Ages, refuse to wait; they want to see their dead right away. For those whose powers are adequate, there is no need of magic: "The calmest, the busiest individuals, however distracted they may be by the preoccupations of life, have strange moments. On a dark, foggy morning, or on an evening that steals upon us swiftly and engulfs us in its shadows; ten, twenty years later, I know not what feeble voices rise in our hearts: 'Hello, friend, it is we. . . . You do not suffer so much from our loss, you can do without us. [This is the cruelest reproach the dead can make. "The dead, the poor dead suffer greatly," Baudelaire was to say. They suffer from the forgetfulness of the living.] But we cannot do without you. Never. . . . The home that was ours is full, and we bless it. All is well, all is better than it was in the days when your father spoke to you, in the days when your little daughter said to you, "Carry me, papa!" But you are weeping. Enough! Farewell.'. . . Alas, they are gone! Sweet and fading cry. Is it true, what they say? No, may I forget myself a thousand times before I forget them!" But forgetfulness comes of necessity, like the inevitable erosion of time. To avoid or postpone it, Heathcliff reopens the coffin of his beloved. Others, in the neo–Middle Ages imagined by Michelet, resort to sorceresses: "And yet, painful as it is, one is obliged to admit that certain shapes disappear, are already blurred, certain features of the face are not so much erased as obscured, faded. It is bitter and humiliating to feel oneself so weak and changeable. . . . Bring him back, I beg you, I am too much in love with this rich source of tears. Retrace, I beg you, those dear lineaments. . . . If you could only make me dream of them at night."

At this point the sorceress intervenes. She has made a pact with Satan, who is "the king of the dead." She knows how to bring them to life. Satan has pity where the Church has none. "The evocation of the dead remains expressly forbidden." "Even the Virgin herself, the personification of mercy, does not respond to this need of the heart." Even today I hear the same complaint made against the Church: that it is indifferent to the bottomless sorrow of the bereaved. Satan is more generous. He is "associated with the old Pluto . . . who allowed the dead to return, the living to visit the dead." He "takes after his father or grandfather Osiris, the shepherd of souls." In Michelet's neo–Middle Ages, that is, in the romantic nineteenth century, "one pays lip service to the official hell and its torments [and it is true that these things have no place in the deeply felt religion of the La Ferronays]. But does one really believe in them? For despite the prohibitions of the Church, husbands and lovers return to the beds of their beloveds. The widow puts on her wedding dress on Sunday night, and the spirit comes back to console her."

The Disappearance
of Pious Clauses in Wills

One last fact should be added to this picture: the disappearance from wills around the middle of the eighteenth century of pious clauses regarding choice of burial, charitable endowments, special arrangements, and so on. This is an important phenomenon. In two decades, the space of one generation, a model of the will that had varied negligibly for three centuries was revolutionized.

My research at the Archives Nationales led me to classify Parisian wills of the second half of the eighteenth century and the beginning of the nineteenth century into four categories. The first, which is still voluminous in the middle of the eighteenth century but then tapers off, is consistent with the traditional model of the sixteenth and seventeenth centuries.

The second is an abridged or simplified version of the first. The religious preamble has been shortened, sometimes to a few words, but it is still present: "I commend my soul to God and beseech his Divine Majesty to forgive my sins" (1811).[44]

Sometimes the preamble is omitted, but the instructions concerning the service are retained: ". . . who in view of her approaching death, after commending her soul to God, made her will. . . . I leave the arrangements for my funeral to my son. I want everything to be as simple as possible, with only one High Mass in the presence of my body" (1774).[45] This shortened version reflects a desire for simplicity in the service.

In the third category there are no longer any specific instructions. The author expresses his desire for simplicity, but does not go into detail. He leaves everything to his heir, a close relative who serves as his executor. The dominant feeling is the testator's confidence in his heirs, his family.

The association between the desire for simplicity in the funeral and the decision to leave everything in the hands of the executor is an old one. We have found it in wills since the fifteenth century. In the early wills the emphasis was on the affectation of simplicity: Let my executor do as he likes; I have more important things to think about, that is, the salvation of my soul. In the eighteenth and nineteenth centuries, the desire for simplicity has become a commonplace, and the emphasis has shifted to the author's affectionate confidence in his survivors. "I leave everything to the discretion of my children" (a vine grower, 1778). "As for my funeral service and prayers, I leave everything to the piety of my sister" (a seamstress, 1778).[46] This category is the largest in the second half of the eighteenth century.

The fourth category includes wills in which all references of a religious nature have disappeared. It is not rare at the end of the eighteenth century; it is increasingly common at the beginning of the nineteenth and becomes the standard will of that century. One is tempted to interpret this, as Michel Vovelle does, as evidence of the decline in religious belief, the advance of de-Christianization. However, there are other causes, for as early as the 1770s it is not unusual to find wills in this category that include the religious among the heirs or legatees.[47]

If one compares the last two categories, one notices that in the third category the testator has expressed his confidence in his heir and in the fourth category he has not. That is the only difference between the two. He has failed to express this confidence in so many words either because he no longer felt it, a hypothesis that contradicts everything we know, or because it was understood. Around the middle of the nineteenth century, a time of exaggerated demonstrations of affection within the family, it sometimes happened that a testator felt the need to express his affection more solemnly. Sometimes he did this in the traditional and now archaic form of the holograph will, recorded in the presence of a notary. Some cases were recorded in aristocratic families; an example is the will of Comtesse Molé in 1844: "I wish my remains to be laid next to those of my beloved daughter and these words to be engraved on my stone: 'Buried next to her daughter, according to her wishes.' I leave to my daughter a portrait of my mother painted by Mme. Le Brun. I also leave her the object most precious to me in the world, a small box of dark wood that I took everywhere with me and that belonged to Elizabeth. It contains the letters she wrote me, her portrait drawn by herself, and several papers in her hand. I also wish to leave her a large box of citrus wood that contains letters from my friends written at different periods of my life. She will save any that interest her and burn the rest. *My confidence in her is total* [italics added]. I leave her my toilet case, which was given to me by my brother-in-law, her godfather."[48]

In the nineteenth century, instructions of this sort were not generally given in the will. When they were written down, which was seldom the case, they were contained in a personal letter or note separate from the will. I have an example of this practice in my own family papers. My great-grandmother died in 1907, leaving four daughters and one son. Her "last wishes" were contained in an envelope addressed to her son. This envelope contained three documents: (1) the will, which covered the distribution among her children of her personal and real estate, that is, a will of the fourth category, without any religious or sentimental references, a purely legal document; (2) a note in which she gave instructions regarding her burial, her funeral service, religious services, and charitable gifts; and (3) a letter to her son in which she explained some of her decisions, expressed her affection, and stated the principles of religion and morality in which she believed and which she wanted her children to carry on.

In the seventeenth century these three documents would have been combined into a single one, the will. From now on, personal instructions and suggestions regarding property of purely sentimental value, or moral or personal messages, were usually communicated orally. Shortly before her death, Mme. de La Ferronays transmitted instructions of this kind to her daughter Pauline. Nothing remained of the will except the legal instrument that the notary needed to determine the transmission of property; indeed, the will itself became much less common than in the seventeenth and eighteenth centuries.

For these reasons we assume that the change in the will in the second half of the eighteenth century is due to the change in feelings between the writer and his heirs. Once, these feelings were rather suspicious; now they have become trusting. A purely legal relationship has been replaced by an affectionate one. It seemed intolerable to give legal form to exchanges between individuals bound by mutual affection in this world and the next.

Everything that had to do with the body, the soul, salvation, friend-ship—including, therefore, religion—was removed from the sphere of the law and regarded as domestic business, family business. The transformation of the will can thus be seen as one indication among many others of a new type of family relationship in which affection outweighed every considera-tion of self-interest, law, or propriety. This affection, which was cultivated and even glorified, made the separation of death more painful and invited the bereaved person to compensate for his loss through memory or some more or less precise form of survival.

The Revolution in Feeling

These devout or secularized Christians and mild skeptics are creating a new paradise—Vladamir Jankélévitch calls it an anthropomorphic paradise—which is not so much the heavenly home as the earthly home saved from the menace of time, a home in which the expectations of eschatology are mingled with the realities of memory.

In the nineteenth century everyone seems to believe in the continua-tion of the friendships of life after death. The only variations in this common background of belief are the degree of realism of the representa-tions and, above all, the relationship between the afterlife and religious faith. These two notions still coincide in Christians of the nineteenth century, but they are separate in non-Christians, positivists, and agnostics. The latter may have abandoned the doctrines of revelation and salvation, the affirmations of the *Credo*, but they cultivate the memory of the dead with an emotional intensity that ultimately creates as vivid an impression of objective reality as the faith of the believers.

By the middle of the twentieth century, this dissociation of the after-life from faith spread to Christians themselves, if we are to believe statistical studies. Even when belief in the afterlife is obscured by respect for industrial rationalism, it remains the great religious fact of the whole contemporary era.

In the second half of the twentieth century, belief in an afterlife declines or becomes less respectable, but studies have shown that it reappears at the end of life in the old and the sick, those who no longer have anything to lose or to hide (see chapter 12).

The various beliefs in a future life or in the life of memory are in fact so many responses to the impossibility of accepting the death of a loved one. This is one piece of evidence among others of that great modern phenomenon, the revolution in feeling. Affectivity dominates behavior, especially at the end of the century, when good breeding requires a show of indifference. I do not mean to imply that affectivity did not exist before the eighteenth century. That would be absurd; but we must be careful not to confuse an idea that is more or less constant with the particular value it has in the collective consciousness at a given moment in history. It is the quality, intensity, and objects of affection that have changed.

In our former, traditional societies, affectivity was distributed among a greater number of individuals rather than limited to the members of the conjugal family. It was extended to ever-widening circles, and diluted. Moreover, it was not wholly invested; people retained a residue of affectivity, which was released according to the accidents of life, either as affection or as its opposite, aggression.

Beginning in the eighteenth century, however, affectivity was, from childhood, entirely concentrated on a few individuals, who became exceptional, irreplaceable, and inseparable.

"One person is absent, and the whole world is empty." The sense of the other now takes on a new primacy. The history of literature has long recognized this quality of romanticism, and made it a commonplace. Today there is a tendency to regard romanticism as an aesthetic and bourgeois mode, without depth. We now know that it is a major objective fact of daily life, a profound transformation of man as a social being.

The Retreat of Evil;
the End of Hell

Since death is not the end of the loved one, however bitter the grief of the survivor, death is neither ugly nor fearful. On the contrary, death is beautiful, as the dead body is beautiful. Presence at the deathbed in the nineteenth century is more than a customary participation in a social ritual; it is an opportunity to witness a spectacle that is both comforting and exalting. A visit to the house in which someone has died is a little like a visit to a museum. How beautiful he is! In the bedrooms of the most ordinary middle-class Western homes, death has come to coincide with beauty. This is the final stage in an evolution that began very quietly with the beautiful recumbent figures of the Renaissance and continued in the aestheticism of the baroque. But this apotheosis should not blind us to the contradiction it contains, for this death is no longer death, it is an illusion of art. Death has started to hide. In spite of the apparent publicity that surrounds it in mourning, at the cemetery, in life as well as in art and literature, death is concealing itself under the mask of beauty.

At this point the history of death intersects the history of evil. In Christian doctrine and in ordinary life, death had been seen as a manifestation of evil, an evil that insinuated itself into life and was inseparable from it. For Christians, death was the moment of a tragic confrontation between heaven and a hell that was itself the most banal expression of evil.

But in the nineteenth century, people scarcely believe in hell anymore: except halfheartedly—and then only for strangers and enemies, those outside the narrow circle of affectivity.

No doubt the La Ferronays would have been indignant if anyone had told them that they did not believe in hell. For them, hell was a remote place without reality, reserved for great and unrepentant criminals, especially heretics. This is why Albert on his deathbed tries to keep his wife away from his Protestant mother-in-law. All that remained of hell was the legacy of the Inquisition.

The saint of the seventeenth century was still afraid of hell, no matter how great his virtue, his faith, and his good works. He imagined hell in his meditations. For the pious believer of the nineteenth century, hell is a dogma that is memorized in catechism but is alien to his sensibility. With the decline of hell, one whole dimension of evil has disappeared. Another remains: suffering, injustice, unhappiness; but Helen Burns, Charlotte Brontë's heroine, knows that this residual evil is bound to the flesh and will disappear with the flesh. In the beyond, in the world of spirits, there is no more evil, and that is why death is so desirable. Baudelaire writes:

It is death that consoles and makes us live, alas!
Death is the goal of life, death is our only hope,
Which like an elixir cheers and intoxicates
And gives us heart to live another day. . . .
It is the famous inn inscribed in the book,
Where we can eat and sleep and take our ease.[49]

Some people will soon decide that it may not be necessary to wait so long to "eat and sleep and take our ease." And there will be an attempt to banish evil from the world of the flesh. This impulse will be examined in the last chapter. But the fact remains that the first great step in the retreat of evil is the end of hell.

The end of hell does not mean the death of God. The romantics were often fervent believers. But for those for whom death was hidden under the mask of beauty, the God of the Bible often took the form of nature. For death is not merely the separation from the other. Death may also be —less commonly, it is true—the miraculous approach of the unfathomable, a mystical communion with the sources of being, the cosmic infinity. Images of vastness, whether terrestrial or marine, express this attraction.

Romanticism may have been a reaction against the philosophy of the eighteenth century, but its God inherited something from the deism of the Enlightenment. This God merges here and there with that universal nature where everything is lost and everything renewed. It is a conception that is not limited to intellectuals or aesthetes, since it became a part of actual religious experience.

II

The Visit to the Cemetery

A large part of our knowledge of antiquity is based on tombs and the objects that were stored in them. The more remote the period, the more important the role of funerary documents. As different groups superimposed their cultures on the same sites, they obliterated the traces of their predecessors but left more or less intact the isolated graves that contained a microcosm of the culture of the living. Thus, the role of cemeteries, or what took the place of cemeteries, is very important to our understanding of ancient civilizations.

Cemeteries and Topography

We have seen that the role of cemeteries declined and disappeared in the Middle Ages, when the tombs huddled against the churches or filled them. In urban topography, the cemetery is no longer visible; it has lost its identity. It merges with the outbuildings of the church and the public park. Gone are those long rows of monuments that extended in every direction from Roman towns like the points of a star. Artists may carve or paint naked skeletons on the floors and walls of churches or in the galleries of cloisters, but the signs of death are no longer apparent, despite the high mortality rate and the presence of the dead. A few bones protrude slightly from the dust or mud; but for the most part, the dead are hidden. They reappear —and rather late, at that—only in a few rare visible tombs. The role of funerary documents in our work as historians has become quite negligible. The civilizations of the Middle Ages and the early-modern era, at least until the seventeenth century, have granted the dead neither space nor monuments. These civilizations do not find expression in the cemetery.

But in the early nineteenth century the cemetery reappears as part of the topography of civilization. A panoramic view of the modern landscape reveals some empty spots in the meshes of the urban fabric that are more or less green. Vast necropolises for the large cities, small cemeteries for the villages, these oases are sometimes nestled around churches, and usually outside heavily populated areas. The cemetery of today is no longer the underground replica of the world of the living that it was in antiquity, but we have a clear sense of its identity. The medieval and early modern landscape was organized around the parish church. The more urbanized landscape of the nineteenth and early twentieth centuries has tried to give the cemetery or funerary monuments the role once filled by the parish church. The cemetery has been—and may still be—the identifying sign of a culture. How are we to explain the return of the cemetery, and what does it mean?

The Devil and the Cemetery

We have seen that the maintenance of graveyards had not changed since men began burying bodies in the church or next to it, laying them in wooden coffins or simply in their winding-sheets instead of in stone sarcophagi. There was a constant shifting about of cadavers, flesh, and bones in the churches, with their uneven and gaping floors, and in the cemeteries. The man of today immediately realizes what odors and emanations, what an insalubrious atmosphere these manipulations must have created, but it is only too apparent that the man of yesterday did not mind them at all.

There came a time in the late sixteenth and seventeenth centuries when a few people began asking questions about the phenomena observed in tombs. Then, all at once, in the eighteenth century, a state of things that had gone on for several centuries became intolerable.

Long before doctors became involved in the matter, people were intrigued by the noises heard in tombs. Today we explain these noises as explosions caused by the gases given off by decomposition. At first they were regarded as supernatural warnings. Garmann recorded that crackling noises emanated from the tomb of Sylvester II (Gerbert d'Aurillac) every time a pope was about to die. In Bohemia, the tombstone of a certain saint rose and fell whenever there was danger of a plague. There was a language of tombs, just as there was a language of dreams.[1]

The doctors of the sixteenth and seventeenth centuries devoted some attention to these noises. They were interested in the stories of gravediggers who had heard sounds like the hissing of geese or had seen masses of foam form around bones and then burst, producing a great stench. It is remarkable that people started paying attention to these kinds of phenomena a century before they became a public issue.[2]

Garmann reported another type of manifestation, which the doctors of the eighteenth century attributed to the credulity of a superstitious believer. During an epidemic of plague, noises were heard coming from a coffin. When the coffin was opened, it was found that the cadaver had devoured part of its shroud. It was observed that this miracle occurred only in time of plague, and that the plague was arrested when the cadaver was decapitated and the head thrown out of the grave. One could ward off the danger at the time of burial either by placing a coin in the mouth of the cadaver, as the ancients did, to prevent it from chewing or by making sure the shroud did not touch the mouth, as the Jews did.

The important idea here is the relationship between the noises that come from tombs, the "emanations" of cemeteries, and the plague. For example, an epidemic in the region of Agen was caused by a well in which bodies had been piled to the depth of an ell.

Public officials and police were quite familiar with this danger, and in time of plague they recommended that the bodies of victims be quickly buried outside the towns and the graves be disinfected with quicklime. Why didn't they burn the bodies, as the ancients did, for hygienic reasons?

The truth is that doctors like Garmann, convinced as they were of the connection between cemeteries and epidemics, confined themselves to observation. They did not attempt to alert public opinion or present a program of reform. They were embarrassed because they were not sure of the real causes of phenomena that might very well be the work of the devil. For, in addition to the relationship of natural causality between the cemetery and epidemics, there are also the devil and his witches. Witches take from the dead those elements they need for their potions. Those cadavers that, in time of plague, are caught in the act of devouring their shrouds and squealing like pigs are those of witches. That is why magistrates are obliged to refuse them burial. For the devil extends his power in time of plague, becoming, in Luther's phrase, quoted by Garmann, *"Dei carnifex"* (the tormentor of God). In a general way the devil is delegated authority over the dead; there is a kind of kinship between him and them. The cemetery is his domain; it is a vestibule of hell. In the cosmic struggle that the Church wages against Satan, it has had to wrest the cemetery from him by an act of solemn consecration, and must defend the holy graves from him; but he prowls around its walls. He is kept at bay by the power of exorcism and of the sacred, but let there be one chink in the fortifications of the sacred and he will return, so strong is the attraction between dead bodies and the devil. The plague, the devil, and the cemetery form a kind of unholy trinity of influence.

One is struck by the ambiguity of the sacred quality attributed to the cemetery. Intrinsically diabolical, the cemetery has been won over by the Church, but it may revert to the devil. It is still sacred, and as such, man cannot defile it with profane hands.

Hence the hesitation to move the cemeteries, to separate them from the towns, even to disinfect them with quicklime. A doctor and astrologer, de Misnie (1557–1636), objects that such a practice would be "unworthy of Christians." Garmann says that generally speaking, the dead are sacred. Like altars and temples, they should not be moved; they must be treated with *reverentia* and *religio*.

Never, I believe, had canonists or theologians compared the cemetery as such to the altar. The dead had been buried in and around the church, and had profited somewhat unfairly from a sacred quality that was not intended for them and that had nothing to do with their presence. Here, on the contrary, the sacred quality originates in the very fact of the graves. It is an ambiguous conception of the sacred. It is curious to find from the same Ciceronian pen, which is erudite in its own way, on the one hand observations on the insalubriousness of the cemetery and its effects on epidemics and on the other hand the idea that the cemetery, as the land of the dead, belongs to the zone of the sacred and should not therefore be touched. Is this not the same confusion that one finds in witch-hunters? Does it indicate the rise of a popular archaic and pagan conception of the sacred of which one finds very few vestiges in medieval folklore? Or does it rather express a modern conception of the sacred that corresponds to the new scientific categories recently discovered by a more rational spirit? Phenomena that in the eighteenth century will become facts of hygiene, chemistry, and biology are on first encounter immediately attributed to the sphere of the sacred. It is a form of recognition. Thus, in our case, as in the case of the repression of witchcraft, the respect that must be shown not to death or to the funeral ceremony or to the prayers for the souls but to the cemetery as a repository of cadavers, that respect belongs to an elite rather than to a popular conception of the sacred, although this elite conception has revived and reactivated certain old currents of popular religion.

In Garmann one finds no trace of the sense of lineage that awakened the nostalgia for the "cemetery of our fathers" among Sponde's Protestants. It is interesting to note these expressions of respect and above all of reverence; they will be revived in the positivist climate of the nineteenth century. They characterize the scientific conceptions of nature of the sixteenth and seventeenth centuries. It would be a mistake to see them as popular forms of veneration of the cemetery. These forms have never been so clear-cut or explicit.

Sanitation and the Cemetery
in the Eighteenth Century

The unsanitary character of the cemeteries was already known. Administrative reports such as the *Grande et Nécessaire Police* of 1619 suggested preventive measures.[3] Although certain extraordinary precautions were recommended in time of epidemics, there was no question of changing the old order of things.

When in sixteenth- and seventeenth-century Paris the consecrated burial grounds had been relocated, it was only to allow for the expansion of the church and its outbuildings, not out of any concern for sanitation.

But by the mid to late eighteenth century, public opinion was beginning to shift. The phenomena observed by the doctors were once again reported and denounced, no longer as manifestations of the devil but as a natural but deplorable state of affairs that must be corrected.

In 1737 the Parliament of Paris took what was probably the first official step by asking the doctors to make an investigation of the cemeteries. They carried out the study in the spirit of modern science, but it had no effect. They simply recommended "greater care in burial and greater decency in the maintenance of cemeteries."[4]

In 1745 Abbé Porée, in his *Lettres sur la sépulture dans les églises,* described a situation that was beginning to be regarded as disagreeable, especially by people living next to cemeteries and churches. Burial in church came under attack as contrary to both public health and the dignity of religion. The author quoted the legal prohibitions and contested the principle of burial *ad sanctos,* which made no sense whatsoever to the Catholic or Protestant reformers. "A power was attributed to prayers and ceremonies whose effect is purely psychological." He asked that burial in churches be prohibited, for "it is permissible to love health, and the cleanliness that is so important to preserving it."[5] Cleanliness is becoming the virtue that it will be in the nineteenth century. Benoît Labre, a saint who still believed in the virtues of filth, no longer had a place in France (although his squalid poverty did not prevent him from being welcomed in Rome.). Abbé Porée thinks churches should be healthy; he advocates "clean, well-ventilated churches, where one smells the odor of burning incense, and where one is not in danger of breaking one's neck because of the unevenness of the floor," because the slabs are continually being shifted about by gravediggers. Finally, he proposes that the cemeteries be transferred outside the towns. This is "the surest way to procure and preserve the freshness of the air, the cleanliness of the temples, and the health of the inhabitants, considerations of the utmost importance."

Actually, such transfers were in no way revolutionary; church councils had already been considering creating new cemeteries and systematically locating them outside the towns. But for Abbé Porée, this relocation not only satisfied a necessity for public sanitation, it also restored a separation between the living and the dead that the ancients had always respected. The dead "remained forever separated from the living. . . . The dead, for fear of harming the living, observed not only a quarantine but an interdict that would not be lifted until the end of time." It is an ambiguous passage, in which it is tempting to identify the roots of the modern rejection of the dead by the living in our postindustrial societies; that is Madeleine Foizil's interpretation.[6] The tendency is already there, and we shall see its influence presently on the members of Parliament who composed the Decree of 1763. But just as during the 1770s the radical naturalism of the authors of the decree will give way and be gradually transformed into a new religion of the dead, so Abbé Porée does not believe that the separation of the living and the dead will harm the dead or condemn them to oblivion. This separation is intended to restore decency to the places of worship of the living and to the abodes of the dead. The visiting of cemeteries continues to be recommended. "It is of the utmost importance for mortals to listen to the lessons of the dead. It is to their tombs that they must go to be convinced of the fragility of all things human. Sepulchers are schools of wisdom." The advice is reminiscent of the *memento mori* and the vanities of the seventeenth century, but is not yet quite the cult of the souvenir that became so popular later.

The 1760s were decisive. When the community of Saint-Sulpice wanted to open a new cemetery near the Petit-Luxembourg, the owner, who was the prince de Condé, opposed the plan. Although both parties withdrew, the procurator general felt that the case was not closed. "If the private interests of the opposing parties have been protected, what of the public interest? Should not this example of an attempt to build a new cemetery in one of the most highly populated quarters of this city, and the alarm caused by this enterprise . . . call the attention of our magistrates to this area of public administration? . . . There are certain abuses that are perpetuated only through a kind of neglect. . . . Must we not classify in this category the excessive complaisance with which we have suffered the noisome abodes of the dead amid the habitations of the living? The fetid odor emitted by cadavers is a sign from Nature, who is warning us that they should be removed to a distance. Those peoples of antiquity who most excelled in public administration relegated their graves to isolated places." Besides, the towns have grown, the houses have become taller. "Formerly, the impure exhalations were dissipated by the air; today they are contained by buildings, which prevents the breezes from dispersing them. They cling to the walls, which they impregnate with a noisome essence. Who knows whether, by penetrating into the neighboring houses along with the air that is breathed there, they may not carry unknown causes of death and contagion?" And the doctors will put it even more straightforwardly than the magistrate.

Following this statement by the procurator general, the court decided that the commissioners of Châtelet and the church councils would each make an investigation of the cemeteries of Paris. The written reports of this investigation, which was conducted with great dispatch and precision, provide a detailed description of funerary practices in Paris in the mid-eighteenth century.[7]

These administrative actions, and especially the Decree of 1763, brought on a veritable publicity campaign, with petitions from owners of property bordering on cemeteries, memoranda, and printed books, especially by doctors, who are now the leaders of public opinion.[8] Their observations are not very different from those of the doctors of the seventeenth century, but their interpretations are. They exclude supernatural intervention, and are based on a scientific theory of air that was immediately accepted by the public and became a commonplace.[9]

We shall take our examples from three works that appeared almost simultaneously and that reflect the ideas of the 1760s and 1770s. They are: Hughes Maret, *Mémoires sur l'usage où l'on est d'enterrer les morts dans les églises et dans les enceintes des villes* (Notes on the present practice of burying the dead in churches and inside the walls of towns, 1773); P. T. Navier, *Réflexions sur les dangers des exhumations précipitées et sur les abus des inhumations dans les églises, suivies d'observations sur les plantations d'arbres dans les cimetières* (Reflections on the dangers of premature burial and on the abuses of burial in churches, followed by observations on the planting of trees in cemeteries, 1775), a communication to the Académie des Belles-lettres, Sciences, et Arts, in Châlons-sur-Marne; and finally, by the celebrated Vicq d'Azyr, a translation of an Italian work, *Essai sur les lieux et les dangers des sépultures* (Essay on the locations and dangers of graves, 1778), in which the decisions of the enlightened prince who reigned in Modena were presented as models.

Maret writes that "on the fifteenth of January last, according to Père Cotte, priest at the Oratoire, a gravedigger who was digging a grave in the cemetery of Montmorency struck a cadaver buried a year before with his shovel. There emerged a noisome vapor that made him shudder. . . . As he was leaning on the shovel to fill in the hole he had just made, he fell dead."[10]

These dangerous burials could also take place during a religious service or a catechism lesson: "On April 20, 1773, in Saulieu, in the nave of the

Saint-Saturnin church, a grave was being dug for a woman who had died of a putrid fever. [The cadaver of someone who died of a disease is considered to be still contagious.] The gravediggers uncovered a coffin containing a body that had been buried the previous March 3. As they were lowering the body of the woman into the grave, the coffin opened, the body was uncovered, and there immediately issued from the grave an odor so foul that everyone present was forced to leave. Out of 120 young people of both sexes who were being prepared for their First Communion 114 fell dangerously ill, as did the priest, the vicar, the gravediggers, and more than 70 other persons, of whom 18 died, including the priest and the vicar, who were the first to be carried away."[11] A veritable hecatomb! Children in catechism classes ran a high risk of exposure. At Saint-Eustache in Paris in 1749, "almost all of them fell at once into a faint and a weakness. The following Sunday, the same accident happened to about twenty children and other people of all ages."[12]

The best story is about a burial in the vault of the Pénitents Blancs of Montpellier that caused three deaths among the gravediggers and their assistants. A fourth gravedigger narrowly escaped, a circumstance that caused the townspeople to nickname him le Ressuscité.[13]

Apparently it is the air that is contaminated. Death is not always instantaneous. The air carries the disease to distant places. The decomposition of bodies is related to epidemics and what we now call infectious diseases. "Such exhalations [the putrid emanations from decaying animal substances], having become contagious, are communicated by degrees and, regenerating themselves from their own ashes, as it were, or from one animal to the next, become highly contagious and capable of devastating entire provinces." "Ramalzini claims that the majority of contagious diseases are caused by the putrid exhalations of dead bodies or the pestilential vapors of stagnant waters."[14] As early as 1559, Vicq d'Azyr notes, "The celebrated Fernel and Houllier assure us that in times of danger the houses adjacent to the cemetery have always been the first to be infected and the longest to suffer from the contagion of the other houses of the town."[15]

When cadavers are transported from their original places of burial to the charnels, the air is poisoned: "By transporting pieces of recently buried cadavers to the charnels, they daily defile the purity and wholesomeness of an air that must maintain health and life."

Fire, and the draft that it creates, "purifies and removes the bad air." In 1709 in Paris huge fires were lighted in the parks to drive away scurvy —with success. For this reason fires were kept burning during exhumations; for example, at les Innocents in 1785. The same results may be obtained by exploding gunpowder.[16]

Contaminated air carries disease and thus infects living things. It has been observed that persons living next to cemeteries can keep nothing in their pantries. In the neighborhood of les Innocents, for example, "Steel, silverware, and gold braid lose their shine very quickly." "M. Cadet declares that cauterized wounds suppurate more profusely there than in other quarters of Paris." The doctors are not the only ones to support these ideas. There is no lack of testimony from people living next to cemeteries, and the investigators of 1763, both laymen and clergymen, quote this testimony in their official reports. The author of a petition against the cemetery of the parish of Saint-Merri writes, "Everything necessary to sustain life spoils; it is no longer possible to keep anything fresh for a few days." And the widow Leblanc, who owned a jewelry shop, lodged a complaint against the council of Saint-Gervais. She had to close her casement windows, which looked onto the cemetery, because "she can keep neither meat nor soup . . . the noxious humors have penetrated into the wine cellar and spoiled the wine and beer." In the latter case, the church council agreed that the complaint was justified. They looked for a site outside the city walls to which to transfer their cemetery.[17]

There is no longer any doubt: Almost everyone is now convinced of the unhealthy condition of the cemeteries. The only wonder is how, in the superstitious Middle Ages, people could have abandoned the reasonable customs of the ancients, how for centuries they could have endured these centers of pestilence and spectacles of horror right in the heart of the towns, surrounded by the habitations of the living.

The Decree of 1763

The first people to be convinced were the most enlightened: officers of the royal court, lawyers, judges, shopkeepers, and so on.

The Decree of the Parliament of Paris of March 12, 1763, which followed the investigation of the commissioners and church councils, was the first attempt to modify the ancient practice of burial *ad sanctos et apud ecclesiam.*

The preamble to the decree quotes the arguments of doctors and people living next to cemeteries. "In the majority of the large parishes, especially those located in the center of town, complaints are made daily about the infection that is spread in their environs by the cemeteries of these parishes, especially when the heat of summer increases the exhalations. It is said that at this time of year the putrefaction is so great that those foods most necessary to life cannot be kept for a few hours in neighboring houses without becoming spoiled. This situation is caused either by the nature of the soil, which is too rich to consume the bodies [the doctors had made chemical analyses of the soil of the cemeteries, especially noting those that were too rich to permit decay without meanwhile causing desiccation or mummification], or by the inadequacy of the area to accommodate the annual rate of burial." It also notes that some church councils had already made arrangements to acquire large cemeteries outside the town, a point well calculated to disarm traditionalists.

The program proposed by the decree is interesting and audacious. Here, in 1763, we are very close to the secular cemetery. The role of the clergy has been reduced to one of supervision and protocol. Rather than a field of repose, what the cemetery will become forty years later is a sort of dump, but clean, hygienic, correct, and well maintained. The tone is extraordinarily matter-of-fact and functional. The idea is to close down the existing cemeteries and to create outside and around Paris eight large cemeteries (four in the first draft) for as many groups of Parisian parishes. Each parish would have its own common grave in the collective cemetery. In the town itself nothing would remain but the repositories near the churches, where the dead would be placed after the religious service. They would be picked up every day by hearses, which would collect "the coffins and winding sheets," marked with the identifying number of the parish, and convey them to the common cemetery, where they would be placed in the ground.

According to this conception, the service in the church in the presence of the body would be the only remaining public religious ceremony. Although the members of Parliament conceded that the priest might accompany the funeral procession, in their eyes this was more for the purpose of overseeing the drivers and gravediggers than of performing a religious duty.

Although the decree itself was never applied, these suggestions were actually adopted. To be sure, the notification of death (which after the end of the seventeenth century had replaced the public proclamation), the service in the church, and the conventions of mourning and condolence continued to be observed; but after the service was over, the public dispersed, and the body was conveyed to a repository, as suggested by the decree. Burial was losing its familial and public character and becoming a simple function of the municipal government.

Moreover, the decree included no arrangements for making the cemetery a public place; indeed, visitors were rather discouraged from making the trip. The cemetery was a space enclosed by walls and large enough so that the common graves could be rotated frequently without exhausting the soil. The lawmakers retained the age-old principle of piling the bodies several layers deep, despite the objections of doctors and priests. They even tried—and this is the most curious feature of their plan—to extend this practice to a whole segment of the population to whom it was unknown. In order to discourage burial in churches without abolishing it altogether, they made it subject to the exorbitant fee of 2,000 French pounds. (Together with the price of the service and the monument, this must have brought the total expense to about 3,000 French pounds. Some of the church councils that participated in the investigation thought that at this price they would have only one customer a year.) Those who could or would not pay this fee had two alternatives. Either they could go to the common grave with everyone else (they could avoid the stop at the repository by paying twice the fee for transporting the body), or else for 300 pounds, still a rather large sum, they were entitled to a private grave along the wall, an area reserved for this type of burial. But in no case could they cover the tomb or erect a monument, although they did have the right to place an epitaph on the wall of the cemetery. The cemetery was to be absolutely bare, without monuments or even trees, since the latter were believed to prevent the circulation of the air. Several council members remarked that there would probably not be many customers willing to pay 300 pounds for a piece of ground as anonymous as that.

Perhaps the members of Parliament thought that their own dead, those of their rank, would either be able to pay the 2,000 pounds or would continue to be buried in the chapels of their châteaux, untouched by the decree (although some of them also had a preference for simplicity). It is interesting to note that the first draft of the decree contained the general prohibition against burial in towns and the fee of 2,000 pounds for the right to be buried in a church, but provided by way of compensation that the new common cemetery *extra muros* might contain monuments: "Ecclesiastics, nobles, and citizens in comfortable circumstances [in later drafts it will read "distinguished citizens"] who shall desire a private grave shall be assigned locations in each of the new cemeteries, where they may be buried privately in exchange for the sum of 50 pounds. . . . They shall be free to embellish these graves as they see fit and to exhume the bodies and bones of their ancestors and transport them to the places assigned to them along with all the distinctive attributes of their birth." We recognize here the cemetery of the nineteenth century, of which Père-Lachaise will be one of the models. It corresponds to an idea that is not yet widespread and that rarely appears in the literature on the subject.

But in the final version of the decree this clause has disappeared, which shows the determination of its authors. The fee for the right to a private grave has been raised from 50 to 300 pounds, and the right to erect a monument has been eliminated. The other drafts insisted on the necessity of "not allowing any epitaph except along the walls and not on the graves," an idea that was adopted and amplified in the final version: "No one shall construct any other edifice [except a devotional chapel or a concierge's hut], or even erect any epitaph, except on the walls and not on any grave."

If the decree was not put into effect, it was probably because of its radicalism. But the fact that it was framed, approved, and recorded, is interesting in itself. To understand its radicalism, we must remember what was said earlier about the distancing of death, the affectation of simplicity in funerals, the tendency toward nothingness and indifference to the body. I see the text of 1763 as the culmination of this tendency and an attempt to impose it on society as a whole. But society did not accept it, and we shall now consider the reactions encountered by the propositions of the lawmakers and by the decree itself.

Almost everyone now recognizes the unhealthiness of the cemeteries and of burial in the churches and agrees that something must be done. But there are reservations, as we know, on the part of the clergy and the church councils. Their financial interests are affected by the decision of Parliament, since the tombs represent a substantial share of their income. (Of course, the decree in no way affects services in the churches.) Some church councils have already established new cemeteries. Others, aware of the dangers of burying bodies directly in the ground under the floors of the churches, have provided for burial vaults, but some are wondering whether the remoteness of the new graves will not bring about a general secularization. What would become of the unbeneficed priests who make their living by taking part in funeral processions, if these processions were reduced or eliminated? The embarrassing position of the parishes is clearly seen in this rather naïve statement of the church council of Saint-Sulpice: "There is no denying that in very hot weather there may be certain disadvantages to this cemetery, but these disadvantages are not sufficient to outweigh its extreme usefulness to the parish of Saint-Sulpice." The only victims would be the priests themselves, and they would not complain. "Generally speaking, it would only be the community of priests of this parish (and a few neighbors) who would suffer from these disadvantages, but one can state confidently that it is very easy to prevent them." One need only take a few precautions at the time of burial and curb the negligence of gravediggers.[18]

The council of Saint-Germain-l'Auxerrois has a "respect for the public welfare, which is so closely related to the physical qualities of the air: air, that inquisitive element that insinuates itself everywhere." The council accepts the principle of the repository and of the common cemetery but foresees that one must allow for "the weaknesses and traditions of the people and the vanity of the rich." "Distinctions" must be maintained; why "should distinguished persons not continue to be buried in the churches, provided they are placed in vaults, such as were just built?" By 1757 Saint-Jean-en-Grève had also decided to discontinue burials except in stone vaults. But Saint-Merri, despite the complaints of the neighbors, maintained its preference for a cemetery next to the church, "which is most convenient for burial and draws the attention of the faithful and inspires them to pray for the dead." This allusion to the prayer for the dead should be noted, for it is very rare in the memoranda of the investigation.

Generally speaking, clergymen and church councils accept the inevitable, while nevertheless attempting to keep as many tombs as possible in the vaults of the churches and to maintain the shortest possible distance between the new cemetery and the church. The officials of the hôpital de la Charité, however, are frankly enthusiastic. They believe that the new arrangement is in keeping with the Christian tradition of funerals. Today "after the last prayers, the body is carried processionally to the site of the grave"; but in future "after the final *Requiescat in pace,* the funeral procession and the people [will leave], as is customary at a service in which the body is not present. After everyone has left, even the clergy, the body will be carried *unattended* [emphasis added] to a repository. . . . The following night it will be placed in a wagon with the bodies of others who have died the same day." Of course, "the people will be upset by this practice at first," but we need fear no violence. "They will soon become accustomed to it," because they will not feel excluded, for "persons of reputation would be subject to the same law." The cemetery will be bare, without anything to indicate distinctions of fortune or birth, or to give importance to the remains. The clergy need have no cause for alarm: "The new arrangement . . . would in no way alter the funeral ceremony. The same munificence would exist," but the ceremony would stop at the church. "The only thing being eliminated is the ceremony of burial."[19] But if the reservations of those who took part in the investigation appear discreet, there are certain anonymous memoranda that disagree violently with the ideas of Parliament and whose tone is not always that of the Enlightenment. One such document is the *Mémoire des curés de Paris.*[20]

The authors of this memorandum do not mince words. They are not at all impressed by the scientific rhetoric of the parliamentarians who wrote the decree; all that is nonsense. Contrary to popular belief—and at that time it took audacity to state it so strongly—they do not agree that the neighborhoods of the cemeteries are unhealthy. "Priests do not deny the fact that in the heat of summer the common graves of the cemeteries of large parishes sometimes give off unpleasant vapors. But they also dare to maintain, and their records confirm, that there are no more illnesses or deaths, and often fewer, in houses that look onto cemeteries, . . . that of les Saints-Innocents as well as those in other parts of town; and that in fact there are a number of persons in those neighborhoods who live to the most advanced ages." Epidemics do not affect cemeteries any more than they do other places. "During two maladies only too well known for the ravages they caused in Paris, this neighborhood [les Innocents] was affected last, and so lightly that one may regard it as having been spared." The vicinity of a cemetery is no more unhealthy than that of a tannery, a starchery, or any other place whose activities involve putrefaction. . . . The people there are robust, and one never sees epidemic diseases." Do butchers become sickly because they frequent slaughterhouses?

Finally, burial in churches, or near them, is a very old practice. These priests make no reference to the canonical prescriptions forbidding or limiting such burial. "Have not Saint-Séverin, Saint-Gervais, and Saint-Paul, parish churches of the sixth, eighth, and twelfth centuries, always had charnels? This is proof positive of the ancient custom of burying there, a custom that would seem more likely to arouse fear than the use of cemeteries [because of the transfer of the remains] but that has never had disagreeable consequences. We must conclude either that the evil has been festering for centuries without anyone's realizing it or that it was known all along but that it took several centuries before anyone thought of complaining or correcting it." The historical problem is well stated here.

Besides, priests have always done what was necessary to avoid the disadvantages inherent in such burial; they are also concerned with hygiene. They bury within twenty-four hours after death, and "every cadaver that was likely to be contagious was exempted from the law of 24 hours. . . . Often the body was buried as soon as it entered the church, before the service began." They know, alas!, that "despite these precautions, the thought of a cadaver already causes our churches to be deserted." The parliamentarians also believed that the public was impressed by the spectacle of death, which was not so certain. The procurator general wrote in pencil in the margin of a memorandum claiming the right of each parish to have its own cemetery outside of town, "The objection has been made that in that case one would see nothing but funeral processions in Paris."

According to the priests, the obligation to store bodies in the repository will actually delay burial and thus increase the possibility of infection! Especially since they have taken the precaution of relocating the common graves and limiting private tombs in churches to those in burial vaults. These projects have "been a financial burden to several parishes and will prove to be ineffective."

The priests also threaten the Parisian officials with public discontent. "The new regulations are disgusting to the people." This is strong language. "Despite the prudence and restraint with which the decree was presented to the public, it caused a general commotion among the two largest classes of society, which are also the ones that should be treated most carefully, the people and the bourgeoisie. The commotion mounted and unleashed a storm of protest against the magistrates that did not begin to die down until it was rumored that the decree would not be carried out." Why this commotion? "The general cry was that Parliament is treating us like Huguenots. They are sending us to the garbage dump."

The priests tried to calm the people and restore their respect for authority, but they were not surprised. "All peoples in the world, especially the French, have always respected the mortal remains of those who were dear to them. For them it is a real consolation, albeit a sad one, not to be separated from those remains until the moment when the tomb conceals them from their eyes." The clandestine nature of burial is the principal criticism made against the decree. "The provision for repositories and general cemeteries dispossesses the son of the remains of his father before he is really buried and adds to his grief that of seeing him taken away without being able to pay his last respects."

It is a popular idea. The priests are not so sure of the attitude of the upper classes. Indeed, they are afraid that people of quality may pride themselves on their simplicity—we have seen that there was a tendency in this direction—and ask to be buried like the poor. "Should a qualified person begin to rank himself with the common class—and this will certainly happen—he will set the tone, and his example will soon be followed" —and the church council will no longer collect either the 2,000 pounds or the price of a solemn funeral service.

But the issue goes beyond popular discontent or financial loss. "The new regulation violates the funeral service as a form of worship." The most serious criticism is that it cuts the ceremony in two: first, the service in the church in the presence of the body, which is still public, and second, the burial, which is not. "The sequence of the main ceremonies will be interrupted and not resumed until 3 o'clock in the morning."

In short, either the people will revolt or they will resign themselves and forget. The second hypothesis was the more likely, and I suspect the priests of exaggerating the emotional reaction of the poor. What they really feared was their indifference. "Given the current decline in faith and morals, this change will have grave consequences. Before long, piety for the dead will be destroyed." And here the priests challenge the actions and propaganda of the *philosophes*, who describe "interest in the dead" as "prejudice" or "weakness." The trouble begins in the upper classes, which is exactly where the *philosophes* are recruited. "It is unfortunately a proven fact among certain classes. . . . Among those who still avail themselves of the intercessory prayers of the church, how many do so purely out of propriety? How many only out of expediency?" This is why the religious services are being abandoned. Could it be that people were already losing interest in funerals and burial services? It is tempting to believe that they were. The bitterness of the priests would confirm the hypothesis of a transition from a once-ascetic meditation on nothingness and vanity to real indifference. The priests seemed to realize that the people and the petite bourgeoisie were more attached to custom. They feared the contagion of the example of the "first estate." "But if faith and charity have reached such a state of decline in an order of citizens whose rank and fortune should and do make such a vivid impression on society, what does this presage for the consequences of the new plan?"

In fact, the priests fear the clandestine nature of burial less than they do the consequences of relocation, not for the cult of the tomb and the cemetery, of which they are unaware, but for the traditional devotions for souls in purgatory. The sight of the tomb had two functions in the eyes of the pastors: the *memento mori* and the *ora pro nobis;* the invitation to conversion and the invitation to pray for the dead. If the priests of 1763 seldom allude to the *memento mori,* which was so important to Abbé Porée in 1735, they are preoccupied with the invitation to prayer: "The distance between the church and the cemetery, by introducing or encouraging indifference, will lead to neglect, and will infallibly and quickly accustom Christians to believing that the dead no longer exist or that they no longer have need of anything." The *philosophes* will then have triumphed, along with the "new systems that reduce everything to matter, thus extinguishing all practice of religion, including the Catholic practice of the prayer for the dead."

The originality of the *Mémoire des curés* lies in the fact that its authors relate the cemetery to the prayer for the dead, see them as mutually dependent, and try to defend one in order to save the other. The argument is new. It certainly expresses a mistrust of the philosophy of the Enlightenment and the forms of worship it proposed. Madeleine Foizil also sees it as a reaction in favor of the traditional attachment to family tombs. But I think this is a projection by the historian onto the past of an idea that did not yet exist in 1763. The priests invoked against the *philosophes* the popular distaste for being treated "like Huguenots" and for the clandestine nature of burial rather than for its anonymity, which was still common.

However, in recognizing this vocation of the cemetery and in defending it against a decree that devalued it, the *Mémoire* was indirectly and unconsciously expressing a new and unformulated idea that did not spring from the common people, an idea that will later be expressed openly for the first time in a lay milieu hostile to the Church, as we shall see presently. In reality the authors of the *Mémoire* favored a status quo that would already include "measures to relocate the common graves." For example, a special cemetery would be created for Saint-Eustache and the Hôtel-Dieu, which would mean so many fewer bodies for les Innocents, "about which it is so fashionable to complain." "This would be the object of the preliminary procedures, before discontinuing this cemetery altogether." In the other cemeteries, each church council would introduce "alterations . . . that by imperceptible degrees would lead to the eventual execution of the decree."

Another memorandum, which seems to have come from the same conservative milieu, advances other arguments. It makes concessions; it abandons les Innocents, whose conditions are inexcusable, but asks, "Why close down the other cemeteries indiscriminately?" There are some that are perfectly salubrious and not at all overcrowded. The same is true of churches. "The churches are also foul when one opens the vault. The odor is bad, but it only lasts a quarter of an hour." Besides, "in some churches each body has a private grave. If there were a grave for each body, the cemeteries would smell less."[21] Neither the parliamentarians nor the priests or church councillors had dared to criticize the common grave and the practice of piling up bodies.

An idea appears here, perhaps for the first time, that will become prevalent in the early nineteenth century in France and throughout the West: "If one makes a grave for each body, it will hardly smell at all." This hygienic argument will later become a principle of dignity and piety.

The Relocation of the Cemeteries

Although the decree of the Parliament of Paris was not put into practice, the campaign to move the cemeteries out of town continued. A dozen years later, the archbishop and the Parliament of Toulouse drew up some plans, which were carried out and in fact were extended to the whole kingdom by a declaration of Louis XVI on May 10, 1776.

A letter by M. Molé on the logistics of transferring the cemeteries outside the city walls clearly shows the ideological shift that has occurred in the interim. The reasons for relocating the cemeteries are the same, but the politics have changed and the goals are different.[22]

Molé, who comes out of the radical circles steeped in philosophy that had drawn up the Decree of 1763, reviews the history of the superstitious abuses that made it possible to bury the dead in the towns and churches. He shows how the cemeteries have been improperly "subjected to a kind of consecration" and "regarded as ecclesiastical dependencies," which they are not. Let no one therefore speak of the cemetery as a sacred place.

Molé's originality consists in the fact that he contested the ecclesiastical character, not only of the cemetery but of the funeral itself, that is, the funeral procession and burial. He attempts to prove that the presence of priests at funeral services is a recent development. The Jews forbade it. "Priests as a body appeared at first only at the funerals of persons distinguished by Christian virtues. . . . These convoys were more like triumphal marches than funeral processions"; for example, the two thousand monks in the funeral procession of Saint Martin. "This attendance, originally voluntary, became imperceptibly a traditional ceremony, a mark of deference to rank and superiority. . . . Later the custom was observed for all persons of established reputation. . . . Gradually, the clergy came to have the privilege of attending the funerals of all Christians." This arrogation was the work of the regular clergy. "The mendicant friars were the last to attend funeral processions. They filled the places now occupied by the poor and the children from the asylums. [In the early nineteenth century the poor and the children reappear with the revival of the large funeral. The four mendicant orders, however, have ceased to perform their age-old function.] . . . After the withdrawal of the regular clergy, the clergy of the parish churches retained the right to appear in funeral processions, although there is no indication that this custom was ever required or authorized by the Church."

It was as the result of an abuse, therefore, that the Church clericalized the funeral service. It is time to return to normal by secularizing the funeral procession and burial. The priests do not belong there.

The secularization of the funeral procession also implies that of the cemetery. Not only will the cemeteries be located outside the towns, but their administration will become a municipal function. "By sparing the priests and church councils the burden of the new cemeteries and all that they entail, we are placing this administrative function in the hands of the municipal authorities, in other words, restoring things to their proper state." A public officer called the master of funerals will be responsible for keeping the records of deaths and burials; that, too, will be secularized.

"In the cemeteries there will be neither chapel nor altar"; and Molé assures us sanctimoniously that this is "so as not to draw the faithful away from their parish churches."

So far Molé is even more radical than the parliamentarians of 1763. He adopts their prohibition against burial in churches and their plans for the creation of general cemeteries outside town (four for Paris) and repositories for local districts. Three hearses will provide transport to the cemetery.

But his ideas on the architecture and general conception of the cemetery differ from those of the decree. The cemetery is more secular, less ecclesiastical, but the impulse to eliminate social distinctions and the desire for anonymity have disappeared. The high wall is lined with an inner gallery at whose four corners there are four pyramidal monuments called *Repos*. As in the text of 1763, the center of the cemetery is reserved for the common graves, but the galleries and the space that runs along the walls are intended not only for private graves but for personal monuments. In these galleries we will recognize the images, inscriptions, and architectural elements that had invaded the churches and cloisters. "For burial in the galleries the authorities will charge what is now paid for burial in churches." Molé proposes a feature found in an early version of the Decree of 1763 that had been eliminated from the final text: "Plots in the south gallery will be granted to families who presently have burial vaults in the secular or regular churches of the district. . . . Each family will be permitted to designate its plot by inscriptions, epitaphs, and other monuments. The four *Repos* will be devoted to the high nobility and to all the famous dead . . . whom the government shall choose to honor in this manner." There will be a place for non-Catholics "behind the gallery opposite the entrance [in other words, very clearly separated]. Another burial place will be provided for foreigners and others who do not follow the Roman rite."

This cemetery will be, therefore, a gallery of great men. "Ranks and distinctions will be preserved, and the hope of being laid to rest in the company of illustrious and useful men will exalt genius, promote patriotism, and glorify the virtues."

Molé's recommendations correspond closely to the prevailing ideas that we find in the great texts of Toulouse and in the Déclaration Royale.

The Decree of the Parliament of Toulouse of September 3, 1774, is interesting, especially the preamble, which repeats the now-classic arguments of the doctors: "The doctors assure us that the putrid vapors that emanate from cadavers fill the air with salts and corpuscles [the language is precise and scientific] capable of impairing health and causing fatal disease." But we enlightened men, devoted to the public interest, have adversaries: "We know that we must combat a certain number of persons who, on the basis of false titles acquired by outright extortion or by the payment of the most nominal sums, imagine that the right of burial in churches has been transmitted to them." From this it would appear that the opposition to the Decree of 1763 came from families who had acquired, or wished to acquire, the right of burial in church, rather than from the people. The archbishop of Toulouse, Monsignor Loménie de Brienne, mentions the same social categories in his edict of March 23, 1775: "Nothing can check the vanity of the great, who always wish to be distinguished, and that of the small [the petite bourgeoisie], who always long to equal the great."23

The archbishop absolutely forbids the burial in church of "any person, ecclesiastic or layman . . . , even in public or private chapels, oratories, or any other enclosed spaces where the faithful gather together." Those who presently have the right to be buried in churches will be buried in cloisters, on the condition that they provide "burial vaults that shall be lined with large stones on the bottom as well as on the top." The archbishop refuses what the Parliament of Toulouse still tolerated a year before.

In future, even the right to be buried in a cloister will be granted only to the titulars of a few ecclesiastical functions or prebends. "All the faithful without exception shall be buried in the cemeteries of their parishes." The churches will take this opportunity to renovate their floors. (One cannot read this passage without shuddering. How many slabs, how many epitaphs must have disappeared in the course of these restorations!)

The new cemeteries are designed according to standards that later became commonplace.

The Déclaration Royale of 1776 adopts the ideas, and sometimes even the words, of the edict of the archbishop of Toulouse. In it one finds the same transfer to the cloister of graves previously placed in churches. But since many churches did not have cloisters, those who had the right to be buried in church "shall be permitted to choose in the cemeteries of said parishes a separate place for their graves, and even to build a vault or monument on the spot, provided the spot not be enclosed; and in future such permission can be granted only to those who are legitimately entitled to be buried in the churches, so that there will always remain in the cemeteries sufficient land for the burial of the faithful."

The proposed cemetery is therefore composed of two spaces: one space for the common graves or graves not covered by monuments and another space for graves covered by monuments and provided for those who have inherited the right to be buried in churches. This right may not be extended to others. In practice this restriction must have disappeared, resulting in a model very close to the nineteenth-century cemetery. The only difference is that the largest and consequently the most visible space is the one devoted to the common graves, the graves of the poor.

Between 1763 and 1776, then, there was a change of model. The cemetery of 1776 is no longer merely a hygienic and functional storage place for bodies. It also satisfies those urges that from the Middle Ages to the eighteenth century impelled families to fill the churches with funerary monuments. It has inherited some of the funerary decor of the churches, as if this decor had been transplanted there. It has become a place of commemoration that may also be one of piety and meditation. The French radicalism of the 1760s has given way to a feeling that, albeit opposed to a clerical tradition, may also have been of a religious nature.

The Closing of les Innocents

Meanwhile, in late 1779, some air from one of the large common graves of les Innocents leaked into the cellars of three neighboring houses in the rue de la Lingerie. These houses had two-story cellars. "So far the mephitis had only reached the lower cellars, which lie beneath the charnel." The door of the cellar nearest the cemetery was boarded up. The Chapter of Notre-Dame ordered the construction of a counterwall, "an operation whose only result was to expose the workers to some rather serious accidents" (troubles of the nervous system). The mephitis filtered through the rock; nothing could stop it. One could not keep lamps lighted. The stench reached the upper cellars, and then the ground floor, where it was "particularly noticeable on Sundays and holidays, when the shops were closed and the circulation of the outside air was reduced. . . . The same was true when the doors were opened. Many times the wife of the barkeeper felt ill when she walked downstairs to her counter in the morning."

In spite of the closing of the cellars, in the summer of 1780 the pestilence spread to the neighboring houses. It was like a contagious disease or an epidemic. There was a public outcry, and the chapter decided to attack the roots of the problem: the large common grave, which was fifty feet deep. The grave was opened and the workmen tried to disinfect it by digging deep trenches all around and filling them with quicklime. The grave was covered with a layer of lime. It was no use, for the mephitis passed underneath!

But the operation was accompanied by hygienic precautions and a theatricality that were impressive. It was a sort of dress rehearsal for the great romantic spectacle that would be performed a few years later over the entire length and breadth of the cemetery: "Bonfires lighted at intervals inside the walls created drafts and helped to purify the atmosphere. . . . The silence of the night, disturbed for the first time in centuries in this mournful sanctuary; the ground piled several feet high with the debris of the human species; walls and ceilings lined with bones; lighted torches; scattered fires feeding on the remains of coffins, their flickering light lengthening the shadows of the tombs and funerary crosses scattered here and there; these epitaphs, these monuments, the pawns of time, which betrays the filial piety or, more often, the pride that has erected them; here, a habitation for a few of the living, surrounded by several thousand dead; over there, in one corner of this lugubrious enclosure, a well-kept garden, a bower of roses where nothing should be growing but cypress." But life goes on, the life of yesterday, in which the living and the dead mingled without uneasiness or distaste, to the surprise of the enlightened spectator of today, who is moved in spite of himself. "Soon the neighbors wake up and rush to the scene, which is one no longer of death but of romance."[24]

The police took advantage of these circumstances and the sentiments they aroused to close the cemeteries of Paris once and for all, starting with les Innocents in 1780, and proceeding to Chaussée-d'Antin (Saint-Roch), rue Saint-Joseph (Saint-Eustache), and Saint-Sulpice in 1781, and to l'Île Saint-Louis in 1782. These cemeteries had to be replaced with others located outside the gates of Paris—either old cemeteries that had been enlarged or new ones. After 1783 processions that formerly went to les Innocents were redirected to the cemetery of Clamart; most of these bodies were from the Hôtel-Dieu or the hospice de la Trinité. In 1784 Saint-Sulpice transferred its two urban cemeteries to the new cemetery of Vaugirard, between the gates of Vaugirard and Sèvres. In 1787, Saint-Roch moved its cemetery from Chaussée-d'Antin to the foot of Montmartre (Sainte-Marguerite). Saint-Eustache enlarged its cemetery in the faubourg Montmartre. Thus, after years of tergiversation, a new topography of Parisian cemeteries was rapidly established. It was the topography of the nineteenth century: for the Left Bank, Clamart and Vaugirard, and for the Right Bank, Montmartre and Sainte-Marguerite, which would be replaced in 1804 by Père-Lachaise. Paris passed expeditiously from a medieval geography of the cemetery, quietly modified in the seventeenth and eighteenth centuries by a few shifts from the churches toward the periphery, to the concentrated extraurban geography that had been proposed by doctors and parliamentarians since the middle of the eighteenth century; from the small courtyard of the local parish church to the large general cemetery.

A New Style of Funeral

After the closing of the old cemeteries, the parishes found themselves in the situation foreseen by the Decree of 1763. The new cemeteries were so far away that it was no longer possible for the procession to accompany the body from the home to the church and from the church to the cemetery without interruption. The ceremony had to be divided into two stages: first from the home to the church and next from the church to the cemetery. It was for this reason that the repositories had been proposed. They had to be prepared under pressure of necessity by the parishes themselves.

The first part of the ceremony was still public and consistent with ancient tradition, but the second part, the journey from the church repository to the cemetery, was solitary and performed quickly and without much dignity. Louis-Sébastien Mercier describes it as follows: "The official permit for the procession states that the body will be buried in the church, but this is no longer the case; the body is merely left there for a time. All bodies are transported to the cemeteries at night. The body is accompanied only as far as the church; today friends and relatives are excused from setting their feet on the edge of the damp grave. A small ordinary hallway receives the dead indiscriminately before they are taken to the open air of the countryside." This was the procedure recommended by the parliamentarians of 1763 and by Molé in 1776. The author of the *Tableaux de Paris* approved it, with a satisfaction that is somewhat sardonic: "This sensible new arrangement reconciles the respect that is owed to the dead with a regard for public sanitation. Appearances are saved; the body seems to have been buried in the church, or at least in the parish, but actually it rests in the open country."[25]

This "sensible new arrangement" brought about a profound transformation in customs and had the unexpected consequence of accentuating the ecclesiastical character of the ceremony, thereby continuing an evolutionary process that already had a long history. Indeed, it was not until well along in the Middle Ages that the funeral cortege became a religious procession. It took a long time for the itinerary of the body from home to tomb to include a stop at the church for the service celebrated at the altar in the presence of the body. In Paris it was not until the 1760s that this custom was extended to charity burials. For a long time the essence of the ceremony had been the act of burial, whereas in the period we are talking about it was concentrated in the church.

After the service, the body was entrusted to the grace of God and the goodwill of men. But what men? In Paris the transport of bodies had formerly been performed by a corporation of town criers, whose job was to announce the disposal of bodies and the arrival of wine while ringing a little bell. Elsewhere the function was performed by confraternities. But these communities were not always prepared or qualified for the tasks imposed by the "new arrangement," whence a makeshift system that lasted until the organization of the funeral services by the Decree of August 10, 1811.[26] This situation is denounced in a memorandum preserved among the Joly de Fleury Papers prior to the Revolution: "It was at the time of the closing of les Innocents and of all the other cemeteries inside the town that [the priests], forced to have the bodies carried great distances from their parishes, were obliged to simplify the religious ceremony. It was no longer possible to have the body accompanied by the clergy of the parish. It was necessary to reduce to one or two [and perhaps soon to none] the number of priests who escorted it to the place of burial. The distance it had to be carried made it impracticable for beadles and other persons who served the churches, and they had to be replaced by porters picked on the street at random, with the result that every day indecency was substituted for religion."

This situation was certainly aggravated by the Revolution, insofar as its religious policy and the general confusion reduced and even eliminated the church service, which was now the only public part of the funeral ceremony.

It is important to understand that for about thirty years a style of burial existed that was very different from anything before or since. It was a style inspired by the model of the enlightened and radical parliamentarians of the 1760s, which left burial proper to the discretion of unsupervised porters.

The Detachment of the Parisians

The fact that this situation was possible tells us a great deal about the state of the collective sensibility in the middle of the eighteenth century and the general indifference toward the dead and their burial, at least in Paris. The final proof is provided by the destruction and transformation of the cemetery of les Innocents in 1785, after several years during which the deconsecrated cemetery formed a zone of silence and emptiness near the great markets in the heart of Paris.

By the investigation of 1763 it had already been proposed that the cemeteries be transformed into markets—which they already were, more or less—and parks. So les Innocents was turned into a park. What progress! The physician Thouret expresses his satisfaction in a report on the exhumation of the cemetery and church of les Saints-Innocents read at a meeting of the Royal Society of Medicine on March 3, 1789. What a horrible place the old cemetery was: "Its lugubrious surroundings, its silent and sinister walls, its low, dark porches, its ancient arches, and in the midst of its impressive funerary monuments, the numerous centers of infection that it harbored in its bosom. [With all this] let us compare the preseι.t condition of the place, open on all sides to the free circulation of the air [no more covered parks, as in the cities of the seventeenth century], its foundations reinforced, its entire surface purified and leveled, embellished by the nearby monuments, graced with a gushing fountain, the first the capital has seen inside its walls, and combining all the sources of life where formerly there gaped all the pits of death."

But in order to arrive at this state, it was necessary to undertake a formidable work of exhumation the like of which had never been dreamed of before. It was not enough to raze the cemetery; it was necessary to disinfect it, which meant removing an enormous volume of cadavers, earth, and bones. The exhumations required two winters and one autumn: December 1785 to May 1786, December 1786 to June 1787, and August to October 1787. A layer of earth over ten feet thick "infected with the debris of cadavers" was removed, eighty vaults were opened (not many for such a large cemetery), as well as some fifty large common graves, "from which over twenty thousand bodies, with their coffins, were exhumed." A group of doctors, including the reporter Thouret, had followed the operations, which provided them with a very unusual subject for research. They took advantage of the opportunity to "add a new chapter to the history of the decomposition of bodies in the bosom of the earth," a fascinating science that had begun with the miracles of the dead and improved with the advance of chemistry. In this gigantic laboratory they discovered a new form of mummification that was distinct from both total decomposition and desiccation, since it involved preservation of the fatty tissues.

Although the presence of the doctors and the few priests who were with the gravediggers ensured that a minimum standard of decency was respected, the fact remains that the "cemetery of our fathers," as Sponde's ridiculous Protestants had called it two centuries before, was excavated, plowed, and harrowed at night by the light of torches and bonfires, which were kept burning to promote the circulation of air. It took more than one thousand carts to transport the bones to the quarries of Paris.

Admittedly, these quarries had been prepared with care and skill; they were christened *catacombs* from the association with the catacombs of ancient Rome, and the word came to mean "cemetery." Thouret was enthusiastic about "a new order of things that will put an end to the intolerable use of the charnels in the various parishes." In these catacombs the bones were not deposited in the disorderly manner of medieval charnels, but in the baroque style of the cemeteries of mummies of Rome and Palermo. They can still be seen, and they attract more visitors every day.

But if the underground cemetery was prepared with respect and elegance, the cemetery above the ground was destroyed with violence, at least according to our modern point of view.

Thouret realizes that there was reason to fear the discontent of the people—the same discontent that the priests of Paris in 1763 brandished as a threat—if anyone touched their cemeteries. The passage is significant: "This cemetery had long been an object of public worship to the people. This respect had not completely disappeared, and although the cemetery had been concealed from view for several years [since 1780], the wall that enclosed it was still an object of veneration. [One could not demolish this cemetery secretly.] The slightest imprudent action could antagonize them."[27]

But in point of fact, nothing happened at all. The people of Paris accepted the destruction of the "cemetery of their fathers" with total indifference and took very little interest in the catacombs. More than half a millennium of Parisian dead had disappeared; a soil that had been venerated so profoundly that sometimes, like the soil of Palestine, a person asked that a handful of it be added to his grave when he could not be buried there, had been scattered without pity or honor.

When we consider the lack of concern of the Parisians on this occasion and the offhand way they entrusted the responsibility of burying their dead to hired porters, we may conclude that there was a certain lack of piety if not toward the dead, at least toward their bodies. I am speaking here of a popular attitude. The Decree of the Parliament of 1763 and the reflections of Molé in 1776 revealed, in another milieu, a similar detachment. In the case of the parliamentarians, we recognize the culmination of a tendency—now spiritualist and religious, now materialist and libertine—that we have been observing since the seventeenth century. The philosophy of the Enlightenment no doubt played a part, but its role was ambiguous, since it also laid the groundwork for the opposite tendency, that is, the cult of cemeteries and tombs, as we shall see. How are we to explain the casual attitude of the people? Was it an imitation of the example of lay and ecclesiastical elites who professed contempt for the body? Or was it a reaction to a clericalization of the funeral service, which had once reduced the role of the grave in favor of the soul and the prayers for the soul, which had concentrated the whole of the public ceremony in the church, and which was now becoming suspect?

Models of Future Cemeteries

The Edicts of 1763 and 1774, the Declaration of 1775, and the decisions to close down the old cemeteries by the chief of police after 1780 called for the creation of new cemeteries. These new cemeteries were to be very different from the old ones, which had been churchyards and continued to resemble churchyards even when they were no longer adjacent to churches. What would these new cemeteries be like? Who would build them? Who would maintain them? These questions were of interest to artists and financiers. During the 1770s and 1780s the office of the procurator general of Paris received several memoranda containing plans and offers of services regarding the new catacombs. These memoranda tell us something about the ideal image of the cemetery at that time. Here are three examples.[28]

The first, which retains some of the audacity of the great visionary architects of the late eighteenth century, is a plan for a circular catacomb. It consists of a central obelisk and five concentric galleries, which divide the space into six zones, each of which is reserved for a certain category of graves. The base of the obelisk contains eight burial vaults reserved for "persons of distinction"; another compartment is intended for ecclesiastics; the central compartment is reserved for the common graves. The last two peripheral galleries "will be open without charge to those who have paid in their parishes the same fees that they would pay today to be buried separately and in the church" (Article 5 of the Declaration of March 5, 1776). They are therefore like a continuation of the funerary decor of the church. The last peripheral gallery will be "a sort of colonnade running along and supported by the outside wall of the catacomb. It will serve as a burial place for those whose memory is to be eternalized by means of epitaphs or other remarkable monuments."

The author adds that the Bureau of Cemeteries will also serve as a Bureau of Records. He proposes a centralized organization of cemeteries and records for the whole kingdom, with an annex for the colonies, the military, "those who die on board ships," and for "all French citizens who die in foreign lands."

The second memorandum, which is the work of Renou, places even greater emphasis on the civic function of the cemetery. The purpose of the catacombs is to honor the dead, as was done in antiquity. The cemetery consists of two galleries, a circular gallery and a square gallery, the circle being inscribed inside the square. In the center is a chapel, in place of the obelisk of the first memorandum, which also contained a chapel. Between the circular gallery and the chapel will be the graves of ecclesiastics. The circular gallery, a porch with mausoleums, is reserved for the nobility and the upper classes. The square gallery, which runs along the outside wall, is intended for the middle classes, "citizens of lesser rank," who, like the nobles of the circular gallery, also have private graves, but whose monuments are more modest.

In both of these plans one notes the persistence of the idea of the mural tombstone. It is still assumed that an outdoor tomb may be against a wall, under a porch. We know that this was not the case in the English churchyard, where the headstones were planted in the ground. It took time for the French to abandon the idea that the noble model was mural.

Between the square galleries and the circular gallery is a large open space planted with flowers and trees. Here are the common graves, delicately referred to as the "tombs of the poor." Outside the walls of the cemetery, two charnels in the form of small cloisters will accommodate the bones from the common graves.

The spaces between the galleries are also planted with trees, shrubs, and flowers. The harmonious appearance of the cemetery is assured by the beauty of the funerary monuments and the gardens. The galleries will protect "mausoleums and other monuments, which will be all the more lasting because they will be sheltered from the ravages of the elements. One may even dare to suggest that arts of this kind, summoned by human vanity [but this vanity is no longer to be criticized; it is in a class with the ancient idea of glory and fame] to erect superb mausoleums, will have many opportunities to be practiced and consequently will flourish in France as never before. In time to come, these catacombs will be an object of curiosity to all foreigners and will be visited as a breeding ground of masterpieces in which each artist has sought to distinguish himself above the rest." Here we see the seed of the idea of the visit to the cemetery. The cemetery is no longer a municipal repository but a place to be visited. One does not yet visit it to preserve the memory of the dead, but as a museum of fine arts and a gallery of famous people.

The poor will no longer be objects of pity, for their common graves will be allotted ample space, which will be planted with flowers and trees. "A large number of trees in keeping with the character of the place [the plan specifies Italian poplars, great maples, plane trees, yews, laurels] will create a unified effect and at the same time will make the air more wholesome." Twenty years earlier, trees were not allowed in the new municipal cemeteries because they kept the air from circulating. Now they contribute to the wholesomeness of the air: an advance in the belief in the goodness of nature?

In short, this cemetery consists of a series of galleries full of monuments in a large garden.

The third plan, which was designed for the plains of Aubervilliers, also features enclosed areas for various social categories within a large garden. The first way in which it differs from the other plans is the original idea of transferring to it the remains of the royal family. The tombs of the kings and queens of France are to occupy a vast central temple, which will replace Saint-Denis. This temple will be surrounded by the tombs of the highborn, the nobility, and then, in a third enclosed space, those who are great by reputation: "the great men of the nation who shall deserve this glorious distinction, as in England's Westminster Abbey. Their tombs will be decorated with statues." The fourth enclosure includes "two small churches" for "private funerals, six pyramids, and approximately 2,000 small chapels designed to contain private graves for all families who shall wish to acquire such graves in perpetuity." The fifth enclosure is for "public graves," of which there are thirteen.

It is the sixth enclosure that is really new and reveals another conception of the tomb: the tomb isolated in nature. It is not really an enclosure but a park, "an intermediary space, very large, perhaps in the shape of the Champs-Elysées, where anyone who is so inclined may build a picturesque tomb by buying the necessary amount of land at so much a fathom."

"This vast enclosure would be surrounded by poplars, cypress trees, and evergreens of all species so as to conceal the monument as a whole from view, which would create a very unusual effect. This tableau would be enriched by transferring all well-known tombs to this space. [The idea of a museum of tombs was realized when the tombs of Abélard and Héloïse, Molière, and others, were transferred to Père-Lachaise.] It would bring together in one place the memorials of great men and the masterpieces of famous artists. Monuments that are now scattered in various places and known to few would become available to the whole world."

An analysis of these three plans helps us to form an image of the cemetery in France in the years just before the Revolution. In the first place, the topography of the cemetery reproduces the society as a whole, just as a relief map reproduces the contours of a piece of land. All are brought together in the same enclosure, but each has his own place: the royal family; the clergy; then two or three categories of persons distinguished by birth, achievement, or wealth, since the sites are for sale; and finally, the poor. The primary purpose of the cemetery is to present a microcosm of society. The cemetery is also a gallery of famous persons, where the nation preserves the memory of great men, as at Westminster Abbey, in England, which is specifically mentioned in one of the plans, or later at the Panthéon, in France.

Finally, the cemetery is a museum of the fine arts. The fine arts are no longer reserved for the contemplation of individual aesthetes. They have a social role; they are to be enjoyed by everyone, publicly.

But neither society nor art should be separated from nature and its immortal beauty. The cemetery is also a park, an English garden planted with trees. Familial piety, the relationship between the deceased and his family or friends, is neglected; the cemetery is the image of public society.

We have come a long way from the first plan of the Parisian parliamentarians of the 1760s. Between 1760 and 1780 the emphasis has shifted from a purely administrative function, a concern for public health and sanitation, to a sense of civic responsibility: the city of the dead as an enduring symbol of the society of the living. It should be noted that this quasi-religious evolution has occurred outside of the Church. Not that priests are absent: They have a place of honor in the hierarchy of burial spaces, and they serve the cemetery actively as ministers of worship, but their role is discreet, comparable to that of a public official. And above all, the ideological conception is alien to the metaphysics of traditional theological Christianity, or indeed of any religion of salvation.

The Sordid Reality
of the Cemeteries

Of course all these beautiful plans were swept away by the tide of Revolution. After Thermidor, however, things returned to normal, and the national and departmental assemblies of the Convention, the Directory, and the Consulate were constantly preoccupied with the state of the cemeteries.

The lawmakers were aware of their indecency and declared it to be no longer tolerable. In the public cemeteries created after the closing down of les Innocents and the old charnels, no provision had been made for private graves, and all those who died in Paris were buried in a common grave that was every bit as squalid as those of les Innocents.

"Having been commissioned by you to inspect the cemeteries of Paris," writes Citizen Cambry, administrator of the department of the Seine, in 1799, "and to ascertain their condition, I have examined them all. I shall spare your sensibilities the picture that I might draw. No other people, no other age shows man after his death in such a cruel state of abandonment. . . . What! Is that sacred creature, the mother of our children, the dear companion of my life . . . to be taken from me tomorrow and thrown into a foul sewer, to lie next to, nay, on top of, the vilest, the most loathsome scoundrel?"[29]

In 1801 a writer has several of his characters discuss the subject. The conversation takes place under two cypress trees that mark the grave of the landowner's brother. We are in the country, in a valley far from Paris where such burial was possible. Euphrasine is not so fortunate: "Happy is she who can come and weep on the tomb of the one she loved! Alas! I am deprived of that melancholy pleasure. My husband was buried in the common grave. He was torn from my arms. I was not allowed to follow his body. A few days later I wanted to visit the place where he had been buried. . . . I was shown an enormous pit with bodies piled up. . . . I still tremble at the thought. I had to abandon the idea of discovering the last resting-place of his remains."[30]

As for the transfer of the body to the cemetery, the same author writes, "I must describe a scene that will inspire you with a righteous horror. These men who transport the dead of the town to the common cemetery often become intoxicated along the way and quarrel, or what is even more revolting, sing gaily, and the public official who goes with them is unable to impose silence."

Two years earlier, in his report for the Year VII, Cambry described a funeral procession as if he had seen it with his own eyes: "When a body is being transported to its place of burial, I have seen our porters go into a bar. Throwing by the door the pitiful remains that have been entrusted to them, they quench their thirst with copious libations of spirits," forcing "the stricken relatives of the deceased," when they were there, which was not always the case, to drink with them and "to pay the price of this sacrilegious beverage."[31] Actually the anecdote was part of the folklore of the time. The actor Brunet of the Palais-Royal was said to have exclaimed at the sight of a funeral procession, "God! If I had to be buried like that, I would rather not die at all!"[32]

The main cause of the problem was that those hired to transport the body were left alone and unsupervised. Consequently, when one wanted to be sure that a minimum of decency was observed, one had to assemble a group of people capable of keeping the porters under control. But the porters were not easily impressed. For example, on 7 Fructidor Year VII, Citizen Cartier, a deputy in the Council of Elders, died. *Le Messager* reported, "A deputation from his department and several representatives of the people attended his burial, which took place in the cemetery in Montmartre with the indecency that characterizes funerals today. This lack of reverence for the remains of the dead is a sacrilegious neglect of morality and religion unprecedented in the history of civilization." The previous year, 1798, the Institute had decided, despite the reluctance of some of the confreres, to accompany deceased members to the cemetery.[33]

At the time of the Thermidorian Convention it was decided to remedy the lack of discipline by having funeral processions accompanied by an important personage—a magistrate, as Citizen Avril suggests, or one of the local public commissioners: "Such an honorable and important function should be entrusted only to a citizen who has demonstrated the highest virtues."[34]

This state of affairs was generally blamed on the Revolution, that is, the Reign of Terror. A report to the General Council for the fifteenth of Thermidor, Year VIII (August 3, 1800), reads, "Henceforth the respect due to the dead was destroyed. . . . Henceforth the procedures of burial were degraded and custom violated with a shamelessness that aroused even the most barbarous. . . . Several of these abuses still exist today. You are already aware of the indecency of these cemeteries, which would more accurately be called pens for the dead, barely walled in as they are by a few miserable boards and abandoned to all the ravages of chance and the elements." Blame was laid on the revolutionary impulse to obliterate distinctions, the pursuit of equality: "That unfortunate equality . . . had extended its influence even to the empire of death, and deprived filial piety or conjugal affection of all that innocent display by which the bereaved seek to beguile their grief."[35] Note the emphasis on the pain of bereavement and the consolatory function of mourning and the visit to the cemetery.

But it was probably Chateaubriand who saw most clearly when he said, "During the revolutionary period, we know how burial was performed and how, for a few pennies, a father, mother, or wife was taken to the dump. . . . But these things should be left to heaven; they were the natural consequence of the first violation under the monarchy." The Revolution had merely aggravated a situation that was at least twenty years old. The only difference is that the situation was no longer tolerated.

The Contest of 1801

A few measures were taken following the Cambry report. In Paris it was decided to discontinue the repositories; henceforth bodies were to be picked up at the home. There was also a new attempt to reorganize the cemeteries, which failed.

In 1801 the minister of the interior, Lucien Bonaparte, invited the French Institute to conduct an essay contest on the following subject: "What ceremonies should be performed at funerals and what regulations should be adopted regarding burial?" In these ceremonies, "no form may be introduced that belongs to any religion"; the intention was to create a secular model.

The Institute received forty entries, and the prize was awarded to Amaury Duval and Abbé Mulot, former deputy to the Legislative Assembly. The winning essays help us to assess the changes that have taken place since 1763.

The principle of burial outside the towns for hygienic reasons is now taken for granted. The issue is no longer discussed, except to deplore once again the state of the old parochial cemeteries.

Another principle, which had appeared in the *Mémoire des curés de Paris* of 1763 but was then forgotten, is now unanimously accepted and proclaimed: "Every individual must be able to render to the spirits of his relatives appropriate tributes of his sorrow and regret. The sensitive person who survives a loving mother, a beloved wife, or a close friend must be able to find consolation for his grief in the respect that is paid to their remains."[36] The essential element is now the affective relationship between the deceased and the survivor. It is in terms of this private relationship that contestants discuss what measures should be taken.

J. Girard's *"Des tombeaux et de l'influence des institutions funèbres sur les moeurs"* (Of tombs and of the influence of funeral institutions on morals), one of the unpublished essays, gives a clear analysis of the dominant ideas on the subject. It defines death from the outset not as the loss of life but as the separation of individuals who love each other. It is as much the death of the other as the death of the self, and in fact the death of the self is conceived only in terms of the other: "One day I shall mourn for those who are dear to me, or I shall be mourned by them." The idea of death is no longer, as in the time of Horace or of the *arte moriendi,* an invitation to the enjoyment of things: "At the thought of death, the oppressed soul longs to open itself completely and envelop the objects of its affection. . . . How many attentions, how many marks of love one longs to lavish on them! How many times one reproaches oneself for the unhappiness one has caused them, for the moments one has spent apart from them."

Such are the sentiments of a man of 1801. Such, also, are the sentiments that nature normally inspires. But these natural sentiments have been distorted by religion. "This touching devotion that the first men rendered to the dead became a principle of error, a source of evil. Superstition was born in the graveyard." In two forms. The first is the irrational fear of the dead, of ghosts, "of hideous specters and larvae"; the horrible and imaginary face of death. The second is the belief in the prayer for the dead. "Man abandoned the light of reason. . . . It was no longer by sublime invocations that he honored the gods but by difficult attitudes, painful mortifications, or cruel sacrifices. The priest lost his divine character. Religion became a profanation of the holiest laws, and the voice of heaven became a cry of terror and greed. If one added up all the countless evils caused by the superstitious fear of death and of the existence said to follow death, one would see man enslaved to bloodthirsty gods. . . . The funeral institutions [of our Christian past] arose from the same source as these superstitions." There is no question of reviving them. Some even believe that these institutions are just as much to blame as the Revolution for the indecency of burial. The Church diverted the ancient cult of the dead toward the immortal soul as an object of intercessory prayers, and abandoned the body to the garbage heap.

But the materialism that is replacing the Church as a foundation for morals is no better. "An even greater danger is that of a cold and humiliating materialism that would destroy the influence of morality and the effectiveness of government and paralyze one of its principal means of power. . . . Superstition may serve to unite the people, to consolidate the authority in the hands of a leader, but materialism destroys all the magic of the social order . . . , it breaks that sacred chain that descends from heaven for the happiness of earth. Then there is no more hope for virtue, no more restraint for crime, no more consolation for grief. . . . Materialism and superstition are equally to be feared."[37]

Toward a Cult of the Dead

Some of the essayists wanted no separation between "sects," that is, religions: "Men of all sects shall lie side by side in this peaceful refuge, where it would seem that differences of opinion should no longer keep them apart"[38] And in the ideal cemetery, there must be no crosses.

And yet it is a cult that must be established: "You will not establish the cult of the dead" unless you take certain precautions. This cult "must inspire salutary fears without inspiring empty terrors." The ceremonies must be "both simple and moving." They must arouse the emotions and direct them "toward a moral and religious purpose."[39] These ceremonies will be secular. Although denominational services may also be held, they will merely be tolerated.

The authors provide for the exhibition of the body after death. Duval and Girard believe that the body should be exhibited with the face uncovered, according to a custom that had been abandoned for centuries except in the south of France, in order to permit and prolong "communication with the dead." The ancient ceremonies must be replaced by public exhibition in the home and in a temple of a nondenominational kind.

Embalming is also recommended, for the same reasons as exhibition with the face uncovered. "The arts record the features of those we have loved. It would be even sweeter to use their magic power to restore the appearance of life to organs chilled by death and to beguile the grief that would revive these mute bodies in order to converse with them and have them as witnesses of our chaste memories." The desire to prolong the appearance of the features as long as possible will inspire all the techniques of preservation. One wonders whether these techniques were not intended to avoid burial, to keep the deceased always visible, to preserve him in order to converse with him.

One of the characters in the dialogues of Amaury Duval, a woman whose mother has disappeared into one of those pits that had become a scandal, expresses everything she owes to "modern chemistry": "A month later, my son died. Ah! Him, at least, I still possess, although he no longer returns my kisses or responds to my voice. Thanks to the discoveries of modern chemistry, it has been possible to preserve my son's features and almost the color of his skin."[40] The process is not new; we remember how Necker and his wife had been preserved at Coppet in two vats of alcohol. Here again we encounter the interest that was accorded to the dead body and its preservation in the eighteenth century, but this time for another purpose: to prolong the physical presence of a loved one.

In this context, the exhibition of the embalmed and lifelike body in the temple makes us think of an American funeral home or of Forest Lawn, the cemetery in Los Angeles. There is probably no connection between these utopias of the late eighteenth and early nineteenth century and American embalming, which is said to have begun during the Civil War, but the resemblance is disconcerting.

The temple will be the scene of a ceremony organized by the public officials who have replaced the priests and are the keepers of the public records and the directors of a sort of national honor roll. There was a plan to combine in a single institution the official records of deaths, the cult of the dead, and the national order of merit. The ceremony was to begin with the announcement of death. After that the name of the deceased would be posted on an honor roll for a specified period of time, say a month.

The announcement would be followed by a eulogy and the solemn reading of the will. This was a curious attempt to revive the will, whose sentimental and religious importance had declined after the middle of the eighteenth century.

Next, the coffin would be carried by porters either in the country or in the towns, placed on a hearse whose "lugubrious aspect shall indicate the purpose for which it is designed," and preceded by a guide on foot.[41] From this moment, there is a choice between the public cemetery and the private estate.

The public cemetery does not resemble the elaborate architectural plans of the 1770s. The "fields of repose" will be large green spaces without buildings or monuments. The authors discourage the builders of tombs; at most they will accept, and with an ill grace, an inconspicuous inscription marking the location of the body, for they know that there can be no cult of the dead "unless the son can find his father's grave." "Let the laws prohibit the erection of any sort of stone monument; but there is no objection to a mound of greensward." Behold the lawn cemetery! Amid these graves covered with sod, "there will be paths where one may stroll, lost in a melancholy reverie. These paths will be shaded by cypress trees, poplars with trembling leaves, and weeping willows. . . . There will be flowing streams. . . . These places will become a terrestrial Elysian fields, where those weary of the sorrows of life may find perfect peace." Or an English garden: "Here one will see the rose fade each fall on the grave of a young virgin, another rose who lived only for a season."[42]

"The husband will abandon himself freely to all the charm of his grief; he will be able to visit the shade of the wife he adores. Finally, those who cherish the fond memory of their benefactors will find a place of peace in this refuge devoted to meditation and gratitude."[43]

Generally speaking, the cemetery is open to all, but remains "under the protection of the government." Some would like to close the cemetery to the public except for certain times, which would be devoted "to the memory and worship of the dead." But even then a son, a parent, or a friend could "come from time to time and water the beloved grave with his tears."[44]

In these plans one is struck by the lack of emphasis on the role of national pantheon, gallery of famous men, or public museum, which inspired the plans of 1780. The private function of the cemetery has prevailed over its public function, which is tolerated only as a necessity in the large towns, and there simply for the sake of the poor. If one were living in the happy days of the Golden Age, in the peaceful countryside, one could dispense with the communal cemetery altogether.

For everyone has the right to dispose of his own body. "If we have the right to dispose of our property, how should we not have the right to dispose of ourselves!" The ideal "last resting-place" is the family estate. Society "must encourage the ordinary man to place his tomb in his father's fields," unlike those illustrious citizens whom it claims for its own. It erects monumental tombs to them in order to keep them alive in the memory of posterity. But even these national tombs must be isolated, like private graves: "Society must assign private locations to the graves of great men, near . . . the former scene of their accomplishments": Rousseau in Ermenonville, La Fontaine in the middle of a wood, Boileau on a promenade. Everyone has his own place. "Why should the peaceful laborer not look forward to resting in the fields he has cultivated? Ah! Let him mark the place where he will one day sleep, whether he prefers the foot of the ancient oak . . . , or wishes to be laid beside a wife, . . . a father, or a son."[45]

Such sacred groves would be the best means of instilling in men a deep-rooted love for their native land. One might assume that men value their dead because they value their fields, but it is just the opposite: They value their fields because they value their dead, and in time there develops a universal and powerful love of the earth and the dead. Here, in the midst of the Thermidorian Convention, the Directory, and the Consulate, among an elite steeped in the philosophy of the Enlightenment and suspicious of, if not hostile toward, the Church, its influence, and its history, we are witnessing the birth of a Barrèsian, Péguyist, Maurrasian, but above all, positivist concept of the earthly fatherland. The affinity is obvious. "How much dearer to him will be the fields" when they contain the graves of his fathers! "Would you recall men to purer manners, to those real affections from which love of one's land is derived? I do not mean that enthusiastic and frenzied love that feeds only on abstractions or proud fancies, but that true and simple love that cherishes the land as a protective divinity, that maintains order and tranquillity. Then bind them to the soil that gave them birth. He who cherishes his father's land is more attached to his country by that simple bond than the proud philosopher. . . . Such are the elements of which true love of country is composed. We love our fields because they provide sustenance for our families. Our town is dear to us because it contains our father's house, the temple where we go to pray, the place where we go to converse with our friends. We love our province because our town is part of it, and finally our country is important to us only because it contains the whole circle of our affections and because it is our protection and our support. . . . Private graves will bind us closer to the paternal fields with a sense of gratitude and honor." Fields containing tombs will not be sold; they will be defended against the enemy. "Thus, private graves will have the additional advantage of binding us to family, land, and country."[46]

These quotations are from the essay by Girard. Amaury Duval's essay suggests the same policy, with fewer sociological arguments: "I need not say that after the body has been exhibited in the temple, each family will have the right to dispose of the one they have lost. The family may have the body of the deceased taken to the land that he possessed, and may even erect the most ostentatious monuments." Duval dreams of a private grave for himself, but without these "ostentatious monuments" that he scorns and whose popularity he fears; that is why he excludes them from the communal cemetery. He will lie in nature: "When I return to my birthplace, I want to dig my own grave in the little field that my father will leave me. I shall make it under the poplars that he planted—I can still see them on the banks of the little stream that waters their roots. Lilacs and violets will bloom around it. To this spot, several times a day, I shall bring my friends and even her who will be my beloved companion. . . . How dear to [our children] will be this spot, if they have our tastes, if they have my soul. Often, after my death, they will kiss the nearby trees, for under their bark will flow the substance that composed my body." Dissolution in nature is no longer the return to nothingness that it was for the libertines of the eighteenth century, but a kind of metempsychosis: It is the same beloved being who continues to exist in other, vegetable forms. Nature—that is, the paternal soil—is composed of the substance of the dead parents and friends; it reproduces them indefinitely.

Once the public ceremony in the temple and the burial in the communal cemetery or paternal field has been arranged, there remains the institution of mourning. This word was understood to mean both expressions of sympathy and the style of life that custom imposed on survivors. The practice of mourning had been contested by the same milieu of *philosophes* from which the drafters of the Parliamentary Decree of 1763 had been recruited, and the decree had in turn been denounced by the *Mémoire des curés de Paris* of the same date.

It was also in response to the decree that Abbé Coyer had written *Etrennes aux morts et aux vivants* (New Year's gift to the dead and the living) in 1768. Born in 1707, a former Jesuit who had left the Society in 1736, private tutor to a Turenne, head chaplain to the cavalry, author of a plan of public education and a *Traité de la noblesse marchande,* Coyer is a good representative of the ideas of the enlightened intelligentsia. He is hostile to the institution of mourning, which perpetuates a "cruel image of death" that is several centuries old, whereas it is necessary to "make death agreeable."[47] I can understand why Madeleine Foizil has been tempted to see the *philosophes* of the late eighteenth century as the precursors of a mid-twentieth-century modernism in which death is no longer either horrible or agreeable but nonexistent.[48] For Abbé Coyer death is "agreeable," as it was to the La Ferronays and the Brontës. This agreeable death foreshadows both the romantic death of the nineteenth century and the unmentionable death of today, and their common origin suggests some secret affinity between the two. The romantics loved and longed for death, and good Christians and Catholics that they were, they did not fear it. They would have agreed with this remark of Coyer's, which is the denial, or rather the reversal, of the old *ars moriendi:* "The fear that one shows must be relative to the sort of life one has led; privileged souls have more reason to desire the end of their pilgrimage than to dread it." Here one puts one's finger on the complexity of this culture that combined a reformed Christianity, a rationalism hostile to all churches, a tendency to hedonism, and the seething passion of romanticism.

When Coyer discusses the customs of mourning, he adopts a bantering tone: "In affliction one should surround oneself with objects capable of cheering the eyes and the imagination. But we bury our grief in crepe and in rooms resembling tennis courts [an allusion, I assume, to the stripping of rooms during the period of deep mourning]. Is this not an unreasonable prejudice? Because a man has died, it does not therefore follow that others must die with him. . . . True grief is found in the heart, not in those drab garments whose use is traditional with us."

It is quite possible that Coyer had disciples, at least in Paris, and that the decline in decorum that we have observed in funeral processions at the end of the century was accompanied by an abandonment of mourning. But there was also a reaction. Duval complains that people are "deserting" the rooms of the dead; Girard would like to "revive the almost forgotten custom of mourning . . . and extend the period out of gratitude. In France the period of mourning was generally set at one year. In some provinces it was extended for another six months. Today everything has changed, and mourning is nothing but a sentimental affectation."

By 1800 it was no longer permissible to speak of mourning in the light and bantering tone that Abbé Coyer used in 1768. In the interval new worlds of affectivity had been discovered. Accustomed as we are to the age-old slowness of psychological change, we are surprised by the extraordinarily rapid emergence of a new sensibility. No doubt it had been developing below the surface, and the changes in family relations in the late seventeenth century had anticipated it, but everything accelerated during the last third of the eighteenth century.

In the last chapter we observed not only the return to deep mourning, but also the affectation of spontaneity. People do not observe the conventions. They follow the impulse of their grief, going further, or in different directions, from those prescribed by custom. Even among the aristocracy, the widow is no longer willing to remain in the house during the funeral; she attends the service. At first she is hidden in a corner of the church or gallery, but tomorrow she will lead the mourning, invisible under her veils and black crepe, as is already the custom among the bourgeoisie.

Mummies of Glass

The proposals I have just analyzed express the opinions of people who are serious, well balanced, reasonable, respectable, and representative of the sensibilities of their age.

The subject was fashionable, and along with this respectable literature there also appeared some pamphlets that we find rather mad. As a matter of fact, so did their contemporaries. But there is a method in their madness.

Pierre Giraud is obviously not a nobody. He is the architect of the Palais de Justice; he risked his life to save some of the victims of the Year II; by the Year IV he had already drawn up a plan for a cemetery, and in the Year VII he submitted it to the department of the Seine. He reissued it in a little book published in 1801 on the occasion of the French Institute competition. He called it *Les Tombeaux, ou essai sur les sépultures:* "In which the author recalls the customs of ancient peoples, mentions briefly those observed by the moderns, and describes procedures for dissolving flesh and calcining human bones and converting them into an indestructible substance with which to make portrait medallions of individuals." We spoke earlier of dissolution in nature. The procedure proposed here consists in substituting science for nature in order to preserve the memory of the dead.

The technique is not new; it is found in the seventeenth-century literature on the miracles of the dead. Becker, the inventor mentioned by Giraud, was already known to Thouret, who speaks of him in his *Rapport sur les exhumations des Innocents.* The "fatty substances" of the large communal graves eventually turned into a sort of glass; thus, mummies of fat could be transformed into mummies of glass! Becker is the author of a *Physica subterranea,* published in Frankfurt in 1669 and reprinted in Leipzig in 1768. By experimentation he discovered that the soil produced by the decomposition of human bodies is the most easily vitrified and "that it produces a very fine glass; but he would not reveal the process because he was afraid of committing a sacrilege." Giraud comments, "For the time that the celebrated Becker was writing, his weakness was excusable." The vitrification brought about naturally by a period of time spent in the common graves can also be achieved by human industry. In this way one can "avenge [the sacred shades] forever from the ravages of time and the caprices of men. May all humanity be imbued with this enduring truth: that anyone who does not respect the dead comes close to murdering the living."

The cemetery proposed by Giraud is similar to the type described in the plans of the 1770s: an enclosure with a portico around a central pyramid. But here the resemblance ends, because the base of the pyramid is a crematory oven, and the columns of the portico are of glass, a glass "made of human bones taken from abandoned cemeteries. . . . If it should prove unfeasible to make such a noble use of these precious remains of humanity, one could substitute the bones of domestic animals." Under the gallery would be monuments, also of glass: portrait medallions and commemorative tablets.

The crematory oven consists of "four boilers large enough to contain up to four cadavers immersed in a caustic lye of the kind used by soapmakers. . . . After the animal substances have been reduced first to a jelly and then to ashes, they may be placed behind the portrait medallion or even added to the vitrifiable materials." An appendix to the plan includes "Directions for Making a Good Soapmaker's Lye Capable of Dissolving Human Flesh" and "The Art of Vitrifying Bones," by Dartigues.

The glass thus obtained is a new form of the human body, rendered incorruptible and imperishable. It is a raw material; but what is to be done with it? "The first method, the one most pleasing to the religious imagination, . . . would be to make a small portrait by pouring the glass into a mold made during the person's lifetime. One need only have a heart to understand how consoling it would be to a sensitive soul to possess a bust of a pleasing material that would have the inestimable advantage of being both the portrait and the actual substance of a father, mother, wife, child, friend, or any other individual who was dear to us." Unfortunately, the glass is not sufficiently fluid. The best technique would be to "make a bas-relief portrait of the individual, to make a mold from this bas-relief, and then to pour the glass into this mold."

These medallions would be displayed in the galleries with epitaphs.

One can imagine their effect on visitors: "How many children would spontaneously, from their earliest youth, be turned away from the path of crime and dissipation at the mere sight of the portraits of their virtuous ancestors?"

There would be enough glass to make two medallions, one for the cemetery, the other a portable object that the family would take with them when they traveled, like a mourning picture. "I also suggest that the child who deserved the most from his parents, his peers, and his country would be the natural heir of the bones, ashes, or medallions of his ancestors. He could take them with him everywhere with the understanding that he was responsible to the rest of the family and would present them to the others upon demand."

The only disadvantage is that the process is expensive. What about the poor, who will not be able to afford it? Our author has thought of that, too; his ingenuity knows no bounds. "Persons in modest circumstances who could not pay the cost of vitrification but who would like at least the skeleton of their loved one could obtain it by paying the price of the dissolution of the flesh." Some would not even pay this price or would not feel the need to keep the skeletons of their dear departed at home, but these bones need not therefore be wasted: "Unclaimed skeletons would be taken to the catacombs, and the remaining flesh would be deposited in one of the eight common graves in the field of repose. After a year their bones would be converted to glass and could be used in the composition of the monuments under the gallery indicated above. In this way an interesting material would be made out of the very substance of the dead, and in a few years [thanks to the large number of unclaimed skeletons of the poor] a monument would be achieved that would be unique of its kind."

In spite of his enthusiasm, Pierre Giraud had some doubts about the fate of his plan, and he offered his own body as a subject of experiment. "I am so convinced of the infinite good that would result from this plan that if it is not carried out before my death, I have proposed in advance . . . that I be used as an example. I have asked that my survivors arrange with a soapmaker or surgeon to separate my bones from the rest of my remains, to burn the flesh and fat, and to place the resulting ashes, along with my skeleton, in a tomb that I have had built especially in my garden, until such time as my descendants can have my bones converted to glass."[49]

Sometimes a humorous caricature tells us more about life than pages of lofty analysis. Here the caricature is unintentional and the humor is nonexistent, but the picture is still significant. The purpose of all this extravagance was to save the remains of the loved one from "the horror of the tomb" and from corruption, and to combine the image of his features and the substance of his body into a single object. The idea would not have seemed absurd to Raimondo di Sangro, in his eighteenth-century Neapolitan anatomy room, or to Frankenstein. But these men, like the alchemists of the Renaissance, were investigating the principle of life, whereas Pierre Giraud is seeking the presence of the other. If he sounds ridiculous, it is simply because he is confusing the languages of two distinct periods: the period when the cadaver promised to reveal to anyone who dissected it the secrets of life and the period when the cadaver gave to anyone who contemplated it the illusion of a presence.

The Decree of 23 Prairial, Year XII

Throughout the second half of the eighteenth century, there was a continuing preoccupation with the burial of the dead. The apparent motives for this interest varied, but the interest and its seriousness remained constant. Burial, once a religious and ecclesiastical act, had become a function of civic administration and public health. Finally, it became a religious act again, but it was a religion without denomination or church, a religion of memory; in extreme cases, a religion of non-Christian forms of survival. In France, this long debate ended with an official decision. With a few alterations, the Decree of 23 Prairial, Year XII (June 12, 1804), determined the rules for cemeteries and funerals until our time. The administration, under all regimes, has steadily decreased the moral and religious importance of the decree and reduced it to a simple program of public health, which it certainly was not in the minds of its originators. More than a legal text, it is a sort of "Ten Commandments" of a new cult, the cult of the dead. However, this becomes apparent only if one sees it as the culmination of half a century of uncertainty and reflection.

The decree definitively confirms the prohibition against burial in churches and towns; cemeteries must be at least forty to fifty yards beyond urban limits. It goes beyond the plans of 1801, which retained the principle of the old common graves. It establishes the principle that bodies may never be superimposed but must always be juxtaposed. This represents a complete break with the past. Private graves, which until now had been reserved for those who paid for them, are henceforth the rule. Even the graves of the poor must be separated from one another. (Later this principle was reconsidered for reasons of economy. The separation between graves was eliminated in the case of the poor, but the obligation to have a coffin was retained. Gone were the days of winding-sheets and communal litters.) So the poor are henceforth buried next to one another in a continuous trench. The required distance between the pits and their depth are specified precisely. No pit is to be opened or reused before an interval of five years has elapsed. "Consequently, the area to be used for burial will be five times larger than the area needed to contain the estimated number of bodies that can be buried in a year." As a result of this provision, the cemeteries grew until they occupied the large surfaces characteristic of the urban landscape of the nineteenth century.

This cemetery will be a garden: "Trees and shrubs will be planted, with appropriate precautions so as not to interfere with the circulation of the air."

In this communal cemetery it will be permissible to buy a gravesite and erect a monument. But it is interesting to note that such permission is subject to restrictions: "When the size of the area reserved for burial permits, grants of land may be made to persons desiring to possess a distinct and separate place to establish their grave and that of their parents or successors and to build vaults, monuments, or tombs. However, such grants will be made only to those who shall offer to make endowments or donations to the poor and the hospitals, in addition to a sum that shall be given to the community." It is the principle of the grant in perpetuity. No doubt the authors thought such cases would be the exception, as burial in church was still the exception under the *ancien régime*. They treated them like the pious endowments of traditional wills, and it is true that in the beginning not many commoners claimed what still seemed a privilege. For reasons of money and prestige, when the new cemetery of Père-Lachaise was created, it was designed as a deluxe cemetery, reserved for grants in perpetuity. Lanzac de Laborie remarks in 1906, "Incredible as it may seem, the rich segment of the Parisian population showed a singular reluctance to adopt the new cemetery," an attitude "explained by its remoteness . . . and by the fact that the practice of grants in perpetuity had not yet become customary."[50] This practice was only recommended by a new species of prophet, the initiators of the cult of the dead, the authors and readers of the plans and proposals being analyzed here.

But the community of the faithful soon came around. Their initial reticence merely serves to emphasize the infatuation that followed. Grants in perpetuity became so numerous that by the first half of the nineteenth century they were creating space problems in the cemeteries: "Grants in perpetuity, whose number and proportion increased with the rise of public affluence and the decline in the value of silver, steadily reduced the available surface of the cemetery."[51] By the end of the nineteenth century, grants in perpetuity occupied three-quarters of the surface of Parisian cemeteries. The five-year grants and the free trenches were pushed back and reduced to a minimum, and perpetual grants, instead of remaining the exception to the rule, were extended to persons in modest circumstances.

Another custom spread on a scale that was not foreseen by the originators of the Decree of Prairial. The decree recognizes the right "of each
individual, without need of authorization, to place over the grave of his
parent or friend a tombstone or other mark of burial, as has been customary
up to the present."

The use of the tombstone spread rapidly. In Père-Lachaise, in
1804, 113 tombstones were laid that had been recovered from the
abandoned cemeteries of Paris. In 1805, 14 new stones were laid, and
thereafter:

1806	19
1807	26
1808	51
1810	76
1811	96
1812	130
1813	242
1814	509
1815	635
1814–30	30,000 (1,879 per year)

In 1889 a former caretaker of a cemetery wrote, "We may assume that
in 1804 no one foresaw how popular this type of burial would become.
. . . This extraordinary increase was beyond anyone's expectation."[52]

It became humiliating not to possess a long-term grant. The grant in
perpetuity was comparable to real estate, except that it could not be sold
and was transmitted only by inheritance. Moreover, each gravesite was
covered by a monument that in countries like France or Italy was often
enormous. There was a reluctance to leaving an anonymous and invisible
tomb.

The customs that became established in the cemeteries following the
Decree of Prairial are the opposite of those of the *ancien régime*. As soon
as superimposition of bodies was abolished, personalization of the burial
place became the absolute rule.

Hereditary ownership of the grave, which had existed only in rare cases
involving the granting of chapels, was extended to the whole middle class.
The monument, which had been the exception, became the rule.

In this system we recognize the ideas of the authors of the plans and
proposals of the 1800s regarding the communal cemetery. They also recommended private burial at home. The Decree of Prairial follows them on this
point too: "Any person may be buried on his property, provided said
property is outside of and the prescribed distance from the walls of cities

and towns." In this case no authorization is required, although in later regulations the decision will be left to the discretion of the municipal authorities, subject to the supervision of the prefect. By the beginning of the nineteenth century, every man has the choice of being buried either in the communal cemetery or on his own property.

All that remained was to organize the ceremony and to indicate who would be in charge of it. The plans of 1800 had called for a secular ceremony to be performed by magistrates rather than priests. They described rituals that are still performed today in secular funerals, such as the offering of "flowers and green branches," which are thrown into the grave.

Before Prairial Year XII there was an attempt to reform the funeral procession by turning it over to a private company. But this private company was soon felt to be taking unfair advantage of its position, and the Decree of Prairial restored exclusive control over funeral rites to the church councils. In 1806 a new decree established a price scale and a division into social classes, to the indignation of Senator Grégoire, who wrote on his copy, "Scandalous division into classes of creatures who come before God clothed only in their good and evil deeds!"[53]

In Paris the church councils subcontracted funerals to a commercial company. Later, the town governments inherited the monopoly of the church councils and ownership of the cemeteries. Unlike the United States, France had no private cemeteries. All the cemeteries were—and still are —public. Things might have turned out differently. This municipalization is the result of a twofold mistrust, of the Church and of the private entrepreneur.

But France was moving toward the restoration of Catholicism and its recognition as a state religion. And all the plans for a secular—national and municipal—ceremony outside the churches that had been proposed since the 1770s were abandoned in favor of a return to the traditional practices observed before the Revolution. Once again burial became a religious ceremony. A decree of August 18, 1811, provided that in Paris all bodies must be taken to the church, in the absence of written orders to the contrary. As early as 1802 the elaborate funeral procession reappeared with all the pomp of the *ancien régime,* to the delight of the Parisians, who attended these events as theatrical spectacles and thought they were good for business. "Today [February 9, 1802] the duc de Bouillon was buried with a magnificence that has not been seen in a long time. Fifty paupers dressed in black and carrying torches escorted the hearse, which was drawn by six horses and followed by ten carriages draped in black and twenty bourgeois carriages." The carriages were an innovation, introduced because of the remoteness of the extraurban cemeteries. At the funeral of Junot's mother-in-law there were three hundred poor and fifty servants.[54]

Was this a return to the religious traditions and ecclesiastical splendors of the *ancien régime?* One is tempted to see it as such, but the people of the early nineteenth century thought exactly the opposite. For the author of a guide to Père-Lachaise published in 1836, the era of the Church was a time of perfunctory funerals, and the cult of the dead was an innovation of the revolutionary period: "Where once there was little order, respect, or decency in the funeral procession of the poor, today there is ardor, dignity, and reserve." In the days when the clergy were in charge, the prayers were rushed through and the dead were piled on top of one another in the common graves. "This revolting state of affairs has fortunately ceased to afflict our eyes. . . . The accursed Revolution, which our scribblers of today blame for all the evil that has been done for the past forty years, without giving it credit for the little good it has managed to accomplish, is the cause of the change that has occurred in Paris in this interesting area of civil administration."[55]

Private Burial
in the Nineteenth Century

Jacques Delille died on May 1, 1813. His body lay in state for six days at the Collège de France with the face lightly painted and the head crowned with laurel. In his book of poems, *Des Jardins,* Delille had celebrated the tomb in nature:

> Come here, all you whose meditative hearts
> Love the sad joys that melancholy imparts.
> Behold this tombstone where the bending birch
> Like the Chinese willow, but more solemnly,
> With its long branches and sad falling leaves
> And hanging arms weeps upon the grave.

And if you have neither friends nor relatives to bury in your garden, you may adopt the grave of a poor peasant:

> Would you blush to decorate their humble graves?
> If you would comfort their lives, then honor their deaths.
> Honor his tomb with a more decent stone,
> Inscribe his virtues, the grief of his town . . .

The result will be a charming place to stroll:

> . . . *Often an involuntary charm*
> *To these sacred confines will draw your eyes.*

The tomb has become the indispensable ornament of a garden, the center of a meditation. It is here that Delille arranged to be laid to rest, and not in a public cemetery. He confides to his wife:

> *Listen, then, before you close my eyes,*
> *To my last prayer and my last good-byes.*
> *You know that when this brief life shall expire*
> *It is my dearest hope and fondest desire*
> *Beside some clear stream to lie sleeping*
> *In the shade of an old oak or young sapling.*

This will be in the country:

> *In the peaceful fields, place my humble tomb.*

This is not the wish of an anti-Christian; the chosen spot has been blessed like a cemetery:

> *And let this spot not be on profane ground,*
> *Let religion sprinkle holy water around.*

The cross, which has become the symbol of the tomb, will be there:

> *And let the glorious symbol of our religion*
> *Assure me of my glorious resurrection!*[56]

If one scans the literature, one has the distinct impression that everyone wanted to be buried on his own property. The communal cemetery must have become the burial place of the poor and of those unfortunate citizens who possessed neither fields nor gardens far from the towns.

In France today there are still examples of these domestic tombs. In a suburb of Aix-en-Provence there is the tomb of Joseph Sec, a carpenter who made a fortune in real estate and built his future tomb near his house. It is an extraordinary monument, a mausoleum whose iconography is of Masonic origin, as Michel Vovelle has demonstrated.[57]

Chateaubriand's idea was "to buy a little plot of land twenty feet long by twelve feet wide at the western tip of Grand Bé. . . . I would have this space surrounded by a low wall surmounted by a simple iron grille. . . . Inside I would put nothing but a granite base carved out of the cliffs along the beach. On this base there would be a small iron cross. No inscription, no name or date. . . . I wish the priest of Saint-Malo to bless my future place of rest, for above all I want to be buried in holy ground."[58]

The practice of private burial is not a French invention, of course. It must have started much earlier in England, where it was no doubt limited to the aristocracy. In 1729 the Howard family built in the garden of their castle a mausoleum, which was modeled after that of Tempietto di Bramante in San Pietro, in Montorio.[59] But in the English colonies of America, especially in Virginia, private burial became common in the eighteenth century. Every family buried their dead on their plantation. In 1771 Jefferson left plans for his tomb in his garden at Monticello, where it remains today. Washington's tomb at Mount Vernon must have served as a model for many whose tastes ran to rural funerary landscapes. From Virginia the practice spread to New England, where the churchyard had originally been the rule.

Although most of these little family cemeteries have been buried under the suburbs of the nineteenth and twentieth centuries, some of them still exist *in situ*. In Hyattsville, in the suburbs of Washington, D.C., there is the cemetery of the Deakins family; the oldest tomb is that of a soldier in the American Revolution (1746–1824). But a great many have either been destroyed by later inhabitants, or else their headstones, which are often beautiful, have been transported to churchyards for safekeeping.

One wonders why the practice disappeared during the first half of the nineteenth century in France. There are at least three areas, however, where it has persisted to our own time. Two of these are Protestant (Charente and Cévennes) and the third is Catholic (Corsica).

The existence of Protestant graves in fields is generally explained by the refusal, after the revocation of the Edict of Nantes, to bury Protestants in the Catholic cemetery, the only one authorized by law. But this explanation does not hold for Corsica, about which Angelo Rinaldi wrote in 1971, "I come from a country where people build very expensive tombs beside the roads the way they buy cars: in order to show off the importance of their social position."[60] But in Corsica this is not an ancient custom. Before the Revolution, people buried the dead in and around the churches, as they did everywhere else. It was in the period of Joseph Sec and Delille that the old habits changed. What is remarkable is that the new practice persisted.

Not far from Bordeaux, among the vineyards of Entre-deux-mers, by the side of the road, there is a broken column surrounded by a grille: the tomb of the X family, 1910. Among the offerings is a souvenir of a First Communion. Were they Protestants? Converts? A Catholic family following the Protestant custom because it was fashionable among people of distinction?

But is this practice of French Protestant regions really specifically Protestant? Would it not be a mistake to regard it as a continuation of the clandestine burials of the eighteenth century? In the early nineteenth century, Protestants had the same choice as Catholics, between the communal cemetery and private burial. If they chose private burial, as did a great many others, it was for the same reasons, with perhaps an added concern, peculiar to themselves, not to be buried next to Catholics. (The cemeteries were not "neutralized" until 1881.) In the case of Corsica the problem remains unsolved. Corsica and the Protestant regions are, therefore, survivals.

Everywhere else, in England and the United States, private burial was abandoned. The principal reason was the uncertainty of preserving the tomb in cases of change of ownership, which became increasingly frequent in a period of social mobility like the nineteenth century in France, and even more so in the United States.

The administration, which had never approved of the right to private burial recognized by the Decree of Prairial, exerted pressure on the municipalities for restrictive legislation. But the mayors closed their eyes. The author of *Jacquou le croquant* tells us that Curé Bonal, a priest who was out of favor with the reactionary clergy of the early nineteenth century, wanted to be buried "at the end of the path [in his garden], under the big chestnut tree that his father planted the day he was born." The union of birth and death, of the native soil and the burial ground, is one of the favorite themes of the romantic era. It was not altogether legal, but the mayor "was not a man to worry about a little technicality of which he may even have been unaware."[61]

It was not until the Decree of March 15, 1928, that the prefect took over the mayor's function of granting authorization to bury the dead outside the public cemetery. The mayor officially delegated his power to the municipalities in those places where the custom was widespread and of long standing. Elsewhere, he generally refused permission, except in very unusual cases. But the popularity of the custom was already declining. Today I know a case of an old widow whose husband had been buried in a family tomb, in Charente, in the middle of a field. For years the poor woman had a terrible time getting to it, and on rainy autumn days she would come home exhausted and covered with mud. She was also under pressure from the new owners of the field, who objected to the presence of the tomb in the middle of their property. She finally requested that the tomb be transferred to a town cemetery so that she could visit it more conveniently.

This is the same reason that had been invoked a century before in New England for the creation of a private cemetery for several New Haven families. It was felt that private tombs on one's own property lacked the proper conditions for maintenance and preservation, and were in danger of disappearing. The cult of the dead brought the private tomb back to the public cemetery, which was "sacred and inviolable."[62]

Sometimes the lay of the land made it possible to place the tomb both in one's garden and in the cemetery. Thus, the tomb of General Chanzy is located on the family estate in Buzancy, but looks onto the cemetery. It is embedded in the wall. Similarly the château of George Sand's family, at Nohant, shared a wall with the church. The part of the garden reserved for family graves is a sort of annex to the public cemetery.

The Visit to the Cemetery

So the public cemetery becomes the focus of all the piety for the dead. In the nineteenth century, according to the American historian S. French, it becomes "a cultural institution"; I would even call it a religious institution.

Actually, this movement began earlier in England. We have seen that in the eighteenth century there were already outdoor cemeteries there with visible tombs and monuments. Another important practice was the elegy, the poem in honor of the deceased. It was printed on a slip of paper and seems even to have been pinned to the catafalque during the funeral ceremonies. It was related both to the long epitaph and to the eulogy. (It corresponded to the French *"tombeau littéraire."*)[63]

Gray's "Elegy" seems to belong to this genre. However, the deceased is anonymous; the poem is not occasional; the author has obviously borrowed the form of the genre and adapted it to his own purposes. He has replaced the traditional theme of the tomb or the deceased with that of the rural cemetery or country churchyard. The cemetery and its poetry are making their entrance into the world of literature. They have already played a part in baroque theater, but only in order to express the fascination or the fear of the horrible. Here the cemetery is a place of serenity and consolation. It is imbued with the peace of evening, when man leaves the fields and Nature prepares for sleep.

If we omit the end of the poem, that is, the elegy proper, the eulogy of the deceased, a young solitary walker without much relevance to our subject, we can distinguish four themes. The first is nature. The little cemetery is located in nature; the time is the evening Angelus, when "all the air a solemn stillness holds." The poet remains alone when the fading light of day "leaves the world to darkness and to me."

The tombs are buried in the grass, beneath the young elms and ilexes.

The second theme is the regret for life, a traditional theme that is treated here in a new way. The life that is regretted is not that of an individual but of a whole community of villagers. This life can be summed up in the words *work, family,* and *nature.* The dead will no longer enjoy nature, they will no longer inhale the fresh scents of dawn, they will no longer hear the crow of the cock. They will no longer know the pleasure of driving the team, of conquering the stubborn earth. They will no longer sit by the fire, their wives will no longer take care of them, their children will not rush to greet "their sire's return" or climb up on his knee to receive his coveted kiss.

The third theme is the golden mean, the middle way, a simplicity that might well resemble happiness. Here we find a distant echo of the *ubi sunt,* the *contemptus mundi,* the vanity of wealth and honors, but in reverse, in negative. The poet recognizes that "the paths of glory lead but to the grave," but only in order to glorify a life of obscurity, far from both great deeds and crimes. Outside of history, his peasants "kept the noiseless tenor of their way."

The last theme is the tomb and its poetry; communication between the living and the dead. The cemetery is first of all the resting-place of one's ancestors. This is an idea that we have sought in vain in the French documents of the later eighteenth century and that does not appear there until about 1800. Here the idea is contained in two superb lines, which have a Barrèsian ring:

> *Each in his narrow cell forever laid,*
> *The rude forefathers of the hamlet sleep.*

These were poor, simple men who did not always know how to read, but they had a dignity of their own. There are no trophies on these tombs; yet they are not bare. Each has its memorial, its headstone decorated with a rude sculpture and an epitaph with the name, the date, an elegy, and a passage from Scripture, carved there by "some illiterate muse."

These monuments have two purposes. One is traditional and didactic: to teach the rustic moralist to die. The other is an invitation to the passerby, not to pray to God for these dead but to weep for them. Here (again) is this completely new idea: the visit to the cemetery.

For the dead have not lost all sensibility. They are asleep, and in their sleep they have need of us. Their "parting souls" hope for a loving heart, but their closed eyes under the ground claim our tears. The tomb is not empty: "From the depths of the tomb, nature raises her moan." The fire of life smolders in the ashes:

E'en from the tomb the voice of nature cries,
E'en in our ashes live their wonted fires.

Memory and immortal soul on the one hand; vague subterranean survival on the other. The first could dispense with the tomb; the second turns the tomb into the scene of a physical presence. When the two are combined, the tomb becomes a place to go to in order to remember, meditate, pray, and mourn. The cemetery of the nineteenth century has become a place to visit, a place of meditation. Delille says to his wife:

> *Visit me, then, in my dark retreat:*
> *There where bending branches gently wave*
> *Sweet illusion will show you my ghost*
> > *Sitting on my grave.*
> *There sometimes, doleful and desolate,*
> *To beguile me again in my abode of gloom*
> *At the end of a lovely day, you will come to visit*
> > *My poetic tomb.*
> *And if ever you should chance to linger*
> *In this place of peace, love, and mourning*
> *And shed a tear or two upon my coffin*
> *From each falling drop would roses spring.*[64]

A little later, Lamartine will visit the tomb of Elvira in the hope of seeing her again. The poet addresses the moon:

> *Come, guide my steps to the tomb*
> *Where your beam a path has traced*
> *Where every evening my knee falls upon*
> *A blessed name, all but erased.*[65]

The dead may reappear anywhere, but especially in the houses they have lived in and loved, in their old rooms. In the nineteenth century, however, they show a distinct preference for the cemetery, which, in the twentieth, they will abandon for the bedroom. But in 1873, the pastors of American consolation literature go to the cemetery to evoke the memory of their dead. "Passing an afternoon at New York's Greenwood Cemetery near the grave of his son, 'Little Georgie,' the Reverend Cuyler bid his son a by-no-means final adieu. 'The air was as silent as the unnumbered sleepers around me; and turning toward the sacred spot where my precious dead was lying, I bade him, as of old, "Goodnight!" ' Greenwood was to him 'simply a vast and exquisitely beautiful dormitory.' "[66]

We have no reason to believe that Edgar Linton, unlike his rival Heathcliff, had any intention of making his dead wife reappear. However, he went to the cemetery every day, "usually in the evening or early in the morning, before anyone else arrived. . . . He remembered her, he recalled her memory with a passionate and tender love, full of hope, he aspired to that better world where, he had no doubt, she had gone." On the anniversary of her death he remained in the cemetery until after midnight.

At the turn of the century in France the characters of Léon Bloy spend part of their lives in the cemetery. Of course, they are not regarded as very well balanced people. But life is not always reasonable, and I once knew an old bachelor who married late in life who went every day to visit the grave of his mother. He took his wife with him, and on Sundays they also brought the baby.

In Léon Bloy's *La Femme pauvre* (1897), "She spent whole days in church or by the grave of the unfortunate Garcougnal, her benefactor, whose death had plunged her into misery."

Léopold and Clotilde go to the cemetery of Bagneux, where their child is buried. "It is always a consolation for them to walk there. They talk to the dead, and the dead answer them in their own way. Their son Lazare and their friend Marchenais are there, and they tend the two graves with love. Sometimes they go to pray in another cemetery, where Garcougnal and L'Isle de France are buried. But it is a long trip, and they like the large dormitory of Bagneux, which is only ten minutes from their house, especially since it is the burial ground of the poor. Beds in perpetuity are rare there, and every five years the guests are taken out of their coffins and thrown pell-mell into an anonymous ossuary. Other inhabitants follow on their heels, equally impatient to find shelter under the ground. The two visitors hope that before this lease has expired, they will be able to provide a more stable resting-place for those they have loved so well." And yet these are Catholics of an absolute and aggressive orthodoxy, who believe in the resurrection of the dead! "Of course they themselves may die in the meantime. God's will be done! There will always be the resurrection of the dead, which no legal regulation can either predict or prevent." But their faith does not lessen their concern for "a stable resting-place." This "integrist" Catholic visited the cemeteries with all the piety of the men of the Enlightenment, the revolutionaries whom he detested, almost a century before. Several times a week, Léopold goes to their favorite graves, cleans them, lays flowers on them, "delighted to find a new rose, a nasturtium . . . , watering them with an unhurrying hand and forgetting the universe, lingering for hours, especially over the little white tomb of his child, to whom he speaks tenderly and softly sings the *Magnificat* or the *Ave Maris Stella*."[67]

The writers of epitaphs spoke the same language as the authors of books. Ever since the sixteenth and seventeenth centuries, but especially in the eighteenth century, we have noted a tendency to add an expression of regret to the eulogy, biography, and genealogy. In the first half of the nineteenth century, as in the preceding century, epitaphs were long, loquacious, and personal.

There are enough tombs left from this period in the new cemeteries created after the Year XII so that we may read the words of survivors on the stone itself. Contemporaries were also interested in this epigraphic literature, not for genealogical reasons, like their predecessors of the *ancien régime*, but because it satisfied the taste of the age for sentimentality in general and the macabre in particular. The authors of guides to the cemeteries made a little collection of the genre.

Here are a few examples taken from the *Véritable Conducteur aux cimetières du Père-Lachaise, Montmartre, Montparnasse et Vaugirard*, published in 1836.[68] "We shall make here for the tenth time the rather singular observation that the majority of the epitaphs we shall encounter are almost entirely devoted to wives or children."

As in the lines of Lamartine quoted earlier, the ghost of the deceased is believed to haunt the funerary grove, the little bit of nature that surrounds the tomb:

> *For the first time, O mother, you fly from us!*
> *Relentless death has chilled your eyes,*
> *But your shadow trembles among the cypresses;*
> *We have given you back the husband whom you mourned.*

The presence of this shadow invited the living to visit her and converse with her.

One long epitaph is devoted to a child of four who died in 1823:

> *In this sad tomb, you sleep, O my child!*
> *Listen, my only hope, your mother speaks!*
> *Wake up! You never slept this long before.*

And another to a child of twelve:

> *Go, take your place in the celestial choir,*
> *Alphonse, God calls, he needs another angel.*

These Parisian epitaphs have the same style and inspiration, the same hope of heavenly reunion as American consolation literature. Usually a phrase alludes to the imminent and longed-for reunion: "I live to mourn her and to join her in the grave;" or: "He built this modest tomb in memory of his worthy and respectable wife, in the hope that he will be reunited with her for eternity" (1820).

Sometimes the author of an epitaph was moved to record on lasting granite some old family grudge. In 1819, for example, an unhappy father proclaimed to all the world that his daughter had died "the victim of an unhappy marriage." The son-in-law, furious at this publicity, received permission from the authorities to have the inscription changed.

When the subject was a man, his professional merits were added to his domestic virtues, and the regrets of his subordinates were combined with those of the family. A hirer of carriages was mourned by both his family and his drivers:

> *Best of sons, fondest of husbands,*
> *Paragon of fathers, may you hear our words!*
> *Your family, friends, and subordinates*
> *Will carry their devotion to the grave.*
> *They weep along with us, they water your dust,*
> *But, alas! our tears will not disturb your rest,*
> *Believe, dear Bagnard, in our cruel pain.*
> *Your dying breath lives in our hearts again.*

This for a small businessman; the epitaph of a great industrialist, M. Lenoir-Dufresne, who died April 22, 1806, is more concise, but more "sublime": "More than five thousand workers who were nourished by his genius and inspired by his example came here to mourn a father and a friend."

In their naïve and garrulous manner, which we tend to find ridiculous and hypocritical, the epitaphs of the nineteenth century express a real and profound feeling, which the historian has no right to deride. The Latin language imposed a simpler tone, when it was still used, as on this Roman tomb of 1815 in Santo Eustachio: *"Quos amor et pietas junxit dum vita manebat, aeternum coeli jungat et alta domus"* (May those whom love and piety have joined in life be united forever in heaven).

For a long millennium, out of a mixture of shame and indifference, people had hesitated to display their feelings in this way except at the actual moment of death (in the early Middle Ages), and (later, in southern and rural cultures) at the moment of mourning. Since the thirteenth century these excessive demonstrations had been repressed or ritualized. But after the eighteenth century we sense a rising need to proclaim one's grief, to advertise it on the tomb, which now becomes something it was not, the privileged place of memory and regret.

Throughout the nineteenth and early twentieth centuries this sentiment persists, but the style gradually changes. The apostrophe is retained, but there are no more long poems, no more interminable eulogies, fewer personal details. The genre was vulgarized as more and more people insisted on inscribing farewells on the tombs of their dead. Dealers in tombstones offered families ready-made formulas that expressed, in a style that was inevitably conventional and banal, sentiments that were nonetheless authentic and personal. "Eternal regrets" painted on enamel plaques were simply laid on the tomb, sometimes along with a photograph of the deceased and some filial or parental apostrophe. Our modern cemeteries are full of them, and in France, Italy, Spain, and Germany, the practice persists in popular circles.

It attests to a feeling that must be the stronger for being frowned on by the churches. In the nineteenth century the churches had accepted and assimilated the attachment of the living to their dead and to the rituals of mourning. Tombs were decorated like little chapels and loaded with pious objects, crosses, candles, souvenirs of Lourdes or of First Communions. The cult of the dead seemed to the priests perfectly natural for a good Christian, and the redundant and pathetic epitaphs were regarded as so many evidences of faith, composed in the style of the religious literature of the time. A few priests of the most reactionary type, however, became alarmed in the name of orthodoxy. They rightly suspected the influence of the deism of the Enlightenment in these overly secular demonstrations. Around 1880 Monseigneur Gaume was already expressing his irritation with these epitaphs "in which nonsense contends with naturalism."[69] But their rhetoric was so closely associated with piety toward the dead that it was impossible to attack one without attacking the other. It was not until the middle of the twentieth century that clergymen no longer hesitated to root out what they had once accepted and even encouraged. In England in 1962 a woman of seventy-five was ordered by a court of the Anglican church to remove from the tombstone of her husband the words "Forever in my thoughts," which were actually quite mild in comparison with romantic eloquence. "I thought the inscription appropriate," she observed. "My husband was everything to me." But the Reverend D. S. Richardson, who was acting as attorney, replied, "In this age of the increasing paganization of funerals, the Church must adopt a firm Christian attitude. It is our opinion that strong expressions of affection or grief are out of place."[70]

During the same period in France a Catholic priest was making a collection of epitaphs of this kind in order to show their absurdity and their underlying paganism.[71] The sentimentality of the nineteenth century was thus held up to ridicule and even denounced as a mask for bourgeois vanity and snobbery. The spontaneous alliance of the nineteenth century between the clergy and the secular cult of the dead was now called into question.

The Rural Cemetery vs. the Cemetery of Monuments

The new cemeteries had become places to visit where relatives and friends liked to gather around the graves of their dead. It was therefore necessary to adapt them to this function and plan them accordingly. Two models were created that were rather similar in the minds of their originators but that later diverged until they characterized two vast cultural domains.

The first is well known: it is Père-Lachaise. The site of Mont Louis had been acquired in 1803 to replace the cemetery of Sainte-Marguerite. Of course it was then located outside Paris, and was conceived as a sort of Elysian fields or rolling English garden in which beautiful monuments were dominated by greenery. To it were transferred some illustrious remains, such as the presumed bodies of Abélard and Héloïse. From the beginning Père-Lachaise, along with the other new cemeteries of Montmartre and Montparnasse, figured in the guides to Paris among the curiosities of the capital. Even today it has retained its romantic charm in the older, wilder section. Its history is well known and is found in all books on Paris. It is the natural culmination, in the early nineteenth century, of all the different ideas and plans that were proposed in the second half of the eighteenth century and that we analyzed above.

The second model is American and a little later: Mount Auburn in Massachusetts dates from 1831. Its history is less well known than that of Père-Lachaise but is well covered in S. French's essay "The Cemetery as a Cultural Institution: The Establishment of Mount Auburn and the Rural Cemetery Movement," in D. E. Stannard's *Death in America.*

From the first decades of the nineteenth century, the Americans of New England were concerned about the state of their cemeteries, the indecency of burial, and its dangers to public health, just as the French had been in the eighteenth century. Some individuals joined together to found private cemeteries that would avoid the disadvantages of burial both on private estates and in the public cemetery, both of which were subject to violation. The cemetery was not under the exclusive control of municipal governments, as it was in France, so these individuals were free to form nonreligious associations to found and run cemeteries as nonprofit institutions in an orderly manner and with perpetuity guaranteed.

The original reasons of decency and sanitation soon gave way to the grand design of transforming the abode of the dead into a "cultural institution" for the living, a place for people to come and meditate. It was then that the word *cemetery* came to replace *churchyard* and *graveyard*. At the dedication of Mount Auburn Justice Joseph Stom said, "Our cemeteries . . . may be made subservient to some of the highest purposes of religion and human duty. They may preach lessons, to which none may refuse to listen, and which all that live must hear. The cemetery has become a school of religion and philosophy." This type of cemetery is first of all philosophical. It teaches that death is not only destruction "but is made subservient to some purpose of reproduction, and the circle of creation and destruction is eternal" (1831). This is why the cemetery is a natural landscape. It is called the *rural cemetery*, and the term will serve to designate all cemeteries created in imitation of Mount Auburn.

Next, this cemetery is patriotic and civic; this function is repeatedly stressed in dedication speeches. As French puts it, the cemetery must provide "a sense of historical continuity, of social roots," or, in the phrase of an orator of 1848, "a sense of perpetual home." "No one will ever forget the place where his father and friends are buried, if this place has a charm that touches the heart and satisfies the senses; and if the ground that contains them had no other attraction, it would always be dear to the living for this reason" (1855).[72]

Finally, the rural cemetery is a school of morality. It will make everyone wiser and more serious, especially the young.

Actually, the plans of the founders of the rural cemetery were not so far removed from those of the French planners of the early nineteenth century, and Mount Auburn is not so different in its fundamental conceptions from Père-Lachaise. Both are gardens with monuments. But the two models will evolve separately and give birth to two different lines.

The relationship between nature and monuments was to be reversed. In the old Mount Auburn, as in the rural cemeteries of the period, the tombs were either neoclassical steles or headstones, often grouped inside a metal grille, as in country churchyards or private cemeteries, or carved monuments with realistic figures similar to the ones erected after the middle of the century in French and Italian cemeteries: busts of men, sleeping children in the arms of sad mothers, angels, women praying, and so on.[73]

In the beginning the rural cemeteries looked very much like Père-Lachaise and the European cemeteries. The monuments dotted the landscape here and there . But during the later nineteenth and early twentieth century, the American cemetery evolved toward nature and away from art. The metal grilles that had been so popular fell into disfavor. Headstones, which were believed to be indigenous, were preferred to monuments, which were regarded as pretentious. All this happened gradually. In the twentieth century even the modest headstone and footstone were replaced by a discreet stone slab or metal plate that simply marked the location of the grave.

After that nothing of large volume arrested the eye or broke the continuity of greensward. The rural cemetery of the nineteenth century evolved into the lawn cemetery of the twentieth century, a huge expanse of green in which the small funerary plaques are barely visible. In America, the cemetery looked less and less like a churchyard and more and more like a garden. Indeed, it has served as a model for city parks such as Central Park, in New York (1856).[74]

At Père-Lachaise, however, it was nature that gave way before the invasion of art. In the beginning the park areas were extensive, as at Mount Auburn, but even then the monuments were undoubtedly more conspicuous. Although in the older, steeper part, with its rougher terrain, the design and spirit of the park were preserved, in the flatter and lower areas the tombs were crowded together, and nothing could bear less resemblance to a park.

The invasion by stone was already well under way toward the middle of the century. Contemporaries were quite aware of the difference between the two models, and partisans of the rural cemetery criticized Père-Lachaise for the pretentiousness of its monuments.

Mount Auburn was immediately imitated in America and England, giving general currency to the type of the rural cemetery, in which the tomb is eclipsed by the landscape until it disappears in the greensward. Abney Park was founded in London in 1840. This model perpetuates—or revives and re-creates—Thomas Gray's churchyard. A lovely painting in the new museum in Brest shows a visit to the tomb of Shelley in the marvelous Protestant cemetery in the Piazza Ostiense, in Rome. The tomb is a romantic oasis in the baroque and classical city, a miniature rural cemetery.

The visit to the cemetery is a subject not unknown in American painting. At the Walters Gallery, in Baltimore, a primitive from the middle of the century shows people strolling through a lawn cemetery with vertical steles.[75] Mount Auburn has also been represented in lithography and painting, as for example in a fine canvas by Thomas Chambers.

The model of the rural cemetery predominates in England and North America. The newer part of Père-Lachaise and the Parisian cemeteries of Montmartre and Montparnasse that resemble it served as general models for the new urban cemeteries of continental Europe, which were also subject to other influences, such as that of the Italian *campo santo* with its persistent flavor of the cloister. Throughout this whole vast geographic area, which was both Catholic and Protestant, stone monuments, both large and small, invaded all available space.

These "built-up" cemeteries were more inspiring to the sculptors of monuments, who decorated them, than they were to painters, who preferred the rural cemetery. The most popular images of the genre in French nineteenth-century art were of families in mourning hurrying through an autumn drizzle on All Saints' Day or Breton widows praying after Sunday Mass before the empty graves of sailors lost at sea.

The difference between the two geographic areas may reflect a difference in attitudes toward nature. In America and England, nature retains emotional power, and its connections with death are real and profound. In France, however, although people were affected by nature for a time in the eighteenth and early nineteenth centuries, it was by accident; later, nature lost its impact, and all emotion was completely absorbed by the monument. The French cemetery is a little stone village with houses crowded together, where two transplanted cypresses are as conspicuous as feather dusters. Such is often the appearance of French rural cemeteries, at least north of the Loire, when they have been moved out of the village in accordance with the law and into a sort of depressing suburb.

It is not easy for the Frenchman or "European" of today to understand the relationship to nature of a man of the late eighteenth century. He tends to suspect it of artificiality, aestheticism, or—and today this is the crowning insult—romanticism.

A passage from *Jacquou le croquant* (1899) shows this idea in its nascent state in a Frenchman born in 1836. Eugène Le Roy becomes a witness to the ideas of his age in a Republican milieu hostile to the Church. Death and burial occupy an important place in his book. His peasants regard them as important moments that must be described if one wishes to be a faithful observer. "La Bertille was distressed that her mother was buried without prayers," because she could not afford to pay for them. Jacquou's mother was turned away by the priest at the door of the church on the pretext that she was a Huguenot. Her body was thrown into a hole. Later, Jacquou attends a funeral and takes advantage of the opportunity "to walk toward the place where my mother was buried. What can I say? It makes no difference, does it, whether there are flowers or wild grasses on top of the six feet of earth that cover the bones of a poor creature? But we are easily influenced by our eyes without listening to our reason. So when I saw this corner full of rocks . . . and invaded by brambles . . . I stood there for a moment, grief-stricken, staring at this desolate spot from which all traces of the burial of my poor mother had disappeared. On my way back I passed a tomb crumbling with age : . . and I thought to myself what a vain thing it is to seek to perpetuate the memory of the dead. Stone lasts longer than a wooden cross, but time, which destroys all things, destroys that, too."

Here we recognize the ancient theme of vanity. What follows is newer and, I think, more deeply felt: "Is it not inevitable that the memory of the deceased be lost in that vast and boundless sea of the millions upon millions of human beings who have disappeared since the beginning of time?" This is the image of "the incessantly renewing sea" that we noted in the poems of Emily Brontë and the journal of Albert de La Ferronays. "Abandonment to Nature, who covers everything with her green mantle, is better than these tombs in which the vanity of the heirs lurks beneath the pretext of honoring the dead."[76]

This is almost the language of the American partisans of the rural cemetery in their indictments of Père-Lachaise. The man of the nineteenth century will not allow the dead to be abandoned like animals. Since he wants to meditate on the sites of the graves, he must be able to identify them by some mark, however discreet. If one renounces art, the solution is the rural or lawn cemetery, in which nature is asked to take the place of art.

In the rural cemetery, the visible tomb makes less and less sense. In continental Europe, however, the tomb is charged with meaning. We saw in chapter 5 that the once-rare cross had now spread everywhere. Whether of stone or of wood, the cross was the symbolic image of death, a death distinguished in varying degrees from biological death, a death surrounded by an aura of hope and uncertainty.

The first funerary monuments to assert themselves were modeled after either the beautiful tombs of churches or the few private structures to be found in cemeteries. Both styles were inspired by antiquity and neoclassicism: steles with urns, pyramids, obelisks, whole or broken columns, and pseudosarcophagi.

These types persisted for a long time; the funerary art of the nineteenth century is very diverse, rejecting the massive conventionality that characterizes both the Middle Ages and modern times.

However, the early 1800s saw the birth of one new style that became very popular and remained so until the end of the century. This was the chapel tomb. (We will recall that in the seventeenth and eighteenth centuries lateral chapels served as places for worship for the living and as tombs for the dead. The coffin was buried just below in a vault, but sometimes there was a monument in the chapel as well. The chapel actually constituted the real visible tomb.)

With a very few exceptions, such as certain private chapels in châteaux (for example, the La Trémoille château, in Niort), or confraternity chapels, there were no funerary chapels outside of churches.

But when it was no longer permitted to bury the dead in church, the lateral funerary chapel was transferred to the cemetery and turned into a tomb. One of the first of these chapel tombs was built in Père-Lachaise about 1815. The "sepulchral chapel of the Greffulhe family" was described and pictured in the guides of the period. This remarkable monument was like a small church. It soon became fashionable to have a miniature chapel in the cemetery, built to the usual dimensions of a grant in perpetuity. These chapel tombs were popularized and vulgarized in the later nineteenth century, and there are a great many in existence. Each little cell has an altar surmounted by a cross and covered with an altar cloth, candlesticks, and porcelain vases; before the altar there are one or two prie-dieux. The names of the deceased and the epitaphs are on the interior walls of the cell, which is surrounded by a grille, originally glazed. The chapel is generally in the neo-Gothic style, with the name of the family inscribed over the door; for, like the lateral chapels of churches, these tombs were not individual, but familial. The tomb now bears scant resemblance to a commemorative monument. It has become a place to visit, the goal of a pilgrimage designed for prayer and meditation, with places to sit or at least to kneel.

In such tombs there is no place of honor for the portrait unless the deceased is famous, like General Chanzy, who is depicted as a recumbent figure in the medieval manner with his face looking toward the altar of his chapel.

Portraits and Genre Scenes

But in the second half of the nineteenth century, portrait statues became more common and were sometimes organized into actual genre scenes. The most pathetic are now the tombs of children or adolescents. There are a great many of these because the mortality rate among children and young people was still high. When we look at them today, as when we read the American consolation literature of the same period, we realize how painful the death of the young had become. These long-neglected little creatures were treated like famous personages, and with a realism and naturalness that gave the tearful visitor the illusion of their presence.

The cemetery in Nice is a wonderful museum, with tombs dating from 1835. On one of these from the late nineteenth or early twentieth century a girl of eight is welcoming her little brother, who has come to join her in the beyond. The two children, who are life-size, are holding out their arms, as the little boy in his nightshirt rushes toward his waiting sister. I found the same scene dating from the same period in the cemetery of San Miniato, outside Florence. One wonders whether they are the work of the same artist or whether the subject was commonplace. Emma and Bianca are meeting in heaven. They run toward one another with arms outstretched. The younger sister is surrounded by roses and has been half transformed into a rose. An inscription tells us that the two little girls left this world within a short time of one another. In a second inscription, to one side, Emma and Bianca tell their parents not to weep for them, for they are now with the angels in heaven, where they sing the glory of God and pray for the living.

It is true that these little girls came from rich families who could afford to commission good sculptors; but one finds popular examples of the same sentiment. In the cemetery of Aureilhan in les Landes, in Gascony, on your left as you enter the little church, you are struck by a very small clumsy or primitive statue of a child without a tombstone. The child is kneeling and holds a crown in his hands as an offering. There is no date, but the work is undoubtedly from the end of the last century or the beginning of the present one.

Another scene frequently represented on tombs by nineteenth-century sculptors is the deathbed. This image, which is very rare before the end of the eighteenth century, must be seen in connection with the glorification of the last moments as we found it among the Brontës and the La Ferronays. In Santa Maria Novella, in Florence, a tomb dated 1807 shows a young girl who is no longer dead but has already entered the beyond. She is sitting up in bed and holding out her arms toward the blessed eternity that is promised to her. She has overcome death, whose skeleton and scythe were lying in wait for her.

This is the good death. In San Clemente, in Rome, an 1887 tomb shows the count of Basterot lying on his deathbed. A woman who represents human frailty weeps, while a cherub who symbolizes immortality smiles and takes the count's unresisting hand.

On the cover of the first issue of the magazine *Traverses*, in 1975, there was a superb photograph by Gilles Ehrmann, taken in some *campo santo* of the nineteenth century, that is better or more lifelike than the original. The work, which must date from around the turn of the century, shows a deathbed scene. The family is grouped around the bed. The dying man is calm and peaceful; his wife is leaning over him and gazing into his eyes. A daughter is resting her head on the pillow in a tender gesture. She is the only one who does not look at the dying man; no doubt she is the youngest. Another daughter holds out her arms as if to embrace her father for the last time. In the background a son-in-law represents conventional grief and the discretion of the virtual stranger.

However tastes and fashions may have changed, this is a very beautiful sculpture. But this sort of quality is not found everywhere. In the second half of the nineteenth century, local artists depicted the deceased in scenes that lacked this animation or pathos, but had the immobility of primitives. In Loix-en-Ré (Ile-de-Ré) there is a family tomb of this period, the Fournier tomb, known locally as the "famous tomb." It certainly deserves its reputation! It consists of a central pillar surmounted by a naked figure kneeling with joined hands and covered by a little pseudo-Gothic aedicula. Around the central pillar are four steles, like Roman altars, which are connected to the central pillar by long carved arms. On the central pillar and the peripheral steles, epitaphs are engraved, and in front are placed busts or full-length statues of members of the family. The father is superb. He has his arms folded and holds a notebook in one hand and a pencil in the other. To one side is a simple slab and a cross for the faithful servant.

Fournier is still a notable, albeit a local one. In the twentieth century the role of statuary declined, and even among great families the fashion of the portrait passed. In Dreux, in the chapel of the d'Orléans family built by Louis Philippe, the most recent tombs are bare. Photography, however, enabled the portrait, which was abandoned by the upper classes, to gain popular acceptance. The photograph was rendered inalterable by glazing. In France I suspect that the oldest images of this kind are those of soldiers who "died on the field of honor" in World War I. Their heroism had saved them from anonymity. Later the practice became general, although it was more common on the tombs of women and children, who were the objects of a particular solicitude already observed in the 1836 guide to Père-Lachaise. It is particularly widespread in Mediterranean countries, where the tombs often resemble the drawers of a bureau in which each drawer is illustrated. One walks from one to the other as if one were turning the pages of a photograph album.

Paris Without a Cemetery?

It would seem that by the beginning of the twentieth century the question of burial had been definitively settled in France, what with the three decisions to create new cemeteries outside the towns, to juxtapose graves instead of superimposing them, and to grant the dead an extended right to occupy the ground. But in fact the problem arose again in Paris at the end of the nineteenth century, although in a very different emotional climate from that of the eighteenth century.

A memorandum from the prefect of the Seine in 1844 describes the problems resulting from the Decree of the Year XII. He attacks the system of the grant in perpetuity, "whose effects could not have been foreseen in the beginning," and the pressures "of a population that is constantly increasing and every day more infatuated, even among the humbler classes, with the cult of the dead."[77] This system results in tying up land both by the length of the grants and by encumbering it with monuments and grilles. Les Innocents had withstood an accumulation of several centuries; the new cemeteries had already run out of space after thirty years. The reason for this was the extraordinary craze for visible and lasting tombs.

Moreover, the town had grown so fast that it had now caught up with the cemeteries that had been moved out with so much trouble. When the suburban communes were annexed to the capital in 1859, Père-Lachaise and the cemeteries created at the beginning of the century found themselves inside the present Paris of twenty *arrondissements*. This was a catastrophe for the administration. The situation of the *ancien régime* had been re-created: The dead were once again in the midst of the living. This was intolerable to the prefect and the administrators, who had inherited the preoccupations and attitudes of their predecessors of the eighteenth century.

Consequently Préfet Haussmann wished to repeat the operation of les Innocents: close the cemeteries created around 1800 and take steps to remove the new cemetery to a distance where it would no longer risk being overtaken by urban development. As a site he proposed Méry-sur-Oise, nineteen miles from Paris. This was too far for the horses that pulled the hearses, and the new cemetery would have to be connected to Paris by a railroad that was soon nicknamed "the train of the dead."

We have seen how at the end of the eighteenth century les Innocents was ripped apart in a climate of general indifference. That was before the appearance of the cult of the dead. In 1868 the mere idea of closing down the cemetery—not to mention moving the bodies—raised a storm of protest. The ordinary people of Paris "like to visit the cemeteries with their families. . . . It is their favorite excursion on their days of rest. It is their consolation in times of distress."

Public opinion was aroused. A letter to *Siècle* for January 7, 1868, expresses the general feeling: "The people's instincts are revolted at the idea of the dead being transported by the dozen in railway cars. . . . They will be treated like so much luggage."[78]

The Parisian administration returned to the attack at the beginning of the Third Republic, from 1872 to 1881, but encountered the same opposition. The history of these debates at the municipal council is preserved in newspapers and pamphlets. "Paris is not a town of skeptics; the cult of the dead has been perpetuated from one age to the next. Under the Empire there was an attempt to create an enormous necropolis at Méry-sur-Oise. All Paris was outraged, and protested against a measure that would have ended the ancient custom of accompanying the dear departed to their place of rest on foot, and substituted a train" (1889).

The administration gave up when they realized that they no longer had the support of the educated elite. In 1879 the municipal council appointed a committee of experts, in the tradition of the doctors and parliamentarians of the eighteenth century, to determine how the sanitary conditions of existing cemeteries could be improved. Everyone was prepared for new denunciations of centers of pestilence. But the answer of the engineers quietly annihilated a century of scientific arguments. The experts stated positively that "the alleged dangers to the areas surrounding the cemeteries are imaginary, . . . that the decomposition of bodies is completely achieved within the legal period of five years."

As early as 1850 certain experiments had been carried out that had contradicted the established ideas. Guérard, who had analyzed the water from a well in the cimetière de l'Ouest, observed that it was capable of "producing beneficial effects. . . . Instead of being hard, as the calcareous matter in the soil might lead one to believe, it made suds and cooked vegetables. It was clear, odorless, and had a pleasant taste."[79]

Professor Colin of the veterinary school at Alfort killed some animals by injecting them with anthrax and septic fluids, and buried them at depths of six to fifteen inches. "Then he penned live animals on the land where they were buried for a period of four to fifteen days. These animals were weighed every twenty-four hours. The weight of the adults remained stationary, while that of the young increased at the normal rates."[80]

M. Miguel "has established that, contrary to the opinions of several authors, the water vapor that rises from soil, flowers, or bodies in a state of putrefaction is always micrographically pure. . . . The gases given off by buried matter in the process of decomposition are always free of bacteria. . . . As far as the cemeteries of Paris are concerned, saturation of the soil by cadaverous matter does not exist with respect to either gases or solids. . . . If neither the soil nor the atmosphere of Paris is poisoned, this is because of the marvelous purifying power possessed by the earth, which may be regarded as a permanent filter."[81]

We are far from the days when the food in the pantries of people living next to les Innocents was spoiled on contact with the air and gravediggers died like flies. "Gravediggers, too, far from being more susceptible than other men to various maladies or occupational diseases, have always been reputed, rightly or wrongly, to enjoy a kind of immunity to infectious disease."[82]

"One need have no fear, then, about walking over to these humble crosses planted in the ground and reading the naïve expressions of the grief of the poor. There is no need to perfume one's handkerchief or to hold one's breath, as certain delicate persons are accustomed to do."[83]

The cemeteries are no longer insalubrious; the "engineers" have proved it. No doubt they worked with scientific objectivity. But it happened that their science coincided with the opinion of the age, an opinion that was religious as well as moral.

The Positivists and the Catholics Join Forces

The controversy about the Méry proposal sheds light on the current attitude toward the cult of the dead. The literature reveals two different points of view, which ultimately joined forces: that of the "positivists" and that of the Catholics. We shall analyze them both.

To whom did the term *positivists* refer? To the disciples of Auguste Comte, of course. However, these men were not pure theorists, but the leaders of a political movement. They addressed themselves if not to the masses, at least to popular or bourgeois elites, and invited them to engage in an action that was both civic and religious.

As early as 1869 one of them, Dr. Robinet, replied to Haussmann in a book significantly entitled *Paris sans cimetière*. Without a cemetery, "Paris would no longer be a city, and France would be decapitated. . . . Without a cemetery, there is no city."[84] In 1874 Pierre Laffitte, "the director of positivism," published his *Considérations générales à propos des cimetières de Paris*, in which he stated that the cemetery "constitutes one of the basic institutions of any society. . . . Every society resulting from the continuous evolution of a series of generations presupposes a past, a present, and a future." Together with the town hall, "the cemetery is the expression of the past."[85]

"Man," Dr. Robinet says with some emotion, "prolongs beyond death the existence of those who have succumbed before him. . . . He continues to love them, to imagine them, to converse with them after they have ceased to live, and establishes in their memory a cult in which his heart and his intelligence strive to assure them perpetuity. . . . This property of human nature . . . makes us affectionate and intelligent enough to love creatures who are no more, to rescue them from nothingness, and to create for them in ourselves this second existence, which is, no doubt, the only immortality." There could be no better expression of the attitude of secular France in the nineteenth and early twentieth centuries. The intensity of memory and its constant preservation had created for the dead, in the minds of the living, a second existence, which was less active than, but just as real as, the first. Laffitte asserts, "The tomb prolongs the moralizing effect of the family beyond the objective existence of its members."

Whence the cult of tombs: "It is fundamentally independent of the state of dogma or the form of government. It has arisen from the depths of our nature as the principle that best distinguishes us from animality. . . . It is the stamp of humanity." Here Robinet is developing an idea of Vico's.

Laffitte gives a popularized version of Auguste Comte's theory of the historic avatars of this original sentiment.

The first fundamental stage is fetishism. "Death is simply the transition from an active life to an inactive life. The preservation of the remains becomes necessary. . . . In these cultures neither death nor the dead body becomes the object of the sort of horror peculiar to theological [and Christian] populations." The tomb is "the representative and striking symbol of those whom we have lost. Consequently, if the memory of our dead is a condition of all social existence because it gives us a sense of continuity, the tomb remains a necessary institution."

A spontaneous fetishism still exists today. This is the basis for "the preservation of objects that remind us of persons we love and respect": souvenirs, bracelets made of hair, and later, photographs. "The material object is for us, and for the whole human species, both the symbol and the substance of the deceased." How does the tomb or the souvenir bring back the deceased, the disincarnate being? "The new scientific spirit repudiates all this, but the true and complete scientific spirit, which embraces and understands all things, accepts and utilizes this disposition of our nature."

Fetishism must therefore be incorporated into positivism. Positivism "sanctions the great inspiration that has made the tomb not only a personal or family institution but also a social institution by the founding of the cemetery, which gives it a collective character. The cult of the dead thus acquires a public character, which enormously increases its utility; for the tomb develops the sense of continuity within the family, and the cemetery the sense of continuity within the city and the human race."

For this reason the cemetery "must be . . . in the city itself, so as to facilitate the worship of the dead, which is an element of civic life of the utmost importance." This is exactly the opposite of the ideas of the parliamentarians of 1763, Loménie de Brienne, and the philosophical clergymen of the eighteenth century. How pale and equivocal the *Mémoire des curés de Paris* seems beside the positivist theory of cemeteries! But it took more than half a century of evolution and meditation to lay the groundwork for this theory, which expresses and conceptualizes the opinion of the majority.

Those who believed in positivism knew that since the golden age of fetishism, the cult of the dead had declined through the fault of theism and the Church. The theological era marks a retreat from "fetishist spontaneity." "The theological theory consists in placing the tomb and the cadaver under the protection of the infernal gods and in obtaining their respect by fear of divine wrath."[86]

Our authors emphasize the responsibility of Catholicism for the decline in popularity of the cult of the dead: "As for Catholicism, it was merely a continuation of polytheism; in fact, its preoccupation with eternal salvation was even more intense than that of polytheism. The Catholic church actually encouraged the abandonment of the dead."[87]

Bertoglio, a former custodian of the cemetery of Marseille writing in 1889, is also amazed at the indifference of the medieval Church: "We have good reason to believe that [the clergy] deliberately abstained [from showing reverence toward the cemeteries]. They were convinced that the horror of the communal burial ground would increase the number of those seeking a place in the vaults of the monuments dedicated to God."

It was the people of Paris who were the first to rehabilitate their dead: "The striking progress that has been achieved especially in France in two generations in the cult of the dead is due to the admirable influence of Paris. For, as we have observed, theology, especially monotheistic, does not in itself encourage reverence for the dead or concern for their cemeteries. After all, why bother to care for the tombs of those whose destinies have been determined for eternity?"

This is the charge that has constantly been made against the Church since the late eighteenth century. Not only has the cult of the dead not been encouraged by the great religions, but it actually increases as the number of the faithful declines. When God is dead, the cult of the dead may become the only authentic religion. It is "constantly observed that two generations ago the cemeteries were very poorly cared for in France, and that in the south, which is said to be so Catholic, their abandonment was almost total. . . . But a profound change has taken place, and every day sees new developments in the care of cemeteries and the cult of the dead. It was in Paris, about two generations ago, that this movement began. This continual and admirable development of the cult of the dead in the great religious (but not theological) city of the West has eventually come to the attention of all observers. But what is even more striking is the apparent contradiction between the increasing theological emancipation of Paris and the growing cult of the dead. As God is steadily eliminated and even forgotten, the cult of the dead is constantly spreading and becoming a part of the humblest lives." We must acknowledge the accuracy of this historical analysis; it agrees with everything we have observed since the middle of the eighteenth century. In one century the cult of the dead has become the great popular religion of France.

However, the positivists are aware of a danger. Laffitte admits that the sudden increase of wealth is attended by an abandonment of the traditions of communal life. Here, in this rationalist and innovative milieu of technicians, engineers, and craftsmen, we perceive a dawning uneasiness about the new forms of industrial life. "The result," writes Laffitte, "is an enormous city whose center is made up primarily of the rich and whose peripheries are inhabited mostly by the poor [the model of the nineteenth-century and early twentieth-century city, which will be reversed after World War I with the advent of the automobile], an arrangement that is just as politically and socially dangerous as it is genuinely immoral. . . . One of the serious disadvantages of this rapid development right now is that it has provided an excuse for raising the question of the cemeteries. . . . The sense of continuity has been damaged by these upheavals, and as a result the level of humanity has declined. . . . The question of the cemeteries of Paris is intimately related to the question of her transformation."[88]

Chardouillet goes further in his book, Les Cimetières sont-ils des foyers d'infection? He establishes a correlation between the relocation of the cemeteries, industrialization, and an idea about happiness, an analysis that was undoubtedly premature for his time but that may be true for ours. Was the engineer a prophet? "Let us hear no more of these arguments that the cemeteries are veritable centers of infection." This is not the real reason that people want to move the cemeteries out of sight: "Let them admit, if they do not have the courage to endure it, that the spectacle of death is distressing; that in a world of happy industrialism, no one has time for the dead." But the psychological effects of "happy industrialism" are still avoidable: "We hope that in a matter of such importance, questions of sanitation aside, concern for the perfect material well-being of modern industrialism will be subordinated to the moral benefits . . . provided to all of us by the cult of our venerated dead."[89]

On May 29, 1881, before the municipal council of Paris, Laffitte made an address in which he summarized the positivist theory of a familial, civic, and popular religion of the dead: "For the second time, the municipal council of Paris is about to vote on one of the gravest questions that could be placed before it, that is, the establishment of a definitive necropolis for the capital at Méry-sur-Oise, outside the department of the Seine, seven leagues from the center of the city. For the second time the undersigned members of the positivist group have come to appeal solemnly to those who represent the city's interests to preserve her places of burial." The address was signed P. Laffitte, director of positivism; F. Magnin, joiner; I. Finance, house painter; Laporte, mechanic; Bernard, accountant; and Gaze, president of a professional organization of Parisian cooks.[90]

The Catholics joined the positivists in this struggle against those whom today we would call the technocrats of the administration. The good republicans criticized this unnatural alliance. Laffitte had no trouble defending his position. He observed that the Catholics were now asking for the preservation of the city's burial grounds. "We maintain that for serious republicans [in 1881 Catholics were not reputed to be republicans], the consideration of finding themselves in agreement with the Catholics on this essential point should by no means cause them to change their minds." Moreover, "the wisdom of priests . . . with their empirical knowledge of human nature" corrects the theological risks of Catholic doctrine. This already smacks of Maurras! If the archbishop of Paris has undertaken the defense of the cemeteries, his reasons "are purely humane or positivist."[91]

The fact is that the Catholics had also adopted the cult of the dead and were defending it as if they had always practiced it, as if it were a traditional aspect of their religion. In 1864 there was an Oeuvre des Sépultures, a burial society whose purpose was not only to say Masses for souls, but also to help families bury their dead, purchase grants, and maintain tombs. "Among the most meritorious good works of religion are the burial of the dead [a traditional function of the confraternities] and the care of tombs [a new activity]."[92]

The cult of the tomb is henceforth regarded as an element of Christianity. "For the Christian it is a consolation to see with what religious attentions the civilized nations surround the remains of the dead. In this cult of the tomb he finds sure evidence of that respect for human life that religion inspires."[93]

I shall not repeat the arguments, for they are almost the same as those of the positivists, with the addition of a few references to Christian tradition. But the reader who has followed me thus far will be surprised at the shamelessness with which the Catholic authors of this period rewrote the recent history of attitudes toward burial. The Church now Christianized (or Catholicized) a devotion that had been quite alien to it, just as it had assimilated certain pagan cults in the early Middle Ages. It did so spontaneously, thus proving that it had lost none of its capacity to create myths and then to believe in them.

In a book entitled *Le Cimetière au XIXe siècle,* written around 1875 in the fulminating style of the clergymen of that time, Monseigneur Gaume maintains that the early Christians buried their dead in churches.[94] What about the catacombs? He dismisses the argument: "The practice of burying the dead at the gates of towns [that is, outside them] was not of long duration, at least among Christians." Adequate parcels of land were purchased or donated, and the bodies of the faithful were laid in the ground that surrounded the holy edifice, but more often inside the churches. Not a word about the prohibitions of canon law! In the ninth century the churches were reserved for the great. Later, "little by little, primitive custom was revived, and almost without distinction the dead were buried in churches and chapels. . . . But if the temples, cloisters, and vaults were inadequate for the burial of large populations, the Church . . . always desired their tombs to be as close to the sacred edifices as possible."

Burial *ad sanctos* is presented as an absolute rule, an immutable custom, and the author confuses it with the veneration of the tomb in the nineteenth century. For him the two ideas are identical. This association of divine worship with piety for the resting-place of the dead lasted, according to him, throughout the Middle Ages and the *ancien régime*. "It was not until the last century that the war against the cemeteries began. True to their pagan education, the sophists of that shameful age demanded loudly that the cemeteries be banished from the habitations of the living. Concern for public health was the mask behind which they hid. . . . The banishment of the cemeteries, demanded by the ungodly of the last century, was then, as now, nothing but an empty excuse. . . . Concealed under the guise of public hygiene was an attack on the Catholic church," which was supposedly guilty of improvidence. "The banishment of the cemeteries was a good way promptly to extinguish the sense of filial piety toward the dead. . . . To separate the cemetery from the church was to disturb one of the finest and most salutary harmonies that religion ever created. In one small space the three churches were united, the Church Triumphant, the Church Militant, and the Church Suffering: what a moving lesson in fraternity!"

With the Decree of Prairial, Year XII, "with two strokes of the pen, the pagan mind abolished the custom of centuries." One might think the ancient cult had been revived in what another Catholic author was to call, after secularization, "the rehabilitated cemetery"; rehabilitated, that is, by the visits of pious survivors. Our author implies that it has, but the danger reappears with the Méry-sur-Oise plan. It is Freemasonry that demands "the banishment of the cemetery to ten leagues from the capital and the establishment of a railroad for the dead." When his opponents cite the customs of the ancients, he expresses his irritation at the influence of antiquity on epitaphs: "And people persist in denying the disastrous influence of classical studies. . . . The nineteenth-century cemetery is the last arena of the desperate struggle between satanism and Christianity." The Revolution, or philosophy, "rides roughshod over all that is most sacred, most touching, and most moral, not only among Christians but among the pagans themselves. What becomes of ancestor worship, or filial piety for the dead, when in order to pray on their tombs one must make a special trip to a remote place? . . . A nation that forgets its dead is a nation of ingrates."

All this ecclesiastical wrath was to subside. The Christian need no longer desert the cemeteries, even if they are secularized. "Let us rehabilitate our cemeteries. Although they are no longer consecrated according to the rules of the Church, in this month of November let us remember that each blessed tomb is like a sacred monument lost in a pagan temple, and that it is all the more worthy of our prayers because of the attempt to keep us away. Let us, therefore, decorate our graves with greater zeal than ever; let us multiply our visits as a protest against the neglect the authorities would impose." The struggle is not only against atheism and secularization but against the neglect of the dead, who were revered by all of nineteenth-century society.[95]

Monuments to the Dead

In the preceding pages I have placed the emphasis, as did contemporary writers, on the private and familial aspect of the cult of the dead. But from the beginning the cult of the dead had another, a national and patriotic, aspect. The first plans for cemeteries of 1765–80 wanted to present a microcosm of the whole society and of its illustrious men. The revolutionary regimes retained the idea, and transformed the Parisian abbey of Sainte-Geneviève into a Panthéon dedicated to national glory. It is still there, but is hardly ever visited by the French as a sanctuary anymore. During the first two-thirds of the nineteenth century the private aspect of the cemetery, which we have analyzed in some detail, was the dominant one, although the collective function was not altogether neglected.

The collective function begins to inspire genuine emotion (which was never true of the Panthéon, except at the funeral of Marat) for the tombs of soldiers who died in combat. Formerly, their fate was not enviable. Officers were buried in the church nearest the battlefield or brought back to the family chapel, where their heroism was commemorated by a long epitaph. The chapel of the hospital in Lille kept a list of officers who had died in combat in the seventeenth century. This was a memorial that corresponded to the sense of honor in a military society in the making. As for the troops, they were buried on the spot after being stripped of their clothing and personal effects. A collective and perfunctory absolution was all that distinguished this operation from being thrown on the dump. An eighteenth-century gouache in the musée de Grasse shows such a scene after a battle.

Of course history records a few attempts to honor slain soldiers on the site of their death. On January 6, 1477, Charles the Bold perished miserably with his Burgundians in the marshes near Nancy. It was his enemy, the duc de Lorraine, who built a chapel, Notre-Dame-de-Bon-Secours, on the site of the battle and the common grave, in gratitude to Our Lady for delivering Nancy from her enemies. In 1505 the chapel received a Lady of Mercy, which soon became an object of veneration, and it became a place of pilgrimage for the people of Lorraine. Stanislas Leszczyński restored the chapel and erected sumptuous tombs for himself and his wife. The site was more that of a providential victory than that of a collective grave, and pious visitors soon forgot the origins of its founding in their enthusiasm for the popular cult of Our Lady of Mercy. The memory of the dead was quickly erased in the minds of the living.

Even during the wars of Napoleon III the bodies of soldiers were treated with the same indifference as those in the common graves of the *ancien régime*. Those bodies that had not been removed by their comrades and quickly claimed by their families were always buried on the spot, and these mass burials aroused the same fears about insalubrity as the graves of les Innocents at the end of the eighteenth century. After the Battle of Sedan, which brought on the flight of Napoleon III, "the graves, which were filled to overflowing, began to emit pestilential fumes. The Belgian government, whose neighboring populations were in the greatest danger, sent to the site a committee that . . . found nothing more expeditious, safe, or economical than the use of fire." They called in a chemist, M. Creteur, who was very sure of himself and who certainly must not have been a positivist. He opened the graves, poured in tar and kerosene, and set fire to everything. The whole process took an hour. It was a pity that they had waited so long; it would not have cost them more than fifteen centimes if the cremation had been done immediately after the battle. The Germans also wished to purify the battlefields of Lorraine. "It seems that they felt greater distaste for this method of disposing of the dead, for since they were still in command at Sedan when M. Creteur was carrying out his operations, they expressed their formal intention of opposing the cremation of the bodies of their compatriots . . . and M. Creteur, in spite of the support of the government and the people, was forced to abstain." Dr. F. Martin, from whom I have borrowed these quotations, would have preferred a more decent but just as efficient burial. "By using a layer of soil three feet thick, sowing alfalfa, and planting some young acacias, one can avoid all disadvantages. By using two layers of bodies, one can bury twenty thousand men in one hectare without danger or serious difficulties."[96] Why deprive oneself of something more decent? Besides, one can add the homage of art to that of nature and erect a monument.

The first slain soldiers who were honored with a memorial tomb were undoubtedly the victims of the civil wars of the French Revolution. Examples are the monument in Lucerne to the Swiss massacred on August 10, 1792, and the expiatory chapel and cemetery of Picpus, in Paris. But the most significant monument is the one in Quiberon. The emigrés who tried to land were shot and buried on the spot, according to custom. At the time of the Restoration the burial ground was bought, withdrawn from cultivation, and transformed into a place of meditation. The bones had already been removed and placed in a nearby convent, in a chapel engraved with the names of the martyrs. The ossuary, which is visible, is a cross between the charnels of the eighteenth-century cemeteries of mummies and the ossuaries of World War I. The tomb at the site of the martyrdom is the object of a worship that is no longer familial and private but now collective.

Tombs are becoming monuments, and monuments are forced to be tombs. Rémusat tells us how in July 1837 the remains of the Parisians who died in the Trois Glorieuses were transferred to the base of the column commemorating the event.

But no one will be surprised to learn that it was in France after 1870 that the memory of the dead came to be more precisely preserved and the dead venerated. Everyone knows how traumatic this period was for all of French society. The collective sensibility received a wound that did not heal until the "revenge" of 1914. In the beginning, of course, this did not prevent the French from burying the slain soldiers without much respect, although they were not proud of the way it was done. But they also had the new idea of drawing up honor rolls on stone or metal, as at Quiberon, and posting them, usually in the church but sometimes in the cemetery. In Père-Lachaise there is a monument to the dead dated 1870. It is an empty tomb that serves as a memorial.

It is very significant that the church and the cemetery were the two places that welcomed the first monuments to the dead: the church, because the Catholics and the clergy regarded those who had died in such a just war as comparable to martyrs and because the Church considered it her vocation to honor the dead and maintain their cult; the cemetery, because it was the place where the living went to remember and had actually been a kind of competitor of the church since the time the two had been legally separated.

On All Saints' Day in 1902 there were some 350,000 visitors to the cemeteries of Paris. A "republican" stresses the unanimity of national feeling toward the dead, especially the war dead: "Let us examine this pilgrimage to the cemeteries, so that we may judge whether superstition has some part in this universal commemoration. . . . People are drawn primarily to those monuments that bear some celebrated and popular name from government, art, or literature, or that reveal some great and noble idea. It is the survivors of our memorable conflicts [veterans of the Franco-Prussian War or the colonial wars] and even of our civil wars [revolutions, Commune of Paris] who, putting aside their differences of opinion, come to salute the remains of their comrades of yesteryear. It is the local authorities themselves who come to pay homage to all the heroes."97

World War I gave the civic cult of the dead "of our memorable conflicts" a popularity and prestige that it had never known before. The idea of burying or burning the dead on the field of honor was no longer tolerated. Entire cemeteries, conceived as architectural landscapes, were devoted to them, with endless rows of identical crosses. The cross was chosen as the common symbol of death and hope, even by people who had not adopted it until then, such as the Americans.

And in each commune of France, in each *arrondissement* of Paris, a tomb was erected to the slain soldiers. An empty tomb, the "monument to the dead," was generally located opposite the town hall. It was an emotional center of the town comparable only to the church. It really was the symbol of unanimous national feeling, almost until our own time.

After the unknown soldier was buried there, the Arc de Triomphe, which Napoleon I built at the Etoile, also became a tomb. The anniversary of the victory of 1918, instead of being celebrated as a day of triumph, has become a day for the dead. In each town or village the local authorities and patriotic associations gather around the empty tomb, the monument to the dead. The bugles sound, as they also do on that day in church, the lament *"Pour elle, un Français doit mourir"* (For her a Frenchman must die). In places where there is no monument to the dead, there can be no commemoration and therefore no celebration.

This convergence of the cult of the dead and national sentiment in the late nineteenth and early twentieth centuries is found in the United States as well as in France. If Washington, D.C., had been built in the seventeenth and eighteenth centuries, it would be a city of royal statues, like Paris: statues of the presidents of the Union. But it grew in the nineteenth and early twentieth centuries, and that is why it is a city of empty tombs, memorials to the country's statesmen, such as the Washington Monument, the funerary obelisk that dominates it from afar. It was the desire of Washington's descendants that kept his tomb on his plantation in Virginia; the American people would have preferred it to be moved to the capital. The vast green carpets that the architect of the capital, Major L'Enfant, designed are punctuated by the memorials of Lincoln and Jefferson, the latter very recent, dating from the Roosevelt era. Both are veritable mausoleums, conceived in the manner of the great classical monuments. From the eminence of Arlington, the tombstones descend on the city, row upon row. The cemetery in which the great servants of the Union are buried forms the backdrop of the urban landscape.

It is these tombs that masses of Americans visit every year from spring to fall, just as the Catholics make pilgrimages to Saint Peter's, in Rome.

Minot: A Country Cemetery

In the preceding pages we have very seldom left the large towns. It was there that the new religion of the dead was born and began to develop. But what was happening in the country? A few villages imitated the towns and moved their cemeteries outside the populated center. The old cemetery was obliterated and covered over by the public park that was next to the church. Many others, however, retained their cemetery at its former site, next to the church; but in these cases no tomb is older than the early nineteenth century, proving that a new cemetery, built in accordance with the new rules, had replaced the old one on the same site.

We can follow what happened in the country in Francoise Zonabend's excellent study of the cemetery of Minot, in Châtillonnais. Her work shows how the different models that I have distinguished in this book are combined in a single country village, from the early Middle Ages to our time.[98]

First there is the Merovingian necropolis, which predated the practice of burial *ad sanctos* and was therefore located outside the original town. A chapel was built there, and a *castrum* erected beside it. It was a very large space, like the necropolis of Civaux in Poitou. The people of the surrounding area were buried there; most of them had been baptized in the chapel. (The situation is similar to Saint-Hilaire with its little church and its old cemetery near Marville, in Meuse; see chapter 5.) When a new church dedicated to Saint Peter was built in 1450 in the neighboring hamlet of Minot, the Merovingian necropolis was abandoned in favor of the church and its yard. But for many years victims of the plague continued to be buried in a corner of the old cemetery, precisely because they had to be kept at a distance from the houses.

After the fifteenth century, or rather late, the classic medieval and modern model of the church and its adjacent cemetery was established in Minot. Around the church and the cemetery were the rectory, the tithing barn, the public bakehouse, the market, and the auditorium where the lord's justice was dispensed and inhabitants assembled. The lord's château was at a distance, on the site of the *castrum* and the old abandoned necropolis. Lords of the manor were buried in the choir, in front of the altar.

The parish records examined by Zonabend indicate that in the seventeenth century, notables were buried outside the church but against its walls, the privileged location being in niches or galleries. Priests had their place at the foot of the large Calvary cross, which was the only cross in the cemetery. The other graves were scattered at random in the field, without visible markers. The field had been blessed on the day the church was consecrated, of course, but it was not enclosed by walls until the middle of the nineteenth century. "Open to all comers, both people and animals, and of vast proportions, located on the village green [and indistinguishable from it], next to the other public buildings, the cemetery was at the center of the life of the parish. Not far from the graves, people met, held their markets, and danced, and the flocks sometimes wandered among the tombs. The dead were intimately associated with life." Here, in an independent study by an author not familiar with my categories, I recognize my first model of the tame death. The fact that the second model, the death of the self, is not represented in this rural community should surprise no one.

But at the end of the seventeenth century we witness the arrival of the Tridentine and reforming priest. He reduced the cemetery to its present dimensions and decided to have it enclosed. Actually, the wall was not completed until 1861, but the desire was already there to separate the cemetery from the public square, to make it a space apart, not accessible to animals, cleared of all the objects that encumbered it, and rid of all the profane gatherings that took place there. It was a question of restoring to church and cemetery their compromised respectability. In the Middle Ages, people had built onto the church storage places where valuables and furniture could be kept safe in time of trouble; the new priest did away with these vestiges of the right of sanctuary. On the other hand, he had the idea of providing a special place for the burial of small children, those "little angels." Here we recognize the purifying influences and the desire for simplicity that marked the seventeenth and eighteenth centuries and that I have grouped, along with other less moral but ultimately harmonious characteristics, in Part 3 under the heading "Remote and Imminent Death."

The cemetery of Zonabend's ethnological study is no longer that of the *ancien régime,* nor is it quite the cemetery of today. In some ways it corresponds to my fourth model, which reflects the invasion of affectivity and the cult of the dead.

Of course, it remained next to the church; the municipal council refused to move it outside the walls. "There was talk of moving it to Fontaine-Condrez, but if that happened, people would not often go there." Here is a small-scale version of the resistance to the Méry-sur-Oise project and Haussmann's "train of the dead."

However, if the cemetery was not moved physically, it was placed at a distance psychologically, removed from everyday life by the new respect it inspired. People no longer dare dance in the covered markets as in the old days, because they are too close to the dead: "It's not right, one must show some respect." The old are amazed at this severity, of which they do not approve. As Zonabend puts it, "Instead of a calm cohabitation, today we find grounds for conflict [if the room where parties are held is too close to the cemetery]. The old familiarity with the sacred has become a respectful separation, a distancing." In Paris and other large towns, the cult of the dead appeared after a long and confused intermediary period in which the medieval familiarity changed imperceptibly into a callous indifference. But here the people passed directly from the age of familiarity to the age of respect, unless one considers the actions of the reforming priests of the seventeenth and eighteenth centuries. The respect of the nineteenth and twentieth centuries was accompanied by a distance and a fear. An old house contiguous with the church remained unsold for a long time. "It was too close to the cemetery," people said. Fear was born of respect. The respect declined, but the fear grew. But I am anticipating.

"This walling in of the dead," Zonabend observes, "this vague desire to put them at a distance, . . . does not correspond to a depreciation of the cemetery or an indifference to the memory of the dead." On the contrary! The old familiarity knew nothing of the cult of memory, the visit to the tomb. "Every day the old come to sit near the grave of a spouse or child. . . . The women stroll there on Sundays or on fine summer evenings. . . . Passing from tomb to tomb, the old read the inscriptions and recall the lives of the deceased. It is during these walks that the memory of the community is forged, and the history of the village families is transmitted to all."

For the space of the dead is divided into "family sections," to use the phrase of a founder of 1912, reported by Zonabend. Each tomb is the counterpart of a house. People say "at our tombs" as they would say "at our house" or "at home." I have made the same observation myself.[99] In a small town outside of Paris an old laundress had prepared a fine tomb for herself and her family, who may not have had a tomb of their own. On the day she quarreled with her son-in-law, she turned him out of his tomb, as if she were turning him out of her house.

Zonabend writes, "Sometimes there is a clause in the deed of sale of a house requiring the new owners to maintain the tombs of the previous owners." These house tombs were grouped in family sections, approximately by lineage. The cemetery is a schematic image of the society, organized by family groups. Such an organization of space is altogether remarkable in that it is absolutely new. The cemetery of the *ancien régime* ignored these family relationships; the dead were entrusted indiscriminately to the Church and to the saints.

Thus, the rural community had the force to create a system of symbols so similar to the codes of traditional cultures that one is tempted to confuse it with them and to believe it to be just as old, whereas in fact it dates only from the nineteenth century.

In this Châtillonnais village we recognize our Parisian model of the cult of the dead. Positivism, with its theory of fetishism and of the cult of the dead, gave conceptual coherence to a group of commonplace feelings and ideas that invaded our societies at the end of the eighteenth century and penetrated them to their roots.

However, there is something in the description of the funerary customs of Minot that does not correspond to our Parisian model and that even seems to contradict the famous Decree of Prairial. In Minot they never stopped superimposing bodies, not, of course, piling them up in common graves, which can never have existed in the village, but in a re-creation of the intimacy of early childhood. "The mama was laid on the grandmama, Albert [the son] was laid on the mama, and when Germain's granddaughter died, she was laid on top of them." A pretty pile that would have horrified the hygienically minded philosophers of 1800.

Contrary to the situation created by the Decree of Prairial, in Minot the grave is not granted on an individual basis. It is a communal property to which everyone has a temporary right. This is very like the situation during the *ancien régime,* except that the mayor and the commune play the role of the priest and the church council. As in the old days, the grave is not a permanent property; in fact, it is not a property at all. So in this cemetery of the nineteenth and twentieth centuries there are some age-old characteristics that coexist peacefully with the innovations of the nineteenth century. Like the old cemeteries, this one is in a constant state of flux. In order to bury a new body, you "reuse a tomb," which is against regulations. The gravedigger explains, "To reuse a tomb, I reopen it. If the old coffin is intact, I leave it as it is and put the new one on top of it. But usually I find bones and pieces of metal and wood. I remove all this debris and put it aside in a little pile, and then, when the new coffin has been lowered into the grave, I put everything on top of it." So the mama was not exactly on top, but underneath. In order to facilitate this reshuffling, it was necessary for the bodies to be rapidly consumed; so in Minot one finds the old language of the Middle Ages: "It is not desirable to remain intact. It is a sign that the funerary ritual was not performed correctly, or the mark of an unusual destiny. The deceased is either a saint or he is damned."

The result was a confusion of bones quite incompatible with the new respect. The predecessor of the present gravedigger "dug the graves at random, and when he found bones, he put them on a nearby tomb. He put the heads on the monuments [as in the first version of Poussin's *Ego in Arcadia*]; the people who came to the funeral saw all this." They laughed. And Zonabend concludes, "In Minot there is a language of death. People talk about it without restraint or reserve; they describe the earthly destination of bodies simply and easily. Here silence has not buried this final phase of the life cycle as it has in the town, among other social groups. In the village, death remains familiar, always present."

It is as if the romantic model has been grafted onto the archaic. The latter has not disappeared altogether, but the former has not developed all its possibilities. The medieval cemetery has been rehabilitated rather than destroyed by the religion of the nineteenth century, which is both ancient and Christian at the same time. The naïve and unselfconscious familiarity between the living and the dead that the medieval cemetery presupposed has a new meaning. It has become more conscious and more ritualized, a symbolic and conventional language that has made it possible to express publicly but discreetly, without pathos or improvisation, the new sentimental relationships between members of a family or between families of a community.

We have used the present tense because that was the grammatical tense of the study. But this present becomes the past under the scrutiny of the investigators. It is decided that the cemetery will be divided up and sold in grants like any urban cemetery of the nineteenth century. The tombs will no longer be reused. Eventually whole vaults will be brought from Dijon "like septic tanks." And Zonabend concludes on a melancholy note: "The dead will then be totally isolated, protected from the earth that once, generation after generation, they formed, they fertilized."

Burial at Home

The cult of cemeteries and tombs is the liturgical manifestation of the new sensibility that, beginning in the late eighteenth century, rendered the death of the other intolerable. The feeling still prevails in France and Italy, especially among ordinary people, as we can see from these two French news items.

The first story appeared in *L'Aurore* for September 19, 1963. It takes place in a village in upper Provence that was to be evacuated to allow the army to set up a shooting range. "When my father found out about this, he died of it, and he did not want to be buried here because he did not want to remain alone in the abandoned cemetery. 'You will send me to X,' he said. 'I do not want to stay here.'"

The other story appeared in *Le Monde* of April 30, 1963. Sergeant

Aimé Druon was killed in Indochina on January 18, 1952. A 1946 law provided that the army furnish to their families free transport and delivery of the bodies of soldiers and victims of the war. After World War II the French people refused to turn their dead soldiers over to the large national cemeteries like those of World War I; they preferred to keep them in family graves.

In the case in question, the body of the sergeant was being contested by two families, the family of his natural parents and the family that had taken him in at the age of fifteen without legally adopting him. In 1959 the court of appeals of Douai ruled against the foster parents, although a judicial investigation showed that the dead man's comrades regarded them "as the real parents, and [testified] that he corresponded only with them." In April 1963 the decision was reversed by the supreme court of appeals. It is possible, therefore, that the body was turned over to the foster parents. The point is that for over ten years two families carried on a legal battle, with all the expense that that entails, in order to obtain custody of a body and to be able to bury it "at home."

Curiously enough, the cult of the dead and the attachment to the dead body have passed from western Europe into other contemporary cultures. This is proved by a story found in an article by Josué de Castro, "Seven Feet of Earth and a Coffin": "In 1955 Joao Firmino, a tenant farmer on the Galileo estate, founded the first of the peasant leagues in the northeast of Brazil. His primary objective was not, as many people believe, to improve the living conditions of the peasants . . . or to defend the interests of this human residue that was being ground by the wheel of destiny as the sugarcane is ground by the wheels of the mills. The leagues were originally formed to defend the interests of the dead rather than those of the living, to give peasants who had died of hunger and poverty . . . the right to seven feet of earth in which to lay their bones . . . and the right to be lowered into their graves inside a wooden coffin that belonged to them, so they could rot slowly along with it." Formerly the coffin was collective, like the charity coffins of the *ancien régime,* and was used only for transportation. "Why this desperate desire to have a coffin of one's own in which to be buried, when during their lifetimes these outcasts of destiny had never been the owners of anything?" asks de Castro. His answer may also be true for the poor and humble of nineteenth-century Europe, who were also eager to possess a coffin and a tomb of their own:[100] "For the counties of the northeast, it is death that counts, not life, since for all practical purposes life does not belong to them." The possession of their death is "their right to escape someday from the grip of poverty and the injustices of life."[101] Death gives them back their dignity.

Part V

THE INVISIBLE DEATH

12

Death Denied

In the early twentieth century, before World War I, throughout the Western world of Latin culture, be it Catholic or Protestant, the death of a man still solemnly altered the space and time of a social group that could be extended to include the entire community. The shutters were closed in the bedroom of the dying man, candles were lit, holy water was sprinkled; the house filled with grave and whispering neighbors, relatives, and friends. At the church, the passing bell tolled and the little procession left carrying the *Corpus Christi.*

After death, a notice of bereavement was posted on the door (in lieu of the old abandoned custom of exhibiting the body or the coffin by the door of the house). All the doors and windows of the house were closed except the front door, which was left ajar to admit everyone who was obliged by friendship or good manners to make a final visit. The service at the church brought the whole community together, including latecomers who waited for the end of the funeral to come forward; and after the long line of people had expressed their sympathy to the family, a slow procession, saluted by passersby, accompanied the coffin to the cemetery. And that was not all. The period of mourning was filled with visits: visits of the family to the cemetery and visits of relatives and friends to the family.

Then, little by little, life returned to normal, and there remained only the periodic visits to the cemetery. The social group had been stricken by death, and it had reacted collectively, starting with the immediate family and extending to a wider circle of relatives and acquaintances. Not only did everyone die in public like Louis XIV, but the death of each person was a public event that moved, literally and figuratively, society as a whole. It was not only an individual who was disappearing, but society itself that had been wounded and that had to be healed.

All the changes that have modified attitudes toward death in the past thousand years have not altered this fundamental image, this permanent relationship between death and society. Death has always been a social and public fact. It remains so today in vast areas of the Latin West, and it is by no means clear that this traditional model is destined to disappear. But it no longer has the quality of absolute generality that it once had, no matter what the religion and the culture. In the course of the twentieth century an absolutely new type of dying has made an appearance in some of the most industrialized, urbanized, and technologically advanced areas of the Western world—and this is probably only the first stage.

Two characteristics are obvious to the most casual observer. First is its novelty, of course, its contrariness to everything that preceded it, of which it is the reverse image, the negative. Except for the death of statesmen, society has banished death. In the towns, there is no way of knowing that something has happened: the old black and silver hearse has become an ordinary gray limousine, indistinguishable from the flow of traffic. Society no longer observes a pause; the disappearance of an individual no longer affects its continuity. Everything in town goes on as if nobody died anymore.

The second characteristic is no less surprising. Of course, death has changed in a thousand years, but how slowly! The changes were so gradual and so infinitesimal, spread out over generations, that they were imperceptible to contemporaries. Today, a complete reversal of customs seems to have occurred in one generation. In my youth, women in mourning were invisible under their crepe and voluminous black veils. Middle-class children whose grandmothers had died were dressed in violet. After 1945, my mother wore mourning for a son killed in the war for the twenty-odd years that remained to her.

The very rapidity and suddenness of the change have made us take stock of it. Phenomena that had been forgotten have suddenly become known and discussed, the subjects of sociological investigations, television programs, medical and legal debates. Shown the door by society, death is coming back in through the window, and it is returning just as quickly as it disappeared.

The change is rapid and sudden, there is no doubt of that; but is it really as recent as it appears to the journalist, the sociologist, and to ourselves, dazed as we are by the acceleration of pace?

The Beginning of the Lie

After the second half of the nineteenth century, an essential change occurred in the relationship between the dying man and his entourage.

Obviously, the discovery that one's end was near has always been an
unpleasant moment. But people learned to overcome it. The Church saw
to it that the doctor carried out the role of herald of death. The role was
not a coveted one, and it required the zeal of the "spiritual friend" to
succeed where the "earthly friend" hesitated. When the warning did not
happen spontaneously, it was part of the customary ritual. But in the later
nineteenth century it became more and more problematical, as we see from
a story in Tolstoi's "Three Deaths," which appeared in 1859.

The wife of a rich businessman has contracted tuberculosis, as happened so often at that time. The doctors have pronounced her condition
hopeless. The moment has come when she has to be told. There is no
question of avoiding it, if only to allow her to make her "final arrangements." But here is a new element: the distaste of the entourage for this
duty has increased. The husband refuses "to tell her about her condition,"
because, he says, "It would kill her. . . . No matter what happens, it is not
I who will tell her." The mother of the dying woman is also reluctant. As
for the dying woman, she talks about nothing but new treatments; she
seems to be clinging to life, and everyone is afraid of her reaction. However,
something has to be done. Finally the family enlists an old cousin, a poor
relation, a mercenary person who throws herself into the task. "Sitting
beside the sick woman, she attempted by a skillfully maneuvered conversation to prepare her for the idea of death." But the sick woman suddenly
interrupts her, saying, "Ah, my dear! . . . Don't try to prepare me. Don't
treat me like a child. I know everything. I know that I haven't much longer
to live." Now they can begin the classic scenario of the good death in
public, which has been momentarily disturbed by the new reluctance regarding the warning.

Behind this reluctance, even when it grates under the satirical pen of
Tolstoi, there is the love of the other, the fear of hurting him and depriving
him of hope, the temptation to protect him by leaving him in ignorance
of his imminent end. No one questions the idea that he ought to know,
yet no one wants to do the dirty work himself; let someone else take care
of it. In France the priest was all ready, for the warning had become part
of his spiritual preparation at the last hour. Indeed, the priest's arrival will
be interpreted as the sign of the end, without it being necessary to say
anything else.

As for the patient, and Tolstoi describes this very well, he does not really need to be warned. He already knows. But his public acceptance would destroy an illusion that he hopes to prolong a little longer, and without which he would be treated as a dying person and obliged to behave like one. So he says nothing.

And everyone becomes an accomplice to a lie born of this moment which later grows to such proportions that death is driven into secrecy. The dying person and those around him continue to play a comedy in which "nothing has changed," "life goes on as usual," and "anything is still possible." This is the second phase in a process of domination of the dying by the family that began among the upper classes in the late eighteenth century, when the dying man chose not to impose his last wishes in a legal document but entrusted them directly to his heirs.

A new relationship had been established that brought the dying man and his entourage closer on an emotional level; but the initiative, if not the power, still belonged to the dying. Here the relationship persists, but it has been reversed, and the dying man has become dependent upon the entourage. It is useless for Tolstoi's heroine to protest that she is being treated like a child, for it is she who has placed herself in that position. The day will come when the dying will accept this subordinate position, whether he simply submits to it or actually desires it. When this happens—and this is the situation today—it will be assumed that it is the duty of the entourage to keep the dying man in ignorance of his condition. How many times have we heard it said of a husband, child, or relative, "At least I have the satisfaction of knowing that he never felt a thing." "Never feeling a thing" has replaced "feeling his death to be imminent."

Dissimulation has become the rule. These feats of imagination inspired Mark Twain to write a story about the tissue of lies maintained by two nice old maids in order to conceal from each of the two invalids they are taking care of, a mother and her sixteen-year-old child, the fact that the other is dying.[1]

This dissimulation has the practical effect of removing or delaying all the signs that warned the sick person, especially the staging of the public act that once was death, beginning with the presence of the priest. Even in the most religious and churchgoing families, it became customary in the early twentieth century not to call the priest until his appearance at the bedside of the patient could no longer come as a surprise, either because the patient had lost consciousness or because he was unmistakably dead. Extreme Unction was no longer the sacrament of the dying but the sacrament of the dead. This situation already existed in France by the 1920s and '30s, and became even more widespread in the 1950s.

Gone are the days of the solemn procession of the *Corpus Christi*, preceded by the choirboy ringing his bell. Gone, long gone, the days when this procession was welcomed sadly by the dying man and his entourage. It is clear that the clergy finally had had enough of administering to cadavers, that they finally refused to lend themselves to this farce, even if it was inspired by love. Their rebellion partly explains why, after Vatican II, the Church changed the traditional name of Extreme Unction to the "anointing of the sick," and not always the terminally sick. Today it is sometimes distributed in church to old people who are not sick at all. The sacrament has been detached from death, for which it is no longer the immediate preparation. In this the Church is not merely recalling the obligation to be fully conscious when one receives the unction. It is implicitly admitting its own absence at the moment of death, the lack of necessity for "calling the priest"; but we shall see that death has ceased to be a moment.

In the nineteenth century the disappearance of pious clauses from the will had increased the importance of the final dialogue: the last farewells, the last words of counsel, whether in private or in public. This intimate and solemn exchange has been abolished by the obligation to keep the dying man in ignorance. Eventually he left without saying anything. This was almost always the way the very old, even the conscious and the pious, died during the 1950s and '60s in France, before the influx of new modes of behavior from America and northwestern Europe. "She didn't even say good-bye to us," murmured a son at the bedside of his mother. He was not yet accustomed to this stubborn silence, or perhaps to this new modesty.

The Beginning of Medicalization

But let us turn to Tolstoi's "The Death of Ivan Ilyich," which was written twenty-five years after the "Three Deaths." Here we enter a new world, a world on the brink of "medicalization." Ivan Ilyich is a man of forty-five who has been married for seventeen years to a mediocre woman. He has had four children, one of whom is still alive; the other three have died at an early age without his being particularly affected by it. He has led the dull and ordinary life of a capable and ambitious civil servant obsessed with advancement, anxious to appear correct. He wears a little medal with an inscription unusual for Russia, *"Respice finem";* a *memento mori* of the sort that was popular in the West from the late fifteenth to the seventeenth century. But his religion seems superficial and has no effect on his egoism. It is an "easy existence, pleasant, happy, always correct, socially acceptable," but marred by money worries and the domestic scenes they provoke. However, success comes with a promotion, and the subsequent choice of a new house, in which he will be able to receive "the best society," "important people."

It is then that the trouble begins: bad breath, a pain in the chest, nervousness; in short, he needs a consultation. By the 1880s, going to a doctor has become a necessary and important step, which it was not fifty years before, in the days of the La Ferronays. It was only *in extremis* that Albert's wife wanted to know the name of her husband's illness. Illness and health, although worthy of attention, were not yet necessarily associated with the action or power of the doctor. The journal of a *bourgeois de Paris*, written at the time of the French Revolution, shows how concerned a man could be with his body. Every day the author notes both the weather and his physiological state, whether he is blowing his nose or spitting, whether he has a temperature: external and internal nature. But it never occurs to him to consult (or to record that he has consulted) a doctor or surgeon, although there are several among his good friends. He takes care of himself; in other words, he puts his confidence in nature.[2]

In the novels of Balzac the doctor plays an important social and moral role. Along with the priest, he is protector of the humble and counselor to rich and poor alike. He prescribes treatments, but he does not cure his patients; he helps them to die. Or perhaps he foresees a natural course of things that it is not his responsibility to alter. We are told that when Albert de La Ferronays reaches thirty, he will recover naturally. He will be sick until then—and perhaps the doctor adds under his breath, "If he lives!" But when the disease grows worse and one feels helpless, one calls in a personality who is no longer a dispenser of treatments and good advice but a man of science, who arrives from Paris in a carriage with a team of fast horses, like a *deus ex machina.* Perhaps science will attempt the impossible. The doctor now appears as a last resort, one reserved for the rich. He is only very rarely, and very late in the day, the one who reveals the nature and name of the illness. He is interested in the symptoms (fever, expectoration), he prescribes treatment (bleeding, enemas), but he does not try to classify the case. For that matter there is no such thing as a case, there is only a series of phenomena.

For Ivan Ilyich, his illness is suddenly a case that has a separate existence and must have a name. What name? It is up to the doctor to say it, and then he will know whether or not it is serious. For there are categories of illness that are dangerous and others that are benign. Everything depends on the diagnosis.

After this first consultation, Ivan Ilyich clings to the doctor like a parasite. His mind embraces the physician's uncertainty. "The life of Ivan Ilyich was not in danger, but there was a struggle between the floating kidney and the appendix." He tries to interpret the words of the practitioner, to guess what he is concealing. "He concluded from the doctor's summary that things were going badly. For the doctor, for everyone else, perhaps, this was of no importance, but for him personally, things were going very badly." His destiny depends henceforth on the diagnosis, a difficult diagnosis that has not yet been made.

When he comes home, he tells his wife about the visit. She feigns indifference and optimism. She is stupid and selfish, but even a more affectionate wife would have behaved the same way outwardly. The main thing is to reassure him. "After she left, he heaved a deep sigh. 'Well,' he said, 'maybe it's really nothing, after all.'"

From this point forward Ivan Ilyich has entered the medical cycle. "Since his visit to the doctor . . . his main concern was to follow his recommendations concerning hygiene and medicine to the letter and to observe his pain closely. All of Ivan Ilyich's attention was concentrated on sick people and health." He is interested in sick people whose cases resemble his own. He reads medical works, consults other doctors. In the course of his consultations, anxiety takes root in him along with knowledge, or the uncertainty of knowledge. "He tried to convince himself that he was better. He succeeded in lying to himself as long as nothing happened to upset him." But as soon as there is some disagreement at home or at the office, the vague anxiety reappears.

His state of mind is dependent on two variables: the diagnosis of the illness and the effectiveness of the treatment. He observes the effects of the treatment, and his mood depends on its ups and downs. Sure knowledge provides security. But when the doctor begins to doubt whether the appendix or the kidney is the cause, Ivan Ilyich, the well-educated and rational government official, despairs and turns to some charlatan who heals with icons. Ivan Ilyich is trapped by his illness like a squirrel in a cage.

The Progress of the Lie

Meanwhile, the pain is getting worse. "There was no doubt about it, something terrible was happening inside him, something new and more important than anything that had ever happened to Ivan Ilyich. And he was the only one who knew about it." He does not give way; he guards his secret suffering, for fear of worrying those around him and also of giving the thing he feels swelling inside him greater reality by naming it. Just as the diagnosis removes some of the anxiety, confiding in someone else might add to it. Such is the power of words in the psychological isolation of the invalid! "The people around him did not understand him, or did not want to understand him, and imagined that everything was the same as usual."

Indeed, it is important to avoid opportunities of showing feeling, emotional encounters; it is necessary to maintain an atmosphere of everyday banality. On this condition, the sick man may be able to maintain his morale. He needs all his strength to do this.

So those around him become part of the farce: "His friends begin to laugh at his fears, as if this horrible and nameless thing that had taken root in him, gnawed at him constantly, and was drawing him inexorably no one knew where, were some sort of amusing joke." His wife pretends to believe that he is sick because he does not take his medicine, because he does not follow his diet. She treats him like a child.

This might have gone on for a long time, but then Ivan Ilyich overhears a conversation between his wife and his brother-in-law. "But don't you see that he is dead?" the brother-in-law exclaims brutally. This is something new. Ilyich did not know, nor did his wife, probably, that this is how people see him. Will he collapse? No, at first he reacts as if he has not really understood the meaning of the warning. Without betraying his presence, "he went back to his room, lay down, and began to think." About what? About the death that he carries with him and that everyone can see? Not at all: about the floating kidney. "The kidney, the floating kidney," he repeats to himself, as if to cover the sound of the little venomous phrase that has infiltrated his consciousness. "He remembered everything the doctors had explained to him, how it had come loose and how it was floating. And by an effort of the imagination he tried to get hold of it, to keep it in place."

He gets up and immediately goes to see another doctor. This is his reaction: He denies death by masking it with disease. "In his imagination the longed-for healing of his appendix took place, . . . the functioning of his organs was restored." He felt that he was better.

This time the warning is given by chance, but there will always be just such a warning. The isolation of the sick man is never so complete that he cannot intercept some sign. The doctors of today know this, and count on chance to spare them the job of direct intervention. The warning is rejected, but it worms its way into the embattled consciousness, and as soon as the pain returns, the illusion is destroyed and the truth becomes obvious. Ivan Ilyich suddenly understands that he is going to die. "The kidney, the appendix," he thinks. "No, that's not the point, it's a matter of life . . . or death. . . . It is death, and here I am thinking about the appendix! . . . Yes, I was alive, but now my life is leaving; it is leaving, and I cannot hold it back. Yes, why lie to myself? Isn't it obvious to everyone, even to myself, that I am dying, and that it is only a matter of weeks, days, perhaps even minutes?" He has reached this point in his reflections when his wife comes in. She knows, but she does not know that he knows. Ever since her brother has opened her eyes, she has looked at Ivan Ilyich with "a singularly sad and sweet expression that was not characteristic of her." These two people might now come together in a shared truth. But Ivan Ilyich no longer has the strength to climb over the wall that he himself has built with the complicity of his family and his doctors. "Desperate, panting, he fell back on the bed, waiting for death," and to his wife, to explain his distraught attitude, he says only, " 'It's nothing. . . . I . . .' What's the use of telling her? She wouldn't understand." The lie has fallen between them forever.

The doctor lends himself to the farce. "He seems to be saying, 'You are upsetting yourself over nothing. We'll fix you up in no time!' " Even after the final consultation with important specialists, and in spite of the aggravation of his condition, "everyone was afraid to suddenly dissipate the correct lie and to let in so much reality."

Then begins a long night, in which Ivan Ilyich must endure in silence the pain and ugliness of the physical disease, as well as the metaphysical anguish. No one helps him through the tunnel except the young *muzhik* who is taking care of him. "The worst torment was the lie, this lie that for some reason was accepted by everyone, that he was only sick, and not dying, and that if he would only remain calm and take care of himself, everything would be fine; whereas he knew very well that no matter what was done, the result would only be even worse suffering and death. This lie tormented him. He suffered because no one was willing to admit what everyone, including himself, could see very clearly. He suffered because they lied and forced him to take part in this deception. This lie that was being told on the eve of his death, this lie that degraded the formidable and solemn act of his death, . . . had become horribly painful to Ivan Ilyich." Curiously, he is frequently on the point of crying out while they are telling their little stories around him, " 'Enough lies, we all know that I am dying! Stop lying to me, at least!' But he never had the courage to do this." He is himself the prisoner of the character he has allowed them to impose on him and that he has imposed on himself. The mask has been on so long that it is stuck, and he cannot take it off. He is condemned to live out the lie. Compare Tolstoi's phrase, written in the 1880s, "This lie that degraded the formidable and solemn act of his death," with the last words of Père F. de Dainville to Père Ribes in 1973 when he was lying in an intensive-care unit with tubes all over his body: "They are cheating me out of my own death!"[3] How close they seem, although they are almost a century apart.

The Dirty Death

After the concealment of death by illness and the establishment of the lie around the dying man, the other new element that appears in Tolstoi's writing is the dirtiness and indecency of death. In the long accounts of deaths of the La Ferronays or the Brontës there is no mention of the uncleanness of the great terminal diseases. Why? A Victorian modesty, which shrank from mentioning bodily excretions, as well as long habituation to disagreeable smells and to the disfiguring effects of pain.

But in Tolstoi, death is dirty. Remarkably enough, it was already dirty in Flaubert, who in 1857 spares us no detail of the hideous death of Mme. Bovary, disfigured by poison. The attacks of nausea were so sudden "that she hardly had time to take her handkerchief out from under the pillow. . . . Charles observed that there was in the bottom of the basin [in which she had vomited] a sort of white gravel clinging to the porcelain walls. . . . He placed his hand on her stomach; she gave a shrill cry. . . . She became paler than the sheet into which she was digging her clenched fingers. . . . Drops of sweat ran down her bluish face . . . , her teeth chattered, her enlarged eyes stared vaguely into space. . . . Little by little her groans became louder. A muffled scream escaped her. . . . Her lips were drawn, her limbs were contracted, her body was covered with brown spots, and her pulse eluded his fingers. Then she began to scream horribly. . . . With her chin against her chest, Emma opened her eyes very wide, and her poor hands plucked at the sheets with that hideous and pathetic gesture of the dying, who seem to want to wrap themselves already in their shroud. . . . Her chest began to heave rapidly. Her whole tongue protruded from her mouth; her rolling eyes grew as dim as two lamp globes being extinguished."

The agony of Emma Bovary is described in merciless detail, but it is brief. The illness of Ivan Ilyich, however, is long, and the odors and the nature of the treatments make it disgusting and—something death never was with the La Ferronays, the Brontës, or Balzac—indecent, improper. "He saw clearly that the hideousness of his agony was degraded by his entourage to the level of a simple irritation, almost a breach of manners (a little like the reaction to a man who emits a bad odor when he walks into a drawing room), and this in the name of that 'correctness' that he had served all his life."

Cleanliness has become a bourgeois value. The war against dust is the first duty of the Victorian housewife. Christian missionaries require their catechumens to have cleanliness of body as well as the purity of soul of which it is the outward sign. And even today, the war against long hair on young men is waged in the name of hygiene and morality.

During the second half of the nineteenth century, death ceases to be always seen as beautiful and is sometimes even depicted as disgusting. It is true that Ronsard and the other macabre poets of the fifteenth and sixteenth centuries had felt a sense of repulsion in the face of the decrepitude of old age, the ravages of disease, the devastating effects of insomnia, decaying teeth, and bad breath. But they were only amplifying the theme of decline in an age when a more brutal and realistic imagination was discovering the decomposed cadaver and the unspeakable interior of man. This interior seemed more repellent than the exterior of the old man and the invalid.

In the eighteenth and early nineteenth centuries, the decrepit old man of the late Middle Ages was replaced by the handsome patriarch of Jean-Baptiste Greuze, an image more suitable to the romantic theme of the beautiful death. But in the late nineteenth century, we see a return of the hideous images of the era of the macabre, which had been repressed since the seventeenth century. The difference is that now everything that had been said in the Middle Ages about decomposition after death is transferred to the period before death, the agony.

Death no longer inspires fear solely because of its absolute negativity; it also turns the stomach, like any nauseating spectacle. It becomes improper, like the biological acts of man, the secretions of the human body. It is indecent to let someone die in public. It is no longer acceptable for strangers to come into a room that smells of urine, sweat, and gangrene, and where the sheets are soiled. Access to this room must be forbidden, except to a few intimates capable of overcoming their disgust, or to those indispensable persons who provide certain services. A new image of death is forming: the ugly and hidden death, hidden because it is ugly and dirty.

Beginning with the already consistent preliminary treatments of Flaubert and Tolstoi, the theme will be developed in three directions, which are so different that it is difficult to accept their common origin. The first culminates in an exceptional and scandalous model that would have been limited to protest literature had not the wars and revolutions between 1914 and our own time presented it rather literally to men in combat. It is a model of men of letters and soldiers.

In Flaubert and Tolstoi it was the disease that was dirty in a death due to disease. In the model of war writers such as Remarque, Barbusse, Sartre, or Genêt, the idea of death and the fear that it inspires open the sphincters and thus re-create in a completely healthy body the sordid realities of disease. The cell of the condemned man or the torture victim becomes just as nauseating as the bedroom of the chronically ill. The model is born of the impossibility of applying the conventions of the beautiful, patriotic death to the hecatombs of the twentieth century, the massacres of the world wars, the manhunts, the slow deaths by torture. The would-be heroes "shit in their pants," and the true heroes are primarily concerned with not doing the same, as in Sartre's *Le Mur*.

In the dramatic literature of the 1960s, the officer in Genêt's *Paravents* dies of the flatulence of his men, and the hermit in a play by James Saunders dies while releasing his own wind. The model culminates in the literature of outrage and defiance. But it also belongs to a folklore of old soldiers by which the writers may have been inspired.

The Transfer to the Hospital

The second direction indicated by Tolstoi leads to the hidden death in the hospital, which began very discreetly in the 1930s and '40s and became widespread after 1950.

In the early twentieth century it was not always easy to defend the bedroom of the dying from awkward expressions of sympathy, indiscreet curiosity, and all the other persistent manifestations of the idea of the public death. It was difficult as long as the sickroom remained in the home, a little private world beyond bureaucratic discipline. And yet the occupants of the home, the family and servants, were less able to endure the promiscuity of disease. The further we go into the twentieth century, the more difficult this promiscuity becomes. Rapid advances in comfort, privacy, personal hygiene, and ideas about asepsis have made everyone more delicate. Our senses can no longer tolerate the sights and smells that in the early nineteenth century were part of daily life, along with suffering and illness. The physiological effects have passed from daily life to the aseptic world of hygiene, medicine, and morality. The perfect manifestation of this world is the hospital, with its cellular discipline.

The burden of care and unpleasantness had once been shared by a whole little society of neighbors and friends, which was more extended among the lower classes and in the country but continued to exist in middle-class circles as well. But this little circle of participation steadily contracted until it was limited to the closest relatives or even to the couple, to the exclusion of children. Finally, in twentieth-century cities, the presence of a terminal patient in a small apartment made it very difficult to provide home care and carry on a job at the same time.

Furthermore, recent advances in surgery, long and elaborate medical treatments, and the use of heavy equipment have generally led the terminal patient to stay in the hospital. Although it is not always admitted, the hospital has offered families a place where they can hide the unseemly invalid whom neither the world nor they can endure. It also gives them a good excuse to let someone else deal with all those awkward visitors, so that they can continue to lead a normal life.

The dying man's bedroom has passed from the home to the hospital. For technical medical reasons, this transfer has been accepted by families, and popularized and facilitated by their complicity. The hospital is the only place where death is sure of escaping a visibility—or what remains of it—that is hereafter regarded as unsuitable and morbid. The hospital has become the place of the solitary death. In a study of English attitudes conducted in 1963, Geoffrey Gorer showed that only a quarter of the bereaved in his sample had been present at the death of a close relative.[4]

The Death of Mélisande

After the dirty death and the death in the hospital, the third direction takes us from Tolstoi to Maeterlinck, Debussy, and their modern commentator, Vladimir Jankélévitch. This third death is modest and discreet, but not shameful. It is a death as remote from the death of Socrates or Elvire as it is from that of the hero of *"Le Mur."* It is the death of Mélisande.

Jankélévitch does not like the beautiful death of the romantics. "In the romantic musicians who celebrate the majesty of death, exaggeration and emphasis expand the instant of death until it becomes an eternity. . . . The great ceremony of the funeral, with its solemn processions and its magnificence, enables the instant to overflow its instantaneity, to radiate like a sun around its sharp point. Instead of an imperceptible instant, there is a glorious instant." Exactly; and Jankélévitch has also understood the historical relationship between this glorification of death and an anthropomorphic eschatology that "peoples the void with shadows, makes the mortal window as transparent as a moonlit night, makes the beyond a pale *duplicatum* of this world, and imagines all sorts of absurd exchanges between the living and ghosts."[5]

We also find in Jankélévitch the now commonplace idea of the indecency of death, which we first met in Tolstoi. But the nature of this indecency has changed. It is not a recoiling from the signs of death, which he does not ignore; it is not something that is "not done," that offends the proprieties and that must be hidden; it has become an occasion for modesty. "The sort of modesty that death inspires springs largely from the unthinkable and untellable quality of the lethal state. There is a modesty attached to metempiric cessation, just as there is a modesty attached to biological continuation. If the repetition of periodic needs is somehow indecent, the fact that a blood clot suddenly interrupts life is also improper." This impropriety, softened into modesty, seems to him to be the source of the contemporary taboo regarding death. The relationship is a fascinating one for the historian. "Is not the taboo word *death* above all others the unpronounceable, unnameable, unspeakable monosyllable that the average man, conditioned to compromise, is obliged to shroud modestly in proper and respectable circumlocutions?" One need not force the meaning to assume a relationship between contemporary taboo and romantic emphasis. The first attempt to mask unnameable reality made use of rhetoric; the second has resorted to silence.

The indecency of the death of Ivan Ilyich has therefore become modesty, and the model of the modest death is the death of Mélisande. It is not a solitary death. There are people in the room by the sea. The old king, full of wisdom and eloquence, speaks at length; he is inexhaustible, like the real living. During his speech Mélisande dies without his noticing: "I saw nothing. . . . I heard nothing. . . . She went so quickly, so quickly! . . . just like that . . . without a word."

Mélisande was no doubt one of the first to leave, as Jankélévitch puts it, "*pianissimo*, on tiptoe, as it were." "To die makes no sound. A heart that stops beating makes no sound. For Debussy, poet of *pianissimo* and extreme concision, the instant was truly the fleeting moment."[6] This was true for Debussy yesterday; it is true for Jankélévitch and the agnostic intellectuals of today, but also for some of our contemporaries, average people, believers or nonbelievers, who find their courage in silence.

The time was the early 1960s. A son was expressing his concern to the priest who was attending his mother, a woman in her seventies in the last stages of cancer. He was not aware of the change in attitudes toward death, the rise of the taboo. He remembered the still-public deaths of his grandparents, which he had witnessed in the 1930s, and he was worried about the silence in which his mother seemed to be taking refuge. There was no sign that she knew about her condition. He did not understand this silence, and he never came to understand it completely. He reminded the confessor of the traditional duty to give the warning. But the priest, a former doctor, replied, "I can see that you have no experience with old women like the ones I have known at the nursing home, who spend their time moaning and crying because they are going to die." He thought that her silence should be respected, that it was courageous, and that there were ways of communicating indirectly without breaking the tacit conspiracy. Later, after the old lady's death, some papers were found that proved that she had had no illusions. At her bedside, her son complained, "She never said good-bye to us," just like the old king, who sighed after Mélisande had taken her last breath, "She went . . . without a word."

The Last Moments Remain Traditional

At the time Tolstoi was writing, the bourgeoisie was beginning to discover the indecency of death beneath the romantic rhetoric. It was still too soon for distaste to overcome the tradition of the public death and succeed in isolating the dying to the very end, as later happened, especially in the hospital. In the late nineteenth century a compromise was struck between the public death of the past and the hidden death of the future, a compromise that was to last for the first third of the twentieth century and that is rather well illustrated by the death of Ivan Ilyich.

In the solitude in which the lie imprisoned him, as in a studious retreat, Ivan Ilyich had time to think. He played back through the film of his life; he thought about his death, which he could not bring himself to accept but which gradually forced itself on him as a certainty. Even today when the silence prevails to the end, the dying go through the same stages as Ivan Ilyich.

Recent sociological studies show that belief in an afterlife is declining at a much faster rate than faith in God among people of Christian cultures, especially among the young. And yet a survey of 360 dying persons made between 1965 and 1972 showed that 84 percent of them accepted the possibility of an afterlife compared to only 33 percent of the control group.[7] It must be during this silent period of review that the hope of an afterlife reappears.

For Ivan Ilyich, this period is long. He suffers, but he does not show it. He buries himself in his solitude and his reverie, and stops communicating with those around him. He turns toward the wall, lying on his side with one hand on his cheek, instinctively imitating the classical attitude of the dying when they had had enough of the world. The Jews of the Old Testament lay like this; in sixteenth-century Spain, this attitude was the mark of the unconverted marranos; Tristan "turned his face to the wall." But today the nurses in the California hospitals studied by B. G. Glaser and A. L. Strauss see this ancestral gesture merely as a hostile refusal to communicate with them.[8]

It is true that Ivan Ilyich's attitude becomes aggressive. His condition grows worse, his pain increases. One morning when his wife walks in and starts talking about remedies, he turns to her and answers with a look filled with hate, "In the name of Christ, let me die in peace." Medical psychologists, such as Elisabeth Kübler-Ross, who are studying the behavior of the dying recognize the existence of this aggressive phase, which they try to channel and utilize. Ivan Ilyich sends away wife, child, and doctor, and abandons himself to the pain that he had once tried to hide.

"He screamed constantly for three days, it was unbearable," his wife admits to a friend. And then comes a period of calm, which is also recognized as a general phenomenon. Doctors who work with the dying observe today, "Immediately before death the need for analgesics decreases. At this time many patients exhibit a brief remission, an increased vitality, and a renewed appetite for food, and their general condition seems to improve."[9] During his solitary passion, Ivan Ilyich realizes, like the dying man of the fifteenth-century *ars moriendi,* that "his life had not been what it should have been," but he convinces himself that "there was still time to make amends."

Emma Bovary experiences a similar respite. She "seemed delighted" to see the priest. "In this extraordinary period of calm she probably rediscovered the lost pleasure of her first mystical transports, with visions of eternal beatitude." The priest administers Extreme Unction. "Her face had an expression of serenity, as if the sacrament had cured her."

Similarly, when Ivan Ilyich emerges from his aggressive silence of several days or weeks, he reopens his eyes, turns to his entourage, sees his son kissing his hand and his wife with "her mouth open, her cheeks and nose wet with tears." The situation is now the reverse of what it was in the early nineteenth century. It is he who feels sorry for them. He understands that he must go away. He asks that his son be taken out of the room, for the sight of suffering and death may be upsetting to children, and their presence at this hideous and almost obscene spectacle is no longer acceptable. (When Emma Bovary asks for her little girl, the child says, "I'm afraid," and shrinks back when her mother tries to kiss her hand. "Enough! Take her away!" cries Charles.)

Ivan Ilyich tells his wife, "I feel sorry for you, too." He wants to add, "Forgive me," but he can no longer speak. His agony lasts two hours. Tolstoi assures us that he is happy. All of this last stage of the death, except for a few details such as the removal of the children, is consistent with the romantic model.

The psychological contradiction between the two models of the hidden death and the public death, which are juxtaposed here before and during the agony, appears clearly in the attitude of the survivors. During the first phase, they take part in the farce and hide the truth from Ivan Ilyich. Nowadays they would have persevered, and regretted that Ivan Ilyich was later conscious enough to know that he was dying and to observe the final phase. By the middle of the twentieth century this unconsciousness would be seen as desirable. "At least we have the satisfaction of knowing that he knew nothing," in other words, that the agony of death was spared him.

But when friends come to present their condolences, Ivan Ilyich's wife quickly assures a visitor who asks whether Ivan Ilyich remained conscious, "Yes, until the end. . . . He said good-bye a quarter of an hour before the end, and he even asked us to take Valadi out of the room."

Very Discreet Funerals

The beginning of the twentieth century saw the completion of the psychological mechanism that removed death from society, eliminated its character of public ceremony, and made it a private act. At first this act was reserved for intimates, but eventually even the family was excluded as the hospitalization of the terminally ill became widespread.

There were still two periods of communication between the dying— or dead—man, and society: the final moments, in which the dying man recovered the initiative that he had lost, and mourning. The second great milestone in the contemporary history of death is the rejection and elimination of mourning. The first complete analysis of this phenomenon was made by Geoffrey Gorer, who was led to the subject by a series of personal experiences.

Gorer lost his father and his grandfather almost at the same time. His father died on the *Lusitania* in 1915, so Gorer was not able to see his body, as was then the custom. Indeed, he did not see his first dead body until 1931. He did observe the conventions of mourning, although he says that these had started to break down during the war because of the high mortality at the front, and also because women were working in men's jobs. The death of a sister-in-law and in 1948 the death of a friend introduced him to the new situation of the bereaved, their behavior, and that of society toward them. He realized that the social function of mourning was changing, and that this change revealed a profound transformation in people's attitude toward death. It was in 1955 that he published in *Encounter* his famous article, "The Pornography of Death," in which he showed that death had become as shameful and unmentionable as sex was in the Victorian era. One taboo had been substituted for another.

In 1961 his brother died of cancer. He was survived by a wife and children. Gorer took charge of the burial and looked after his sister-in-law and nephews, and again he was struck by the rejection of traditional ways of behaving and by the harmful effects of this rejection. He told the whole story in a book. Then he decided to study the phenomenon, no longer as a memorialist but as a sociologist, in a scientific manner. In 1963 he began an investigation of mourning, which resulted in his major work, *Death, Grief, and Mourning in Contemporary Britain*.

His first observation was that death has been removed to a distance.

Not only are people no longer present at the deathbed, but burial has ceased to be a familiar sight. Among those interviewed, 70 percent had not attended a funeral in five years. Children do not even attend the funerals of their parents. Of his nephews, Gorer writes, "Their father's death was quite unmarked for them by any ritual of any kind, and was even nearly treated as a secret, for it was very many months before Elizabeth could bear to mention him or have him mentioned in her presence." When Gorer went back to his sister-in-law's house after his brother's cremation, she told him very naturally that she had had a good day with the children, that they had gone on a picnic and after that they had watched the grass being cut.[10]

Children have been excluded from death. Either they are not informed or they are told that their father has gone on a trip or that Jesus has taken him. Jesus has become a kind of Santa Claus whom adults use to tell children about death without believing in him themselves.

A questionnaire published in 1971 by the American magazine *Psychology Today* elicited the following letter from a woman of twenty-five: "When I was twelve, my mother died of leukemia. She was there when I went to bed and when I woke up the next morning, my parents were gone. My father came home, took my brother and me on his knee, and burst into screeching sobs and said, 'Jesus took your mother.' Then we never talked about it again. It was too painful for all of us."[11]

In most of the surveys the proportion of those who believe in an afterlife is between 30 and 40 percent. This is only an indication, for it is very difficult to confine in the words of a questionnaire notions that are more sensed than defined. The belief decreases in the young, whereas we have seen that it increases among the very ill.

It is rather remarkable that in 1963, in Gorer's investigation, and only among the old, one encounters the anthropomorphic eschatology of the nineteenth century. The subjects interviewed see their dead again and talk to them. "They are able to watch over us here and give us help and guidance." "Just before my brother died, he saw Mother standing at the foot of the bed." "He was killed in the Air Force, in the war, my youngest boy, and he often comes back and speaks to me." One day when the subject was in bed thinking and worrying about him, a voice said, "It's all right, Mum," and she thought, "Thank God he's all right; but he'd gone. Still, I think I'll see him again someday. In fact it's kept me going." Heaven is "a place where there are no worries, and where we meet all our relatives and friends."[12]

One notes also the complete disappearance of hell. Even those who believe in the devil limit his power to this world and do not believe in eternal damnation. This will not surprise us; we have already noticed the phenomenon since the beginning of the nineteenth century.

The answers to Gorer's survey also show that the clergy have abandoned their traditional role. It is not that they are being dismissed; it is now they who are reticent.

But the most important phenomenon brought out by Gorer's study is the decline in mourning and in the dignity of funerals. From now on, cremation is more popular than burial. Out of sixty-seven cases, there are forty cremations and twenty-seven burials. The most remarkable aspect is the meaning attributed to the choice. To choose cremation is to reject the cult of tombs and cemeteries as it has developed since the beginning of the nineteenth century. "In many cases, it would appear, cremation is chosen because it is felt to get rid of the dead more completely and finally than does burial."[13] Some subjects refuse cremation as being too final. This attitude does not depend on the nature of the act itself (the ancients worshiped the ashes of their dead) but on the comparison with the tomb. For despite the efforts of the directors of crematoria, the families of the cremated generally avoid erecting a monument. Out of the forty cremations in the survey, only one was accompanied by a memorial plaque and fourteen by an inscription in the "Book of Remembrance," which is available for the consultation of visitors. But there are no visitors. Some, and this is even more radical, have their ashes scattered.

But the cemetery remains the place of memory and visits. Of the twenty-seven who were buried, only four have no monuments. The survivor goes to the tomb to lay flowers on it and to remember.

It would be a mistake, however, to interpret the disappearance of the body in cremation as a mark of indifference or neglect. The relative of the cremated person rejects the physical reality of the site, its association with the body, which inspires distaste, and the public character of the cemetery. But he accepts the absolutely personal and private nature of regret. For the cult of the tomb he has substituted a cult of memory in the home: "I'm not one to keep going to the cemetery—I believe in helping the living. On birthdays, I put a bunch of flowers by their photographs" (a woman of forty-four). "I think that's the finish as far as the body goes. I mean, I think you can preserve their memory more at home than where they're actually buried. I'll tell you one thing I always do—perhaps it's silly, but I always buy her a little present at Christmas of some azaleas or flowers of some description; I feel that she's still in the house, you see" (a widower of fifty-five).[14] Sometimes the cult may tend toward mummification: The house, or the room of the deceased, is left exactly as it was during his lifetime. Thus, a profound sense of loss is perfectly compatible with the neglect of the tomb, which is sometimes the hated place of the body.

From now on there are two places to cultivate the memory of the dead: at the tomb, a custom that is disappearing more rapidly in England than on the Continent; and in the home. The Canadian sociologist Fernand Dumont reports the following anecdote, which must have taken place in the early twentieth century: "When I was a child, the whole family used to pray together at home. . . . After the prayer, . . . my father would remain alone for a while, kneeling with his head in his hands. This intrigued me in a man who had never been 'pious' in the usual sense of the word. When I asked him about it, . . . my father admitted that at these times he often spoke to his father, who had been dead for a long time."15

The Indecency of Mourning

After the funeral and burial comes mourning in the true sense of the word. The pain of loss may continue to exist in the secret heart of the survivor, but the rule today, almost throughout the West, is that he must never show it in public. This is exactly the opposite of what used to be required. In France since about 1970 the long line of people offering their condolences to the family after the religious service has been eliminated. And in the country the death notice, which is still sent out, is accompanied by the dry, almost uncivil formula, "The family is not receiving," a way of avoiding the customary visits of neighbors and acquaintances before the funeral.

But generally speaking, the initiative for the refusal to mourn is not taken by the survivors. By withdrawing and avoiding outside contact, the family is affirming the authenticity of its grief, which bears no comparison with the solicitude of well-meaning relatives; it is also adopting the discreet behavior that society requires.

Geoffrey Gorer distinguishes three categories of bereaved: those who succeed in completely mastering their grief, those who hide it from others and keep it to themselves, and those who allow it to appear openly. In the first case the bereaved forces himself to behave as if nothing had happened, to pursue his normal life without interruption: Keep busy, he has been told by the few people he has spoken to, the doctor, the priest, a few friends. In the second case, almost nothing shows on the outside, and mourning goes on in private, "as one undresses or goes to bed in private." Mourning is an extension of modesty. This is probably the attitude most acceptable to common sense, which realizes that one must tolerate some release of emotion, provided it remains private. In the last case, the obstinate bereaved is mercilessly excluded as if he were insane.16

Gorer had occasion to experience the judgment of society firsthand after the death of his brother. "A couple of times I refused invitations to cocktail parties, explaining that I was in mourning; the people who invited me responded to this statement with shocked embarrassment, as if I had voiced some appalling obscenity. Indeed, I got the impression that, had I stated that the invitation clashed with some esoteric debauchery I had arranged, I would have had understanding and jocular encouragement; as it was, the people whose invitations I had refused, educated and sophisticated as they were, mumbled and hurried away." They did not know how to behave in a situation that had become unusual. "They clearly no longer had any guidance from ritual as to the way to treat a self-confessed mourner; and I suspect they were frightened lest I give way to my grief, and involve them in a distasteful upsurge of emotion."[17]

Death Is Excluded

Indeed, the transition from the calm and monotonous world of everyday reality to the inner world of the feelings is not made spontaneously or without help. The distance between the languages is too great. In order to establish communication it is necessary to have an accepted code of behavior, a ritual that is learned by experience from childhood. Once, there were codes for all occasions, codes for revealing to others feelings that were generally unexpressed, codes for courting, for giving birth, for dying, for consoling the bereaved. These codes no longer exist. They disappeared in the late nineteenth and twentieth centuries. So feelings too intense for the ordinary forms either do not find expression and are held in, or else break forth with intolerable violence because there is no way to channel them. In the latter case, they threaten the order and security necessary to daily activity. Therefore they must be repressed. It is for this reason that everything having to do first with love and then with death became forbidden. This taboo became necessary after the gates and dams that had contained these wild forces for thousands of years were abandoned. A model was born, especially in the English public schools, of virile courage, discretion, and propriety, which forbade public allusion to romantic feelings and tolerated them only in the privacy of the home.

As Gorer says, "At present, death and mourning are treated with much the same prudery as the sexual impulses were a century ago." One must learn to dominate them: "Today it would seem to be believed, quite sincerely, that sensible, rational men and women can keep their mourning under complete control by strength of will and character, so that it need be given no public expression, and indulged, if at all, in private, as furtively as if it were an analogue of masturbation."[18]

It is quite evident that the suppression of mourning is not due to the frivolity of survivors but to a merciless coercion applied by society. Society refuses to participate in the emotion of the bereaved. This is a way of denying the presence of death in practice, even if one accepts its reality in principle. As far as I can see, this is the first time that the denial has expressed itself so openly. For some time this denial had been rising from the depths where it had been thrust, moving toward the surface without yet reaching it: from the fear of apparent death, to the time when one concealed the death of the other out of love and concealed the sick person from others out of disgust. From now on, the denial of death is openly acknowledged as a significant trait of our culture. The tears of the bereaved have become comparable to the excretions of the diseased. Both are distasteful. Death has been banished.

A new situation appears around the middle of the twentieth century in the most individualistic and middle-class parts of the West. There is a conviction that the public demonstration of mourning, as well as its too-insistent or too-long private expression, is inherently morbid. Weeping is synonymous with hysteria. Mourning is a malady. This disparaging attitude begins to appear in subtle form in the postromantic sarcasm, still mingled with romantic beliefs, of Mark Twain. Twain is both annoyed and moved by theatrical demonstrations, and defends himself from antiquated sentiments with humor. Today this attitude has become common. The period of mourning is no longer marked by the silence of the bereaved amid a solicitous and indiscreet entourage, but by the silence of the entourage itself. The telephone does not ring. The bereaved is in quarantine.

The bereaved is not the only object of this exclusion. The denial of death has gone beyond the bereaved and the expression of mourning. It has extended to everything that has to do with death, which has become infectious. Mourning or anything resembling it is like a contagious disease that one is in danger of catching in the room of a dying or dead man, even if he is a stranger, or in a cemetery, even if it contains no beloved tomb.

It is significant that when this attitude began to emerge, psychologists immediately pronounced it dangerous and abnormal. They have never stopped insisting on the necessity of mourning and the dangers of its repression. Freud and Karl Abraham went to some pains to show that mourning is different from melancholia, or depression. Today there are many studies on the subject: Colin Murray Parkes and quite recently Lily Pincus, in two fine books full of case studies.[19] Their view of mourning and its role is exactly the opposite of the attitude of society. Society regards mourning as morbid, whereas for the psychologists it is the repression of mourning that is morbid and pathological.

This contradiction shows the force of the feeling that drives people to exclude death. All the ideas of psychologists and psychoanalysts on sexuality and child development have been popularized and assimilated by society, whereas their ideas about mourning have been completely ignored and excluded from the orthodoxy disseminated by the media. Society was ready to accept the first, but rejected the second. Its denial of death has not for one moment been mitigated by the criticisms of the psychologists.

The psychologists have unwittingly made their analyses of mourning into a historical document, a proof of historical relativity. Their thesis is that the death of the loved one is a deep wound, but one that heals naturally, provided one does nothing to delay the healing. The bereaved must become accustomed to the absence of the other, must transfer the libido still obstinately fixated on a "living" person, must "internalize" the deceased. The bad effects of mourning occur when this transference is not made, and there is either "mummification" or inhibition of memory. The mechanisms do not concern us here. What interests us is that our psychologists describe them as if they had always been a part of human nature. Like any natural phenomenon, death is believed to inflict on the immediate survivors a trauma that can only be healed by a series of stages. It is up to society to help the bereaved go through these stages, because he is not strong enough to do it alone.

But this model that seems so natural to the psychologists is no older than the eighteenth century. It is the model of the beautiful death of the romantics and of the visits to the cemetery that we have called "the death of the other." The style of mourning of the nineteenth century—although too theatrical, of course—corresponds rather well to the requirements of the psychologists. The La Ferronays had every opportunity to release their libido and internalize their memories, and they had all the help they could possibly expect from their entourage.

There was no way these torrents of mourning could be checked without risk in the twentieth century. This the psychologists have understood very well. But the state to which they refer is not a state of nature; it dates only from the nineteenth century. Before the eighteenth century the model was quite different, and it is this model that might, because of its extreme age and stability, be compared to a state of nature.

In this other model, affectivity did not play the role it acquired in the nineteenth century. It is not that the death of the loved one went unregretted. The first shock was dulled by the traditional solicitude of the group that was present at the death, but after that it was often quickly overcome. It was not unusual for a widower to remarry a few months later. This did not mean that he had forgotten, but that his grief was quickly assuaged.

But sometimes the threshold was exceeded, and the bereaved could not overcome his grief. Such abnormal cases anticipated the nineteenth-century model and the great revolution in feeling. Thus, H. de Campion could not bear to remain in the memory-filled house of a wife who had died in childbirth in 1659; he did not return until a year later, still inconsolable.[20]

But in general, although one was unhappy, one did not lose one's head. In the first place, all the available affection of each individual was not concentrated on a very small number of heads, as in the nuclear family, but was divided among a more extended group of relatives and friends. The death of one person, even one of the closest of this group, did not destroy one's whole emotional life; substitutions were still possible. Finally, death was never the complete surprise it became in the nineteenth century, before the spectacular advances in longevity. It was one of the risks of daily life. From childhood, one more or less expected it.

Under these conditions, the individual was not prostrated, as he was in the nineteenth century. He was not expecting as much from life. The prayer of Job belonged as much to a popular wisdom, an ordinary resignation, as it did to an ascetic piety. "Death took away what life had given: That was life!"—to reduce this poem to the most banal level.

The individual was not overwhelmed, and yet mourning existed, in a ritualized form. Medieval and early modern mourning was more social than individual. Helping the survivor was neither its sole nor its primary purpose. Mourning expressed the anguish of a community that had been visited by death, contaminated by its presence, weakened by the loss of one of its members. The community protested loudly so that death would go away and not come back, just as the great prayers of the litany were designed to ward off catastrophes. Life came to a halt here, slowed down there. People took their time over things that were apparently useless and unproductive. Condolence visits repaired the unity of the group and re-created the human warmth of holidays; the ceremonies surrounding burial also became a holiday from which joy was not absent, in which laughter was often quick to take the place of tears.

It was this kind of mourning that in the nineteenth century imperceptibly took on another function. It retained its social role for a while, but it appeared increasingly as a means of expressing great pain, an opportunity for the entourage to share this pain and to help the bereaved. This transformation of mourning was so profound that its novelty was quickly forgotten. It soon became part of human nature, and it is as such that it served as a reference for the psychologists of the twentieth century.

All this has been going on under our eyes. Whether we like it or not, we have all been transformed by the great romantic revolution in feeling. It has created ties between us and other people, ties whose destruction seems inconceivable and intolerable. It is this first romantic generation that was the first to deny death. It exalted death, it deified death, and at the same time it transformed not just anyone, but the loved one, into an inseparable immortal.

This attachment is still with us, despite an apparent relaxation that has to do with a more discreet language, a greater modesty—the modesty of Mélisande. At the same time, for other reasons, society no longer tolerates the sight of things having to do with death, including the sight of the dead body or weeping relatives. The bereaved is crushed between the weight of his grief and the weight of the social prohibition.

The result is dramatic, and sociologists have particularly emphasized the case of widowers. Society avoids them, whether they are young or old, but especially if they are old, for in that case they are doubly distasteful. They have no one to talk to about the only subject that matters to them, the person they have lost. There is nothing left for them to do but die themselves, and that is often what they do, without necessarily committing suicide. A study conducted in 1967 in Wales showed that the mortality rate among close relatives of a deceased person was 4.76 percent in the first year following death as compared with 0.68 percent in the control group, whereas in the second year after death it was only a little higher than the control group (1.99 percent as compared with 1.25 percent). The mortality rate among widowers rose to 12.2 percent in the first year as compared with 1.2 percent for the control group; in other words, it was ten times higher.[21]

The Triumph of Medicalization

Everything proceeds as if the romantic model as it existed in the middle of the nineteenth century underwent a gradual dismantling. First, in the late nineteenth century, there were the changes that occurred in the early stages of dying, the period of very serious illness during which the patient is kept in ignorance and isolation: the case of Ivan Ilyich. Then, in the twentieth century, beginning in World War I, came the taboo against mourning and everything in public life that reminded one of death, at least the so-called natural (i.e., nonviolent) death. The image of death was contracting like the diaphragm of a photographic lens being stopped down. There remained only the actual moment of death, which at the time of Ivan Ilyich, and long afterward, retained its traditional characteristics: the reviewing of the life, the public quality, the scene of the farewells. But after World War II even this last survival disappeared, owing to the complete medicalization of death. This is the third and final stage in the process of reversal.

The essential fact is the well-known advance in surgical and medical techniques, which bring into play complex equipment, competent personnel, and frequent interventions. These techniques can only be fully effective in the hospital, at least so it has been believed until our own time. The hospital is not only a place of medical expertise, observation, and instruction, it is a focal point where auxiliary services such as pharmaceutical laboratories and rare, costly, and delicate equipment are concentrated, giving the hospital a local monopoly on death.

As soon as an illness seems serious, the doctor usually sends his patient to the hospital. Advances in surgery have brought parallel advances in resuscitation and in the reduction or elimination of pain and sensation. These procedures are no longer used only before, during, or after an operation; they have been extended to all the dying, in order to relieve their pain. For example, the dying man is given food and water intravenously, thus sparing him the discomfort of thirst. A tube runs from his mouth to a pump that drains his mucus and prevents him from choking. Doctors and nurses administer sedatives, whose effects they can control and whose doses they can vary. All this is well known today and explains the pitiful and henceforth classic image of the dying man with tubes all over his body.

By a swift and imperceptible transition someone who was dying came to be treated like someone recovering from major surgery. This is why, especially in the cities, people stopped dying at home—just as they stopped being born at home. In New York City in 1967, 75 percent of all deaths occurred in hospitals or similar institutions, as compared with 69 percent in 1955 (60 percent for the United States as a whole). The proportion of deaths in hospitals has risen steadily since then. In Paris it is common for an old man with a cardiac or pulmonary condition to be hospitalized so that he can have a painless death. It might be possible to provide the same care by hiring a visiting nurse, but home care is less well covered, if at all, by Social Security. It also imposes on the family a burden that it can no longer bear, especially when the wife works and there is no child, sister, cousin, or neighbor available.

At the beginning of this chapter I talked about the indecency of serious illness, the physical distaste it inspires, the need to conceal it from others and from oneself. To square their conscience, the family confuses their unconscious intolerance for the sordid aspects of disease with the requirements of cleanliness and hygiene. In most cases, especially in large cities like Paris, the family has made no attempt to keep the dying at home or to bring about social legislation less favorable to their departure.

The hospital is no longer merely the place where one is cured or where one dies because of a therapeutic failure; it is the scene of the normal death, expected and accepted by medical personnel. In France this is not true of the private clinics, which do not want to frighten their clientele, and also perhaps their nurses and doctors, by the presence of death. When death does arrive, when one is unable to avoid it, they immediately send the body home; one is regarded as having died in the eyes of the state, the medical expert, and the world.

This dispatching of the body is not possible in public hospitals, which tend therefore to be crowded with the very old, the incurable, and the dying. In some countries there is a movement to keep these patients in places that specialize in painless death and preparation for it, places where they could avoid the disadvantages of a medical organization designed for another purpose, to keep the patient alive at all costs. This is the new conception of the "hospice," the model for which is the Hospice of Saint Christopher, in the suburbs of London.

Today Ivan Ilyich would have been sent to the hospital. Perhaps he would have been cured, and there would be no novel.

This transfer of death to the hospital has had profound consequences. It has accelerated an evolution that began in the late nineteenth century and pushed it to its logical conclusion. Death has been redefined: It has ceased to be the instant that it became in the seventeenth century, but whose punctuality it had not until then possessed. In the traditional mentality, the sense of the moment of death was softened by the certainty of a continuation: not necessarily the immortality of the Christians, but a subdued prolongation of some kind. After the seventeenth century, the more widespread belief in the duality of the soul and the body and in their separation at death eliminated the margin of time. Death became an instant.

The medicalized death of today has restored this margin, but by borrowing time from this life, not from the beyond. The time of death has been both lengthened and subdivided. Sociologists have the satisfaction of being able to apply their classificatory and typological methods; thus, there is brain death, biological death, and cellular death. The old signs, such as cessation of heartbeat or respiration, are no longer sufficient. They have been replaced by the measurement of cerebral activity, the electroencephalogram.

The time of death can be lengthened to suit the doctor. The doctor cannot eliminate death, but he can control its duration, from the few hours it once was, to several days, weeks, months, or even years. It has become possible to delay the fatal moment; the measures taken to soothe pain have the secondary effect of prolonging life.

Sometimes this prolonging of life becomes an end in itself, and hospital personnel refuse to discontinue the treatments that maintain an artificial life. The world will remember the Shakespearean agony of Franco, surrounded by his twenty doctors. The most sensational case is no doubt that of Karen Ann Quinlan, an American girl of twenty-two who, for thirteen months, was kept on a respirator and fed and given antibiotics intravenously. No one expected that she would ever regain consciousness. In spite of the pressure of the family and a court order, the hospital persisted in keeping her alive artifically because she was not in a state of brain death, that is, her electroencephalogram was still registering. It is not our purpose here to discuss the ethical problems raised by this rare case of "therapeutic tenacity." What interests us is that medicine can cause someone who is almost dead to remain alive almost indefinitely: and not only medicine but the hospital itself, that is, the whole system that turns medical activity into a business and a bureaucracy that obeys strict regulations regarding method and discipline.

The example of Karen Ann Quinlan is exceptional, a borderline case caused specifically by the persistence of cerebral activity. Today doctors usually discontinue treatment when brain death has been determined, thus allowing vegetative life to be extinguished as well. In 1967 there was a public outcry when it was discovered that in a certain hospital in England the staff was marking the beds of certain old people NTBR, that is, "not to be resuscitated."22

The duration of death may therefore depend on an agreement involving the family, the hospital, and even the court, or on a sovereign decision of the doctor. The dying man, who had already formed the habit of confiding to survivors wishes he no longer included in his will, abdicated gradually, abandoning to his family the control of the end of his life, and of his death. The family, in turn, passed this responsibility on to the scientific miracle worker, who possessed the secrets of health and sickness and who knew better than anyone else what should be done.

It has been noted that the doctor is less mysterious and less absolute in the home than he is in the hospital. This is because in the hospital he is part of a bureaucracy whose power depends on discipline, organization, and anonymity. These hospital conditions have given rise to a new model of medicalized death.

Death has ceased to be accepted as a natural, necessary phenomenon. Death is a failure, a "business lost."23 This is the attitude of the doctor, who claims the control of death as his mission in life. But the doctor is merely a spokesman for society. When death arrives, it is regarded as an accident, a sign of helplessness or clumsiness that must be put out of mind. It must not interrupt the hospital routine, which is more delicate than that of any other professional milieu. It must therefore be discreet. What a shame that Mélisande did not die in a hospital! She would have made a good patient. The doctors and nurses would have made a fuss over her and remembered her fondly. It may be desirable to die without being aware of it, but it is also correct to die without anyone else being aware of it either.

If death is too noticeable, too dramatic, and too noisy, most especially, if it is also dignified, it arouses in the staff an emotion quite incompatible with their professional life, still less with hospital routine. For death has been brought under control in order to reconcile an accidental, sometimes inevitable phenomenon with the psychological security of the hospital.

Hospital personnel have defined an "acceptable style of facing death." This is the death of the man who pretends that he is not going to die. He will be better at this deception if he does not know the truth himself. His ignorance is more necessary than it was in the time of Ivan Ilyich. His ignorance is for him a factor in his recovery, and for the hospital staff a necessary condition of their efficiency.[24]

What today we call the good death, the beautiful death, corresponds exactly to what used to be the accursed death: the *mors repentina et improvisa*, the death that gives no warning. "He died tonight in his sleep: He just didn't wake up. It was the best possible way to die."

But today, with the advances in medicine, such an easy death has become rare. It takes skill to bring the slow death of the hospital closer to the *mors repentina*. The surest method is no doubt the ignorance of the patient. But this strategy is sometimes foiled by his diabolical cunning in interpreting the attitudes of the doctor and nurses. So, instinctively, unconsciously, the staff forces the patient to feign ignorance. In some cases the silence takes the form of a conspiracy; in others, fear of a confession or a call for help cuts off all communication.

The patient's passivity is maintained by sedatives, especially at the end, when the pain becomes unbearable and would otherwise produce the "horrible screams" of an Ivan Ilyich or a Mme. Bovary. Morphine controls the great crises, but it also diminishes a consciousness that the patient then recovers only intermittently.

Such is today's "acceptable style of facing death." The opposite is the "embarrassingly graceless dying," the bad death, the ugly death without elegance or delicacy, the disturbing death. This is always the death of a patient who knows. In some cases he is rebellious and aggressive; he screams. In other cases, which are no less feared by the medical team, he accepts his death, concentrates on it, and turns to the wall, loses interest in the world around him, cuts off communication with it. Doctors and nurses reject this rejection, which denies their existence and discourages their efforts. In it they recognize the hated image of death as a phenomenon of nature, whereas they had turned it into an accident of illness that must be brought under control.[25]

In the case, fortunately more frequent, of the good death, one sometimes ends up not knowing whether the patient is dead or alive. This is the most desirable situation. Thus, David Sudnow tells us that a young student nurse in an American hospital could not get a seriously wounded man to drink through a straw. She called her supervisor for help. "Why, honey, of course he won't respond. He's been dead for twenty minutes!" It would have been a beautiful death for everyone if the young student nurse had not had an attack of hysterics.[26]

In charity hospitals the staff takes advantage of this uncertainty to select the most favorable moment for certain procedures. For example, they close the eyes of the dying a little while before they die; it's easier. Or they arrange to have them die in the early morning, just before the night shift leaves. These are presumptuous and extreme acts in unsupervised and obscure places, the refuges of the old and abandoned. Yet their very crudeness reveals some aspects of that bureaucratization and "management" of death that are inseparable from the hospital as institution and the medicalization of death, and are to be found everywhere. Death no longer belongs to the dying man, who is first irresponsible, later unconscious, nor to the family, who are convinced of their inadequacy. Death is regulated and organized by bureaucrats whose competence and humanity cannot prevent them from treating death as their "thing," a thing that must bother them as little as possible in the general interest.[27]

The Return of the Warning; The Demand for Dignity; Death Today

This was the situation at the end of the 1950s. It has changed, especially in the Anglo-Saxon world, in one essential respect: the ignorance of the dying. But in France, the attitude of the early twentieth century still exists. In 1966 the journal *Médecine de France* published a discussion between the philosopher Jankélévitch and three doctors, J.-R. Debray, P. Denoix, and P. Pichat. "The liar is the one who tells the truth," declared Jankélévitch. "I am against the truth, passionately against the truth." (It is a position that is accompanied by a scrupulous respect for life and its prolongation: "Even if you should prolong the life of the patient by only twenty-four hours, your efforts would be worthwhile. There is no reason to deprive him of this day. For a doctor, life itself has value, no matter how diminished or pathetic the person who is living it.")

Robert Laplane understands the complexity of the problem: "M. Denoix was right to stress that there are cases in which the truth must be told in order to relieve the patient. I have said that most patients ask only not to be confronted with the truth about their condition. This is true in the majority of cases, but it also happens sometimes that we doctors are afraid of this truth, that we take refuge behind our authority, that we play hide-and-seek. . . . There are doctors who never say anything. The lie of convenience very often takes the form of silence."

But in the United States in the past few years a complete reversal of attitudes has been taking place. The change was not initiated by the medical fraternity; it has been imposed on them by a group of psychologists, sociologists, and psychiatrists who became aware of the pitiful situation of the dying and decided to defy the taboo. It was not easy. Before 1959 when Herman Feifel wanted to interview the dying about themselves, no doubt for the first time, hospital authorities were indignant. They found the project "cruel, sadistic, traumatic." In 1965 when Elisabeth Kübler-Ross was looking for dying persons to interview, the heads of the hospitals and clinics to whom she addressed herself protested, "Dying? But there are no dying here!" There could be no dying in a well-organized and respectable institution. They were mortally offended.

But this resistance on the part of hospital personnel could not discourage the interest and sympathy of a few pioneers, who rapidly gained adherents. The first manifestation of the new attitude was an anthology edited by Feifel in 1959, *The Meaning of Death.* [28] Ten years later another collective work, *The Dying Patient,* contained a bibliography of 340 titles published after 1955, all in English, on the subject of dying, as distinct from funerals, cemeteries, or mourning. The quantity of this literature gives some idea of the movement that shook the little world of the social sciences and that eventually reached the medical and hospital establishment. It was a woman who played a vital role in this effort, because she was a doctor and knew how to talk to her colleagues, in spite of many discouragements and humiliations. I refer, of course, to Elisabeth Kübler-Ross, whose fine book *On Death and Dying,* published in 1969, has had a profound impact in America and England, where more than a million copies have been sold. [29]

The new trend, born of pity for the alienated dying, was directed toward the amelioration of the actual process of death by restoring to the dying man his forgotten dignity. Banished from medical expertise except in cases of legal medicine, regarded as a temporary failure of science, death had not been studied for its own sake; it had been dismissed as a subject of philosophy that had nothing to do with science. Recent research is attempting to restore its reality and reintegrate it into medical study, from which it disappeared after the end of the nineteenth century.

The doctor, who along with the priest had long been the witness and messenger of death, these days has no experience of death outside the hospital. But it is now believed that a better-informed doctor will be able to prepare his patients better and will be less inclined to take refuge in silence.

It is the dignity of death that is at issue. This dignity requires first of all that death be recognized, not only as a real state but as an important event, an event that should not be conjured away.

One of the conditions of this recognition is that the dying man be informed of his state. English and American doctors have yielded to the pressure very rapidly, no doubt because it enabled them to share a responsibility that they were beginning to find intolerable.

Are we on the eve of a new and profound change in attitudes? Is the rule of silence becoming obsolete?

On May 13, 1976, an American television network broadcast an hour-long film called *Dying*, which received considerable attention, especially in the press, although many Americans ignored it.

The director, Michael Roemer, observed death in postindustrial America the way an ethnologist might study a primitive society. He took his camera into the homes and hospital rooms of terminal cancer patients and their families and lived intimately with them over a period of time. The resulting documentary is extraordinary and upsetting. It reveals the present state of public opinion better than all the literature published in the last few years.

One trait is common to the four cases presented and corresponds closely to the traditional death with which we are familiar. The patient and his family are given very specific notification by the doctor of the diagnosis and the probable course of the disease.

The first case is presented in the form of a monologue, in which a young woman in her thirties tells about the illness and death of her husband. They both knew what was happening. Indeed, the awareness the couple had of the situation, far from traumatizing them, brought them closer than ever. Surprising as it may seem, the wife said that the very last days were the happiest and most beautiful of her life. More than a century later, I seem to hear the accents of Albert or Alexandrine de La Ferronays. Here in the middle of the twentieth century, I recognize the romantic model of the beautiful death.

The fourth and last case is the long passion of a black preacher in his sixties. This time the camera takes us inside his modest home, among his large and harmonious family: his wife, whose simplest gestures have the natural nobility of a great tragedian; his married children; his grandchildren, still very young. He has cancer of the liver. We attend the consultation during which the doctor tells him and his wife that he is going to die. We sense what is going through their minds: a mixture of sadness and resignation, pity and tenderness, and faith. We are in church on Sunday when the minister makes his farewells to the congregation, who punctuate his sermon with short cries of response. We accompany him and his son on a pilgrimage to his childhood home in the Deep South, to visit the grave of his parents. When death approaches, we are at his bedside in the crowded room in which the whole family is gathered, the old and the young; we see the children come to kiss his deeply lined but peaceful face for the last time. Finally, we attend the funeral ceremony in the church, we watch the congregation file by the open coffin, we hear the singing and the tears. There is no mistaking it: This is the tame death, the familiar and public death.

The other two cases have nothing in common with our ancient or known models. On the contrary, they are typical of the new death of today among young adults in the comfortable milieu of the golden suburbs.

First there is the case of a young woman of thirty who has cancer of the brain and who lives with her mother. Her shaved head has been disfigured by the operation she has undergone, her body is half paralyzed, her speech difficult. However, she speaks to us very openly, in a detached manner, about her life, and about the death she expects any day now. She is not afraid of it; one must die; she doesn't care when it is, as long as she is unconscious, in a coma.

She impresses us by her courage, but also by a complete absence of emotion, as if death were something of no importance, *mors ut nihil.* This resembles the *omnia ut nihil* of the seventeenth century, except that here the *nihil* has lost its tragic sense and has become quite ordinary.

The patient would be very much alone without the silent and attentive presence of her mother. As the disease grows worse, it reduces her to the state of dependence of a young child or animal who must be fed with a spoon and who can do nothing except open her mouth. Outside the complicity that binds mother and daughter beyond tears or confessions lies the solitude of beautiful empty houses and large deserted gardens. They are totally alone.

The other case takes place in a similar setting. A man of about the same age also has cancer of the brain, but he is married and the father of two teenage sons. His wife, who is traumatized (and perhaps upset by the presence of the camera), is trying to avoid all emotion and to convey an air of realism and efficiency. One afternoon she calls her husband in the hospital to inform him that she has succeeded in obtaining a plot in the cemetery. She speaks in a detached tone, as if she were talking about a hotel reservation. She has not even bothered to send the children out of the room, and they play on as if they were oblivious to everything.

But beneath this facade, the poor woman is ready to crack. One day, at the end of her rope, she goes to see the doctor—still on camera—in revolt. Her husband is so weak that he has become indifferent and takes no part in the life of the family. And yet the interminable prolongation of his life makes it impossible for her to remarry, to find another father for her children. And tomorrow it may be too late! One senses her wishes, but the doctor refuses to understand.

In the last images we see the patient, after he has left the hospital for the last time, back in his beautiful house and garden, imprisoned in a silence from which he will never emerge. The nonverbal communication that existed between mother and daughter in the preceding case is absent. Here the solitude is total.

The new phenomenon revealed by *Dying* is not so much this solitude as the desire to divulge things having to do with death and to speak about them naturally instead of hiding them. But the difference is not as great as it appears, and the exhibition achieves the same purpose as the silence of the taboo: to stifle emotion, to desensitize behavior. Indeed, the audacity of *Dying* seems more effective than the shame of the taboo. It succeeds even better in ruling out all possibility of communication; it ensures the most perfect isolation for the dying. Both attitudes, which are really very close, are responses to the uneasiness caused by the continued existence of death in a world that is eliminating suffering: moral suffering—hell and sin —in the nineteenth century; and physical suffering—pain and disease—in the twentieth (or twenty-first) century. Death should have disappeared along with disease, but it persists; it is not even any longer in retreat. Its persistence is a scandal whose presence calls up two possible attitudes. One is the attitude of the taboo, which consists in behaving as if death did not exist by banishing it from daily life. The other is the attitude of *Dying:* accepting death as a technical fact but reducing it to the state of an ordinary thing, as insignificant as it is necessary.

But even in the second case, some people think that the state of the dying has become intolerable. Dying must be made bearable, either by allowing the natural dignity of the dying to reappear, as in the case of Mélisande, or by means of a training which is learned like an art, a training such as Elisabeth Kübler-Ross gives at the University of Chicago. There students behind a one-way mirror are able to observe dying persons who have agreed to talk about themselves with men of feeling and science, the new masters of the art of dying. Those who receive this training may be able to alleviate some of the effects of death in the world of technology, but this does not mean that they will be able to eliminate death itself.

In the current debate, those who are not satisfied by such alleviations and who reject them as ambiguous compromises are led to contest the medicalization of society. Such is the case of Ivan Illich, who has the courage to take his idea to its logical conclusion. For him, the medicalization of death is only one case, albeit a particularly significant and serious one, of the general medicalization of culture. For him, the improvement of death would necessarily involve its demedicalization and the demedicalization of society as a whole.[30]

But Ivan Illich is only one man. On the whole, the debate opened in 1959 by Feifel has remained confined to an intelligentsia, albeit a large one. Now and then this intelligentsia has contact with a wider public, which on these rare occasions reveals its underlying uneasiness and anxiety. For the reopening of discussion on death has not shaken society's determination to repress the real image of death. I have some recent examples that show the persistence of the rejection of mourning. When a young European woman living in the United States suddenly lost her mother, she went abroad to attend her funeral, but she came back as soon as she could, dazed and suffering, to be with her husband and children. She hoped to have the support of her friends, but the telephone did not ring. Like Geoffrey Gorer's sister-in-law, she was in quarantine: mourning in reverse. This is a very unusual attitude in a society where people are quick to feel pity and are always accessible.

Some people want to improve death in the hospital, provided death does not *leave* the hospital. However, there is a breach in the medical defense system through which life and death, so carefully separated, may well come together in a flood of popular protest. This is the question of euthanasia and the power to discontinue or prolong treatment.

Today nobody is really consciously concerned about the manner of his own death. But the image of another person dying in a tangle of tubes all over his body, breathing artificially, is beginning to break through taboos to galvanize a sensibility that has long been paralyzed. Perhaps public opinion will be aroused and will seize on the subject with the passion it has shown for other vital issues, notably abortion. Many things would be changed. Claudine Herzlich asks, "Are we about to witness a resurgence of the problems of death that will go beyond professional circles and eventually bring about a social movement as important as that of abortion? We know today that in some cases, at least, people die [or do not die] because someone else has decided it was time. Are people going to demand to die when *they* are ready to die?"[31] We have no idea yet, but the very fact that the question is being raised in this way is significant. The most recent model of death is associated with the medicalization of society, that is, with the segment of industrial society in which the power of technology has been most widely accepted and is still least contested. For the first time, people are questioning the unconditional benevolence of this power. It is in this area of the collective conciousness that a change in contemporary attitudes might well occur.

The Geography of the Invisible Death

We have described the model of the invisible death and its gradual advance in time. It also has a geographic and social distribution of its own. It has an early history, of course, in the bourgeois and cosmopolitan European society of the late nineteenth century, which encompassed the Russian aristocracy, despite its strong ethnic flavor. That is why we find it in Tolstoi. But it is most solidly represented in the twentieth century in the United States and in England. There it has become established, because there it has found the conditions most favorable to its development.

Continental Europe, on the other hand, is like a bastion of resistance, in which the ancient attitudes still persist. In the last decade or two the taboo of the invisible death has spread beyond its birthplace, claiming vast provinces from the traditional and romantic death. It would be interesting to draw the present frontier. A large part of northern Europe has been won over. Funeral homes of the American type are appearing even on the shores of the French Mediterranean.

However, parts of England were still free of the taboo at the time of Gorer's investigation. In Presbyterian Scotland, for example, the bodies of those who die in the hospital are always brought home for a traditional ceremony. This shows how wrong it would be to regard the Anglo-Saxon model as a Protestant model, as opposed to a traditional Catholic one.

Its social space is as clearly defined as its geographic space. In 1963 Gorer's study demonstrated the bourgeois or middle-class quality of the invisible death. Mourning was more prevalent among the working class.

In the United States a study conducted at the University of Chicago and reported by John. W. Riley also shows great differences according to social class. The traditional image of *requies,* which was assumed to be outmoded, was chosen by 54 percent of the sample.[32] In 1971, a survey conducted by the magazine *Psychology Today* found that among its readers, who belong to the American liberal intelligentsia, the image of *requies* was chosen by only 19 percent.[33] The difference between the two figures reflects the weight of the working class.

Another subject of the same Chicago study was the active or passive nature of attitudes toward death. It is easy to distinguish two categories. The richer and better educated are both active (they make wills and take out life insurance policies) and unconcerned (they provide for their families, but only in order to forget). The lower classes hesitate to make commitments that imply their disappearance; they are passive and resigned; but for them death is still something real and serious, regardless of whether one has accepted it or not. In them we recognize vestiges of the traditional death.

This geographic and social distribution suggests certain correlations. It is remarkable that the contemporary taboo has its origins in a territory corresponding to that of the rural cemetery, whereas the bulwark of resistance coincides with the urbanized cemeteries where monumental tombs, sometimes illuminated in the evening, line the paths like houses on a street. In the last chapter we saw that these two types of cemeteries corresponded to two different attitudes toward nature. The rural cemeteries bear witness to a de facto religion of nature, while the urbanized cemeteries betray a de facto indifference. It seems to me that a vague but powerful belief in the continuity and goodness of nature has penetrated religious and moral practices in English-speaking countries and popularized the idea that suffering, poverty, and death should and could be eliminated.

There is a second correlation between the geographic distribution of the invisible death and what might be called the Second Industrial Revolution, that is, the world of white-collar workers, big cities, and complex technology.

In the last chapter we saw that the term *happy industrialism* was used by a positivist of the 1880s to define and denounce a hedonistic denial of death that seems to anticipate the mid-twentieth century. The Saint-Simonians and positivists sensed a relationship between the advance of technology, the rise of prosperity, and the virtual elimination of death from daily life. But in the 1880s the relationship was strictly theoretical. It appeared only in isolated and extreme cases, and it required considerable perspicacity to perceive it.

This relationship became more real with the growing influence of technology, not only over industry and production, but over public and private life in general after the first third of the twentieth century—a little earlier in the United States. People began to believe that there was no limit to the power of technology, either in man or in nature. Technology erodes the domain of death until one has the illusion that death has been abolished. The area of the invisible death is also the area of the greatest belief in the power of technology and its ability to transform man and nature.

Our modern model of death was born and developed in places that gave birth to two beliefs: first, the belief in a nature that seemed to eliminate death; next, the belief in a technology that would replace nature and eliminate death the more surely.

The Case of America

But the cultural area thus formed is not homogenous, even in its Anglo-Saxon birthplace. There is a great difference between England and the United States.

In England, the goal was the complete effacement of death from the visible surface of life: the suppression of mourning, the simplification of funerals, the cremation of bodies and the scattering of ashes. A few pockets of resistance remain in Presbyterian Scotland, among Roman Catholics and Orthodox Jews, and also among a few individuals regarded as abnormal; but on the whole the goal has been reached. Death has been evacuated efficiently and completely.

In the United States and Canada, the elimination is less radical; death has not completely disappeared from the urban landscape. Not that one sees anything resembling the old funeral processions, but large signs right on the street advertise funeral homes or funeral parlors, words that were supposedly forbidden.

It is as if one whole part of the culture were pushing America to erase every vestige of death, while another part is holding on to it and keeping death in a place that is still quite visible. The first trend we know, for it is the one we have been analyzing. It is the one that is spreading the taboo about death or the idea of the insignificance of death throughout the modern world. The second trend is none other than the old romantic attitude, the death of the other, in modern dress.

Between these two contradictory tendencies a compromise had to be reached. The period of death has been divided between them. The prohibition reigns, as in England, up to and including death, and resumes after burial, since mourning is also taboo. But between death and burial the taboo is lifted and the ancient ritual still exists, although it is unrecognizable in its present form: so unrecognizable that it has deceived observers as perceptive as Roger Caillois[34] or as traditionalist as Evelyn Waugh in *The Loved One*. They see this ritual as purely modern, whereas what is modern is merely a veneer over a very old background.

The analysis of American funerary practices is easy, for funerals are an industry and the leaders of this industry, the funeral directors, are communicative. Their remarks have been reported honestly, if critically, by Jessica Mitford in *The American Way of Death*.[35] One has only to read them to realize that they derive directly from nineteenth-century consolation literature, which we explored in chapter 10. Funeral directors have taken over where the ministers of those days left off.

Take the coffin as an example. The coffin has received attention only in very special cases: the vaguely anthropomorphic coffins of England in the late sixteenth century; the sarcophagus-coffins of the Hapsburgs in Vienna, which were still made of lead; the Polish coffins of the eighteenth century, which were sometimes decorated with painted portraits of the deceased. But most lead coffins were simple boxes designed solely to provide better preservation or to allow transport over long distances.

One of the books Ann Douglas cites in her contribution to Stannard's *Death in America* is entitled *Agnes and the Key of Her Little Coffin* (1857). This "little coffin" is no ordinary coffin. By 1857 children's coffins no longer had "broken lines and angles. . . . They look like other things, and not like that which looks like nothing else, a coffin. . . . You would be willing to have such a shape for the depositing of any household article." It closes with a lock and key, not with sinister screws and screwdrivers. It is not made of wood but of metal. In short, this coffin is still called a coffin, but it is already a casket.[36]

The old coffin belonged to the traditional arsenal of the macabre along with the skeleton, the death's-head, the scythe, the hourglass, and the gravedigger's spade. It had played the role of *memento mori.* Its symbolism became unbearable in a world in which death was no longer regarded as fearful but as beautiful and fascinating.

The luxuriousness of the new coffin, the casket, made up for the banality of the tombstone, which was reduced to a small stone slab or an even smaller bronze plate in the lawn cemeteries that were beginning to replace the rural cemeteries. Like the tomb of yesterday, the coffin of today had to be an object of art. Nothing sad could be associated with death. This attitude of the romantic nineteenth century anticipates the attitude of the technological twentieth century, except that it is still associated with the regret of the living. Mourning was not yet incompatible with the beautification of the happy death. Happy the dead, but unhappy the living, deprived of their loved ones until the (theoretically) long-awaited day of the eternal reunion.

It was also around this time that embalming reappeared. If I read Jessica Mitford correctly, embalming was often used during the Civil War to allow the bodies of slain soldiers to be brought home. Rich families no longer accepted collective burial on the battlefield.[37] It is said that a certain Thomas Holmes embalmed 4,028 soldiers in four years at one hundred dollars per body. We may assume that embalming was regarded as a way not only to transport but to honor the remains of a loved one, and that the practice persisted after the war because people were so attached to their dead and desired to remain in communication with them.

The new needs to which this piety gave rise were met by the creation of a new industry. The trappings of death occupied such a large place in the sensibility of the late nineteenth century that they became one of the most valuable and profitable objects of consumption. The phenomenon is characteristic of the whole Western world. In France, funeral companies have replaced the criers, confrères, and councillors of the *ancien régime*. But their activities have been more discreet—if no less lucrative—than in the United States, where they have more openly adopted the aggressive methods of the business world, with everything this implies in the way of competition and publicity. Thus, on New York City buses in 1965 one could read advertisements praising the services of one such firm and inviting the passengers to use them.

The profession underwent a change at the end of the nineteenth century. The first undertakers were undoubtedly craftsmen or hirers of carriages who provided transportation and procured coffins. They became important businessmen—those funeral directors whom we have already mentioned. But even though they studied the death market like any other economic market and adopted the methods of capitalism, they presented themselves, from the first, as a species of priests or doctors with a moral mission. The National Funeral Directors Association, created in 1884, adopted a deontological code that states that "there is, perhaps, no profession, after that of the sacred ministry, in which a high-toned morality is more imperatively necessary than that of a funeral director's. High moral principles are his only safe guide."[38]

As we see, funeral directors replaced the ministers and authors of the books of consolation analyzed by Ann Douglas. They left communication with the beyond to spiritualists and took over the material ceremonies that expressed a desire to prolong the presence of the dead. At this time, or so it seems, the churches, even the Protestant ones, began to criticize the excessive importance of the dead in religious sentiment. This attitude served the funeral directors; they stepped into the shoes of the priests to exploit neglected psychological needs.

Then, with remarkable agility, they began to capitalize on the advice of the psychologists of mourning. Since Freud, psychologists had been insisting on the natural necessity of mourning and the importance of a collective consolation that middle-class urban society was refusing to survivors. So the funeral directors took up the slack. They appointed themselves doctors of grief, and called their vocation grief therapy. From now on they were responsible for assuaging the pain of the bereaved. They removed mourning from daily life, from which it had been excluded anyway, and concentrated it in the brief period of the funeral, where it was still accepted.

In this way they came to provide a special space entirely devoted to death, a death that was no longer shameful and secret, as in the hospital, but visible and dignified. The church had never been the place of death. The dead passed through the church and sometimes remained there, not without irritating purist clergymen. The first mission of the church was divine worship, the second to welcome the community when it needed to restore itself at the milestones of life and death.

This secular space reserved for death is called the funeral home or funeral parlor. This specialization freed the clergy, the family, and the doctor or nurses of responsibility for the deceased in the church, the home, and the hospital. The deceased was assured a place where he would continue to receive the respect that society refused him and that the churches hesitated to render him. This house of the dead was sometimes associated with a cemetery, as in Los Angeles. In the United States cemeteries are private; they are maintained by such nonprofit organizations as churches, or by commercial establishments. There are also municipal cemeteries, but until now these have usually been reserved for the poor ("potter's field").

The funeral home has nothing to hide. Its name is quite visible. As you enter a town or locality there is sometimes a big sign advertising its advantages, with a photograph of the funeral director.

In the funeral home the rites have evolved in the last decades under the influence of the dominant ideas, but without breaking away from the spirit of the nineteenth century. The customs of the nineteenth century (such as the use of the casket, the practice of embalming, and the visit to the deceased) have been preserved, but they have been supplemented by new customs brought by recent immigrants of Mediterranean and Byzantine origin (customs such as leaving the face of the deceased uncovered until burial, which permits the sale of very ingenious caskets which open only at the top). But all of these customs have been adapted to the tastes of an age in which death has ceased to be beautiful and theatrical and has become invisible and unreal.

All activities center on the visit to the deceased, which is referred to as "viewing the remains." Often the deceased is exhibited in a room of the funeral home just as he was in his own home, and people come to pay a final visit according to the traditional rite, which is simply being performed in a different place. Sometimes he is presented in a tableau as if he were still alive, at his desk, in his armchair, and (why not?) with a cigar in his mouth. This image or caricature occurs more frequently in the cinema or literature than in reality. But even apart from these exceptional cases, the impulse is always to use the skills of the mortician to erase the signs of death, to make up the deceased until he looks almost alive.

It is of paramount importance to create the illusion of life. This illusion enables the visitor to overcome his intolerance, to behave as if the deceased were not dead and there were no reason not to approach him. In this way he is able to circumvent the prohibition. Thus, embalming serves less to preserve or honor the dead than it does temporarily to maintain the appearance of life in order to protect the living.

The same desire to reconcile the traditions of death with the prohibitions of life has been the inspiration of the proprietors of cemeteries such as Forest Lawn, in Los Angeles. Here the cemetery remains what it was in the nineteenth century, a peaceful and poetic place where the dead are laid to rest and one can visit them, a beautiful park where one strolls and communes with nature. It will also become a museum, a commercial center of art and memory, and the scene of serene and joyous celebrations: baptisms and marriages.

The services of the funeral home, the preparation of the bodies, and the accessories are expensive, and the business provides good profits to a well-organized industry. Today this situation arouses considerable criticism, not only in the United States. Critics are denouncing the commercial exploitation of death and grief, not to mention superstition and vanity.

In the *tableaux vivants* of the funeral parlor, people have recognized the effects of a systematic denial of death in a society dedicated to technology and happiness. They have not always seen that these apparently futuristic rites incorporate traditional elements: for example, the visit to the deceased and the visit to the tomb. In this society that has banished death, half the people who died in the year 1960 had ordered their own tombs while they were alive (in the same spirit in which they had taken out life insurance policies, that is, immediately putting it out of their minds). Funeral directors are probably afraid that cremation will become as popular in America as it is in England. Cremation is much less lucrative, but fortunately for them, the American public finds it distasteful.

The most ridiculous and irritating aspects of the American ritual, such as the making up of the body and the simulation of life, express the resistance of romantic traditions to the pressures of contemporary taboos. But undertakers have exploited this resistance and presented commercial solutions whose extravagance recalls some of the French proposals of the 1800s.

Their adversaries, Jessica Mitford and the American intelligentsia, have proposed reforms that would simplify funerals and eliminate both the traditional and perverted survivals and the speculators who have exploited them. These reformers are inspired not by the religious rites of yesterday but by the English model of today, which is the most radical version of the invisible death. They would extend the practice of cremation and reduce the social ceremony to a memorial service. At a memorial service, friends and relatives of the deceased gather together without the body to pronounce the eulogy, console the family, indulge in a little philosophical speculation, and, if the occasion warrants, perhaps say a few prayers.

As for the churches, in recent years they have been trying to bring about the compromise that commercial extravagance has delayed. The priests and the agnostic intellectuals of the memorial associations share a mistrust of superstition, whether it involves the body or an overly realistic notion of survival. They abhor a sentimentality that they find irrational and un-Christian, but that has been powerful enough to support the funeral industry.

Even today it is in its American version that the model of the invisible death is being introduced in France. "Atheneums" are being built near cemeteries. Except for the unusual hum of the air conditioning, they resemble ordinary houses, unlike the vulgar American model. In northern Europe, it is the English variety that is catching on; its success reflects the growing popularity of cremation.

Conclusion

Five Variations on Four Themes

In the preface, I explained how I was gradually led to select certain kinds of documentation: literary, liturgical, testamentary, epigraphic, and iconographic. I did not study these documents separately or in any particular order. I studied them simultaneously, in the light of a question that arose in the course of my first explorations. My hypothesis, which had already been proposed by Edgar Morin, was that there was a relationship between man's attitude toward death and his awareness of self, of his degree of existence, or simply of his individuality. This is the thread that has guided me through a dense and confusing mass of documents; this is the idea that has determined the itinerary that I have followed to the end. It is in terms of these questions that the information contained in the documents has taken on a form and a meaning, a continuity and a logic. This has been the key that has helped me to decipher facts otherwise unintelligible or unrelated.

In *Essais sur l'historie de la mort,* I held to this system of analysis and interpretation. I have also used it in the general organization of the present work. It has inspired the titles of three of the five parts: "The Tame Death," "The Death of the Self," and "The Death of the Other." These titles were also suggested by Vladimir Jankélévitch in his book on death.

But my research for that gave me a greater familiarity with the facts, which slightly altered my original hypothesis, raised other questions, and opened up other perspectives. Awareness of one's self or one's destiny was no longer the only possible point of departure. Other systems of analysis and interpretation appeared along the way, systems that were just as important as the one I had chosen to guide me and that would have served just as well to give some order to the formless mass of documentation. I have allowed them to take shape in my text as I discovered them in the documents, while I continued my research and reflection. I hope that the reader has noticed them in passing.

Today, at the end of this seemingly endless itinerary, the assumptions I started out with are no longer exclusive. Having abandoned my preconceived ideas along the way, I turn and cast my eye over this thousand-year landscape like an astronaut looking down at the distant earth. This vast space seems to me to be organized around the simple variations of four psychological themes. The first is the one that guided my investigation, *awareness of the individual.* The others are: the *defense of society against untamed nature, belief in an afterlife,* and *belief in the existence of evil.*

By way of conclusion I shall try to show how the various models defined in the course of this book (the tame death, the death of the self, remote and imminent death, the death of the other, and the invisible death) can be explained in terms of variations on these four themes.

The Tame Death

All four themes appear in the first model of the tame death, and all are of equal importance in defining it.

Death is not a purely individual act, any more than life is. Like every great milestone in life, death is celebrated by a ceremony that is always more or less solemn and whose purpose is to express the individual's solidarity with his family and community.

The three most important moments of this ceremony are the dying man's acceptance of his active role, the scene of the farewells, and the scene of mourning. The rites in the bedroom or those of the oldest liturgy express the conviction that the life of a man is not an individual destiny but a link in an unbroken chain, the biological continuation of a family or a line that begins with Adam and includes the whole human race.

One kind of solidarity subordinated the individual to the past and future of the species. Another kind made him an integral part of his community. This community was gathered around the bed where he lay; later, in its rites of mourning, it expressed the anxiety caused by the passage of death. The community was weakened by the loss of one of its members. It expressed the danger it felt; it had to recover its strength and unity by means of ceremonies the last of which always had the quality of a holiday, even a joyous one. Thus, death was not a personal drama but an ordeal for the community, which was responsible for maintaining the continuity of the race.

If the community feared the passage of death and felt the need to recover itself, this was not only because it was weakened by the loss of one

of its members. It was also because death—the death of an individual or
the repeated deaths caused by an epidemic—opened a breach in the defense system erected against the savagery of nature.

From the earliest times man has refused to accept either sex or death
as crude facts of nature. The necessity of organizing work and maintaining
order and morality in order to have a peaceful life in common led society
to protect itself from the violent and unpredictable forces of nature. These
included both external nature, with its intemperate seasons and sudden
accidents, and the internal world of the human psyche, which resembles
nature in its suddenness and irregularity; the world of the ecstasy of love
and the agony of death. A state of equilibrium was achieved and maintained
by means of a conscious strategy to contain and channel the unknown and
formidable forces of nature. Death and sex were the weak points in the
defense system, because here there was no clear break in continuity between culture and nature. So these activities had to be carefully controlled.
The ritualization of death is a special aspect of the total strategy of man
against nature, a strategy of prohibitions and concessions. This is why death
has not been permitted its natural extravagance but has been imprisoned
in ceremony, transformed into spectacle. This is also why it could not be
a solitary adventure but had to be a public phenomenon involving the
whole community.

The fact that life has an end is not overlooked, but this end never
coincides with physical death. It depends on the unknown state of the
beyond, the solidity or ephemerality of survival, the persistence of memory,
the erosion of fame, and the intervention of supernatural beings. Between
the moment of death and the end of survival there is an interval that
Christianity, like the other religions of salvation, has extended to eternity.
But in the popular mind the idea of infinite immortality is less important
than the idea of an extension. In our first model, the afterlife is essentially
a period of waiting characterized by peace and repose. In this state the dead
wait, according to the promise of the Church, for what will be the true end
of life, the glorious resurrection and the life of the world to come.

The dead live a diminished life in which the most desirable state is
sleep, the sleep of the future blessed who have taken the precaution of
being buried near the saints. Their sleep may be troubled owing to their
own past impiety, the stupidity or treachery of survivors, or the mysterious
laws of nature. In this case they cannot rest; they wander and return. The
living do not mind being close to the dead in churches, parks, and markets,
provided they remain asleep. But it is impossible to forbid these returns;
so they must be regulated, channeled. Society permits the dead to return
only on certain days set aside by custom, such as carnivals; then it can
control their presence and ward off its effects. The Latin Christianity of

the early Middle Ages reduced the ancient risk of their return by installing them among the living, at the center of public life. The gray ghosts of paganism became the peaceful recumbent figures, whose sleep was likely to remain untroubled thanks to the protection of the Church and the saints; later, thanks to the Masses and prayers said in their behalf.

This conception of life after death as a state of repose or peaceful sleep lasted much longer than one might believe. It is surely one of the most tenacious forms of the old attitude toward death.

Death may be tamed, divested of the blind violence of natural forces, and ritualized, but it is never experienced as a neutral phenomenon. It always remains a misfortune, a *mal-heur*. It is remarkable that in the old Romance languages physical pain, psychological suffering, grief, crime, punishment, and the reverses of fortune were all expressed by the same word, derived from *malum,* either alone or in combination with other words: in French, *malheur, maladie, malchance, le malin* (misfortune, illness, mishap, the devil). It was not until later that an attempt was made to distinguish the various meanings. In the beginning there was only one evil that had various aspects: suffering, sin, and death. Christianity explained all of these aspects at once by the doctrine of original sin. There is probably no other myth that has such profound roots in the collective unconscious. It expressed a universal sense of the constant presence of evil. Resignation was not, therefore, submission to a benevolent nature, or a biological necessity, as it is today, as it was no doubt among the Epicureans or Stoics; rather it is the recognition of an evil inseparable from man.

The Death of the Self

Such is the original situation, as defined by the relationship of our four themes. Later, as one or more of these fundamental elements varied, the situation changed.

The second model, the death of the self, is obtained quite simply by a shift of the sense of destiny toward the individual.

We recall that the model was originally limited to an elite of rich, educated, and powerful persons in the eleventh century, and still earlier to the isolated, organized, and exemplary world of monks and canons. It was in this milieu that the traditional relationship between self and other was first overthrown, and the sense of one's own identity prevailed over submission to the collective destiny. Everyone became separated from the community and the species by his growing awareness of himself. The individual insisted on assembling the molecules of his own biography, but only the spark of death enabled him to fuse them into a whole. A life thus unified acquired an autonomy that placed it apart; its relations with others and with society were transformed. Friends came to be possessed like objects, while inanimate objects were desired like living beings. No doubt the balance sheet of the biography should have been closed at the formidable hour of death, but soon it was carried beyond, under the pressure of a desire to be more—something death could not touch. These determined men colonized the beyond like some new continent, by means of Masses and pious endowments. The chief instrument of their enterprise, their guarantee of continuity between this world and the next, was the will. The will served both to justify the love of earth and to make an investment in heaven, thanks to the transition of a good death.

Individualism triumphed in an age of conversions, spectacular penitences, and prodigious patronage, but also of profitable businesses; an age of unprecedented and immediate pleasures and of immoderate love of life.

So much for awareness of the individual. It was inevitable that such an exaltation of the individual, even if it was more empirical than doctrinal, would cause some changes in the third theme, the nature of the afterlife. The passion for being oneself and for being more than was manifested during a single lifetime spread by contagion to the afterlife. The strong individual of the later Middle Ages could not be satisfied with the peaceful but passive conception of *requies*. He ceased to be the surviving but subdued *homo totus*. He split into two parts: a body that experienced pleasure or pain and an immortal soul that was released by death. The body disappeared, pending a resurrection that was accepted as a dogma but never really assimilated at the popular level. However, the idea of an immortal soul, the seat of individuality, which had long been cultivated in the world of clergymen, gradually spread, from the eleventh to the seventeenth century, until eventually it gained almost universal acceptance. This new eschatology caused the word *death* to be replaced by trite circumlocutions such as "he gave up the ghost" or "God has his soul."

This fully conscious soul was no longer content to sleep the sleep of expectation like the *homo totus* of old—or like the poor. Its immortal existence, or rather its immortal activity, expressed the individual's desire to assert his creative identity in this world and the next, his refusal to let it dissolve into some biological or social anonymity. It was a transformation of the nature of human existence that may well explain the cultural advance of the Latin West at this time.

So the model of the death of the self differs from the older model of the tame death with respect to two of our themes, that of the individual and that of the afterlife. The second and fourth parameters, on the other hand, have hardly moved. Their relative immobility protected the model from too sudden a change. It gave it a centuries-old stability that can be deceptive and that can give the impression that things had not changed at all.

Our fourth theme, belief in evil, remained virtually unchanged. It was necessary to the economy of the will and to the maintenance of a love of life that was based partly on an awareness of its fragility. It is obviously an essential element of permanence.

The second, defense against nature, might have been affected by the changes in the sense of the individual and of the afterlife. It was certainly threatened, but its equilibrium was restored.

The desire to assert one's identity and to come to terms with the pleasures of life gave a new and formidable importance to the hour of death mentioned in the *Ave Maria,* a prayer for a good death that dates from the end of this period. This could very well have upset the relationship of the dying man to his survivors or to society, making death pathetic, as in the romantic era, or solitary, like the death of the hermit, and abolishing the calming ritual that men had created as a defense against natural death. Death might then have become wild and terrifying, because of the force of emotion and the fear of hell. But this did not happen, because a new and totally opposite ceremony took the place of what had been threatened by individualism and its agonies.

The deathbed scene, which had once been the most important part of the ceremony, persisted, sometimes with just a touch more pathos, until the seventeenth and eighteenth centuries, when the pathetic element declined under the influence of an attitude of mingled acceptance and indifference. A series of ceremonies was inserted between death and burial: the funeral procession, which became ecclesiastical in character, and the service at the church in the presence of the body, which was the work of the urban reform movement of the late Middle Ages and the mendicant orders. Death was not abandoned to nature, from which the ancients had claimed it in order to tame it. On the contrary, death was more concealed than ever, for the new rites also included a fact that may seem negligible but that is highly significant. The face of the cadaver, which had been exposed to the eyes of the community and which continued to be for a long time in Mediterranean countries and still is today in Byzantine cultures, was covered by the successive masks of the sewn shroud, the coffin, and the catafalque or representation. After the fourteenth century, the material covering of the deceased became a theatrical monument such as was erected for the decor of mystery plays or for grand entrances.

The phenomenon of the concealment of the body and face of the deceased is contemporaneous with the attempts we find in the macabre arts to represent the underground decay of bodies, the underside of life, which was all the more bitter because this life was so well loved. This interest was transitory, but the concealment of the body was permanent. The features of the deceased, once calmly accepted, were henceforth covered because they might be upsetting, that is, frightening. The defense against untamed nature was invaded by a new fear, but this fear was immediately overcome by the taboo to which it gave rise. Once the body was conjured away by the catafalque or representation, the old familiarity with death was restored and everything returned to normal.

The definitive concealment of the body and the prolonged use of the will are the two most significant elements of the model of the death of the self. The first balances the second, maintaining the traditional order of death against the pathos and nostalgia of the individualism illustrated by the will.

Remote and Imminent Death

This model of the death of the self, with all that it preserved in the way of traditional defenses and a sense of evil, influenced customs until the eighteenth century. However, profound changes were beginning to take place by the end of the sixteenth century, to some extent in actual customs and conscious ideas, but more especially in the secret world of the imagination. These changes, although barely perceptible, are very important. A vast transformation of sensibility was under way. The beginning of a reversal— a remote and imperfect adumbration of the great reversal of today—was starting to appear in representations of death.

Where death had once been immediate, familiar, and tame, it gradually began to be surreptitious, violent, and savage. Already, as we have seen, the old familiarity had been maintained only by means of the artifices of the later Middle Ages: more solemn rites and the camouflage of the body under the representation.

In the modern era, death, by its very remoteness, has become fascinating; has aroused the same strange curiosity, the same fantasies, the same perverse deviations and eroticism, which is why this model of death is called "remote and imminent death."

What was stirring in the depths of the collective unconscious is something that had hardly moved at all for thousands of years, our second theme, the defense against nature. Death, once tame, was now preparing its return to the savage state. It was a discontinuous movement, made up of violent jolts, long imperceptible advances, and real or apparent retreats.

At first sight it may seem surprising that this period of returning savagery was also characterized by the rise of rationalism, the rise of science and technology, and by faith in progress and its triumph over nature.

But it was at this time that the barriers patiently maintained for thousands of years in order to contain nature gave way at two points that are similar and often confused: love and death. Beyond a certain threshold, pain and pleasure, agony and orgasm are one, as illustrated by the myth of the erection of the hanged man. These emotions associated with the edge of the abyss inspire desire and fear. An early manifestation of the great modern fear of death now appears for the first time: the fear of being buried alive, which implies the conviction that there is an impure and reversible state that partakes of both life and death.

This fear might have developed and spread and, combined with other effects of the civilization of the Enlightenment, given birth (over a century ahead of time) to our culture. This is not the first time that the late eighteenth century seems to lead directly into the twentieth. But instead, something happened that could not have been foreseen and that restored the actual chronology.

The Death of the Other

If the momentum really did carry from the eighteenth to the twentieth century, it hardly seems that way to the unsophisticated observer. The continuity exists on deeper levels, but only rarely does it show above the surface. This is because in the nineteenth century, which saw the triumph of the industrial and agricultural techniques born of the scientific thought of the previous period, romanticism (the word is convenient) gave birth to a sensibility characterized by passions without limit or reason. A revolution in feeling seized the West and shook it to its foundation. All four of our themes were transformed .

The determining factor was the change in the first theme, the sense of the individual. Up to now this theme had alternated between two extremes: the sense of a universal and common destiny and the sense of a personal and specific biography. In the nineteenth century both of these declined in favor of a third sense, formerly confused with the first two: the sense of the other. But this was not just any other. Affectivity, formerly diffuse, was henceforth concentrated on a few rare beings whose disappearance could no longer be tolerated and caused a dramatic crisis: the death of the other. It was a revolution in feeling that was just as important to history as the related revolutions in ideas, politics, industry, socioeconomic conditions, or demography.

An original type of sensibility now came to dominate all others, a type that is well expressed by the English word *privacy*. It found its place in the nuclear family, remodeled by its new function of absolute affectivity. The family replaced both the traditional community and the individual of the late Middle Ages and early modern times. Privacy is distinguished both from individualism and from the sense of community, and expresses a mode of relating to others that is quite specific and original.

Under these conditions, the death of the self had lost its meaning. The fear of death, born of the fantasies of the seventeenth and eighteenth centuries, was transferred from the self to the other, the loved one.

The death of the other aroused a pathos that had once been repressed. The ceremonies of the bedroom or of mourning, which had once been used as a barrier to counteract excess emotion—or indifference—were deritualized and presented as the spontaneous expression of the grief of the survivors. But what the survivors mourned was no longer the fact of dying but the physical separation from the deceased. On the contrary, death now ceased to be sad. It was exalted as a moment to be desired. Untamed nature invaded the stronghold of culture, where it encountered humanized nature and merged with it in the compromise of "beauty." Death was no longer familiar and tame, as in traditional societies, but neither was it absolutely wild. It had become moving and beautiful like nature, like the immensity of nature, the sea or the moors. The compromise of beauty was the last obstacle invented to channel an immoderate emotion that had swept away the old barriers. It was an obstacle that was also a concession, for it restored to this phenomenon that people had tried to diminish an extraordinary glamour.

But death could not have appeared in the guise of the highest beauty if it had not ceased to be associated with evil. The ancient and intimate relationship between death and physical illness, psychic pain, and sin was beginning to break down. Our fourth theme, the belief in evil, which had long been stationary, was preparing to withdraw, and the first stronghold it deserted was the heart and the mind of man, which was believed to be its original and impregnable seat. What a revolution in thought! It is a phenomenon as important as the return of untamed nature within the human psyche, and indeed, the two are related; it is as if evil and nature had changed places.

The first barrier that fell in the eighteenth century—perhaps as early as the seventeenth in England—was belief in hell and in the connection between death and sin or spiritual punishment. (The necessity of physical illness was not yet questioned.) Scholarly thought and theology raised the problem as early as the eighteenth century. By the beginning of the nineteenth century, the debate in Catholic and Puritan cultures was over; belief in hell had disappeared. It was no longer conceivable that the dear departed could run such a risk. At most, among Catholics, there still existed a method of purification: time in purgatory, shortened by the pious solicitude of survivors. No sense of guilt, no fear of the beyond remained to counteract the fascination of death, transformed into the highest beauty.

If hell is gone, heaven has changed too; this is our third theme, the afterlife. We have followed the slow transition from the sleep of the *homo totus* to the glory of the immortal soul. The nineteenth century saw the triumph of another image of the beyond. The next world becomes the scene of the reunion of those whom death has separated but who have never accepted this separation: a re-creation of the affections of earth, purged of their dross, assured of eternity. It is the paradise of Christians or the astral world of spiritualists and psychics. But it is also the world of the memories of nonbelievers and freethinkers who deny the reality of a life after death. In the piety of their love, they preserve the memories of their departed with an intensity equal to the realistic afterlife of Christians or psychics. The difference in doctrine between these two groups may be great, but it becomes negligible in the practice of what may be called the cult of the dead. They have all built the same castle, in the image of earthly homes, where they will be reunited—in dream or in reality, who knows?—with those whom they have never ceased to love.

The Invisible Death

In the nineteenth century the psychological landscape was completely transformed. Neither the nature of the four themes nor the relationships among them were the same. The situation that resulted did not last more than a century and a half. But the model of death that came next, our model, which I have called the invisible death, does not challenge the underlying tendency or the structural character of the changes of nineteenth century. It continues them, even if it seems to contradict them in its most spectacular effects. It is as if beyond a certain threshold, these tendencies produced the opposite effects.

Our contemporary model of death is still determined by the sense of privacy, but it has become more rigorous, more demanding. It is often said that the sense of privacy is declining. This is because today we demand the perfection of the absolute; we tolerate none of the compromises that romantic society still accepted beneath its rhetoric—or beneath its hypocrisy, as we would say. Intimacy must be either total or nonexistent. There is no middle ground between success and failure. It is possible that our attitude toward life is dominated by the certainty of failure. On the other hand, our attitude toward death is defined by the impossible hypothesis of success. That is why it makes no sense.

The modern attitude toward death is an extension of the affectivity of the nineteenth century. The last inspiration of this inventive affectivity was to protect the dying or the invalid from his own emotions by concealing the seriousness of his condition until the end. When the dying man discovered the pious game, he lent himself to it so as not to disappoint the other's solicitude. The dying man's relations with those around him were now determined by a respect for this loving lie.

In order for the dying man, his entourage, and the society that observed them to consent to this situation, the protection of the patient had to outweigh the joys of a last communion with him. Let us not forget that in the nineteenth century, death, by virtue of its beauty, had become an occasion for the most perfect union between the one leaving and those remaining behind. The last communion with God and/or with others was the great privilege of the dying. For centuries there was no question of depriving them of this privilege. But when the lie was maintained to the end, it eliminated this communion and its joys. Even when it was reciprocal and conspiratorial, the lie destroyed the spontaneity and pathos of the last moments.

Actually, the intimacy of these final exchanges had already been poisoned, first by the ugliness of disease, and later by the transfer to the hospital. Death became dirty, and then it became medicalized. The horror and fascination of death had fixed themselves for a moment on the apparent death and had then been sublimated by the beauty of the Last Communion. But the horror returned, without the fascination, in the repellent form of the serious illness and the care it required.

When the last of the traditional defenses against death and sex gave way, the medical profession could have taken over the role of the community. It did so in the case of sex, as is attested by the medical literature on masturbation. It tried to do so in the case of death by isolating it in the scientific laboratory and the hospital, from which the emotions would be banished. Under these conditions it was better to communicate silently in the complicity of a mutual lie.

It is obvious that the sense of the individual and his identity, what we mean when we speak of "possessing one's own death," has been overcome by the solicitude of the family.

But how are we to explain the abdication of the community? How has the community come to reverse its role and to forbid the mourning which it was responsible for imposing until the twentieth century? The answer is that the community feels less and less involved in the death of one of its members. First, because it no longer thinks it necessary to defend itself against a nature which has been domesticated once and for all by the advance of technology, especially medical technology. Next, because it no longer has a sufficient sense of solidarity; it has actually abandoned responsibility for the organization of collective life. The community in the traditional sense of the word no longer exists. It has been replaced by an enormous mass of atomized individuals.

But if this disappearance explains one abdication, it does not explain the powerful resurgence of other prohibitions. This vast and formless mass that we call society is, as we know, maintained and motivated by a new system of constraints and controls. It is also subject to irresistible movements that put it in a state of crisis and impose a transitory unity of aggression or denial. One of these movements has unified mass society against death. More precisely, it has led society to be ashamed of death, more ashamed than afraid, to behave as if death did not exist. If the sense of the other, which is a form of the sense of the self taken to its logical conclusion, is the first cause of the present state of death, then shame—and the resulting taboo—is the second.

But this shame is a direct consequence of the definitive retreat of evil. As early as the eighteenth century, man had begun to reduce the power of the devil, to question his reality. Hell was abandoned, at least in the case of relatives and dear friends, the only people who counted. Along with hell went sin and all the varieties of spiritual and moral evil. They were no longer regarded as part of human nature but as social problems that could be eliminated by a good system of supervision and punishment. The general advance of science, morality, and organization would lead quite easily to happiness. But in the middle of the nineteenth century, there was still the obstacle of physical illness and death. There was no question of eliminating that. The romantics circumvented or assimilated it. They beautified death, the gateway to an anthropomorphic beyond. They preserved its immemorial association with illness, pain, and agony; these things aroused pity rather than distaste. The trouble began with distaste: Before people thought of abolishing physical illness, they ceased to tolerate its sight, sounds, and smells.

Medicine reduced pain; it even succeeded in eliminating it altogether. The goal glimpsed in the eighteenth century had almost been reached. Evil was no longer part of human nature, as the religions, especially Christianity, believed. It still existed, of course, but outside of man, in certain marginal spaces that morality and politics had not yet colonized, in certain deviant behaviors such as war, crime, and nonconformity, which had not yet been corrected but which would one day be eliminated by society just as illness and pain had been eliminated by medicine.

But if there is no more evil, what do we do about death? To this question modern society offers two answers.

The first is a massive admission of defeat. We ignore the existence of a scandal that we have been unable to prevent; we act as if it did not exist, and thus mercilessly force the bereaved to say nothing. A heavy silence has fallen over the subject of death. When this silence is broken, as it sometimes is in America today, it is to reduce death to the insignificance of an ordinary event that is mentioned with feigned indifference. Either way, the result is the same: Neither the individual nor the community is strong enough to recognize the existence of death.

And yet this attitude has not annihilated death or the fear of death. On the contrary, it has allowed the old savagery to creep back under the mask of medical technology. The death of the patient in the hospital, covered with tubes, is becoming a popular image, more terrifying than the *transi* or skeleton of macabre rhetoric. There seems to be a correlation between the "evacuation" of death, the last refuge of evil, and the return of this same death, no longer tame. This should not surprise us. The belief in evil was necessary to the taming of death; the disappearance of the belief has restored death to its savage state.

A small elite of anthropologists, psychologists, and sociologists has been struck by this contradiction. They propose not so much to "evacuate" death as to humanize it. They acknowledge the necessity of death, but they want it to be accepted and no longer shameful. Although they may consult the ancient wisdom, there is no question of turning back or of rediscovering the evil that has been abolished. They propose to reconcile death with happiness. Death must simply become the discreet but dignified exit of a peaceful person from a helpful society that is not torn, not even overly upset by the idea of a biological transition without significance, without pain or suffering, and ultimately without fear.

NOTES AND INDEX

Notes

Abbreviations

AD   Archives Départementales.

ANMC   Archives Nationales, Paris, Minutier Central.

Gaignières   Gaignières Collection, prints division, Bibliothèque Nationale, Paris.

Joly de Fleury Papers   Joly de Fleury Papers, French manuscripts division, Bibliothèque Nationale, Paris.

Tenenti, *Il senso*   Albert Tenenti, *Il senso della morte e l'amore della vita nel Rinascimento* (Turin: Einaudi, 1957).

Tenenti, *La Vie*   Alberto Tenenti, *La Vie et la mort à travers l'art du XVe siècle*, Cahiers des Annales, no. 8 (Paris: Armand Colin, 1952).

Tuetey   A. Tuetey, *Testaments enregistrés au Parlement de Paris sous le règne de Charles VI* (Paris: Imprimerie Nationale, 1880).

Chapter 1

1. See Jacques Le Goff, "Culture cléricale et traditions folkloriques dans la civilisation mérovingienne," *Annales: Economies, sociétés, civilisations*, 22, no. 4 (July–August 1967): 780–91.

2. Modern editions of these works cited: J. Bédier, ed. and trans., *La Chanson de Roland* (Paris: H. Piazza, 1922); J. Boulenger, ed., *Les Romans de la Table Ronde* (Paris: Plon, 1941); J. Bédier, ed., *Le Roman de Tristan et Yseult* (Paris: H. Piazza, 1946); J.-C. Payen, ed., *Les Tristan en vers* (Paris: Garnier, 1974).

3. Raoul Glaber, cited by George Duby, *L'An mil* (Paris: Julliard, 1967), pp. 78, 89.

4. Musée des Augustins, Toulouse, No. 835.

5. Duby, *L'An mil*, p. 76.

6. Gilbert Grimaud, "Liturgie sacrée," in Gulielmus Durandus, *Rationale divinorum officiorum*, trans. Charles Barthélémy (Paris, 1854), 5:290.

7. Tenenti, *Il senso*, p. 170, n. 18.

8. Mme. Dunoyer, *Lettres et histoires galantes* (Amsterdam, 1780), 1:300.

9. Henri Troyat, *Vie de Tolstoï* (Paris: Fayard, 1965), p. 827.

10. Jean Guitton, *M. Pouget* (Paris: Gallimard, 1941), p. 14.

11. Durandus, *Rationale*, 5:xiv.

12. See Johan Huizinga, *The Waning of the Middle Ages* (Garden City, N.Y.: Anchor Books, 1954), p. 83.

13. Louis Thomassin, *Ancienne et nouvelle discipline de l'Eglise* (1725), vol. 3, col. 580.

14. Jacques Hennequin, *Henri IV dans ses oraisons funèbres* (Paris: Klincksieck, 1977), p. 30.

15. Durandus, *Rationale*, 5:xiv.

16. Balbulus Notker, Responses for Septuagesima, in the Roman Missal of the Council of Trent.

17. Durandus, *Rationale*, 5:xxxviii.

18. Guyot Marchant, *Danse Macabre* (Paris, 1485), cited in Emile Mâle, *L'Art religieux de la fin du Moyen Age* (Paris, 1931), pp. 364ff. On the originals in les Innocents see John Gerson, *Oeuvres complètes* (Paris: Desclée de Brouwer, 1966), s.v. "Danse macabre," 7:286–300.

19. Alexander Solzhenitsyn, *Cancer Ward* (New York: Farrar, Straus & Giroux, 1969).

20. Saint-Simon, Louis de Rouvroy, duc de, *Mémoires* (Paris: Les Grands Ecrivains de la France, 1901), 15:486.

21. Jean-Pierre Peter, "Malades et maladies au dix-huitième siècle," *Annales: Economies, sociétés, civilisations,* 22, no. 4 (July–August 1967): p. 712.

22. Mme. Augustus Craven, née La Ferronays [Pauline Marie Armande Aglaé Craven], *Récit d'une soeur: Souvenirs de famille* (Paris: J. Clay, 1866), 2:197.

23. Lily Pincus, *Death and the Family* (New York: Vintage Books, 1975), pp. 4–8.

24. Pierre-Henri Simon, "Discours de réception à l'Académie française," *Le Monde* (Paris), 20 November 1967.

25. Mathilde Pomès, trans., *Le Romancero* (Paris: Stock, 1947), p. 191; cf. A. Duran, ed., *Romancero General* (Madrid, 1924).

26. Pomès, *Romancero*, p. 158.

27. Isaac Babel, *Contes d'Odessa* (Paris: Gallimard, 1967), pp. 84–86. All Slavic countries with a Byzantine tradition are conservatories. See M. Ribeyrol and D. Schnapper, "Cérémonies funéraires dans la Yougoslavie orthodoxe," *Archives européennes de sociologie* 17 (1976): 220–46.

28. Vladimir Jankélévitch, *La Mort* (Paris: Flammarion, 1966), p. 57; Georges Bataille, *L'Erotisme* (Paris: Minuit, 1961).

29. Philippe Labbe, *Sacra sancta concilia* (Paris, 1671), vol. 5, col. 87; *Dictionnaire d'archéologie chrétienne et de liturgie* (Paris: Letouzey, 1907), s.v. "Ad sanctos," vol. 1, col. 479, "Mort," vol. 12, col. 28.

30. Jacques de Voragine, *La Légende dorée*, trans. J.-B. Roze (Paris: Garnier-Flammarion, 1967), 2:12ff.

31. ANMC, 8:369 (1559).

32. *Dictionnaire d'archéologie chrétienne*, s.v. "Mort," vol. 12, col. 28.

33. See Ribeyrol and Schnapper, "Yougoslavie orthodoxe."

34. Nicole Castan, "Criminalité et subsistances dans le ressort du parlement de Toulouse (1690–1730)" (Mimeographed *troisième-cycle* thesis, University of Toulouse–Le Mirail, 1966), p. 315.

35. Paul Bourget, *Outre-mer* (Paris: A. Lemerre, 1895), 2:250.

36. This chapter was completed before the publication of V. Thomas, *L'Anthropologie de la mort* (Paris: Payot, 1975).

Chapter 2

1. Cited by Louis Thomassin, *Ancienne et nouvelle discipline de l'Eglise,* 1875 ed., vol. 3, cols. 543–44; *Dictionnaire d'archéologie chrétienne et de liturgie* (Paris: Letouzey, 1907), s.v. "Ad sanctos," vol. 1, cols. 479–509.

2. Thomassin, *Discipline de l'Eglise,* vol. 3, col. 550.

3. Charles Saumagne, "Corpus christianorum," *Revue internationale des droits de l'Antiquité,* 3d series, 57 (1960): 438–78; 58 (1961): 258–79.

4. Saint John Chrysostom, *Opera* (Paris: Montfaucon, 1718–38), Homily 74, 8:71.

5. J. D. Mansi, *Sacrorum conciliorum: Nova et amplissima collectio* (Paris, 1901–27), vol. 1, col. 842.

6. See *Dictionnaire d'archéologie chrétienne,* s.v. "Ad sanctos."

7. M. Meslin and J.-R. Palanque, *Le Christianisme antique* (Paris: Armand Colin, 1967), p. 230.

8. Jacques Le Goff, *La Civilisation de l'Occident médiéval* (Paris: Arthaud, 1964), p. 239.

9. *"Insepultus jaceat, non resurgat. Si quis hunc sepulcrum violaverit partem habeat cum Juda traditore et in die judicii non resurgat* [etc.]." *Dictionnaire d'archéologie chrétienne,* s.v. "Ad sanctos," vol. 1, col. 486.

10. Tertullian, in Jacques-Paul Migne, ed., *Patrologiae cursus completus, series latina,* vol. 2, col. 856.

11. Como, late sixth century. See *Dictionnaire d'archéologie chrétienne,* s.v. "Ad sanctos."

12. Maximus of Turin, in *Patrologiae (l.),* vol. 57, cols. 427–28.

13. *Dictionnaire d'archéologie chrétienne,* s.v. "Ad sanctos."

14. Ibid.

15. Ibid.

16. E. Salin, *La Civilisation mérovingienne* (Paris: Picard, 1949), 2:35.

17. Robert Dauvergne, "Fouilles archéologiques à Châtenay-sous-Bagneux," in *Mémoires des sociétés d'histoire de Paris et de l'Ile-de-France* (Paris, 1965–66), pp. 241–70.

18. See J. Siral, *Guide historique de Guiry-en-Vexin* (Guiry: Musée Archéologique de Guiry, 1964).

19. Françoise Zonabend, "Les Morts et les vivants," *Etudes rurales,* no. 52 (1973).

20. *Monumenta germaniae historica* (Hanover, 1875–89), Leges 5, Capitula de partibus Saxoniae, year 777, p. 43.

21. *Dictionnaire d'archéologie chrétienne,* s.v. "Ad sanctos."

22. See E. Lesne, *Histoire de la propriété ecclésiastique en France* (Lille: Desclée de Brouwer, 1936), 3:122–29.

23. See Siral, *Guiry-en-Vexin.*

24. See F. Eygun and L. Levillain, *Hypogée de Dunes à Poitiers* (Poitiers: La Ville de Poitiers et la Société des Antiquaires de l'Ouest, 1964).

25. Humbert of Burgundy, *Maxima bibliotheca veterum patrum* (1677), 25:527.

26. "*Antiquos patres ad vitandam urbium frequentiam quaedam solitaria loca elegisse, ubi ad honorem Dei fidelium corporum honeste potuissent sepeliri.*" A. Chedeville, *Liber controversiarum Sanct Vincentii Cenomannensis,* or *Second Cartulaire de l'abbaye Saint-Vincent du Mans* (Paris: Klincksieck, 1968), no. 37, pp. 45, 1095–1136.

27. H. Sauval, *Histoire et recherches des antiquités de Paris* (Paris, 1724), 1:359.

28. Humbert, *Maxima bibliotheca,* 25:527.

29. Aeneas Sylvius, *De origine Boemorum,* chap. 35, cited by Henri de Sponde, *Les Cimetières sacrez* (Bordeaux, 1598), p. 144.

30. Sponde, *Cimetières sacrez,* p. 112.

31. Thomassin, *Discipline de l'Eglise,* vol. 3, cols. 543ff.

32. Saint Julian of Toledo, in *Patrologiae (l.),* vol. 96, col. 474.

33. See *L'Elucidarium et les Lucidaires: Mélanges d'archéologie et d'histoire des écoles françaises d'Athènes et de Rome,* ed. Y. Leferne, fasc. 180 (Paris: de Boccard, 1954).

34. See Lesne, *Propriété ecclésiastique.*

35. Dom H. Morice, *Mémoires pour servir de preuves à l'histoire civile et ecclésiastique de Bretagne* (Paris, 1742), 1:559.

36. Fauveyn, cited in Frédéric Godefroy, *Dictionnaire de l'ancienne langue française* (Paris, 1881–1902), s.v. "Aître."

37. Charles Dufresne du Cange, *Glossarium mediae et infimae latinitatis* (Paris: Didot, 1840–50), s.v. "Imblocatus."

38. Alain Chartier, cited in J.-B. de Lacurne de Saint-Palaye, *Dictionnaire d'ancien français* (1877), s.v. "Aître."

39. A. Tuetey, ed., *Journal d'un bourgeois de Paris au Moyen Age* (Paris: Champion, 1881), entry dated 12 November 1411, p. 17; entry dated 15 September 1413, p. 44.

40. Jan Potocki, *Manuscrit trouvé à Saragosse,* ed. Roger Caillois (Paris: Gallimard, 1958), p. 51.

41. See Louis Chevalier, *Classes laborieuses et classes dangereuses à Paris* (Paris: Plon, 1958).

42. Gabriel Le Bras, oral communication.

43. Mansi, *Sacrorum conciliorum,* vol. 5, col. 842.

44. Gulielmus Durandus, *Rationale divinorum officiorum,* trans. Charles Barthélémy (Paris, 1854), vol. 5, chap. 5, p. xii.

45. Mansi, *Sacrorum conciliorum,* vol. 34, col. 648.

46. Ibid.

47. Ibid., vol. 34, col. 698.

48. Thomassin, *Discipline de l'Eglise,* vol. 3, col. 554.

49. Jean Charles-Picard, *La Carthage de Saint Augustin* (Paris: Fayard, 1965), pp. 204–5, 210.

50. *Armes parlantes:* rebus-like arms which refer to the name of the bearer; also called canting arms and allusive arms.

51. Boymans–van Beuningen Museum, Rotterdam.

52. Thomassin, *Discipline de l'Eglise,* vol. 3, col. 555.

53. John Gerson, *Opera* (Antwerp, 1706), 2:440.

54. Thomassin, *Discipline de l'Eglise,* vol. 3, col. 563.

55. "*Ecclesia ut ibi cimeterium esse mortuorum.*" Cited in Lesne, *Propriété ecclésiastique,* 3:122–29.

56. "*Ecclesia in qua humantur corpora defunctorum.*" Du Cange, *Glossarium,* s.v. "Cimeterium."

57. "*Nullo tumulorum vestigio apparente, ecclesiae reverentia conservetur. Ubi vero hoc pro multitudine cadaverum difficile est facere, locus ille coemeterium et polyandrium*

habeatur, ablato inde altare, et constituto sacrificium Deo valeat offeri." Cited by Auguste Joseph Bernard, "*La Sépulture en droit canonique*" (law thesis, Paris, 1933), pp. 20–21, n. 7.

58. See *Patrologiae (l.),* vol. 99, col. 983.

59. In 1059 a Roman council fixed the *confina cemeteriorum* for main churches at sixty paces *per circuitum,* for chapels at thirty paces *per circuitum.* See Lesne, *Propriété ecclésiastique.*

60. Gabriel Le Bras, *Dictionnaire d'histoire et de géographie ecclésiastiques* (1930), s.v. "Asile," vol. 4, cols. 1035–47.

61. Godefroy, *Dictionnaire,* s.v. "Aître"; see also C. Enlart, *Manuel d'archéologie du Moyen Age* (Paris, 1902–32), s.v. "Cimetière," pp. 909ff.; P. Duparc, "Le Cimetière séparé des vivants," *Bulletin philologique et historique du Comité des travaux historiques et scientifiques,* 1964, pp. 483–509.

62. Du Cange, *Glossarium.* s.v. "Stillicidium" and "Paradisum."

63. See Eugène Emmanuel Viollet-le-Duc, *Dictionnaire raisonné de l'architecture française* (Paris: B. Bance, 1858–68), 9:23.

64. Mathieu de Coucy, *Histoire de Charles VII,* cited in Lacurne, *Dictionnaire,* s.v. "Charnier."

65. Antoine Furetière, *Dictionnaire universal* (Rotterdam, 1690), s.v. "Charnier."

66. R.-J. Bernard, "L'Alimentation en Gévaudan au XVIIIᵉ siècle," *Annales: Economies, sociétés, civilisations,* 24, no. 6, (Nov.–Dec. 1969): 1454, n. 1.

67. "*In carnario qui locus intra septa ecclesiae illius ossa continet mortuorum.*" *Chronique de Marigny,* cited in Lacurne, *Dictionnaire.*

68. Guillaume le Breton, "Description de Paris sous Charles VI," in L. Leroux de Liney and L. Tisserand, *Histoire générale de Paris* (Paris, 1867), p. 193.

69. Aimar de Ranconnet (Jean Nicot), *Thrésor de la langue françoyse* (Paris, 1606), s.v. "Charnier."

70. César-Pierre Richelet, *Dictionnaire françois* (Genève, 1680), s.v. "Charnier."

71. See Valentin Dufour, "Le Cimetière des Innocents," in F. Hoffbauer, *Paris à travers les âges* (Paris, 1875–82), vol. 2, pt. 1, pp. 1–28.

72. Sauval, *Antiquités de Paris*, 1:359. This tomb is today at the musée de Cluny.

73. "The area surrounding the church of Saint-Gervais [Paris] was thus probably in antiquity and in the Merovingian period a vast cemetery which remained in existence, albeit diminishing in size, until the Middle Ages." Abandoned upon the creation of the parish of Saint-Jean-en-Grève, its memory subsisted in the name "Place du Vieux-Cimetière-Saint-Jean": *Platea veteris cimeterii*. See M. Vieillard-Troïekoufoff et al., "Les Anciennes Eglises suburbaines de Paris du IVᵉ au Xᵉ siècles," *Mémoires de la Fédération des sociétés d'histoire de Paris et de l'Ile-de-France* (Paris, 1960), p. 198.

74. Gilles Corrozet, *Antiquités de Paris*, cited by Valentin Dufour, *La Danse macabre des Saints-Innocents de Paris* (Paris, 1874), p. 59.

75. F. de Lasteyrie, "Un Enterrement à Paris en 1697," *Bulletin de la Société d'histoire de Paris et de l'Ile-de-France* 4 (1877):146–50.

76. *Bourgeois de Paris*, Oct.–Nov. 1418, p. 116.

77. Sauval, *Antiquités de Paris*, 2:557.

78. See L.-M. Tisserand, "Les Iles du fief de Saint-Germain-des-Près et la question des cimetières," *Bulletin de la Société d'histoire de Paris et de l'Ile-de-France* 4 (1877): 112–31.

79. See Joly de Fleury Papers, no. 1207.

80. Ibid.

81. Corrozet, cited in Dufour, "Cimetière des Innocents," p. 29.

82. Anatole Le Braz, *La Légende de la mort chez les Bretons armoricains* (Paris: Champion, 1902), 1:313.

83. See M. Pillet, *L'Aître Saint-Maclou* (Paris: Champion, 1924).

84. Le Braz, *Légende de la mort*, 1:286.

85. *Preseutoirs*: the spaces over the galleries where the bones were displayed.

86. Le Braz, *Légende de la Mort*, 1:262.

87. See T. Ducrocq, "De la variété des usages funéraires dans l'Ouest de la France" (Paper delivered 18 April 1884, 22ᵉ Congrès des Sociétés Savantes, Section des Sciences Economiques et Sociales [Paris: E. Thorin, 1884]).

88. Le Braz, *Légende de la mort*, 1:115.

89. See Bernard, *Sépulture en droit canonique*.

90. Le Bras, *Dictionnaire*, s.v. "Asile"; see also Duparc, "Cimetière séparé des vivants."

91. Gaignières, *Répertoire Bouchot* (Paris: Bibliothèque National, 1891), nos. 5186 (Evreux Cathedral), 5650 (Saint-Etienne de Beauvais), and 5879 (Saint-Armand de Rouen).

92. E. Raunié, *Epitaphier du vieux Paris* [*Histoire générale de Paris*, vol 22., 5 vols (Paris: Imprimerie Nationale, 1890)], vol. 3, p. 87, n. 3.

93. See Le Bras, *Dictionnaire*, s.v. "Asile"; Duparc, "Cimetière séparé des vivants."

94. Du Cange, *Glossarium*, s.v. "Cimeterium."

95. Richelet, *Dictionnaire françois*, s.v. "Cimetière."

96. "Azylus circum ecclesiam." Lesne, *Propriété ecclésiastique*, 3:122–29.

97. G.-A. Prevost, *L'Eglise et les campagnes au Moyen Age* (1892), pp. 50–51. At Minot-en-Châtillonnais, within the cemetery and alongside the church, were depositories set aside for the safekeeping of inhabitants' valuables during times of strife. These depositories were abolished in the eighteenth century. See chapter 11 below and Zonabend, "Morts et vivants."

98. Du Cange, *Glossarium*, s.v. "Cimeterium."

99. See Lesne, *Propriété ecclésiastique*, 3:122–29.

100. Du Cange, *Glossarium*, s.v. "Cimeterium."

101. *Cartulaire Saint-Vincent*, No. 153.

102. Champeaux, *Les Cimetières et les marchés du vieux Dijon*, p. 6, cited by Bernard, *Sépulture en droit canonique*, p. 60.

103. "Such profane activity seemed natural to the people of the time because the sanctuary

was a common house." A. Dumas, "L'Eglise au pouvoir des laïques," in Fliche and Martin, *Histoire de l'Eglise* (Paris: Presses Universitaires de France, 1940), 7:268.

104. *Bourgeois de Paris*, p. 234

105. See A. Vallance, *Old Crosses and Lynchgates* (London: Batsford, 1930), p. 13.

106. Sauval, *Antiquités de Paris*, 1:354.

107. Corrozet, cited in Dufour, "Cimetière des Innocents," p. 10;

108. *Bourgeois de Paris*, pp. 366–67.

109. Dufour, "Cimetière des Innocents," p. 5

110. Le Braz, *Légende de la mort*, 1:123 and n.

111. *Cartulaire Saint Vincent*, No. 285.

112. Le Braz, *Légende de la mort*, 1:259, n. 1.

113. Du Cange, *Glossarium*, s.v. "Cimeterium."

114. See Bernard, *Sépulture en droit canonique*, p. 55; Dom E. Martène, *Veterum scriptorium . . . collectio* (1724–33), vol. 4, cols. 987–93.

115. Le Braz, *Légende de la mort*, 1:xxxv.

116. See Bernard, *Sépulture en droit canonique*, p. 67.

117. Dufour, "Cimetière des Innocents," pp. 1–28.

118. Berthaud, *La Ville de Paris en vers burlesque, 1661*, cited by Raunié, *Epitaphier du vieux Paris*, vol. 1, "Preface."

119. *Journal d'un voyage à Paris en 1657* (Paris: A. P. Fougère, 1862), p. 46.

120. Raunié, *Epitaphier du vieux Paris*, vol. 1, "Preface."

121. Ibid.

122. Bernard, *Sépulture en droit canonique*.

123. Dufour, "Cimetière des Innocents," pp. 1–28.

124. See Jacques Le Goff, "Culture cléricale et traditions folkloriques dans la civilisation mérovingienne," *Annales: Economies, sociétés, civilisations*, 22, no. 4 (July-August 1967): 780ff.

125. Jean du Berry, will dated 24 August 1411, Tuetey, no. 282.

126. See Le Braz, *Légende de la mort*.

127. Tuetey, no. 105 (1403).

128. AD Haute-Garonne 11 808, no. 19 (1648).

129. Cited by Lesne, *Propriété ecclésiastique*, 3:122ff.

130. Tuety, no. 282 (1411); Médéric=Merry, ANMC, 75 (1663); 26:24 (1604); 51:112 (1609); 75:87 (1654).

131. AD Haute-Garonne 11 808, no. 19 (1600); ANMC, 75:54 (1644).

132. ANMC, 75:372 (1690); 119:355 (1787); 78 (1661); Tuetey, no. 217 (1407).

133. ANMC, 75:94 (1657).

134. ANMC, 75:97 (1659).

135. Jean Régnier, in André Mary, ed., *Anthologie poetique française du Moyen Age* (Paris: Garnier-Flammarion, 1967), 2:201.

136. Tuetey, no. 323 (1413).

137. ANMC, 8:328 (1574), cited by Antoinette Fleury, "Le Testament dans la coutume de Paris au XVIe siècle" (Thesis, Ecole Nationale des Chartes [Nogent-le-Rotrou: Imprimerie Daupeley, 1943]), pp. 81–88. Mlle. Fleury has kindly allowed me to consult the manuscript of her thesis. ANMC, 75:48 (1642).

138. ANMC, 75:76 (1651).

139. See Fleury, "Testament."

140. ANMC, 75:62 (1644).

141. ANMC, 26:25 (1606).

142. "Anniversarium G. A. canonici limovicensis qui est sepultus in claustro nostro in pariete *sive* in pila claustri." Obituaire de Solignac, AD Limoges, H. 9180 *bis* (supplied to the author by J.-L. Lemaître).

143. Tuetey, no. 211 (1407); see Fleury, "Testament"; ANMC, 3:507 (1608); 16:30 (1612); 75:146 (1669); 76:112 (1661).

144. Tuetey, no. 211 (1401); no. 217 (1407); see Fleury, "Testament"; Tuetey, no. 132 (1404).

145. ANMC, 75:94 (1657); 75:80 (1652).

146. Tuetey, no. 337 (1416).

147. Tuetey, no. 55 (1400); no. 264 (1410); see Fleury, "Testament"; ANMC, 75:117 (1662); 75:142 (1669).

148. Tuetey, no. 323 (1413); see Raunié, *Epitaphier du vieux Paris.*

149. Tuetey, no. 337 (1416); ANMC, 78 (1661); AD Haute-Garonne, 11 808, no. 19 (1600).

150. ANMC, 3:533 (1628); 78 (1661).

151. See Fleury, "Testament"; ANMC, 3:532 (1621).

152. ANMC, 26:24 (1604).

153. Tuetey, no. 80 (1402); ANMC, 75:372 (1690); 75:109 (1660); Saint-Julien parish, will dated 20 May 1560, AD Seine-et-Oise, cited in Fleury, "Testament"; ANMC, 75:78 (1649).

154. ANMC, 26 (1602).

155. ANMC, 3:516 (1622); 75:146 (1669); 26:26 (1607); 3:533 (1628).

156. E. Magne, *La Fin troublée de Tallemant des Réaux* (Paris: Emile-Paul Frères, 1922), 342.

157. Tuetey, no. 122 (1404); ANMC, 75:142 (1660).

158. ANMC, 75:46 (1641); 75:66 (1648); 49:179 (1590).

159. ANMC, 75:117 (1660); 75:137 (1667); Tuetey, no. 185 (1406); Archives Nationales (Paris), Y86, F°68 n V° (1539), cited in Fleury, "Testament."

160. Parisian wills have been subjected to systematic quantitative study by P. Chaunu and his pupils. See P. Chaunu, "Mourir à Paris," *Annales: Economies, sociétés, civilisations,* 31, no. 1 (Jan.–Feb. 1976), pp. 29–50, and the report by B. de Cessole cited therein, p. 48, n. 4.

161. Furetière, *Dictionnaire,* s.v. "Cimetière."

162. Archives de la Ville de Toulouse, Parish Registers.

163. ANMC, 3:522 (1624).

164. C. W. Foster, *Lincoln Wills* (Lincoln, 1914).

165. Ibid., p. 54.

166. Ibid., p. 558.

Chapter 3

1. See Vladimir Jankélévitch, *La Mort* (Paris: Flammarion, 1966), p. 174, n. 2.

2. See J. Ntedika, *L'Evocation de l'au-delà dans les prières pour les morts* (Louvain: Nauwelaerts, 1971), pp. 55ff.; also Salvador Vicastillo's unpublished thesis (Madrid, 1977) on Tertullian's view of death.

3. See J. Hubert, "Les Cryptes de Jouarre" (Contribution to the fourth Congrès de l'Art du Haut Moyen Age [Melun: Imprimerie de la Préfecture de Seine-et-Marne, 1952]).

4. Cf. Jerusalem Bible, 1 Cor. 15:51–2.

5. See J. Dupont, "La Salle du Trésor de la cathédrale de Châlons-sur-Marne," *Bulletin des monuments historiques de la France* (1957), pp. 183, 192–93.

6. See Emile Mâle, *La Fin du paganisme en Gaule* (Paris: Flammarion, 1950), pp. 245ff.

7. See R. P. Feder, *Missel romain* (Tours: Mame), pp. 1623–24.

8. Jean Lestocquoy, *Les Villes de Flandres et d'Italie sous le gouvernement des patriciens* (Paris: Presses Universitaires de France, 1952), p. 194.

9. See Emile Mâle, *L'Art religieux du XIIe siècle* (Paris: Armand Colin, 1940).

10. Mathilde Pomès, trans., *Le Romancero* (Paris: Stock, 1947), p. 111; cf. A. Duran, ed., *Romancero General* (Madrid, 1924).

11. Saint Michael is often honored in the higher parts of churches. In one chapel dedicated to the saint, at Saint-Aignan-sur-Cher, are the remains of two frescoes portraying the slaying of the dragon and the weighing of souls in the balance.

12. *Confiteor* of Chrodegang of Metz (d. 766), in J.-A. Jungmann, *Missarum solemnia* (Paris: Aubier-Montaigne, 1964), 2:41.

13. See Tenenti, *Il senso,* fig. 40 and p. 443.

14. See Tenenti, *La Vie*, fig. 17 and p. 103.

15. See Gaby and Michel Vovelle, "Vision de la mort et de l'au-delà en Provence d'après les autels des âmes du Purgatoire, XVᵉ–XXᵉ siècles," Cahiers des Annales, no. 29 (Paris: Armand Colin, 1970).

16. *Miroir de l'âme du pécheur et du juste pendant la vie et à l'heure de la mort: Méthode chrétienne pour finir saintement la vie* (Lyons: F. Viret, 1736, new ed., 1752), p. 15.

17. Ibid., p. 35.

18. See Tenenti, *La Vie*, pp. 98ff.

19. Ibid., p. 108.

20. *Manuscrits à peinture du XIIIᵉ au XVIᵉ siècle* (Exhibition catalogue [Paris: Bibliothèque Nationale, 1955]), no. 115.

21. Tenenti, *La Vie*, p. 55.

22. *Manuscrits à peinture du XIIIᵉ au XVIᵉ siècle*, no. 303.

23. Tenenti, *La Vie*, pp. 50 (n. 16), 55.

24. Pierre de Nesson, "Vigile des morts, paraphrase sur Job," in André Mary, ed., *Anthologie poétique française du Moyen Age* (Paris: Garnier-Flammarion, 1967), 2:184.

25. See also Johan Huizinga, *The Waning of the Middle Ages* (Garden City, N.Y.: Anchor, 1954), p. 141.

26. Ibid., p. 139.

27. Ibid.

28. Pierre Michault, "Triomphe de la Mort," in *Anthologie poétique . . . du Moyen Age.*

29. Metropolitan Museum of Art, New York.

30. See J. Baltrusaitis, *Le Moyen Age fantastique* (Paris: Armand Colin, 1955).

31. See Emile Mâle, *L'Art religieux en France* (Paris: Armand Colin, 1931–50); Erwin Panofsky, *Tomb Sculpture: Four Lectures on Its Changing Aspects from Ancient Egypt to Bernini* (New York: Harry N. Abrams, [1924]).

32. Cf. Jean Adhémar, "Les Tombeaux de la Collection Gaignières," in *Gazette des Beaux-Arts* 1 (July–Sept., 1974): 343–44.

33. Domenico Capranico (1513); cf. Tenenti, *Il senso*, pl. 19 and pp. 192–93.

34. Gaignières, *Répertoire Bouchot.*

35. Original in Memling's Workshop, Strasbourg Museum; see also Tenenti, *La Vie*, pl. 8–10.

36. See J. Saugnieux, *Les Danses macabres de France et d'Espagne* (Paris: Les Belles Lettres, 1972); "La Danse macabre des femmes," in *Anthologie poétique . . . du Moyen Age*, 2:353–55; E. Dubruck, *The Theme of Death in French Poetry* (London and Paris: Mouton, 1964).

37. Pierre Michault, "Raisons de Dame Atropos," in *Anthologie poétique . . . du Moyen Age*, 2:323–29.

38. Nesson, "Vigile les morts," pp. 183–86.

39. Eustache Deschamps, "Ballade des signes de la mort," in *Anthologie Poétique . . . du Moyen Age*, 2: 151.

40. Pierre de Ronsard, *Oeuvres complètes* (Paris: P. Laumonnier, 1967), 28:176.

41. See Tenenti, *La Vie*, p. 99.

42. François Villon, "Les Regrets de la Belle Heaumière," in *Le Testament* (Paris: La Cité des livres, 1930), pp. 82–5.

43. Michault, "Raisons de Dame Atropos," in *Anthologie poétique . . . du Moyen Age*, 2:328.

44. See Johan Huiziuga, *The Waning of the Middle Ages*, p. 38.

45. Michault, "Triomphe de la Mort," Anthologie poétique . . . du Moyen Age."

46. See Josse Lieferinxe, *St. Sebastian Interceding for the Plague-Stricken*, Walters Gallery, Baltimore; François Perrier, called Le Bourguignon, *The Plague in Athens* Dijon Museum.

47. Jacques Heers, in *Annales de démographie historique*, (1968), p. 44.

48. Antoinette Fleury, "Le Testament dans la coutume de Paris au XVIᵉ siècle" (Thesis: Ecole National des Chartes [Nogen-le-Rotrou: Imprimerie Daupeley, 1943]).

49. Jean Delumeau, *La Civilisation de la Renaissance* (Paris: Arthaud, 1967), p. 386.

50. Huizinga, *The Waning of the Middle Ages*, p. 151.

51. See P. Mesplée, *La Sculpture baroque de Saint-Sernin* (Exhibition catalogue [Toulouse: Musée des Augustins, 1952]).

52. In England, toward the end of the sixteenth century, lead coffins permitted the practice of preserving the general form of the body. This practice constitutes a peculiar exception to a general rule, and may in a sense be understood as a rejection of that rule. See Lawrence Stone, *The Crisis of the Aristocracy* (Oxford: Oxford University Press, 1965), chap. 8.

53. Tenenti, *Il senso*, p. 430.

54. Tenenti, *La Vie*, p. 38.

55. Tenenti, *Il senso*, p. 165.

56. Ibid., pp. 48–79, 81.

57. Tenenti, *La Vie*, p. 38.

58. Tenenti, *Il senso*, pp. 48–79.

59. Tententi, *La Vie*, p. 38.

60. Tententi, *Il senso*, p. 52.

61. Tenenti, *La Vie*, appendix, pp. 98–120.

62. Hieronymus Bosch, Museum of Fine Arts, Boston.

63. Charles Sterling, *La Nature morte* (Exhibition catalogue [Paris: Orangeries des Tuileries, 1952]), p. xxx.

64. P.-A. Michel, *Fresques romaines des églises de France* (Paris: Editions du Chêne, 1949), p. 69.

65. *Manuscrits à peinture du VIIe au XIIe siècle* (Exhibition catalogue [Paris: Bibliotheque Nationale, 1954]), no. 222, pl. 23.

66. Master of Flémalle, *Annunciation*, Musée des Beaux-Arts, Brussels.

67. *Manuscrits à peinture du XIIIe au XVIe siècle*, no. 110, pl. 21.

68. Sterling, *La Nature morte*, p. 8.

69. Huizinga, *The Waning of the Middle Ages*, p. 141.

Chapter 4

1. See J. Ntedika, *L'Evocation de l'au-delà dans les prières pour les morts* (Louvain: Nauwelaerts, 1971), pp. 68ff.

2. Gulielmus Durandus, *Rationale divinorum officiorum*, trans. Charles Barthélémy (Paris, 1854), 5:xxxviii.

3. Jacques-Paul Migne, ed., *Patrologiae cursus completus, series graeca*, vol. 57, col. 374.

4. E. de Martino, *Morte e pianto rituale nel mondo antico* (Turin: Einaudi, 1958), p. 32.

5. Charles Dufresne Du Cange, *Glossarium mediae et infimae latinitatus* (Paris: Didot, 1840–50), s.v., "Reputatimes."

6. See Ntedika, *Evocation de l'au-delà*.

7. *Dictionnaire d'archéologie chrétienne et de liturgie* (Paris: Letouzey, 1907), s.v. "Diptyques," vol. 4, cols. 1046ff.

8. Migne, *Patrologia cursus completus, series latina*, vol. 85, cols 114ff.

9. Ibid., cols. 175, 195, 209, 221, 224–25.

10. Ibid., col. 224.

11. See Ntedika, *Evocation de l'au-delà*, p. 133 and nn.

12. J.-A. Jungmann, *Missarum solemnia* (Paris: Aubier-Montaigne, 1964), 3:77, 24; see also vols. 1 and 2 (French trans.).

13. Ibid.

14. Ibid.

15. Raoul Glaber, cited by George Duby, *L'An mil* (Paris: Julliard, 1967).

16. Jungmann, *Missarum solemnia*, 1:267, 273.

17. See Jean Charles-Picard, "Etude sur l'emplacement des tombes des papes du IIIe au Xe siècle," *Mélanges d'archéologie et d'histoire*, vol. 81 (Ecole Française de Rome, 1969), pp. 735–82.

18. *Monumenta Germaniae historica: Epistolae selectae*, 1:232–33.

19. Gabriel Le Bras, *Etudes de sociologie religieuse* (Paris: Presses Universitaires de France, 1955), 2:418.

20. Jungmann, *Missarum solemnia*, 1:269.

21. M. de Moléon, *Voyages liturgiques en France* (Paris, 1718), pp. 151ff.

22. A. Van Gennep, *Manuel du folklore français contemporain* (Paris: Picard, 1946), 2:674–75.

23. See Moléon, *Voyages liturgiques*.

24. Van Gennep, *Folklore français*, 2:715–16. Many English and Dutch tombs of the sixteenth and seventeenth centuries depict the corpse laid out on a straw mat.

25. Mathilde Pomès, trans., *Le Romancero* (Paris: Stock, 1947), p. 102.

26. See Tenenti, *Il senso*, pp. 55–58.

27. Tuetey, no. 233 (1410).

28. F. Autrand, "Offices et officiers royaux sous Charles VI," *Revue d'histoire*, December 1969, p. 336.

29. ANMC, 3:533 (1628); 75:63 (1647); 49:179 (1590).

30. Tuetey, no. 105 (1403).

31. ANMC, 75:74 (1650).

32. ANMC, 3:490 (1611).

33. Comte de Voyer d'Argenson, *Annales de la Compagnie du Saint-Sacrement* (Marseilles: Dom Beauchet-Filleau, 1900).

34. ANMC, 119:355 (1769).

35. ANMC, 75:78 (1652).

36. ANMC, 17:30 (1612); See F. de Lasteyrie, "Un Enterrement à Paris en 1697," *Bulletin de la Société d'histoire de Paris et de l'Ile-de-France*, 4(1877): 146–50.

37. See R. E. Giesey, *The Royal Funeral Ceremony in Renaissance France* (Geneva: Droz, 1960).

38. Pinacoteca, Vatican, No. 233.

39. In eighteenth-century Poland, for instance, a portrait of the deceased would be painted on an outer side of the coffin.

40. A bas-relief on a fourteenth-century Spanish tombstone now in the Cloisters Museum, New York, shows a priest spreading the *pallium*.

41. ANMC, 8:369 (1559).

42. ANMC, 8:343 (1532).

43. ANMC, 75:66 (1648).

44. ANMC, 75:82 (1655).

45. ANMC, 75:74 (1650); 75:109 (1660).

46. ANMC, 75:62 (1646); 75:78 (1652); 75:46 (1641); 75:89 (1606).

47. ANMC, 75:137 (1667); 75:72 (1650).

48. ANMC, 119:355 (1780).

49. Tuetey, no. 131 (1394).

50. ANMC, 75:72 (1650).

51. ANMC, 75:137 (1667); 3 (1661); Tuetey, no. 356 (1418).

52. ANMC, 3:533 (1628); 26:25 (1606); 8:343 (1582).

53. ANMC, 75:101 (1658).

54. ANMC, 75:989 (1812).

55. ANMC, 75:603 (1812).

56. ANMC, 8:383, 292 (1545).

57. ANMC, 16:30 (1612).

58. See P.-M. Gy, "Les Funérailles d'après le rituel de 1614," *La Maison-Dieu*, vol. 44 (1955).

59. ANMC, 3:533 (1628).

60. ANMC, 75:54 (1644); AD Haute-Garonne, 3E 11 808 (1600); Michel Vovelle, *Piété baroque et déchristianisation au XVIIIᵉ siècle: Les attitudes devant la mort d'après les clauses des testaments* (Paris: Plon, 1973), p. 119.

61. Tuetey, no. 45 (1399).

62. Tuetey, no. 337 (1416).

63. ANMC, 26:44 (1612).

64. ANMC, 3:533 (1628).

65. In this connection for England, see W. K. Jordan, *Philanthropy in England, 1480–1660* (London: Allen and Unwin, 1959).

66. ANMC, 75:137 (1667).

67. AD Haute-Garonne, 3E 11 808 (1678).

68. Tuetey, no. 55 (1400); ANMC, 54:48 (1560).

69. ANMC, 3:533 (1628).

70. Vovelle, *Piété baroque*, pp. 114ff.

71. ANMC, 75:137 (1667).

72. Maurice Agulhon, *Pénitents et Francs-Maçons dans l'ancienne Provence* (Paris: Fayard, 1967), p. 86.

73. See L. Reau, *Art chrétien* (Paris: Presses Universitaires de France, 1955–59), vol. 2, pp. 759–60.

74. Voyer d'Argenson, *Compagnie du Saint-Sacrement*, p. 43.

75. Agulhon, *Pénitents et Francs-Maçons*, p. 110.

76. ANMC, 8:451 (1560).

77. Tuetey, no. 523 (1413).

78. Tuetey, no. 131 (1394).

79. ANMC, 8:451 (1560).

80. ANMC, 3:533 (1628); Jean Regnier in André Mary, ed., *Anthologie poétique française du Moyen Age* (Paris: Garnier-Flammarion, 1967).

81. Jacques Le Goff, *La Civilisation de l'Occident médiéval* (Paris: Arthaud, 1964), p. 240.

82. Ibid.

83. Jacques Heers, *L'Occident aux XIVe et XVe siècles* (Paris: Presses Universitaires de France, 1966), p. 96.

84. See J. Schneider, *La Ville de Metz aux XIIIe et XIVe siècles* (Nancy, 1950).

85. See Jean Lestocquoy, *Les Villes de Flandre et d'Italie* (Paris: Presses Universitaires de France, 1952).

86. Paul Veyne, "Panem et circenses: L'Evergétisme devant les sciences humaines," *Annales: Economies, sociétés, civilisations*, 24, no. 3 (May-June 1969):805. Veyne has taken the problem up at greater length in a very fine study which appeared after the present chapter had been completed: *Le Pain et le cirque* (Paris: Seuil, 1976).

87. The Hôpital de Cavaillon, now a museum, houses a collection of foundation records, *donatifs*, showing that donations were consistently made from the seventeenth century through the mid-nineteenth, with but a brief interruption during the Revolutionary period.

88. Max Weber, *The Protestant Ethic and the Spirit of Capitalism* (New York: Scribner, 1977).

89. See André Vauchez, "La Pauvreté volontaire au Moyen Age," *Annales: Economies, sociétés, civilisations*, 25, no. 6 (November-December 1970):1566–73.

90. Cited in Lestocquoy, *Villes de Flandre et d'Italie*, p. 200.

91. Gaignières, Tombs, B.2518: Grégoire Vidame de Plaisance; cf. Jean Adhémar, "Les Tombeaux de la Collection Gaignières," in *Gazette des Beaux-Arts* (Paris, 1974), n. 122.

92. Tuetey, no. 323 (1413).

93. ANMC, 16:30 (1612).

94. ANMC, 75:78 (1652).

95. See *Miroir de l'âme du pécheur et du juste: Méthode chrétienne pour finir saintement sa vie*, 2 vols. (Lyons, 1741, 1752).

96. ANMC, 75:69 (1649).

97. Vovelle, *Piété baroque*, p. 56.

98. Régnier, in *Anthologie poétique . . . du Moyen Age*, 2:201.

99. François Villon, *Le Testament* (Paris: La Cité des Livres, 1930).

Chapter 5

1. Erwin Panofsky offers a fine analysis of these two aspects—commemorative and eschatological—of the funerary art in his *Tomb Sculpture: Four Lectures on Its Changing Aspects from Ancient Egypt to Bernini* (New York: Harry N. Abrams, [1924]).

2. "The bodies of slaves, or of those too poor even to lay their hands on the few coins needed to pay for pyre or burial place, were treated as refuse. In such cases death was attended by no religious trappings, for no form of solemnization existed short of the full funeral ceremonial." Paul Veyne, *Le Pain et le cirque* (Paris: Seuil, 1976), p. 291.

3. Charles Lebeuf, *Histoire de la ville et de tout le diocèse de Paris* (Paris, 1954), 1:241.

4. See M. Labrousse, "Les Fouilles de la Tour Porche carolingienne de Souillac," *Bulletin monumental,* 159 (1951).

5. Antoine Furetière, *Dictionnaire universal* (Rotterdam, 1690), s.v. "Cercueil."

6. Enguerrand de Monstrelet, *Chroniques,* 1:96.

7. César-Pierre Richelet, *Dictionnaire francois* (Geneva, 1680), cited in H. Sauval, *Histoire et recherches des antiquités de Paris* (Paris, 1724), 1:376.

8. See Y. Christ, *Les Cryptes mérovingiennes de Jouarre* (Paris: Plon, 1961); J. Hubert, "Les Cryptes de Jouarre" (Contribution to the fourth Congrès de l'Art du Haut Moyen Age [Melun: Imprimerie de la Préfecture de Seine-et-Marne, 1952]).

9. Christ, *Cryptes mérovingiennes,* pp. 20–21.

10. See Jean Charles-Picard, "Etude sur l'emplacement des tombes des papes du IIIᵉ au Xᵉ siècle," *Mélanges d'archéologie et d'histoire,* vol. 81 (Ecole Française de Rome, 1969), pp. 735–82.

11. See Abbé Roze, trans., *La Légende dorée* (Paris, 1900). This translation was incorporated into the Garnier edition of 1967. See, in that edition, "Notice" concerning Saint Gregory, 2:231.

12. Musée des Augustins, Toulouse, No. 818.

13. Musée des Augustins, Toulouse, No. 197.

14. M. R. Lida de Malkiel, *L'Idée de la gloire dans la tradition occidentale* (Paris: Klincksieck, 1969), p. 98.

15. See Jacques Le Goff, "Culture cléricale et traditions folkloriques dans la civilisation mérovingienne," *Annales: Economies, sociétés, civilisations,* 22, no. 4 (July–August 1967):780–91.

16. Aimeric de Perguilhar, *Chant de croisades* (in Provençal), cited in Lida de Malkiel, *Idée de la gloire,* p. 113.

17. *Récits de croisades* (in Provençal), known as *Labran conquista d'Ultra Mar,* cited in Lida de Malkiel, *Idée de la gloire,* p. 114, n. 21.

18. Bernard de Cluny, cited in ibid., p. 142.

19. See Tenenti, *Il senso,* pp. 21–47.

20. M. Vieillard-Troïekoufoff et al., "Les Anciennes Eglises suburbaines de Paris du IVᵉ au Xᵉ siècle," *Mémoires de la fédération des sociétés d'histoire de Paris et de l'Ile-de-France* (Paris 1960), p. 151.

21. Gaignières, Tombs, *Répertoire Bouchot,* B.6950; cf. Jean Adhémar, "Les Tombeaux de la Collection Gaignières," in *Gazette des Beaux-Arts* (Paris, 1974), pp. 35, 37 (tomb of the first Abbé d'Ardennes). The ownership of these uninscribed tombs must have been known within the monastery through oral tradition.

22. Gaignières, Tombs, *Répertoire Bouchot,* B.6696, B.6698, B.2273; Adhémar, "Collection Gaignières," p. 11, no. 2.

23. Tombstone of Chevalier Burchard de Guiberschwihr, founder of the Abbey of Mahrbach, Unterlinden Museum, Colmar; see Museum Catalogue (1974), p. 24, no. 7.

24. Musée des Augustins, Toulouse.

25. E. Raunié, *Epitaphier du vieux Paris* [*Histoire générale de Paris,* vol. 22, 5 vols. (Paris: Imprimerie Nationale, 1890)], vol. 1.

26. Sauval, *Antiquités de Paris,* 1:415.

27. Raunié, *Epitaphier de vieux Paris,* vol. 1.

28. Sauval, *Antiquités de Paris,* 1:415.

29. Raunié, *Epitaphier de vieux Paris,* vol 1.

30. Ibid.

31. Ibid., 2:364–65.

32. Ibid.

33. Ibid.

34. Pierre Taisan de L'Estoile, *Memoires Journaux de L'Estoile* (Paris: 1875–96).

35. J. Marmier, "Sur quelques vers de Lazare de Selve," *Revue du XVIIᵉ siècle,* 92 (1971):144–45.

36. Raunié, *Epitaphier de vieux Paris.*

37. Ibid.

38. Ibid.

39. Paul Flamand, personal communication.

40. Tomb of Canon Aymeric. Musée des

Augustins, Cloister, Toulouse. This tomb is described later in the present chapter.

41. See Panofsky, *Tomb Sculpture*, p. 53.

42. Albert Erlande-Brandenburg, in "Le Roi, la sculpture et la mort: Gisants et tombeaux de Saint-Denis," *Bulletin des Archives départementales de la Seine–Saint-Denis*, no. 3 (June 1975), p. 12.

43. See Emile Mâle, *L'Art religieux en France* (Paris: Armand Colin, 1931–50).

44. See Panofsky, *Tomb Sculpture*.

45. Panofsky, *Tomb Sculpture*, fig. 227 and p. 58.

46. *Marranos* were Spanish Jews forced to convert to Christianity; they sometimes remained secretly faithful to the Hebrew religion. See C. Roth, *A History of the Marranos* (Philadelphia: Jewish Publication Society of America, 1941).

47. Jean-Claude Schmitt, "Le Suicide au Moyen Age," *Annales: Economies, sociétés, civilisations*, 28 (1973): 13.

48. Panofsky, *Tomb Sculpture*, figs. 235, 236.

49. Originally from Royaumont, this tomb is now exhibited at Saint-Denis. There is also a cast of it at the Trocadéro, Paris.

50. Jean-Pierre Babelon, in "Le Roi, la sculpture et la mort," pp. 31–33.

51. Ibid., p. 36.

52. Gaignières, Tombs, *Répertoire Bouchot*, B.2513.

53. Ibid., B.2258.

54. Albert Erlande-Brandenburg, in "Le Roi, la sculpture et la mort," p. 26.

55. Ibid.,

56. Cited in Raunié, *Epitaphier de vieux Paris*, 1:87, n. 3.

57. Antoinette Fleury, "Le Testament dans la coutume de Paris au XVIᵉ siècle (Thesis, Ecole Nationale des Chartes [Nogent-le-Rotrou: Imprimerie Daupeley, 1943]).

58. ANMC, 8:299 (1557).

59. Tuetey, no. 288 (1411).

60. Tuetey, no. 132 (1404).

61. See "Cimetière de Vauvert," Joly de Fleury Papers.

62. See A. P. Scieluna, *The Church of Saint John in Valletta* (Malta, 1955).

63. I make an exception in the case of English cemeteries, where crosses are rarer. This question is dealt with in chapter 11.

64. Tuetey, no. 55 (1400).

65. Tuetey, no. 122 (1404).

66. Tuetey, no. 244 (1409).

67. ANMC, 3:516 (1622).

68. Tuetey, no. 288 (1411).

69. ANMC, 3:490 (1611).

70. ANMC, 3:533 (1628).

71. ANMC, 3:502 (1616).

72. A case in point is Notre-Dame de Paris, whose pillars were laden with tombstones and altars until these were demolished on the orders of the eighteenth-century canons; see Orest Ranum, *Les Parisiens du XVIIᵉ siècle* (Paris: Armand Colin, 1973), p. 15. Such tombstones were in the choir of Notre-Dame as early as the reign of Louis XIV; see also Raunié, *Epitaphier de vieux Paris*, vol. 1, "Preface."

73. Gaignières, Tombs, *Répertoire Bouchot*, B.3427.

74. Raunié, *Epitaphier de vieux Paris*, 3:359.

75. Lenz Kriss-Rettenbeck, *Ex-voto* (Zurich, 1972), p. 130.

76. Ibid., p. 60.

77. Ibid., pp. 58–59.

78. Ibid., p. 62.

79. On ex-votos, see also M. Mollat, Preface to *Ex-voto des marins du Ponant* (Exhibition catalogue [Nantes-Caen, 1975–76]).

80. Tuetey, no. 55 (1400).

81. ANMC, 26:23 (1603).

82. ANMC, 26:33 (1617).

83. ANMC, 3:516 (1622).

84. ANMC, 42:407 (1745).

85. ANMC, 26:25 (1606); 75:66 (1650).

Chapter 6

1. A. Corvisier, "Les Danses macabres," *Revue d'histoire moderne et contemporaine*, (1969), pp. 537–38. In France, five out of eleven danses macabres are from the sixteenth and seventeenth centuries; in Germany eighteen out of twenty-six are from the sixteenth to eighteenth century, and one is even dated 1838.

2. This chapter was completed before the publication of two relevant articles: R. Chartier, "Les Arts de mourir (1450–1600)," *Annales: Economies, sociétés, civilisations*, 31, no. 1 (January-February 1976): 51–75; and D. Roche, " 'La Mémoire de la mort': Recherche sur la place des arts de mourir dans la librairie et la lecture en France aux XVIIᵉ et XVIIIᵉ siècles," *ibid.*, 31:76–119.

3. Cited in Tenenti, *Il senso*, pp. 268 (n. 47, 49), 269 (n. 55), 242–43.

4. Saint Robert Bellarmine, *De arte bene moriendi*, in *Opera omnia* (Paris, 1875; Frankfurt, 1965), 8:551–662.

5. Cited in Nancy Lee Beaty, *The Craft of Dying* (New Haven and London: Yale University Press, 1970), p. 150.

6. Cited in Tenenti, *Il senso*, p. 312, n. 61.

7. Nathalie Z. Davis, *Holbein: Pictures of Death and the Reformation at Lyons*, Studies on the Renaissance, no. 8 (1956), p. 115.

8. Cited in Tenenti, *Il senso*, p. 312, n. 56.

9. Jean de Vauzelles, cited in Davis, *Holbein*, p. 115.

10. Ibid.

11. See Beaty, *Craft of Dying*, p. 68.

12. Cited in Tenenti, *Il senso*, p. 315, n. 107.

13. See Erasmus, "The Shipwreck," in *The Colloquies of Erasmus*, trans. Craig R. Thomson (Chicago and London: University of Chicago Press, 1965), pp. 139–46.

14. Jeremy Taylor, *The Rule and Exercises of Holy Dying* (London: R. Royston, 1651), pp. 189–90, cited in Beaty, *Craft of Dying*, p. 215n.

15. See *Miroir de l'âme du pécheur et du juste pendant la vie et à l'heure de la mort: Méthode chrétienne pour finir saintement sa vie*, new ed. (Lyons: F. Viret, 1752), pp. 22, 60, 188.

16. Cited in Tenenti, *Il senso*, p. 361, n. 99.

17. See Gaby and Michel Vovelle, *Vision de la Mort et de l'au-delà en Provence d'après les autels des âmes du Purgatoire, XVᵉ–XXᵉ siècles*, Cahiers des Annales, no. 29 (Paris: Armand Colin, 1970).

18. See Philippe Ariès, *Essais sur l'histoire de la mort* (Paris: Seuil, 1975), pp. 115–22.

19. ANMC, 75:78 (1652).

20. ANMC, 75:372 (1690).

21. In the second half of the eighteenth century, in France, however, there is a return on the part of the Christian apologists and their adversaries, the atheist or deist *philosophes*, to the *hora mortis* (see R. Favre, *La Mort au Siècle des Lumières* [Lyon, Presses Universitaires de Lyon, 1978], pp. 86ff.). This return can be explained by the new meaning that was found in the good death, the peaceful death, when the new opposition between the believer and the nonbeliever replaced the traditional one between the good man and the sinner. Both the good man and the believer claim the good death for themselves and reserve the angry or defiant death for their adversary, whoever he may be.

22. See Tenenti, *Il senso*, pp. 268 (nn. 47, 49), 269 (n. 55), 242–43.

23. See Bellarmine, *De arte bene moriendi*, 8:551–662.

24. Ibid.

25. Cited in Tenenti, *Il senso*, p. 291.

26. Cited in Tenenti, *Il senso*, p. 364, n. 124.

27. Francesco Barbara to his daughter, 30 November 1447, cited in ibid., p. 264, n. 125.

28. Denis Meadows, *Elizabethan Quintet* (London: Longmans, Green, 1956), pp. 173–75, cited in Beaty, *Craft of Dying*, p. 183 *n.*

29. Giovanni Battista Gelli, cited in Tententi, *Il senso*, pp. 213, 227 (n. 134), 211ff, 227 (n. 137), 228 (n. 140).

30. See Bellarmine, *De arte bene moriendi*, 8:551–662.

31. Henry Suso's view, according to Tenenti, *Il senso.*

32. Cited in Henri de Sponde, *Les Cimetières sacrez* (Bordeaux, 1598).

33. Joly de Fleury Papers, no. 1209.

34. On the matter of a single parish having two cemeteries, see the discussion in chapter 2 of the two cemeteries of La Daurade, Toulouse.

Chapter 7

1. Archives Nationales, Paris, Dossier d'Alençon, S 6160, cited in Antoinette Fleury, "Le Testament dans la coutume de Paris au XVIᵉ siècle" (Thesis, Ecole Nationale des Chartes [Nogent-le-Rotrou: Imprimerie Daupeley, 1943]).

2. ANMC, 75:364 (1690).

3. ANMC, 119:355 (1708).

4. ANMC, 55:1156 (1723).

5. Will of Louis de Rouvroy, duc de Saint-Simon (1754), in A. Dupouy, ed., *Extraits des Mémoires de Saint-Simon* (Paris: Larousse, 1930), 4:199.

6. ANMC, 75:109 (1660).

7. ANMC, 75:94 (1657).

8. ANMC, 75:66 (1648).

9. ANMC, 120:355 (1708).

10. ANMC, 75:80 (1652).

11. See Jacques-Bénigne Winslow, *Dissertation sur l'incertitude des signes de la mort et de l'abus des enterrements et embaumements précipités,* trans. from Latin with commentary by Jacques-Jean Bruhier d'Ablaincourt (Paris, 1740).

12. See E. de Martino, *Morte e pianto rituale nel mondo antico* (Turin: Einaudi, 1958).

13. Coraly de Gaïx, *Oeuvres* (Paris, 1912).

14. The comte de Latresne versus his sister-in-law, the marquise de Noé. Will dated 1757. AD Haute-Garonne, SE 11808.

15. Marin Le Roy de Gomberville, *La Doctrine des moeurs* (Paris, 1946).

16. Jan Molenaer, *Family Portrait*, Rijksmuseum, Amsterdam, 1635 A3. In another painting in the Rijksmuseum, Dierik Jacoby's *Portrait of Man with Death's Head*, children play with fruit and animals, a young woman holds a flower crown, and the paterfamilias holds a death's head.

17. Gerard Dou, Geneva Museum, No. 1949–12.

18. André Chastel, "L'Art et le sentiment de la mort," *Revue du XVIIᵉ siècle*, nos. 36–37 (1957), p. 293.

19. See Frederick Parkes Weber, *Aspects of Death* (London: T. Fisher Unwin, 1918), cited in Theodore Spencer, *Death and Elizabethan Tragedy* (Cambridge: Harvard University Press, 1936).

20. For a reproduction of such mourning rings, see David E. Stannard, *The Puritan Way of Death* (New York: Oxford University Press, 1977), fig. 7, p. 114.

21. Emile Mâle, *L'Art religieux de la fin du Moyen Age* (Paris: Armand Colin, 1931), p. 353.

22. See Michel Vovelle, *Mourir autrefois* (Paris: Gallimard, 1974), pp. 163ff.

23. Louis de Rouvroy, duc de Saint-Simon, *Mémoires,* ed. A. de Boislisle (Paris: Hachette, 1927), 39:59–62.

24. See Jacques-Bénigne Bossuet, *Sermon sur la mort pour le Samedi Saint* in *Oeuvres* (Paris, Pléiade, 1961), pp. 1073ff.

25. Joly de Fleury Papers.

26. Orest Ranum, *Les Parisiens au XVIIᵉ siècle* (Paris: Armand Colin, 1973), p. 320.

27. Viviers, AD Haute-Garonne B, *procédure* 497. Reference supplied by Yves Castan, personal communication.

28. F. Burgess, *English Churchyard Memorials* (London: Lutterworth Press, 1963), p. 50

29. Ibid.

30. For Virginian tombs and cemeteries I have drawn on Patrick Henry Butler's unpublished thesis "On the Memorial Art of Tidewater Virginia," Johns Hopkins University, June 1969.

31. See David E. Stannard, ed., *Death in America* (Philadelphia: University of Pennsylvania Press, 1975).

32. See Max Fumaroli, "Les Mémoires du XVIIᵉ siècle," *Revue du XVIIᵉ siècle*, nos. 94–95 (1971), pp. 7–37.

33. R. Balton (London, 1635), cited in Stannard, *Puritan Way of Death.*

34. Cited by Chateaubriand in *La Vie de Rancé* (Paris, 1844).

35. Reproduced in Emile Mâle. *L'Art religieux de la fin du XVIᵉ siècle* (Paris: Armand Colin, 1951), p. 221.

36. See A. Bulifon, *Guida de foresteiri* (Naples, 1708).

37. Gomberville, *La Doctrine des moeurs*, pp. 100–102.

38. Samuel Steward, cited in Stannard, *Puritan Way of Death.*

39. See Pierre Muret, *Cérémonies funèbres de toutes les nations* (Paris, 1679).

40. *The Colloquies of Erasmus*, trans. Craig R. Thomson (Chicago and London: University of Chicago Press, 1965), p. 70.

41. *La Grande et Nécessaire Police* (Paris: Nicolas Alexandre, 1619), extracts in Dr. Gannal, *Les Cimetières de Paris*, vol. 1 (Paris, 1884).

42. Montapalach, July 1758, AD Haute-Garonne B, *procédures* 360 and 375.

43. See F. Lebrun, *Les Hommes et la mort en Anjou* (Paris and The Hague: Mouton, 1971), p. 480.

44. Reproduced in E. Hugues, *Histoire de la restauration du protestantisme en France au XVIIIᵉ siècle* (Paris, 1875), 2:424. Supplied by P. Joutard.

45. Cited in Gilbert Lély, *Sade, étude sur sa vie et son oeuvre* (Paris: Gallimard, 1967), pp. 350–52.

46. Jan Potocki, *Manuscrit trouvé à Saragosse*, ed. Roger Caillois (Paris: Gallimard, 1958), p. 235.

Chapter 8

1. See L. C. F. Garmanni [Christian Friedrich Garmann], *De miraculis mortuorum* (Dresden and Leipzig, 1709).

2. See Michel Foucault, *Naissance de la clinique* (Paris: Presses Universitaires de France, 1963).

3. See Philippe Ariès, *Essais sur l'histoire de la mort en Occident du Moyen Age à nos jours* (Paris: Seuil, 1975), pp. 123ff.

4. See R. E. Giesey, *The Royal Funeral Ceremony in Renaissance France* (Geneva: Droz, 1960).

5. Lawrence J. Stone, *The Crisis of the Aristocracy* (Oxford: Oxford University Press, 1965), p. 579. The "brann" in question is matting.

6. ANMC, 75:80 (1652).

7. ANMC, 119:355 (1771).

8. Jean-Antoine Chaptal, *Mes Souvenirs* (Paris, 1893), cited in L. Delaunay, *La Vie médicale des XVIᵉ, XVIIᵉ, XVIIIᵉ siècles* (Paris, 1935).

9. ANMC, 75:142 (1669).

10. M. Aymard, "Une Famille de l'aristocratie sicilienne," *Revue historique*, January–March 1972, p. 32.

11. Will of Louis de Rouvroy, duc de Saint-Simon (1754), in A. Dupouy, ed., *Extraits des Mémoires de Saint-Simon* (Paris: Larousse, 1930), 4:199.

12. Cited in David E. Stannard, *The Puritan Way of Death* (New York: Oxford University Press, 1977).

13. ANMC, 75:489 (1712).

14. ANMC, 105:1156 (1723).

15. Denis Diderot et al., eds., *Encyclopédie, ou Dictionnaire raisonné des sciences, des arts, et des métiers*, 28 vols. (Paris, 1759–72), s.v. "Anatomie."

16. See R. Aubert, ed., *Journal de Célestin Guittard de Floriban, bourgeois de Paris sous la Révolution* (Paris: France-Empire, 1974).

17. Diderot, *Encyclopédie*, s.v. "Anatomie."

18. Antoine Furetière, *Dictionnaire universal* (Rotterdam, 1690), s.v. "Anatomie."

19. Cited in Jean Rousset, *La Littérature à l'âge baroque en France* (Paris: José Corti, 1954), p. 10.

20. André Chastel, "L'Art et le sentiment de la mort," *Revue du XVIIe siècle*, nos. 36–37 (1957), pp. 288–93.

21. Marquis de Sade, *La Marquise de Gange* (Paris: Pauvert, 1961), p. 238.

22. I. Ringhieri, *Dialoghi della vita et dello morte* (Bologna, 1550), cited in Tenenti, *Il senso*, pp. 327 and 357, n. 52; see also André Chastel in *Le Baroque et la mort* (The Third International Congress of Humanist Studies, Rome, 1955), pp. 33–46.

23. Marquis de Sade, *Juliette* (Paris: Pauvert, 1954), 4:21.

24. Joly de Fleury Papers.

25. Louis Sébastien Mercier, *Le Tableau de Paris* (Paris, 1789), 9:177ff., 139–41.

26. René de Chateaubriand, *Mémoires d'outre-tombe*, ed. E. Biré (Paris: Garnier, 1925), 2:122.

27. *Journal de Barbier* (Paris: Charpentier, 1857), 2:453, see "March 1734."

28. Dierik Bouts, *The Martyrdom of Saint Erasmus*, Saint Peter's Church, Louvain. The same peculiarly placid attitude of both executioner and victim may be seen in Bouts's *Martyrdom of Saint Hyppolite* (Bruges), as well as in Gerard Dou's portrayal of the meticulous flaying alive of the unjust judge, also in Bruges.

29. Rousset, *L'Age baroque*, pp. 82–83.

30. Ibid., p. 88.

31. See R. Gadenne, "Les Spectacles d'horreur de P. Camus," *Revue du XVIIe siècle*, no. 92, pp. 25–36.

32. Rousset, *L'Age baroque*, p. 84.

33. Pierre-Jean Jouve, *Paulina 1880* (Paris, 1925).

34. Cited in Leo Spitzer, "The Problem of Latin Renaissance Poetry," in *Studies in the Renaissance* 2 (New York: Renaissance Society of America, 1955), pp. 118–38.

35. Bologna Museum.

36. Cited in Mario Praz, *The Romantic Agony* (London: William Collins, Fontana Library, 1960), p. 120.

37. See Rousset, *L'Age baroque;* also Theodore Spencer, *Death and Elizabethan Tragedy* (Cambridge: Harvard University Press, 1936).

38. See Rousset, *L'Age baroque.*

39. See Jacques-Bénigne Winslow, *Dissertation sur l'incertitude des signes de la mort et de l'abus des enterrements et embaumements précipités*, trans. from Latin with commentary by Jacques-Jean Bruhier d'Ablaincourt (Paris, 1740).

40. Ibid., 1:61.

41. Sade, *Juliette*, 6:70ff., 270–71.

42. Jan Potocki, *Manuscrit trouvé à Saragosse*, ed. Roger Caillois (Paris: Gallimard, 1958).

43. Mme. Dunoyer, *Lettres et histoires galantes* (Amsterdam, 1780), 1:275.

44. Ibid., 1:313.

45. L. Lenormand, *Des Inhumations précipitées* (Macon, 1843), p. 34; see also E. Bouchot, *Traité des signes de la mort* (Paris, 1883).

46. See Joly de Fleury Papers.

47. See A. P. Scieluna, *The Church of Saint John in Valletta* (Malta, 1955), p. 161.

48. *Extraits des Mémoires de Saint-Simon.*

49. Dunoyer, *Lettres et histoires galantes;* see also Lawrence J. Stone, *The Family, Sex and Marriage in England 1500–1800* (London: Weidenfeld and Nicolson, 1977), p. 250, on Lord Spencer's visit to the crypt.

50. See Spencer, *Death and Elizabethan Tragedy*, p. 225.

51. J.-C. Herold, *Germaine Necker de Staël* (Paris: Plon, 1962), pp. 561, 137, 484.

52. See Michel Vovelle, *L'Irrésistible Ascension de Joseph Sec, bourgeois d'Aix* (Aix-en-Provence: EDISUR, 1975).

53. See *Journal de Barbier*, see "1723."

54. Mary Shelley, "Author's Introduction," in *Frankenstein: Or, The New Prometheus* (New York: New American Library, 1965).

55. Potocki, *Manuscrit trouvé à Saragosse*, pp. 74–75.

56. Sade, *Juliette*, vol 4; on the remarks of Pope Braschi 6:170, 269.

57. See Georges Bataille, *L'Erotisme* (Paris: Minuit, 1961).

Chapter 9

1. Deschambre, *Dictionnaire encyclopédique des sciences medicales* (Paris, 1876), s.v. "Mort."

2. See H. Sauval, *Histoire et recherches des antiquités de Paris* (Paris, 1724), 1:415.

3. Jacques-Bénigne Winslow, *Dissertation sur l'incertitude des signes de la mort et de l'abus des enterrements et embaumements précipités,* trans. from Latin with commentary by Jacques-Jean Bruhier d'Ablaincourt (Paris, 1740).

4. Ibid., 1:151. L. G. Stevenson discusses the relationship between apparent death and anaesthesia in "Suspended Animation and the History of Anaesthesia," *Bulletin of the History of Medicine,* 49 (1975): 482–511.

5. Foederé, *Dictionnaire médical* (Paris, 1813), 3:188.

6. Mme. Dunoyer, *Lettres et histoires galantes* (Amsterdam, 1780), 1:177–78.

7. Winslow, *Signes de la mort,* 1:49–50.

8. ANMC, 75:117 (1662); 75:146 (1669).

9. ANMC, 119:355 (1768).

10. ANMC, 75:364 (1690); 42:399 (1743).

11. ANMC, Paris, S6160 (1696); vol. 119, will dated 21 June 1790.

12. ANMC, 12:635 (1855).

13. *Dictionnaire des sciences médicales en soixante tomes* (Paris, 1818), s.v. "Inhumation."

14. See Deschambre, *Dictionnaire . . . des sciences médicales,* s.v. "Mort" and "Cadavre."

15. E. Bouchot, *Traité des signes de la mort et des moyens de prévenir les inhumations prématurées* (Paris, 1883), p. 402.

Chapter 10

1. Coraly de Gaïx, *Oeuvres* (Paris, 1912), p. 112.

2. René de Chateaubriand, *René* (Geneva: Editions du Milieu du Monde), p. 143.

3. Gaïx, *Oeuvres,* p. 61.

4. Denis Diderot et al. eds., *Encyclopédie, ou Dictionnaire raisonné des sciences, des artes, et des métiers,* 28 vols. (Paris, 1759–72), s.v. "Mort."

5. Alphonse de Lamartine, *Méditations* (1820).

6. Mme. Augustus Craven, née La Ferronays [Pauline Marie Armande Aglaé Craven], *Récit d'une soeur: Souvenirs de famille,* 11th ed., 2 vols. (Paris: Didier, 1867).

7. Mme. Fernand de La Ferronays, *Mémoires* (Paris, 1899), p. 212.

8. Craven, *Récit d'une soeur,* 1:224.

9. Ibid., 1:35.

10. Ibid., 1:63.

11. Ibid., 1:103.

12. Ibid., 1:308.

13. Ibid., 1:335.

14. Ibid., 1:365.

15. Ibid., 2:21–22.

16. Ibid., 2:125.

17. Ibid., 1:446.

18. Ibid., 2:317.

19. Ibid., 2:327ff.

20. Ibid., 2:400–403.

21. Alphonse de Lamartine, "Le Crucifix," in *Nouvelles Méditations poétiques* (1823).

22. Craven, *Récit d'une soeur,* 2:414–15.

23. Gaïx, *Oeuvres,* pp. 252–53.

24. Emily Brontë, *Complete Poems* (New York: Columbia University Press, 1941).

25. See Charlotte Brontë, *Jane Eyre* (Harmondsworth, England: Penguin Books, 1966), pp. 108–14.

26. Emily Brontë, *Wuthering Heights* (Harmondsworth, England: Penguin Books, 1965).

27. Alphonse de Lamartine, *Harmonies poétiques et religieuses* (1830).

28. See Mario Praz, *The Romantic Agony* (London: William Collins, Fontana Library, 1960).

29. Emily Brontë, *Wuthering Heights*, Introduction, p. 14.

30. Ibid., pp. 319–22.

31. See Lewis O. Saum, "Death in Pre–Civil War America," in David E. Stannard, ed., *Death in America* (Philadelphia: University of Pennsylvania Press, 1975), pp. 30–48.

32. Ann Douglas, "Heaven Our Home: Consolation Literature in the Northern U.S., 1830–1880," in Stannard, *Death in America*, pp. 49–68.

33. Mark Twain, *Huckleberry Finn* (New York: Harper & Row, 1962).

34. Charlotte Brontë, *Jane Eyre*, p. 346.

35. Ibid., p. 444.

36. Ibid., see pp. 108–14.

37. Maurice Lanoire, *Réflexions sur la survie* (Paris: Debresse, 1971); see also "Transcendances" (Mimeographed, 1975).

38. ANMC, 75:95 (1657).

39. Gilbert Grimaud, "Liturgie sacrée," in Gulielmus Durandus, *Rationale divinorum officiorum*, trans. Charles Barthélémy (Paris, 1854), 5:290.

40. ANMC, 75:94 (1657).

41. See Gaby and Michel Vovelle, *Vision de la mort et de l'au-delà en Provence d'après les autels des âmes du Purgatoire, XVe–XXe siècles*, Cahiers des Annales, no. 29 (Paris: Armand Colin, 1970).

42. François de Salignac de La Mothe-Fénelon, *Lettres spirituelles*, no. 224 (12 November 1701), *Oeuvres complètes* (1851), 58:591, cited in Vladimir Jankélévitch, *La Mort* (Paris: Flammarion, 1966).

43. Jules Michelet, *La Sorcière* (Paris: Julliard, 1964), p. 33, 93–95.

44. ANMC, 75:987 (1811).

45. ANMC, 119:355 (1774).

46. ANMC, (1778).

47. See ANMC, (1775).

48. ANMC, 12:635 (1844).

49. Charles Baudelaire, *Oeuvres complètes* (Paris: Gallimard, 1951).

Chapter 11

1. See L. C. F. Garmanni [Christian Friedrich Garmann], *De miraculis mortuorum* (Dresden and Leipzig, 1709).

2. Philippe Ariès, *Essais sur l'histoire de la mort* (Paris: Seuil, 1975), p. 116.

3. See *La Grande et Nécessaire Police* (Paris: Nicolas Alexandre, 1619), extracts in Dr. Gannal, *Les Cimetières de Paris*, vol. 1 (Paris, 1884).

4. Cited in Madeleine Foizil, "Les Attitudes devant la mort au XVIIIe siècle: Sépultures et suppression des sépultures dans le cimetière parisien des Saints-Innocents," *Revue historique*, April–June 1974, pp. 303–30.

5. Abbé C. G. Porée, *Lettres sur la sépulture dans les églises* (Caen, 1745).

6. Foizil, "Attitudes devant la mort."

7. Joly de Fleury Papers, no. 1207.

8. The Joly de Fleury Papers and the medical literature upon which I rely here have recently informed the researches of a number of American historians: R. A. Etlin, "Landscapes of Eternity: Funerary Architecture and the Cemetery, 1793–1881," *Oppositions*, no. 8 (1977); "L'Air dans l'architecture des Lumières," *Dix-huitième siècle*, no. 9 (1977); O. and C. Hannaway, "La Fermeture des Innocents," ibid.

9. See O. and C. Hannaway, "Fermeture des Innocents."

10. Hughes Maret, *Mémoire sur l'usage où l'on est d'enterrer les morts dans les eglises et dans l'enceinte des villes* (Dijon, 1773), p. 36.

11. P. Toussaint Navier, *Réflexions sur le danger des exhumations précipitées et sur les*

abus des inhumations dans les églises, suivies d'observations sur les plantations d'arbres dans les cimetières (Paris, 1775).

12. Félix Vicq d'Azyr, *Essai sur les lieux et les dangers des sépultures* [*Oeuvres complètes*, vol. 6 (Paris, 1778)]: a translation from Scipione Giovanni Buonagiunta Piattoli.

13. Ariès, *Essais*, p. 123.

14. Navier, *Danger des exhumations.*

15. Vicq d'Azyr, *Les Lieux et les dangers.*

16. Navier, *Danger des exhumations.*

17. Joly de Fleury Papers.

18. Ibid.

19. Ibid.

20. *Mémoire des curés de Paris*, Joly de Fleury Papers.

21. *Réflexions au sujet de l'arrêt des cimetières*, Joly de Fleury Papers.

22. *Lettre de M. M[olé] à M. J[amet le jeune] sur les moyens de tranférer les cimetières hors de l'enceinte des villes* (Paris: November 1776).

23. Order of Loménie de Brienne, archbishop of Toulouse, 23 March 1775, cited in Gannal, *Cimetières de Paris.*

24. M. Cadet de Vaux, *Mémoire historique sur le cimetière des Innocents*, read at the Académie Royale des Sciences in 1781, cited in Gannal, *Cimetières de Paris*, p. 86.

25. Louis Sébastien Mercier, *Les Tableaux de Paris* (Paris, 1789), 10:190.

26. See Maxime du Camp, *Paris*, vol. 3 (Paris, 1875); M. Agulhon, *Pénitents et Francs-Maçons dans l'ancienne Provence* (Paris: Fayard, 1967).

27. Michel Augustin Thouret, *Rapport sur les exhumations du cimetière et de l'église des Saints-Innocents*, read at the meeting of the Société royale de médecine at the Louvre March 3, 1789 (Paris, 1789).

28. Joly de Fleury Papers.

29. *Rapport sur les sépultures présenté à l'Administration centrale du département de la Seine par le citoyen Cambry* (Paris, Year VII [1799]).

30. Amaury Duval, *Des Sépultures* (Paris, Year IX [1801]).

31. See *Rapport sur les sépultures.*

32. See François Valentin Mulot, *Vues sur les sépultures à propos d'un rapport sur les sépultures de Daubermesnil*, read at the Council of Five Hundred, 21 Brumaire, Year V (Paris, 1796). This was the report which led to the Departement of the Seine's passage, on 4 Floréal, Year VII (1799), of its decree on funerals.

33. François Victor Alphonse Aulard, *Paris pendant la réaction thermidorienne et sous le Directoire*, 5 vols. (Paris, 1898–1902), 5:698–99.

34. *Rapport de l'Administration des travaux publics sur les cimetières*, read to the Conseil général by citizen Avril.

35. Report to the Conseil général of the Departement of the Seine, 15 Thermidor, Year VIII (3 August 1800).

36. *Sépultures publiques et particulières* (Paris, Year IX [1801]).

37. J. de Girard, *Des Tombeaux et de l'influence des institutions funèbres sur les moeurs* (Paris, Year IX [1801]).

38. Duval, *Des Sépultures.*

39. Girard, *Des Tombeaux;* Dr. Robinet, *Paris sans cimetières* (Paris, 1869).

40. Duval, *Des Sépultures.*

41. *Sépultures publiques.*

42. Girard, *Des Tombeaux.*

43. Duval, *Des Sépultures.*

44. *Sépultures publiques.*

45. Girard, *Des Tombeaux.*

46. Ibid.

47. G. F. Coyer, *Etrennes aux morts et aux vivants* (Paris, 1768).

48. See Foizil, "Attitudes devant la mort."

49. Pierre Giraud, *Les Tombeaux, ou essai sur les sépultures* (Paris, 1801).

50. Léon de Lanzac de Laborie, *Paris sous Napoléon: La Vie et la mort* (Paris, 1906).

51. See Préfecture de la Seine, Directions des Affaires Municipales, Bureau des Cimetières, *Note sur les cimetières de la Ville de Paris* (1889).

52. L. Bertoglio, *Les Cimetières* (Paris, 1889),

53. Lanzac de Laborie, *Paris sous Napoléon.*

54. François Victor Alphonse Aulard, *Paris sous le Consulat*, 4 vols. (Paris, 1903–09), 2:735.

55. MM. Richard and XXX, *Le Véritable Conducteur aux cimetières du Père-Lachaise, Montmartre, Montparnasse et Vaugirard* (Paris, 1836).

56. Abbé Jaques Delille, *Les Jardins* (Paris, 1782).

57. See Michel Vovelle, *L'Irrésistible Ascension de Joseph Sec, bourgeois d'Aix* (Aix-en-Provence: EDISUR, 1975).

58. René de Chateaubriand, *Mémoires d'outre-tombe*, ed. E. Biré (Paris: Garnier, 1925), 1:xiv, 445.

59. For the Howard mausoleum, see J. Summerson, *Architecture in Britain, 1530 to 1830* (Harmondsworth, England: Penguin Books, 1953), pl. 106 and pp. 177–78. The existence of this mausoleum and the discussion of it just cited were brought to my attention by I. Lavin. Lawrence J. Stone evokes a similar case in West Wycombe, Buckinghamshire, England, in his *The Family, Sex and Marriage in England, 1500–1800* (London: Weidenfeld and Nicolson, 1977), p. 226 and p. 712, n. 3.

60. Angelo Rinaldi, cited in J. Piatier, *Le Monde* (Paris), 30–31 May 1971.

61. Eugene Le Roy, *Jacquou le croquant* (Paris, 1899).

62. S. French, "The Cemetery as a Cultural Institution," in David E. Stannard, ed., *Death in America* (Philadelphia: University of Pennsylvania Press, 1975), p. 75.

63. See J. W. Draper, *The Funeral Elegy and the Rise of English Romanticism* (New York: Octagon Books, 1967 [1929]).

64. Delille, *Les Jardins.*

65. Alphonse de Lamartine, *Méditations poétiques* (1820).

66. Ann Douglas, "Heaven Our Home: Consolation Literature in the Northern U.S., 1830–1880," in Stannard, *Death in America*, p. 61.

67. Léon Bloy, *La Femme pauvre* (1897).

68. MM. Richard and XXX, *Le Véritable Conducteur.*

69. Mgr. Gaume, *Le Cimetière au XIXᵉ siècle* (Paris, n.d. [late nineteenth century]).

70. London correspondent, *Le Monde* (Paris), 18 December 1962.

71. P. Ferran, *Le Livre des épitaphes* (Paris: Editions Ouvrières, 1973).

72. French, in Stannard, *Death in America*, pp. 68–91.

73. See E. V. Gillon, *Victorian Cemetery Art* (New York: Dover, 1972).

74. French, in Stannard, *Death in America.*

75. Walters Gallery, Baltimore, no. 1520.

76. Le Roy, *Jacquou.*

77. Memorandum on the cemeteries of Paris presented by the préfet de la Seine at the hôtel de Ville, 1844.

78. See Chenel, *Sur un Projet de cimetière et de chemin de fer municipal ou mortuaire* (Paris, 1868).

79. Guérard, *Visite au cimetière* (Paris, 1850).

80. Bertoglio, *Les Cimetières.*

81. J.-F.-E. Chardouillet, *Les Cimetières sont-ils des foyers d'infection?* (Paris, 1881).

82. Ibid.

83. Bertoglio, *Les Cimetières.*

84. Robinet, *Paris sans cimetière.*

85. Pierre Laffitte, *Considérations générales à propos des cimetières de Paris* (Paris, 1874).

86. Ibid.

87. Ibid.

88. Ibid.

89. Chardouillet, *Les Cimetières . . . ?*

90. J. Brunfaut [a partisan of removal to Mery-sur-Oise], *La Nécropole de*

Méry-sur-Oise: De Nouveaux Services à créer pour les inhumations parisiennes (Paris, 1876).

91. Ibid.

92. A. Lenoir [of the Institut], *Cimetières de Paris. Oeuvre des sépultures* (Paris, 1864).

93. Ibid.

94. Gaume, *Cimetière au XIXᵉ siècle.*

95. Although in the foregoing I have taken Paris as my example, any of the principal provincial cities of France would have served as well. R. Bertrand, working under the direction of P. Guiral, has taken the same situation in Marseilles as the subject of a master's thesis. Bertrand's thesis has been summarized as "Une Contribution à l'histoire du sentiment. Cimetières et pratiques funéraires à Marseille du milieu du XVIIIᵉ siècle à la fin du XIXᵉ," *Les Conférences de l'Institut historique de Marseille,* January–February 1970, pp. 264–67. "Thus what was a place of horror in the eighteenth century," notes Bertrand, "had been transformed within less than a century into an object of pride and reverence."

96. See F. Martin, *Les Cimetières de la crémation* (Paris, 1881).

97. See Faucheux and Revel, *Les Tombes des pauvres* (Lyons, 1903).

98. Françoise Zonabend, "Les Morts et les vivants," *Etudes rurales,* no 52 (1973).

99. Ariès, *Essais sur l'histoire de la mort,* pp. 141–42.

100. Compare this attitude also with that of the slaves and poor of ancient Rome: "When a man of the people had been able to provide the most urgent necessity, that of his daily bread, the two next most imperious needs were the need for banquets [the indispensable luxury] and the need for tombs." Paul Veyne, *Le Pain et le cirque* (Paris: Seuil, 1976), p. 291.

101. See Josué de Castro, "Sept Pieds de terre et un cercueil," *Esprit,* 1965, p. 610.

Chapter 12

1. See Mark Twain, "Was It Heaven? Or Hell?" in *The Complete Short Stories of Mark Twain,* ed. Charles Neider (Garden City, N.J.: Doubleday, 1957), pp. 472–88.

2. See R. Aubert, ed., *Journal de Célestin Guittard de Floriban, bourgeois de Paris sous la Révolution* (Paris: France-Empire, 1974).

3. P. Ribes, "Ethique, science et mort," *Etudes,* November 1974, p. 494, cited in Philippe Ariès, *Essais sur l'histoire de la mort en Occident du Moyen Age à nos jours* (Paris: Seuil, 1975), p. 208.

4. See Geoffrey Gorer, *Death, Grief and Mourning in Contemporary Britain* (Garden City, N.J.: Doubleday, 1965).

5. Vladimir Jankélévitch, *La Mort* (Paris: Flammarion, 1966), p. 229.

6. Ibid., p. 202.

7. L. Witzel, *British Medical Journal,* 1975 (no. 2), p. 82.

8. See B. G. Glaser and A. L. Strauss, *Awareness of Dying* (Chicago: Aldine, 1965); Ariès, *Essais sur l'histoire de la mort,* p. 173.

9. Witzel, p. 82.

10. Gorer, *Death, Grief and Mourning,* p. 13; see also Ariès, *Essais sur l'histoire de la mort,* pp. 180–89.

11. *Psychology Today,* June 1971, pp. 43–72.

12. Gorer, *Death, Grief and Mourning,* pp. 35–36.

13. Ibid., p. 45.

14. Ibid., pp. 77–78.

15. Fernand Dumont, in *Les Religions populaires* (Quebec: Presses de l'Université Laval, 1972), p. 29.

16. Gorer, *Death, Grief and Mourning,* p. 128.

17. Ibid., p. 111.

18. Ibid.

19. See Colin Murray Parkes, *Bereavement: Studies of Grief in Adult Life* (New York: International Universities Press, 1973); Lily Pincus, *Death and the Family* (New York: Vintage Books, 1975).

20. See H. de Campion, *Mémoires,* ed. Marc Fumaroli (Paris: Mercure de France, 1967).

21. See W. D. Rees and S. G. Lutkins, "Mortality of Bereavement," *British Medical*

Journal 4 (7 October 1967): 13–16, cited by
Louis Lasagna, in Orville G. Brim, Jr., et al.,
eds., *The Dying Patient* (New York: Russell
Sage Foundation, 1970), p. 80.

22. S. Harsenty, "Les Survivants," *Esprit,*
March 1976, p. 478.

23. See Robert S. Morrison, Preface to Brim,
Dying Patient.

24. See Glaser and Strauss, *Awareness of
Dying.*

25. Ibid.

26. David Sudnow, "Dying in a Public
Hospital," in Brim, *Dying Patient,* p. 197.

27. Sol Levine and Norman A. Scotch,
"Dying as an Emerging Social Problem," in
Brim, *Dying Patient,* p. 214.

28. H. Feifel, *The Meaning of Death* (New
York: McGraw-Hill, 1959).

29. Elisabeth Kübler-Ross, *On Death and
Dying* (New York: Macmillan, 1969); see also
V. Thomas, *L'Anthropologie de la mort*
(Paris: Payot, 1975).

30. See Ivan Illich, *Medical Nemesis: The
Expropriation of Health* (New York:
Pantheon, 1976).

31. Claudine Herzlich, "Le Travail de la
mort," *Annales: Economies, sociétés,
civilisations,* 31, no. 1 (January–February
1976): 214.

32. John W. Riley, Jr., "What People Think
About Death," in Brim, *Dying Patient,* p. 36.

33. *Psychology Today,* June 1971, pp 43–72.

34. See Roger Caillois, *Quatre Essais de
sociologie contemporaine* (Paris: Perrin, 1951).

35. See Jessica Mitford, *The American Way
of Death* (New York: Simon & Schuster,
1963).

36. Ann Douglas, "Heaven Our Home:
Consolation Literature in the Northern U.S.,
1830–1880," in David E. Stannard, ed., *Death
in America* (Philadelphia: University of
Pennsylvania Press, 1975), p. 61.

37. See Mitford, *American Way of Death,*
pp. 200–201.

38. Ibid., p. 233.

Index

abbey. *See* monastery and abbey
Abraham, bosom of, 26, 153–4
absolution and benediction, 140–2, 152, 176, 178, 248
acceptance of death, 8–9, 15–16, 27–8, 118. *See also* indifference: to death
ad sanctos. *See* burial: *ad sanctos*
afterlife, beliefs about, 22–5 *passim*, 95–6, 106; as flower garden, 25–6; pause between earth and paradise, 147–8; uncertainty about salvation, 150–4, 160; popular vs. clerical, 161; expressed in funerary figures, 266–8; in American settlers' letters, 449–50; in American consolation literature, 453; in C. Brontë and the La Ferronays, 458; 19th–20th c., 471–2; modern decline of belief in, 573, 576; and tame death, 604–605; and death of self, 606; and romantic death, 611. *See also* hell and damnation; Last Judgment; paradise; purgatory
Ages of Man, 299, 329
alms: to children and poor in funeral procession, 165–8; on anniversary of death, 178. *See also* endowments and legacies: charitable
altars, multiple, 159–60, 173–81 *passim*, 187–8
Amat, Françoise, marquise de Solliers, 323, 363
American attitudes toward death: as expressed in cemeteries, 339–40, 531–3, 534, 550; in settlers' letters, 446–50; in consolation literature, 450–4, 457, 526, 528, 596; of children, 447, 460, 597; private burial, 522; dignity of dying, 589–93; and social/economic classes, 594; overview, 596–601

American cemeteries: Mount Auburn (Mass.), 531–3; Arlington (Va.), 550–1; Forest Lawn (Calif.), 600
anatomy, 364–9. *See also* dissection
"antiepitaph," 228–9
apparent death, 396–404. *See also* burial: premature; fear: of being buried alive
artes moriendi: and moment of death, 105; iconography of, 107–10; and macabre, 112, 127; and *transi*, 114; new phase (14th–15th c.), 129–30; and wills, 196; new style (16th c.), 303–305; and beautiful death, 310. *See also* death: moment of
Arthur, King. *See* Round Table, stories of
art of dying well. See *artes moriendi*
ashes: and dust, as theme of macabre, 111–12; dead exhibited on, 162; of cremation, scattered, 577
aspersion with holy water, 141–2
asylum, right of in cemeteries, 62–4, 68, 552
Augustine, Saint, 41, 96, 188
avaritia, 130–1, 194–5, 308, 309; and still life (art form), 132–7, 332; and *odium Dei*, 310; end of, 333. *See also* temporalia
Ave Maria, 18, 301, 607
Aymeric, Canon of Toulouse, 251–2, 255

Balzac, Honoré de, 448–9, 564
basilicas, 34–40. *See also* saints: burial of
Bataille, Georges, 22, 393
Baudelaire, Pierre Charles, 468, 473–4
beautiful death, 310–12, 374, 409–11, 460, 473, 610; in La Ferronays family, 419, 427, 430; in America, 449, 451; gives way to "dirty death," 569–70; in Jankélévitch, 571–2; in film *Dying*, 590

Begon, Abbot of Conques, 212, 247
Bellarmine, Robert, on: preparation for death, 299, 304; *mors repentina*, 307; death of criminals, 308; *temporalia*, 309; position for dying, 311; indifference to death, 313; *De arte bene moriendi*, 443
benediction and absolution, 140–2, 152, 176, 178, 248
benefactors of the Church: burial in church (early Middle Ages), 46–7; prayers for, 149, 151; and general economic situation, 191–3
bequests. *See* alms; endowments and legacies
Bernini, Gianlorenzo, 333, 377
biography: life as, 103–106, 138; and funerary inscriptions, 217, 222–30
Blair, Robert: "The Grave" (1743), 347
body [Used in reference to individual dead. For collective sense, *see* dead, the. For medical and scientific sense, *see* cadaver]
concealment of, 168–73, 206, 607–608. *See also* body: exhibition of; shrouds; winding sheet
dismemberment of, 145, 205–206, 208, 261–2, 361, 387. *See also* dissection
exhibition of, 127, 245, 246, 381, 508–509. *See also* body: concealment of; funeral home
presence of in church during service, 172, 176–8
preservation of: and preservation of soul, 261; concern for, 292; natural, 359, 360; delays "absolute death," 404; commended by Duval and Girard, 508–509. *See also* cremation; embalming; mummies; vitrification
sensibility of, after death, 355–61 *passim*, 381, 389, 390
separation of, from soul. *See* soul: separation from body
transportation of, 145, 169–70, 205–206, 261–2, 361, 497, 504–506. *See also* funeral procession
wrapping of, 145, 164, 261. *See also* body: concealment of; shrouds; winding sheet
bones: exhibition of, 59–61; separate burial of, 262, 382; curative powers, 358. *See also* exhumation; ossuaries
biography and funerary inscriptions, 217, 222–30
book (as symbol), 103–106, 149, 151
book of hours, 114–15; of Rohan, 114–15, 248–9; of Jean, duc de Berry, 134–5
Bosch, Hieronymous, 106, 131
Bossuet, Jacques-Bénigne, on: acceptance of death, 21; tombs of the great, 335; contemplation of death, 342–4; opening tombs, 385
Bourget, Paul: *Outre-Mer*, 27–8
Bouts Dierik, 135, 370, 371

brain death, 585, 586
Breton burial customs, 60–1
Brontë, Charlotte: *Jane Eyre*, 434–6, 455–6, 457–8, 462
Brontë Emily, 433, 436–42; *Wuthering Heights*, 341, 360, 433, 436, 442–6, 456–7, 527
Brontë family, 431–46
brotherhood, universal, 149–51 *passim*
Burgundy, dukes of, 166, 187, 235
burial:
ad sanctos, 32–40; antecedents of, 32–3; inscriptions attesting to, 33; for outcasts, 45; and Church law, 46; replaced by burial *apud ecclesiam*, 71–3, 289; takes on a function of the visible tomb, 215–16; only for the rich, 320; disputed (18th c.), 479; and Decree of 1763, 483; modern interpretation (19th c.), 546. *See also* basilicas; saints: burial of
as charitable act, 184–7, 207
choice of, 17, 190; of early Christians, 31; hierarchy of desirable locations, 72–4, 78–92; for women, 74, 75, 76, 77; with family, 74–7, 289–92 (*See also* family burial places); for servants, 77; in Parisian wills, 125–6; in Régnier and Villon, 200; at frequented site, 220; by French Protestants, 315–17; *See also* burial: site of; will
in church, 45–51, 71–7; location within church, 78–82; vs. cemetery, 82–92 and *tables;* and Decree of 1763, 485; and edict of Archbishop of Toulouse (1775), 493–4
of criminals, 42–5
depth of, 235–6, 359–60
double, 54, 58, 208, 262, 382–3, 482
family areas. *See* family burial places
fees: 9th c., 39; and Church canons, 50; 17th c., 55–6; to parish churches, 74; 16th–17th c., 86–7; in Decree of 1763, 485; in 1806 decree, 519. *See also* death: tithe; endowments and legacies: to abbeys
nonpublic (after Decree of 1763), 484, 487, 489–90, 496–8, 504–506
orientation of body in, 14
of poor. *See* poor, the: burial of
premature, 375–6, 377–8, 397–9, 402–404; provisions against, in wills, 399–401. *See also* apparent death; fear: of being buried alive
private: on family land, 39, 510–11, 518–19, 521, 522–3; pagan, 40–1; in cemeteries (18th c.), 320–1; in England and America, 522, 523
of saints. *See* saints: burial of
secularization of, 484, 492, 519
site of, 29–92; cathedral vs. cemeterial church, 37–40; in churchyards, 52–6; on

burial (*cont'd*)
wall of church, 54, 58; hierarchy of
desirable locations, 72–4, 78–92. *See also*
burial: choice of; burial: in church;
cemetery
of soldiers, 547–51
See also cemetery; funeral; grave; tomb

cadaver [Used in medical and scientific sense.
For individual dead, *see* body. For
collective sense, *see* dead, the], 354–74;
sensibility of, 355–61 *passim*, 381, 389,
390; remedies derived from, 357–8;
danger of contact with, 358–9; natural
preservation of, 359 (*See also* mummies);
theft of, 366, 368–9, 380–1. *See also*
dissection; embalming
Calvin, John, 299–300, 302
Camus, Jean-Pierre, Bishop of Belley, 372,
377
capitalism, 136–7, 191, 331
casket, 170, 597
"catacombs" of Paris, 499
catafalque, 169, 172, 173, 246, 258
cemeteries:
Alyscamps, Arles, 48, 58
Antigny, 61–2
Châtenay-sous-Bagneux, 37, 38
Civeaux, 37
Cordeliers, les, Toulouse, 360
Dalbade, la, Toulouse
Daurade, la, Toulouse, 83–90
Guiry-en-Vexin, 38, 39
Immaculate Conception, Rome, 360
of Knights of Malta, at Valletta, 271–2, 321
Minot-en-Châtillonais, 38, 551–5
Pénitents-Blancs, Montpellier, 482
Saint-Etienne, Toulouse
Saint-Hilaire, Marville, 274–6
Saint-Hilaire, Poitiers, 34
Saint-Maclou, Rouen, 59
Saint-Ouen, Rouen, 67
Saint-Rémy, Rheims, 34
Saint-Sauveur, Toulouse, 86
Saint-Savin, Basses Pyrénées, 66
Séléstat, 64
Souillac, 204–205
See also American cemeteries; Paris
cemeteries; Saints-Innocents, les,
cemetery, Paris
cemetery:
in America, 338–40, 531–3, 534, 550. *See
also* American cemeteries
commercial activity in, 68–70
communal, 30, 33–4
death depicted in, 114–15
in England, 271, 273, 338–41, 350
family groupings in. *See* family burial places
large, 61–2, 496, 517
location of: in antiquity, 30; in town or

cemetery (*cont'd*)
country, 37–42; with church, 34–5,
37–42, 51–6, 61, 320–1; in churchyard,
51–6
of mummies, 381–5, 406
nonfunereal functions of, 37, 62–71
pagan, 33–4, 38, 40–1
as park or garden, 503, 517; "lawn"
cemetery," 509, 533, 597; Forest Lawn,
600
private, 321, 531
prostitutes in, 66, 70
and public health. *See* public health and
cemeteries
recreational activities in, 69–70
relocation of, 478, 491–4; of Paris
cemeteries, 317–20, 337–8, 479–96
rural, 349–50, 532–3, 535, 595
sanctity of, 41, 478, 491, 524
secularization of, 484, 492–3
social functions of, 62–71
urban (modern), 533–4, 595
visit to, 502, 506, 509, 525–31, 533, 577
See also burial; cadaver: theft of; charnel;
decrees on cemeteries and funerals;
exhumation; ossuary; tomb
Chanson de Roland, ritual aspect of death in,
16, 17–18; death of Roland, 5, 6, 12,
14–15, 17, 22–3; prayers for dead, 25,
98–9; burial in churchyards, 52; use of
charnier and *aître* in, 52–3; burial with
comrades, 74–5; absolution at death,
140–1; gestures of mourning, 142; eulogy
for the dead, 143–4; treatment of dead
body, 145–6; Roland as secular saint, 213
chapel, funerary, 39, 188, 268, 535–6. *See also*
family burial places: chapel
chapel tomb, 535–6
charity. *See* alms; burial: as charitable act;
confraternities; endowments and legacies:
charitable; poor, the: burial of
charnel (*charnier*), 52–6, 59–61, 208; history
of word, 52–3, 54; named for businesses,
69–70; as chosen burial site, 82;
anonymity of, 382; of mummies, 383;
decorative, 384
Chateaubriand, vicomte François René de, 8,
341–2, 409, 506, 521–2
children: burial site of, 85 *table*, 88, 90, 207,
552; in funeral processions, 165, 167–8,
492; funerary inscriptions of, 231, 528;
death of, 447, 460; funerary portraits of,
536–8; excluded from death of others,
576; coffins of, in America, 597
church: location of cemetery with, 34–5,
37–42, 51–6, 61, 320–1; parish, 39, 74,
77, 83, 84 *table*. *See also* burial: in
church
Church councils:
Angers (1423), 68

Church councils (*cont'd*)
Attigny (762), 160
Braga (563), 30, 46
Mayence (813), 46
Nantes (1405), 68
pseudo-Nantes (900), 46
Rheims (1683), 47
Rouen (1231), 69
Rouen (1581), 47
Trent (1545–64), 77, 318
Tribur (895), 46, 51, 74
churchyard (*aître*) and cemetery, 52–6
class distribution of burials, 82–9, 84 *table*
Clemens, Samuel Langhorne (Mark Twain),
401, 562, 580; *Huckleberry Finn*, 451–2
clergy: Extreme Unction reserved for, 18,
23–4; burial in church reserved for, 46;
and veneration of saints' tombs, 72; effort
to arouse fear of death/hell, 124, 405;
and absolution, 142; and mourning, 146,
161–4; and funeral, 146, 165–8, 183;
pastoral functions limited, 319–20; and
spiritualism, 458; and relocation of
cemeteries, 486. *See also* Knights of
Malta; *Mémoire des curés de Paris*;
mendicant orders
clothing of mourning, 164, 325–6; robes, 165,
167, 187
coffin: in trees in cemetery, 45; 13th c. and
following, 169–70; portrait on, 171;
wooden, 205–206; lead, 216, 336, 359;
and vertical and mural tombs, 235–6;
required for the poor, 516; individual (in
Brazil), 556; in America, 596–7; stone
(*See* sarcophagus)
commemorative inscription, 217, 222–30
Commendations, 17, 98–9
common graves. *See* grave: common;
cemetery: communal
communication with the dead, 386, 420,
444–6, 453, 455–8, 576; spiritualism,
454–5, 458–60; and purgatory, 463; in
elegy, 525; *See also* dead, the:
reappearance of *conclamatio*, 397, 398
confraternities, 183–8; burial in chapel of,
76, 88–9; patron saints of, 80; burial
of poor, 185–6, 207; modern, 465, 497,
545
consolation literature in America, 450–4, 457,
526, 528, 596
contamination by the dead, 13, 29–30, 36. *See
also* fear: of the dead and ghosts; public
health and cemeteries
contemplation of death, 227, 298, 301, 342.
See also *artes moriendi*
contemptus mundi, 15, 111, 191, 218, 525
contracts with churchwardens, 181–2, 280–1,
284, 290
convent. *See* monastery and abbey
corpse. *See* body; cadaver

councils of Church. *See* Church councils
courtyard of church. *See* churchyard
Craven, Pauline. *See* La Ferronays family:
Pauline
cremation, 577, 600
criminals: victims of, 11–12, 355, 356; death
of, 12, 307–308; burial of, 42–5;
imprisoned in cemeteries, 66
cross: monumental, 62, 65, 71, 270; site of
tribunals and orations, 67–8; as chosen
burial site, 80–1, 91, 92; and tombs,
269–74, 275–6; public, 270, 271; stele,
273–4; symbolism of, 276, 287, 521, 535,
550; in ex-votos, 287; held by the dying,
430–1; omitted from secularized
cemetery, 508
Crusades and Crusaders, 194, 214. *See also*
Knights of Malta
cult of the dead: antecedents of, 161, 206,
208; 19th c., 508–13, 516, 517, 520, 524,
530, 539, 542–3, 545, 611; and national
sentiment, 550; in rural setting (Minot),
553, 554; extends beyond Europe, 556
cult of the tomb, 545, 546, 577; antecedents
of, 208, 216

Dalbade, la, church, Toulouse, 83–90
damnation. *See* hell and damnation
danse macabre, 15, 65, 110, 116–18, 297; of
Holbein and J. de Vauzelle, 300; erotic,
369–70
Dante Alighieri, 25, 43
Daurade, la, abbey church, Toulouse, 83–90
dead, the [Used in collective sense. For
customs with reference to dead
individual, *see* body. For medical and
scientific sense, *see* cadaver]:
anonymity of, 53, 203–209, 216–17
burial of. *See* burial
communication with. *See* communication
with the dead
cult of. *See* cult of the dead
fear of, 29, 30, 36, 507
list of, read during Mass, 150–1, 155, 160
masses for: 5th–7th c., 142, 146;
development of, 154–9 *passim. See also*
prayers for the dead
memorials of. *See* biography and funerary
inscriptions; funerary jewelry; hair; heart;
mourning: pictures; tomb: as memorial
perceived by the dying, 7–8
reappearance of, 29, 107, 526–7, 604–605.
See also communication with the dead;
dead, the: perceived by the dying
repose of. *See* repose of the dead
sanctity of, 40–1, 46. *See also* cemetery:
sanctity of
transportation of. *See* body: transportation
of
wax or wooden image of. *See* effigy

death:
    acceptance of, 8–9, 15–16, 27–8, 118. *See
        also* death: indifference to
    agony, 299, 409–10, 569; of Emma Bovary,
        568. *See also* death: indecency of; death:
        moment of
    apparent, 396–404. *See also* burial:
        premature; fear: of being buried alive
    beautiful. *See* beautiful death
    contemplation of, 227, 298, 301, 342
    by criminal action, 11–12, 355, 356
    of criminals, 12, 307–308
    and eroticism. *See* eroticism and death
    fear of, 22, 124, 128, 130, 303, 403,
        405–406, 410, 569, 609, 610
    indecency of ("dirty death"), 568–70, 612
    indifference to, 312–13, 322, 591
    invisible, 560, 575–6, 578–83, 600–601,
        611–14; in hospital, 571, 586–8;
        geographic incidence, 594–5
    in life, 128–9, 300–305, 308, 331–3
    mask, 127, 170, 261, 262
    medicalization of, 563–5, 583–8, 612
    moment of: devaluation of, 297–300; and
        the Church, 314; duration, 585–6. *See
        also artes moriendi;* beautiful death;
        death: agony; deathbed scene
    premonition of, 6–10, 13
    public aspect of, 18–19, 108; modern, 19–22
    reunion after. *See* reunion after death
    of saints, 13–14, 370–3
    as separation from loved ones, 609–11; in
        Brontës, 435, 436, 437–8; in American
        consolation literature, 452–3; in 19th c.
        literature, 456–7; and the Church, 466;
        and wills, 471; and beliefs in afterlife,
        471–2, and form of funerals, 507. *See
        also* communication with the dead;
        reunion after death
    as sleep, 22–4, 354, 420, 440–1, 525, 605.
        See also repose of the dead
    of soldiers, 12–13, 569
    sudden. *See* sudden death
    symbols of: horsemen of the Apocalypse,
        110; *transi,* 114; mummy, 115, 116–18;
        funeral procession, 166; recumbent figure,
        244–5; praying figure, 256, 259; cross,
        276, 287, 521, 535, 550; in vanities,
        328–32; burial vault, 347; sea, the, 416,
        441, 535
    tithe, 189
    unmentionable, 560; antecedents of, 512;
        "the lie," 21, 562, 565–7, 587, 612 (*See
        also* warning of death); word a taboo,
        572; social dynamics, 578–83, 614; vs.
        acknowledgment, 590–3
    warning of. *See* warning of death
    and wealth. *See temporalia*
deathbed scene, 14–21, 107, 108, 299–300,
    327, 447–9, 537, 607; in La Ferronays

deathbed scene (*cont'd*)
    family, 412–31 *passim. See* also *artes
        moriendi;* death: moment of
death's-head, 329–31, 340
decrees on cemeteries and funerals: of March
    12, 1763, 480, 481, 483–91, 493;
    Parliament of Toulouse, Decree of Sept.
    3, 1774, 491, 493–4; Déclaration Royale
    of 1776, 491–4 *passim;* of Aug. 10, 1811,
    497; of 23 Prairial, Year XII (1804),
    516–20; of March 15, 1928, 523
de Gesvres family, 224–6
Delille, Jacques, 520–1, 526
denial of death. *See* death: invisible; death:
    unmentionable
despair, 123, 130, 303, 405. *See also* suicide
devil, 105, 115, 123, 130; fear of, 151, 158;
    and cemeteries, 476–8; limited modern
    belief in, 576–7
dismemberment of body, 145, 208, 261–2,
    361, 387
dissection, 361, 363; private, 366–8
doctor: as spokesman for popular beliefs, 353,
    361; and forensic medicine, 353–4;
    reluctance to verify death, 401; and
    apparent death, 402–404; lack of
    confidence in, 416, 417, 431, 434; as
    herald of death, 561; consultation with,
    as important, 564; attitudes of, toward
    death (20th c.), 586–7. *See also* death:
    medicalization of; hospital
du Cange, Charles, 51, 63, 68, 144
Durandus, Gulielmus, Bishop of Mende: on
    sudden death, 11, 12–13; on orientation
    of dead, 14, 246; on sanctity of burial
    site, 41; on burial in churches, 46; on
    holy water and incense in grave, 142;
    tomb of, 254
dying: art of (*See artes moriendi*); fear of (*See*
    fear: of death and dying)
Dying (film), directed by M. Roemer, 590–2
dyptichs. *See* "reading of the names"

Edict of Nantes, 315, 350–1, 522
effigy, 170–2, 233–4; as recumbent figure,
    240–7; as praying figure, 247, 252–60; as
    portrait, 260–6, 267, 536–8
elegy (*tombeau*), 232, 524. *See also* Gray,
    Thomas: "Elegy . . ."
embalming: early practice of, 261–2; 15th c.
    and following, 361–4; delays moment of
    "absolute death," 404; recommended by
    Duval and Girard, 508; in America, 509,
    597, 599–600
endowments and legacies: to abbeys, 73,
    181–2, 191; charitable, 181–3, 188–97
    passim, 279–80, 517; and development of
    wills, 190–6; effect on economic
    conditions, 192–3. *See also* alms; Mass:
    endowment; tomb: "of the soul"

endowment tablets, 181–2, 277–86
England: burial in church, 91–2; cemetery in,
271, 273, 338–41, 350; burial vault in,
347; burial practices (17th c.), 348–9;
embalming practices, 361–2; private
burial in, 522, 523
epidemics: common graves for, 56–7, 58; and the
macabre, 124–5; and cemeteries, 349, 477;
omens of, 357, 476, 477; and the devil,
477; burial of victims, at Minot, 551
epitaph:
formula, 217–18, 233; appeal to passerby,
218–21, 225–6; age given, 218, 220, 221;
pious exhortation, 221–3; family
inscription, 222, 230–3; biographical
account, 222–30
as identification, 217–18, 219–20; of entire
family, 222; on tombs of ordinary people,
273
for wife or child, 528, 538
See also inscription
Erasmus: on preparation for death, 298,
302–303, 312; on *mors repentina*, 307; on
tomb of St. Thomas of Canterbury, 349
Eros and Thanatos. *See* eroticism and death
eroticism and death, 369–74, 392–5, 404;
necrophilia, 374–81; in *Wuthering
Heights*, 443–6
eschatology. *See* afterlife; hell and damnation;
Last Judgment; paradise; purgatory
Escorial, the, 254; Pantheon, 334–5; double
burial in, 282–3
eulogy for the dead, 143–5, 163; in
inscriptions, 226–7, 230. *See also*
biography and funerary inscriptions
euthanasia, 585–6, 593
exhumation, 45; to make room for new bodies,
54, 57–8; clandestine, 375–80; of
Saints-Innocents (1785–7), 498–500. *See
also* cadaver: theft of; eroticism and
death
Extreme Unction, 18, 19, 23–4, 303, 562–3
ex-voto, 286–8
Eyck, Jan van: Last Judgment of, 106, 112

face: concealment of, after death, 127,
168–73, 206, 401, 508, 607; as feature of
commemoration, 266. *See also* death
mask; portrait
failure, sense of, 137–9, 611. *See also* despair
fame: and salvation, 214–15, 228; and epitaph,
220–1, 229; and tomb of J. van
Wassenaer, 264
family, depicted on tombs, 257
family burial places, 39, 74–7, 289–92, 553
chapel, 224–6, 289–92, 316, 321; tomb,
535–6
estate or land, 39, 510–11, 518–19, 521,
522–3
(near) family pew, 82, 291

family burial places (*cont'd*)
royal, 205, 241, 333–6, 347
vaults, 30, 255, 289–92
faubourg sanctuaries, 34–5, 36, 40
fear:
of being buried alive, 362, 386, 396, 397–9,
402–404, 609. *See also* apparent death;
burial: premature
of the dead and ghosts, 29, 30, 36, 507
of death and dying, 22, 124, 128, 130, 303,
403, 405–406, 410, 569, 609, 610
of the devil, 151, 158
of hell and damnation, 110, 124, 151–4,
458, 473–4
of solitary grave, 42
fetishism, 542
Flaubert, Gustave: *Madame Bovary*, 568, 574
Fleury, Antoinette, 87, 125, 269
Freemasons, 387, 521, 546
funeral: simplicity desired, 322–4; women's
attendance, 419, 513; and Decree of
1763, 484, 487, 489–90, 496–8;
American, 596, 598–601. *See also* burial;
cemetery; decrees on cemeteries and
funerals
funeral home (or parlor): antecedents, 401;
American, 509, 596, 598–600; European,
594
funeral procession: depictions of, 49, 186–7,
245, 250; early forms, 145–6; 13th–18th
c., 165–8; for the poor, 186–7; in Villon,
200; and importance of coffin, 206;
secularization of, 492; evolution of, 497
funerary chapel, 39, 188, 268
funerary jewelry, 388, 460–2
funerary statue. *See* effigy
Furetière, Antoine, 53, 82, 205, 365

Gaignières, François-Roger de, 115, 195, 217,
282
Gaïx, Alexandrine de, 431–2
Gaïx, Coraly de, 326, 409, 431–2
Gallican liturgy, 23–4, 148–51, 154–5, 156
Garden of Torments, 370
Garmann, Christian Friedrich, 354–9, 398,
476–8 *passim*
Girard, J.: *Des Tombeaux* . . . , 506–507, 508,
510–11
Giraud, Pierre: *Les Tombeaux* . . . , 513–16
Glaber, Raoul, 6, 7, 56, 159
Gomberville, Marin Le Roy de, 327, 346–7
Gorer, Geoffrey, 571, 575–7, 578–9, 594
grants in perpetuity, 517–18. *See also* family
burial places
grave:
common: of the poor, 56, 57, 58, 207, 320,
502; during epidemics, 56–7, 58; chosen
in humility, 82; in relocated cemeteries,
484, 491, 494, 504. *See also*
superimposition of bodies

grave (*cont'd*)
private: origin of, 40–1; fees for (Decree of 1763), 485; on family land, 510–11, 518–19, 521, 522–3
violation of, 32
See also tomb
graveyard. *See* cemetery
Gray, Thomas: "Elegy . . ." (1751), 341, 346, 347, 524–6
Gregory the Great, Pope, Saint: on burial in church, 49; in frescoes at Brinay, 133; concept of purgatory, 153; and intercession for the dead, 158; and "Gregorian" (30 Masses), 174; concept of death, 188; funerary inscription of, 211–12; his "lasting glory," 214
grief. *See* mourning
Grimaud, Gilbert, 7–8, 464

hair, preserved as memento, 388, 462, 542
health. *See* public health and cemeteries
heart: preserved, 145, 261, 387–8; buried separately, 205–206, 208, 261–2, 362, 387; of corpse, and macabre eroticism, 376; Sacred Heart of Jesus, 387
heaven, images of, 25–6. *See also* afterlife
hell and damnation, 25, 99–101, 109–10, 123–4, 473–4, 576–7, 610; fear of, 110, 124, 151–4, 458, 473–4
Holbein, Hans, the younger, 300, 330, 331–2
holy water, aspersion with, 141–2
Homer, 15, 23, 25, 313
homo totus, 247, 266, 277, 286, 394. *See also* soul: separation from body
Honorius of Autun, 26, 42; *Elucidarium*, 41–2, 49; on number of Masses a day, 158; on works of mercy, 185
hospice, 585
hospital, death in, 570–1, 584–8. *See also* death: medicalization of
hour of death. *See* death: moment of
Huizinga, Johan, 124, 126, 137
humility, expressed in: choice of burial site, 82, 88, 92, 337; simplicity of inscription, 229; tomb style, 239, 258, 271; simplicity of burial, 322–4, 327
hygiene. *See* public health and cemeteries

Ignatius of Loyola, Saint: *Spiritual Exercises*, 301, 315, 342
Illich, Ivan, 592–3
incense, 140, 141, 142
indifference:
to death, 312–13, 322; in film *Dying*, 591. *See also* acceptance of death
to remains of the dead, 29, 30–2, 321, 322, 348–52, 498–500; by the Church, 398, 543
indulgences, 154, 158, 160

Innocents, les, cemetery. *See* Saints-Innocents, les, cemetery of, Paris
inscription: early practice of, 78; on Roman tombs, 202–203; lack of, 5th–18th c., 203–209, 215–16; of saints' tombs (Middle Ages), 209–15; reappearance (12th c.), 216–17. *See also* endowment tablets; epitaph
inscriptions, cited in reference to: protection of saints, 33; commemoration of saints, 210–12; identity, 217–18; prayers for the dead, 219–21; biographical accounts, 222–30 *passim*; family (15th c. and following), 222, 230–3; military exploits, 225–6; posthumous eulogy, 226–7, 529; family feeling, 231–3; endowments, 282–4; trend toward nothingness, 345; regret and hope of reunion, 528
inscriptions, on tombs of:
Barberini, Cardinal Antonio (17th c.), 345
Beaudoin, Charlotte de (17th c.), 232
Begon, Abbot of Conques (12th c.), 212, 247
Blosset, Pierre (17th c.), 226, 231
Burgundy, dukes of, 235
Capelletus, Flaminius (17th c.), 231–2
Chartier, Mathieu (16th c.), 227, 231
Fouilloy, Edouard de (13th c.), 221
Le Maistre, Pierre (16th c.), 223–4
Marle, Anne de (16th c.), 222–3
Potier, Léon, duc de Gesvres (18th c.), 224–5
Theodechilde, Saint, 210
See also tablets; endowment epitaphs
intercession for the dead. *See* prayers for the dead

Jankélévitch, Vladimir, 22, 23, 121, 128, 471, 571–2, 588, 602
jewelry (commemorative), 388, 460–2
Jouarre, Crypt of, 97, 103, 151, 209–10
judgment: of the dying, 106–10, 112, 131; and concept of hell (*See* hell and damnation); Day of (*See* Last Judgment)
justice: administration of, in cemeteries, 66–7; earthly and heavenly, 102–103

Knights of Malta, 223; cemetery at Valletta, 271–2, 321; church at Valletta, 239, 336; burial customs, 382
Kübler-Ross, Elisabeth, 573, 589, 592

La Ferronays family, 412–31; Fernand, comptesse de 19, 413, 429–31; Pauline (Craven), 412–31 *passim*; Auguste Marie (compte) de, 412–14, 423–4; Albert, 414–19, 421–2; Alexandrine, 414–22, 427–9, 457; Eugénie, 424–5; Olga, 425–7
Laffitte, Pierre, 541–2, 544, 545
La Fontaine, Jean de, 9, 15–16

Lamartine, Alphonse de, 411, 439, 454–5, 526

Last Judgment, 31–3, 96–110, 150, 152, 153, 184–5; artistic representations of, 99–101, 104–105, 106, 110, 112, 184–5, 248, 257–8, 465

last rites, 303. *See also* Extreme Unction

lavatio corporis, 161–2

Lazarus, 248, 258

Le Bras, Gabriel, 44, 61, 160, 351

Le Braz, Anatole, 59, 60, 61, 67, 69, 72

legacies and endowments. *See* endowments and legacies

letters of American settlers, 446–50

Libera, 13, 152, 154, 188

liber vitae. See book (as symbol)

life: death as part of, 128–9, 300–305, 308, 331–3; remnant of, in cadaver, 355–61 *passim*, 381, 389, 390; after death (*See* afterlife); love of (*See* love of life)

liturgies. *See* Gallican liturgy; Mass; Mozarabic liturgy; Roman Mass (old liturgy); Serapion: Prayer Book

love and death. *See* eroticism and death

love of life, 128–32, 191–2, 197, 310. *See also avaritia*

macabre, the, 110–29; and exhibition of bones, 61; meaning of word, 110, 116; and plagues, 124–5; and effigies, 172; and turning away from death, 308; artistic expression of, 328–32; return of images (19th c.), 569. *See also* danse macabre; eroticism and death

Mâle, Emile, 113, 117, 241–2, 243, 331

marteloyge, 182

martyrs, *see* saints

Mary, Virgin, 18; burial near images of, 80, 92; pardoning role, in iconography, 101–102; in iconography of *artes moriendi*, 108–109; death of, iconography, 141, 250, 311; Dormition of, iconography, 250; as Our Lady of Mercy, 258, 548. *See also Ave Maria*

mask of death, 127, 170, 261, 262

Mass: burial near celebration of, 72, 79, 81, 92; for the dead, 142, 146, 152, 154–9 *passim;* cemeterial (early), 147–8; and Gallican liturgy, 154–6; private, 158–60; burial, 173–5; "service," the, 175–81; Requiem, 178; endowment, 179–80, 282–4; reduction in, 183. *See also* Gallican liturgy; prayers for the dead; Roman Mass (old liturgy)

materialism, 137, 507

Maurras, Charles, 306, 387, 545

medicine. *See* death: medicalization of; dissection; doctors; hospital

meditation on death. *See* death: contemplation of

memento mori, 127, 218, 257, 330, 368, 377, 461, 490, 563, 597

Memento of the Dead, 25, 155, 156–7, 158. *See also* "reading of the names"

Mémoire des curés de Paris, 487–91, 506, 511

memoria. See tomb: as memorial

memorial services, endowed, 282–4. *See also* Mass: endowment

mendicant orders: as specialists in death, 83; in England, 91; as preachers, 114, 123–4; on images of death, 138; in funeral processions, 165, 166, 492; promoting fear of death, 302; Franciscan techniques for preserving body, 383. *See also* monastery and abbey

Mercier, Louis-Sébastien, 368, 369, 496–7

mercy, works of. *See* alms; burial: as charitable act; legacies and endowments: charitable.

Méry proposal (1844), 539, 541, 544, 546

Mexico, 328, 387–8, 465

Michael, Saint, 100, 101, 103, 105, 108, 115, 249

Michault, Pierre, 112, 118, 119, 124

migration of the soul, 248–52

miracle: depicted in *ex-votos*, 286–7; relating to the dead, 311, 357, 359–60, 404. *See also* remedies derived from cadavers

Missa privata, 158–60

Mitford, Jessica: *American Way of Death, The*, 596, 597, 600

moment of death. *See* Death: moment of

monasteries and abbeys:

Saint-Gall, 159–60

Celestines, les, 224–5

Centula, 159

Chaise-Dieu, la, 117

Cluny, 159–60, 161–2

Daurade, la, Toulouse, 83–90

Sainte-Geneviève, Paris, 203

Saint-Sernin, Toulouse, 75

Souillac, 204–205

monastery and abbey: burial in church of, 73–4, 83; legacies to, 73, 181–2, 191; and development of private Masses, 157–60; prayers for lay benefactors, 183; retirement to, before death, 191. *See also* mendicant orders

Mornay, Philippe de, 300–301

mors improvisa. See sudden death

mors repentina. See sudden death

mortuary (donation to priest), 91

mortuus sepellitur. See burial: as charitable act

mourners, paid, 144, 163, 165–6, 325–6

mourning, 142–5; extreme gestures of, 142–3, 530; Church's attitudes toward, 144–5, 468, 530–1, 601; clergy involvement in, 146, 161–4, 577; restrained gestures of, 162–4, 578–83; clothing of, 164, 165, 167, 187, 325–6; impersonality and ritualization of, 325–7; social acceptability

mourning (*cont'd*)
    of expressions of grief, 326–7, 578–83;
    rings and gloves, 330; flowers as part of,
    419; picture, 451, 461, 515; 19th c.
    customs, 511–13; rejection and
    elimination of, 575, 577–83, 612–13;
    organized by funeral directors, 598–600
Mozarabic liturgy, 149–51 *passim*, 154
mummies: and danse macabre, 116; cemeteries
    of, 381–5, 406; privately preserved,
    385–8; naturally preserved, 499; of
    "glass," 513–16
mural (vertical) tomb, 234–7, 256, 501

nature, 346–8, 390, 393–5; Sade's view,
    391–2; and cemetery, 503, 524–5, 532–4;
    and tame death, 604; and death of the
    self, 608; and romantic death, 610; and
    invisible death, 612
Necker, Jacques and Suzanne, 386, 508
necrophilia, 374–81
Nesson, Pierre de, 119–21
nihilism, 238. *See also* nothingness
nomina. See "reading of the names"
nothingness, 322, 341–6, 591; and nature,
    346, 348. *See also* nihilism

obituary (medieval), 78, 161
Office of the Dead, 114, 165, 177, 178
Orléans, Elisabeth d', 323, 363, 400
ossuary (*charnier*), 53–4, 58–60;
    decorative, 384; at Quiberon, 549. *See
    also* bones
Our Lady of Mercy (cult), 258, 548

pall, 172
Panofsky, Erwin, 113, 202, 238, 241, 242,
    243–4, 330
Paracelsus, 355, 389
paradise, images of, 25–6. *See also* afterlife
parapsychology, 459–60
Paris cemeteries: relocation of, 317–20, 337–8,
    479–96; 18th c., 318; disappearance of,
    318–19; and public health, 348–50,
    479–88, 495, 540–1, 544; guarded from
    theft, 368; investigations of, 479, 481,
    540–1; guidebook to (1836), 528–9;
    Clamart, 496
    Innocents, les. *See* Saints-Innocents, les,
        cemetery, Paris
    Montmartre, 496
    Saint-André-des-Arts, 318
    Saint-Eustache, 368, 482, 496
    Sainte-Geneviève, 203, 547
    Saint-Germain-l'Auxerrois, 486
    Saint-Germain-le-Vieil, 319
    Saint-Gervais, 318, 319, 483
    Saint-Jean-en-Grève, 86, 87, 278–9, 280–1,
        292, 318, 319, 368, 487
    Saint-Louis-en-l'Ile, 56, 337–8, 496

Paris cemeteries (*cont'd*)
    Saint-Marcel, 216–17
    Sainte-Margarite, 496
    Saint-Nicolas-des-Champs, 318
    Saint-Roch, 318, 319, 496
    Saint-Sulpice, 58, 69, 318, 337, 480–1, 486,
        496
    Trinité, la, 57
    Vaugirard, 496
    See also cemeteries; decrees on cemeteries
        and funerals; Méry proposal;
        Père-Lachaise cemetery, Paris;
        Saint-Denis, Paris
parish church: origins of, 39; burial in, 74, 77,
    83, 84 *table*
Père-Lachaise cemetery, Paris, 459, 485, 496,
    503, 517, 518, 531–6 *passim*, 539;
    guidebook to (1836), 520, 528–9, 538
pilgrimage: cemeteries as resting-places, 65;
    posthumous, 72
Pincus, Lily, 19–20, 580
plague: common graves for victims, 56–7, 58;
    and the macabre, 124–5; and cemeteries,
    349, 477; omens of, 357, 476, 477; and
    the devil, 477; burial of victims, at
    Minot, 551
planctus. See eulogy for the dead
pollution by the dead, 13, 29–30, 36. *See also*
    public health and cemeteries
poor, the:
    burial of: in common graves, 56, 57, 58,
        207, 320, 502; by confraternities, 185–6,
        207; anonymity of, 207; in cemeteries,
        271–2, 502, 521; in individual graves,
        516–17
    in funeral processions, 165–8 *passim*, 492
    See also alms; endowments and legacies:
        charitable
portrait: on Roman tombs, 202; family, 257;
    in funerary effigies, 260–6, 267, 536–8; as
    commemorative statue, 265–6; in vanities,
    328–9; group, centered on anatomy
    lesson, 366. *See also* death: mask; effigy
positivists, 541–7 *passim*
possessions. *See temporalia*
Potocki, Jan: *Manuscrit trouvé à Saragosse*, 44,
    379, 389, 392
Poussin, Nicolas, 330, 374
prayers for the dead, 146–8; in Gallican
    liturgy, 23; in Prayer Book of Serapion,
    25; St. Augustine on, 41; Honorius of
    Autun on, 42; reading of the names,
    148–51, 154; and uncertainty of salvation,
    152–3, 154; among religious communities,
    160; in epitaphs, 218–21; in 18th c., 487,
    as superstition, 507. *See also*
    Commendations; Mass: for the dead;
    Office of the Dead; purgatory: devotions
    for souls in; *refrigerium*
Prayers from the Pulpit, 156–7, 182, 280

praying figure (effigy), 247, 252–60; and migration of the soul, 249; and recumbent figure, 252–4, 256; eschatology of, 266–8; in *ex-votos*, 286–8

premonition of death, 6–10, 13. *See also* warning of death

prostitutes in cemeteries, 66, 70

Protestants: choice of burial site, 82, 315–17; moralists, 301–305

public health and cemeteries, 477, 493; in Paris, 348–50, 479–88, 495, 540–1, 544; in America, 531. *See also* contamination by the dead; epidemics

purgatory: origins of doctrine, 107, 148, 153–4, 201, 306; represented in *ex-votos*, 288; devotions for souls in, 305–306, 462, 465–7, 490; development of doctrine, 462–7. *See also* indulgences; *refrigerium*

Rabelais, François, 53, 70

"reading of the names," 148–51, 154. *See also* Memento of the Dead

recumbent figure *(requiescens)*, 240–7; as image of paradise, 26; and effigy, 170; examples, 241, 244; and separation of soul and body, 248–9; and praying figure, 252–4, 256; eschatology of, 266–8; imitated in life, 311; in funerary jewelry, 461

refrigerium, 25, 26, 147–8, 154, 274. *See also* paradise; purgatory

Régnier, Jean, 76, 190, 198–200

regret: for life, 15–16, 21, 521; for the dead, 143–5, 163, 326, 506, 528

relics. *See* saints: relics of

remedies derived from cadavers, 357–8

repose of the dead *(requies)*, 24, 150; and recumbent figure, 241–3; in American settlers' letters, 449; and purgatory, 463–4. *See also* sleep: death as

Requiem Mass, 178

requies. See repose of the dead

resignation to death. *See* acceptance of death

resurrection, 31–3, 106–107

reunion after death, 409; in La Ferronays family, 420–1, 428; in Brontës, 435, 436, 439; in American consolation literature, 452–3; as aspect of romantic death, 611. *See also* death: as separation from loved ones

Revelation, Book of, 97–8, 100, 101, 103

robe of mourning, 165, 167, 187

Roland. *See Chanson de Roland*

romanceros, 21, 102, 63

Roman Mass (9th c. and following). *See* Mass

Roman Mass (old liturgy), 25–6

romantic concepts of death: antecedents of, 293, 512, 555; and triumphant death, 448–9; and purgatory, 465; death of a few others as intolerable, 472, 555,

romantic concepts of death *(cont'd)* 609–10; and deism, 474. *See also* beautiful death; death: as separation from loved ones; reunion after death

Ronsard, Pierre de, 121–3, 569

rosary, 167, 305–306

Rostang family, 224, 230–1

Round Table, stories of: sudden death in, 10–11; death scenes in, 13–18; burial with comrades, 74–5, 76; gestures of mourning, 142–3; eulogy for the dead, 143–4; transportation of dead to burial site, 145

Rousset, Jean, 370–2

royal burial places. *See* family burial places: royal

Rubens, Peter Paul, 116, 374

rural cemetary, 349–50, 522–3, 535, 595

Sade, Donatien Alphonse François, marquis de: will, 351–2; on private dissections, 367, 368; necrophilia in work of, 378–9; on man and nature, 391–2

sadism, 370, 377

Saint-Denis, church, Paris, 59; tombs of royal line, 241, 333, 334, 335; plan to replace (18th c.), 502–503

Saint-Etienne, church, Toulouse, 83–90

saints:
burial of, 30, 34–5; iconography of, 141; tombs, 209–15
communion of: development of dogma, 160
death of, 13–14; martyrdom, 370–3
devotion to, 71–3
list of, read during Mass, 149–50
protection of, 29–33, 73
relics of, 35; placed in others' tombs, 39–40; devotion to, 71, 171; transfer of, 382
See also basilicas; burial: *ad sanctos; ex-votos*

Saint-Simon, Louis de Rouvron, duc de, 18–19; will (1754), 324, 363–4; on the Escorial, 334–5, 382–3

Saints-Innocents, les, cemetery, Paris; relation of church to cemetery (les Clampeaux), 51, 86; early descriptions of, 54, 55, 57; boundaries of, 55; common graves at, 57, 495; crosses in, 62, 269; large ceremonies at, 65–6; recluse of, 66; prostitution in, 70; description (16th c.), 269; dead of other churches buried at, 318; reputation for decomposing bodies, 360; fires lit to purify air, 482; health problems in area, 483; closing of (1780), 495–6; destruction and transformation of (1785), 498–500, 539

Salutati, 163–4, 307, 310

sanctuary, right of, 62–4, 68, 552

Sangro, Raimondo di, Prince: palace, Naples, 336, 367, 380–1, 516
sarcophagus, 202–206, 288; of saints, 209; and lead coffin, 216; as mural tomb, 234–6
Satan. *See* devil
Saum, Lewis O., 446–9, 455
Savonarola, Girolamo, 109–10, 114, 330
Scroll of the Dead, 160–1, 183
secularization, 129, 216; of death, 161; and relocation of cemeteries, 486. *See also* burial: secularization of; cemetery: secularization of
Serapion: Prayer Book, 25
"service," the (series of Low Masses), 175–81
Seven Sleepers of Ephesus: legend, 24; awaiting Day of Judgment, 32, 97, 248; and liturgy, 241; as *homo totus*, 247; and concept of afterlife, 267
sexuality. *See* eroticism and death;
shadow of death *(umbra mortis)*, 24
Shelley, Mary Wollstonecraft: *Frankenstein*, 389–90
shrouds, 113, 145, 169–70, 172, 205, 206, 207, 216, 235
Simon Stock, Saint, 305, 465
sin. *See* absolution and benediction
skeleton, 104, 110, 118, 328–9, 331, 345, 381
skull (and crossbones), 328–31, 340
"skull box," 60–1
sleep, death as, 22–4, 354, 420, 440–1, 525, 605. *See also* repose of the dead
Society for Psychical Research (SPR), 459
soldier: death of, 12–13, 569; burial of, 547–51
sorcery, 309–10, 467, 468
soul:
   separation from body, 219, 277, 285–6, 300, 342; and migration of soul, 248–52; artistic depictions, 248–9, 251; and recumbent and praying figures, 266, 268; and sensibility of cadaver, 354–6, 360; and communication with the dead, 456
   "tomb" of, 181–2, 281–6, 293
spirits, disembodied, 455–60, 462. *See also* communication with the dead
spiritualism, 454–5, 458–60; and purgatory, 463, 466. *See also* communication with the dead
Sponde, Bishop Henri de, 315–17, 320
statue, commemorative, 265–6. *See also* effigy; praying figure; recumbent figure
still life (art form): development of, 132–7; and vanity, 330, 332
Stoicism, 15, 163, 164, 299
stone coffin. *See* sarcophagus
straw or ashes, dead exhibited on, 162, 264
sudden death, 10–13, 108, 118; as desirable, 123, 587; no longer seen as dangerous, 307
suicide, 44, 123, 130, 438. *See also* despair

superimposition of bodies, 56–9, 491, 516, 518, 554
sweetness of death. *See* beautiful death
synods. *See* Church councils

tame death, 28, 142, 162, 201, 243, 267, 293, 394, 410, 552, 603–605; and beautiful death, 312
temporalia, 130–2, 136–7, 308–309, 333; and distribution of inheritance, 190–6. *See also avaritia*
Tenenti, Alberto, 109, 128–9, 163–4, 308, 310, 312–13
Thanatos and Eros. *See* eroticism and death
Thomas Aquinas, Saint, 306, 463
Thomassin, Louis, 12, 49–50
Tolstoi, Leo, 9–10; "The Three Deaths," 10, 561–2; "The Death of Ivan Ilyich," 21, 563–7, 573–5
tomb, 202–93
   and cemetery (Middle Ages), 53
   cult of, 208, 216, 545, 546, 577
   family. *See* family burial places
   as memorial, 202–203, 207–209, 229–30, 263; of saints and important persons, 209–16; to express grief, 529–30; for soldiers and heroes, 549
   multiple, 277; for parts of body, 208, 261–2
   noises in, 357, 476–7
   proximity to burial site, 207–208, 277, 288–9
   Roman, 202–203
   of saints and important people, 209–15
   "of the soul," 281–6, 293
   types: epitaph, 233–4; vertical, mural, 234–7, 251–2, 257; horizontal, 237–40; with cross, 271–4; box, 340; chapel, 535–6
   words for, 237–8
tombs, of:
   Adon, Saint, 210
   Agilbert, Saint, 210
   Aguilberte, Saint, 210
   Altieri (18th c.), 344
   Aymeric, Canon of Toulouse (13th c.), 251–2, 255
   Barbara, Saint, 171
   Begon, Abbot of Conques (12th c.), 212, 247
   Bourbon dynasty, 333–4
   Burgundy, dukes of, 166, 187, 235
   Bussière, la, Abbot of (12th c.), 217
   Charles Barromeo, Saint (16th c.), 239
   Dagobert I (7th c.), 249
   Durandus, Gulielmus, Bishop of Mende (13th c.), 254
   Gisleni (17th c.), 344–5
   Hapsburg dynasty, 205, 335, 347
   Hattstadt, Conrad Werner von (14th c.), 244

tombs (*cont'd*)
Isabel of Aragon (13th c.), 261, 262
Jean de Montmirail, 253
Lonati, Cardinal Bernard (16th c.), 169
Louis XII (16th c.), 253
Maria Christina, Archduchess (19th c.), 347
Marigny, Enguerrand de (14th c.), 254
Penthagothus (6th c.), 38–9
Pot, Philippe (15th c.), 166, 187
Sernin, Saint (12th c.), 209
Theodechilde, Saint, 210
Valois, dukes of, 254, 263
Venice, doges of, 264
Wassenaer, Admiral J. van (17th c.), 264
William I, the Conqueror (11th c.), 261–2
William I, the Silent (16th c.), 263–4
tombstone: "literary," 228, 467; popularity in 19th c., 518; inscriptions (*See* endowment tablets; epitaphs; inscriptions)
torture, 371–3
Toulouse, 379–80, 398–9; class distribution of burials, 82–9, 84 *table*; age distribution of burials, 89–90; burial of children, 85 *table*, 90; relocation of cemeteries (18th c.), 491, 493–4
transi, 113–14, 242, 244, 253, 328, 368
transportation of the body. *See* body: transportation of
Tristan and Isolde: death of Tristan, 6, 14, 18; attitudes toward death, 21; disposal of those dishonored, 44–5; treatment of dead body, 145
Triumph of Death, 118–19, 124, 127
Turpin, Archbishop of Rheims, 25; death of, 6, 14, 15, 17

umbra mortis, 24
undertaker, 598–600
underworld. *See* afterlife
universa fraternitas, 149–51 *passim*

Valois, dukes of: tombs of, 254, 263; chapel of, 289, 333, 334
vanities (art form), 327–32, 366
vault (burial), 289, 292, 318; family, 30, 255, 289–92
Vauzelles, Jean de, 300, 301, 304
vertical (mural) tomb, 234–7, 256, 501
vestigium vitae, 355–61 *passim*, 381, 389, 390
Vicq-d'Azyr, Félix, 17, 402, 481, 482
vigil, 161, 165
Villon, François, 121, 123, 198–200, 208
violation of grave, 32
Virgil, 11, 23, 25

Virginia, cemeteries in, 339–40; Arlington, 550–1
Virgin Mary. *See* Mary, Virgin
vitrification of body, 513–16
Vovelle, Michel and Gaby, 182, 187, 305, 324, 333, 387, 465, 470, 521

warning of death: role diminished, 298–9; reluctance about, 561–2, 572; provided by chance, 566; contemporary practice of, 590. *See also* premonition of death
wax image of the dead. *See* effigy
wealth, attitudes toward. See *temporalia*
Westminster Abbey, London, 170, 263, 502, 503
will, the:
antecedents of, 18
and endowments, 279–80, 285, 517
effort to revive (19th c.), 509
functions of, 188–93; pious clauses, 189–90, 469–71 (in Régnier and Villon, 199); redressing wrongs and injuries, 190, 199–200; expression of affection, 324, 470–1; transmission of property, 471
as literary genre, 198–200
as moral obligation, 196–8
as personal document, 197–8
required by Church, 189
simplicity expressed in, 322–4, 469. *See also* humility
and veneration of saints, 72
See also burial: choice of; endowments and legacies; *temporalia*
wills, cited in reference to: posthumous pilgrimages, 72; burial in church, 72–3, 277; burial near other persons, 75–7; burial site, 78–82, 91–2, 277, 291–2; the macabre, 125–6; funeral procession, 166–8; Masses to be said/sung, 173–81 *passim;* charitable endowments, 181–2, 279–80; pious clauses, 189–90, 469–71; redressing wrongs, 190; sense of stewardship, 195–6; crosses and tombs, 269–71; tablet, 277–81; anxiety about Last Day, 306–307; simplicity desired, 323–5, 469; contempt for immortality, 351–2; preservation of body, 362; opening and dissection of body, 363–4; precautions against premature burial, 399–401; purgatory, 463; affection for survivors, 470–1
winding sheet, 205, 516
Winslow, Jacques-Bénigne, 397–8, 402

Zacchia, Paul, 353–4, 359–60